The Psychodynamics of Race:

Vicious and Benign Spirals

The Psychodynamics of Race:

Vicious and Benign Spirals

RAE SHERWOOD
Formerly Senior Research Fellow,
Columbus Centre, University of Sussex

THE HARVESTER PRESS · SUSSEX

HUMANITIES PRESS · NEW JERSEY

First published in Great Britain in 1980 by
THE HARVESTER PRESS LIMITED
Publishers: John Spiers and Margaret A. Boden
16 Ship Street, Brighton, Sussex

and in the USA by
HUMANITIES PRESS INC.,
Atlantic Highlands, New Jersey 07716

© Rae Sherwood, 1980

British Library Cataloguing in Publication Data

Sherwood, Rae
  The psychodynamics of race
  1. London – Race relations – Case studies
  2. Family – England – London – Case studies
  I. Title
  301.45' 1042' 09421   DA676.9.A1

ISBN 0–85527–996–6

Humanities Press Inc.
ISBN 0–391–01804–3

Printed in Great Britain by
Redwood Burn Limited, Trowbridge and Esher

To Nicholas and John

CONTENTS

EDITORIAL FOREWORD

Following a proposal originally advanced by Mr David Astor, a research centre was set up in the University of Sussex in 1966 to investigate how persecutions and exterminations come about, how the impulse to persecute or exterminate is generated, how it spreads, and under what conditions it is likely to express itself in action. The Centre was originally called the Centre for Research in Collective Psychopathology, but later adopted the more neutral name of the Columbus Centre, after the Trust which financed it.

The Centre's work resulted in a series of books on the pre-conditions – ideological, social and psychological – of some of the great persecutions which have occurred in the course of European history. These books were published under the rubric of Studies in the Dynamics of Persecution and Extermination (Sussex University Press in association with Heinemann Educational Books). The Centre was however also able to give some attention to the cognate field of inter-ethnic tensions. *The Psychodynamics of Race*, which is based on field-work and is concerned with interethnic perceptions and misperceptions in contemporary Britain, is the result.

Like the work which resulted in the various volumes in the series on persecution and extermination, the field-work on which the present volume is based was financed by the Columbus Trust, under the chairmanship of the Rt Hon the Lord Butler of Saffron Walden. A full list of Trustees, of members of the various financial and advisory committees associated with the Trust, and of those who contributed to its funds, will be found in the earlier volumes. It would however be wrong not to mention again the massive donations made by Mr David Astor, by the late Lord Sieff of Brimpton and Sir Marcus Sieff, and by the Wolfson Foundation. It would be equally wrong not to mention that during the long period required for writing up the results Dr Sherwood financed herself; and I should like to pay tribute to the determination and devotion which have enabled her to carry the task to a successful conclusion.

During the planning and carrying-out of the fieldwork very substantial assistance was received from Miss Pearl King and

Professor Marie Jahoda. At a series of committee meetings Professor Max Beloff, Mr Nicholas Deakin and Dr Martin James contributed valuable suggestions. And I should like to associate myself, most emphatically, with Dr Sherwood's expression of gratitude to Dr Robert Gosling. Throughout the extraordinarily difficult enterprise which has borne fruit in this book, Dr Gosling has given most generously of his time and energy, and has never failed to provide expert guidance, constructive criticism and moral support as and when they were needed. As general editor of the books sponsored by the Columbus Centre, I am deeply indebted to him.

Norman Cohn
Director of the Columbus Centre,
University of Sussex, England.

FOREWORD

The making of assumptions about oneself and about others is ubiquitous; in this sense prejudice is endemic. Moreover there appear to be many factors at work that lead to these assumptions or stereotypes being fortified and generalized and to their being resistant to change even in the face of vivid experience. Some of these factors arise from within the individual himself, in his struggle to maintain his identity for instance; while others are engendered in consort with his human environment, the need to find a satisfying scapegoat being a well known example. Some of these factors are relatively stable, such as those arising from the impact of an individual's past experience or those that have become enshrined in legalized custom; while others are constantly changing, such as those arising from biological changes within the organism, the impact of current behaviour, or the shifting sands of shared attitudes and myths within the community. This dynamic field is daunting in its complexity; in the case of racial prejudice it is also daunting in its urgency.

There are many approaches to the study of this highly emotive field. They range, on the one hand, from those that attempt so far as possible to detoxify the subject and, as in a medical student's training, to dismember it in a deliberate and thoughtful way and so to control some of the variables that have so far been identified. When this approach leads to observations that can be replicated one of our major contemporary paradigms of science has been honoured and we draw apparently justified satisfaction from this fact alone. What the meaning or the relevance of our findings is for the practical affairs of men often remains obscure.

At the other end of the range are those studies that lay emphasis upon the simultaneous interaction of a large number of factors, known and unknown, that can best be appreciated, though certainly not measured, by immersing oneself in the dynamic field as deeply as possible. Such a method of study makes painfully obvious the shortcomings of the observer's conceptual equipment and even more the embarrassing flounderings of his own participation in a value-laden field, At best he can try to do some justice to the field of forces he is caught up in, rather in the manner of a clinical observer in an anxiety-ridden hospital setting or an ethologist on some rocky crag.

What such an observer has to tell us can all too easily be dismissed as unreliably subjective or too cramped by his working concepts, his preferred unconscious gestalts and his values, to say nothing of the way his field of observation is materially altered by his presence in it as an observer in a manner that cannot be identified with any certainty. But all these objections are a matter of degree and every methodological simplification carries with it its own distortion. Given some readiness on the part of the observer, however, to be transparent in the methods he is using so that the quality of his perceptiveness and his interpretations are readily betrayed, a document may be put into our hands of great import for the dilemmas that beset our society.

Rae Sherwood's study is an heroic effort in this latter tradition. The published text makes plain the dogged determination and the moral rigour that both she and her research assistant, Mrs Sylvia Hutchinson, have been able to call upon. As someone playing only a small part behind the scenes, I can only express my admiration. In so far as the part I have played, however, has contributed to the array of conceptual tools that Dr Sherwood has found herself using, I should both own my responsibility and in turn acknowledge my sources.

First of all I have been concerned to remember that the human mind from infancy onwards is replete with assumptions and more or less fixed ideas of both a good or idealizing kind as well as a bad or vilifying kind: the imagination is replete with both good fairies as well as grotesque monsters. An individual's evaluation of his experience, in addition to conscious and more or less rational considerations, cannot help but resonate to archaic residues of earlier experience that have long since been lost to consciousness. Falling in love, religious ardour and political idealism are as much dependent on splitting processes within the psyche as are blind rages that lead to murders within the family circle, the infamy of the Inquisition and the easy dismissal of those who oppose us as being less than human.

Sophisticated people who have read their Freud by their very knowingness are in danger of forgetting how ludicrous and horrifying and offensive some of the resonances are that none can escape. The dark night is still peopled with terrors. Excreta is still to be execrated. Food that is good for you and food that is bad is a distinction that is still so agitating that new rituals are for ever being established. It is therefore no help to contemplate evil prejudice without acknowledging its kinship with all that we believe is best in the world and that both of them have their roots in craziness.

From psychoanalytic studies, particularly those that have followed the stimulus of Melanie Klein's work, we have learned how the balance between self-love and love-of-another is in jeopardy from the earliest days of life. At one moment self-esteem demands that all others shall be denigrated; at the next it demands that the self be identified with a highly valued other or group of others; and finally, and sometimes only fleetingly, self-esteem is gained through the work of repairing or putting to rights what has in phantasy or in fact been wantonly damaged in the other by wilful expropriation or exploitation.

But who, one might ask, would have any sympathy for an individual who buys his self-esteem at the expense of another, or achieves it by being a parasite on someone else's achievements? Altruistic concern is surely a far more worthy pathway to self-respect. But, alas, what choice do we have in this matter? Some, perhaps. Yet I doubt if there is anyone who has not at some time found himself wondering if his own sanity or 'his society' is to be saved from falling apart, who is it he is going to hate? This is a horrifying question with horrifying implications. Only an idolator of social or psychological science could dismiss it as unnecessary or avoidable.

As these propensities within an individual are derived from the interpersonal experiences of an infant's upbringing, small wonder that group life as an adult is strewn with their manifestations. As, moreover, many of them were first lived through long before the child had developed the capacity for speech, it is again small wonder that as adults we are sensitive to messages from others and are skilled at informing others of our feelings far beyond what we have learned to say with our words or to hear with our ears. Groups are suffused with non-verbal communications that we have all practised unthinkingly from our earliest days.

The second source I wish to acknowledge, therefore, is that scattered band of psychotherapists who have interested themselves in the mutual influencing of members of long established small groups who have learned, often unconsciously, to play on each other with consummate skill, such as members of a marital dyad, or members of a nuclear family. It was Henry Dicks in his teaching and his book "Marital Tensions" who first brought home to me how much in an established married couple there was a sharing of internal objects (or ghosts), a mutually collusive enactment of shared unconscious preoccupations from the past and a system ideally suited for the operation of the intrapsychic processes of splitting and projection.

In my view one of the notable achievements of the author of the present book is that despite the ideological sway such emotional involvement makes inevitable, in her studies of individuals in their social contexts she has been able to hold on to the interactive processes of reciprocity, mirroring, collusion and so forth. In such a system there is no successful projection without a willing, or an eager, or at least an acquiescent receptacle, whether for the projection of good things or bad.

The other notable achievement, to my mind, is her beginning to chart the characteristics of what she has felicitously called benign and vicious spirals. I am sure that further study of the factors that promote these spirals or play a part in switching one into the other will prove both theoretically fruitful and socially invaluable.

R. Gosling
Consultant Psychotherapist and Chairman of the Professional Committee,
The Tavistock Clinic, London

ACKNOWLEDGEMENTS

The original idea for this research emanated from the Columbus Centre of the University of Sussex and I am grateful for the opportunity afforded me to undertake this project and for my association with the Centre.

To the Director of the Centre, Professor Norman Cohn, I am deeply indebted for his unwavering moral support, sustained interest and meticulous editorial guidance as well as for helpful comments on portions of the manuscript. I also wish to record my sincere appreciation to Professor Marie Jahoda and to Miss Pearl King, who, as Committee members of the Columbus Centre provided useful ideas in the early phase of the study. To Miss King, who thereafter served for a very short period as a part-time consultant to the project, I am happy to record my appreciation for her contribution to some of the early theoretical conceptions underlying aspects of the study.

But above all, my greatest single debt is to Dr Robert Gosling which I gladly take this opportunity of acknowledging. Despite heavy responsibilities as Chairman of the Professional Committee of the Tavistock Clinic, London, he always made time to study the manuscript and contribute important clarifications. He was supportive throughout and I am deeply grateful to him for adding to my grasp of aspects of the research and for creative ideas, generously shared.

I was most fortunate to have as my co-interviewer in the field, Sylvia Hutchinson, whose sensitive and skilled work contributed not only to the good relationships with subjects but also to the quality of the interview material with the adolescents. I owe a great deal to colleagues and friends who have been prepared to serve, on occasions, as my sounding boards and have been generous with time, guidance and criticism and would like to express my thanks to Rhona and Robert Rapoport, Anne Hayman, Selma Gillman, Maryann Phillips and Jean Stewart.

The task of analysing the material and writing this book was carried out over a long period and much of it was done without any financial backing. I could not possibly have completed this study without the practical help and generous assistance as well as the warm interest of Edward Sherwood, Evelyn and Felix Schiff, Jean and Harold Bernstein and my sons, Nicholas and John, all of whom I wish to thank.

The diagrams of the *spirals of prejudice* in the final chapter of the book were clarified and enhanced by the technical skill of John Sherwood. The preparation and checking of the manuscript was made much less of a chore with the help of Louise Harris and Susan Loppett. Mrs Sherry Zeffert worked patiently and most efficiently on the typing of the manuscript. To all of these I express my thanks.

A great debt is owed to the twelve subjects from the three families, all of whom must remain anonymous. I wish to express my deep thanks to each of them for their confidence, their generosity in giving so freely of their time and for their hospitality. It was a rich and rewarding experience to know them. It is my hope that their courage and openness in being prepared to share their deepest feelings and experiences may one day bear fruit in the shape of greater insight and tolerance between the races. Should this book in any way have offended them, or if I have inadvertently appeared to betray a trust, I ask their forgiveness.

And finally, a debt of gratitude is owed to the three National Health doctors in Athol who facilitated contact with these three families; they too must remain anonymous.

London   Rae Sherwood
October 1978

Chapter 1

PERSPECTIVES

This book is about the inner and outer worlds of race. We live in a world increasingly exposed to inflammatory racial issues but despite an extensive amount of important research on the psychology of race relationships, we have little insight into how ordinary people, living in racially mixed neighbourhoods come psychologically to use and to misuse people of other races as well as those of their own race and how, in turn, they too are used and misused by others. We know little of why these relationships take the forms which they do, or why they shift and change. We are also ignorant of the deeper functions these relationships serve to the individuals concerned and how the target racial groups so used and misused are affected. And yet, these are the vital issues affecting many who live in multi-racial areas where people of different races mutually experience each other, and each is also the object of the other's experience.

Little attempt has yet been made to explore in psychological depth the dynamic and changing patterns of inter-relationship between several racial groups where each is studied as intensively as the other, each in its own right, and their dynamic and reciprocal interplay elucidated. The psychological studies already done have either contributed to understanding the roots of prejudice,[1] or explored the consequences for those who have been its targets.[2] Most studies have concentrated separately on one of two contrasting groups: either those known to be prejudiced against specific groups and seen as the persecutors, or those racial groups who are identified as the victims. What seems to be lacking is an exploration in depth of the ways in which ordinary people of different races, who share a common neighbourhood, come to feel about each other, both consciously and unconsciously, and in the process the use and misuse made by each group of the other.

There are also very few studies which look at the psychological unfolding of racial feelings and attitudes among ordinary people of different races, people who are neither undergoing psychotherapy nor those who have been especially selected for their known views

1

on race. We know little of the personal events and inter-racial experiences which have occurred in the lives of others and the meanings, both conscious and unconscious which these have for them. People of all races tend to assume that what seems real and convincing to them is also real to other racial groups. This is not necessarily so. But we are even more ignorant when it comes to examining the incessantly reciprocal interplay *between* racial groups where individuals and groups not only perceive each other differently but in the process affect each other in perpetual spirals of interaction.

Although such ideas of mutual interaction have not yet been applied to the empirical study of race relations, these ideas are not new and have been used to explore processes at work in a variety of other settings. In trying to understand both marital happiness as well as marital discords, for instance, the relationship between the partners has been looked at not only from the point of view of each party, but it has included their dynamic interaction and those normal processes, both conscious and unconscious, which are at work between them.[3] Each may be seen, for example, to project into the other feelings which are painful to tolerate as part of the self; sometimes these are experienced as the less worthy or even deplorable parts of the person and are attributed to the partner. But in other cases, these may be positive and good aspects which the individual feels unable to claim as belonging to the self because self-esteem has been severely undermined. These qualities are kept alive by being put into the partner by the unconscious process of projection. Partners can unconsciously combine with such an interplay between them, colluding with what may be going on under the surface while consciously denying it. These processes may move and change but also, under certain conditions, they may remain rigidly fixed.

In more strictly controlled contexts too, these same ideas of unconscious interactive processes have also been explored. Laboratory experiments[4] for instance, have shown how behaviour or attitudes which experimenters may expect from others, and unconsciously predict, can operate silently and subtly to convey hidden expectancies which potently affect the behaviour and achievements of others. If each subject had been studied solely as an individual unit, the dynamic, interactive effects of the experimenter's covert attitudes and expectations would have been overlooked and a partial and distorted picture obtained.

In each of these settings the task for the researcher has been a dual one: to study the individual in his own right, from his own centre looking out on his world, and also to explore him as a person in the world of the other, picking up the feelings of both about each other and how these impinge in both conscious and unconscious ways. The inner world of each is affected, which in turn generates chains of reaction.

In the relations between racial groups, where passionate and powerful currents of feeling are resonated, empirical studies are lacking on this interface between the groups. A dynamic, interactive model is used in this book to throw light on how racial groups, sharing a common neighbourhood, come to use and to misuse each other. The point of view taken here is that throughout development we all unconsciously use a variety of social groups in various socially acceptable ways to serve different, normal developmental functions. This is as true of individuals growing up in racially and culturally homogeneous communities as of those who live in racially mixed communities. For all of us, social groups (such as social class, religious, racial, ethnic, occupational, as well as informally constituted groups which local lore may designate 'goodies' or 'baddies', 'drop-outs' etc.) serve as ways of differentiating and distinguishing between people and their characteristics and these, in turn, enable an individual to locate and identify himself in relation to others. This is part of the process of identity development, a sorting-out and categorizing process. But groups also serve in other more dynamic ways. For all of us at times, there are aspects of reality which arouse feelings of conflict and anxiety, and at such times social groups can be misused as *repositories* for aspects of the self which are felt to be too painful to face. By the process of projection, by which aspects of the self are unconsciously attributed to other groups and then imagined to be located in these groups, the individual seeks a way out from experiencing painful and deep inner conflicts. Some of this may be socially sanctioned by one's social groups, for prejudice, as we know, is unfortunately a universal human experience.

Racial groups, while sharing in common with other social groups the general features already mentioned, have certain distinctive aspects which make them more especially seductive as repositories for individuals experiencing such conflicts. It is the task of this book to clarify what these issues are which make racial groups especially inviting and vulnerable to the use and misuse by others of different races.

Before proceeding further, I wish to clarify how I am using the words *racial use* and *misuse*. By *racial use*, I mean the fleeting and transitory functions served by racial groups as repositories, which, while affording an individual a temporary safety valve providing a breathing pause, does not in any way harm the group used. By *racial misuse*, I refer to all those forms of biased and harmfully pre-conceived judgements about racial groups which deny the in-dividuals in the group their rightful identity. Racial misuse covers all those instances where the group is used as a repository for denied, disallowed and negative aspects of the self but it also includes those instances where the group is used to keep alive idealized, 'perfect' qualities. Where individuals are unable to hold onto anything good inside themselves, by putting these into a racial group the individual is able to keep in touch with these qualities while distancing them beyond his present reach. All of these projections, both the negative and the idealized ones, act as impingements on the target racial groups, infringing the sense of identity of members of these groups. In all these cases the racial group is *being misused*.

Living within a quarter-mile radius of each other, in the same densely crowded, multi-racial neighbourhood in London are an English family, whose roots in this part of London extend back through two generations, and two coloured immigrant families, one West Indian and the other Indian.[5] This book is a study of two generations in each of these families, mother, father and two adolescent children. It explores microscopically, and in depth, the personality dynamics of these twelve people and traces through the intricate pattern of their life stories how each has become the person he or she is, their perceptions, feelings and phantasies about people of other races and those of their own race, and the interactive spirals of use and misuse which move incessantly between the three groups. No empirical generalizations are advanced in this book about *the* English family, or *the* West Indian, or *the* Indian family. In no sense are these three families considered a representative sample of their respective groups. In the following chapter who the families are and how they were contacted is dealt with as part of a full discussion on the field approach adopted and the methodological issues connected with the study.

The method chosen for the study involves the detailed analysis of unstructured life history interviews collected over a considerable period. The twelve life stories to which these interviews gave rise throw light on the human experiences of the subjects in relation to race and are intrinsically valuable in their own right. These appear in Chapters 3, 4 and 5. Nonetheless, it is largely in the use made of this material and the conceptual approach adopted for its analysis that the contribution of this book must lie. Clearly, the book is unable to answer questions as to how general or atypical the attitudes or experiences of these individuals may be. The scope of the study and the questions it raises are of quite a different order. They arise from an attempt to throw new light on the underlying psychodynamic and psychological processes which are at work in the interactive spirals of relationships between these people of different races. The same kind of study could have been undertaken on any family, from any social-class background, and with any set of beliefs with regard to race. It should be emphasised that the families were not chosen because of their known views on race; their attitudes and experiences were completely unknown in advance of the study and were, in any case, of no relevance in their *selection* for the study. How they came to develop their attitudes and to be the people they are, and how race figures in their inner and outer lives, these are the concerns of this book.

It is, of course, possible to analyse the relations between racial groups from this chosen interactive point of view at any time in the life-cycle. The psychological and social processes which are involved by which one racial group humanizes or dehumanizes another are continuing processes. Studies on crises, however, have shown that whether these arise from broad social and environmental sources as in migration, social mobility or economic depression,[6] or from normal developmental transitions in the life cycle,[7] or from loss or bereavement,[8] they provide a valuable vantage point for the investigation of ways in which people mobilize their anxieties and defences in the face of stress. Crises can act as challenges and spurs to the constructive and creative mobilization of latent resources which increase an individual's capacity to deal with reality and to value his own worth and that of others. On the other hand, they can also go the other way and push the individual back on less mature ways of coping, involving the use of various defence-mechanisms such as projection, introjection (the process by which aspects of others are taken into the self) and scapegoating.

The context of this study explores individuals within families who are under the pressure of various normal and predictable forms of stress, in order to throw into relief how anxiety is handled in relation to race. By selecting families with two adolescents, not only can the potentially turbulent stage of adolescence be explored but also the parents can be observed struggling with a wide range of inner conflicts and interpersonal problems thrown up by their mid-life crisis.[9] In these ways, normal developmental transitions which we all experience are built into the study and the subjects' reactions to these are explored, especially in relation to the use and misuse of racial groups.

There are other sources of stress encompassed within the net of the study by virtue of having chosen indigenous English, as well as immigrants, as subjects. Little is known of how the impact of immigration affects the anxieties and ways of trying to keep emotionally secure of the uprooted. There is also little information concerning the psychological impact of coloured immigrants on English members of this society.

Migration is certainly a stressful experience involving the loss of a home and the search for a new one. The relinquishing of their country was a decision taken for different reasons by both the West Indian and the Indian father. By uprooting themselves, they stretched themselves away from all that previously bound them to their early beginnings and the familiar faces of their past. Once embarked on the transition from one society to another, from one home to another, each of the immigrants in their personal ways experienced stress arising from the break in continuity of their habitual life patterns. In the process of beginning again, each of the immigrants brought with them phantasies and hopes for what each might become and realize in themselves. These colour and distort the windows through which each looks at the new society and the racial groups within it.

But what of the indigenous English? Certainly the particular English family analysed in this study feels uprooted. Instead of leaving their roots behind them as the immigrants have done, they have stayed in the same place while familiar aspects of their neighbourhood, their psychological tap-roots, have been changing around them as the steady influx of immigrants with different cultural patterns has made them feel loss and dismay, a sense of being impinged upon and invaded. Their phantasies and longings are trapped in the community as they knew it before it changed, and what they take forward with them are altered hopes, disappointments and feelings of frustration. The close confrontation between different groups has threatened their view of life and their sense of who they feel themselves to be.

The research context of this study therefore focusses on interactions between the races when people are under the pressure of various forms of stress. Taking individuals in families as the unit of study rather than isolated individuals is also intrinsic to the approach adopted. It is in the family that an individual acquires his attitudes and values and the family is the matrix within which the most fundamental relationships leave their mark upon later personality development and growth. It is also in the family that individuals develop their early feelings in regard to their racial identity. Family members reflect to the growing child the wider patterns of racial feelings, both conscious and unconscious, which reverberate in their society. A young child even before becoming aware of his race, picks up and responds to the tensions or doubts, or the feelings of pride and self-esteem which the parents feel in relation to their race. Race relations, in common with other forms of early learning, are communicated to each generation at the 'gut' level – a deep sense of being at peace, or feeling uneasy about oneself, one's body and one's own race, which, in turn, affects feelings towards other races as well.

Studying individuals in the context of the family enables processes to be traced as they move both from the family towards the neighbourhood and *vice versa*. Neighbourhood tensions or excitements between the races may intrude into the heart of the family and there affect the inner pattern of relationships between family members. Conversely, what originates within a family in the shape of unresolved problems in family relationships may generate more tension than is manageable within the confines of the family and these can then spill over into the racial area. These fluid intrusions and extrusions, into and out of the family, open up additional ways of looking at inter-racial patterns and their dynamics.

Having adopted a dynamic and interactive point of view for the study, and taking the reciprocity and circularity of the process seriously, there is always a question of where in the continuous process to start. There are points for and against any choice. Furthermore, the process is an exceedingly complex one as between individuals and families within the same racial group, between an individual and diverse individual members of other racial groups, and between an individual and his racial group as a whole.

In this study the formation of an individual's sense of his own *identity* and the impediments that lie in his path in doing so has indicated the point of entry, because a key concept chosen for exploring the racial interface is that of identity conflicts. Previous theoretical work suggests that there is a link between *unresolved identity conflicts* and racial prejudice and hostility,[10] but how exactly these are connected or how generally they may occur is unclear. It seemed fruitful to use unresolved identity conflicts as a major analytical tool to explore in depth how these might relate to the use and misuse of racial groups, and how, as part of an interactive spiral, such use and misuse of target racial groups might, in turn, affect *their* unresolved identity conflicts.

Identity is not a neatly definable concept and different writers have approached it in various ways.[11] Erikson's usage is the one followed here.[12] This focusses on what people's lives mean to them, and deals with the life-long processes by which a person comes to feel not only who he is but also what he can do with his inner resources. Since much of our deeper nature is unconscious, identity not only includes the hidden forces which underlie our defences but because people are influenced to think about themselves in the light of how others who are relevant to them relate to them, it cannot be fully understood without reference to social relationships. Conscious and unconscious communications, conveyed directly and indirectly by others, play a vital role in determining an individual's sense of identity. Furthermore the individual's role and position within various groups and social structures also bear on identity development, as do changing political and social events.

Identity conflicts are a necessary and normal part of each individual's development and from adolescence onwards and throughout the life cycle, we all confront a variety of such conflicts. These conflicts are viewed as the high spots in the continuing processes of everyday life. In facing the changing inner and outer tasks which steadily confront us, we repeatedly re-anchor and re-clarify our identity although we may not be fully aware of doing so. Some of these conflicts are especially intense and are of major importance to the individual, while others may press upon the individual with less insistence and be less critical in terms of further development. But all of these unresolved identity conflicts are seen as constituting particularly vulnerable areas within the personality.

In each of three chapters (Chapters 7, 8 and 9) the detailed analysis of current unresolved identity conflicts among the four members of each family is presented, these being looked at as part of the total patterning of each individual life. From these analyses, a striking relationship emerges between unresolved identity conflicts and patterns of racial misuse. Why one race rather than another is chosen for the unconscious working through of these conflicts, and what each person would have to face in himself if he did not resort to the misuse of race are both explored.

Since it is identity which each of us brings to our encounters with other racial groups, the study suggests that some individuals, when hurt or angered, respond in ways which further inflame and exacerbate racial tensions, so becoming caught up in and perpetuating behaviour of a *vicious spiral* type, characterized by mounting intolerance and escalating hostility; while others manage to deal with their hurt and anger by setting in motion constructive behaviour constituting *benign or virtuous spirals*. These inter-racial encounters have a developmental character arising from the inter-action. Vicious spirals produce self-perpetuating cycles of behaviour and response which are likely to take fixed and rigid forms which increasingly lie out of the range of reality-testing, whereas benign spirals progressively feed goodwill and mutual respect, and are open to reality-testing.

Present knowledge suggests that most of us have some degree of racial prejudice which can be evoked in certain circumstances and also that most of us have areas where our sense of racial identity has been bruised or irreparably damaged. Why is it then that some individuals are able to set in motion benign cycles and others only vicious ones and what are the factors at work to make for such crucial differences in inter-racial behaviour? Furthermore, why is it that some individuals when caught up in inter-racial encounters which are potentially destructive are able to switch them around into benign cycles while others implacably act to shift the potentially benign into the destructive? The final chapter, Chapter 10, takes up these issues and examines them in detail.

It is also in the final chapter that the general theoretical processes, accounting for the reciprocal and interactive nature of race relationships, is conceptually depicted as a spiral and a theoretical model is developed showing how the ferment of unresolved identity conflicts in interaction with a range of important social, psychological and environmental *activators* and *constraints*, either propels people towards racial misuse and prejudice, or constrains them from doing so. Specifically what these activators and constraints are and how they interact with these unresolved identity conflicts is dealt with in depth. Chapter 10 pulls together the main theoretical findings of the book and considers their implications for an understanding of racial prejudice.

BIBLIOGRAPHY AND NOTES

1 Allport, G. W. *The Nature of Prejudice*, Doubleday, New York (1958); Kris, E. 'Roots of hostility and prejudice', in *The Family in a Democratic Society: Anniversary Papers of the Community Service Society of New York*, Columbia University Press, New York (1949); Ackerman, N. W. and Jahoda, M. *Anti-Semitism and Emotional Disorders: A Psychoanalytic Interpretation*, Harper & Row, New York (1950); Adorno, T. W., Frenkel-Brunswick, E., Levinson,

D. J. and Sanford, R. N. *The Authoritarian Personality*, Harper & Row, New York (1950); Jahoda, M. *Race Relations and Mental Health*, UNESCO, Paris (1960); Reiser, N. 'On origins of hatred toward negroes', *American Imago*, 18 (1961), 167–172; Bettelheim, B. and Janowitz, M. *Social Change and Prejudice*, Free Press, New York (1964); Wangh, M. 'National socialism and the genocide of the jews', *International Journal of Psychoanalysis*, 45 (1964), 386–395; Kubie, L. S. 'The Ontology of prejudice', *Journal of Nervous and Mental Disorders*, 141 (1965), 265–273; Hamilton, J. W. 'Some dynamics of anti-negro prejudice, *Psycho. Anal. Review*, (1966), 5–15; McDonald, M. *Not By the Colour of Their Skin*, International Universities Press, New York (1970); Katz, P. (ed) *Towards the Elimination of Racism*. Pergamon, Oxford (1976).

2 Dollard, J. *Caste and Class in a Southern Town*, Harper & Row, New York (1937); Davis, A. and Dollard, J. *Children of Bondage: The Personality Development of Negro Youth in the Urban South*, American Council on Education/Harper & Row, New York (1964); Kardiner, A. and Ovesey, L. *The Mark of Oppression: A Psychosocial Study of the American Negro*. Norton, New York (1951); Coles, R. *Children of Crisis*, Little, Brown, Boston (1964); de Vos, G. and Wagatsuma, H. *Japan's Invisible Race*, University of California Press, Berkeley and Los Angeles (1966); Fanon, F. *Black Skin, White Masks: The Experience of a Black Man in a White World*, Grove Press, New York (1967); McDonald, M. *Not By the Colour of Their Skin*, International Universities Press, New York (1970).

3 Pincus, L. (ed) *Marriage: Studies in Emotional Conflict and Growth*, Methuen, London (1960); Family Discussion Bureau, *The Marital Relationship as a focus of Casework*, Codicote Press, London (1962); Laing, R. D. and Esterson, A. *Sanity, Madness and the Family*, Penguin, Harmondsworth (1970).

4 Rosenthal, R. *Experimenter Effects in Behavioral Research*, Appleton-Century Crofts, New York (1966); Friedman, N. *The Social Nature of Psychological Research: The Psychological Experiment as a Social Interaction*, Basic Books, New York (1967).

5 The community, which I have named Athol, has a high density of immigrants, West Indian, Indian and Pakistani, as well as an indigenous English population. Workers are largely semi-skilled and skilled and the social class of all three families was gauged to be roughly equivalent in terms of occupational status of parents, and general socio-economic standards, although the placing of immigrant families within the social class structure of modern English cities is, at best, an arbitrary and inaccurate judgement aggravated by the fact that their original social class positions within their countries of origin cannot easily be equated.

6 Fried, M. *The World of the Urban Working Class*, Harvard University Press, Cambridge, Mass. (1973); Marris, P. *Loss and Change*. Routledge & Kegan Paul, London (1974).

7 Erikson, E. H. 'Identity and the life cycle' *Psychological Issues*. 1. (1959), 1; Rapoport, R. 'Normal crises, family structure and mental health', *Family Process*, 2 (1963), 1; Rapoport, R., Rapoport, R. N. and Strelitz, Z. *Fathers, Mothers and Others*, Routledge & Kegan Paul, London (1977).

8 Pincus, L. *Death and the Family: The Importance of Mourning*, Faber & Faber, London (1976).

9 Jaques, E. 'Death and the midlife crisis', *International Journal of Psycho-analysis*,

46, (1965), Part 4, 502–514; Neugarten, B. *Middle Age and Aging*, University of Chicago Press, Chicago (1968); Levinson, D. K. 'Middle adulthood in modern society: a socio-psychological view' in DiRenzo, G. (ed) *Social Character and Social Change*, Greenwood, Westport (1976).

10 Jahoda, M. *Race Relations and Mental Health*, UNESCO, Paris (1960); Dicks, H. V. *Licensed Mass Murder*, Sussex University Press/Heinemann, London (1972); Erikson, Erik H. *Identity: Youth and Crisis*, Faber & Faber, London (1968); Bettelheim, B. and Janowitz, M. *Social Change and Prejudice*, Free Press, New York (1964).

11 Abend, S. M. 'Problems of identity', *Psychoanalytic Quarterly*, XLIII (1974), No. 4, 606–637; Greenacre, P. 'Early physical determinants in the development of the sense of identity', *Journal of the American Psychoanalytical Association*, 6 (1958),612–627; Strauss, A. *Mirrors and Masks: The Search for Identiy*, Free Press, Glencoe, Ill. (1959); Rainwater, L. 'Crucible of identity: the negro lower class family' in Handel, G. (ed) *The Psychosocial Interior of the Family* (1966); Jacobson, E. *The Self and the Object World*, International Universities Press, New York (1964).

12 Erikson, E. H. 'Identity and the life cycle', *Psychological Issues*, 1 (1959), 1; Erikson, E. H. *Identity: Youth and Crisis*, Faber & Faber, London (1968); Erikson, E. H. 'Psychoanalysis and ongoing history: problems of identity, hatred and nonviolence'. *American Journal of Psychiatry*, 122 (1965), 241–250; Erikson, E. H. 'The concept of identity in race relations: notes and queries', *Daedalus*, 95 (1966), 145–171; Erikson, E. H. 'Autobiographic notes on the identity crisis', *Daedalus* (1970) Fall, 730–759.

Chapter 2

METHODOLOGY AND FIELD APPROACH

Research methods must be appropriately chosen for the type of problem under investigation. How did the research objectives described in the first chapter guide the choice of research method and help to determine the field approach?

Since the aim of the study is a complex one and is about inner worlds and social contexts in relation to race, to pursue the aim it is necessary to disclose the inner reality which each person experiences. It is basic to our approach therefore that the focus be on the whole individual rather than on specific attitudes or attributes of people treated as isolated variables. Equally important is the requirement that whatever research method is chosen it should be capable of producing data which throw light on both conscious and unconscious processes, and that each individual should be studied both within the context of the family and within his cultural, social and broadly historical contexts.

By focussing on the whole individual, two different objectives of the study are facilitated: firstly, racial attitudes and experiences can be appraised as a part of each person, and their salience, intensity and importance within the total personality become capable of assessment; secondly, the relationship between different parts of the whole personality can be investigated, notably identity processes and unresolved identity conflicts on the one hand, and racial attitudes and ways of using and misusing racial groups on the other.[1]

For these reasons the most appropriate method seemed to be a series of unstructured life history interviews constituting case studies on each of the twelve subjects. In the fields of psychology and psychiatry, the intensive study of the individual has had an important place. Gordon Allport argued most persuasively in the early 1960s that psychological research should be concerned with the unique features that distinguish each man from his fellows.

> Why should we not start with individual behaviour as a science of hunches (as we have in the past) and then seek out generalisations (also as we have in the past) but finally come

12

back to the individual, not for the mechanical application of laws (as we do now) but for a fuller and more accurate assessment than we are now able to give?[2]

And recently Liam Hudson has urged psychologists to look at 'the way people think and the way they run their personal lives. Quite simply, I think one should look at what matters to people in life and illuminate that and eventually help refine it too'.[3]

Unstructured life history interviews were chosen as the method for studying individuals of different racial groups, so that the research material yielded could be looked at both at the conscious surface level and in order to provide insights into the unconscious motivations and defences.

Essentially the study is a naturalistic one in that feelings and attitudes are not deliberately contrived nor studied within the artificial settings and constraints of a laboratory, clinic, classroom or university. On the contrary, people are studied within the familiar surroundings of their own homes. Despite an increasing emphasis by some psychologists on the need to study social-psychological phenomena in their natural settings and with a minimum of control or manipulation, the proportion of field studies of any kind in psychology is exceedingly small.[4,5] This study joins that small group.

Taken together, the decision to study people within their own social settings, and also to use unstructured interviews as the research tool, possessed certain advantages. By going to people where they live, and entering their homes, families and personal space, and at the same time ensuring by the choice of method that respondents are given maximum freedom to talk about whatever they wish, in their own time and in their own ways, important attitudes are being implicitly communicated: firstly, that the researchers see and recognize some of the dimensions of their social world as an intrinsic part of them; secondly, respondents are able to feel valued as individuals in that they are free to talk about their life experiences in their chosen ways. This combination facilitates the development of relationships in the field and increases the possibilities for fruitful research. In addition, that which is being researched, is minimally altered or modified by these research methods, although, as I discuss later in this chapter, all research relationships and every research method affects and modifies human behaviour which is under study. It is all a matter of direction and degree.

The study is seen as an initial exploration of issues at the forward edge of established lines of enquiry, so that fresh ways of thinking about questions may be generated and new hypotheses advanced. It is hoped that these, in turn, may stimulate others to conduct further studies, using more systematic and rigorous techniques in order to refine or refute the findings of this study. But that which emerges from such a second stage of the research process should ideally also later be re-scrutinized and explored within real-life settings within the field. This study has of course built on a great deal of work which has gone before, but it also represents a fresh beginning.

Essentially the concern of the book is with ordinary people and with the normal range of everyday feelings. A great deal of our understanding of the psychology of race relationships has been derived from the study of people who have extreme views on race, or have been exposed to known degrees of racial discrimination. The subjects in this book are not selected on these grounds. Much previous research has also concentrated on 'captive' groups, such as school children, university students or patients undergoing psychotherapy. By contrast this study is based on ordinary city-dwellers who willingly agreed to become subjects of the enquiry.

Because of the complex and interlocking processes which are under analysis and the need to work microscopically and in depth, the study necessarily had to be on a small scale. It was decided to focus on three families, one from each of the major racial groups in Athol, namely English, West Indian and Indian, and within each family to study both parents and two adolescent children, one to be at school and one at work, and the two to be of opposite sex. This brought the number of subjects to be studied to twelve individuals, comprising three racial groups, two generations and both sexes.

Hudson has recently put the case for very small samples which allow for study in depth, noting that

> most of science has been based on the particular study of the particular . . . and the most influential psychology has been based on tiny samples – like Freud and Piaget. Skinner himself uses tiny numbers. I would like us to go back to the idea of building up our samples, from individual studies, one at a time – to understanding the integration of forces within each individual life, because what can be said about large numbers of people, considered as a whole, is usually rather trivial.[6]

Our sample can be said to be both very small but also overwhelmingly large in relation to the volume of interview material it was to produce, the microscopic analysis attempted and the complexity of the interactive processes to be given conceptual shape.[7]

THE FIELD APPROACH

The research team

Psychological research with human subjects always involves a social interaction between researchers and their respondents. This is so whether the research setting is a laboratory, an analyst's couch or field conditions such as those in our study. The impressive research studies of Rosenthal and also of Friedman[8] have demonstrated that research findings are modified by the interpersonal nature of these relationships: even under rigorously controlled conditions, as in laboratory experiments and despite pre-suppositions to the contrary, there are experimenter effects which are unintended, frequently remain unrecognized and yet potently affect the research data. This is of course, equally true of all other psychological research methods.

This interactive process between researcher and respondent has been taken seriously in this study. In order to examine the nature of the interactive process between our subjects and the interviewers, I will first discuss who we are and our general orientation, then move to consider the criteria for the selection of families, how contact was initially made and who our subjects are, and finally proceed to discuss field procedures and the research method in the light of the relationships between interviewers and subjects.

Before deciding on the composition of the field research team, a decision was reached in relation to the race of the interviewers. There are two possibilities: either to attempt to match race of respondents to race of interviewers and so recruit and train a team of three pairs of interviewers, equivalent in skill, experience, personality and style of approach, or to use the same interviewers with all three families, recognizing that for two of those families there would be cross-racial – and hence cross-cultural – combinations of interviewers and respondents. The second alternative was chosen. There are of course evident advantages and disadvantages in either course but the course adopted provided the best opportunity, in our view, of selecting an experienced pair of interviewers who could be sensitive to the large range of ways in which they influence and affect the research results, of which race would only be one variable, however important.

As the senior psychologist in charge of the project and having considerable experience in psychodynamic and cross-cultural research, I was familiar with the issues and problems involved in working within the sensitive area of inter-racial studies. I naturally chose to be one of the two interviewers in the field. It seemed desirable to divide the interviewing in each family along generation lines, and being middle-aged myself, I decided that I would interview the three pairs of parents. The adolescents required a younger interviewer and Sylvia Hutchinson joined the team and subsequently interviewed all the adolescents. Although near the beginning of her research career, nonetheless she also had experience of working on a cross-cultural study.

The fact that both interviewers were female, white and middle-class meant that even before we communicated with our subjects, we would be perceived as all of these things. Each of these factors adds its own weight to the relationships and modifies the types of responses. There is of course, no norm or ideal solution to this problem. If we were male, black and working-class, that too would affect outcome. There is no way of defining the researcher out of the study – we exist – and some of us have different characteristics from others. What matters is that these should be consciously recognized as the attributes which we presented to our subjects throughout the study and to note the implications. Other highly relevant attributes relate to personality and personal style; in general, both of us tend to relate to people in ways which could be described as friendly and informal rather than stiff and formal, and we also belong at the 'warm' end of the continuum 'cold to warm' in our personal styles of relating to respondents. Although by no means sought as a criterion of selection, nonetheless neither of us was born or educated in this country,[9] so our accents had the advantage that, while not obviously revealing that we were not English (except to trained ears), they made it difficult to place us within a specific regional area of the country or within any very specific social class—although, by virtue of our roles as scientists, we were seen as upper middle class by our respondents.

The selection of the families
Who are the three families and how did they come to be studied? Certain criteria guided our selection. At the racial level (and at the ethnic level) we sought a family from each of the three racial groups – the indigenous English, the West Indians and the Indians. Both of the parents in the English family were required to be English and not Irish, Scots or Welsh, to have been born in London, and to have roots in the neighbourhood of Athol where the study was to be done. We did not wish to study very recent immigrants, to allow time

for the interlocking patterns to be discernible and also to avoid the possibility of language difficulties, particularly within the Asian family. So we sought immigrant families who had lived in England for some eight to twelve years. One of the primary criteria for selection was that each family should contain two adolescents who should be the biological offspring of these particular parents. Although we could not, of course, ensure in advance that members of such families as might be chosen would not in the course of the study reveal psychological or social pathologies, nonetheless we decided to exclude families known in advance to have any members in psychiatric treatment or to be under the surveillance of the social service departments. At the social class level, the families to be selected should be roughly equivalent in social status and to be drawn from the ranks of skilled workers.

Having chosen the neighbourhood of Athol and established our criteria, how were such families to be located and approached? We experimented for some months with trial runs using various contact approaches, none of which were satisfactory. If we had used schools to help us locate families with two adolescents, for example, we would then have been seen by the subjects as having some kind of link with the existing school system, and since we were aware that immigrant families especially might have strong feelings about schools and about certain aspects of the educational system we at all costs wished to avoid such an association. Through personal contacts and networks we also tried to find families who might meet our criteria, but this proved difficult and our relationships with such individuals were influenced by the type of personal network through which we had located the family in the first place. We even started knocking on doors to find families but quickly abandoned that method of approach.

Finally, I wrote a letter to every doctor working within the National Health Service in Athol, describing the scope of research financed by the Columbus Trust at the University of Sussex, indicating my position on its staff and the Trust's concern with research into the causes of man's inhumanity to man. In the letter I briefly indicated that we wished to study some psychological and social patterns among the indigenous English and among minority groups and hoped to locate a small number of families in each of these three groups. I asked whether they might be interested to spare some time to meet me personally in order to discuss the project, in the hope that they might assist us in introducing suitable families. The response to the letter was small but gratifying in the genuine interest aroused, and in the research experience and research orientations of the doctors who replied, six of whom I subsequently met. I explained the study to each doctor, and asked whether among his patients there were families which met the basic criteria outlined above. I also requested that, should such a family come to visit the doctor in the near future, he should tell them we were going to study a few families, vouch for our *bona fides* as scientists of integrity, and ask whether they would be prepared to receive us both by appointment? If the answer was affirmative, we would then discuss with the family what we proposed to do and ascertain whether they would like to take part or not. It was made clear to the doctors that they were a means of *contacting* relevant families, and ensuring that such families knew something of our professional affiliations and standing, but that this in no way committed the family to participation. Several of the doctors kindly offered to help in this way.

Within the space of two months, one doctor sent us the name and address of a West Indian family who were willing to have us contact them with a view to making an appointment to visit them one evening; later a different doctor sent us an Indian family's name and address, followed by a third doctor who supplied us with the name and address of an English family.

Initial approach

The next move was to write to the family concerned, mentioning the contact doctor's name and asking whether we could call and meet with all four potential subjects by appointment. We stressed that this was no more than an opportunity to meet them and tell them about ourselves and what we were doing, and that there was no commitment whatsoever on their side beyond receiving us.

In all three cases appointments were made to meet at their homes in the evening, where on each occasion we spent approximately two hours discussing what we were doing and what would be involved for each of them if they chose to come into the study. (See Appendix I for the notes used to guide us informally and flexibly in these contact interviews). Since the commitment of time, psychic energy and efforts on all our parts was to be a considerable one and to extend over a considerable time, it was vital that each one of the family members should individually decide whether he or she wished to join the project. Throughout the discussion we tried to involve the adolescents as much as we sought to involve their parents. We made it easier for the members of the family to refuse participation than to accept it in order to ensure, that if they accepted, it would be a deeply thought-through commitment which would not be abandoned lightly. We therefore preferred that they should not commit themselves on that same evening. We contacted them after a day had elapsed in order to learn of their decision.

The only families which Mrs Hutchinson and I approached were these three families and after reflection and discussion each one accepted and came into the study. It is about these three families that this book is written.

Introducing the families
The three families are only briefly introduced here. In each of the next three chapters, the four verbatim edited life histories of the members of each of these three families are presented so the reader can form his own impressions of the subjects from their first-hand accounts. Following after these chapters, the next four chapters (Chapters 6, 7, 8 and 9) are devoted to the analysis of this material and to the theoretical findings.

To protect the anonymity of the subjects, each family chose new names.

The West Indian family.   Frederick James, his wife Geraldine, their daughter Johanna (aged 18) and their son Adrian (aged 15), come from Barbados. Mr James is a bus driver with London Transport, his wife a machine operator in a small sweet factory, Johanna a secretary receptionist to a large group medical practice in the West End and Adrian is at school. Mr James came to this country in 1958, followed some nine months later by his wife. Johanna, aged 6 and Adrian aged 2, stayed in Barbados with their paternal grandmother. Johanna rejoined the family when she was 13 years old, while Adrian came five years later than his sister, when he was 15. The family have twins who are under two years of age.

The English family.   Charles Chattaway, a foreman fitter and welder, his wife Rebecca, a housewife who does some part-time cleaning in the evenings, their son John (aged 18) an apprentice gas-fitter and their daughter Elaine (aged 15) who is still at school. The family has lived in Athol for the past eight years and Mrs Chattaway's mother has lived in Athol for many years. Both the Chattaways were born in London and in addition to John and Elaine they have a small son of three.

The Indian family.   Mr Baldev Singh, superintendent of technical supplies for an airline company, a Sikh from India, his wife Tara, a housewife from Delhi, their daughter Vera (aged 18) a teller in a bank, and their son Eric (aged 14) who is still at school. Mr Singh came to England in 1953, his wife followed four years later, bringing with her their young daughter Vera, who was born shortly after her father left for this country. Eric was born in England. In addition to the two adolescents they have three other children, the youngest of whom is five.

It will be clear from all that has been said above about how these families were chosen, that in no sense were they intended to be, nor are they a representative sample of their respective racial groups.

Why the families came into the study
We are often asked why the families agreed to participate in this study. It is an important question and several reasons suggest themselves as to why they initially decided to say 'yes'. (Once the study began, of course, other satisfactions accruing from the developing relationships with the interviewers and the research task added further sources of satisfaction, to be discussed later).

Firstly, our initial contact with the families had come through their doctors and facilitated a solid, professional introduction. We came with status, partly our own as scientists – vouched for by their doctors – and our association with the University of Sussex, but also the doctor's status had, by association, also rubbed off on us. Our method of approach, stressing the privacy of relationships, the confidentiality of the material and the anonymity of respondents made a good fit with some of the ethics of the doctor–patient relationship. This, I believe, afforded some sense of security to the family from the outset.

Secondly, at the time of the initial contact interview, a personal relationship between both the interviewers and the four members of the family was initiated and their decision may have been in part prompted by the desire to continue this relationship.

Thirdly, I believe that the relative isolation of families living in large metropolitan cities, not only in this country but in the Western world generally, is such that no one has much time to 'tell it as it is', nor to find good listeners with time and inclination to care enough about *this* individual and to be interested in what he may wish to tell. The invitation to talk freely about their lives, feelings and experiences, without interruptions, comments or criticisms and the absence of explicit and prominent value judgements on our parts, could have been a potent motivation.

Fourthly, to be asked to join a study focussed on the life experiences and feelings of family members recognizes and bestows on each member a sense of being valued and of having intrinsically something of importance to contribute.

Finally, by focussing on the life experiences of family members, it recognizes not only the individual but the importance of the family and so supports in-group or family narcissism.

While all or some of these motivations could be generally shared by all three families, the immigrant families might have come into the study for reasons specific to their situation within the country. To be able to address the host society through the medium of this study (they all knew a book would be the final outcome of the project) allowed them to share their minority experiences in a way otherwise not ordinarily available to them. Since we were seen as representing the host society, by talking to us they were communicating aspects of their inter-racial experience to the English.

Field procedures

Within the familiar confines of their own homes, all four members of each family were interviewed, individually and privately by appointment at times which suited their convenience. In order to ensure privacy, various rooms in each home were used, including bedrooms and kitchens. Although at times there were unexpected interruptions caused by small children, unexpected guests or the odd telephone call, for the most part there was privacy and uninterrupted quiet.

Throughout the study none of the respondents defaulted in keeping their appointments with each of the interviewers. There were two occasions when appointments had to be re-arranged because of unexpected changes in working schedules and the death of Mr James' mother in Barbados. But these were dealt with in a responsible manner by the respondents.

Although not rigid, both interviewers worked to a duration of approximately one hour for each of the interviews so that subjects knew what the time expenditure was likely to be and as far as possible factors of fatigue, for both respondents and interviewers, were not brought into play. As it was, each of the subjects were interviewed in the late afternoons, early evenings or after the evening meal and each had already faced long hours of work, study and travel by the time the interviews began.

All of the subjects were interviewed individually for about seven to eight hours, spread over a period of some three to five months. In addition on two occasions all four members of the family were interviewed jointly by both the interviewers. The purpose of the first of these interviews has already been given, namely the *contact interview*. The second of the family interviews took place when the individual study was complete and this *terminal interview* sought additional information, to be described in a later section of this chapter. About a year after the study was complete a final visit was made to each subject during which the individual subject played an active role in working through some of the interpretations, and in participating in decisions on which aspects of the material required disguise with a view to final publication.

From the outset the research was a collaborative field effort between the twelve subjects and the interviewers. They not only gave of their time but entered into the strangeness of the situation, each in their own way. At the first contact family interview, it was pointed out that since the aim of the study was to learn how each felt and what life looked like through their eyes, it was essential to record the way in which they thought about things, and exactly how they told us of their feelings. There was a choice between writing their words down as fast as possible or using the convenience of a small tape recorder. At the first of the individual interviews, each person was asked for their preference and all twelve chose the tape recorder. The first interview was usually preceded by some informal and inconsequential 'play' with the recorder during which they learnt how to control the recording of their own voice and were allowed to play these recordings back – which to some of them was a novel and amusing experience. Once the novelty had worn off, the interview proper commenced; it was our experience that the use of the tape recorder both enhanced the concentration of the interviewer and facilitated the establishment of rapport between interviewer and respondent. In no case did the recorder appear to worry the respondents, and they became apparently indifferent to its presence. Its greatest advantage lay in providing us with an accurate transcript of everything which was said, the inflections and intensities of the words, the silences and pauses, the hesitations and repetitions, the changing rhythms and emotional overtones, the sighs, the laughs and the changes in volume. But against these evident advantages, the use of a tape recorder for lengthy interviews of this type involves large expenditures of time and money if the interviews are to be transcribed accurately.

The transcripts were combined with two additional sources of information: informal observation of all non-verbal expressive behaviour by the subjects which was noted as soon as we entered the home until our departure; and notes made after each interview by the interviewer on a face sheet (see Appendix II) giving information on the feelings and the interactive processes between the interviewer and the respondent throughout each interview. All three, taken together, constitute the research data.

At the outset it was emphasised that although the real names of the subjects would be known to the two interviewers, even the audio-typists transcribing the tapes would not know their real names and from the outset these never appeared on the transcripts. During the terminal interview each family chose a new surname and each subject chose a new given name. It has been relatively easy to protect the anonymity of these individuals and families from recognition by their friends and neighbours, by obvious changes of names, occupations and other distinguishing events. But since each family can recognize itself, there have been areas where discretion and consideration for the subjects required that material be withheld from publication lest it upset relationships within the family.

It was vitally important that since the subjects had voluntarily agreed to let us enter their family lives and had come into an unknown research situation, the skewed relationship between the interviewers and the subjects should be balanced by putting back as much power in the hands of the subjects as possible. I have therefore refrained from divulging details which could damage the family members; and both researchers took whatever precautions we could to minimize the disturbances which the study might produce within the family.

Unstructured interviews as the research tool
Each subject was asked to tell us about his or her life experience and his or her feelings, attitudes and preoccupations, starting wherever he or she wished either in the present or at any point in the past. Each was free to range from past to present or *vice versa* and back again, and to move from topic to topic as free associations determined. If respondents blocked and had difficulty in knowing how and where to begin it was suggested that they might like to start with their very earliest childhood memory, however trivial, sad, amusing or ordinary it might now appear.

Each subject used the interview time in the ways of his or her choosing so that natural frames of reference emerged and the content, form and emotional quality of the data reflected not only individual preoccupations but also inner defences against anxiety and the unique relationship with the interviewer.

The interviewers refrained verbally and non-verbally, as far as possible, from revealing any signs of agreement or disagreement with the respondent in relation to any point of view or line of behaviour which was being discussed; no advice, interpretations or moral judgements were made or signalled.

Questions were minimal and served several functions: firstly, to understand and clarify the material and encourage the free expression of attitudes and feelings; secondly, to open up content areas which, by the fourth and fifth interviews, had not yet been touched upon. Before the field work began, the research team developed a guide to the major research areas about which it was hoped respondents would spontaneously provide information. Gaps in the data were opened up by open-ended questions, incorporated into the last two interviews (for example 'You've talked very little about the time when you first went to school. Could you tell me something about that time in your life and how you felt?'). Most of these questions were directed at broadly defined developmental periods or at relationships with key family figures, friends, neighbours, employers and fellow employees. Questions on racial attitudes and experiences therefore, fell into either of these two categories. Sometimes it was necessary to establish the racial identity of people who figured in the life history where this was unknown, and at other times it was important to open up areas which offered the potential for inter-racial experience. For example, we asked 'Who are your neighbours?'.

A third function was served by questions. In the last individual interview each subject was asked to quickly say how he saw himself, followed by a brief description of how he imagined a good friend might see him and finally how someone who might not like him would describe him. These were valuable adjuncts to the identity analyses.

The interview series therefore comprised:

1   A family interview jointly handled by both interviewers meeting with all four subjects – the *contact* interview.

2   Six to eight individual unstructured interviews, the last of which incorporated the brief self-descriptions.

3   A family interview jointly conducted by both interviewers with all four subjects – the *terminal interview*.

4   Follow-up individual interviews, a year after the field work was complete, to work through with each subject broad lines of possible interpretations which were then shaping up, and ascertain what material each subject would like to withhold from

publication in case this might embarrass or harm their relationships with other family members – *the working-through interview*.

The processes and dynamics involved in multiple research interviews with four members of a family are exceedingly complex and require methodological analysis in their own right. A recent paper by Laslett and Rapoport[10] explores some of the components of multiple interviews with several members of a family using more than one interviewer, and also points out how little attention these problems have received in the methodological literature. One of the research issues which we faced was the sequence of the interviews. By doing the series in the way indicated above we hoped to achieve the following: by starting with one family interview, and by ending with another, we hoped to minimize the disturbances within the family which might be produced by our individual interviews, in privacy, with four of its members. But at the same time, we ensured that the main bulk of the interviews were individual ones; this was basic to the gathering of the research material. In addition, by placing the unstructured interviews first we aimed to make the best possible use of them as a projective measure, each individual revealing not only conscious attitudes but also disclosing re-occurring patterns which threw light on unconscious processes and defences. Such questions as then followed, the open-ended ones and the self-descriptions, only came after at least four or more hours of unstructured interview material had already been recorded. A third consideration related to the privacy of the disclosures. By restricting family interviews to the beginning and the end, subjects had no cause to fear that we might advertently or inadvertently betray confidences which they might not wish to be shared with other family members at that time. When we commenced the terminal interview we emphasised that we were not going to refer to anything which had been said to date by any of them but that the family interview was the occasion for asking them quite different questions.

The terminal interview opened up two additional areas of research study. Firstly, how had the research process affected the family as a family and the extent to which its members were consciously aware of any changes in relationships within the family, shifts in communication patterns between themselves, the stimulation of family reminiscences about the past and the sharing of these or not, changes in emotional climate between them, and so on? (See Appendix III for the questions asked.) Secondly, we wanted some feedback on how they viewed the way we had handled our role as interviewers and to obtain insights into how, in the complexities of these cross-cultural contexts, we might have inadvertently offended our subjects, been stupid, clumsy or insensitive to specific feelings or attitudes, or not. In addition we tried to obtain material on some of the transference effects by which each respondent might have perceived the interviewer as evocative of former relationships. (See Appendix IV for the questions asked.)

Although the data derived from this terminal interview are incorporated as part of the identity analyses in Chapters 7, 8 and 9, and also figure in the relevant sections of the theoretical findings of the last chapter, it is worth commenting here that not one of the families was consciously aware of the study having changed their family lives in any way (with the possible exception of the trivia of tidier bedrooms where some interviews had taken place!) This may not be the most appropriate method, of course, for tracing the subtle effects of research intrusions into a family. Or it may well be that the study did not alter *family* processes, although – a matter I will discuss later – I believe that it led to changes within the individual subjects.

When it came to feedback questions on ourselves as interviewers although this was not the best way of exploring respondents' attitudes towards us, we tried them out. The questions invited criticism and expression of negative feelings to be volunteered but in all cases very positive views were expressed, feelings of liking for us as individuals and comments on our capacities as good listeners. The literature is meagre on similar studies, but this appears to be a general response in studies of this type, where respondents have not only voluntarily decided to come into a study but in addition have stayed the course and in the process derived growing satisfaction from the process of the research itself.[11] Such satisfactions would include the deepening relationship with the interviewer, the freedom to reminisce and 'tell it as it is', the sense of being recognized as an individual, the feeling of being noticed and of being important to the interviewer and through her to the project and its sponsors as a whole, and the capacity to use reminiscence for the catharsis of dammed up emotional experiences and the growth of self-insight. All of these, while all mediated by the particular relationship between subject and interviewer, lead, on termination, to an overflow of good feelings, perhaps excessively positive to conceal the impending sense of loss and the anger which this must arouse.

Some recognition of past irritations and negative feelings towards the project and ourselves emerged in this terminal interview from one or two subjects who were able to contrast their early feelings about the research interviews with their later ones. For example, one or two subjects said that at the beginning they would suddenly remember that we were due to arrive and in tones of voice which clearly betrayed irritation and impatience recalled how they'd say 'Oh God, its Wednesday and those women are coming' or something similar. These views were openly expressed because of the positive views which had preceded them. The transference material, very revealing in some cases, is also dealt with in the identity analyses chapters.

The selection and editing of the life history material

Since the individual series of interviews ran to more than 2,000 pages of typescript, I have edited this material by concentrating upon extracting what seems fundamental to the major research interests of this book; but even here, a great deal of detail has been sacrificed by rigorous selection. However, I have retained as much verbatim material as relevance and space permit, so that the reader may be able to obtain the feeling for the whole person rather than confront too many fractured bits. It is impossible however to do full justice to the richness and subtlety of much of the material. All unusual accents or pronunciations have been dropped but otherwise the language is left exactly as it was spoken.

Since each interview was free-ranging and time sequences ranged back and forth from past to present, the life history is re-arranged to fit the continuity of each person's experience and not retained in the actual chronology of the interview sequence. In the theoretical chapters, however, psychological interpretations are made, at times, in relation to the actual sequence of the research material. This verbatim life history material appears in Chapters 3, 4 and 5, each chapter comprising four life histories of the family members.

The core interactive relationship: subjects and interviewers

The relationship between subjects and interviewers is not fortuitous nor to be regarded as 'unscientific' but is the very medium through which the study proceeds and the research data are gathered. The research data are enhanced and deeper meanings are yielded if there is a full, conscious attempt to recognize the dynamics of this mutual interaction.

The subject's conscious and unconscious attitudes towards us as interviewers are only in part determined by the kinds of people we are and the role which we are enacting. They are also influenced by past relationships, especially with parents and siblings and others who have been of deep emotional significance to them, and these, in turn, become unconsciously associated with us as interviewers. These transference effects, familiar in psychoanalysis, are crucially important in research which continues over a period of time and uses unstructured interviews. Too little is known of transference effects within the inter-racial context of research such as this. Are the transference effects derived from previously important persons in the inner life of the subjects, irrespective of race – or is race an overriding criterion for transference phenomena? And what of other variables such as social class? Would we, as interviewers, be likely to resonate in the immigrant subjects previous emotional feelings to figures in the past who had been perceived as both white and middle class? Or is the relationship itself, that of subject and interviewer, more likely to revive parental or sibling relationships, in which race is of no relevance?

The process is also a two-way one. Counter-transference accounts for what the interviewer brings to the encounters in the field, affecting emotional attitudes and unconscious feelings both towards the respondents and the research material.

Robert Gosling has distinguished three components in the counter-transference;[12] firstly, the feelings stirred up in the interviewer of which he or she is aware, provided attention is drawn to these; secondly, unconscious factors stirred by the material which betray their presence to the interviewer because they are touching on his or her previously sensitized areas; and thirdly, the stirring of factors in the interviewer of which he or she is unconscious and which have unknown effects on the interchange, constituting blind spots and projections, that remain undetected and influence the relationship. The first two of these components throw light on certain features of the relationship and of both parties to the interaction and can therefore be used to elucidate more about the respondent. Such information may make bias potentially correctable. It is only by becoming increasingly conscious and aware of these counter-transference effects that a researcher is able to take them into account. But the third component, unfortunately remains unrecognized and operates under cover. To use a different language, experimenter effects are compounded of all three factors.

The study had originally been planned to include working on transference and counter-transference effects with the help of an outside, part-time consultant.[13] Unfortunately by the time the field work began, the collapse of adequate funding for the study made this impossible; later, for the same reason, the field work had to be completed under some pressure. We were able to compensate for this loss only by our own efforts and only to a small extent. Transference and counter-transference effects in the research material and in the analysis of it are less well worked through than we had originally planned. Nonetheless the identity analyses chapters incorporate insights into those of which we were aware and of which we subsequently have become conscious.

The effects of race of interviewers on the research material. The effects of the race of the interviewer on the research material requires an examination of the historical and social context of the enquiry. What does it mean to *this* subject, at this moment in *historic* time and set within this *society* and this *community* to be interviewed by *this researcher* in relation to *this research task*? Again, the subject will wonder: What is the study about? What is it about *really*? Are there hidden aims? How will the material be used? By whom? And why?

If, within the wider social context of the society at that point in time, race differences evoke images of manipulation, power politics and covert attempts to prove or disprove theories or facts pertaining to racial groups within the society, the response to the race of the investigator will be influenced heavily by these factors. It is almost meaningless, in my view, to isolate the race of the investigator and attempt to trace what influence this solitary variable may have on research findings. In a recent and comprehensive review on racial experimenter effects in experimentation, testing, interviewing and psychotherapy, Sattler[14] has commented on how sparsely investigated the field is and particularly on the methodological inadequacies of such studies as there are. In many of these studies factors other than race are either uncontrolled or so inadequately controlled as to render the findings relatively meaningless.

In reviewing this extensive literature, Sattler concludes by saying that the extent and direction of the influence of the race of the researcher depends on many factors and that instead of asking whether the researcher's race influences the findings, we should be asking 'What are the conditions in which the experimenter's race affects subjects' performance?'[15]

This is a point of view I endorse. The interaction of Mrs Hutchinson and myself as white interviewers with the West Indian and Indian subjects involved complex and interacting variables, each of which modified the influence of the other. The research task, unlike many others, did not involve performance which could be judged as either good or bad, right or wrong. It also was a task which only *that* individual could perform. The researcher was not therefore either in the role of an examiner or an evaluator but rather of an interested listener and spectator. The power to perform the task or not lay in the hands of the respondents only, facilitated by the researcher. To this extent, the situation by which white researchers may be seen to be equated by immigrant subjects with greater access to power within the society was balanced in the research setting by the creative control vested in the respondents.

The setting of the study within their homes, the choice of unstructured interviews, the style of approach characteristic of both interviewers – all of these taken together implicitly conveyed to the immigrants that they were thought of as individuals, given a familiar space within which to operate and freedom to choose how they wished to perform. These factors taken in the context of the wider roles within society of whites and immigrants, also might be seen to constitute a different equilibrium.

Taking race as a mechanical variable, unlinked with the deeper personal attitudes of the investigator towards specific racial groups, can be grossly misleading. Different researchers of any race vary in their experiences, attitudes and sensitivities of approach to others and in their inner capacities to tolerate differences in their subjects. These, whether intentionally conveyed or not, are nonetheless signalled in all sorts of verbal and non-verbal ways. It is the combination of racial attitudes and experiences as well as research task, research setting, method, and broad historical-social contexts which need to be considered in relation to each other.

On the evidence of this study, it would seem that previous experiences which the respondents have had in relation to race – including the unconscious meanings attached to those experiences – determine whether an investigator of another racial group will be reacted to with suspicion, hostility and angry distrust, or with flexibilities which open the way to a good beginning.

There is no way of knowing how other West Indian or Indian families might have reacted to the combination of our research task, methods, personal approach and other factors specific to our study. All we know is that both immigrant families appear to have accepted both of us as representing good internal objects. Having now studied their life histories in detail and having become familiar with the dynamics of their personalities, it seems that most of them had had early good relationships with white people in their past and we, as white researchers, were given the chance to endorse these earlier internal figures.

In the social interaction of subject and researcher, where these are of different race, a methodological enquiry is needed to trace in depth the antecedents in both of previous significant encounters. Taken together with the other variables, the conditions under which race may affect research findings can then be more relevantly gauged.

Age, sex and social class are three other important variables which combine with race and cannot easily be disentangled. In our relationship with the English family, where race was not the issue, social class variables were much more prominent; and at the terminal interview, it was solely this family which became engrossed in the ethnicity and national origins of both Mrs Hutchinson and myself. In the research material, too, social class figures prominently in their transference effects.

There is some similar evidence in the literature to suggest that when Negro therapists were used for Negro clients, social class and other intragroup tensions modified the material.[16]

In conclusion, every variable in a research study modifies the research findings. It is a question of how and why these do so, the direction they take and the extent to which the effects can be minimized. But, most important of all, since they cannot be abolished they require to be discerned and acknowledged.

The research process as a modifier and an agent of change.   The experience of being a subject in this study was unique and complex in the psychological demands it made and in the inner rewards it incidentally bestowed. It was also a stressful experience. Reflections on the past as well as the present stir up and activate areas of doubt and conflict as well as guilt and pain, and bring to the fore current unresolved issues with their attendant anxieties.

The family agreed to something unknown in participating in the study and accommodating itself to the intrusion into its private world of two researchers. On our side, we took various precautions to modify our influence and to leave disturbances as much in their control as was possible, by putting back into their hands whatever power we could. Each had the chance of determining omissions in the published material, and participated in changes to secure anonymity. And analysis of family relationships at a depth level has been excluded from this book as too intrusive and likely to be painful and potentially damaging to the family members.

How did the relationships with us alter (over time) the expressed and experienced attitudes towards white people of the immigrant subjects? Initially, they related to us in ways, at least partly determined by their past feelings towards whites. As time wore on, however, and the relationships with us deepened, and became more relaxed, their race attitudes towards the English may well have shifted in the direction of greater tolerance and acceptance.

Changes in self-insight also apparently occurred in many subjects. By giving each the opportunity of re-creating and re-living meaningful parts of past and present experience, each was able to re-integrate these in their own ways and in the process self-insights occurred. This is often a subtle and unrecognized reward for participation in such research ventures.

The life history material

The life history material represents what each person at a specific time was willing and able to reveal to us as interviewers.[17] To a certain extent the material can be seen as a fiction since there is no way of knowing whether events were, in fact, as they are being depicted. All that is known is how the individual views these events and experiences, and cares to reflect upon them to a particular interviewer at that particular moment. Of course, life history material reflects to a greater or lesser extent actual experiences, but the way these are remembered and woven together is a personal creation of each individual. This material is approached in this book as, in part, a personal myth which embodies and expresses how each person has re-created aspects of his life, a sense of who he has been, who he now is and why he feels himself to be as he is.

But the life histories are also a product of a number of factors acting as *elicitors*, selectively drawing on a storehouse of unconscious and pre-conscious memories, feelings and experiences. These give a particular content and shape to the life stories and imbue them with a unique set of meanings.

Four main types of elicitors, all of them inter-related, can be artificially distinguished for our purposes and most of these have already been mentioned; those emanating from *intrapsychic* sources within the individual; *interpersonal* elicitors arising within the interview situation and revealing the changing nature of the relationship between the interviewer and the subjects; *research task and setting* elicitors, stimulated by the nature of the undertaking and the subject's understanding of it, the phantasies regarding the purpose of the research and how the material is to be used as well as all the aspects of the research setting where the interviews have taken place (e.g. time, place, psychological climate surrounding the interviews etc.), and finally those elicitors arising from current personal experiences and environmental impingements acting as *current environmental elicitors*.

What the objective life experience of any of our subjects has been is both unknown and unknowable. The life history material yielded in this study would have differed as a result of variations in any of the elicitors. All that we can work with in this book is the research material as given by each subject – a very small sample of an individual's life, exposing the sense and meaning which each person has made of their experience and which they felt free to relate at a given time and place as a response to the here-and-now of the present, which included at its centre a focal relationship with the interviewer.

The research material discloses the personal myths which each person has created from their past, from the separate episodes of their lives. In revealing parts of these personal myths, past and present become dynamically interwoven, the past affecting the recollections of the present, the present acting as a magnet eliciting past memories. Current experiences and feelings related in the interviews, may consciously or unconsciously resonate past experiences associated within the inner world of the person. And when talking of the past and re-living some of its emotional impact, an individual may unconsciously become selectively attentive in the present to people or events which such past recollections revive.

Conceptual approach
The basic conceptual approach used in this book is an inter-disciplinary one since the psychological, sociological and cultural aspects of our lives are interdependent in determining our re-lationships, feelings and actions. But the emphasis is a psycho-dynamic one so that the search for meaning in the research material is largely in terms of individual depth processes.

BIBLIOGRAPHY AND NOTES

1 A recent overview of psychological studies on racial prejudice suggests that unanswered questions and ambiguities result from two aspects of such research: that prejudice has not been adequately considered in terms of the social context in which individuals exist, and that prejudice has been treated as an isolated variable . . . rather than as an interactive aspect of an individual's complete self-system. See Ashmore, R. D. and Del Boca, F. K. 'Psychological approaches to understanding intergroup conflicts', in Katz, P. A. (ed) *Towards the Elimination of Racism*, Pergamon Press, Oxford (1976), p. 100.

2 Allport, G. W. 'The general and the unique in psychological science', *Journal of Personality*, 30 (1962), 405–422.

3 Cohen, D. *Psychologists on Psychology*, Routledge & Kegan Paul, London (1977). Interview with Liam Hudson, p. 158.

4 Bickman, L. and Henchy, T. *Beyond the Laboratory: Field Research in Social Psychology*, McGraw Hill, New York (1972).

5 Fried, S. B., Crumper, D. C. and Allen, J. C. 'Ten years of social psychology. Is there a growing commitment to field research?' *American Psychologist*, 28 (1973), 155–157.

6 Hudson, L. in Cohen, D. *op. cit.* (1977), p. 158.

7 At a time when to my knowledge neither David Cohen nor Liam Hudson knew of this study, and the book was in its final stages, Cohen asked Hudson: 'Would you object to a study of say, ten or twelve people which was almost like a series of long interviews?' to which Hudson replied 'I'd say the sample was rather large but otherwise excellent'. Hudson, L. in Cohen, D. *op. cit.* (1977), p. 158.

8 Rosenthal, R. *Experimenter Effects in Behavioural Research*, Appleton Century Crafts, New York (1966); and Friedman, N. *The Social Nature of Psychological Research: The Psychological Experiment as Social Interaction*, Basic Books, New York (1967).

9 We were both born in South Africa. I left there permanently in 1958 and lived in the United States before coming to this country in 1961. Mrs Hutchinson arrived in this country more recently.

10 Laslett, B. and Rapoport, R. 'Collaborative interviewing and interactive research', in *Journal of Marriage and the Family* (November 1975), 968–977.

11 Bott, E. *Family and Social Network*. Tavistock Publications, London (1957); and Rapoport, R. personal communication (1978).

12 Gosling, R. personal communication (1978).

13 Miss Pearl King.

14 Sattler, J. M. 'Racial "experimenter effects" in experimentation, testing, interviewing and psychotherapy'. *Psychological Bulletin*, 73 (1970), 137–160.

15 *Ibid*, p. 155.

16 Seward, G. *Psychotherapy and Culture Conflict*, New York, Ronald Press (1956).

17 I am greatly indebted to Dr R. Gosling for suggesting this way of looking at life history materials.

Chapter 3

THE WEST INDIANS REFLECTING: THE JAMES' LIFE HISTORIES

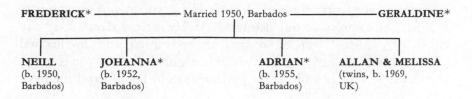

FREDERICK* —————————— Married 1950, Barbados ——————————**GERALDINE***

NEILL
(b. 1950,
Barbados)

JOHANNA*
(b. 1952,
Barbados)

ADRIAN*
(b. 1955,
Barbados)

ALLAN & MELISSA
(twins, b. 1969,
UK)

IMMIGRATION TO UK

Mr Frederick James: March 1958
Mrs Geraldine James: December 1958
Johanna James: January 1965
Adrian James: July 1970

* The research interviews were conducted from 10 December 1970 to 20 April 1971 and the research
subjects are indicated by an asterisk.

MR FREDERICK JAMES: HIS STORY

I will start with the past when I was a little boy about four
years old. I can remember my grandmother died and when she
took sick they summoned the doctor and they put me outside to
look for him. I was on the step of the door as a marker and I
could see when he was coming and tell him to stop. Later, I was
sitting having a bowl of soup when the doctor told my mother
that my grandmother has not too long to live. I couldn't carry
on drinking soup. I just had to leave it. I felt very sad and she

35

just lingered on in my mind and I lived with it for a long time
before I got over it. She was so kind to me.

Mr James sits on the sofa in his comfortably furnished and attractive
living room, his legs stretched out before him, relaxed and at ease. He
talks to me relatively freely and his earliest memory of his
grandmother's death comes spontaneously to his mind, bringing to
his sensitive and good-looking face a wealth of expressions, sadness,
humour, warmth and gratitude. His voice is quietly expressive and
he responds to me conversationally and with no great inner press and
uses silence comfortably for reverie or the re-experiencing of
emotional events of the past. He is of medium build with a slightly
humorous face, carrying himself well. His gestures and movements
are deft and expressive but also reserved. He is tired after a long day
of driving buses, but he retains an emotional and intellectual
aliveness and a capacity to be *there*. It is night and the house is quiet,
the day drops away and his thoughts return to his life and the past.

My father worked for an English gentleman doing gardening. We got on very well with this Englishman – it was very
nice. I used to visit his place and he had butlers and maids and all
sorts of things like chauffeurs.

I was born in Barbados and we lived in a small village – the
church and everything was near at hand. I was a pretty happy
boy. We weren't among the richest but my mother tried her best
for all her eight children and we all went to school.

My father used to keep two or three sheep and goats. We had
to take them to the pastures to graze and while they were
grazing we would have a game of cricket with other boys and
when the sun went down we took the sheep back home.

I loved my mother so much – she was very kind and she was
fond of all her children. She would do things for us. She
wouldn't mind if she didn't have anything to eat – if she had a
biscuit, she would give it to us and she would go hungry – our
mother! She would look out for her children all the time and
make sure that we each had something, however small it might
be. She would make sure we had something.

My father was not as nice as her. He would be sharp, was
always quick with the belt. Sometimes she would say to me, 'I'll
tell your Dad', but she wouldn't because she knew he believed
in the corporal punishment way of life.

His father would accuse him of not grazing the sheep adequately and this often led to a flogging. He was also required to be home by 9.00 pm in the evenings and even when he was seventeen years old he was still flogged for coming in at 10.30 pm. His mother, on occasions, covered up for him even when she knew he was in the wrong.

He was one of those fathers who was very severe, you know. But apart from that I loved him because I did my best for him when he was sick. He died young when he was forty-two – I was about twenty-one at the time. I didn't feel that he was more severe than other fathers, because I never really complained.

Coloureds and whites

At the elementary school we were all coloured children. There were no white kids at my school only four half-castes – which had nothing to do with them, they just happened to be that way – and we were all friends with them.

Most of the white children went to private schools because they could afford to pay for their education. I felt – how is it, or why is it that all the coloured people seem not to have any money? It was always the white man who seemed to have the best of everything – got the best of things. I suppose we found it that way. But things have changed a lot since then. When I left, the ordinary person was improving his position and more coloured people were able to send their children to paying schools.

When the school day was finished, we would go to the sea and have a bathe. We would be together on the sand – playing cricket and so forth, and making ourselves happy among the white people.

We were friends as we played with them. We did not take the white boys home to tea or anything of that sort – it was just that we played with them, you know.

The closest friendship I had with a white boy was with the nephew of a white lady for whom I worked at weekends. He was younger than I and he could ride a bicycle before I could, so he said to me one day, after having come to look for me, 'Come on', he said 'Can't you ride?' I said 'No'. He said 'I can ride and you are bigger than I am. Come on, let me teach you to ride'. We were at her house. It was a big house and you could ride right the way around it. He put me on the bicycle and held the saddle while I pushed off. He did that a couple of times until I caught my balance and then when I thought he was still holding me, he wasn't! He said 'You see, you can ride by yourself'. [Laughs]

From the time that I knew my father, he was working for white people. I knew white people from the time I was born. I remember seeing them, as I went backwards and forwards, and when I went out working with my father I saw them. And my brothers worked with them and I worked with them. In fact, it was a white lady who taught me how to drive! The aunt of the boy who taught me how to ride a bicycle.

Working for white people

When I was still at school, I would go and clean her car at the weekends and also tend the garden. Then one day she said to me: 'Well, my husband has a bike and he doesn't use it'. So she gave me this bicycle and that was my first bike.

Then she wanted someone to look after her car for her because her husband was at sea and she, a woman, didn't want to clean the car herself. She got very fond of me and I used to have dinner there. And then she said to me 'Would you like to learn to drive a car?' And I said 'Yes' and she gave me my first lessons and I took my driving test on her motor car and I got my licence. She started me off.

And then later on, if she was going out she would say to me 'Take the car and drop me at the party, then take the car back and come for me when the party is finished'.

And every Christmas, I used to get my gift from her. And when her husband used to return from Guyana, he would give me about four pints of rice and a dollar or two. He treated me very well. He was a generous man and whatever they had at their table, I would also partake of some of it. It was very nice, you know, they had coconut trees and all sorts of fruit trees in their garden and I would have some of whatever they had. They shared things with me.

When I left school at fourteen, apart from the weekend work with this white lady, I was learning to be a motor mechanic and I did that for two years. Then I became a coach-painter and continued to do that until I came here in 1958.

In the West Indies, I had to do the dirty part of the work and the white man was only walking with his hands in his pockets, showing me what to do and telling me what to do. And the white men would just come along – yes, I remember! One white man fresh from school came to the workshop where I was working. He was looking around to get ideas and then he got ideas and they sent him off for a course to England. And he came back and they made him a foreman and he stayed there for three years and then he left and he took over another garage. But the ordinary people, you see, we West Indians, we could be there for all our lives. They wouldn't think of sending us on a course! But we just took it for granted at that time. It was just the way we found it, I suppose. We thought it was the way things were . . . .

Marriage and children

When I was about twenty, I used to see Geraldine pass. As a boy you cast your eyes. [Laughs] The first time I got close to her was when I went to a fair and I arranged to take her out and the next Saturday I took her to the pictures and then we started going out regularly after that. She visited my parents and I visited hers. Then her mother died and we got married – just before my father died.

I had one or two girl friends before her, but she was the girl I felt most serious about. You can go with plenty of girls – see plenty of girls, but somehow there is *one* that you go to more than the others – that you *cling* to.

Geraldine was in domestic work at that time. And we married, and Neill, our first son was born. Later we had Johanna and then Adrian.

Considering emigration

People started about 1953 saying 'We're going to England!' Going to England, I thought, well, if so many people are going to England it must be very good there, so I will try also. So I decided to come to England to see.

I made this decision when I was doing piece-work as a coach painter. One week I would have plenty of money and the next three or four weeks I might not – just plenty of bills! So I said, this is not good enough. I want to do better than this. Having young children, you know, I want to get somewhere. So then I heard everybody was coming to London and I heard there were very good jobs with London Transport. So I said 'I will go and try'. So that's how I came here.

I had friends at the garage where I worked who had come here before me and they wrote back to say they were doing all right. And others also wrote to their friends who told me what they had said, and that's what made me come, though I would have preferred to go to America because it was near. England sounded so far, you know. But there are always some disturbances in America so I thought that since we were a British colony, it would be more suitable here. I thought we would be treated better here.

The white lady was not too pleased when she heard I was coming to England. She said it is too cold over here and she didn't think that I could stick it, because . . . well, I was thin then and she said people go to England but they don't like it, as it's too cold for them. But I wanted to see what it looked like because everybody was coming to England and I said – 'I will see what it looks like'. I wrote to her when I first came here.

I didn't feel so downhearted about going away first and leaving my wife because there were so many thousands who had gone before me and they had sent for their wives and relatives, so I thought it might only be a matter of a few months before I saw my wife again. So I always said that she would be with me soon.

It was difficult to leave the kids though, not knowing when I was going to see them again, but I wanted to make a better living. That's why we all do things – with hope.

I did not have to save for the fare, because we borrow from our friends and our family. They helped me and then when I got over here I paid them back. After nine months in England I sent the money to my wife. It was not enough but it helped her and she got some more from her family, and later I sent money for my two children.

Leaving and arriving

When I was coming out to this country on the ship, I met an Englishman. He was a Minister returning to England after time in the West Indies. He was very nice indeed and he said to me that I will meet some very nice people in England and some who will be horrible, but just try to get on with them. He said that I would find it different over here. He told me the things the English like, and the things they don't like, like being loud and playing our grams too loud and having plenty of parties. 'They like a bit of peace and quiet, particularly your landlady', he said, and 'She will want you to be home at such-and-such a time and she will like you to keep your room nice and tidy'.

Oh! It wasn't that nice when I arrived here. It was shocking!

They said there will be a liaison officer here to look after you, so he will get you somewhere to live because you have come from a strange country. And then you have this man to look after you, but he was looking after *himself*, because if he knew someone with a house, he would say to that person, 'Well, I've got some people coming from the West Indies, and they don't know the conditions, but this room may hold one or two people. Let's put *four* people in here and add two bunk beds'. As the room might be valued at £3, he could then charge £3 each from the four of us. So he was making a fortune, you see. So those were the conditions I came to and four of us were put in a room and we each paid £3.10.0, but it had nothing in it. We had no saucepans and no stove. He then fitted a little gas-ring but we had to go out and buy saucepans and cups and everything. He was a West Indian living in London, and *he* was the liaison officer supposed to find us accommodation! We were quite surprised. And that night, I remember, [laughs] one of the fellows said – 'If I could swim, I would start swimming now'. [Laughs again] 'Look at the conditions they have put us in!' But then we moved around the next day and we saw that it was not all like that. You see, other people were managing differently. So we thought – well, all we must do is to get ourselves another room, move out and things will be better.

I didn't stop in that room – I wouldn't stop in that room. I got a better place.

He got a job as a bus conductor with London Transport, and then set about arranging accommodation for himself. At first he had a double room and then a small flat where he and his wife lived for six years.

My first landlord was only interested in the rent and lived away from the place. I was fortunate in my second landlord – he was Polish and was very nice and friendly. When I was about to leave, he was very sorry because he liked the way I used to keep the place clean. He liked me for that. I wasn't noisy. I knew what he liked, well, then I did it, you see. I remembered the advice I'd been given on the ship. I also had a couple of friends here and they were living with landladies and I heard from them what they liked and didn't like. So I never gave anyone any trouble. And if they didn't like anything, I wouldn't do it, you know. If I had a party, I'd ask the landlord and he'd say yes. I'd just play the gram within reason so that everybody could enjoy it. You don't have to have it blaring – and then everything is all right.

This has been a problem for others and will be, because a lot of our people won't try to compromise. They won't say to themselves 'Well, if they don't like it loud, we will still have a party but respect their reasons'. But some people don't seem able to enjoy music unless it's up to full volume. Then someone will come and say 'Would you mind lowering the gram?' and the lad might say 'All right', and lower it, but be the type of person who might start to create a row – you know those sort of things. I don't go out of my way to annoy people, I never have. All the years I have been here I have never had any objections. Everyone says I am very friendly and very quiet, easy to live with. I know of some people who got objections but I have never had any. But then, I myself don't like loud noise; I like quiet and peacefulness. [Laughs gently]

He and his wife did not share a flat until some months after her arrival as she was accommodated in a railway hostel in another part of London. As soon as they could, they moved in together. He did not find it difficult picking up his relationship with her again. They then steadily worked toward the day when their children could join them.

Acquiring a home
The reason I took so long about getting the children with me was that I wouldn't have enough room to take them where I was living since it was a one-room flat. So I decided they must stay until I could manage to get my own place. And I always thought of my mother. If I should take them and leave her alone, – well, I said to myself, she's brought them up all this time. She is getting older and they can help to make her happy. That's why I let them stay so long.

But he had another major set-back which delayed the reunion between himself and his children. He wanted to buy a house and a few years after his arrival a West Indian friend suggested to him that they combine their resources and buy a house which could be divided into two flats for the two families. He and his friend went to a West Indian estate agent, 'Being new we didn't know our way about', and they each deposited a sum of £200 with the agent. Months elapsed and despite vigorous pressure on their side, they were only sent to one derelict house. They finally went to the police – the man was brought before the court and found to have defrauded twenty-four people, blacks and whites; he was declared bankrupt and they lost their hard-earned savings.

He was a fool. A friend had told us about him – he said someone had told him he was all right – but he wasn't all right – he turned out to be a crook. I had to start all over again . . . . Everybody has problems – many of my friends have had setbacks – but considering the amount I lost and everything, I think I got off fairly well.

Six years after his arrival in London, Mr James bought his present double-storied, detached house. It is very well maintained and attractively decorated and furnished.

I liked this house and I got a Council mortgage. I had to borrow from others to buy furniture, and bit by bit we paid them back. This is how West Indians manage. If you are in need and come to me and you say 'Could you help me? Could you lend me £100 or so?' If I have it, I say 'Yes' and when you get it, you pay me back.

About Indians

There are Indian neighbours on both sides of my house whom I speak to in the yard. At first they couldn't speak English – the children would say 'Hello' but now they speak a little better and the woman next door says 'Hello, how are you?' and so forth and when it's Christmas she drops in a card.

I've never been inside any Indian homes. Johanna had a school friend and visited her once or twice. You can't seem to get through to them. It's strictly Indian – you must be Indian, you see.

What makes me annoyed is if you're in a car with them, though they can speak English, they don't do so. You may be with five or six of them in a car and they have given you a lift and they *can* speak English but they won't speak it. They always 'nat, nat, nat' in their language and you are the odd man out. It's so annoying and not polite.

When I first came here I didn't like shopping on a Saturday because you would see all the Indians congregating on the pavement and you couldn't get past them. If I was standing on a pavement and saw you coming, I would step aside and give you freedom to pass. They wouldn't move and you would have to push them, push right through them. Well, you don't see so much of that now.

Another thing, when I was first here – you would see three or four Indian men meeting another four, and they would be hugging and kissing and all sorts of things like that. But I don't see that now either – they seem to have got out of that habit.

I think the change has come because they have learnt English and some people may have told them that they don't like this kind of thing and so they have tried to break it.

Well, the way they appear to me, I don't know if it's in their natures, but they seem so *different* as if they never try to get on with people or try to get to know people. They seem so cast away, as if they want to be by themselves – entirely different, you know. Most of them don't seem friendly at all. Apart from the few neighbours who speak to you, you meet others in the streets and I'll say 'Good Morning' but they just don't want to know! They just skin their noses up and go by. It's only the ones whom you meet at work and who know you, who are not like that.·

I just don't know why this is. They seem to stay *beneath*. Or maybe they've got an idea that they are going to stick to Indians or Pakistanis and they don't want anything to do with West Indians. I don't know if that's their belief, or if that's the way they were brought up. But I suppose it's a lot to do with their culture because their parents tell them what to do and whom to marry and they pick husbands for the girls and so forth.

I think it will change – in time. But they should learn to speak more English and speak it amongst people in crowds. If you can speak it, *speak* it! I don't think it is nice to carry on in a different language in a crowd when you can speak the language others speak.

But the other day an Indian gave me a lift. He works at my place and there were two of them in the car and he was talking to me and speaking to his friends in Indian and then everytime he said something he would turn to me and say in English what he had just talked about. So I said to myself – this is the first time this has ever happened! He was an ex-policeman too!

On living with the English
If there are troubles or incidents between people of different

races, I think it is mostly brought on by the people themselves. If you see someone who wants to pick an argument, it's best to ignore him and don't retaliate because that's when the trouble comes.

I have never seen any fights or quarrels in this area between people of different races.

I felt good and very happy when I came here because in my country you see only white people with their cars, their servants, and their elaborate homes. But when I came here, I saw they all have to work. It's only the few who might have servants. We will all be walking with our own kids here, and will all be going to work. At home, in Barbados, they employ coloured people to look after the kids while they work and they would pay them a salary – not much, but I suppose they're glad to get it. It was very surprising to see everyone here, more or less working, or having to work, not like in the West Indies. I can remember the same white lady who befriended me – she had a cook and a maid who did the dusting, and then she had a washerwoman and a gardener. Well, she didn't have a chauffeur because she used to drive herself and afterwards I used to drive her a bit. So some of the white people had six servants and the more wealthy ones had a butler and also a nurse. Here, in this country, I feel a kind of equality.

Being a bus driver
What keeps me working as a bus driver is that I like security – it eases a bit of burden . . . . Sometimes I get a bit bored and fed up, you know, the same thing everyday. When it comes to long weekends and holiday periods all the family are off and go to the park or stay with other members of the family while I have to work. And others have nice holidays in the summer but I'll be working then – and then I'll have my holidays in the winter. But there's a good side to the job as well. Because it is shift work, someone is always at home. When my wife is away during the day I'm on late shift. I'm at home most of the day and can do something around the house. But if we all go out at one time, and all come home together, we bump into one another. We get in each other's way. But when she comes home, well, the house is straightened, it's clean and tidy and she can just get on with the cooking. So that's why I have stayed in this job so long. I think it has a *good* side as well as a bad side.

I feel so tired working all the time and sometimes working

overtime and getting up at 4 o' clock in the morning. I don't get much rest what with my shifts and the twins, and the work to be done at home.

When I'm at the wheel of my bus I suppose its got to be very overbearing for me to get out of temper. But I never say anything to anybody even though I may say to myself 'Now, what did you do that for? It's a silly thing to do!' I've seen some drivers stop and get out and go for a fight and all sorts of things. But I've never done that because even when things come into my mind on the spur of the moment, by the time I've got to the next bus stop, I've forgotten about them and maybe I've already started to think of something else. [Laughs]

It is more lonely now that I drive a one-man bus, especially at night when I'm at the terminus and there is no one to talk to . . . but I'm getting used to it.

I haven't made friends at work whom I could bring home because we are all on different shifts and as you are coming out they are going in. So time is more or less spent amongst your friends only while at the garage or in the canteen.

I have worked in the past with plenty of different conductors – different crews – some Irish, some English. I got along well with all of them.

When I was a conductor there was only one unpleasant incident – and at that moment I felt – well, a bit sad. I always try to help people and one day a fat lady was getting on the bus. I held her hand in order to help her and I got out in order to help her in. I rested my hand on her so she couldn't fall backwards if the bus moved. So she said to me 'I don't need your help thank you. I can manage. I can very well manage without'. I felt very annoyed at that because I was only out of my kindness trying to help her. So I thought, well I don't think I will help anybody. But being the type of person I am, I couldn't do that. Since that day I've continued to help people. Some say I shouldn't help them unless they ask but I just couldn't see someone struggling with a pram or push-chair and baby and not help.

When I was still a conductor I was paired for the longest time with an Irish chap who drove the bus. He was my friend and took me to his home on a couple of occasions for tea and so forth. Anything I asked him to do he was always willing to help. Anything I didn't know, he was always willing to tell me.

The worst trouble I've had has been from the white kids. When I go to give them change on my one-man bus they withdraw. So I just put it there on the counter where they can take it for themselves. But other than that, I've never had trouble from snobbery or anything of that sort.

There's a canteen for staff where there are always plenty of people. If the white people have any different feelings towards coloureds they have never shown them, because they will come and sit with me and talk. If I go into the canteen and there's a group talking together, well, I wouldn't go and join them – I wouldn't know what they were speaking about and I think it would be rude to join in and go and sit amongst them. But other than that, if there just happens to be a space, we all have a meal and we talk about everything. I suppose we all feel what things might cause a disturbance. For instance, Powell might have made a speech. We may all sit there and read it – but that is not to say that any of us would stir things up and say things that would annoy others.

We all laugh about the same things. Today I had to laugh! I was at the wheel and I had closed the doors and was ready to move off when a little white kid came running across the road and asked me to hold on a minute, as his friend was inside putting his shoes on [laughs merrily]. So I just laughed and closed the door. I said to him 'What a cheeky thing!' I laughed and everytime I remember it, I laugh.

I have found the English people whom I have met very friendly and nice. They treat me with respect and I treat them with respect. You can also speak to English children when they are *indoors*.

When I was a conductor I was quite shocked by what they used to call the teddy boys. The way some of them behaved! I wouldn't ever have expected it! But when you meet the average person, he's quite nice and you can't judge the English people by the teddy boys.

My children, Johanna and Adrian

Neill, his eldest son, did not want to come to England. His life has proceeded independently in Barbados. Johanna was brought over before Adrian since it was safer to bring in the elder first because of immigration restrictions which limit the entry of children after the age of sixteen. Johanna had been separated from her parents for seven years and was thirteen when she arrived in England. Both parents had written to their children regularly and sent them pocket money and gifts on their birthdays and at Christmas.

I was so happy to see her – though when I saw her she had changed so much. When I left her she was a little girl and when she came here she was so big – just a nice young lady.

Adrian last saw his parents when he was two. Mr James sent money for Adrian's school fees once he went to secondary school. By the time Adrian came to England he was fifteen years old and had not seen his parents for thirteen years, and his sister Johanna for more than five years. Mr James had feelings of conflict about Adrian leaving his grandmother in Barbados in order to join the family in England.

Even when I sent the money to him so that he could come here, I had a conflict. Even the day I met him at the airport, I said – 'I am glad to have you,' I said 'but even now I can't get over the feeling of knowing that *I* am not over there. Whilst I was not there, *you* were there, and I knew that a part of me was with my mother. But now that you are not there, I feel as if I have done a wrong. I have left her all alone, you see'.

When he was there, I felt that he was there. And my mother knew that he was there, so if she felt lonesome, some part of me was there. But when I brought him here, I felt that there was no link at all. I would only have to write to her . . . . Then she took sick, she couldn't write because she had a stroke. And I just couldn't believe it . . . .

I used to get an idea of what Adrian was like from my mother, but seeing a person is a different thing. You know, I hadn't seen him since he was two years old and then when I saw him he had grown up so big and nice, I was very surprised also because he's very polite and nice compared with children of his age and teenagers today. The things we see them up! I'm surprised to see how nice he is . . . .

My mother, at Adrian's departure, felt sad. She said that she knew that she was sick and not getting younger. I asked first if she minded me taking him away? She said she wouldn't mind me taking him because it would be better for him; if she should die it would be best for him to be with me.

During the course of the study, Mr James learnt that his mother had died. He showed open but quiet grief during the next two interviews. He felt very far away from home and continued to mourn her.

Everytime she comes to my mind, I can't help shed a tear or two.

I think, Johanna's that nice! She gets on with everybody – she can adapt herself. I don't think I have any problems with her. Johanna stands out – everyone thinks she stands out. She does what she sees needs doing. You don't have to ask her – she'll help with the twins or she'll help with the cooking or anything. She's so nice a child, that's why she's stayed so long here. I suppose we are also good parents. I try to be nice to her . . . . I think she's a young lady that would make a nice wife for anyone in all respects – in anything, everything.

I feel I haven't done enough for my children. Sometimes if Johanna wants to go somewhere she says 'Daddy, why don't you get a car. Why haven't we got a car?' I say to myself – Well, she must feel all her friends have cars and I should have one. Maybe one day . . . . Sometimes I would like to be better – or do more for my family.

Most West Indians like us, who have left their families back home, have had to save hard to get them over here. So we have done without holidays, cars and things like that. It's the pressure of finding a home that makes people save so hard. Whenever I have holidays, I decorate the house or tend to the garden as I just can't afford to do anything else.

I sometimes say to Johanna and Adrian, 'Three years ago things weren't like that', or 'Such things didn't used to happen', – or 'You wouldn't have done that *then*', and Johanna says, 'Well that was *then*, this is today, Daddy, *today*, Daddy! Things have changed now'.

Most of the young men she knows I have seen . . . and they seem all right. Sometimes she says 'Dad, well such-and-such a person asked me to go out with him! And I may say 'I don't think you should go out with him – or 'I don't think I would like you to go out with him!' She says, 'Why not?' I say 'Well I just don't think . . . he doesn't appeal to me . . . I just don't think he's the sort of bloke . . .' and she might say 'Why not?' But she wouldn't say 'Well I'm going', you know. But if she did I . . . I don't think there's much you can do because it's her life and she's the one that's got to live with him. I can just give her my advice. That's all I can do.

I think she's very influenced by my comments. [Laughs] At times she thinks I'm a bit old-fashioned and says 'That was ages ago', but you know, she only says that, but doesn't really mean it.

I don't try to stop her going out as long as I know she's . . . well . . . in good company. She's the type of girl who would know if a person is trying to lead her into bad company. She'd just say no.

It was funny, but only last week Johanna went to take the twins to the doctor and he said to her 'You have some nice babies' and she said 'They're not mine, they are my mother's'. He said he wouldn't believe it. . . .

Now Adrian, he's a nice – oh, he's such a nice kid! If he asks me for something and I say, well – I can't give it to you now, he doesn't mind, he understands and he waits until he *can* get it. Some kids see what their friends have and decide well – I want that, give it to me, but he's not like that.

The white lady next door said to me only last week 'I don't like teenagers, but he's one teenager I like. When I spoke to him' she said 'I asked him if he liked being here and he said "Yes" but he felt sad leaving his grandmother especially since she was sick'. 'Well', she said 'teenagers today don't think about their grandparents. When they grow big and their grandparents are old, they don't think about them. I think he's very nice,' she said.

My mother brought him up better than I would have done. [Laughs]

He's done very nicely here – very nicely. He goes to church and they are all friendly with him there. He went to a tea-party with all the white church members and they all liked him. He goes to church every Sunday morning at half-past six because he goes to choir practice.

Last week it was his birthday and he turned sixteen. I gave him a small party – really a joint party with Johanna – just a few friends you know . . . . I enjoyed it. [Laughs]

He's still happy to be with the family; he goes to the pictures but he doesn't seem to want to go to discotheques or clubs like other kids do. He watches television and tries to do his work for school – he tries his best to get on . . . . And he's getting on very well at school. His last report said he was doing very nicely.

Sometimes the wife will say to Adrian 'Well, don't do it like that. What kind of a marriage will you make? I wouldn't do it that way!' Well he may frown when she says that, but then he does it the way she says he should do it.

My marriage

One of the things which has made me most happy in life is my marriage to Geraldine. I have no regrets. I think it has been fair and it's been good for me.

He sees his part in the home as being complementary to his wife's. He does most things when she is at work, sweeps and dusts, tidies the rooms and washes up. He often starts the dinner before she comes and then she does the cooking.

About racial issues

When I first heard about this new Immigration Bill [The 1971 Immigration Bill] I was told it was for *all* Commonwealth citizens but the Bill is strictly only about *coloured* immigrants. I knew what Enoch Powell had been saying and expected those things from him, but now this Bill looks as if Mr Powell has been speaking for the rest of the people.

I fear trouble because those coloureds who may have to be sent back from England will get annoyed and feel - why should other people - the patrials - be allowed to stay here?

It affects me very much because I don't quite know where I stand. At one moment I am trying to settle down and be happy and then they start bringing these things up and I start wondering why I came here? Was it a waste of time coming here? I might as well have stayed at home.

The government at home should stop West Indians leaving for England because if Britain says she can't take any more, it'll only be creating difficulties here. There's plenty unemployment here now as it is.

I feel very despairing . . . . It's not so easy when you have a family. If I was on my own, I'd get a passage and go back home.

Even though it's got this far, something can still be done. Even if they don't allow more Commonwealth citizens to come in, they could still try and make it better for all of us who are here, so that we can all live together and it would then be a better place for coloureds and whites - everybody.

Our children may, in future, have more difficulty than we have had because we came here as grown-ups, we accept what we are offered, but children who are born here, might try to stick it out. They might say, 'Well, I was born here, I've got just as much right to have this or that as other people,' and that's the way trouble may come.

I would like my twins to stay here if things remain as they are. But if things become worse, we will have no alternative but to take them to the West Indies. But I would definitely *prefer* them to grow up and be educated here because the education is much better.

But the children now in this area have to get coaches to go to school in neighbouring areas and they are picked up each morning. A few years ago there was not an Indian in this part of London and now there are thousands – going to school and travelling all these distances – so God knows, when it's time for my twins to go to school where they will have to go!

I like living here because it's near to my job and the house was a reasonable buy, but now everything seems to be getting more and more alike because places which never had Indians before are all becoming crowded as they move in. As the Bill says, there are thousands more waiting to be brought in from Kenya – so you can imagine what it will be like!

I don't know . . . . I may be wrong, but the Indians don't seem to get on with others. We all change, you know, but we seem to *face* the English quicker, or better, or more *with* them, than the Indians do. They always seem to be far away from others. Perhaps it's because of their language – the difficulty of the language – or the different customs they have in India. We try to adapt ourselves but they don't – a lot of them don't seem to try.

Self-description

Without thinking too hard about it, how do you see yourself?: Well, I would say that I was very quiet and decent, fairly even-minded and I love everyone – I don't hate or envy anyone. A good friend might even think of me as being an even nicer, quieter, more gentlemanly-like person than I think of myself as being.

How might somebody who doesn't like you, see you?: Well, I've never had that experience but I suppose the most such a person might say is that I'm *so* quiet, you know. Most of the time I just sit and read the paper or read a book though I might laugh or be friendly I might not go so often to the pub as some might like. Some might even say 'He seems a *very* quiet fellow – I don't know – I can't approach him, you know, he seems *that* quiet!' But I think that is all I can say because I have never done anything – to my knowledge – that is a harm or wrong to anyone.

It is so rare for me to be angry that I can hardly remember a time . . . I'm trying to remember . . . . I can't . . . the worst thing that happened to me that made me very annoyed was when the agent robbed us, and took all that money and yes – there was another occasion when there was a friend to whom I lent some money. I was depending on it to get it returned and to this day I haven't got it. Well, I was angry at that time. I said 'Well, I don't think I'll speak to you again,' but a month or so went by and there we were speaking again – and he never said anything to me about the money and never mentioned it to me again. There was also another man who borrowed £3 from me and never returned it and we're friends up to this day and he never remembered.

MRS GERALDINE JAMES: HER STORY

It is a week before Christmas and the tree in the living room has been carefully taken out for the eleventh year in succession. It is gaily lit and decorated and the alternating lights flicker on and off much to the enchantment of the twins who, with Johanna, are waiting with me for their mother to come. I do not wait long; the door opens and in comes a well-built woman of medium height, energetic bearing, and with an open attractive manner and friendly face. Johanna withdraws with Melissa and Mrs James greets me warmly and settles down in a chair facing mine, sighing gratefully. It is 8.00 pm and she has had a long working day, a tiring trip home by bus – two young babies to care for and a family to feed.

The house is quiet. She talks with voluble ease, words coming rapidly and with great crescendos of emphasis and dramatic expressiveness – face, arms and body all revealing the intensity of what she is saying. She brings alive the scenes she is re-living; her voice changes as she finds the words that she remembers – her own and those of others – her face is animated, her manner graphic, her presence demands attention. Sometimes her thoughts and memories tumble out with great speed and she gets temporarily immersed in the drama of her own re-creations. At other times, her attention is concentrated and more focussed. While she talks she manages to give tender care to her twins.

My husband came to England first and then he sent for me

and I came. We had nobody here at all but we made friends quickly. I was afraid of travelling because I had never travelled before – I was scared of sailing. I was scared of . . . I don't really know what! And I was a bit on the scared side to leave the kids. I knew they would be properly looked after by my mother-in-law but then a mother is different. Anyway I had to make a big decision. For months and months my husband was writing about it and I didn't give him the answer [laughs] until in the end he got fed up and said 'If you don't want to come, just don't come . . . ' So I thought, well, I suppose to keep my family together, I'd better go because you never know what will happen. He may talk to somebody for company and then if I am not there he may get somebody to do things for him like cooking a meal and washing his clothes – and well, I mean – he might pay them but they might get closer and closer and in the end, I may be on the outside looking in . . . .

She grew up in Barbados in a neighbouring parish to her husband. She was the seventh child in a family of eight, four boys and four girls. Her father was a foreman of a sugar factory and had white employers and her mother was self-employed making confectionery at home.

My childhood

I didn't have a bad childhood – some had a worse childhood than me. My mother was a woman who was always for peace. She never had rows and she never quarrelled with anybody. Even if somebody tried to pick a quarrel with her, she would just go away, and if she felt like singing she might just sing.

The only time she used to be very strict with us was when she went out and left us to do something and came back expecting it to be done and it *wasn't*. She would get very cross with us and well – give us a few lashes, you know. [Laughs] Sometimes she would say 'I'm running behind you, you know, because although you have got a sweet face now, I won't let it pass'. But then I'd say 'Mummy' and she said 'You want the lashes now?'. [Laughs] And I'd say 'Oh I don't Mummy, I'm sorry', and so she might then let it pass. But if she did lash us, she would give us all the lashes which she owed. She would lash us with anything – an old shoe, a belt, anything she could put her hands on. If she had time she would go out and cut a twig, and she would lash us on our legs or around our feet. But she never stripped us to beat us or anything like that.

But she was a very good woman. Everybody said that about

her and after she died, people would just give me things. 'Oh', they would say 'Have this to carry home to the children, dear. Your old lady was a good woman, a very good woman to me'.

Yes, when I got older I went to the beach to buy things and to get the fish that comes in every day, freshly caught. And sometimes before I could say 'Oh, I want some of this' the fisherman would say 'Have it, you know, because of your mother'.

When I was a little girl growing up my mother always used to say to me that if I and a friend should fall out, she warned me never to talk and drop remarks about that girl. Even if she dropped remarks about me, she always warned me never to answer because she said the only people who drop remarks about one another, are – you must excuse me – prostitutes.

Dropping remarks and walking the street while quarrelling and cursing one another is what whores do, and she said 'You are not to do it and don't ever let me hear you cursing anybody'. I never do it.

When I was a child, I heard my parents say that if anybody speaks to you and calls you by name and makes motions definitely directed towards you, then you can answer them; but if a person talks and even if you hear him talking about your own mother, then if he is *not* talking *to* you, go about your business! Don't worry! And I have always followed that advice. If you are not talking to me, I am not listening to you. And even if I hear what you are saying, I just don't pay it any mind. Really! And I hear a lot of very dirty remarks that people make about the coloured people, but it never bothers me because they aren't talking to me personally.

Where I'm concerned, I don't care what anybody says, because I always say that words are wind and wind is cheap because I don't have to buy it. Anybody can talk but if they aren't hitting me and aren't touching me, I'm not bothered. I just turn my head and I don't hear anybody say anything. I just leave it like that.

My mother taught us that if my sisters or brothers had quarrels, it was nothing to do with us. And if I went past the next morning and saw the lady that had been quarrelling with my sister and did not go up to her and speak to her – my mother said, 'You will see what you will get! She was not quarrelling with *you* and it is no business of yours'. That is always what I practice myself and teach my children to do.

I can remember my father as just a quiet man who was always the same towards us. I never heard him quarrel or swear at anybody.

He was a foreman on a sugar estate. He used to more or less live on the estate, but he did come home often although *we* used to visit *him* more regularly.

He died when I was about ten.

All my sisters and all but one of my brothers have got very different characters from me. They have very bad tempers and if they don't like things, they tell you off with a flash – with high words too – and they hurt one another.

They got involved in endless feuds with people in the community and a lot of her youth and adulthood was spent in extricating her siblings from bitter fights and arguments and fending off confrontations.

I would pass and hear people saying terrible things about my family. But I would also hear them say that the best ones in the family were myself and one of my brothers.

I sometimes used to say to my eldest brother, who was a fisherman and who had plenty of money 'Oh, give me a dress to go to a party tonight'. If he was in a good mood, he'd give it to me but if he wasn't, he'd just chuck me away. Then if I started to cry or became vexed or something – he'd say 'Oh, when is the party?' and would give me the money. I'd go and get the cloth and go to the dressmaker.

My mother never worked for white people but my sisters worked as domestics. By going backwards and forwards to my sisters, people saw us and got to know us and the white people would take us in.

I grew up on white people's doorsteps – we went backwards and forwards and we were one of them.

When I was growing up, the white people's children were growing up also and we all grew together and played and did everything together in the house.

It was not as if I was outside in the yard and they were in the house – no, all the mothers and fathers cherished us in the same way and they more or less used to look upon us as one of them. The whole family got to know us and sometimes I even used to go to different parts where other white families were and spend time with them. So you see when I came to this country it wasn't difficult for me to live with the white people because I have lived with white people all my life, ever since my schooldays.

Working and learning
I went to school with white and coloured people. I finished school at fourteen because I did not want to go any further and everybody at that time was trying to get more money and I wasn't doing anything to help.

A West Indian woman asked my mum if I could come and work in her grocery shop. Well, some of the West Indian people are so wicked [laughs] that they take advantage of you. My mum thought that she really wanted to teach me how to serve and how to weigh things and get me really interested in the work. But she didn't – what she really wanted was someone who would come and cook for her and wash her clothes and her husband's big khaki suits and every day I had to go into the city with her husband's breakfast which she had made me cook. Sometimes I had no time to eat before 3 o'clock . . . I was so stupid because I never went home and told my mother but she saw that I was looking ill and called the doctor. He said if she wanted me to live, she had better stop me from working and he gave me medicine and told my mother to send me to the seaside for a rest. I was very ill and thin.

When I got better the woman wanted me to go back but I wouldn't and my mother also said no and sent my brother who made a big noise with that woman and scared her. Well, he wouldn't have hit her but he was so mad, you know, for the way she had treated me.

I went to work in another grocery shop belonging to a coloured couple. They were nice people and I didn't mind working there because I was learning something. When you leave school, you can't get a job that easily.

I worked there some time and then I thought of trying something else. I had been going to classes in needlework and my mother asked a woman who was a good seamstress whether she would teach me everything she knew. Well, it seems to me that wherever I go there is somebody wanting to make me work because all that woman wanted me to do was a little bit of hemwork and sometimes, as soon as I arrived, she would ask me to go into her kitchen to wash dishes. She never did anything skilled in front of me – she never cut anything out – she always had something ready for me to hem or to overcast. Oh, and then she wanted me to fetch their groceries from the shop and the whole day she might only give me a little dress or two to hem. So I got fed up and bored – it wasn't getting me anywhere since I could already do all those things.

Up till then, I had only worked for West Indian people. I was quite young – only about sixteen – when I became a nanny and worked for white people.

What I liked about being a nanny was that you are more or less in the best position in the family because everybody looks up to you as you are caring for their child. Wherever the mother goes, there the nanny goes too! As long as I was taking the baby, they ended up taking me – and then I take the baby [laughs] and that was very good.

I used to push the pram and I and other friends got together on the beach and talked while looking after the kids of course. Then I'd take the baby back, give him a bath, put him to bed and then go home because I still lived at home.

I also liked a lot of dressing up and things like that and I didn't mind to be seen as a nanny. In the mornings we would wear blue and in the evenings all white, just a pure white uniform you know, with cuffs turned back and just a little pinny in front and a little thing around your head like in the hospital you know. And I liked that really.

In different countries there are people who are poor and others who are average or rich. If you want to hire a maid here in England, well, you would have to hire a white maid because that is whom you have got. Barbados is a mixed place and if people are rich and have the money to hire a maid, they have to hire a coloured maid. And if they take you as a maid, then *you are a maid*! They don't refer to your colour. Sometimes one met uppity people but even then they didn't say anything about my colour. Well, the only place where I've ever heard people referring to my colour is here in England. That's the honest truth.

Marriage, family and work
While I was working as a nanny I met Frederick and we married and soon started having our children.

My mother-in-law took the children when I went back to work which was when the baby was about eight months old. When I'd finished nursing the baby she would then take the baby and would look after it. I would go backwards and forwards carrying baby feeds. She took Neill and Johanna until it was time for them to go to school but in that period they couldn't forget mummy – or daddy – because we were always *there*, you see what I mean? On Sundays and almost every evening we would come so they couldn't miss us. When Johanna was ready for school she came back to me then [laughs] because you see at about four and a half to five years they start school and their grandmother lived very, very far away from the girls' school but near to the boys' school. So Neill and Adrian stayed much longer with their grandmother than Johanna did.

My mother-in-law and I always treated one another with respect. She was very quiet and always very willing to help. She was a woman who didn't worry about herself. She would give you whatever she had and she wouldn't bother whether she had anything for herself or not. And she tried to help everybody in all kinds of ways. When she was a middle-aged lady she would help several old people who lived far from her. She would cook their dinners and send them with the children, packed in a basket.

She brought all my children up, in a way, except the twins, of course. But she mostly brought Adrian up because he was there with her for thirteen years.

When my first white employer left the country she passed me on to a Venezuelan woman. She was a *very* nice woman and she seemed to take a liking to me. I looked after everything for her, you know.

I used to bank her money because she couldn't speak English well and she trusted me to go to the bank each morning. I went every morning to draw money for what I needed and although she never doubted me in any way and never checked me, I still used to count out all the money for her. She always used to say to me, 'It's a waste of time' and I'd say 'No, it's not a waste of time, it's your money and let me check it. You have got to learn. If I leave tomorrow you will have to get another West Indian maid and you will have to know'.

I would go to market to buy the vegetables and she would say cook whatever you like; and whatever I cooked she ate.

She had three children when I came to her and the youngest was a baby. I actually raised him up because when I started working for her he was less than a year old but when I left he was seven.

Every year she and her husband and family went home to Venezuela for three months and she used to leave me to live in her house, with my husband and my children.

She left the house exactly as when she lived there – there was food for three months, the electricity was left on, there was a radio and a good home and she also paid me while she was away. Yes, she was very nice.

Both Johanna and Adrian were born while I was working there and I stayed at home for a while after they were born but she wanted me back so I went and worked every day and she helped me by allowing me to cook for my family in her kitchen and also wash my clothes at her house; she provided food for me and for the children.

When she left for Venezuela she wanted me to go with them. But I decided that I didn't want to travel and I didn't want to go. It was only a couple of months after she left that I decided to come to England and here I am!

I had her address and then I lost it and I cried such a river of tears and did all I could to find it again. I was ever so sorry I lost it.

Before she emigrated, she worked for an English woman who had a small boy of four – she cooked for the family and looked after the child.

He was a very difficult little boy because if he didn't like you, you could not get him to do anything. But they all had taken a liking to me and he used to do anything I said as I knew how to handle him.

Deciding to emigrate

When I decided to come to England I needed to get a reference so I told her. She was very sorry to know I was leaving but she said it was best for me to go to my husband.

She described England to me and gave me two brand new vests of her husband's and told me to keep them on because they were very thick and warm. She also made me some pyjamas out of flannelette, and a skirt.

She was very nice – a very good lady really. I used to write to her and she used to correspond with me but then she left Barbados and returned to England and forgot to give me her home address.

All the time I was in Barbados I remained friends with the white people whom I had known when I was growing up and when we saw each other they would talk to me and would want to know how I am. If I had the time when I was passing near any of them I would stop to say hello and they were always pleased to see me.

When my husband was in London, I had to make a decision – the children or my husband. I decided to give the children to their grandmother and leave them. I said I would come and he decided to send the passage money and I booked my passage. I didn't travel with anyone I knew but while we were booking our passages we all made friends.

Hostel life

A lot of us had our husbands and friends waiting to greet us when we arrived. My husband was there and other friends but we couldn't go home with our husbands but had to go straight to the hostel because it was arranged that I was going to work with British Railways, you see. And this was a Railway hostel somewhere in London.

My husband brought me to the hostel and the lady who was looking after the place gave me a late pass so I could go back with him and he made dinner and everything . . . [laughs]. Then I went back to the hostel and stayed there for two weeks before we were all distributed to work at various stations. I was sent all the way to Maidstone and of course my husband was in London.

I wanted to go and put in for a transfer. I didn't want to leave the job but I didn't want to stay there. But the lady said that I had got to work six months before I got a transfer and you know, believe me, I worked and worked and six months never seemed to end.

Well, my husband and I were so far away from each other that we only saw each other at the weekends and even then sometimes I had to work and then he used to come over and see me – all that way he would come over and see me! And sometimes he would bring me a chicken which he had cooked.

There were mostly English people living in the hostel, one other girl was coloured. All the others were white people from different parts of the world. [Laughs] We were the only two! I got along fine with them but she didn't – you see she was a person who had never mixed, she had never had dealings with whites even in the West Indies, but, as I told you, I actually grew up on the white people's doorstep.

I ate everything and the food never bothered me but my friend was a very funny eater. And then I said to her, 'If you don't want what they give you, just take what you want and leave the rest alone – otherwise have a chat with the manageress of the hostel and tell her what you like. When you say you like rice, they think you mean rice pudding.'

I think the food was only bothering her because she really wanted to get to her husband – that's what! And he was distributed in Reading and I think this was getting on top of her. I said 'Why don't you make yourself happy?' and so we laughed and talked for hours and didn't go to sleep. [Laughs]

We shared a double room with two single beds. It was one of those things. He used to come and see her but I suppose it wasn't good enough. When he came he just spent a couple of hours there and then he had to hustle to catch his train back again.

I think sometimes it is good to be away from our men for a while anyway because I think you can get thought about more.

This girl finally decided to leave and she went to Reading. So I was the only coloured but it didn't bother me because we used to live well and we had girls of all different nationalities there. They would never go out anywhere and leave me. They *never* did and sometimes I had to force them to go – they wanted me to go and I didn't want to go.

When they were going to the pictures and asked me to go I would go – that was alright; but when they wanted me to go into the pub, I used to be so scared. I didn't want to go because at home we never go into the pubs. And then they wanted me to start smoking and I had never smoked at home at all, but I got accustomed to it and would just puff a little.

Anyway I got into the habit of going to the pubs with them and I didn't find it strange afterwards. Well, that really had me! 'Are you going to the pub?' The only coloured in there was me! [Laughs]

Nobody knew me, but even strangers bought me drinks and everybody started talking to me – everybody was quite good, bar tenders, everybody!

The first night I went was when my good friend Jenny had her birthday party. She was my English friend and she and some of the girls and some of the boys who were off-duty all went.

They were all white. I was the only little coloured one [laughs] and everybody seemed happy with their drinks and everybody wanted me, and they also wanted me to drink and I said 'Sorry, I can't drink that much!' They said 'You have to'. There was a table full of drinks and we had such a good time. And when I left there was I tipsy!

In Barbados I only used to drink some wine – or a liqueur which we would drink slowly. But we didn't drink a lot just a little whisky or a small tot of rum.

When we returned to the hostel my English friend, Jenny, had to undress me as I was tipsy. We had a real laugh over it next day. I said I'd never drink again as long as I live.

Working for the railways
I worked in a Railway canteen which also had a bar. Serving beer is the most awkward part of the job. The working man wants to drink before he catches his train and even if its only a couple of seconds he still wants to have his pint to drink and to catch his train. And of course there is a queue and it would start a row if I served the man who was in such a hurry. So I would just say to him quietly: 'Listen, there are only two things you can do mister. Wait for your drink or catch your train. Either one suits me fine!' You know they all just rush in at the same minute 'Oh, can I have so and so?'. I said, 'Yes – you can have anything you like but I have only got two hands, dear, and I'm not against serving you if you can possibly wait.'

But now and again you may meet an awkward one who comes in and starts to talk especially when he sees that I'm coloured you know. They are forever sending me back to Jamaica and I have *never* seen Jamaica in my whole life! [laughs] They start saying they don't know why I don't go back to Jamaica and I say 'Do you know Jamaica?' 'No, I don't know Jamaica'. 'Then if you don't know it, have nothing to say about Jamaica. I don't know Jamaica and I am certainly not going to Jamaica. If I was leaving here, I'd go back to where I came from', I said, 'so shut your mouth and wait for your drink and behave yourself and if you keep annoying me, you won't get one, because the law is that I'm not supposed to serve any man that comes on these premises who is rude to the attendant or has had too much to drink!'

Then one might say 'Oh go on, Geraldine, give us a drink'. I would say, 'I'm not giving you anything – you get on my nerves – go away'. But anyway he stands there, and when he shuts up I give it to him and he drinks.

Oh, they all knew my name there, everybody knew it! They only have to hear somebody call your name once and they always know it.

About five years after she started work there was a white tramp who came to the canteen and tried to sell some fish. Mrs James refused to buy any and the man was angered. They often had arguments and one day:

He and I nearly got away! He came and I was sitting just round the corner on a stool. I was sitting there minding my own business and I felt this thing slung into my lap. When I looked up it was his cap. He wanted me to come and serve him so he took off his nasty cap and slung it in my lap. I was so mad – I didn't say a word, I picked up the cap and slung it but I didn't know where it went. Nobody could find it. So he started kicking up a row and I didn't say a word, I just sat there. When the customers came I served them and he kept on with his swearing and calling me all the bastards and different colours you could think of. He then told the manageress and the chargehand that I had his hat. I said 'If you can see your hat on me then take it off – I'm not against you taking if off'. I then turned to the manageress and the chargehand and said to them 'Look, from the time I have known you two ladies and from the time I've been here, you have always been one way with me and I have never been disrespectful to either of you. I am asking you now, please don't let me be, because I don't want to be.' I said 'I've got no hat'. I then said 'Look, before I have to say anything more, I think you had better give me my card and my money now. Then I'll take off your overall and apron and I'll put it here for you very gently. Because this man can bring me into trouble and the best thing for you to do is to let me get out now'. The Manageress said 'Well you don't have to get so upset!' I said 'Look, I've had enough of him and if I continue having enough of him, one day I'll be rude to you all and I don't want to be – so let me go now. Please let me go now.'

The women told the tramp to go away and stop interfering with her. It was time for Mrs James to clean the front of the showcases and as she started doing so he came around and held her.

I grabbed a knife out of the cutlery tray and said 'If you ever put your hands on me again, I will drop you dead with this knife and I mean it.'

Three policemen came. The manageress supported her, warned the man off the premises and she told the policemen that Mrs James was a very good worker and she could not afford to lose her. There were other coloured workers there, but Mrs James felt that he singled her out because she didn't buy his fish and because he hated her. He hated a white woman who worked there who also had refused to buy his fish. She felt compassion for the man – he wasn't a bad man but a nuisance.

I mean I didn't really want harm done to him but sometimes he upset me.

Mrs James got a severe chill when she was living at the hostel.

The Hostel superintendent said to me 'I should really give you a smack', she said. I said 'What have I done?' 'What have you done?' she said. 'You could have killed yourself. Why did you go out to work?' She phoned the doctor and got me into bed. I was roasting with fever.

The doctor ordered her to bed for two weeks and said that if she moved out of bed she would have to deal with him.

'Else I will have your death on my hands', he said. 'Even if you want a glass of water, don't go for it,' he said, 'Whoever is in this building let them bring it to you'. Everybody was so shocked to hear how ill I was. He told the lady in the hostel that I couldn't move and everybody would have to assist me and do whatever I wanted. She said it was the greatest pleasure. 'We don't want her to move'. Everybody was waiting on me hand and foot. The cook brought up my breakfast you know. You could hear men shouting down to her 'What's happened? No breakfast in bed yet? It's about time we hear from you! . . .'

And the supervisor would bring in the basin and wouldn't let me wash myself. And every morning she would wash my nighties especially when they got soiled, you know.

They really looked after me and the supervisor was really good to me.

She recovered. She stayed almost a year in the hostel; her transfer came through but because they were short-staffed, the superintendent concealed from Mrs James that she had received the transfer.

I wrote out my notice and I took it to her and I said 'This is my notice. I don't want to leave the firm but the transfer never seems to come. You said it would be four to six months. I can't wait any longer. I don't mind doing the job but I want to do it nearer home because it doesn't make sense. I am over here and my husband is over here and he has to pay for his laundry bill and he has to cook his own food when he comes home, dying or dead. It's not right!

It's funny – she had the transfer all the time and she didn't want to give it to me because the white girls used to come and go in that job and she seemed to think I was permanent. But she came one night to my door and she said she was sorry and she explained all to me.

Married life in London

So I went to live with my husband. We got a double room in Nottinghill Gate, and I went to work at Euston Station canteen. I wanted to be nearer to him you know, because I was here and he was still doing for himself – so it didn't make sense.

Later on, I had to have an operation. They had coloured nurses but I was the only coloured patient. Everybody makes a fuss you know, when its like that (laughs).

I was so ill when I came in that they thought I wasn't going to live another minute.

I was very sick one evening when I still had the ether on my chest and the white lady in the next bed had her husband visiting her. He came in a bit early and was sitting there and I was being sick and he held my sick cup for me. He was there attending to me as a nurse.[Laughs] So the next day I was feeling a lot better and had just done myself up and he said, 'That's how I like to see you. You look like you are going to get married tonight. I had to be both doctor and nurse to you last night and praise God, I pulled you through. I thought you were going to pass out on me', he said. I said 'Thank you for helping me'. He said 'That's all right darling, that's what we are all here for, to help one another'. He was quite nice really.

He continued to come over to chat to her and she was teased in the ward about having two 'husbands'.

On another occasion when she got a fish bone stuck in her throat, she spent a day at the hospital. The white sister said,

> I'm not going to send you home in a bus because I will have to take the responsibility for your death. [Laughs] She said 'You sit down there and wait', and I kept saying 'Can I go now?'. She said 'No, you can't. [Laughs] Sit down or lie down there'.
>
> The white ambulance driver was ever so nice and made a great old fuss of me. He lifted me up and put me in the ambulance. I said I could walk but he said no, he wasn't going to let me fall down.
>
> He brought me to the door and he said to my husband, 'Have you got the dinner cooked because she's not to do any work, you know'. 'You go and lie down', he said. He was quite nice really.

Mrs James spoke very little about the separation from her children or their reunion with her. She re-joined her husband in a room of their own in London. He was at that time on night shift. When Johanna re-joined the family in London she seemed to fit in easily with her mother's patterns and everything went smoothly.

Johanna arrives

I was prepared to talk to Johanna when she arrived about sex and explain things to her. I never scared her off from talking to boys or from making friends but I explained things to her. They told her about sex at school over here – and every book and paper you pick up has something in it – I think its better this way because it gives the mother a more basic ground with the child when she realises she already knows these things from school.

So when Johanna comes home and says 'Mom, what we have been learning at school today is where the baby lives inside you and how it lives' then I can't back away because if I do she knows definitely that I'm lying. So all I have to do is come and meet her if not fully at least half-way.

I come from a different world. If I said it's not true, the baby comes by aeroplane – well she knows it can't be true because they've been told it all from beginning to end. So you can't escape it.

Mrs James was incredulous when she discovered from the doctor that she was pregnant. There was an interval of fourteen years between Adrian's birth and the new pregnancy. She had a white doctor under the National Health Service.

You know I have a habit of saying 'Yes, sir', and 'No, sir'. Well, for me a man is 'Sir'. I couldn't say 'Yes Dr Musgrave'. He said '*Don't* call me sir – don't keep saying "Yes sir and No sir" call me Dr Musgrave!' But you know, I couldn't and everytime I said 'sir', he got mad with me and he said 'If you call me "sir" once more, I shall do something'. And he was sitting there for hours talking to me, you know – this man. Honestly, he didn't mind if he had other patients waiting, he just kept talking. He was ever so nice really.

The doctor said he preferred to have me go into hospital because it was such a long time since I'd had a baby and now I was going to have twins. He said 'Excuse me saying so but you are not very young and now if anything happens I want you to be near me not I to be near you'. I said 'That's understandable and I'm a bit scared myself'. He said 'I know you are, but we will look after you very well'.

If labour had begun and I needed to telephone, my next door neighbours have a telephone and there is one at the shop right across the road from me. My neighbours are Indians, and they are very good and mean well and are all right in things like this. They are very concerned you see. The husband can understand English and the son goes to college and the little boys go to school and understand English. I think the only one who doesn't understand it is the mother. She gets a few words here and there like 'Hello', 'Morning', 'How's the baby?' 'How are you?' but to talk to her otherwise means getting one of her children to tell it to her in her language and then she will answer 'Yes' or 'No'. If I was here alone and labour started I could call out to them and they would hear me and they're very good.

The shop owners are white people and they are very good to us as well, and if I had to call up, they would let me use their phone.

When labour started, I had a horrible time with pains and I said I'm not going through with it and the doctor said 'Oh yes, you have to go through with it; we are not going to help you, you are very strong'. I said 'That's what you think!' You know, it was funny that I answered him back. They didn't give me any sedation or anything like that because he said 'You've had your others normally so you can have these just as well – there's nothing wrong with you.' I said 'I'm tired', and he said 'Go on, push just a little bit more – for me'.

She had two healthy babies – Allan and Melissa and the sister brought them to her and said 'Look at this beautiful little girl and this buxom boy'. She breast fed them for a short time and then put them both onto bottle feeds.

I wanted to look after the twins myself and I did that until they were eight months old. I didn't really want to give them out to anybody and it hurt my heart to do so at eight months. I have found a very nice West Indian woman who takes them during the day. She only looks after the twins – no other children – and she takes very good care of them. We pay her and give her the food for the babies.

Working with West Indians
I took a night job at an ice cream factory during those eight months – and left the twins with Johanna and with my husband.

The supervisor was a bit of a hard nut to crack. She used to drive us like slaves. She was getting a certain amount of money for the quantity of ice cream she could get packed – and one thing I couldn't stand was the shouting – she would shout. 'Come on so-and-so – get the ice cream out!' and she would start bawling and hollering you know and it used to get on my nerves. I suppose its her job and she felt that if she shouted she could get it done.

She was a West Indian – a Jamaican. There were so many West Indians there and only a few whites. I don't hold a grudge but I don't think that I like working in places where West Indians work. They are my people but if you work with a group of them, especially if they are all from the different islands – there's always something wrong. Some of them are so touchy – they can't hear anything and let it slide, but they have to answer it and then one starts and then the other starts and there goes! There were always rows and confusion, bad behaviour and language. They used to get on my bloody . . . on my nerves you know. I would pass and I would hear things and I would just go on as if I had never heard. Working with a group of touchy people, I didn't like the atmosphere.

If we got a break during work, I would just sit in a corner and do some knitting, and if I felt like eating I would just go all the way over to the gallery where there might be one or two fellows and girls, quiet people, who didn't really like the row.

Although I worked there I don't think they even knew me there. I left, and I don't think they missed me either because they never knew I was there. Somehow I couldn't bring myself to join in with them.

They just think they own the place and they can do what they like and you can't comment or say anything. I just wanted to do the work and get my money and get out. I left after three months.

Adrian re-joins the family

We left Adrian at two years of age and when he came here he was fifteen. He has exactly the ways of his grand-mother – nothing really bad or anything like that. He can cook, iron and wash clothes but he is lazy and expects me to do everything for him. I do when I feel like it and when I don't, I make him get up and do it.

If I tell him to do anything and he forgets, I tell him off because he's big enough to remember.

My children have never used rude words to me at all although some children, much younger than mine, will talk with rudeness and back talk to their parents.

If you have a child – you should tell him what to do that is right and you don't expect him to do what is wrong. But if he does something wrong he must have a good excuse otherwise he will be punished. Now Adrian when he goes out I tell him to take the direct road and not to stop for anything until he gets what he went for and then come back. 'If anybody tries to stop you', I say, 'You don't have the time. You've got your mummy and she's told you you can't stop. You go and come back to me'.

I say to Adrian, 'When you go to school, I expect you to be back home after school, never fool about the streets or anything like that. If you have to remain at school and you haven't told me beforehand, then when you come home you let me know exactly where you were, you see'. I don't beat my children but I want them to *understand*. I don't want them to mix with bad company. I don't want them to do things that they may see other children doing in the street.

I tell him that if he thinks any of the girls and boys at his school are his friends, as long as their parents let them come to me, then he can be friends with them. They can come to me sometimes, but he can go to them at other times. But no street business or anything like that. And he has to go to Sunday school. I sometimes go to church when I'm not too tired.

When Adrian comes home from school, he fetches the twins home for me.

Well, when Johanna comes in from work, I'm cooking and looking after Allan and Melissa. They won't sit quietly but walk up and down, and I have to give them a toy and keep them in the kitchen, watch that nothing hot drops on them and they are maliciously interfering with everything. [Loud laughter] I only pray to God to let Johanna come. Lord, let Johanna come; Lord, let Johanna come! And then I hear the door open and in she comes. She takes them over. Then one of us does the nappies and the other prepares the food.

And about my husband

I don't really regret my marriage – I wouldn't tell my husband that because I'm always telling him off and telling him that I'm going to walk out and leave him, and he can look after the children himself because I'm finished and fed up and all sorts of rubbish like that'. [Laughs] Then he says to me 'You were going to do that a long time ago. You should be coming back by now'. [Laughs] I say 'Never mind, nothing happens before its time and when the time comes, you'll get the shock of your life – because I'll be *gone* when you come'. [Laughs]

My husband – I don't think I would find anyone better, really.

He gives us all he has — and he even tries to give us what he has not got. He's had to work for everything and money has been a bit scarce for us. Things would have been better if he had had a bit more money. Even now he spoils me and brings things for me for the household you know. If I just say I want something he brings it home and says 'Oh, I've just bought so-and-so for you', and I'm so surprised to see it you know. He's like that. How he is – thank God for him'.

Working for Mr Rabinowitz

I'm a machine operator in a small sweet factory and I've worked there for about six years. My employer is a very nice gentleman. I've known him now for three years and I've never heard him say a cross word. His name is Mr Rabinowitz. And you can talk to him – you can you know – and he listens and if he can help you, he will help you. If you want anything, you tell him and he can get it. He always jokes with me. He always understands everything I say.

She is called upon to make sense of what is said by two other coloured women who work there. Nobody seems able to understand their accents.

Yes, I understand them but sometimes when I want to pull the chargehand's leg I say 'I didn't hear what they said because I wasn't listening.' She then says, 'I know you weren't listening but you heard'. I say 'Well, look, you will have to pay me for interpreting'. [Laughs]

I was doing some work for Mr Rabinowitz this evening when I put my hand to my ear and I found one of my earrings was missing. Just then he came up to talk to me and I said to him, 'I think you are in debt to me'. He said 'What for? What have I done now?' I said 'You haven't taken anything from me but I lost my earring on your property and I can't find it now'. [Laughs] He said 'Well, I will have to buy you one', and I said 'Yes, and I want good ones too'. Then he started looking all over the place. I was only joking you know, but he went on looking for it all day.

During the course of the study, Mrs James' mother-in-law died in Barbados.

Oh, I felt very sad and hurt for the lady. We couldn't go to the funeral because we only knew days afterwards. We might have got credit for a passage and gone to see her, even though she couldn't see us. It would have made us feel a bit better.

Race prejudice in England

When I left Barbados I didn't expect to come across race prejudice in England because I wasn't accustomed to it. I thought that after all these years whites and coloured people in England would be mixed and accustomed to each other. If a person comes suddenly upon you it is understandable that you may be annoyed, but I mean after all these years, you should be accustomed to it.

It is not as bad now as it was when we first came. The first thing people referred to was your colour – you know – you black so-and-so. It didn't happen to me personally, but I sometimes overheard conversations in the buses and in queues. You might be waiting to be served and an awkward person would come up and say 'Don't worry about her – she's black, so don't bother about her.'

It made me feel awful; the coloured person is not living in your house, they are not living with you and don't have contact with you – and even if they *have* and a coloured person asks you something or other, all you need say is 'Yes' or 'No' or 'I'm sorry, I can't help you'. You don't have to pass all sorts of remarks about their colour because whether we are white, black or blue, we are all human you know.

If you cut me and I cut you, it's the same red blood. In those days if I found awkward people who said things which were not called for, well – I just ignored them and didn't bother about them. But they don't do these things much any more – it was much worse in '58 and '59.

It's very seldom now that I hear anybody talking about the coloured race because everybody is happy, everybody is together now, more or less. In the streets, if four people are walking together two will be coloured and two will be white. Now everybody is hand in hand. Even if they feel anything, they don't say it and don't show it. Now everybody is one.

But in years gone by when we first came, if you pass *here*, as you pass they wash it away with water because they feel you have left something on it. Do you know what I mean? When we came to this country, we couldn't get a drink in a pub without the server then breaking the glass right under our eyes. It never happened to me, but to people I knew. My husband and I are not pub people. But these things don't happen now – we are all one big happy family. White people come to our parties – wedding parties and birthdays. You invite them and they come and they eat whatever you have got and they like it *ever so much*! So now it's different.

When we first came here our church was the Anglican church. But there was a bit of an upset when we arrived as they didn't want coloured people in the church – and we thought a lot about that situation – believe me! Yes – and sometimes the white people wouldn't go to church because there was a coloured person there. It didn't happen to me personally but people to whom it happened told me, you see.

But things have changed now and the churches are full of all colours. I go to the Baptist Church now, when I go – because of what happened in years gone by.

In those early days things were not difficult for me. If you don't have anything, you can't lose it. So since I didn't choose to go and mix with people, they couldn't do anything to me. You see, every coloured person looks alike to the English so if I do something which they don't like – I'm coloured! But you can be coloured also and you didn't do what I did, but because you are coloured you have to suffer for it also. So when I found that things were like that, I just kept to myself. I only rarely went to parties or weddings – my friends used to beg me to come; but I used to go to work and come back home and just sit there and watch television or knit. And even in the summer I used to say 'I just don't feel like walking out – I just don't feel like going out'. At home, in Barbados, that just wouldn't happen as you wouldn't find me in the house one minute. I think the cold has a lot to do with it, but even if this country was a more or less warm country, I don't think I would have fallen back like that. The people didn't *do* anything to me – they couldn't stop me going anywhere I *wanted* to. If I went somewhere and you didn't want to mix with me, well, I didn't care.

She didn't have time to watch television or read the newspapers in the weeks during which the Immigration Bill was being discussed. She had heard no discussion of any of Enoch Powell's speeches either at work or at home. 'I don't know Mr Powell'.

If I try to be friendly to you and I see that you don't want my friendship and you aren't polite to me, then I wouldn't come a second time to you. And if you were coloured wouldn't you feel the same way? I wouldn't call your name again. I always say that respect is due a dog. If you've got a dog, you'll treat it with respect and that dog will then always respect you and it will always know you. But if you have a dog and you keep hitting it and kicking it about, whenever that dog sees you, he will bark and will be ready to jump on you, because you were always hitting it. Right?

As long as we're here, you must accept us for what we are because we don't change. Our customs are the same as yours, the only difference is colour. We're not going anywhere. We're here to stay – and starting from *now* we must learn to live together and settle down. It's no use trying to bring back the past. It doesn't happen that way.

On Indians

You know Indians don't bother me and don't trouble me. If I want anything I ask them, and if they want anything – well they hardly want anything of me – but sometimes they want to know something and they ask me and I tell them. They are people who don't meddle with others or mix with others. They just go their way and mind their own business. It leaves you feeling a bit nosey!

They talk in their own language, but what you don't know, doesn't hurt you.

The Indians I think are a good people really in certain ways and certain things. I mean, in domestic things they are very lacking, most of them – lacking in tidiness in their homes. They throw things here and there and don't care. Well, I wouldn't do that because, well, you've never been into my back garden – it is the same as my front garden, just as tidy and well kept.

Coping with impingements

All around our house, on the pavements, where the government should sweep, we sweep. Either I do it myself or my son or my husband does it, whoever has time. I don't like things littering the garden – you don't have to have a garden but if you do have it, then keep it clean and pick up the leaves. What makes me very angry is when people throw things from the street over into my garden.

I was at the window one day and a coloured boy came past, and as he finished drinking Coke, he threw the tin right into my garden. By the time I came out he was down at the shop and I went and called him. I said 'Come here – I want to show you something'. And he came back. I said 'Open that gate and look at that – pick up that tin!' I said 'Would you like me to pass down the street with all my rubbish and throw it into your mother's house?' I said. 'No, you wouldn't like that because your mother's house is kept clean.' I said, 'Well, so is this front garden. I want you to put your rubbish in the bin that the government provides, or you can put it at the side of the road, but don't throw it in here'. He said 'I'm sorry', and I said 'All right, but don't do it again because it's not nice. Don't forget this is a private house and not a public'.

A big coloured man sat on the wall over there and threw bottles over into the garden. I said to him 'First of all this is not a park bench, you know. I look after this place and we pay taxes for it and we expect to work to keep it clean. I'm not against you resting against the wall, I'm not against you staying there – but fancy you drinking and throwing bottles over my fence'. I said 'Pick it up, man. I wouldn't come and do that to you, why do you do it to me?'

Self-description

Without thinking too hard, how do you see yourself?: Well, I would describe myself as pleasant and kind, sometimes I get upset but it passes off quickly. I wouldn't say I was a bad person, not really. I mostly do as I'm told and you can ask any favour of me as long as I've got the power to do it. That's what goes on at work every day. You know I can't – I just can't say no. Even if I'm fed up and tired – I'm just like that. I wouldn't say I'm a wicked person because everybody – both here and at home in my own country, always has a good word to say about me.

How do you think somebody who doesn't like you might see you?: I wouldn't say I've got any enemies at all. I don't think there's anything about me which I would change. I mean, in this world you have got to have a little bit of spirit and a little bit of pluck. You have to know when, where and how to show them. Sometimes I just have to lose my temper; often I don't bother to. But sometimes I just let go.

MISS JOHANNA JAMES: HER STORY

I remember when my dad left for England and my mom took us down to the harbour when the boat left and I waved to him and my hanky dropped into the harbour and I saw it sail away. And I remember crying and I said 'When is daddy coming back?' And my mom said 'Next week.' So I started to quieten down a bit; I wasn't old enough to think logically that he just could not come back the next week. We went home and every night we would lie in bed and we would say, 'When is daddy coming back?' because we missed him an awful lot, you know. She said 'Don't you want to go to a nice school?' We said 'Yes' and then we got over it after a while. When she got letters from him she would read them to us. Neill understood them better because he was older than me but I got a general idea.

Then she said to us 'Well, I'm going over there.' Sometimes I think back and remember all these things and I can remember where we were at the time she said this to us. We always seemed to be in bed because she would always take us to bed and read to us. We had quite a lot of toys and books because everyone felt sorry for us because Dad had gone away and we always seemed to take all these things to bed! My mother never went out anywhere – she used to stay at home with us all the time – but if she did go out we went with her. And then she told us she was going away as well. That upset us a great deal. We cried and then we thought we had no one really. I thought it over to myself and felt that this was going to mean an awful lot of loneliness – what you can do with your mother you can't do with anyone else. She obviously understood us better. And we were quite worried about her going. But you know, when she left we got such good attention that we probably didn't think about it – I can't remember thinking about it. If I was specially upset at any point, then I'd wish my mom was there, but it didn't happen very often. I went through all the stages of growing up and sometimes I'd just wish she was there, you know, because she was so nice to us. But then, of course, when I understood that I was coming over here when I was older, I realised it was all for the best and it was done to help us.

She sits on the double bed in her parents' bedroom – an extremely attractive, vivacious young woman, simply but elegantly dressed in a black mini-dress. She is lithe and slim, carries herself well with head borne high, quick deft movements of her long slender arms and hands emphasise and express a wide range of feelings. She is animated, talks quickly and becomes deeply absorbed, finding it difficult to draw an interview to a close because of her intense involvement in what she is saying. She relates warmly and easily to Sylvia Hutchinson and needs little prompting to start talking of her life – a lively intelligence is at work and a range of passionate feelings are aroused.

My Dad always used to bring me toys. He had a little briefcase which he took to work with him when he was in the

West Indies. When he got paid he would always buy me dolls and I said to him only the other day 'Do you remember that briefcase?' and he said 'Yes – that was when you were a little girl.' I can remember him coming home and we were all glad to see him and I'd jump up and sit on his lap and be ready to open the case. I was so small. I can also remember that he used to take me out in the car – because we had a car then – and he'd take me to the seaside and he taught me to swim. It was great being with him.

I remember my mom from funny points of view. She used to make me take horrible medicines which I didn't like and I can remember thinking 'Oh! I don't like her for this!' I can also remember that when I didn't want to go to Sunday school, she would insist that we went every Sunday and she used to bathe us and dress us and I had long hair then and she would plait my pigtails and then take us to church. She would walk us there and see us to the door because she was worried about the traffic. And she would then come back and wait for us, you know. She gave us money to buy lollipops. [Laughs] I can also remember how she would take us to bed early and sing to us and tell us about when she was a little girl. I can remember her as being a fantastic mom.

She used to work with some people from Venezuela and she often took me round to their house. They were wonderful people. She took us out a lot during the school-holidays and would leave us with our grandparents for a while – never for very long because she didn't think we were able to do without her! So she came back for us after a week-end. She also didn't leave us long because she missed us really – and liked having us around.

Neill is the oldest one – he's living on his own in Barbados now. I was close to him as a child but I was much closer to Adrian. Neill was always with his own friends and they were too old for me and I don't think that we had a lot in common. We weren't together much because of this and often we would stay with different relatives since it was an awful lot for any member of the family to have three children at the same time, so Adrian would come along with me wherever I was, and Neill would often be with someone else.

I can remember one thing about Adrian when he was a small baby. He was very tiny and my mother was cooking one day and he was crying in his cot. Oh, and I tried to pick him up and I dropped him. [Laughs] I can remember struggling to lift him and he was crying you know and I can remember saying 'Why doesn't he stop crying? I've picked him up!' And then my Mom got mad with me and she said 'You should have left him in his cot', and we were worried about him, and she got the doctor to see him. He always seemed to be crying and I asked her one day 'Why do babies have to keep crying all the time?' But I can't remember more than that until he grew up a bit.

Then I used to take him to school and to Sunday school. He was just a sweet little boy you know and we got on fantastically well. I was almost his favourite. We used to go to the beach together and I'd take him on picnics; we were always together because he was very close to me and we preferred to be together. I understood him better than Neill did – he pushed him around quite a bit and was too bossy. I wouldn't worry Adrian – I'd give him money to buy sweets and he'd adore me for that.

When I left to come to England, he cried his eyes out at the airport and I just didn't want to leave when he started crying. He kept saying 'I want to go with my sister.' He was really crying and screaming and my poor granny was trying to keep him quiet. We kept in touch by letters and I kept all his letters and I could tell how he was growing up from those letters.

My mother's mother died before I was born so I never knew her. My father's mother – my grandmother – was very close to us and I stayed with her for a long time. I adore my grandmother – today she is very ill and old. I really love her and have always loved my grandmother.

When my mother left we stayed with my grandmother and next door there were uncles, aunts and cousins, and there were family all around us – you didn't have to look very far to find the James' – they were all over the place.

I had a very special aunt who is very dear to me still – I've just had a letter from her. We were very close. She would take me shopping and buy me clothes and would spend quite a bit of money on me. She loved me and she didn't have any children of her own, so I was her favourite. She looked upon me as her daughter. We write to each other now and although she has children of her own now, she is still fond of me. When I was small she was always ready to give. Now I feel that I owe her quite a lot, and I send her something at times.

It was great fun being at home. We weren't lonely because

there was too much of a family gathering to be lonely. There was always somebody willing to look after us and although our parents weren't with us and we obviously missed them and wished we were with them, we were never really unhappy children. And if you're happy you can get on all right and settle down.

But despite this, I sometimes wish we had all come over here together and that we had grown up as a family together without having had all this splitting up. I try not to think about it but it would have been better if we had been all together from the beginning – it would have been different and we'd feel more of a family.

Although I loved Barbados it just didn't have the opportunities for us there and my parents had obviously come over here to make life better for us in the future. So I grew up understanding that it was for the best and done to help us, and that one day we would join them again.

Discovering white and black

My mother worked for a very nice couple. She was Venezuelan and he was Canadian and they had two little girls and my mom would take me there. The woman was very nice to me and she used to buy me dolls. I can remember being very tiny and playing with her kids and her husband would take us out in the car. I can remember them being different because I'd look at them and think – they're white and I'm black, and it sort of registered that we were different by looking at each other's hands. But I was too small to even think about prejudice.

I think I asked my grandmother one night as we were going to bed. She always used to say to me 'Say your prayers before you go to bed', and I can remember asking her why families were different colours. She said 'It's to do with different races, they're white and we're coloured you know.' I can remember asking her 'Why? why? why?' [laughs] and she said 'Well, it's just that they're the European race and we're the African race.' I was just too young – it didn't mean anything to me.

At school with whites

I was older when I became aware that people were prejudiced because of colour. When I went to secondary school the headmaster was Canadian and was very nice to me when I entered the school. He said to me, 'Well, in this school Johanna, you mix with all sorts of people from all over the world. I hope you will like it and settle down.' I was in a class which was half white and half coloured and my great worry was that I hope that they would like me. I didn't worry so much about my liking them.

The headmaster took me by the hand and introduced me to my teacher who was English. And he was so charming, he said he was pleased to meet me and he introduced me to the girls – he said this is Kathy, and this is Marjory and they got up and said 'Hello Johanna and welcome to the Lincoln High'. They were mostly Canadian girls and boys since it was a mixed sex school.

My seat was next to a Canadian boy. I felt frightened and kept thinking – I hope he likes me [laughs]; I hope I get on all right with him. I sat there sort of day-dreaming, looking round the class at everybody and then at lunchtime they were all so nice. I hadn't remembered to bring my swimming suit to school and a Canadian girl lent me hers because she wasn't well.

It was so nice and I kept on thinking that I'd expected them to be different and to treat me differently because I'd heard grown ups say what had happened to them and I'd listen and think well, as long as they're white, they're going to be nasty to me.

But I never had any trouble with anybody at that school.

The first evening my grandmother was going to come and fetch me from school as I probably would not have found my way home. But Paul, the Canadian boy who sat next to me, asked his father whether he could give me a lift home in his car – and told his father I was a new girl.

His father said 'Well, where is she?' So Paul said 'She's standing over there.' And I heard his father say 'That coloured girl?' So he said 'Yes' and then his father thought about it and I don't know, but something inside me went funny. Then Paul came and said to me 'We'll give you a lift' and I can remember saying 'No thanks.' 'Why not?' he asked and I said, 'No, I'll wait for my Grandmother'. Then the father got out and said 'Oh come on, we'll take you home.' So I went and he took me home and I remember Paul's father said to me 'Not that I didn't want to take you, but – er – you're too young to understand anyway.' But he took me right to my grandmother's house and after that he called for me every morning and took me home each evening.

I got on very well with the white girls in my class. We were in the Brownies and Guides together and went on holiday together and I'd go to their houses and they came to mine. I just never felt left out and they made me feel I was one of them. I knew I wasn't, you know, but I just never gave it a thought.

When I used to visit their houses, they weren't rude to me or anything like that. They were all very nice and they had coloured maids and I would go there and meet the coloured maid.

When I left for England the girls bought me presents and they wrote to me for the first few months but then we all gave it up – we just couldn't keep it up.

If I'd stayed there any longer, Paul's parents might have got worried. They probably didn't worry then because we were very young but I should think now if I went back and met him they would probably be afraid that we might get too involved. I think when it's a girl and a boy relationship they don't want their son to marry a coloured girl – or a daughter to marry a coloured man.

I asked myself why do they object so much – if English girls want to marry, say a Greek, well, he's foreign but he's white, and it's alright. I always think 'Why the difference?' And I always come back to the same thing – if you are black they don't want to mix with you – why does this always have to be the great reason?

White Barbadians were of two sorts – one half thought that we were inferior to them and the other half did not look down upon coloureds. The prejudiced half thought we were just stupid and they looked down on us as in the days of slaves. The black Barbadians ignored them because they felt that in time they would come around to another way of thinking.

Although, whites and coloureds lived in the same neighbourhood we didn't have white neighbours. Whites didn't do any 'dirty jobs' – you would always find them in offices and banks – the smart jobs that they wouldn't dream of giving to anyone who was coloured.

Now, since independence, it's all changed, it's fair play now and all are equal. I know that they're mixing now and although you probably wouldn't find white people doing dirty jobs, the coloured people are being well treated since independence.

Going to England
When I was twelve, my mother and father decided to send for

me and I was quite excited about it. Of course, Neill being the eldest had the opportunity to come first but he didn't want to come. He didn't think he'd like England – he was afraid of the cold. So I said I'd like to come and I arrived here in January 1965. I was so thrilled you know but I was a bit scared of the plane as there was fog and we had to stay in Dublin a while. I got quite worried about it and I kept thinking 'Gee! is it always this cold?' I was really freezing. Anyway, my mother met me at the airport – my father couldn't as he was working. I hadn't seen her for such a long time, but I still remembered what she looked like and she remembered me of course. We came home and I met my dad that night. He was so glad to see me. They were living in this house and my father explained to me that they bought this house for the family. And they showed me my room. It was the first time I'd had a room of my own and I was quite thrilled and excited about it, and there was this toy white poodle on the bed and my Dad had bought me a nightdress case as a welcome-home present.

School experiences

I started school soon after I got here and I was a bit worried about it as I wasn't sure what English girls were like. I went to school the first morning and the headmistress took me round and introduced me to the girls. They were all very nice and I settled in pretty quickly because by the end of the week I was great friends with all the girls – all except one.

I always remember her. Her name was Susan. I was the only coloured girl in the class and she was horrible to me but the others would be sort of on my side and told me to leave her alone. She would say that I smelled and other ridiculous things and I remember one day I sat at my desk and questioned myself. I said 'I'm sure I don't smell.' And then I asked one of the white girls about it and they said 'No, it's just a thing some people say about coloured people.' And I can remember feeling very depressed about it and then I thought I would not take any notice of her because I was sure that I didn't smell. She kept it up and at break when I might sit at my desk reading, she would come and throw things at me and hit me and she would say really rotten things. I just didn't like it and I thought 'Oh, why did I come over here – why did I?' And then I couldn't take it any longer and I told my form teacher and she told Susan off but Susan then accused her of taking up with 'that wog'. The teacher gave her a detention and she told her mother who came down to the school to see me and gave me a lecture. 'You little black thing' she said 'Why don't you leave my daughter alone?' And I explained to her what her daughter had said. The headmistress then told her that I seemed a very nice girl and I would not say these things if her daughter had not said them. So Susan's mother said 'Oh! It's that blacky's word against my daughter's!' The headmistress said 'Please don't bring colour into it. You know they are growing up and are both teenagers and they'll sort themselves out, you know.'

So anyway that was that, but she still went on being horrible. One day I just couldn't believe my eyes! It was Easter time of the next year, and there was a card on my desk and it was from Susan. I said to the form captain, 'I'm seeing things.' And I showed her the card and she said 'Susan's obviously decided to see sense', because the others didn't encourage her. So when she came in I went to her and said thanks. She said, 'Oh, you are welcome' And from that day on we were the best of friends [laughs] . . . It was really strange and I had to ask her why. It was really worrying me. 'Why did you decide I am nice?' She said, 'I'm sorry about all the things I've said but it was just that I wasn't really very happy at home and I was trying to take it out on you.' And, you know, I went right through school and never had a problem with anybody and I finished school being friends with all the girls – and happy.

All the time she was at school (more than three years) she was absent three times – she got the trophy for good attendance and awards for good conduct. She was also a school prefect and never once had a detention. She got on 'fantastically well' with the teachers.

My headmistress did go on and on about what I'd achieved and I wish that she hadn't as I felt horrible. I was quite pleased but it was making it difficult for me because it was so embarrassing. That's what I don't like. People have got an opinion that I can't do wrong and I don't like that sort of thing, because if you do wrong, then no one believes that it might be you. [Laughs]

Race discrimination and despair

She left school when she was sixteen and started looking for a junior office post. She was sent to the Gas Board. The man who was to

interview her seemed surprised and said that with a name like James
he had expected someone English. She was however tested and when
she was turned down she said 'Don't think I'm rude, but why didn't I
get the job?' He said he thought she was too young but on the way
out, when told by an employee that they never employ coloureds in
the office, she said 'Oh well, that's life.' She came home and told her
parents who said they were very unhappy for her but that she should
keep trying.

I felt hurt and unwanted that they wouldn't give me a try and
didn't want me just because I was a different colour.

She returned to the Youth Employment Officer who was upset at
what had happened and she was next sent to a well-known perfume
firm. When she told the switchboard operator that she had come for
an interview, she said

I don't want to dishearten you, but they don't like coloured
people in this place.

She was interviewed and then turned down.

'Mind you', he said 'it's nothing to do with your colour'; and
I said 'I never said it. I do understand.'

She walked and walked and wondered why she had come to
England. She told her parents and again they said 'Try again.'
She next went to a large vacuum cleaner factory and had the same
experience except that the supervisor was more honest and said that
if a coloured was appointed it would make the staff unhappy.

I never really got angry or said anything rude to them. I just
said I understand and walked out and felt that I wasn't wanted.
Then I gave up and never bothered for about two weeks and
I just stayed at home. I then felt that wasn't good enough and I
would make another try so I was sent off to a large firm and I did
a test and had to fill out a medical form. I was turned down on
health grounds because all I had put in was that as a little girl I
had had measles and that I got colds occasionally. He said that a
member of staff had to be in good health and that it was nothing
to do with my colour. I said 'I'm sure', and walked out again.
I tried another large medical firm. I met the most abrupt, rude

woman who, the moment she saw I was coloured just told me they didn't have coloured people in the office and she was very harsh. I just stood there a while and then she said 'What are you waiting for?' So I just left.

Working in a family setting

It was very depressing. It was nearly driving me out of my mind. So I told the Youth Employment Officer to try and find me something *very* small — I didn't really care what she got me as long as I could type. I went to see a woman who had turned the front room of her home into an office because she had asthma. I thought there couldn't be much opportunity in such a job but at least it would be a job.

I went there. I was so nervous that as I rang the door bell I was shaking. She opened the door and the moment she opened it I thought she seemed such a nice person. She said 'Hello, you are Johanna' and I said 'Yes' and she invited me in. She said to me 'This is our home and you will be working here with me.' She asked me what I could do and then she appointed me and told me she would pay me £6 a week after tax. So I left and came home and I was so happy. I knew it wasn't fantastic — it was just a house, just her home, but I thought at least I might be happy there.

She learnt a lot from the woman about office work, and her employer was very pleased with Johanna and the speed with which she learnt. They worked together very happily for three years and she did the bookkeeping, typing, invoices and correspondence. She was allowed to use their kitchen for her lunch.

I was really happy there and got on well with the entire family, and had great respect for her husband and her two sons. She helped me by taking me on after that period of torment and I helped her in different ways too because she was not strong. In the end I became part of the family.

After three years I felt I had been there long enough and I told her and she asked me why I was leaving. I said 'Well, I don't know — I just feel I want to move on now and I'd like to work up-town.' She said, 'I wish you the best of luck', and the day I left she was crying and I had to leave quickly as I felt the tears coming to my eyes. She said 'I hope this isn't goodbye and that you will come and see me.'

Moving forward

After a few abortive attempts to obtain a post in the West End, she was rejected for a post because of insufficient training. 'I understood that and I accepted it and wasn't disheartened.' She was then told by an employment agency of a post as secretary-receptionist for a large group medical practice in the West End. They wanted someone who had to be 'pleasant, charming and intelligent' and while Johanna was in the agency office the agent telephoned to the practice and said 'We've got just the person you are looking for – she's nicely dressed from the West Indies.' She was interviewed by one of the English partners whom she liked and he then said it was her job if she wanted it. 'We have decided we like you, it's whether you like us.' He had had a long talk to the employment agency while she was enroute and he said 'I think you are charming and don't get upset if I say this, but I think you're beautiful.' She was offered the post with a salary of £17 a week; she works with four girls in the office and is assigned as secretary to one of the senior medical men 'a very nice man.' She has been in this post some five months now. She finds her employers and her colleagues most congenial and pleasant. All four girls with whom she works are white.

Working in the West End

> I was ever so nervous at first but the girls were very nice to me. Bertha remarked on my nervousness and said 'I think I know why you feel a bit conscious of us being English but don't worry about it. I've mixed with a lot of coloured people and have got nothing against coloured people as long as you are nice. I don't really care where you're from or what you look like'. When she said that I felt happier. And now I don't think about it at all.

The men who work with the practice – and other men who come to the office pay rather special attention to Johanna. The girls comment on this.

> They keep saying I'm taking all the men away. There's a man in the next office who had never said a word to the girls before I came and now he's always talking to me and they get quite angry and say 'What do you do to them?' One girl said I gave men the wink and I said 'I don't – I just ignore them.' The girl then said she thought I was too nice to people. So I said 'But I don't go out of my way to be – it's just me!'

All the doctors and staff of the medical practice had a Christmas dinner together at a West End Restaurant and Johanna was the only coloured person there. 'I felt conscious of people looking at me all the time.' But she is now getting used to this kind of situation and the girls with whom she works comment that she doesn't seem to be nervous any more.

One day I went into a restaurant in Oxford Street to have a meal. I usually have sandwiches but I felt a bit hungry and spent some time looking at the menu, unable to decide. The waitress came and said 'Give me the bloody menu' and pulled the menu from me and said 'When you make your bloody mind up, tell me.' A few minutes after that an English couple came in and they were looking at the menu for some time and in the end all they ordered was a cup of coffee and she smiled at them and put it on the table. I sat there eating what I'd ordered and thinking 'Oh God! I'd just love to tell her what I think of her!' But I – er – I just can't be hostile to people – I just can't. I always stop myself. There was an Englishman sitting next to me and he was very upset about it. He told the waitress off about it and he said to me 'I'm surprised at you – you should have said something to her – you shouldn't just sit there and take it.' I said 'Well, I don't know – I just can't be bothered' and he said 'I hope you don't always have to put up with this sort of treatment.' I said 'Well, most of the time, but let's say I'm getting used to it now.' He was really choked about it all and he said 'Stay and finish your food – you've paid for it.' And I was too choked to eat it – I just left it and as I walked out the waitress muttered something about 'bloody foreigners.'

I went back to work and the girls saw something was wrong so I told them and one of the girls was so upset – she had asked me to describe the waitress to her – and she just put on her coat and said 'I'm coming back' and she went and blew her top to the waitress.

When she came back, she was upset 'Bloody nerve', she said. 'I went up to her and I just said to her "I understand you were very rude to a very polite young lady today – a coloured young lady." And she said "Oh yea, that stupid bitch".' So my friend turned to me and said 'I don't know why you don't go home, you know where people respect you and why you come to a country like this.' I said 'Our life is full of why's and but's and if's, but it's no good thinking like that.'

I don't go to that restaurant any more – when the others go there I sit in the office and have my sandwiches. Things like that make me wish I wasn't around, you know – didn't exist. But on the other hand I've been in so many restaurants and had fantastic treatment. I suppose she was in a bad mood and wanted to take it out on me.

If I had answered the waitress back, we would probably have ended up with a big row and the police would probably have come and the waitress would have said that I had said more than I did and I just felt that everybody would have been against me. I've known people to whom things like that happened. I just thought it wasn't worth it anyway to degrade myself to the extent of carrying on in a big restaurant with so many people there.

Many of my friends don't just sit back – they fight back. I suppose it's not a bad thing fighting back but there's no point in fighting if you're not going to get anywhere – it's like hitting your head against a wall. I suppose we're all made differently. Some people can take things and some can ignore them and I'm one of those who can pretend that I never heard things if I want to. But if I really want to take action, I can get pretty worked up about it.

Some weeks after Johanna recounted this incident, she spoke of the waitress coming into the medical practice.

'You don't have to accept my apologies,' she said to me, 'but I'd like you to.' I said 'It's all forgiven and forgotten – it doesn't matter.' 'But what surprised me', she said 'was that you didn't blast off which most coloured girls would have done. I felt terrible afterwards picking on you, but I – I've got a lot of problems at the moment.'

After she went I just sat there and thought people are funny! I don't know whether she was genuinely sorry or if she came in to see the doctor and just saw me there. But I wouldn't be *that* rude to someone unless I had really great cause to be.

A Kenyan secretary who joined the staff, was the first African woman whom Johanna had known. 'I expected her to be thinking at the stoneage level, but she's very westernized and thinks in an English way.' They became friends and compared experiences in relation to job discrimination in London.

Johanna's work requires great patience with members of the public and she has found that she manages difficult people well and her employers also recognise that she has this ability.

Five months before the research study began, Adrian arrived to join the family in London.

Re-union with Adrian

When I first saw him he was definitely changed – he had lost that baby face he had and he was grown-up. Then he was just a sweet little boy but now he is a grown-up brother. I sort of feel he is older than me sometimes.

We get on fantastically well together – we don't have any rows and if anyone says anything about me, he is always on my side and jumps to my defence. I can never do any wrong in his eyes and I love him a great deal. He likes to be with me all the time and he is quite a lot of fun to be with too.

When he first arrived I thought 'We'll have to wait a while to see how we are going to get on together after such a long period of time.' The first week he didn't say much and was quiet. He just answered questions very briefly and I never got much out of him. I think he was just trying to settle in and get used to things. He hadn't seen mummy and daddy for years and the twins were new to him too and I think he felt a stranger and really not part of the family. But then the next week you know, he was in full swing and he felt he belonged then. I think it was because my mom and dad showed him great love and I did as well, but in the first week I think he just didn't seem to be sure if he really fitted in or not.

I was the last person in the family whom he had seen and he remembered what I had done for him and how kind I'd been to him.

When I was here and he was still in Barbados, I always thought of him and wondered how my little brother was getting on. I worried about him a great deal because I thought that he hadn't got a mother or father there and I wasn't there and I had been very close to him.

My father had thought it best to leave him until he could decide whether he really wanted to come. When he got to the right age, he said 'I'd love to come to England to be with you all' and we felt bright because he was coming happily and because he really wanted to and not because we were forcing him to.

He adores the twins you know. He gets on very well with Mom and Dad and we just get along great as a family. I think the only barrier between us all is the very great strictness over me.

My parents

My parents are very strict – I think it's just the West Indian way of life. They treat me like a child and overprotect me. They read things in the papers and keep on saying 'I wouldn't like that to happen to my daughter', and then they start laying down the rules. But I can't stand that! That's how they were brought up and this is a different age altogether.

After school I became a bit rebellious and I found I had to protest to have permission to go anywhere – even to the cinema. And that started breaking it a little.

I hate to be treated as a child and sometimes I have to say 'I'm nineteen years old, you know.' And my mother says 'Well, I'm trying to protect you.' I keep saying to her that I can take care of myself and she says 'Oh, you can't you know.' Oh dear! I go through this all the time. I said to her 'Don't you trust me?' and she said 'Oh, I trust *you*, but I don't trust the people in the world!' And it's an awful way to be really you know. I have to grow up sometime. She and my dad both get worried about me. He tries not to show it but deep down he is just as worried as she is really.

I like to feel free and to be able to go out. I think that provided you go out with nice people and enjoy yourself there's nothing wrong with it.

We sometimes have an argument and they will win – they always do because I have to back down and then I don't say any more. I just – you know – suffer in silence – come to my room and forget all about it. Then if they think they've been a bit too hard, then they'll say to me 'Oh, it's alright, you can go.' But by then I don't want to go anywhere because I've lost interest. I think they're trying to protect me too much actually.

It's typical of West Indian families. You can't get away from it. Unless the girls decide to leave home and break away from the family entirely. They treat sons differently. My West Indian friend Miriam was complaining of the same thing. Her brother is seventeen and can go out and come in at six in the morning and nobody asks him a question but she is nineteen and she can't go out. It's always the girls who suffer in West Indian families – they're not ill-treated but they don't have as much freedom as the boys do. Adrian has more freedom than me and he's only fifteen. It's so annoying, you know. Adrian understands my situation – that I'm a grown-up but am not able to go out. He doesn't even talk about it but I think he doesn't want to say anything against mummy and daddy but you can tell he thinks its ridiculous. Sometimes I can tell he feels sorry for me. English girls have a lot more freedom.

On one occasion Johanna had accepted a date with a West Indian man to go to the cinema and when he came to fetch her, her father didn't like the look of him and wouldn't let her go. She was acutely embarrassed and later when she saw the man, he said that even if he wanted to take her out, he could not go through that again and that he thought her parents should let her grow up a bit. Since then she doesn't accept dates with people because she can't forget what happened. She has a special boyfriend Roger who is an engineer. He is half-Barbadian and half Canadian and she has known him for some years and is deeply fond of him. Her parents like him and trust him and are quite happy when she goes out with him. But he has a social life which includes other girls as well, and Johanna is placed in the situation where she would happily go out with him more often but is not given the opportunity; and on the other hand, her parents restrict her freedom to go out with other men.

It just gets me down and I don't feel like an individual since I'm not free to do as I want. I prefer to have freedom and then if I get hurt well, I've only myself to blame.

It's the way they've been brought up and it's the way they are going to bring us up – but I can assure you it won't be the way I'll bring my children up!

Her parents decide things together but she sees her father as the head of the house and her mother as just agreeing with him.

It's always been like that since we were little. I suppose it's an effective way to be from her point of view but not from ours.

His words carry a lot of weight. It's not two minds working, it's just one.

I've always been close to my dad and able to get through to him. He says – when I want to go out with a man 'Do you think you should go, dear?' and then I say 'Why not?' Then he can't give me a reason for not going but he just doesn't think it's right and I can't stand it. If he wants to lay down the rules, then he should say what the rules are.

At other times he says 'If you want to go, go' and then I don't because I feel he doesn't want me to go.

He can always tell when there's something wrong with me. I just go quiet and live in a world of my own.

Since hearing about my Grandma's death the other day, I just don't feel like doing anything anymore. I don't want to go anywhere and want to be left alone for a while. I really loved her so much.

I try to forget about it because when I think about her then I get a headache – but it's not that easy to forget about her. I keep seeing her, you know.

Moving in wider circles

I find when I go to parties English men always come over to me and ask me to dance and then they say that I'm a great dancer – even if they don't mean it you know. And then for the rest of the evening they talk to me right the way through and I don't even remember that they are different from what I am – I'm enjoying it all. And I'm sure they don't even think of it because everyone is enjoying themselves. We don't have time to think about it. But Roger is the only man I've really been out with individually, and when I tell the girls at the office that, they can't believe it. He's also the only man I've ever kissed and then it was only last year and I was already eighteen. The girls at work think it's incredible. I mix with a lot of boys when I go to parties you know but that's all there is to it. It's only Roger whom I think of in a special way.

If an Englishman asked me out, I'd go and I don't think my parents would stop me. Perhaps at the back of their minds they might not want me to marry an English fellow because they probably think it wouldn't work out but they never say anything. Once I said to my Dad 'If I brought an English chap home, would you say anything about it?' And he said 'No, I wouldn't – it's up to you who you want to go out with, but I'd hope that if you were going to marry him, it would work out because so many of the marriages don't. Even if it works out for the couple, it's the children you must think about.'

Johanna goes to a number of parties which are mixed – coloureds and whites of many different nationalities – Swedes, English,

Germans and Italians. At first she was very self-conscious of her colour because at the first party she went to she was the only coloured person there. But she has gradually become used to mixed parties and 'Now they don't worry me'. She also has asked her English friends to come to West Indian parties and they feel equally self-conscious and she helps them by talking about their feelings and those that she had in the past and says 'You just have to take the plunge'.

> Englishmen love to dance with coloured girls and they always tell us we can dance. I like dancing with English chaps too.
> Coloured girls say it's easier to get on with English men than with English women. I find the men much nicer than the women; they treat me with greater respect. I don't think men worry about colour. On the other hand, West Indian men say they prefer English women to English men as men want to compare their sexual capabilities with the West Indians and all that sort of nonsense.

Each year she goes to a church camp with English girls. She is the only coloured person at the camp.

> I had a great time. They were all so nice to me and for nearly three weeks we were there and we got on fantastically well together. They were all great and they write to me now and my best friend, Vicky, has been down to spend a weekend with me. And another of the girls who is a teacher, has been to visit me. My parents welcome them – they don't worry about colour as long as it is a decent sort of person. I say 'Oh Mommy and Daddy, this is a friend of mine' and they just welcome them and entertain them.
> Some West Indian families may be a bit self-conscious and may think English people come to see how we live and what our homes are like; but we have so many English friends. My mother's employer – well she's really her immediate supervisor, she often comes here. She's crazy about the twins and she really loves them.
> I was on a bus the other day and an English woman accused the coloured conductor of wanting to keep some small extra change and although the conductor showed her the fares chart she said 'You blackies want to tell me what to do with my money!' And then she picked on all the coloured people in the

bus and she said to me 'Why don't you go back to where you came from, you blackies?' It didn't really bother me because by now I am immune to it. I thought it was ridiculous to behave in that manner.

Sometimes when you're talking to an English chap in the street, you can feel the atmosphere around you. You can feel something is happening because everyone walking by looks at you and they're thinking 'Oh yeah! Is he going out with her?'

I was talking to an English schoolfriend whom I met recently in the Co-op. The cashier kept looking at us and I knew she wanted to say something. She said to my friend 'Are you going out with her then?' He replied 'Mind your own bloody business.' You can feel when you are talking to white men that people are looking at you and wondering.

I went with Roger to the Jimmy Talbot show and I was the only coloured person there since Roger although coloured, looks white. Everyone was looking at me – all the cameramen kept staring and you feel so embarrassed. Then the usherette, when we were coming out, said to Roger 'Is that your wife?' and he said 'No – and I think she's very nice.' And I thought 'Oh my God, let's get out of this place!'

About racial prejudice and discrimination
I think laws to make people unite won't work – it has to be something from the heart. We're just looked down upon because of the colour of our skin and although some white people do sincerely feel that what the coloured people go through is terrible, they cannot really feel it to the extent that we do, because they haven't experienced it themselves. When I went through it, I realised what it was like to be rejected because of what you are and who you are.

White people who discriminate are just being very selfish. They want everything for their own race and don't want anybody else of a different race to get on in life.

I know a West Indian girl who when she first went out with an English chap, kept saying to me that if she fell for an Englishman he'd probably only want one thing from her – sex. She was wrong because they're happily married now – she was just frightened that he would take advantage of her because she was coloured.

I've seen some West Indian boys who can't leave girls alone and one night one was pestering an English girl who wasn't interested in him. He said to her, 'Don't you want to talk to me because I'm coloured?' and she said it had nothing to do with it. He really pushed that girl into talking to him and I got really mad and felt like hitting him.

There's a saying that West Indian men are supposed to be highly sexed. They don't like this reputation but the women enjoy talking about it.

A West Indian friend of mine was arrested for assaulting an English girl on the tube because she wouldn't move her bag. The English girl had hit my friend and they had a big fight. I felt terribly embarrassed. They got so worked up about it and shouted and I can't be bothered with that kind of thing. My friends get angry with me if we're all together and I just keep quiet on these occasions. They get really mad.

I know a lot of coloured boys who are before the courts at the moment because they get into arguments and end up fighting. Boys are different from girls, they're always ready to fight if something goes wrong. I would never get involved in anything like that. If I see an argument starting, I get away from there.

I have a Jamaican friend – a man of twenty-one who is finishing a university course. There are sixteen of them completing this course and he is the only coloured and he is the only one who hasn't been placed in a job. When he confronted his tutor with this, he just said 'It's not because of colour – it's – well, just one of those things.'

I feel really hurt when I hear things like that – it just gives me a feeling that I should just hate everybody. But then it's no good doing that, you just have to live with people and close your eyes and forget about it.

I've never seen fighting in the streets of this neighbourhood.

If people want to make things better, they should start by seeing that coloured people who are qualified, should be given the positions which they merit. Job discrimination is what annoys me more than anything else.

There's a huge shop in Oxford Street which is owned by three coloured people but there are no coloureds on the staff because the owner told me that they couldn't dream of employing coloured people because nobody would want to come in and buy. This is not the only instance of this kind of thing because I have a coloured friend who used to own a restaurant in Acton under his own name and he just didn't do any trade at all. He now has another business in Ealing, and although it's run by a coloured man, all the staff are white. It makes me livid to think that you can invest your money and start up a place and you can't even employ whom you want to employ.

I feel things are going to get worse here because people just don't seem to be trying to make it any better. I feel part of the generation of my twin baby brother and sister. I don't know what we'll have to face.

I bought the newspaper with Enoch Powell's speech in it but I haven't read it yet. I don't want to think of Mr Powell. I'd just get myself upset. I'm not very political. If he wants to get up and shout his mouth off about coloured people, well, good luck to him. Some coloured people can be difficult to get on with but if anyone's ruining the chances of us all getting on together, he's going about it in the right way. Actually I don't bother to listen to him anymore – it gets so boring after a while. They talk about it at the office and the African woman who works with me gets very worked up about Powell. I'm interested to know what people think but I always try not to get into any arguments.

I think they shouldn't let any more people into this country – whether they are black or white. Otherwise unemployment will get out of hand.

I haven't discussed Powell's speech with my parents except to remark to dad 'Powell's at it again.'

On Indians

I have an Indian friend who is very nice. I met her at a party once and although she lives on the other side of London we've been friends for some time and we understand each other.

Indian girls often have trouble with their parents because they change their outlook, start wearing modern clothes and cut their long hair. I know an Indian girl who has had to leave home because of this.

The Indians are beginning to see that they have to live here and that means having to change their outlook.

Indian children used to be quiet and afraid to mix with others. But I think they're changing because they are very cheeky now. Even my Indian friend says the same thing; they now have attitudes like the English or West Indian children and they're not quiet anymore. They used to be accused of doing things like smashing shop windows and although they didn't do those things at that time, recently an Indian, West Indian and

English boy all smashed a shop window together 'for kicks.'
They've just gone mad. [Laughs]

I think it's because they live closely together and go to school
together and they've become more friendly with English
boys – they're fitting in better and so they decide to have a 'go'
with the gang. You see them walking home from school now in
groups together – West Indians, Indians and English. Before
the Indians would always be on their own.

Now they speak English together – beautiful English – and
even seventeen and eighteen year old Indian, West Indian and
English boys and girls now mix. You see them at the cinema for
instance. The Indian parents are still strict so there are not many
girls but there are some wearing mini-skirts now and they're
growing up and mixing.

Self-description
My doctor has been talking to me for years about relaxing and
trying to say what I really want to say – not keeping it all inside
me and never talking about it. He said to me 'That's the wrong
way to be.'

If there's the slightest little tension, my head starts to hurt
and I just can't think about anything. I have to keep calm all the
time in order not to get a headache. There's always a tension,
you know.

The doctor with whom I work said to me 'There's no point in
worrying about getting all the work cleared up, you only make
it worse for yourself – just relax and do what you can, you
know.'

From the time I was a little girl of seven, I always pictured
myself with someone saying to me 'Take a letter Miss James'.
[Laughs] I always wanted to work in an office.

I get on well with everybody – I fit in with people and I'm
glad to say I'm happy.

I just can't be hostile to people – I always stop myself. I'm
not a touchy person – if I was touchy, I don't know I – I'd
always be in arguments.

That's the trouble with me, you see, because I feel things and
get hurt inside and I keep them to myself. I just keep it to myself
and feel sorry for myself. I'm not a person to protest a lot.

Without thinking too hard about it, how do you see yourself? : I'm
kind – very generous [laughs] and on the whole, I think I'm

understanding. I expect I've got sympathy. I can always put myself in someone's else's shoes and I think that's why I'll probably never get anywhere in life because I always feel sorry for people and always wish I could help them.

I'm easy to get on with – but I've got moments when people get on my nerves. I let them know – we can still be friendly and I never bear a grudge. We just have it out and get it over with. I don't go round hating people – I never dislike people that much, but sometimes people get on my nerves and get me down.

How do your friends see you? :   Well, one or two of them think I'm too soft and that I should be a bit more hard. And when I'm with one of my friends who has a very quick temper and gets very worked up about things, and I'm just calm, she wants to hit me for not being as worked up as she is. I think it's very childish.

People have got an opinion about me that I can't do wrong and I don't like that sort of thing because I do wrong you know and no one believes that it's me. I say I'm going to get really nasty and do such and such and everybody says 'Oh, you couldn't do it – you haven't got the nerve you know.' My dad was talking the other day and he said that if somebody told him I had done anything drastically wrong, he wouldn't believe it. Well I don't like that.

I wish I could go out and be more free. I never really have the urge to go mad and do really terrible things but sometimes I think if I do something really wrong, I'd just shake them up a bit. They think I'm a goody-goody. Even at work now I've got that image and I really don't like it.

Life would be more interesting in Barbados than here – I'd get more fun from life and there'd be more to enjoy – the sea, the beach, picnics and glorious weather. If you try to be too gay in England something goes wrong. It's very hard really and then the weather doesn't really encourage you to go and do crazy things.

If I ever returned to Barbados I couldn't think of anything I'd miss in England.

ADRIAN JAMES: HIS STORY

It is late afternoon when Sylvia Hutchinson rings the front door bell. Adrian answers the door smiling shyly. He is of medium height for a fifteen year old, sturdily and athletically built with an open, broad, pleasant face and impeccably dressed in his school uniform, white crisp shirt, dark tie and blazer. They sit opposite each other in comfortable chairs. At first he is tense and fidgets nervously pulling at his shoelaces while the interview proceeds but he relaxes a little as he starts to enjoy talking. He has been in London only five months and his manner is still uncertain, somewhat anxious and unsure when silences occur. He usually breaks the silence by asking if there is anything else which she wants to know and it takes patience and tolerance on both sides for the interviews to develop so that Adrian finds his own way of reflecting on himself and his life. His speech is somewhat slow, and at times becomes a mumbled soft blur. But as the interviews proceed Adrian's greater spontaneity emerges as a result of his growing sense of confidence in his relationship with the interviewer.

Well, I'd prefer to start talking about my life back in Barbados. As you probably know my mom and dad were here long before I even knew them because I was two when they left and I lived with my grandmother for about twelve years. I had a few experiences there when I was about ten years old. I had some friends and they used to walk into the school and make trouble and the police came for them. There wasn't much trouble for me really but I just trembled for them. What they had done was to take a match and set light to the grass along the road and then they said I had done it. When the police came, there were two of them against me – their word against my word – and the police wouldn't believe me. But a man had seen these boys light the grass and he said I didn't do it. It was really a shocking thing.

They were summonsed but I was rather lucky and didn't get a summons. After that I used to keep away from boys who got into trouble. At school, you meet some boys who are nice and some who try to beat you up just because they are bigger than you. But that was when I was ten.

The very earliest thing I can remember is when I went to school at three years of age. My aunt took me to school and she took me in to the headmaster and then she left me. All of a sudden I started to cry because I didn't know where I was and she'd gone. And all the teachers tried to lift me up and said 'Hush, hush' and I'm not paying them any mind. I'm crying and crying and want my aunt. And I went to my class, the class for little children and I sat there all day wailing and crying, crying, crying. And the teachers came and looked at me, every hour they came and when my aunt came back for me I was still crying. I didn't want to go back to school but after a few days I settled down pretty well.

That's the earliest thing I can remember. My parents left when I was two but I can't remember that at all.

Staying with my grandmother and aunts and uncles
I was living with my grandmother and also my aunt and an uncle and cousins. I liked my grandmother very much but her ways were different from mine and she'd want me to do things her way. Well, I got a bit annoyed at that but if I didn't do it as she said I'd get a spanking and she'd hit me with the first thing she could get in her hand. For instance when I came home from school, she would want to send me to the shop and I'd feel tired and she would say 'You aren't tired – you've just come home from school'. Well, if I didn't go to the shop, I'd had it. So I had to play safe.

My grandmother used to tell me a lot about my dad. She remembered him as a little boy, you know, and the things he used to do for her. When she used to ask me to go to the shop, she used to tell me how when he was young, what a nice boy he was and how obedient he was and if she asked him to do anything he did it so quickly that if he was not busy doing it he'd finished it already!

She was responsible for my upbringing. She never used to let me miss a day from school. I'm not all that brainy but I know a bit more than some of the boys who are in my form. If I try hard I might come out where I really want to be and then I think it would be a credit to her. If she hadn't encouraged me, I might have just played games instead of going to school. She was one of the most important people in my life.

My aunt took me everywhere when I was small. She was more like a mother to me and I was very sad when she left to come over here. She is now a Sister in a hospital in Newcastle.

I had a lot to do with my uncles, one of whom also left and came over here but one remained there. My uncle tried to help me and was pretty nice, especially when I was a little boy. He gave me what he could afford and would stick up for me if I got into fights with other boys. He was a kind of father to me. He also tried to give me good advice to keep away from the company of bad boys and I tried to follow his advice.

My brother and sister

My brother Neill didn't live with me after my parents left. He lived with another relative and when he got older he left and lived on his own. He was very nice and I liked him a lot but he was a bit selfish and as I got older I realised that he didn't pay much attention to me and didn't come and look for me or visit me at all. When Johanna left, he didn't come near me and after a few years I went into my aunt's shop and I didn't know who he was. If he knew me he should have come and said 'Hello brother, its nice to see you' but he didn't and he then wrote and told my mom that I didn't speak to him. She wrote and asked me why I didn't speak to Neill and I said 'Well, I was in two minds – it could have been my brother or it couldn't and it was hard to know. If he recognised me, he should have said "Well, hello Adrian".'

I like him but he does certain things which I don't like. He should not have just left and gone to live on his own as if he didn't care and could leave his relatives like that. Everbody was vexed with him.

My sister Johanna was a different person altogether to Neill. I liked her a lot and whatever she had she gave me, you know; she still does that now. She used to come and see me whenever she could, because you see she lived with my uncle most of the time.

I felt very bad when Johanna left to come over here. I didn't want her to leave because after she had gone there would only be me left of our family because Neill didn't care much and after Johanna left he didn't come and look for me at all.

At the airport I called out to her because I didn't want her to go. I knew then I wasn't going to see any of my family until I grew big. I was nine when she left and when I saw other children going to the park and I couldn't go, I'd just sit and cry and say 'I wish my sister was here; then I could go'.

Feelings and thoughts about my dad and my mom

I thought a lot about my dad and my mom after they left. They used to write to me and send photographs of themselves. I – I just saw them you know, saw their faces in the picture but I was hoping that sometime my dad would come back to Barbados so that I could really see him and get to know him. My grandmother told me a lot about him.

When I was old enough to write, I wrote as if I was just talking to my dad in front of me. It seemed as if my dad was there and I was talking to him. I loved – loved him a lot although I didn't know who he was. [Laughs]

I know some fathers don't care about their sons but I always saw him as a father who loves his sons – loves his children and will try his best for them. If I needed money and he didn't have it in time, he would try to get it to me as fast as he could. He would write once a month and send money.

When Johanna left, I used to say – 'Well, they don't care about me, they don't like me. They sent for Johanna and they left me here for all this length of time.' But I couldn't give up you know and had to write to them, just to keep in touch. Well, after Johanna had gone, my Dad said 'Don't feel downhearted – I'll have you down here one of these days'. Well, after that I began to cheer up.

I saw my mom more or less the same way as I saw him. I felt she was the same. She used to write every two weeks. And I used to send them cards for their birthdays and Christmas. I had pretty good contact with them but I never heard their voices on the phone. They never got around to calling me, you know, so I never heard their voices. I just read their letters and had to put up with writing.

Schooldays in Barbados
I first went to a boys' school and we had a few white boys but mostly coloured boys there. The bigger boys like to bully you so I used to keep far away from them and they used to call me all sorts of nicknames. These are the sort of boys who are really human but their ways are so different they are more like dogs, they go round making trouble. They go down to the market place on a Saturday night and beat up people there.

These boys came to school one morning. I was form captain at the time and was sitting in my form room and they walked in. I was in the third form and they were in the fourth and fifth forms. As captain, I wasn't allowed to let any person come into the room before the bell went in the morning. I told these boys but they just pushed me out of the way, came inside and did what they liked. I got the blame from the headmaster. I told him it was these boys' fault but he didn't want to believe me because they were bigger than me and it was their word against mine. So I didn't like them very much and they didn't like me.

Then they used to go and interfere with girls and pull at them and touch them in all sorts of places and if anyone asked them their names, they gave my name. The next day the person reported this to the headmaster and he called me and asked me about it. I said I don't know anything about it. So the headmaster took us to the girls' school and asked the girls which boys had interfered with them and they accused the right boys and not me. They were expelled from the school.

That school closed down and I went to another school which had some boys but mostly girls. One of the boys threw a stone and cut someone else above the eye. I was wrongly accused but I said I didn't do it and the whole school was questioned. Then a man came and said he had seen a boy throw a stone and it was a prefect and his prefect's badge was taken away.

There were five boys who were the worst in the school and they were bigger than me. One day our teacher was absent and some of these tall boys were sent to keep us quiet. One of the boys in the class was talking so these big boys came straight to me and said 'Shut up' and I said I wasn't speaking so he said 'Yes, you were' and knocked me on the head. So I said 'Don't do that' and he did it again. I had proof I wasn't talking because I was sitting by some girls and boys and we were all reading books. So I went to the headmaster, and the boy was flogged. The headmaster had to try to get these boys out of the school as they were ruining the good name and reputation of the school.

I think they picked on me so much because I had a reputation as the best behaved boy in the school and they didn't like that. They bore me a grudge for that. And I used to come first in all my subjects and these boys came last and when the teachers praised me and said I was the best behaved boy in the school, they didn't like it. They did a lot of things to make my reputation drop, you see.

I tried to keep out of their reach.

There were no white boys in this school, it was a private school and the white boys went to the government school. At my first school there were a few white boys but I wasn't at the school long enough to get to know them. I didn't meet white boys at all in Barbados. If we passed them on the road as they rode their cycles up and down, they didn't stop to talk. The only white person that I knew at all in Barbados was the priest – he was American. All our neighbours were coloured. I didn't know any white people.

Adrian sang in the church choir for five years and was confirmed. Whites and coloureds both went to the same church and he observed that the white people were very generous particularly one white man who gave large sums of money to the church.

Encounters with adults

I was once in a bus queue full of grown-up people and a middle-aged man jumped in front of me. He pushed me out of line and each time I went in he pushed me out again. The policeman came up and at first he didn't believe my story so I went to him again and I said 'You can ask that lady behind the man.' So he asked the lady and she said yes, I had been there in front of her. So the policeman just took the man away because you're supposed to keep in line. If you are last, well, you are last.

Adrian recounted a number of incidents all involving West Indians in which he was falsely accused. 'I was coming home from the fair and some boys were stealing a lady's coconuts. I was passing that place at that time'. The man accused him, he denied it and 'so he took me up and put me on his shoulder – he was a big strong man and was going to take me to the police station. I let him take me up and went along pretty calmly but near a short cut to my home, I knocked his hand away and jumped off and ran home'. This same man accused him of stealing guavas and loosened a bull and it chased him. He wasn't stealing guavas but had permission to pick them. On another occasion the same man set five dogs onto Adrian for picking fruit in his own uncle's orchard. 'He wants to act as if he owns the village; if anything goes wrong, he's the first to get there and the first to want to take you to the police station. Most people didn't like him'.

'It was pretty rough in Barbados.'

Arrival in England

I kept on saying in Barbados that I wouldn't like to come to England because its so cold but I had to come here to my parents. I wanted to come because I was interested in the place.

Because I didn't know the voices of my mom and dad I thought it was going to be difficult for me because I might not be able to find them. But it wasn't so difficult because the air hostess took me around to the hall where the people were waiting and then she called out 'Mr James! Mr James!' and I saw this man – this gentleman. I say to myself 'He's supposed to be my dad.' The air hostess said 'I don't think we have any more

Mr James's here' and then she asked the question if he knew this boy? He said 'I've never really seen him' So she said 'Is he like your son?' He said 'Yes'. So she asked me if this is my dad? I said 'I don't know if it's my dad because I haven't seen him for twelve years.' Anyhow I saw it was my dad because my mom, she was there also and she was with my dad at the time and I knew her by some pictures I had been sent back home and there were also ones of Melissa and Allan. I saw her with the babies so I said 'That's my mom and my dad'. Then we got in the car and came to this house.

They were glad to see me and I was glad to see them also.

It was strange because not knowing them, anybody could come and say 'Well, he's my son' and I didn't know where I would end up. Anyhow it wasn't as bad as that. I found my dad and mom pretty easily. Then when I got here, after the beautiful airport so different to others back home, there were all these lovely buildings and I said to myself 'Is this where you live?' And then I said 'Yes' and I inspected all round and I thought 'It's gorgeous'. Then I came inside and looked around. It was all nice you know. Back home our houses have walls with a sort of pattern – but not wallpaper like here.

I went to look at different places with my dad. We saw some houses and buildings and I went to cricket with him at Lords. I'd never seen anything like that, it's big and gorgeous and I loved it and wished I could play there.

It was nice seeing Johanna again but she was big and she had changed. When she left home she was just a skinny girl but now she's grown up. We get on pretty well together.

My family got used to me pretty quickly but it took me a bit of time to get used to them because, you see, my ways were different. I did things differently, you know, and then my mom would tell me it's wrong and I would do it her way and try to get used to her.

I found my mom and dad were what I'd thought they'd be like. I thought they'd be nice and I think they were all happy when I came.

School in London

The first time I travelled on a bus was actually when I first went to school and back. My mom asked me if I wanted her to come and meet me after school. I said to her 'Well, I'll find my way'. So she left me and in the evening, the teacher asked some boys if they lived in my part of the city. So she told one boy to take me home. After school, I was looking for the boy. I don't know where he disappeared to, so I decided I'll follow the other boys to the bus stop. I didn't know which bus to take and looked for one with the name of this suburb on it. Well, I stood there all evening because of course you could get any one of those buses and it would have been alright.

Eventually I met a boy and he was going where I wanted to go and he said you have just missed four buses which stopped for you. And I said I didn't know. Anyhow the next bus came and I got on it and I got home. But the first day was pretty difficult.

I was shown around the school by the boys and I tried to pick up their ways. Sometimes I spoke and they didn't understand me and then they spoke and I couldn't understand them. Then we tried to correspond with each other.

The white boys didn't want to play with me and the boys my colour – well they wanted to play but they wanted to bully me and knock me around and I didn't like that.

The best thing that happened to me at school was the teachers all liked me. When I first went to school I was in the third grade – the lowest grade, 3C. and by the end of the term I went up to 4C. At the beginning of this term I then went into 4B. I'll probably go into 4A next term.

When I went to school they were short of cricketers so I got to play cricket for the school and did pretty well. The Headmaster was proud to have a new boy, whom people did not know too well yet playing in the school team.

The work is more or less the same as at home but I also do some different subjects like Technical Drawing, Metal-work and Woodwork.

Some of the things I've heard boys say at school! Fifteen year old English boys here are different to fifteen year olds in Barbados. Here they swear a lot and talk about a lot of rude things – what they did last night and all that stuff. They brought a record to school and just played it and played it and it's a very bad record – it wouldn't be allowed on the radio because of all the words in it. It's all sex – but these boys actually think – they just think it's fun and the songs are very bad. Well I don't know if it's bad to them but it is to me.

They give a lot of trouble to the lady teachers especially in these ways.

I think they are different to me.

They swear a lot and if you pass them and just happen to touch them they swear at you.

These boys probably can't help behaving like this – they're accustomed to it. The only time they behave is when they are scared of a certain teacher or the headmaster. Then they'll be quiet and obedient and once outside they call him this and that. If someone annoys them, even if he's the smallest boy they just kick him.

Some English boys I like, some of them are my friends but they don't do much swearing and we talk, you know. But we watch these other English boys picking on the first years and we can't do anything about it. If we went to the head, we wouldn't know whether they got punished or not.

I'm not so close to my friends. I don't see them often, just sometimes I might see them at the cinema. Some of them live down this road. The boy I like best is not English – he's an American Indian. He's very quiet and when the whole form is in trouble he's usually the one who doesn't join in with these boys. If he sees someone coming to beat him up or interfere with him, he tries to talk him out of it or he may go to the teacher. He tries to avoid fights, that's what I like about him.

He likes this country. People say – I don't know if it's true or not – that this country has the best education. Well, he says he likes to come to school in this country and the teachers like him and he likes them. But he says one thing he doesn't like is the little – can you imagine? When I first came to school I was shocked – little boys with big cigars smoking! I said to myself 'What's he doing?' I went to school and saw the same thing. I asked the fellow if he knew what he was doing. He said 'Yes'. Then he asked me for a sixpence for an icecream and I gave it to him. Then he went and bought two fags – two fags!

This American Indian doesn't smoke or anything like that. He likes this country and enjoys being fifteen.

English, Indians and West Indians at school
In my school I think there are only about six West Indian boys. Three quarters of the school is Indian or Pakistani and about a quarter are white. There must be about 450 boys in the school altogether.

English boys' ways are different to mine. We all do the same sports and work but their ways are different, that's all. Today they passed a post on their way to school and there was glass there and they said 'Go on Bill, go on, knock the glass out' And he goes and knocks it out. Whatever they tell him to do he does – he's actually the 'idiot' of the school. So they tell him to kick other fellows and he goes and kicks them.

Another time these boys went and interfered with women in the maternity hospital and there were a lot of complaints at school from the hospital.

These boys are always making trouble and man, when it hits you, it hits pretty hard. A Jamaican fellow at school got punched in the leg with a red hot metal rod – you know they were all doing metal work. They were playing the fool but this fellow got the thing in his leg.

Last week I saw a lot of things happen which I wouldn't expect to happen. An English boy had a fight with the history teacher – they were pushing each other around the room because the boy was told to go out of the room because he was making such a lot of noise and he wouldn't move so the teacher got hold of his jacket and pulled him up. So he started to push the teacher around. Later that day the boy said to the teacher 'I'm going to beat you up before the day's up' and they started to fight in the classroom, you know. The teacher took the boy to the headmaster and he was expelled but last night when the teacher was leaving school the boy waited for him in an alley to fight. So now the headmaster has stopped the master from staying on at the school late.

I am actually sorry for boys like this – they're out of their minds to go and do things like that – beating up a teacher. I think this boy's a bit mad, because he shouldn't do that. I've never heard of a boy who beat up a teacher.

The same week at school this gang of six white boys came to pick a fight with this Indian friend of mine. They never beat up any English boys but they pick on Indian blokes who are scared; they just go bashing up the Indians. I was so sorry for my Indian friend because he's just a little boy, you know. He's in my form but he's a bit slim and short you know and he's so quiet. He doesn't pick a fight with anybody and when he saw these boys coming to beat him up, he just ran to hide from them; he was afraid he would get hurt. And then when he returned to the school he told the headmaster and the boys concerned were caned. These boys always give trouble in Assembly each morning. Well, this morning the headmaster was talking to the school in Assembly about these two things – the boy and the history master, and the way these boys tried to beat up this Indian. He said that the school had never had anything like this before.

I don't really feel sorry for these boys because they're always doing things like this and they're always getting the cane. They're actually accustomed to it and the cane doesn't mean a thing to them. They come along and bash you up, get their cuts and then they go back and bash you up again.

They don't pick on West Indians but they pick on the Indians and Pakistanis. I think they don't like them, that's all. They call them funny names.

Well, half the prefects and form captains and librarians at the school are Indians and they have a good reputation for behaviour. I think the white boys actually feel a grudge, you know – they feel a grudge against the little Indian boys for what they have accomplished. The Indian boys usually come top in their form, you know. That might be why some of the English boys don't like them.

To me the Indians and Pakistanis are not different from others in the school. In some ways they are even better than some of the white boys. Most of the people who are in the sixth form at school and who have 'O' levels and working for 'A' levels are the Indians. The headboy is the only white boy in the form working at 'A' levels. The Indians actually outclass the white boys in everything at school. I hope no one will dislike them – I don't dislike them.

The white boys feel very bad about the Indians outclassing them. Like if a white boy sees an Indian tomorrow morning with a new pair of shoes on, he would say 'Oh – his shoes – how cheap!' and all that stuff and in this way they actually crush the Indian boys. Its probably that the English boys want what the Indians have accomplished. They can get it if they try hard enough to learn, but they don't. They just come to school and talk about girls.

I won't feel sorry for a white boy if he goes around and bashes another boy because he would be getting the joy of it. But if I saw a West Indian boy beating up a white boy, well I'd probably say he's giving some of his own medicine back. But at this school there are more white boys than West Indian boys so if a white boy saw another white boy being beaten up, he'd join in and help beat the other one up.

I don't like to see people fighting like that – just for nothing. English boys don't play with Indian boys.

The only way in which Indian boys are different from me is that some of them wear turbans. Indians think alike you know and they don't think like the whites.

I think some of the white boys are actually like me – but the majority of them are just out to pick a fight. Like today at school an Indian boy was in a form room having a cup of coffee and this white boy went inside and grabbed him and told him to get out and take the coffee outside. They don't like Indians, that's all.

Last week we had a debate at school about Indians, Pakistanis and West Indians. The English seem to like the West Indians but they don't like the Indians and Pakistanis and I just don't know why. They say some awful things about them and they don't seem to know why they come to this country. But there are millions of people in India and its poor and some of them try to get out to come to this country where it's a bit more free you know and also to get away from their religion. People here don't seem to appreciate this. They want to come to this country – some of them come illegally, some come legally, but some white people don't seem to like them.

About girls

At school in Biology we are doing plant life, insect life and human life. Talking about girls is a subject but I don't hurry the teacher. He teaches what he wants to teach and he starts off on the grounds of Biology. You have to know the plant life and the insect life before you can know about humans and the human body. He is trying to bring this up gradually but the English boys want to start at the top.

If I pass a girl, then a friend might say 'Hey, Adrian, there's a bird for you!' I just smile you know because I don't see much sport in it actually. My ambition is to get my 'O' levels first and probably then I can start thinking about girls. [Laughs]

There's a friend who comes here – my sister's friend – she's nice you know – not in the sense that other boys might refer to a girl friend you know. I just like her, she's nice.

At home with the family

Life in Barbados was pretty good you know, but now with my dad and mom, its a new phase and I begin to enjoy myself. Well, at fifteen – I like being fifteen.

I go to picnics here and to the cinema and on excursions and to parties. I never used to go to parties or anything like that back home. I go to parties with people older then me – my dad's friends and then I go with my dad, mom and Johanna. They're very nice people and they're kind. Sometimes people might say that they're having a party only for adults – or only men or only women – but I go and somebody may say 'What are you doing here?' [laughs] but it doesn't upset me – I am there and I've come along with my family and had a nice time. People dance and have drinks. I don't actually drink, I don't like it. People always give me a sip but all I have is probably a bit of wine. But I love dancing. At first I was a bit shy to go and dance but now I dance and talk to the people. Most of them are my dad's friends and he introduced me to them and we just have a little chat. They ask me how I like the country and I say 'I've only just come and I'll have to wait and see but I think I like it and I'll stay a certain time. I don't know how long I'm going to stay'.

I go to the cinema about once a week. The first time I went with Johanna and a friend but now I go on my own. I usually tell my dad in the morning and when my mom comes home I'll say 'Mom, I would like to go to the cinema. Can I go?' You know, she'd say 'Yes you can go'. They don't say 'No'.

I get pocket money each week which pays for my school dinner and for the cinema and I think it's enough for me.

There are some things I'm expected to do at home. During the summer I have to sweep [laughs] the yard and the back garden and the front porch. I have to sweep the leaves off and when it's dirty I have to wash it. I'm accustomed to doing it and feel alright about it.

My sister sometimes makes my bed for me or I do it myself. But say like Saturday, if my room hasn't been tidied up before watching the telly, I have to go and do it before my mom sees it. If not, I have to do that and double up and do the stairs also and maybe hers too – so I do it you know.

I try to do everything to please you know but sometimes Johanna gets annoyed like when I don't feel like putting the paraffin in the heaters. I just say to her 'Can't you do it?'

I don't do much choosing really. If I can do anything, I do it but I don't choose it. I might say I don't want to do something, but it would be three against one, so I go and do it.

My parents expect me to be doing well at school and I try my best to do well. I'm staying on to do 'O' levels and will probably go on and do 'A' levels also.

I want to become an airline pilot – or an accountant. Every week at the school the careers officer comes and I asked my dad to come to the school. He said to the officer 'Well, my son says he wants to be a pilot' and they gave us a bit of advice and told us about the work a pilot does.

Johanna is a young woman now and she should have the freedom she wants. I think my parents give her actually more freedom than they would give me. I may have a bit of freedom when I'm older, but I don't think they will give me much freedom to do what I want. I want to do something one way and they might want me to do it another way – for instance say I had to water the garden. It's a pretty simple thing but here you aren't legally allowed to water the garden with a hose. Well it's pretty boring watering with a can of water and coming back and carrying it around. I want to turn the water on and just spout it with the hose. But they say 'No you can't – you're not allowed'. But some people do it.

Church

Adrian brought a letter from his church in Barbados when he arrived. He sang in the choir at home and was invited to join the choir in the church here (where the congregation is largely white) but was reluctant to do so as he wanted a bit of a rest from choir practice. One of the head ladies in the Church came to talk to his father to persuade him to join the choir and his father then 'talked me into it.' When he was asked to join the Servers, he said he'd have to think about it but he did join them and the Bishop was present the first time he served. 'I got a lot of praise for it'. He then decided he would continue with it. Later he was asked to become Chief Crucifer 'The priest says he will be glad if I can do the job permanently. So I think I will take the job and do that and sing in the choir'.

On race and Enoch Powell's speech

I read Enoch Powell's speech in the paper this morning but I didn't make much sense of it. If you got on a bus today, you wouldn't notice if the bus conductor was Indian, West Indian or an Englishman. You'd just pay the fare and not take much notice of him.

I haven't talked about this speech to anybody at home yet

because I only read it in the paper this morning and I haven't seen them yet.

I don't hear of any black people causing trouble in this country. If there's any trouble, it's probably some stupid white man. There's no violence going on in this country, no black people are involved in any violence.

Powell wants to see immigrants leave but then the English would have to give up good jobs in order to run essential services. If it weren't for West Indians and Indians, who would run London Transport?

Powell can talk but he can't make people leave. What he's trying to do is get all white people to hate the coloured people. This is what might spoil my future in this country and any coloured person's future.

This colour thing can affect all people and can affect all nations, West Indians, Pakistanis, Indians and Africans.

If it goes on and on, well, the coloured people might not stay around for this any longer and they might leave.

I don't think the coloured people here are being given dirty jobs and find it difficult to find good jobs if they're qualified. If they have the qualifications, they can get anything they want.

Indians are lucky and the white people begrudge them. I don't know where they get their money from but they get money and buy shops. One man would try and get friends and they would join together and buy the store and then they would run the store together.

Self-description

Don't think too hard, just tell me as quickly as you can how you would describe yourself: I'm 5 ft 7 inches tall, coloured with dark hair and eyes which are dark, dark brown. I wouldn't say I was handsome [laughs] but fairly good looking. I'm honest and like to help other people. I think I must have a fairly good conscience.

How would your best friend describe you?: He would say I was sporting, kind, generous, helpful – and that's about it apart from tall and coloured.

And if you had a worst enemy, how might such a person describe you?: Well, she'd probably say I was black and ugly and a vagabond who's no good, who would steal, you know. I'm thinking of a special coloured woman in Barbados who used to think she was white, you know. She would say I was a thief and would steal people's things.

The reason why I want to be a pilot is that a pilot enjoys the dangerous part of it because once you are on a plane everything is dangerous because you are flying this plane and you are the only person who can actually control it. If anything goes wrong with you, well everybody's doomed. I think everybody has to take a risk sometime. And well, I would say the most difficult part of being a pilot is that you have to be bang on target – it's one of the basic parts of the training.

I would like to be in air control, the man who is in the control tower and who contacts all the pilots and directs the planes in to land. He controls everything from the control tower.

But I might change my mind and be an accountant or a pilot. For accountancy you have to be able to count well not only with your eyes but with you brain too and have to be able to count fast and deal with money.

If I do either of these things, I think it's best to be trained at a university and I'd like to go and I'm looking forward to it.

Chapter 4

THE ENGLISH REFLECTING: THE CHATTAWAYS' LIFE HISTORIES

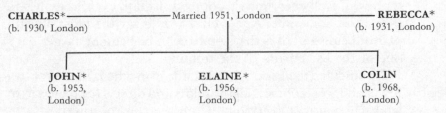

CHARLES*————————————Married 1951, London————————REBECCA*
(b. 1930, London)   (b. 1931, London)

JOHN*   ELAINE*   COLIN
(b. 1953,   (b. 1956,   (b. 1968,
London)   London)   London)

*The research interviews were conducted from 10 January to 15 April 1971 and the research subjects are indicated by an asterisk.

MR CHARLES CHATTAWAY: HIS STORY

It is after dinner and Mr Chattaway is expecting me. He is a tall burly man with dark curly hair, powerful and heavy in his movements. He comes to the door of his double-storied council house, neatly but casually dressed and we walk down the passage to the kitchen. The evening meal has just finished and the aroma of a roast hangs heavy over us. He pulls out chairs for us both and across the small yellow-topped plastic table, we face each other, sitting upright on our kitchen chairs. He leans forward, arms crossed on the surface of the table – a troubled face on which suffering seems to have left a mark. The closeness of the room catches and traps the waves of feeling which come through at times with understated nonchalance, denials of hurt, and at other times with powerful vehemence, anger and force. He is articulate and words come easily and fast. His eyes usually move quickly past mine – darting away from me – evading or avoiding – but at other times he looks at me with great earnestness, seeking to convince me of his point of view and attempting to secure confirmation.

The large living room adjacent to the kitchen is where his eldest son John is talking to Sylvia Hutchinson and intermittently his small son Colin aged two and a half comes through the intervening door and is given a biscuit or a cool drink by his father and encouraged to

116

go upstairs. Mrs Chattaway is at work for a few hours each evening at this time.

I'll start off at the beginning. I was born in Uxbridge and I never lived with my parents. I was told that my mother left my father when I was about six weeks old and I went to live with my grandparents who brought me up. To this day I've never seen my father. My mother was a housekeeper to a doctor in Putney and she used to come over and see me and sometimes she lived with us.

I grew up in Notting Hill you know – I suppose you've heard of that – it's a bit rough – a terrible quarter. They reckon that if you've come from Notting Hill you'll never get a job. The old saying went 'You're either a thief or a prostitute coming from Notting Hill'.

You had to sort of look after yourself or you got a good hiding and that was it. You were on your own, I mean . . . I broke my nose not knowing how to defend myself properly but this hardens you in life and I became independent and had to do my own thinking. I had to think by myself as a child. It was over to me. I had to think things out.

Childhood
I lived with my gran and grandfather and an uncle and two aunts. I was the baby of the family.

It never bothered me that my mother didn't live with me. She was alright. I mean to say she left me a penny a day for sweets and that sort of caper, you know. She always took me on holidays – that's a thing I always had – just with my mother. And I had what gear I wanted.

I never went short of food, nothing like that . . . uhm . . . aaah . . . I have no complaints really.

My gran was a bit of a puritan [laughs]; she came from Staffordshire and was a bit countrified and a bit of a bible puncher [laughs]. Holy Joe, you know! My grandfather was a bit on the severe side too. They were Church of England and I went to a church school once and always had to go to Sunday school. My gran insisted. I don't go now – to tell the truth I haven't got a lot of time for that sort of thing.

I couldn't really bring friends home to my gran's. I used to play with the boys and go out but we never sort of had any one in to play or anything like that.

It didn't bother me not knowing my father – I didn't think about him. I had a good childhood and used to do what I wanted with my grandfather. I mean to say my father never bothered about me. Why should I bother about him? He was on his own and now I'm on my own. That's the way I look at it. I mean I've got hardened. But when I was young it never bothered me.

Once an aunt of mine came on a Sunday afternoon and she said 'Here', she said, 'I thought I saw your father'. And I said 'Oh did you'? [Laughs] She said 'I'll swear it was your father'. And I said 'Oh yeah'. That was a long time ago.

The only picture I've seen of him was when my mum was married.

School in Notting Hill

When I lived with my gran, I used to get up, go to school and have my meals. The kids there were a bit boisterous and a bit sportified. We used to play football and cricket. There were English boys mainly, but we had Jews – a girl Shirley and her brother Saul who used to own the fish-and-chip shop. And there was an Italian bloke and very few coloureds. We didn't know anything about coloureds then, not like now with the masses we've got over here.

When I was about ten, I lost my temper and I crippled a boy. We were in the playground and he started agitating and I didn't take a lot of notice. But he pushed his luck and I don't know how, but I just got him and threw him down and he fell and broke his leg. He had to have irons around it you know and he came up in front of the headmistress and he said I was vicious and all that old caper, and I had to go around and apologise to the boy. I took him some oranges and all that lark. You get a normal amount of scratch when you're a boy you know – I mean good hidings – and you give them too. I don't know if he's still in irons. It's a case of . . . er . . . you hit someone back or you just take a good hiding. It's self-preservation.

Uprooting

My gran's house got bombed out during the war and I was sent to Cornwall for nine months and then when things got a bit quiet in London I went to live in Chiswick with my auntie. My gran stayed in Notting Hill but they thought there were better opportunities for me if I came to Chiswick. My uncle did fence erections and I had a cousin who was about five years younger than me.

I had to think for myself then. I couldn't turn to my auntie and say things like kids say nowadays. My kids have now got their own rooms and can bring their friends in, but when I lived with my auntie I never had that sort of freedom.

Money was tight in those days and I used to go down to the market with a crowd of my mates, and while the man on the barrow wasn't looking, I'd nick apples or oranges or something like that. If I wanted something and I hadn't got the money, well, when nobody was looking I'd take it. It wasn't a crime – nicking you know – the crime was getting caught. [Laughs]

I liked school and started getting interested in Maths, and woodwork. I had a mechanical aptitude. I've always been interested in making things well and the only aptitude I've really had is using my hands.

I've always been a great reader too and I get my nose stuck in a book.

My cousin who lived with us had a good headpiece. Later on when he grew up he went to college and did well. He's got his own house and everything now. I don't know, I suppose his father stood behind him and could read and help him. I suppose with myself, as I say, my mother wasn't very career minded . . . she wasn't the type of person who had been around a lot or knew anything much like sorts of work and things like that.

When I left school at fourteen, I was just average. I wasn't clever or anything like that.

There were very few coloureds in Chiswick but a bloke used to be in our club. He was coloured and a good boxer. I've seen him a couple of times since then and he's married a white girl. And you know it's as if I was talking to one of my own mates. We were all mixed together then and we didn't think of him as black. But I'm more aware of who is black now than I was then because there are so many of them now.

Growing up

Charles left school at 14 and his uncle found him a job working in a machine shop. He started night school, studied mathematics and technical drawing and was later called up and went into the RAF as an engine mechanic. He served largely in England but paid brief visits to Belgium, France and Holland. He was demobilized in 1949.

> At that time I used to do a lot of drinking as most of my mates were in the Merchant Navy. All I used to do was drink, drink, drink and I weighed 14 stone with a big belly out here. I used to gamble a lot too and play cards and all that kind of caper.

He got in with a group of three others whom he met in a pub. One of these men had been in prison for armed robbery. They all started stealing cars.

> I've only done a lot of things which all boys do, you know, like knocking off a few cars. The furthest I took a car was to Bristol and there's a bit of a story about that one. W'd taken the car and then we all went to the cinema but unfortunately someone had spotted us and the law came and surrounded the cinema. We dived down into the stalls, getting down behind the seats. The cinema was then empty and they were going round with flash torches but they couldn't see us. But afterwards, two dashed out one way and two the other, and I went towards the car but as I got there, the copper came out and blew his whistle. He wouldn't tackle me himself, you know, he was a bit nervous. So I shot down the road and two of us managed to escape. The other two got caught and got done for three years. I was single then of course. I don't do that sort of caper now.
>
> I always look at life like this. If I do something I shouldn't do and I get caught – well that's it and I don't quibble about it. If I play for high stakes and I know the penalty, well if I get caught I've got to pay for it but if I get away with it – well, that's my good luck.
>
> When I was in the forces I got punished and I accepted it.

He recounted various incidents when he was in the RAF. He hit an NCO at a dance and got ten days in prison. Then he was accused by a Squadron Leader ('a northerner – he didn't like Londoners') for being 'a disgrace to the King's uniform' and he got another ten days for that, because he had his hands in his pockets and his hat off while in uniform. After night flying, men were usually excused from parades the following morning but he was told to be on parade after night flying and then given a week shovelling coke for having dirty boots. He resented this bitterly.

> That sort of thing gets up my back – silly little things like

that! I mean many of these staff sergeants are right bullies – they punch and hit blokes and knock them around – not around the face, because that would show bruises – but they could hit a bloke and give him a good hiding and you wouldn't see a mark on him. No, they didn't do it to me but they have done it. There are a lot of things that go on that people don't know about . . .

And finally when he was not well, he was unjustly accused of malingering.

It got up my back. I never tried to dodge anything. If it comes my way, well, I take it.

Courtship and marriage
It was about 1950 and I was knocking around with a crowd of young hounds and we all went to a dance hall in Uxbridge. My missus went up the stairs to the dance and so I said 'Hello darling' or something like that and I got a dirty look. [Laughs] Anyway we got into the dance hall and we had a few beers and we had a few dances and then I said 'I'll see you Sunday night down at the Catholic' – that was a dance hall run by the Catholic church but you didn't have to be a Catholic. So we met down there and we started going out then.

Then one day my missus was on the back of my motor bike and the copper came out of nowhere and I had no tax or insurance and I got done for it. I've got done lots of times – motorbikes and doing things I shouldn't do.

It's not the doing of things that matters – it's getting caught – that's what I'm against. If you can get away with things and give them a load of old flannel, that's alright as long as no one's harmed or anything like that.

I was twenty-one when I married Rebecca – and I stopped drinking then and went off beer just like that. I very seldom have a drink now – I don't bother about it any more.

Rebecca and I went to stay with my mother-in-law in Athol and we lived there for two years. She was alright – my mother-in-law was – but Rebecca had her other brothers and sisters there, and I was sort of a bit bombastic you know. I'd been free and my own boss and had been able to do what I liked and please myself and I've always had to think for myself and make my own decisions and everything had only concerned me. I thought I could carry on in the same sort of way but – well, you learn by experience don't you? I had to change my tune.

Having a home

My mother-in-law lived in this part of London where we live now. After two years with her we moved to Notting Hill – we had our own front room and another room and we could do what we liked but we had no water taps. If we wanted water for washing we had to go downstairs, fill a jug, come upstairs and empty it and downstairs again. And when John was a youngster he couldn't run around or make a lot of noise and there was no garden. Rebecca couldn't stick it any longer – it was really bad and we were there for three years.

We went to try and get better accommodation and the people had the audacity to say to me 'Your wife can go into one of those institutions and you can go into lodgings'. Well, you can guess what I said. That was in 1953/4 – but it's twice as bad now. The price of houses is fantastic and there's no chance of buying a house and I think that's all wrong. The government's priority ought to be building houses. But people who complain about council houses don't know how lucky they are. They've never had to rough it like we did – up and down those stairs and having to hold on to your temper with the woman who lived beneath us.

We then went to live with Rebecca's mum for a month and moved into this part of London. We first got a flat on this council estate in 1956 and Elaine was born there and we stayed in that flat for six years and then got this house, on the same estate. It's also a council house.

A lot of people haven't got the ability to go and buy a house. Let's be honest about it – I myself couldn't be bothered to buy when I had a chance. But I've got nothing against this house. I hear people moan about council houses but I flare up sometimes because they've never had to rough it, living in one room where you can't creep about and daren't make a noise at all. I flare up when people talk about 'only having a council house'.

People who are homeless have no incentive to do any better but once you've got a house then this gives an incentive to go to work and also to respect property, because if people are living in a slum house with the paper peeling off and the damp rising and no toilet, well their kids aren't going to grow up to have respect for other people's property. If you went through the background of all the juvenile delinquents, you'd find half of them came from poor families where their parents didn't care – so you can't blame the kids but I think that's the thing which the government has got to tackle – building houses.

When we moved into this house, it was the bad winter of '62/'63 and we had no coal. I never ordered any because I didn't want to move it from the flat to here and we couldn't get any coal. Rebecca was in bed ill for a fortnight and my work meant I had to do the fire boilers so when I was there – well, I'll be honest about this – there was some coal and I loaded a bag up when it was dark and took it on my pushbike home because we had no fuel. It was there so I took it – it wasn't my fault – we couldn't get any fuel. I ordered it but it never came.

My son John

When we had John we lived in those two rooms in Notting Hill and John was a subdued child because he wasn't allowed to make a noise. And I didn't find a lot of time for him because I was away working.

I don't believe in forcing anyone to do anything but we tried to get John to go to Sunday school and he wasn't interested. He didn't even like going to ordinary school and we had a hell of a job taking him to school. I never had much to do with him because I was working all over the place and sometimes I didn't get home until late at night and I very rarely saw John when he was growing up.

My missus thinks I'm too hard on him – I expect too much from him but once I've told him something I expect him to know. I was only told once and that was that. I treat him the same way.

He's got to do his own thinking and solve his own problems. He's always had a free hand. I don't know what he does inwardly but outwardly he gives the impression that he's not really bothered or worried. He's more happy-go-lucky than my generation was. He and others his age speak their minds more and they won't knuckle down, whereas we were frightened to look at the foreman, for instance, but they will go and argue with him which I think is a good thing.

I've had a bit of bother with him with his motorbikes. The police have worn a path up to the front door – they keep walking up here for the least little thing. He gives them a false name and address – he does what the bright hounds tell him to say – but of course the police have his number and can trace him. He doesn't *think* but he's got a bit smarter now and I've wised him up to a few things.

John was driving without L-plates, giving pillion lifts which as a learner he was not allowed to do, and then giving false names and addresses. His father feels very emotionally involved in John's dealings with the police.

They were having a go at him. The copper came in one morning early and started laying down the law and that got up my back. I felt that the police are not going to get away with it.

And I could have killed these coppers. I had it all written down, what I was going to say and the questions I was going to ask. But John had to be tried in the Adult court and so he had to speak for himself. I could have torn those coppers to bits because I couldn't say anything.

John's a bit strong willed. He doesn't say a lot – he's a bit deep, old John and if he's got a problem he'll work it out himself. He doesn't say much to me but mostly to his mother. She's more understanding than I am. I flare up you see and have a go. Now the missus – he sort of says things to her, but he won't say anything to me. He knows there might be a couple of blows or something. I've come to blows with John – oh yeah – but I never hit him really hard because my missus would go potty. But last time the copper came with six charges, I hit him.

John can look after himself. He's quiet though and he's deep and he doesn't tell his mother much either. He had an argument with three blokes round the flats one day and he hammered them and we didn't know anything about it – someone else let it out of the bag.

You know what these boys are – bravado! When there's another war, they'll be pleased the boys do that sort of thing. They wouldn't want the timid ones, they'd want the potty ones.

I never stuck up for John. If he used to have a punch up then that's his problem and he's had a few that we know nothing about – not supposed to know about them anyway. [Laughs]

John has it easy. If his scooter's broken he moans because he's got to walk. I never used to have a scooter or motorbike at his age and that's what upsets me and I flare up at him – I don't blame him for having it easy but when he moans about it – he doesn't realise how much easier he's got it than I had.

I've got my gear out in the shed and I've got loads of tools there and I know where they are. I've had them for years. John comes in and borrows them and slings them here and there, and that gets up my back and I have a row about it. I mean I've got tools now which I bought when I first started work – they're something to me and when people use them I flare up, see? I've looked after them all these years. I had to buy them myself and I mean to say I never had a lot of money.

John is a skinhead.[1] I think these skinheads and rockers[2] are a stupid lot. One crowd has got motorbikes and the others have got scooters and so they punch each other up and cut each other up. Oh, they are *stupid*! While they're fighting amongst themselves, they could rather have a go at these wogs that keep going around looking for bother. Keep them *down*! But while they're fighting among themselves, well I said to John and the other hounds that come around here 'Why are you boys fighting among yourselves? They're all laughing at you – these coloureds – they're the ones you want to have a go at'. I say these boys have got to stick together because if they don't, this other lot of coloureds are going to get the upper hand and they won't be so tolerant to us as we have been tolerant to them.

John's got loads of girls – they've all been around here and there were some nice girls but I don't think he sticks with them long. [Laughs]

About his work, John's a plodder. I've had him out with me working and he won't do anything until he's told, you know, in case he does it wrong, instead of using a bit of initiative. But other people have spoken well of him. I probably expect too much.

My daughter Elaine
When Elaine was little you know, she was all there. She was of slim build. She's a bit timid, you know. If you say 'Boo' like that, she'll jump out of her skin sort of thing. [Laughs]

Elaine, being the girl, is a bit on the plump side now, you know. I'd like to get some of her weight down. She doesn't go out much and I'd like to see her go out more, go to dances and I'm quite prepared to go and pick her up and all that, but I think she's a bit of a stay-at-home girl. She might be different when she goes to work but I think she's a bit immature. You know she's not so fly as some girls. Other girls younger than her, they know all the tricks of the trade and I think she's a bit backward like that, you know, physically I mean. You know you can get that with little girls her age – they know about the facts of life, they talk and they go out and go to these discotheques but Elaine doesn't do that sort of thing. I think she's either a bit shy or she lacks confidence. She's a late starter, you know, and my wife's discussed it with her and with the doctor and he says there nothing to worry about – some are late starters. She may be different when she loses a bit of weight. The doctor says it's nothing to worry about and all of a sudden she might go like a dose of salts. The wife's had a talk to her about these things – I'm not much good at that [laughs], they can have a chat with me, but I'll probably be a bit crude. But I don't like to broach it with her in case it embarrasses her you know. If they're prepared to talk about it well, you know, it's half the battle but if I've got to broach the subject, I'll have to pick and chose my words and start stumbling and end up feeling it was a bad job.

I'm a bit of racialist – no doubt you gathered that but you've got to be either white or black, nobody wants khaki. I wouldn't go out of my way to put the block on Elaine – she knows my feelings now so I don't think that she would entertain coloureds, but there again it's up to her. When she's eighteen and of voting age, she can do exactly as she likes, but I would make it clear that if she did get married to a coloured I wouldn't want to know. I wouldn't go to the wedding, I say that now, but I might change my mind. He might be a nice lad – I mean there are some nice boys among them. They're the same as me if they work for a living. They've also got to earn a crust. But if they marry, there will be children and there you are – it's still that I'm white and they're coloured. It's as simple as that.

I don't think I'd entertain her bringing a coloured friend here. I wouldn't be aggressive to the girl, because I wouldn't want anyone to be aggressive to her, but I don't think I would encourage it.

And Colin

John and Elaine grew up when there were hardly any coloureds here but Colin is unfortunate – he's got to be lumbered with them unless I can move out somewhere, where they haven't got such a mass of immigrants. It depends if I can get something going. Then I shall leave like thousands of other people who want to get out of Athol.

Some kids haven't got anything but Colin's got everything – loads of toys, everything, cars, barrows, swings, he's got a desk and boxes and boxes of toys. All the family bring him toys.

He doesn't miss a thing. He's all there and he's more daring than the others. He's a bit more adventurous and more independent. If he wants to do something and sets his mind on it, he'll do it. Definitely more 'go' than the other two had.

My wife

We get on right well now but we never did to start with. I used to flare up at the least little thing and pack my tools and I was away and that sort of caper. But now I have to think a bit differently and my attitude is a bit different.

Rebecca says I'm not homely and all that silly old caper. Well, I haven't much idea of papering and decorating. I don't bother about colours – things could be pink or green it doesn't bother me. She's different. She's got to live in it all day. It's up to her, I say. She chooses all the colours.

I'd like to go and travel round different countries. As I'm married now Rebecca doesn't like me being away so I've had to turn down lots of good jobs. So I'm home at night and there you are! I mean, that's life!

We don't go out a lot. Before Colin was born we started going out on Saturdays for an evening meal and then we'd go for a drink with friends but the wife doesn't drink and I've gone right off it. I love a game of cards and a gamble but my wife doesn't play cards and that was knocked on the head.

I seem to be getting a bit more domesticated. [laughs] It's only during these past few weeks when I've been out of work that I've said to my missus 'What do you think?' That's the first time I sort of asked her what she thinks. I must be getting soft or something. [laughs]

I accept things as they are – I've settled down into married life – going to work – coming home – I'm resigned to the fact that I'm married.

My work

I've always been interested in engineering and when I left school I went to night school and even when I married I was doing night school three nights a week, learning welding. But when John and Elaine were born I had to give up my course and couldn't be bothered to finish it because I needed the money, and so had to work overtime.

He became a responsible foreman fitter and welder and worked with various large firms. At the beginning of the study he had a chance to start on his own and left his job, but the contract he thought he would get fell through and he found himself without a job for the first time in thirteen years. He was without work for many weeks but got fixed up before the end of the study.

I can get a job – I was offered a foreman's job, but I don't want the responsibility, I don't want all that worry now, I've had enough of it. I've also been offered another four jobs but they don't suit me so I don't want them.

They asked me if I wanted the foreman's job and I said 'No'. I've had enough of it – responsibility of others. I wouldn't mind if you didn't have to chase them. You get these blokes who just don't bother as long as somebody else does it – it's typical of the British disease all through industry – passing the buck – and nobody wants to make a decision about anything.

I don't worry now – I've had enough of it. When I was a foreman and had 100 men under me, there's a hell of a lot of running around to do and I was working twice as hard as anybody else and the other blokes were just standing around doing a job which should take them a couple of hours and instead would take them a day or two. Then I had to account for that time and I knew full well they were loafing so I had to ruck them. Then they said I'm a big burk! I was the go-between between the governor and the men and the blokes would turn around and say they weren't bothered it was my worry but I had to answer for their work. If you sack them, you're a right burk again see – and if you don't get the work out of them, then you're asked what you're doing sitting on your arse. I hate being crude but that's how they talk. So I was the butt of both sides.

I wasn't ruthless enough to be a good foreman – I was a bit soft-hearted, but I've learnt my lesson.

I think I'll just get a job – plod – why should I bother – and that's the attitude of a lot of people nowadays. It's a cut-throat race and it's getting worse – those who are climbing up the ladder are stamping on the feet of those who are trying to get up and the bloke whose trying to get up is pulling the ladder away from the bloke who's up there. It's a rat race and I'm not bothered.

Nowadays people couldn't care if they go to work or not. I've got that attitude now. I'm ashamed to admit it. I always used to be conscientious – be at work on time welding until midnight but it's done me no good.

Well I'm pleasing myself now. I don't want to work all those hours. I can't see any future in it. If I get desperate and have no money then I'll go tomorrow. But I've got 20p in my pocket and I sort of plod along – it doesn't bother me but if I'm really desperate then I'll have to get my fingers out and get something.

There's something wrong with the whole country. I think it's apathy. During the way when I worked in the factory people had an aim and we had a target so everyone worked and then after the war everyone reverted back to looking after themselves and the country went down and down and you're taxed higher now. I was conscientious then but I've changed now.

I think the trouble lies with the general relaxation of discipline not only in homes between parents and teenagers but also discipline has been relaxed in industry.

When you work in a factory and in one spot all the time and you can't get out – there aren't opportunities for making yourself some extra money. On jobs on the outside I can get a few perks. There were some bits of lead and copper which were lying around once and which I just took and flogged for a good price. I saw it lying there – well I mean if people leave it around, well that's their problem. One year we had copper ingots away which were worth over £600 and 'touch wood' – I've never been caught.

That's why I like to work outside – I get opportunities.

Working with coloureds
I've worked with coloureds – there was a boy – Jeff, he was quite a nice lad and he came from Harlesden – there were quite a few coloured welders who worked with me. Another coloured boy there was a good worker and he worked the same as me, day and night the same as me. He wanted his money and he worked for it. He didn't get anything on a plate – he worked for it and I've got nothing against him. He's the same as me – he goes to work in order to see what he can get.

But I can't stand blokes who come over here with no intentions of working – they're a liability. They hang around and make it awkward so you've got to sack them – they don't want to learn – but then they go on the dole and we've got to pay those taxes – they shouldn't have come in in the first place – they're a liability and that's what's getting up people's backs.

I've been in factories where I've seen an Indian hanging around and making it awkward and finally the bloke got sacked. He went to the labour exchange and said 'Oooh, because I'm coloured they sacked me' and he got a form which his governor had to fill in. So the governor said 'Forget it', and brought him back and employed him again. It was a blooming big form to fill in as to why they sacked him and his governor said it wasn't worth it to bother to fill it in. So he went back to work there.

But there's a welder/plater from Guyana who worked with me – he's an asset to this country because he's the same as me – you give him a job and he can do it.

We should be choosey and let in the people who will be some use to us like doctors, scientists, engineers and others who will be an asset to the country not a liability. I'm for that because these people have set European standards and social habits, but you get a lot who come over here straight from the backwoods – they still want to be treated as Europeans but they still want their own culture.

The West Indians physically they're the same as us – if we cut ourselves we all still bleed [laughs] but they're on the boisterous side and noisy. They are alright when they're at work but when they're hanging around talking afterwards they're a bit noisy. But when they're at work they're the same as everyone else. They only go to work to get what they can – same as me. You can't say they're lazy because they're not.

There are a lot of these coloureds who come over with criminal records and have no intention of working. Now if I want to go to Australia and I've done time or nicked something and I've got a police record, I couldn't go, so why shouldn't it apply in both places?

Living with other racial groups
I was working up in Wales on a job and the Welsh people said to me 'Oh, where do you come from?' I said I came from Athol and they said 'Cor, I wouldn't like to live in Athol'. Now you go anywhere and people know about Athol. They seem to think it's just a mass of blacks and coloureds and a place which they

wouldn't want to live in. They've heard so much about it that they are just automatically prejudiced.

The coloureds now represent about one in four people here and as you go along the streets and come out of the cinema, you'll see nothing but coloureds here.

In this council estate there's only one bloke living with a coloured girl but I've got an inkling that something's going to happen because a lot of people have moved out and I think that they will gradually start integrating this estate as houses become empty. They'll bring one coloured family in here in one road, then spread them out a bit and then make it every other house – black, white, black, white. And then they'll be able to say 'Look at integration, black, white, black, white' – but it will be forced on people.

Well, a hell of a lot of white people have moved out of here already and the coloureds are moving in to Athol. Some of my friends have moved out and gone to places where there are fewer Indians because we don't want to live around here with the darkies and see our kids grow up with them. People seem to think that we should accept them but they don't want to be accepted – a lot of them. Or they say we should be kind-hearted and should mix and integrate and all that silly old clap-trap. *They* haven't got to contend with it. They have probably got a flat in Westminster or they live in Surrey miles away and commute to town and they don't live with coloureds and their children don't have to go to school with them. A man like Mark Bonham Carter makes me sick – he's the chairman of the Race Relations board and I mean to say if I wanted to sell a house and I put it up for sale and a darky comes along and he wanted to buy it and I said 'No, I don't want to sell it to a darky', he can take me up in front of the Board. Well, why shouldn't I be able to sell the house to whom I want without being frightened of pro-secution? Do you think that's a good law because I don't?

No one seems to bother that a lot of factories in Athol have been closed down because they've had so much trouble with immigrant labour. They're so slow to grasp anything that they're moving factories now to Plymouth where there won't be coloured labour. The trouble is you get people who may come from the Punjab, from a village where there is no sanitation or water or things like that and you bring them into a society like ours which is developed and you can't blame the people, but they just can't compete in this society.

We're creating problems in this country by having these coloureds here – eighty to eighty five per cent of them are illiterate, straight off the plough. What good are they to this country? We've got enough of our own illiterates without importing them.

I've had a lot of blokes with me – white boys who can't read or write. Well, this is their country, and its not a drawback if they can't read or write because this is their country and they can still make a living.

You could write a book on the things that have happened in Athol. I went to the pictures with my wife and a young lad of eighteen rushed out to get his last bus and must have knocked a darky a little bit so this man shouted 'Man, you push me again and I'll give you six inches of steel'. I thought 'Well if he drew a bit of steel I'm behind him and I'd have had him on the back of his neck, but if I'd done that before he drew his knife, I'd have been held up for assault.'

There are a lot of things that have happened in Athol which don't get into the papers. Now I know a young lad who lived on this estate and he was coming home one night and some coloureds jumped at him and put a knife across his throat. I think he had about twenty-four stitches in his throat. Now his grandfather is a friend of my mother-in-law and all this I'm telling you can be verified but nothing was said about it in the paper. John's mate was coming home one night and a crowd of Indians ran across the road and stabbed him seven times in the back. They rushed him to hospital and they had detectives investigating but nothing was said about it. Knife fights go on here for hours, coloureds fighting but the police don't come near and why isn't that put in the paper? It's because they're frightened of being accused of prejudice against the coloureds.

He relates a series of incidents in which white boys are prosecuted before the courts for misdemeanours, but when the coloureds seem to do exactly the same things the police come along and say 'Oh alright then – on your way'. He vividly describes violence and fights outside the local pub 'The Black Dog'.

You never see the law around there. But these white boys playing around up on the green, playing football, they're done in straight away for the simple reason it's too hard if they take a coloured person – it's too hard to prove anything because there's the automatic reaction of 'It's prejudice – because I'm black'. So it's easier to pull in a white bloke and that's what's getting up people's backs.

The police are frightened – their hands are tied and I've heard something confidential – that the police have been told to lay off coloureds. If they try to get a coloured bloke, they've got so much bother and then they've got to contend with the Race Relations board and they get a smart solicitor or lawyer who says you picked on him because he's coloured, so they shut a blind eye. But if a white man does the same thing, they'll have him away. It's all wrong.

A lot of the people who want these coloureds are these so-called intellectuals like Mark Bonham Carter – and what's his name? – Jeremy Thorpe and all that crowd. They're solicitors, they're the upper crust, the intellectuals. Their children don't go to these coloured schools where half the class is coloured and they can't speak English properly so the white kids are doing silly little things that they've already learnt. These kids are then held back. Now these upper crusts – their children automatically go to preparatory schools, they go to college – Eton – their lives are mapped out for them. So this coloured problem hasn't hit them yet. When that starts, when the coloureds in this country start getting into the professions, become solicitors – well, you've got them now but I mean in masses – *then* it will affect them. Then they'll be saying 'Oh, we can't have this, we can't have that' – but it doesn't matter about the working class because we can't do anything about it.

And another thing – I'll tell you a good thing to read is a pamphlet called *Combat*. I don't know what it's about. It's a bit fascist, it could be the National Front, British Fascist party, or something like that but it brings these things to light – all these little incidents which happen and people don't know about. Things that are hushed up. Well, I didn't want to get involved in that type of organization but I get copies from my mates who are a bit strong on all this. Now there's no country in the world where they've brought in a bill like the Race Relations Bill which is against the native population which includes people like me, the white people, and it's us who are discriminated against.

Indians and Pakistanis
I've got no objections to sitting down next to Indians in a bus – I mean it's public transport.

When you're shopping and walking around the streets in

Athol, the Indians stand holding hands in groups. They stop other people walking because you've got to push your way through the groups which is all wrong. And they also push and shove and that's why I lose my temper if I come up against some of them as they are just standing there on the corner holding hands. If I did that they'd have me up for obstruction. So now I don't go out and walk around the main shopping streets of Athol but go to shop in other parts of London.

I get irritated by Indian motorists. They turn left or right without any indicators and that's what gets up my back. And if the lights are green and I'm going across in my car and they walk in front of me, I drive for them. I know it's wrong. [Laughs] My missus gets scared [laughs] because when the light says green for me I go, and if they walk across then, they're taking a chance. They're in the wrong because they shouldn't cross. I've had some near misses – ooh yeah . . . regularly every morning, down here at the end of my road, I don't stop for them. I tell you my missus gets worried about it and says 'You'll kill one of them one of these days'. As I say I've got the lights in my favour, I've paid my insurance and road tax and I obey all the rules and regulations and they must do the same. What's good enough for me is good enough for them. So if they want to walk in front of me and take a chance, well that's up to them. It doesn't bother me. I go for them. I don't swerve or avoid them. If I hit them, well it's up to them. So far, I've only skinned them. [Laughs] They get away with murder. If the lights are in my favour I do everything I should do. Whites automatically stop, they don't take chances like that, but the Indians just walk across ignorantly as if you have to stop for them. Well, I don't, I'm afraid, I don't. If they want to live in this country, then they've got to do the same things as I do. If the lights say 'Go', I go – if it says 'Stop' I stop. They must do the same instead of just turning left and right without indicators. They just get up my back. You just look at their cars – they've got bashes and bangs on them where people have hit them. It's because they just don't bother – it's like their own country, all run to wrack and ruin.

I wouldn't shop at Indian shops round here – their standard of hygiene is so low.

Indian shops can stay open until late at night and all Saturday and Sunday but if a white bloke wants to do the same, he can't. But the Indians get away with it.

A few streets away from here the Indians have got their temple. They want their own culture and everything which they had in their own country, but they want to be accepted as Europeans too. Well they've got to make the break and accept our ways because they are now in England but they want to still hang onto their own culture and all that.

He cites a case in the paper which he says describes an Indian giving false information about having a wife and children when he had neither wife nor children and that it was all done to evade tax.

The Indians are corrupt and dishonest. They smuggle these immigrants over here – and who's making money out of it? The Pakistanis who are battening down like leeches on their own people. Then these immigrants have to work years and years in this country to pay some of this money just to be allowed to stay here and they're frightened to be out of work or sick because they haven't a National Insurance number with date of entry as to when they came to England. I mean that's not a way for people to live. Someone's making money out of it. And the immigrants hear that England's paved with gold and all that silly old caper.

Now take the schools. Colin's with a lot of Indian kids at nursery school who can't understand a word of English because the parents are talking their own language all the time. Well, when Colin goes to primary school he'll probably be in a class with a load of Indians who can't understand English and so the teacher will have to give them extra tuition or time to learn how to speak basic English – so this will make Colin retarded.

Each school is only supposed to have thirty per cent immigrants but I don't know – I've read the reports round here and some of them have fifty to sixty percent coloureds which is all wrong.

I can foresee in the very near future, the terrible clash in this country. When there's mass unemployment in this country, that's when this race problem will explode – it must do. There'll be gangs of whites, gangs of blacks – well, to be honest with you a girl can't walk down this way without being accosted by coloureds. Even Elaine has been accosted by an Indian. It was about eighteen months ago and this Indian went up to her in the road and said 'You come to bed with me and I'll give you 75p'. Elaine must have gone to the police and they picked this bloke up and they didn't tell me until an hour after they had released him. I demanded his name and address and the copper said to me 'Don't take the law into your own hands because you'll come off second best'. So I said 'What are you going to do about it?' And he said 'Leave it with us, we've got him marked'. So I thought I'd leave it at that.

West Indians

West Indians are on the boisterous side and are a bit aggressive. If West Indians have parties they go on all day and all night and everybody from one end of the street to the other can hear it. They don't conform to our ways because if we have a ding-dong to about 2.0 am that's it, but they continue being noisy and rowdy and really getting aggressive. These West Indians are very undisciplined and can't be disciplined – they won't accept it. I've seen them bring out big juke boxes and blare away and that gets up people's backs.

There was a bit of bother down at Elaine's school dance the other night. I took the washing down to the launderette last night and there was a white woman talking about it. These coloureds had no tickets for the dance and couldn't go in and these people have no sense of discipline and were agitating for a lot of trouble and so they started trouble.

And if you have a go with the West Indians, they seem to have a chip on the shoulders when they come to England – I suppose they think because they're black everyone's against them which is not true. I think there's a lot of resentment among West Indians – more so than among Indians because if you try to help a darky they think that you're having a go at them – trying to take the mickey out of them. They seem to have an idea that in Britain we've always had it easy and we haven't. I mean to say when I was a boy my Gran used to say to me here's threepence. I'd get a twopenny bit of fish and a penny worth of chips and that was my dinner.

I don't suppose the West Indians trust white people. They might feel that if a white man's friendly to them he's trying to get one over on them – that the white man is thinking they are illiterate and treating them as children. They might also feel that they are a bit inferior to the white man and have that attitude. I don't think there's any real love for white people. They're only over here because it's a better standard of living and they can improve themselves and their children can get a better education. They're out to get everything they can, same as everyone else I suppose.

The great majority of West Indians feel that we've exploited them – but that was years ago. I've never exploited any coloured person in my life. But if we hadn't gone out and developed places like Arabia and Libya, the old wogs would still be walking around with donkeys. Look at the millions of pounds of royalties they get for their oil, it's only because we put our money into it and developed it. I mean if they had the brains they would have developed their natural resources but they haven't had the savvy, have they? The great percentage of them are illiterate.

On coloured immigrants in general
If the Indians come to England they have got to accept our ways – it's our country after all and they are immigrants. But they want their own culture and I agree that Indians or Pakistanis have got a culture that's probably older than ours. West Indians, West Africans or Negroes are more European and readily accept European ways more than the Indians do because they've been brought up to sort of respect the Queen and all that silly old caper. I think they are more readily accepted into our way of life than the Indians and that's why I don't think you get so much bother with West Indians or Negroes although a lot of them are more aggressive than Indians. The Indians are more closely knit – more family bonds than the West Indians. It's not so much a question of colour as they want their own ways and won't adopt ours – but 'When in Rome do as the Romans do' – but they don't.

I've worked with Indians and I've worked with West Indians and I've had no bother at work but when they're out, after work, that's when it's different. At work when I was a foreman and had 100 men under me I had to treat each man as an individual.

Indians call us prejudiced but they are more class conscious with their caste system than anybody else.

Enoch Powell
Enoch Powell is saying a lot of things that everybody's thinking. A lot of people in the Tory party are thinking what Powell is saying but nobody's got the guts to say it. Till there's a showdown which must come, especially when there's mass

unemployment in this country. That's when this racial problem will explode – it must.

Self-description

Without thinking too hard, how would you describe yourself?: Uh . . . like an average person . . . well, when you get on in the world, you seem so frustrated all the time . . . Maybe I've been too conscientious on jobs . . . I seem to have to think too long about something if you know what I mean, weigh all the pros and cons up.

That's what I think is a failing with me you know. I think about everything that comes along instead of making a snap decision like some people can. I have to weigh everything up and tread lightly.

How might your best friend describe you?:   As pretty reliable and a plodder . . . I don't know, well, I've mucked about a lot when I was younger and got up to capers. I'm pretty easy with everything and take things as they come but if somebody gets up my back then I have a go. But I've got to be well provoked before I do anything and when I do I just see red and if I lost my temper a bit more often, I wouldn't be so bad when I do lose it. Do you know what I mean? I get vicious and I don't know when to stop. I'm pretty even-tempered until someone upsets me and I'll take a lot of insults from anybody but once it gets on my mind and gets up my back, nothing will stop me and if someone gets in my way – well it's self-preservation. I think I should lose my temper more instead of building it up because – as I said, when I was younger, I lost my temper and crippled that boy.

The things I value most in life are having good qualifications, money and good health. What I dread most is bad health. You've got to sit around and let life go past you and you can't do anything about it. I'm a bit sentimental and seeing blokes who are crippled, it upsets me, you know. It's the same as I can't hold new babies – that's a thing I can't do. I never held any of mine, only Colin, and that was a great struggle. But the others I couldn't hold them. I get nervous – you know what I mean – or I grip them you know and Rebecca says, 'Ooh, it's too hard' and I forget, you know and I'm frightened I could hurt someone so that's why I very rarely pick a baby up. When they get older I do. I'm frightened, you know what I mean, that I might forget myself with babies. I did hold Colin for a little while but he was the only baby I ever held. I've got more relaxed, see, because I'm getting older, so I'm more able to take things a bit easy, you know.

NOTES

1 Skinheads: British working-class tough youths with closely-cropped hair, who dress distinctively (work pants, suspenders and heavy boots), drive scooters and frequently engage in street fighting.
2 Rockers or greasers: The rival gang who wear their hair longer, have tight trousers and ride motorbikes.

MRS REBECCA CHATTAWAY: HER STORY

My childhood wasn't all that good. I was born in Battersea and my mother and father broke up when I was about six years old. I don't remember them breaking up but I then lived with my dad and his mother whom my brother and I called nan. My brother was five years older than me and after a while my mother got married again and she had three children – Jilly, Roger and Jackie. He was marvellous, my second dad, and his three children were never like step-sisters and step-brothers to me but like real sisters and brothers.

My dad and my nan brought me up and I was very lonely as my brother was sent off to boarding school and I was the only child at home. But my mother didn't live far away and when she got married I used to go around and see her and I used to go out with her and my step-dad at Easter times and at Whitsun and when they had children we all used to go out together.

When the war came we had a lot of bombing in Battersea and I was evacuated to Devon. I must have been about nine then and I went to a lovely farm and a lovely family but of course, once again I was the only one. But they were very nice to me and one day my dad came down to see me and I was playing with an imaginary friend. All children do this but my dad didn't realise that and he went to see my mother, who was then living here in Athol because they had been bombed out, and he asked her if she would have me because he felt I was so lonely down there. So I came to my mother when I was about ten and a half.

I didn't like returning to my mother very much because I suppose my dad had spoilt me. Jackie wasn't born yet but Jilly was about six years old and Roger was four. Jilly and I used to argue and clash terribly because she used to say I ran away from her in the park when I was supposed to be looking after her and then I'd get a wallop, you know. We're as thick as thieves now – but then we used to bicker.

My step-dad never interfered. He was very, very good to me and I had no rows with him. But if we used to get told off, my sister used to say to me 'Oh, you're not my sister' and it used to upset me a lot inside.

My older brother went off and joined the Merchant Navy and when he used to come home on leave, he gradually came more and more to my mother and in the end he also came to live with us.

Meanwhile my nan died and my dad, who was a cripple and had a disease of the spine and used to have to wear two sticks, had to go into a home. This happened just before I came up from the country. I used to go and see him now and again but then he got put in a place near Slough. It was like a workhouse and he wasn't very well in health and my eldest brother used to go and see him but it used to upset me to see all those poor people. I went now and again but he died there, but I wasn't really in touch with him then – you know how these things happen and you don't bother although he was very good to me.

But then we were all united with my mum and my step-dad and I had no complaints about him because he was a cracker-nut! And as we got older we all got on alright together.

My mum and step-dad used to go out to shows and I used to have to look after the kids which I did resent really – that's why I don't make my children look after little Colin. Not that I think that it hurt me in anyway, but I used to feel that if I wanted to go to the pictures, I couldn't go because I first had to find out if they were going out. I always used to have to take Jackie out before I could go and play and at night I had to bring him in by half-past seven and then I was allowed out until eight. It didn't make me any better than anyone else, but they were very strict about the times I came in.

My mum always made my friends welcome and they all used to come to us and my step-dad used to show us tricks of cards and everybody came just like everybody comes in here now.

My mum was a cook and she used to cook in pubs, or schools or nurseries and she was always nice and never knocked us about or anything. She's always had a tremendous lot of patience and she never got obedience from us by giving us hidings. Her words were law and she didn't have to knock us about, just as I don't knock my children about. They all know how far to go with me and we all knew how far to go with our mum.

I can't really remember her when I was tiny only my dad and my nan. But she was always a good mother to us and it wasn't like a broken family with two different surnames – but we were a proper family, all treated the same. Even today she never treats me to a plant without buying one for Jilly and she never buys things for my kids without buying things for all the other kids. She'll never talk about one of us to the others and if you told her anything in confidence she would never pass it on to my sisters and brothers. You could go and tell her your troubles – you still can. Well I think she's marvellous. She lives right round the corner from me now and if she doesn't see one of us for two or three days, she's around to see us. She worries over all our kids – in fact she really worries too much half the time. But she was always a good mother.

She gets up from the kitchen table where she has been talking to me, intently absorbed in what she was saying, and moves to the cooker, deftly and quickly takes out a roasting pan and bastes a mass of potatoes and returns them to the oven. Her auburn hair frames her jolly and friendly face with softness, and her green eyes are lively and humorous. She moves around the kitchen with confident ease – sitting down next to me in a relaxed sprawl, leaning across the table to talk with animation – then going to attend to her dinner and with large, generous movements, stirs vigorously and tastes the seasoning of her vegetables. Although she moves back and forth from table to cooker – and sometimes to delve into her cupboards for supplies – there is a comfortable rhythm to it because it seems to be a natural part of her – to talk and express her thoughts and feelings while she busies herself with preparing food for her family. Rebecca Chattaway's air is a confiding one, friendly and outgoing and when her attention returns from her cooking activities she comes back to her kitchen chair next to mine and picks up her thoughts and reflections of the past and the present. She leans forward, her pink blouse neatly clinging to her sturdy but trim figure, and continues:

No one in this world could convince me that I was a drudge

to my mother – no one. I just thought that she worked all day like I did. I used to come home from school and cook the midday meal and the breakfast things were there and the curtains still to be drawn and I had to do all that but I never thought less of my mother – no! I made the dinners and went back to school and then I called in at the nursery at half past three where my mother was a cook and she'd tell me what shopping to get and I had it all prepared by the time she came home from work.

We always had a fortnight's holiday, all of us – mum and my step-dad and all the kids.

She worked all day and so did my step-dad and sometimes they'd go out to the pub and I would look after the children. Jackie would be in bed and so would the others and I'd sit and listen to the wireless. If they came in very late, I went to bed. More often than not, in my sleep I used to think I could hear my Jackie and I'd come out of my bedroom and shush him in the cot and then – my mum's told me this – I'd climb into my mother's bed thinking they weren't in. She told me that she then would say to me 'It's alright Rebecca – we're in now and he's gone to sleep' and then I'd get out and go back to my own bed. You see, I didn't know they had come in.

I loved Jilly and Roger but I had so many dealings with my Jackie, you know – there's no one like him – I loved him very much.

When I was about fourteen, there was a boy – Jimmy Pollard his name was, and I asked my mum if I could go to the pictures with him and she said 'Yes, if you take Jackie with you'. She laughs now but I say 'ooooooooohhh'. Well, I grumbled but I loved my Jackie so I took him.

Courtship and marriage
When she left school, she went to work in the despatch office of a large departmental store where she was a filing clerk. She was staying with her mother in Athol and used to go dancing but was only allowed out until half-past nine.

I was running up the stairs to the dance and Charles was behind me and he said 'That's a fine time to come to a dance' and I said 'Mind your own business' or something like that. Then I went upstairs and forgot all about him and when we had a dance I didn't remember he was the same bloke on the stairs. After another dance together he asked me for the last waltz and invited me to the Catholic dance on Sundays.

They married soon afterwards and went to live with her mother and with her step-father and the other children.

When I was married to Charles, he was always kind to me. We had one room upstairs and he would bring fresh strawberries, a block of ice-cream and two dishes and he'd say 'Go on, eat them up here' and I used to shout down 'Charles has brought some ice-cream. Do you want some Jackie?' and he used to turn green and I couldn't understand why he didn't want to share it because he had been the only child and he made a big thing of having treated me and me only to the strawberries and ice-cream and I could never see that. I just used to take my lump of ice-cream and give them all a bit. Then he'd say 'Don't go downstairs with them. Stay upstairs with me' and we'd look at each other but because I'd been so used to everybody being together and he'd been an only child – although he did live with his aunt and cousins later on – he'd always feel that he was pushed out.

We didn't have a honeymoon – we just stayed at home for a fortnight and went here and there. The first week of the honeymoon we were going to the pictures and Jackie said 'Can I come Rebecca?' and I said 'Yeah, come on'. So we sat in the back row with my Charles's face long as you like, and I've got my little brother with me! He was about ten years old.

We lived with my mother for about eighteen months and John was born there and when he was about six months old we got this room in Notting Hill. She was a very nice lady on top of the house when we moved in there and she said 'Oh, what lovely company it will be to have a little baby', but she then started being nasty and insulting. She painted the step red and then I couldn't bring John's pram in because of the step and then I'd go to hang his nappies out and before I got there she had put out all the tea towels so there was no room. Instead of saying to me 'Well, I'm going to hang my washing today, you do it another day'. I then said to her 'I don't want to be bad friends with you, but if you want to tell me anything that I do wrong, this is your place, so please tell me.' 'Oh there's nothing wrong' she said. Well, I had no sink there in that room, no running water and I was about three stories up. I had a big white jug and I used to come down to her sink and fill the jug with water and she wouldn't let me rinse John's nappies down there so I had to keep on carrying water up and down those three flights of steps. And then in the end the woman used to come behind me with a cloth in case I dropped some water because I had the jug and also John under my arm. And when John started crawling, she'd say 'Stop that noise' and in the end John used to go 'Shooo – I'll walk quietly'. Now that's no good.

We also had a lot of coloureds living on the other side of the road who had Irish girls as prostitutes. They lived in there with them and were on the streets and if they hadn't brought enough money home those West Indians used to give them a hiding so you had all that hollering and shouting up the road.

I couldn't stand another day of being in that room and when I got pregnant with Elaine I knew that the woman in the house wouldn't have another baby in there and she would put me out. So we went to the Kensington Town Hall and stated our case – we had no fireplace and the woman wouldn't let us have an electric fire – but they said we couldn't have a place.

All this time I was also trying to get a place in Athol because they thought I was still living with my mother – they didn't know we had this room. It was a bit of a fiddle but a lot of people do it and I didn't really want to live in Notting Hill because Athol was beautiful. But when the Kensington people said they could put John and I in a hostel and Charles in lodgings, it got to such a pitch that I got the people across the road to keep our furniture and when my husband came home from work I had the cases packed and I was off to my mum. He said 'Does she know?' and I said 'No, but I can't find a place!' The doctor had also told me that the baby was lying wrongly because we were all cramped into one bed and he said if the baby didn't turn I'd have to have a caesarian. So I thought if we went back to my mother there was a bed for Charles and I and we could get John's cot up again.

We came back to my mother and were there only nine months. We were very, very lucky because we were given a council flat around the corner and Elaine was born there and was one of the first children to be born on this estate.

Both John and Elaine were born in hospital and John came so fast that I was standing in the middle of the ward and didn't know that John's head was already showing, but Elaine's birth was a wonderful birth. I had a doctor at each side of me and two nice nurses – talk about the Queen, you couldn't have had better service if you were to pay £100!

Working and caring for children

When John was very small she used to do some house-cleaning jobs and have to take him with her. She worked for English women and when she moved to Athol she started doing part-time work in a despatch department but when that folded up she began evening work cleaning factories and offices. All her working experience has been solely with other white people. As Elaine got older, she worked in a shop and later started evening classes in typing and also in English. She completed two years of the three required but then became pregnant with her third child, Colin. At the time of the study, she has gone back to an evening job of cleaning and working in offices after-hours, but intends to resume her typing work as soon as it is possible.

My son John

John and Colin are a bit alike in that they both are bad-tempered. John when he was tiny used to throw himself all over the place. He was my first baby so I used to just wallop him which made things worse.

I had such a lot of trouble with John. From the time he started school he hated it and I used to take hold of his hand and tug him along. He didn't care how much anybody might have laughed. It wasn't that he was a naughty boy but he just wouldn't settle down at school. I went up to the school and asked the headmaster if anybody was unkind to him. It wasn't that. I used to go up at playtime and stand up on the bridge where he couldn't see me and he used to be just sitting on the window-sill by himself.

He wasn't a good reader and I think that worried him. He isn't one now but he's coming on since he left school. They gave him special lessons at school when he was about ten or eleven and one day he'd try and another day he wouldn't.

His dad and I used to clash over this. At school they used to domineer him over his reading and then he used to come home at night and 'Get that book' his dad used to say and because John was like me, they'd row and then I'd argue and say 'Leave him alone. I'll do it quietly with him later'.

They did try with him at school and he sort of gave up quickly but otherwise he held his own at school. I could push

John and that's why I made him go to school when he was little
and he didn't want to go. But one thing about him, he never
played truant.

He got a bit saucy when he was about thirteen, answering
back. I've always asked him 'Where are you going?' and if he
doesn't tell me then he can't go. I always used to stipulate that
he came in at 9 o'clock if he was playing up the top of the road.
Then as he got older it became 10 and then 10.30 but never
later because I said 'There's nothing doing after half-past
ten – that's when you get into trouble'. As he got older he got
his own key. To this day he says where he's going. I don't
stipulate it. I'm not a nosey mother although the woman down
the road accused me of being nosey. [Chuckles]

He's left school now and doing electrical work. He has to go
to school once a week – I didn't think he'd have the pluck to do
it because of all the writing, but he does and I think he's getting
a bit more confident. But I never made him do anything when
he left school. He didn't know what he wanted to do so I let him
go his own way. He did one thing after another and at night
school he had trouble. There was a teacher there who spoke to
him about his work and he's the sort of boy that once you pick
on him and belittle him, he's had it. So he said he wasn't going
to try and walked out and I said 'Well, you silly boy!' and he
said 'No, he's not pushing me about' and he gave up school and
he left his job. Then he went into this electrical job.

John has had three scooters and has been involved in several
accidents. In one he failed to use his crash-helmet and was badly
concussed and spent time in hospital and was away from work for
five weeks.

He wears his helmet now – he can't go out unless he wears it
and although he's nearly eighteen years old I have said to him
'While you're with me, you do as you're told'. I give him a lot of
rope but it's no good having that worry, is it?

What with the motorbikes and the scooters and the coloureds, it's a real headache it is. The skinheads and
rockers – oh – they've got hold of John many a time. He's a
skinhead because he's got a scooter and the others on the
motorbikes are called rockers. One night he pulled up at the
lights in the main road and three rockers pulled up behind him
and they kept banging his helmet and I said to him 'You should

have put your foot down on the pedal and gone up the road' and he said 'Oh don't be daft Mum, they'd cut me, head me off, you know'. These boys kept on saying to him 'I don't like your helmet, I don't like skinheads', and they started to kick his bike and he punched one with his hand and kicked another and started off on his bike. They chased him for miles and he came home on his own and there were about six or seven of them really roaring around him. Well, it's frightening, isn't it? He's been lucky so far. There's always been another fellow on a scooter who has helped him out.

It annoys me because I said to him 'There's enough trouble in this world without white boys – who prefer a motorbike to a scooter and whose mums let them have their hair long whereas I make you have your's short – fighting and arguing like that. It's silly. I suppose when I was a teenager, there must have been something – I can't really remember – Teddy Boys, I think and spivs – but we never got so really spiteful as this. I mean they kick each other's bikes – and give each other terrible hidings. One of John's mates pulled up one night at a fish shop and four rockers came and gave him a terrible hiding, for no reason. I said to John 'I hope you don't bash a fellow on his own – three or four of you together', and he said 'No, I don't – but if I've been done by two or three of them and I see one of them, I'll tell my mates and we ride around and cut them in and you know – one thing and another'. It's a wonder they don't kill each other on the road.

If he goes to a dance and he's not home by half past eleven and his scooter's out of action and he's waiting for a bus, I lie there worrying that any minute a copper's going to knock on the door and say 'Your boy's been done up'.

The other day in the laundrette, there were two West Indian girls and their wireless was jazzing. They were making such a noise. If I had asked them to turn it down they would have brought a copper – they'd have worked it round so that they weren't wrong. But if my John had been playing his radio and a white woman had said 'Pack it up or turn it down' and even if he hadn't given her any lip, she'd have got a copper and run John in and they would have booked him. I definitely do think that they don't like to pick up coloureds and take them to the police station, because it's so involved. But it's straight-forward when they get the likes of John. I mean if John is taken to court now at seventeen, he doesn't have a leg to stand on. But the coloureds they don't even get brought before the courts.

The police are frightened and they're told not to pick on the coloureds too much or they are quoted as being racially prejudiced. My eldest brother was over here in the main road the other day and he said 'Cor', he said 'A darky over the main road, he had a great big knife down his trousers, all with a jagged edge'. So I said 'Did you tell a copper?' 'No', he said. 'Well, you should have', I said 'If my Johnny had a penknife they'd have had him – they want to have him'. If I told the copper about the darky and his knife, the copper would probably just say nothing to the man – just 'Don't wear it' and he would probably say it was his religion. Well, if it's his religion, he wants to keep the knife done up, not bring it out and sort of frighten people with it.

Some white boys carry knives on them. My Johnny doesn't because I begged him not to, because I said you'll come up against one of those darkies – he'll bring his knife out and you'll bring yours, and you'll come off second best. But he did say 'Alright Mum, I won't carry it, but I don't know what I'll do if one of them starts on me. I must take some protection for myself'. Isn't that terrible that at seventeen you have to have some protection?

Commenting on an incident at Elaine's school dance when coloureds created a disturbance (see later account of this), she says:

It's always the coloureds. I know the white boys can do it. I mean the likes of my Johnny could go to a dance and if they can't get in, they could be a bit funny. I just hope that Johnny never throws a milk bottle through a window, because he'd have to answer to me, let alone the police, if we found him doing things like that.

I saw John speak to an Indian boy a couple of years ago and this boy was thrilled to bits to see Johnny and they shook hands, with great feeling towards Johnny. He shook hands and I said to him 'Who's that boy?' and he said 'Oh, he used to work with me on my first job' and he was so pleased to see John again. As I say, there must be good and bad – but there are definitely, but definitely too many coloureds here in Athol.

John's relationship with his father
I don't think more of Johnny than I do of my other two, but

Charles does seem to shout at John – he did when he was a baby you know. He's got more patience with Colin than he had with the other two but I can't bear him to start on my Johnny. I don't like him to start on Elaine but he doesn't start on her very often. But he has terrible clashes with John. I think, looking back on my married life, I've had more rows over my Johnny and standing up for him than anything.

I think perhaps he feels jealous of Johnny, but my husband's as happy as a sandboy when there's only him and me. But you see I'm his wife but I'm also mum to these three. When we're alone he wants me to sit with him and have a cup of tea and I'm like his number one. It's very nice if you are the type of person who can be selfish to your children – I could have a lovely life – oh yeah, I could have the world. I can't do that, I've got too much of a conscience. I know it's silly, but we've had terrible rows over Johnny. And yet Johnny's not unkind to his father and he toes the line. I mean he's nearly eighteen and when his dad talks to him sometimes you'd think he was about twelve – his dad goes on sometimes and nags him and nags him and he goes on and on and how it hurts me and he says 'Wait until that boy comes in' and my tummy goes right over, right over.

They clash about different things – John's using Charles' tools and John putting his tools in his father's shed. Charles can't possess everything, can he?

She describes a recent upsetting incident when she got up early on a Sunday morning to make tea and toast for John who was off to the seaside for the day with his friends. When she got back to the bedroom she was 'told off'. 'There are always scenes. It doesn't matter if I make tea and toast for the other two, I'm not wrong then but only for Johnny'.

I try and keep the happy medium with the pair of them. Sometimes I could put my fist through that door with both of them . . . . I can't *bear* the way he talks to John – I can't take it. I don't like it. I don't know if it worries John or if it hurts John, but it worries me.

Charles has never got a good word for John and he'll make him look small in a crowd. I don't know whether he means it or not but if the boys are all playing football out here, he'll say 'Go on dummy, kick the ball'. Well, that's his boy and I go out there and I say 'Don't you dare make him look small in front of those boys – you're not so clever yourself'. I can't keep my mouth shut. If I did we'd get on better.

Sometimes when Charles is very angry I tell Johnny to tread lightly as 'Your dad's had an up-and-a-downer with me'.

My relationship with John

I know that John gets my wick at times. He'll come in and throw his coat down and walk upstairs with mud on his boots and we've got no hoover – it's been broken for years and so I have to go and pick all that up with a dust-pan.

If I have words with John I have to get it off my chest. I can't keep lying awake worrying and I say to myself 'Now don't lose your temper – be calm' and I try not to fly off the handle. But I have to sort it out because John and I can have an up-and-a-downer and then he'll say 'We're not bad mates are we, Mum?' and I'll say 'No, I wanted to say it. It's off my chest, you know where you stand with me and that's it'. I can't bottle things up.

I always know when Johnny's doing something under-handed because he can't look me in the face. I know it worries him if I say 'Give up so and so – or try and avoid that place or that boy or girl'. I know he's not doing what I say and he's upset inside and after a few days I'll say to him 'Anything worrying you, son? Because if so, share it with me if you feel you want to'. 'No, nothing's worrying me, Mum' but even if it's a simple thing about work or anything, it comes out in the end. And then he's as right as ninepence. I've always told my children 'If you've got a worry, share it with me, trust me. If you've got a worry, John, it doesn't mean I'm going to tell Daddy'.

And I wouldn't tell Johnny about Elaine or the other way around. I said to them 'I'm here to help if I can but if you think you can sort something out for yourself and then you realise you can't then have a talk. But have a go and sort your troubles out yourself if you can't tell me'.

He's had a couple of girl friends and he goes to dances at the weekends.

She decided against breast-feeding Colin and when the midwife said it was best to breast-feed she said, 'Yes I know, but I feel embarrassed to feed him in front of Johnny anyway and you can't always go and hide yourself'.

My daughter Elaine

Elaine has always been placid as the day is long. She doesn't get overwrought. She's like her dad, placid. They've got bad tempers but it takes a terrible lot to make them mad. They're more quiet-like.

I had no trouble with Elaine when she went to school – unlike Johnny. She watched me pulling him to school and she went into school as good as gold.

Elaine is fourteen and a half during the time of the study and is a late developer. Her mother has taken her to the doctor and been reassured that although her menstruation has not yet started, there is nothing to worry about. Mrs Chattaway was an early developer and 'I thought she'd take after me'. But adolescent changes are now occurring in Elaine's behaviour.

Elaine is just getting a bit bad-tempered and my mum says that girls go through these temperamental stages.

You can't get to her. I think that she's worried and I'm trying to get through to her but I can't. It's so hard – I think 'Now how am I going to get to her?' She's only got like this recently since she's getting older.

She very seldom lost her temper but I think she's having her up-and-downers now – you know she's becoming a teenager – neither one thing nor another and I think that's why we clash. I don't hit her or anything like that but she does make me lose my temper.

I get het up with her at times – I try to plan, so I take her round the shops but you never seem able to please her; you think you're doing her a good turn, you know, but her face is as long as a fiddle when you take her shopping.

I try my best. I haven't got a lot of money but I take her out and buy her a meal, just her and Colin and me which they like but then she says 'Well, it was alright' in a whining kind of way and I think 'Well, there's no one round here her age with whom she could go off for a day, and there's nowhere to go to. So I've got to cater for her and for Colin and do my work at the same time.

Elaine and Johnny are different altogether. You don't know where you stand with Elaine – you may clash, but you don't know whether you've made it up sort of thing.

When we clash we get het up instead of agreeing. You try but she will have it her way. Like when it's time for bed, her response will be 'Alright – you don't have to tell me' and I could blow my top because there's no need to say that to me when I'm just asking. It's that 'hoity-toity'. She'll do it in the end, but she's got to be in the mood and she can't be pushed, like I could push Johnny.

She's one of these fourteen year olds who are slow in developing because she's not like the other girls, you know, dancing and all that, but when she eventually does go out – up to the main street or anywhere like that, when she's coming home she's terrified when the darkies come up to her and start talking to her because they don't say 'Hello' or 'What's your name?' like a white boy would at fourteen, it's more 'Come to bed with us'.

She then recounts an early incident when Elaine was twelve to thirteen and an Indian approached her in this way and she didn't really know what he meant but came home crying.

And of course my husband and Johnny flew over with her to the police but before they got to the police station, they had already released the Indian. He had said 'Me speak no English' but he could talk English alright to ask what's what. He frightened the life out of her. The boy's parents had been to the police station and said that he wasn't that type of boy and he never would have said it. Well, I mean she could never have made it up. She had a mate with her and she hasn't got boy friends yet and if you kid her up about things, she goes as red as a beetroot. She's a good girl and there was no need for that. But it did frighten her. There you are, it's because he was coloured – if it had been my John they'd have run him in and made a court case and it would have been in all the papers. But they dropped it. They said to my husband 'There's nothing you can do – he doesn't even speak English' and all this. Anyway my husband and Johnny found out his address and were going to wait for him and give him a good hiding one night – well, it makes you like that, doesn't it? I mean it's our daughter and why have her spoken to like that? Yes, so they went at the end of the week to give him a good hiding but they'd moved – the police wouldn't give his new address because they said 'Mr Chattaway, if you lay a finger on him, you'll have racial prejudice and you'll be in the wrong, you know'.

Elaine just didn't understand what he was after although I've told her everything. They're no good – no good. So when she starts going out, she's going to remember that.

When Elaine was about nine there was one Indian girl in her class and I said to Elaine 'Ah, be kind to her, don't push her out.' Her mother was very nice. And when I had a party for Elaine, she wanted to invite this girl and I said 'Yes, because she's in your class and she's in your school' and I said to Elaine 'Tell your other friends she's coming'. But everybody came to the party, you know, and she's a very nice girl. She's gone to grammar school now. When this girl was about eleven, she didn't come home from school one day and her mother, who lives in the same road as my mother – although she knows quite a lot of people – came to me and said 'Whatever am I going to do? I can't find her – she hasn't come home from school', and she cried. And I went to the school but she wasn't there – I'm not sure whether this woman had a young child at the time, but I said to her 'Well, you go home and I'll look for her', and she had gone home with another girl instead of going straight home from school and I gave her a good telling-off and took her back to her mum. So she told her off and she said to her mother 'Mrs Chattaway's told me off' you know. I think she's moved away from here now. I saw her once with a new baby and I gave him a little cuddle – I love all new babies.

I definitely think we've got too many coloureds in Athol now – there are definitely too many and I think it's worrying for the kids at school too. They are a terrible lot up at Elaine's school. I think they're ever so fierce. They're not like my John's crowd. I mean John's lot may have a fight but they never bring knives and things out. Now the coloureds don't think anything of having knives. It doesn't worry them at all and I think it's awful when Elaine starts going out because I think they abuse the kids – the coloured boys do. I mean I've been over to the main street and they even talk to me – a married woman with kids, and I don't think they've got any respect for kids of Elaine's age.

It's not the Jamaicans, not the curlies – but the other ones – the Indians.

She is worrying to me – she doesn't go out. She thinks the girls are very forward at school – they're ever so much more advanced than she is – all of the girls, the whites and the coloureds.

Of course I think the coloureds are very aggressive. They don't know how to have a clean fist fight – they always threaten with knives. There are always things in the local papers about coloureds who have broken into people's houses or held up people at garages and they always come out with their knives straight away. Well, I can see my children getting cut up, you know, when they get older. I hope Elaine never brings one home – I'd go potty. There are enough white boys and it doesn't matter how lovely you think they are, you've got to think of what your children will go through – they'll be coffee-coloured. And I said to her 'You stick to your own colour, because there'll be a lot of trouble later on if you have coloured children.' I know that all the girls at school who are a bit older than Elaine go to dances and dance with coloureds. They are at school with them so they are all together at the dance. But I've said to her 'Don't let a West Indian bring you home' because, I mean to say, some of them are lovely looking boys, you've got to admit it – and I mean, I think the girls get flattered to be asked to go out with them because on the one side they have got charm – but underneath that charm, they're more aggressive I reckon than a white man definitely.

I don't know what kind of husbands they might make but they've got a spiteful streak in them. I know that all men want to be the governor but you've got to have a happy medium – you can't push a wife right down but I think underneath these coloured men, they would be really spiteful and knock you about.

I wouldn't like Elaine to go out with coloureds – she's seen how domineering they are at school – but I try to explain to her that she should form her own opinion but I would wish that she doesn't go out with them but rather stick to white boys. It's no life for coloured children – children can be awfully wicked, white and black, can't they? Children against children!

She doesn't make friends very easily – at school she goes with a couple of girls and I encourage her to bring them here but nothing comes of it. I've said to her 'Make arrangements to go out on Saturday with one of them – bring them here and have some lunch – go out on the bus to somewhere nice and have a nice day. I'll give you a couple of bob to have a bit of tea out'. But it never materializes. I don't think she's bad to get on with – she seems to have quite a lot of personality in a crowd at school – she can make them laugh – but she doesn't make a mate. Now our Johnny's got loads of mates, because there are lots of boys who've grown up on this estate but no girls.

So Elaine doesn't go out with anybody. Johnny's no problem at all. She'll say 'Shall we go out somewhere – oh, let's go out', but I can't go out if Charles says he'll be in at 3 o'clock and walks in at 7 o'clock and you're stuck behind the door because you're wanting to give him a fresh meal.

I wish she could find a mate – perhaps she'll break out – she's going to a school dance next week – I'm ever so pleased. She's going with a girl friend and she's going to come and sleep here after the dance as her mother wouldn't let her go because of getting home. They've both got tickets for the dance – and I'd like them to have a dance with a boy, you know. This is her first dance. I used to *love* dancing – I thought I'd never marry someone who wouldn't take me dancing – but I did. Mind you, Charles is a nice dancer and I can follow him well, but it never worried him whether we went to the pictures or for a walk.

I told Elaine 'Now don't forget, before you leave you must *dance*'. And she and her mate said 'Oooh, we can't get up, we don't know how to do those dances.' I said 'Look, the more you sit and watch, the time will be gone'.

Next week – after the dance
She thoroughly enjoyed herself at the dance, but there was a fight between darkies, all West Indians. They couldn't get into the dance so they gate-crashed and threw milk bottles through the school windows and now the headmaster has said that there'll be no more school dances. Well, I wanted to go up and see him and say to him 'That's the first dance she's ever been to and she really enjoyed herself and now they can't have any more because of the coloureds!'

I think it's a shame. Elaine never goes anywhere in Athol because of them. I told you she doesn't go anywhere. There's always trouble. She won't go over to the main street because she's frightened of the coloureds; she used to do old-time dancing and she stopped that because of them, because one of them spoke to her at the bus stop; and now this – I said to her I was going up to see her headmaster and tell him it's not fair and she said 'Oh no, don't go, don't go!' It makes me wild because – well – there's no more dancing. She was so excited.

I asked her if the police were down at the dance and she said 'Yeah' but why can't they have two policemen on the door, all the time the dance is on? I know the police are *outside* but they should be *there*. I mean we've got enough to spare because there are enough of them driving up and down here all night, looking to see if the likes of my Johnny are behaving themselves.

I don't know if the West Indians who did it were at the school – but they didn't have a ticket.

Johnny said the next day that this used to happen when he went to school dances. It's always the coloureds. They're different to us because they're so aggressive, that's why. I mean they're boisterous. They shout, they holler and shout, they fight, the girls fight against each other, and the screaming and shouting before they start fighting – it's really awful.

The youngest son – Colin
When Mrs Chattaway had Colin she had a midwife to help her in labour at home.

> I had the other two in hospital and I was absolutely terrified at having the baby here because if anything goes wrong it's better to be in hospital. I asked my doctor if I couldn't go into hospital and he said there wasn't a bed. Now I know why there wasn't a bed because they've got too many coloureds in there – most of the patients in this hospital nearby are blacks. He said I was a healthy woman but I'd gone twelve years without having a baby and I was thirty-seven at the time.
>
> Funnily enough I had a coloured midwife – she was lovely. She came right away and she said 'Now tell me where the other children are so that I don't walk into the wrong room and frighten them'. She stayed with me.

It was a difficult birth – the doctor had to be called – she felt the midwife was 'marvellous' and showed 'great kindness' but because of the unexpected delivery problems she felt that she should have been in hospital with full medical care.

At the time of the study Colin was two and a half years old. Mrs Chattaway commented that it was like having started another family – having two families – because of the long time interval between the children. He was not a contented baby like her first two, but a very hungry baby. Bottle-fed on demand, he was toilet trained from the age of one month and 'successfully' achieved training at the age of six months according to Mrs Chattaway. She is very concerned about Colin and devoted a lot of time to describing his problems. He came in and out of most interviews with Mr and Mrs Chattaway and much of what she said about her son was readily observable. He goes to play-school twice a week but has only been going for the past month.

He's the most difficult one at the school – he's the one who still cries so when I go all the mothers have dropped their children and I have to stay and have a walk around with him.

He's so emotional and gets het up and bad tempered and the teacher has got a terrible lot of patience with him.

When he goes to the primary school at five, the best part of the class will be coloured, so he's got to be with them now at play-school and learn to accept them. I tell him to say 'Hello' because those babies can't help what they are. I don't let Colin spit and I hope the other mothers don't let their kids, but it seems to me that when the coloureds grow up, they're spitting and got no respect for their mum or dad at all. Whether these little kids are going to be like that, I don't know.

I put Colin in this play-school. For one reason he was lonely and for another there are no coloured children round this estate, but there will be in his class and I don't want him to have such a shock to know that there's another child who is a different colour. So he mixes with them now. He gets on *ever* so well with a coloured little girl. She adores him and she won't leave him. She gives him all the teddies and I don't know her name. I've asked him but he doesn't know.

He does come out of school lately and gabbles like an Indian – oolabella – bella – he's going. I just laugh really but his dad doesn't like it and says 'Ooh, you'll be talking like a woggy next'. But I've definitely got to accept it – they're definitely here. They'll be in his school. I can't say to the teacher 'Don't put my Colin next to him,' can I, because they're all God's children, after all, aren't they?

The coloured mothers are good to their babies – they're good mothers. I've never seen them knock their children about – they seem to have a lot of patience with them. The children are always beautifully dressed and they're always clean. The mothers are all friendly and they always say 'Hello' but we don't have – you know – conversation because we're either settling our children in or we're picking them up and just pleased to see our children.

I don't saddle Elaine with him for long because I don't think it's fair.

Whereas Johnny used to throw himself all over the place

when he was tiny, I try and calm Colin down before he really loses his temper. I'll change the subject rather than let him do all that screaming and exhausting himself.

But he still loses his temper just like that, you know – he gets aggressive – he turns immediately you know. But oooooh he shouts and hollers at you. I mean he wouldn't think anything of kicking you but my other two would never raise their feet. And he's got so much will-power and is defiant and although I never have brought their dad in – I never say 'Wait until daddy comes home' – but this bloke even defies his father. He is an awfully aggressive child.

How cheeky Colin is to me – oh! you'd never believe he was mine, because I was so strict with the other two – I wouldn't have any answering back – but this one – oh! – he says 'Shut your mouth – shut up'[laughs] – he does honestly and I smack his bottom and I try talking him out of it. It's because he's got a big sister and brother and they let him do just as he likes especially Elaine, she spoils him terribly. But he'll go into the garden and be shouting 'Give me a push on the swing' and if I say 'No' or 'Stop shouting' he says 'Shut up mummy'. You'd never believe he was mine because I'd have brained him! He shouts to my mother 'You shut up nanny' and he shuts the door on her as she goes from the kitchen into the other room, he pushes the door and he knocks down my dad and shouts 'Shut up grandad' to him – well my dad is seventy and he's marvellous with patience – but you can't have him going on like that. I just give him two good smacks on the bottom, not hard but with his trousers down and he's as sick as a dog all over the place. Every time I give him a good smack on his bottom, he's sick, well, what can I do? I sometimes sit him in here after he's been shouting and answering back and tell everybody not to go to him but he screams and hollers. What can you do? I mean I don't know which way to turn. Johnny was bad-tempered but he never answered me back like this bloke – never – I don't know whether it's because I'm older that I'm giving in to him but inside I *rave*. He shouts and hollers at you. Sometimes his dad hits him – gives him a smack, he doesn't like it and sometimes he's sick but not like when I smack him – then he's always sick.

He's spiteful to the cat you know – he'll pull its tail as he passes, as it's lying there quietly – ding-dong he goes and I say 'Don't be wicked to Sandy' but he'll go back and do it again. I know children do it but Colin does it more. He's so spiteful, and if you give him a smack he gives the cat a sly kick if you're not watching. And the big boys come round and he won't let them play with his football and he screams and kicks and he speaks so aggressively from the back of his throat – really very spiteful.

He's a real problem to me. If I heard another child talk to his mother like this one does to me, I'd give him such a hiding. You'd never believe he was mine. I think he's so cheeky – he's disgusting. I can't master this problem. I mean, I give him a hiding [laughs] and he brings up all his dinner and I think 'Oh blow that – he's got a bit of calcium in him and now he's throwing all the milk back'. [Laughs]

If he goes to school as lippy as he is now, he'll get disliked.

She details many ways in which Colin is cheeky and aggressive to her, his dad, his gran and his grandad and her anxiety and despair at not being able to cope with him. 'I feel awful . . . . I don't know what to do – he drives me potty.'

I have been severe with him but he's a very, very strong-willed and very, very independent child.

How the three children get along together

Elaine's got a lot of patience with Colin – he's very trying at times; she'll be doing a nice drawing and in a second he'll whip it out of her hands and destroy it. He'll get told off for it but she may say 'Ah well'. Johnny and Colin are alike so that when Colin loses his temper, Johnny can talk him round. Johnny used to throw himself down and bang his head against the wall but Colin doesn't throw himself down and before he gets to such a pitch, I pick him up and take him to the garden.

Before Colin was born, I'd sometimes go out with Charles to Bingo and leave the two children together and then I'd come back and they'd had a row. I was silly really, because my mother said I was making a rock for my own back and shouldn't worry and I should leave the two of them to sort it out, but I didn't – I stepped down and never went to Bingo again or left them alone together. Charles sometimes went on his own.

My husband and I

I liked my husband right from the beginning when we met but he wasn't really like me. He was always kind to me and you remember I told you when we got married, how he'd bring me special things to eat and how I'd bring in my little brother and others to share.

There's nobody like me in his eyes.

Although we both came from broken families – Charles and I had been brought up by our relatives in one way or another, I think that Charles feels he's had nobody to really help him to do things and has a sort of chip on his shoulder. He was very spoilt in one way when he was little but he didn't have his own parents to really look after him and care for him and specially when he went to live with his aunt – he felt kind of left out.

I feel I've had a very happy life and although I lived with my stepfather and stepsisters and brother – I felt I was one of the family.

He's awfully placid – I mean you can go a long, long way before that man loses his temper but when he does, he goes, you know.

I don't think I'm a bad wife – I know I lose my temper sometimes with him – when the children were little I used to work at night until 9 or 10 o'clock and all day I was fed up because I was stuck inside with the kids – so I'd let him have it when he came in. He might come in dead tired and I'd have just put his dinner on the table – and I would be up to here by the time he came in – and he was just like a valve and I'd start with him. But we've now got that little bit of understanding for each other and it's much better.

There's one thing I do dread, rowing with him because he sulks afterwards . . . sulks afterwards and he gets me to such a pitch that each day I wake up and think 'Now what's he going to be like when he comes home from work?' because he does get irritable and he's very hurtful, let's put it like that. He's getting much better but I'm quickly hurt, very quickly hurt and instead of thinking 'Oh, I don't care' inside me I'm unhappy, you know. When he starts he does make my life a misery.

Mind you I'm not frightened of him – I used to be – but now I'll have a go with him, he'll never push me down. But it's the afters – that's when he's going to sulk and come in and eat his dinner and slosh the cat and he's not talking to me, and he's sulking over a simple thing that we've then made ever so big.

One of the last rows we had – I said to him 'I'm not going to have an unhappy life. We're either going to be happy or we're going to part. This is *me* talking this time,' I said 'we're going to come to an understanding. If we can't talk things out or have a little row and forget it, instead of making it in to a great big thing and sulking, I'm not having any more of it. I'd rather go than make my nerves bad so that I'm irritable with the kids. I don't want any more of it.' I'm not saying that anybody can get on with me because they can't but it's just that he's so bombastic with it all, and it's childish to have to act like that.

They go out very seldom together – a drive to Notting Hill to see her mother-in-law each fortnight and an occasional drive with Elaine and Colin. Johnny goes out with his friends.

We keep saying we're going to Bingo but of course Colin doesn't go to bed until late and I can't expect Elaine to be saddled with him when she's got school all day.

She is frightened that her husband may hit an Indian one day in his car.

The Indians don't cross the roads with the lights. You're the one who has to put your brakes on – like my husband, he gets very annoyed. I can see him hitting one of them one day in the car. They plead that they don't understand about crossing the road but if they live here it's about time they learned to know where the crossing is and not just walk across the road anywhere they like.

Living in Athol

I used to like Athol when I first came out here – it was all nice and there was open country and you didn't have to go far to find a lovely place. But now everything's getting to be a run-down dilapidated area which started with the coloureds letting things go and now white people aren't bothering, because they can see that the Indians and the coloureds are getting a lot of their own way and people are just giving up.

We all look after our homes and keep them nice and our windows cleaned but in the main street and in the High Street, it's not nice – the picture palaces are beginning to look very dull and also the shops – when the leases expire they let them to coloureds and they don't keep them nice. You can always tell a coloured house or shop. I know there are some good and some bad – but the majority of them buy a house and let rooms off and it's not nice at all.

On Sundays you used to be able to go for a nice walk in Athol but now it's terrible. There are about four or five coloureds walking abreast going to the pictures. They've taken over the picture palaces, Indians have, and Johnny used to go there on Sunday afternoons but he can't bear the smell of garlic and so he doesn't go any more. He has to go to other parts of London.

I used to go and do my shopping down in the High Street, but the coloureds make me too fed up, they stand and talk, jabber, jabber, jabber and won't move when you want to get by. Once upon a time, you could go along and say 'Excuse me' and they'd move, but they're too ignorant. They look right through you, you know, and you've got to more or less push your pram into them to move them. They've got no manners anyway. And how they spit in the street, I can't bear that! Even the women do it – the Indians and the West Indians but the curly-headed women do it more. There are so many germs in what they're spitting up and they just walk along and do it and I see men even doing it from their noses – Oh! how can they be so rotten?

Not that we're drinkers, but in the summers, we used to have a shandy and sit in the garden of the pubs round here and take the kids but now we don't do that because they're full of West Indians and you go along there on a Saturday afternoon and they are so bombastic and they shout at each other and you'd think there was going to be a fight any minute.

On this council estate we're lucky because there are no coloureds but we've got them living down along the side roads. And they don't keep their places nice, their curtains are rotten. But they do keep their kids clean – the children always look nice at school.

Down across the High Street there's an Indian temple and Indian music's playing all the time. It's quite nice you know, there are cymbals going.

I wish we could win the pools and I'd like to pick this house up and take it somewhere else. I love this house but I want to move out of Athol. I don't know where – I don't really know because everywhere we know is going to be coloured – there are so many of them here – so many . . .

One day I went to the park down here with Colin and there were some Indian youths flicking knives in the grass. I went potty and wanted to go over to them and sort them out but the kids started crying 'Don't Mum – they'll knife you' so I went down to the police station and said they should be at work not throwing knives in a nice park where babies want to run.

You hear about Indians using knives more than the West Indians. But the West Indians are loud and sort of aggressive – the girls are just as aggressive as the boys – their aggression – it's like a streak in them, like Colin's got a bad temper and that's his streak – well the West Indians are bombastic and think they are 'it'. They are very much more mouthy than Indians. They shout and bawl, couldn't be quiet to save their lives.

But the Indians are classed as cunning – they're quiet but they'd also just bring a knife out only to look at you. They're an arrogant lot.

Well I don't go around Athol much – very seldom – but I hear all about it from the boys, people on the estate and so on. I haven't actually seen anyone knifing someone.

Mrs Chattaway arrived a little late for her fourth appointment – and described the reason for it:

I just saw a little girl up the road breaking her heart – she was about eleven and was crying and I said to her 'Come here, what are you crying for?' She said 'I've lost my money and I've got to get some peas with it and my sister's going to hit me if I don't find it and I've looked all over'. 'How much did you lose?' It was two shillings so I said to her 'Here, don't cry any more. Take your two bob and get your shopping.' And I thought 'There's not much in my purse mate,' but I couldn't see her breaking her heart. I've never seen the girl before – she's coloured – I don't know if she was an Indian or curly-headed; she had an anorak all around here. She was breaking her heart! 'My sister's going to give me a smack', she said.

On inter-marriage
The people I know who have married coloureds, seem to fall in love and don't realize the difference. He doesn't look coloured to her, sort of thing. Well, like my husband had a scar on his face I wouldn't notice it for ever, would I?

I had a friend who was courting an Indian and married him and I felt ashamed for her – I felt sorry for her because once you're in love, you can't see anything wrong with them no matter what they got up to. She really thought the world of him and she fell out with her mum and dad because of it.

My health at the moment

My doctor has a partner who is Indian and he is really a very
nice doctor.

She has been told she needs a hysterectomy and is very worried
about it and does not fully understand what is the matter with her nor
what the implications of the operation may be for her and for her
sexual relationship with her husband. She went to her doctor to allay
her anxiety and an Indian doctor was there. She spoke to him at
some length 'He was ever so nice and he did me a drawing of the
womb' and he explained things to her and spent time telling her in
detail about what was happening to her insides and he reassured her.
'Are you worried?' he asked and she said 'Yes I'm ever so worried
about it'. But when she left there, she felt much better and
understood the need for the operation and that it was not serious.

Self-description

Johnny and Colin take after me – my mother used to say I had
a bad temper when I was little.

My friend says that I don't push enough – that I'm alright
sorting out other people's problems but that I don't push for
myself, you know.

*How would you describe yourself in a few words, without
thinking too hard?* Well, I'm a very good mum I reckon – I decided to be a good mother to my kids because they didn't ask to
come and it's up to me to give them a nice little life. I don't think
I'm a bad wife. I know I lose my temper sometimes with them
all – but as a Mum I like to know that they are alright. I'm not
bad to get on with – I don't like my own way all the time in an
argument, but I'll certainly talk someone down if I think I'm
right.

I've always really wanted my own house – we've never been
able to save up enough for the deposit to own our house. I love
this house but I'd like it to be our own.

I'm really quite contented to go on as I do. I've never been
one to want to go out, gadding about, you know. I like to go to
a show now and again but I wouldn't go unless we had enough
money, because I've got to go happy.

The worst thing that could happen to me would be to die and
leave my kids. I think that's tragic.

JOHN CHATTAWAY: HIS STORY

We skinheads don't like the greasers, you know. It's the way they dress really because you know skinheads have short hair and greasers have long hair and a lot of them don't like washing it – they like to grease it. But we wash our hair and want to dress up smartly sometimes and greasers only do that on some occasions. Skinheads have scooters and they aren't built to go fast, you know, but the greasers always want to go fast on their motorbikes. Skinheads play football but greasers, you know, they seem to like to kick someone else around. I mean, when we go down the coast we get on alright together – but you know you've got to have a go at someone, haven't you? If there's no one else we'll have a go at them. But none of us like the Pakistanis, and we join up with the greasers to get them – and once we've got rid of them we start fighting the greasers all over again.

It's quiet now – but you wait until the summer, there will be punch-ups galore and the skinheads will take over all these parts soon because we don't like the Pakistanis and all the skinheads come down here from all over just to get them. Last July there were a couple of skinheads who got done by the Pakistanis – they were stabbed by them and that started everything. There were about seventy skinheads and they just beat up all the Pakistanis – just beat them up and they put loads of them in the hospital and if it wasn't for the police, you know, they would have killed them all if they had the chance. I wouldn't feel anything if I killed a Pakistani but I wouldn't kill anyone else if I could help it. I don't like Pakistanis – and they'd kill you if they had the chance.

If I was walking along with a crowd of my friends – say about six of us – and we get pulled up by the police and get searched, if I've got a comb on me or a sharp pen or something without a top on it, they do me. But I can guarantee that if you pull up practically any Pakistani he's got a knife on him because at school they all used to have knives and stuff that you can stick into someone. I can guarantee that if you walk along here pretty late at night and see crowds of twenty or more Pakistanis walking round the streets, the police don't do a thing, but the six of us get done. If I do carry a knife, I always get rid of it before the police come. I see them coming and there are enough drain holes and fences – you can do anything to it or even you can break the blade. They can't do anything.

I was coming home one Friday night and there were about thirty of my mates and Pakistanis were chucking bricks at them and stuff like that – down the south of Burn Street there were about seventy of them onto these thirty skinheads. We'd all been to a dance and we went back and got the blokes with cars and we really gave them a hacking, you know. We swung one through a shop window and smacked them really up. And the police came down and, you know, we got blamed for it. They said we provoked them you know – we were just walking along the road.

My friend got stabbed with a screwdriver. We were going to the carnival and Indians sort of jumped on him just because they knew he was a skinhead. They got a big screwdriver and stabbed him in the back loads of times, all down his back. Well, he was well in with all the other skinheads and there were loads of us down there – there were about 400 and you might have heard about it! We went along the main street and there were fights and we were beating up every Pakistani we could find. My friend was in hospital for about three to four weeks because he had a punctured lung and loads of stab marks.

John sits tautly in the easy chair in the large living-room. He is a good-looking lad of eighteen with black hair, roughly tousled which is cut short and trim about his ears. His dark eyes dart restlessly around the room, resting on Sylvia Hutchinson from time to time. His speech is quick, words tumble out, ideas are sometimes disconnected so that one event follows another and cannot readily be distinguished. He has a long slender face, drawn and nervous and is tall and wiry, moves fast and fidgets with his hands as he speaks. His manner is nervous and somewhat ill-at-ease. Colin comes in and out from time to time. John responds to his brother with some warmth although the verbal sparring between the two is mostly concerned with threats of being beaten up – each threatening the other.

His childhood
John's memories of his childhood are almost non-existent. 'No, I can't remember anything.' 'I just remember there were trains running in the street at the end of the road – I can't remember anything else'.

He cannot remember Elaine's birth.

His mother
He remembers that when he went to the junior school 'mum had to take me to the school every day and the headmistress had then to take me into the school'.

His father
He has no early memories of his father.

Accidents in his childhood
John's memories of childhood – while meagre in almost every respect – were copious in relation to accidents. His first interview was largely pre-occupied with accidents recounted in great detail.

> I was in a field and some other boys were throwing big stones and I got hit on the head and had stitches in two places.
>
> When I was three or four years old, I drove down a hill on a three-wheeler bike and it toppled over and I conked myself up.
>
> When I was about six, I was driving a pushbike and a dog ran in front of me and I went into bushes of stinging nettles and I had to have my arm in a sling and camomile lotion to stop it burning.
>
> A few years later I rode down to the station bridge on a pushbike and the brakes snapped as I put them on and I span all over the place and had all sorts of scars where the stones went into me.
>
> I ate a cake when I was small and a bee was on it and it stung my tongue.
>
> We were once building sandcastles and a friend of mine had built one and I pushed his down and he picked up a spade and hit me across the head with the sharp part. That's where I got all these stitches across my head here.
>
> A lot of my friends have had accidents but I've just been unlucky.
>
> When I was playing cricket I ran along and tripped over a stone and cut myself up along my leg.

Schooldays
In junior school I always used to get hit with the ruler and used to get a belt of pain every day. I was always in trouble with the teacher and was always hit more than other boys. I used to go to school with my mum and then I used to clear off and play football – I was more interested in going for walks or drawing things than work. 'You ought to be an artist – you're always drawing stuff', the teacher said. He used to sit there gabbling

away and I used to draw the teacher or a car or a motorbike or scooter.

I always used to get into trouble and once I got hit and he cut all my knuckles across here because he hit me with the side of the ruler.

There weren't any coloureds in the junior school – we didn't have any there when I was there.

I did alright in junior school but I didn't want to leave the class I was in. I wanted to stay in the class with all my mates.

When I went to senior school there was a boys' school and a girls' school and then they mixed them together so I used to have some days at one school and some days at another school. We didn't do a lot at school – I didn't like it much.

When I first went to the school there were only two or three coloured pupils there but by the time I left the school was practically all coloured. Yeah, nine tenths of it was coloured because in my class three quarters of the class was coloured and there were three classes that were all coloureds. You know it was busting with coloureds there – mainly Indians and Pakistanis – and a couple of West Indians, about the same number as whites.

They used to come in every day – loads of them you know, and practically take over the school.

I didn't want to do well. I could have, you know, but I just didn't want to go up a class. In mock exams I always used to come near the top – in the top three – but in real exams I used to come about twentieth because I never used to want to go up to the next class. Later when I when to college, we had a mock exam and I got 87 per cent – top of the class but when we came to the exams I didn't want to go up to his A class so I made all the mistakes purposely and so I got 30 per cent and came sixth from bottom. I didn't want to go into another class with different sorts of people but wanted to stay with my mates.

If we had an hour for an exam I finished it in quarter of an hour and went home and I came second in the class.

I finished school when I was just fifteen and left.

The headmaster used to come in and say 'Good morning, to us all and I used to say 'Good morning, governor'. And he said 'Boy, come here – it's not governor, it's sir to you'. And I said 'Well, you don't have to call me sir – we're at school, you know, not outside on the street, so it's alright'. He used to get very narked about it.

A friend of mine at school was climbing over the iron bar fence around the swimming pool and he slipped and spikes went through his leg here and came out the other side. He was screaming and they couldn't pull him off because it was so rusty. They had to hit him about twenty times to knock him out and the ambulance people came and sawed it off. He was hanging by his leg – half off and half on.

I always used to get into trouble. There was a greenhouse and a load of Indians were on top of it and I kicked a ball and it went through the roof and about four Indians went through the roof with it – the ball was rock hard and the roof was glass.

I also once dived for a ball and knocked over rainwater which the teacher had been saving all year.

We had a motor mower at school and I drove it into a fishpond, caught a brick in the blades and broke them.

I knew everyone at school and they all knew me. I've still got some of the same mates from school.

There were some white boys at another boys' school near by, and they were a very bad lot – a rough lot over there. They used to set the school alight up there – they beat the teachers up, they used to have knives, you know, and knife people outside the school. And then they used to come over here and get the Indians. I know loads of them – the big blokes over there you know – they're all part of the gang and I used to go out with them.

Indians, Pakistanis and West Indians at school
We didn't use to get on with the Indians and Pakistanis – we were always getting into fights with them. The West Indians were with us – they never used to like them either. You used to get Indians who had the attitude of reckoning that we ought to do this and we ought to do that but they thought we ought to bow down to them. It's not the colour – it's just their attitude.

Oh, I've been in several fights with them – loads of fights – there used to be one practically every night.

We never mixed with Indians – as I say, you just don't like them – they're not the sort of people you like.

At school they all used to have knives and stuff that you can stick into someone.

I wouldn't ever give a lift to one of them. I'd knock them down rather than give them a lift.

They always reckoned that they ought to be prefects and stuff like that – serve on the counters and do everything that was responsible.

They used to do games and I mean – well you'd get in a team and they wouldn't pass the ball – they'd just try and do it themselves and get beaten.

They're just ignorant, you know, you can't teach them, you can't show them anything. We used to do welding and things like that and they used to hang around and then do it their way – a stupid way they used to go about things, but you can't tell them anything.

If you were making something and you could see someone else was doing it wrong – well, they wouldn't tell you it was wrong but just let you go on and do it wrong. But other sorts of people, you know, would help you and come and show you but they wouldn't. They've always got to do things themselves.

We used to do metal work and none of them used to get it right. And then in a snide way they'd do things behind your back – change the numbers on these jobs, you know. I've seen it done several times, they'd swop their job over and change the numbers – oh, it's happened loads of times.

The teachers all used to favour the Indians, they used to get round the teachers and always got their own way. They all used to favour the Indians – all used to say 'Come here and I'll do this or that for you.'

I don't know why it was.

We used to have gardening lessons and all the class had to go outside. But if the Indians said they couldn't go out they had colds, the teacher used to say they didn't have to go out. But if I said it he'd tell me to go out there – and he'd do the same with my mates. It was just like that and you couldn't do a lot about it.

If there was ever a fight, the teachers used to say it was our fault and we used to provoke it.

Everyone had to play football and the Indians and Pakistanis used to say they can't do it, because some of them have turbans or something like that and they can't do it. But if I let my hair grow long I'd probably get expelled from school. They have their hair long and wear turbans and they can wear coloured jackets and pointed shoes and things like that, but if we wanted to wear boots or bovver hats they just wouldn't let us do it – but they allow them to do it.

They were too lazy to play football and they wanted to play hockey. So they used to give them the pitch and let them do it, but if I said I didn't want to play football and wanted to do something else, I wouldn't be able to do it.

A lot of them don't have to come into assembly because they don't agree with the religion bit, but if we said we didn't agree with it we would probably get the cane or something like that. They always get their own way.

They get let off lessons if someone says he's sick – but if I'm sick I have to bring a note and all that stuff – but they don't have to.

They used to speak in their language and they used to call you names or talk behind your back and you couldn't understand them but in the classroom when they sort of say your name, you know they're talking about you – they can't say your name in Indian – and you get up and belt them one, you know. But it's always you that's seen to start the fight, or so they reckon and they always get their mates – that's two thirds of the class – to say it's not their fault. There's not a lot you can do about it.

If I said something about one of them they'd go straight up and tell the teacher. But because I can't speak their language, I can't go up and tell the teacher – so they get away with everything.

Because a lot of them didn't like potatoes and stuff like that, they used to have curry at school every two months or so and I never used to stop at school when we had curry but used to go up to the chip shop. They used to cook curry just to suit them – a lot of them wouldn't eat meat so they had to make them something different – made especially for them you know – for a couple of them – eggs or something like that. It used to get on your wick.

Some of the Indians and Pakistanis are more European-like – they can't even speak a word of their language, you know, and they used to want to come and muck around with us and they used to be in the football team but none of the others. These few Indians didn't used to go out with the others when they went off home or went to the synagogue or whatever it was – these few blokes came out and played football with us and wouldn't want to go to church and stuff like that. We used to get on alright with those Indians – they would come out with us. I'd give them a lift and they'd give me a lift but I wouldn't give the others a lift. I'd knock them down rather than give them a lift. If there was a fight, these Indians who are English-like, would be on our side.

We used to mix with the Jamaicans – but not with the Indians.

At school with us there was a half caste – half white and half West Indian – and, you know, he used to beat the Indians up and never liked them.

Work

I left school as soon as I could.

At first I worked right near my school with my friends, working with machines, but I left there because the doctor said the oil was bad for my skin. I then went to work doing some welding and also was at college as part of the job. But I got the sack because my teacher started punching me and so I beat him up at the college. He'd been pushing everyone about and I had a compass and he started prodding me with it, you know, telling me how to do something and I just got hold of the teacher and belted him one so did a couple of the other blokes in the class and they all had good reason. The teacher got thrown out and I got sacked the next day. I just got up and lost my temper with him. He sort of fought back but I got the upper hand.

I was sorry to leave there – my grandad used to work at the same place and all my mates from school. We used to have good laughs. Before the holidays they welded me to a bench and I had to cut myself off with a hacksaw. Everyone had gone home and I was there about an hour after they'd locked the shop up. They just left me there.

Before I left college, I was the second youngest in a class of thirty-eight and what used to take most of them six or seven weeks to do used to take me just the afternoon and I used to get good marks.

I chucked out before the exam but I would have come top of the class; all the others used to find it hard – they used to say 'How do you do this or how do you do that?' and I used to do it for them and it was easy.

John recounts the 'larking about' that took place when he still worked for the firm. He was working in a yard with lots of others, and for a lark his mates locked him in a great big tall cupboard which was in the yard and 'in it was a gallon of stuff that's poisonous and can knock you out'. It was knocked over as they put him in there.

It was a redhot summer's day and they could hear me banging

but no one could find me. Then the banging stopped and they thought I was just sitting there but I was sort of knocked out and had gone all funny. A couple of my mates came and got me out and I went home. I was so sick. My dad went up to my mates and had a go at them about it, you know.

He recounted many incidents involving other mates of his who were 'knocked into the canal', 'strung up by a Union Jack and left on the girders of a ceiling', and a mate whose feet were welded to a big ball and chain and had to walk home with it because he couldn't get it off.

He also took part in other 'larks' when cars were jacked up and turned over, and also the wiring of the ignition on cars so that people got electric shocks when they turned the ignition on.

When he left the firm, he worked briefly doing plumbing work and that firm was bought out and he is now an apprentice gas-fitter and back at college as part of his training. He has become friendly with a West Indian at college who calls the Indians 'black bastards and hits them and stuff like that – he never used to like Indians'.

The Indians used to bring my mate some of their food and offer it to him because he was their colour but he wouldn't take it – he'd rather have egg and chips like we have. He played football and he'd come with us and sit on one side in the classroom with us, he'd prefer to sit there – the Indians would be on the other side.

At college, I've proved the maths master wrong each time. I show him the easier ways of doing the sums.

I don't like doing jobs in Indian or Pakistani houses. I go in there and don't say anything but I just don't like working for them. My boss doesn't like them either and he turns some jobs down when it means working for them but he's frightened of them reporting him to the Race Relations Board.

My mate at work goes out in a van and he pulls out over the corners trying to frighten me – and I put my foot down on the accelerator to frighten him. We have a laugh.

Incidents and accidents

John has had many accidents. His scooter caught fire once while he was on it. He was on his scooter and had a head-on collision with a car and he was in hospital for a week or more, had concussion and fractured his arm and was badly cut and scarred on his legs. 'I can't remember anything about it now if someone asks me the story – it's loss of memory. It happened five months ago'. He was lucky to have survived as he was not wearing a crash helmet.

Two years ago he was walking along and suddenly got shot in the head with a rifle. It went into his ear and he had stitches in his ear and 'If I didn't have my mouth open it would have killed me'. The police never found out who shot at him.

One day he went down to where his mates were making something – 'like a bomb' – and it blew up and the metal cut his leg open but nobody else was hurt.

He has had innumerable car accidents, all very detailed and involving bruises, blood and cuts on legs and arms. He has also had many accidents on his various scooters of which he owns three.

His escapes are miraculous 'We had a car with a convertible roof and I was on top of that and it turned over and I shot out. I just had bruises'.

He was walking along the roof of a water-tower with a couple of friends and 'We went through the roof – crunch into it – but it was a bit of a laugh, only had cuts and bruises'.

'I've had quite a few accidents.'

John also recounts countless incidents and adventures, involving falling into an open grave and cutting himself on a tin there – and looking for a ghost in a churchyard and being very frightened. At Blackpool one of his mates 'shoved me off the pier into freezing water – it was horrible and it frightened me a bit – I went under the water and it was horrible and cold there'.

Girlfriends
He knows a lot of girls and seems to be much sought after.

> It's always her who wants to go out with me – so I go out with her – that's Shirley.
>
> Meg came over to me and she got on my scooter and went off with me.
>
> I can tell her anything – to clear off even and she doesn't get insulted. She's very keen on me.
>
> Down at the dance hall, and there's this good-looking girl Yvonne and she just came and asked me to dance. I nearly got beaten up over it.
>
> One day Yvonne was waiting at the zebra crossing and she walked out into the road and I practically hit her – had a big skid. 'Silly cow', I shouted to her as she stood in the middle of the road.

A girl told me that Joan fancied me and always wants to go out with me. I thought, 'Christ! I can't go out with her – she's about a foot taller than me, she's older than me, and she always used to bring me presents and things.'

Once I had three girls going at once and we had a kind of game with my mates as to who could keep going longest without getting caught. It was making me broke.

On Sunday I had to try and avoid one of the girls because I was taking her out and I didn't bother to turn up. I didn't bother to phone until a couple of days later.

If a girl isn't ready when I call for her, I don't bother to wait – don't bother to get off my scooter most times.

They come after me, I don't bother about them.

He goes dancing to the discotheques where they play 'reggae and stuff like that you know – it's a skinhead place'.

My mum and my dad

They don't stop me from doing anything I want – if they said I couldn't go anywhere, I'd still go anyway.

They said to me 'You're not going to have a scooter'. I got a scooter. They said 'We'll put a hammer through it', and I said 'I'll put a hammer through your car if you put a hammer through that' and that was that.

My dad and I sometimes have a punch-up – he punches me maybe once a year – something like that – mostly when the coppers come round and I'm in trouble. I hit him back if he hits me and then he stops when he knows I'm going to hit him back.

I'll go indoors after that if I want to and if I don't I'll go out with my mates.

He says to me 'If you go out, you can clear off and not come back', but my mother always says 'I want him to stay', and she always gets her own way. But I've always got somewhere else to stay – loads of places with my mates.

He gets angry with me because he doesn't want me to get into trouble. He was in trouble, you know, but not really anything for him to worry about.

He sort of just goes to hit me but he doesn't really lose his temper all that much.

Most of us get on alright with our dads – we must muck around.

My scooter's not going – but my dad's been helping me fix it.

The only time my mum gets angry is when the police come round here.

I get on alright with my mum. All my mates come here and they muck about. Some parents don't even ask you in, they let you wait on the step but my mum just tells them they can come round the back for me and call for me.

She doesn't hit me, but if she did, it wouldn't hurt anyway.

John feels that conflicts he may have with his parents are much the same as in other families. She doesn't want him to get a motorbike but 'I'm going to get one'.

Elaine

He has little to say about his relationship with Elaine except that he gets on 'alright' with her. 'I took her out to the fair last week because her friend had gone to Austria and my mum said "Take her out", so I took her up there.'

Colin

He follows me around and plays football sometimes and when I'm doing anything on the scooter he picks up a hammer and starts to play about.

Dialogue overheard during an interview: John to Colin: 'You shut up'. John to Colin: 'I'll beat you up'. Colin: 'Beat me up, beat me up', John to Colin: 'No, I'll beat you up later!'

Skinheads, greasers and Pakistanis

Last summer there were about 400 of us skinheads on scooters all going down to the coast and there were police cars on either side of us, sort of following us. They stopped us loads of times and wouldn't let us go down there – they put up road blocks and made us turn back. But loads of us got down there anyhow.

Sometimes skinheads and greasers fight each other but not often. The greasers don't like the way the skinheads dress – and their music's different – the greasers have rock-and-roll and they like these tight trousers and motorbikes. But the skinheads like heavy brogues and sharman shirts and all flash stuff and fancy stuff like our scooters all done up.

After I took Elaine back from the fair I went back there and there were forty to fifty greasers and a load of skinheads. They jumped on me with sticks and bottles and stuff like that and my crash helmet's all got cracked and I got dents in my scooter where bricks hit it. A big motorbike came roaring at me and my mates and I headed it off with bricks and smashed his bike up. We got him and beat him up and we'd all cleared off before the police came.

We used to go Paki-bashing before but we can't now as there are too many police.

If the Pakistanis decided to get the skinheads, the police grab us but they won't grab them if there's a punch-up because they say it's us causing the trouble. But nine times out of ten it's the Pakistanis who do the provoking.

They walk in crowds and if you go past on a scooter, they shout out to you and have a go at you. If you go along a footpath and you've got boots on and short hair, they'll have a 'go' at you too. They don't particularly worry me because you can normally see them from a distance and it gives you a chance to get away or round the flats.

If I see Indians who have been in my class at school – maybe for three years or so – they still wouldn't say 'Hello' to me on the street and I wouldn't say 'Hello' to them.

I know if I go out tonight and if I see any of them, I'll have a go at them, you know.

You sometimes see one or two Indians in skinhead gear and they've got scooters and stuff like that. But their families don't speak a word of Indian – it's not the Indian curry and stuff like that.

Living in Athol
My mates and I stood on a building in Athol and we counted and in half an hour there's one white person to every ten Indians down the main street.

When I visited someone in hospital down here, there were Indians in every room – a girl I know had a baby and in the ward there were eight Indian or Pakistani women and two who were white. You can't get away from it.

If you're up at the Labour Exchange, all the unemployed are Indian – only about one in fifty is white.

I had to queue up for a passport and all these Indians on the dole – they try to get the sack so they can get the dole. They don't want to work.

Practically every Pakistani has got a knife on him.

If any Indians or Pakistanis move into this housing estate they won't last long, I think.

It's not their colour – they could be green – but it's just their attitude, you know what I mean. They just don't like you so we don't like them. It's something about them.

They can come into our pictures – but on a Sunday evening and you wanted to go to the pictures, they wouldn't let you in. The bloke on the door would tell you to 'clear off'.

There are a few West Indians who are all dressed up in skinhead gear and when the fight comes in Athol, they don't know whose side to be on. They had Indian friends and they didn't know what to do at first and then they all came onto our side.

The police
The police are all over the place now in Athol.

They always pick on skinheads and they booked me for taking someone on the back of my scooter when I had L-plates on.

They've picked me up loads of times. I used to get stopped once a night for just having a scooter. 'Where did you nick it from?', they'd say.

I got done £5 for going the wrong side of a 'keep left' sign – they just picked on me.

They know me and my name – they know every one of my mates.

They know me because of my scooter not because of my fights – I haven't been caught so far anyway.

I've been fined £27 for carrying a passenger while still a learner – they just pick you up – they're alright I don't dislike all of them, some of them are alright.

I got pulled up once for walking along the road – the panda car pulled up and the copper said 'Where did you get the coat you've got on?' and he made me turn out my pockets and then asked whose shoes they were – and said they'd seen me in a house back there or something like that. They took me to the law station just to find out something, you know, kept me there about an hour and a half and brought me home.

There used to be about seven Indian policemen round here but there aren't any now – three have been killed already and another was killed recently in a car crash.

Self-description
John, when asked to describe himself briefly, said he couldn't do so

and could not imagine what a best friend might say about him. When asked how someone who might not like him would describe him, he said he 'didn't know of anyone who didn't like him – or if they didn't, he hadn't been told of it'.

When asked what sorts of things might be frightening to him, he said, 'Never been frightened really – I don't get frightened and don't worry'.

> I don't like accidents but I don't mind them when I'm in them. When you see someone all smashed up, I don't like that – it turns me over – but if I get smashed up that doesn't affect me.

He feels happy when his scooter starts going – he is deeply absorbed with his scooters and devoted a lot of time to technical discussions about them.

> In ten years' time, I think I'll be famous. I'll invent something – I won't be like these others – my mates – I'll do something – I haven't thought about it yet but I'll invent something – but this lot will all be in the same jobs. I'm going to look after myself – it just needs a bit of common-sense and know-how to make loads of things.
>
> I could be famous. You don't have to do anything – just something simple – to be famous.
>
> The future? I say it's going to get more and more tense. It's going to boil over – there will be guns and stuff like that – because people are getting tired of the Indians now – I know they are.

MISS ELAINE CHATTAWAY: HER STORY

The first thing I remember was when I was five years old at the infants' school and there were all these boys who were mucking about and they had put coats on top of a boy and were trying to suffocate him. I took them off because he couldn't breathe and I took him to the teacher and stayed with him until he got his breath back. I had just come out of the classroom into the playground and there they were, sitting on him.

And then I remember once in gym, my friend got on my shoulders and I couldn't move and she sort of stopped me breathing.

I never used to go out when I was very young – only

sometimes down to the park or to my nan's – you know, my grandmother.

I can't remember the first day I went to school but I remember a thunderstorm with lightning one day and I was so frightened and sat right over in the corner waiting for it to be over.

I don't remember much about when I was very young. I remember when Colin was born. I came home and thought 'Oh, her time's near like' and then I woke up one morning and I found a blue car outside and I thought a hostess is here or something and I went downstairs and my dad was boiling things and he said 'Mummy's having the baby', and I went 'Ooh blimey!' and I went upstairs and she had started her labour pains and we had this Jamaican woman to help her. I went and sat with dad on the stairs and then Colin's arms got stuck when he was coming out, see. The midwife said, 'Quick Mr Chattaway, get the doctor', and my dad rushed up the road and phoned the doctor. The doctor came and they asked my dad if he wanted to see it being born but he said 'No' because he can't bear anything like that. And so me and my dad were sitting on the stairs and then I went in there and said 'Can I hold him?' and the doctor said 'Oh, you are a nuisance', but he got him out for me and I was holding him and every time he woke up for his feed, I was sitting at the end of the bed.

My mum said I should go round and tell my aunt and so I went round there with my bike and when I came back I shut my finger in the door. I had it all bandaged up. I shall never forget that.

I thought he would change us all and he does – it used to be worth going on holiday, we'd just sit on the beach but now we've got to keep our eyes on Colin – just sitting there, we can't go anywhere otherwise he'd start moaning.

He gets his own way all the time, you know. We always used to give in to him and now he takes it for granted.

Elaine is talking to Sylvia Hutchinson in the large, comfortable living room which stretches from the front of the house to the rear, with windows looking out on the street down which many Indians, Pakistanis, West Indians and white English are passing. At the other end of the room the green stretch of lawn can be seen, neatly maintained. Elaine is trying to cope with Colin while the interview proceeds. His toys are strewn over the carpet – he turns the radio on loudly and has to be cajoled and enticed to turn it down – he interrupts constantly, screaming, questioning, shouting and Elaine interrupts the flow of her thoughts to tell him to be quiet – orders him to stop being noisy – and at times ignores his screaming which makes it impossible for Sylvia Hutchinson to hear what Elaine is saying. The television is put on and Colin becomes absorbed – but soon he turns the volume up and again interrupts the progress of the interview. Not all interviews included Colin but he was a distracting influence in many of them. Elaine is a fourteen year old with an open, broad face at that stage in early adolescence when her body is starting to mature. She moves and sits with an air of being unsure how to use her changing body – she is on the heavy side and this makes it more difficult for her. Friendly in her manner, she chatters, rarely staying long enough with any subject to become deeply involved. Her attention moves over the surface of her current life and relationships. Her memories of the past are meagre and sparse. It is the present which preoccupies her.

My parents

I sort of get the blame now for things – I can't remember it being like that when I was younger, it's sort of changed as I've got older. But now my dad goes 'Oh you stupid'. I suppose we've all got to go through that stage.

My mum may say 'Oh yeah, we'll see the headmaster about such and such', then I'll say, 'Do you want me to make the appointment then?' and my dad goes 'Don't be cheeky'.

They shout at me sometimes – both of them.

My dad

If I knock something over, he goes 'Clumsy'. And at other times he says 'Oh you stupid . . . stupid mare – always knocking something over'.

I can't use the tin opener. I can't grip it to start with and he goes 'You never learn. How many years have you been?' And I say 'Fourteen'. And he goes, 'You can't do anything, can you?' And he is mad with me because I can't open the tin.

Dad threw my bike out of the shed in our garden. And I go 'Well, where am I going to put it then?' And he goes 'I don't know – you find somewhere to put it'. And I go 'That's nice, isn't it? Everything is for your privilege, everything. How come that we can't put our things in the shed?' My dad said 'Well, build yourself a shed then'.

On another occasion he said he would put the bike in the kitchen for Elaine but left it in the garden and said she could move it herself 'Right old trick that was – I don't think it's fair'.

When I have an exam I say 'Oooh, I won't pass' and I'm all nervous. And my dad goes 'Well, if you don't pass, you don't pass, do you?' It's alright for him to say that, you know, but I get so worried when I get there that it all goes blank in my mind.

My dad goes 'If you don't pass, you don't pass, it doesn't matter if you don't get to Eton'.

If you ask my dad how to do a sum, he goes all around the world to help you get it. We had to draw this kitchen once for domestic science – to plan it – and he goes 'Here's how you do the wall', and I couldn't do it and he goes 'You can't do anything'. He goes all round the world just to get one thing – you can't just draw it, he has to explain it all and then he goes and looks things up in the dictionary so I have to look it up in the dictionary. He goes 'You should learn these things – ask the teacher'.

I ask my dad to help me if I've got a hard problem and I can't do it and he always helps me.

My mum
If ever I'm whistling, she says 'Stop that' and if I didn't, I'd get a clout around my ear-hole. [Laughs] But she larks about with me mostly – if I'm whistling or singing she may say 'Choochee face' or something like that and 'stop doing that'. Even my friend says that when I whistle I sound like a navvy.

I can always talk to my mum – it's easier to talk to her in the kitchen and have a chat with her than to talk to my dad.

They all say I look like my mum. I can't have anybody picking holes in my family – my mum can't stand that either. I can have a joke with my mum and she can have a joke with me – that's all right.

But I'm a bit lazy and the other day my mum and dad asked me to go and get some tobacco and I go, 'No, why should I? I'm going the other way with the dog', and my mother goes 'Alright, don't then – if you want something done, I'm going to say that I'm going the other way'.

She says 'We'll do this and we'll do that'. She's sort of got it planned for me like. The other night my mum said 'You go round to the shops and get this', and I thought 'Oooh blimey' and then my dad goes 'You go and get some stuff in', and I go 'Oooh God, here we go again!'

Being fourteen now, I can sort of talk to my parents.

I don't want to stay at school. I want to work in a shoe shop. My mother says 'We'll have to see about that'.

My dad says 'Well, look at all the opportunities you've got – you could learn a language, be a secretary, do typing and shorthand'. And I say 'I don't want to'.

John

When we were in junior school, Johnny used to give me a bar of chocolate – I used to pay him for it – and then I went to play – that's all I can remember.

I keep having fights with my brother. If I open the door he says it's someone for him and I then say 'All right', and then he calls me nosey and screws my nose round and round.

We're always having fights. He practices judo on me I reckon. He came the first night when he'd first started learning and he almost broke my arm off and he pulled my fingers back. 'Oh don't do it properly – just practice on me', I said. He threw me to the floor and I got my leg caught.

I get my own back because one night I threw some water at him because he showed me up in front of his mates. He said to me 'Old fat, won't slim', so I threw water on him and chased him round the garden.

Yesterday morning he goes, 'Look at all that milk she puts in her tea' and I goes 'Ooh, it's alright, you haven't got to drink it, have you?' My parents just say 'Pack it up' – mostly my dad says it and then he says 'If I have any more of this, you'll go upstairs'.

John's all right, you know. He always says that if anybody starts with me, I'm to tell him. I can always depend on him.

He said to me 'Come on stinker, get your coat on' and he took me to the fair.

He brought me home about nine and when he went back this greaser comes up to my brother's mate with a chain and he goes 'You looking for trouble? You want this round your neck?' And John says 'No' but when he came home he had bashes all over the place and he'd got hit on the top of his head with a bar but he had his crash helmet on. They were looking for trouble – these greasers – and then Johnny got stuck in because you have got to have a bit of trouble. [Laughs] I'm glad I went away when I did, I can't stand the sight of a bit of blood. Johnny just told the greaser to get down and lick his shoes because he had knocked John's bike over.

When Johnny had his accident when that car collided with his bike, I thought, 'Oh blimey, is he going to be all right? Has he damaged himself – an arm or something – so he won't be able to go to work?' It doesn't matter if he's got scars, you know, as long as it hasn't affected him in any way.

Colin

She feels he is attached to her and fond of her. He shares her bedroom and often sleeps in her bed.

> If he wants something, he really screams for it. He shouts and always gets his own way.

She brings him home sweets every evening.

She recounts an incident when he accompanied her parents to her school concert and he saw a West Indian girl there with 'fuzzy hair and big ear-rings'. Colin exclaimed 'Oooh, I've got one of those golliwogs at home'. Elaine commented that no one had told him about West Indians and this was the sense which he had made of his own observations.

School life

Elaine goes to a secondary modern school – the same one which John attended. When she went to infant school there were only a few coloured pupils in each class; then in junior school there were about six in each class, mostly Indians and Pakistanis and she thinks they comprised about a fifth of the class. Now at this school there are considerably more Indians, Pakistanis and also West Indians in each class, and she thinks there are twice as many Indians and Pakistanis who are in the sixth (final) form and also twice as many Indian prefects as whites. When she was in the infants' school she knew an Indian girl who 'was nice' and Elaine went to her house and 'she gave me sweets, apples and all sorts of things and we got on all right at school. You know I don't like to mix with them'.

In the junior school there was an Indian boy:

> We used to have a good old laugh at him – he used to make us laugh the way he talked.

In the junior school, the school laid on a coach for the Indians and they got brought to school. We had to walk to school – everyday, with rain or snow – but they got a coach and got lifts to school and lifts home. Perhaps they think they're just high class, or something. They've got a double-decker bus now.

Elaine is a late developer and during the period of the study she commented that she used to feel physically inadequate and 'not proper' because the rest of the class had reached menarche and she had not yet done so. Her material on events at her present school was copious and detailed and covered four main areas of interest.

Relations with my friends

There is a great deal of material on Elaine's problems with her girl friends at school.

It's always those two – Jean and Barbara – it's never us two, me and her. It's always just them.

Now my friend Jean can have funny turns. One day she's with Barbara and one day with me and the other day I went into the classroom with her and she shut the door and said 'Oh I didn't see you', and I said 'You couldn't miss me, you rotten old cow'.

Barbara is always trying to make me jealous – she goes 'Oooh, Jean and I this, and Jean and I that'. I try and tell her something like what I've been doing at home and she doesn't take any notice of me. I've got to listen to her all the time. She gets on my nerves. It's always for her benefit like.

Jean sees more of Barbara than she does of me – she sees me just here and there for convenience, I reckon. It makes me feel wild. Once for instance, it was her birthday and she didn't know who to have for tea and I go 'I don't care – I don't want to come – take Barbara', and she goes 'All right then I'll have Barbara'.

She goes a bit far sometimes. She goes 'Is my hair alright? And then she says I haven't even looked, and I have. Then she goes 'Have I got anything on my face?' and I go 'No' and she goes 'Yes, I have, I've got a bit of something there'. Oh God, if someone knocks her hair . . .

Jean's going on a skiing trip to Austria with the school next week. And she goes 'Just think of where I'll be this time next week!' and I say 'You'll be in hospital with a broken leg and a broken arm.' I don't want to go. I don't like to leave home. I think she's going just to be able to say she's been abroad, I suppose. She wants to get some suede hot pants over there . . . . I wouldn't wear them.

She has a fight with another girl in the class who ends up calling Elaine 'Old grandma – keep doing your knitting', and Elaine responds 'I couldn't care less and don't talk about me behind my back', and they shout at each other across the room.

She envies a Greek girl at school who she says has three houses, spends about £3 a day, buys presents for everyone and has three ice-creams a day as well as sweets and cakes. In addition to all this, she gets a double helping of pudding at school even if she declines the main course.

That's charming, isn't it? If I don't have my dinner, I'm not given one single pudding – I've never had one single pudding when I don't have my dinner.

She has a deep absorbing interest in food and much of her interview material deals with what she likes to eat and what she dislikes. She buys sweets each day and would like a little job in a sweet shop.

People don't like Barbara. She puts you off when you eat, she sort of eats in a funny way.

A friend takes another friend away from Elaine. This happens often and many similar occurrences were recounted with different girls – and 'I thought – well blow you, mate'.

Elaine goes to her first dance – a school dance. Her friend Jean goes with her and Jean spends the night at Elaine's house. There were about 100 people there, more girls than boys and all races. She's with her friend when an Indian comes to Jean and asks her to dance and Jean said, 'No, I wouldn't touch you'. Elaine wasn't asked but said she would have told him to go away if he had asked her. If an English boy had asked her to dance she would have, 'but I'd be all knees'. [Laughs] They didn't dance with anybody individually but a group of them started dancing to reggae or scottish records – 'just mucking about. We just copied everybody else – just cottoned on like – got all my feet tied up!' The dancing finished at quarter past ten and her dad picked them up by car.

We're not going to have a dance next year because these Jamaican boys gate-crashed and knocked all the front windows out and broke the glass and threw milk bottles from outside the hall. A bloke came to the microphone when we were in the hall and said 'There's been a bit of trouble outside and stay in the hall'. So we stayed there. They had the police outside but they didn't come in. My mum goes 'Oh, you should have had police inside'.

I didn't hear it happening – when we were outside they were asking us to give them our tickets. I don't know if they caught them – Jean's brother says it was a crowd of Jamaicans who did it.

After the dance Jean and I got some chips and Jean didn't want to hang around because she didn't want to be picked up like – at the traffic lights a bloke stopped his car and kept looking at us and I didn't want that and I said 'Blimey – Dad will be doing his nut – I'll go down to the lights to see if he's there', and he was just coming along.

At home she and Jean shared a room and talked about the dance. Jean liked a boy at the dance – someone else's boy friend – and Elaine said that she didn't fancy any of the boys 'they were not my type'. She hasn't gone out with any boys yet but feels that it would do her good and 'It would bring me out'. On the other hand she later comments that she doesn't want to go out with boys now as they would be a lot older than her, and 'I'd feel a drip, you know, walking round as young as I am'. The boys in her class who are her age, she feels are not nice.

They keep nicking our ball and I say to them 'Keep your hands to yourself, keep off our ball'.

She thinks she'll be ready to go out with boys next year because she'd be a 'bit more grown-up'.
She hasn't had any crushes on boys.

Oh, Jean likes going out with boys. She's been out with a boy this time last year. They went to the swimming baths and to the pictures and she said 'He got me in the back row and – his hands! I'm not going out with him any more.' She didn't think he was that sort but she liked him you know. He's older than her.

Jean's also had a crush on another boy and then she found out he was going out with another girl.

When I'm on holiday – like last year at the seaside – there were some boys and we were all in pedal cars and we had a good old time chasing around in them.

Johnny's friends treat me all right – they come in here and sit in here and muck around.

The girls at my school like the skinhead boys – they're in that crowd, you know.

At our school dance there were some hippies in one corner – they had big long dresses and big hats on and long hair and glasses – and there were greasers there too.

Feelings and relationships with Indians and Pakistanis

Whenever you go into the toilets at school there are these Indian girls in there, doing their hair and putting mascara – you know – black stuff on their eyes. And then in shorthand, Miss Pierce goes 'How's that eye shadow Janet then?' Janet's English and she had eyeshadow on – she had on a very little bit, light blue – she had only a very little bit – but these Indian girls smother themselves in it – and have powder too.

This Indian girl at school used to have a different pair of tights every day. She carried them in her bag. She had a ladder in one once, so she took them off in the toilet and put them in a bag, just in the dustbin. Nothing round them or anything, you know – all cheesy-like – and then she put on another pair of tights, just like that. We can't afford tights. I – er – laddered mine once in school. I used to carry a bit of cotton around with me in case I had to sew them up. I can't just take tights off and put them in a bin, just like that. I can't afford it.

The Indian girls at school – well, they sort of overcome themselves. Like this one girl who came to school the other day in a black sort of sparkly dress with sort or silver stuff on it and grey stuff around the arms – and lots of make-up on like this, you know, and up here her hair is tied back. And then they wear tights so that you can see their bums and things like that, you know. And they wear high-heeled shoes you know. But we're not allowed to wear high-heeled shoes in case we fall down and have an accident – that's what we were told in our second year. We're not allowed to wear rings but they can wear lots of rings.

In the second year the teacher said to us, 'We don't like you wearing these Scholls sandals in the summer or high-heeled

shoes because you can easily fall down and break your necks.'
Well, Jean has got these red and blue shoes with a two inch heel
but she can't wear them. But the Indian girls come to school
with their flat-heeled sandals and they go 'click-click-click', you
know, as they walk along and nothing's said.

The Indian girls who dress up like this are younger than me
you know – they're about thirteen years old.

One Indian boy at school has got a car. They've also got these
nice shoes – patent shoes – they have everything nice like. The
Indians have lots of money – they draw the dole and can't get
work and can't speak English and yet you know they get money
for their kids. When I was once in Uxbridge there was this
Indian and he was buying three pairs of girls' trousers and he
spent £21 on them. My dad's got a pair of trousers – crimplene
you know – but he doesn't get anything in bulk, you know.

She recounts how Indian boys at school sometimes push into
queues and when challenged they say 'Oh, no understandee', and
take no notice. 'It's not fair.'

These Indians take all their books home and do homework.
Now if we were told to do homework, we'd do it, but we've
only had homework once and we had one sum to do – that's all
the homework we've had from the teachers, but all these
Indians have it every night.

The teachers help the Indians in our class but if we go up to
the teacher he says 'Oh no, that's all right – you do this like this
and go back and look through page 7.' He won't help us, he
helps them.

I don't talk to the Indians – Indians stick to the Indians and
the whites to the whites. In the playground we play up one end
and we sort of like to get away from them and they hang about
playing football in the other end.

There's a girl Melissa who's Greek and she mixes with the
Indians; she goes about with them and she holds their arms,
brings them sweets and everything.

There's an Indian boy at our school – we call him a dirty old
pig – he's in my class for Maths. Every girl he sees, he goes to
try and sit next to her and then he starts to thump you one and
he says, 'You want to fight?'

I was coming from my friend's and he came up and touched
me so I went for him and threw him against the fence. I can't

stand him. He gets on my nerves. He always gets away with everything. The teacher goes 'Shut up', and he just carries on talking. He gets away with murder.

Some teachers just favour the boys – and then there's one teacher who doesn't like Indians. She says, 'Oh, the smell of curry in here', and things like that and then opens all the windows.

Indian boys wait about for the Indian girls to come out of school. They go out with much older boys than we do. They come round the playground and whistle whenever Indian girls go by and they go off with them. They don't whistle at the white girls. If they did, I'd kick them, but they keep staring at you though.

We were coming out of school one day and a boy shouted, 'Mind your back', and there was this Indian boy and he had a knife. I was frightened and started to run up the road because Johnny's mate got stabbed in the back down in the main street and he was in hospital for a long time. There was a group of them and these Indians started following them and started looking for trouble and they hit him on top of his head and hit the others too and they all fell down and some started running and my brother's mate got stabbed in the back and he fell down and there was blood all over the window of the shop. It was horrible my brother said.

Feelings and relationships with West Indians
There are quite a lot of West Indians at our school but not as many as the Indians – I expect about forty West Indians in the school altogether.

They're lippy, you know, if you look at them they say 'Why are you looking at me?' and they want to start a fight.

There's only one Jamaican in our class and she's ever so funny. She's a good laugh and sort of cheeky really. She's nice.

This girl – Sally – in our class – she's a laugh, she's a caper. We'll be writing our essay and she's sitting at her desk with her legs right outside the desk and the teacher says, 'Sit up properly Sally – that's not the right way to write', and she says 'My gawd' and she'll move her chair out and waddle around and then she sits down and carries on with her work.

West Indians take a different attitude towards us. If you look at them as if to say 'I like that coat – that's nice, isn't it – or I like those coloured tights, you know', then they say 'Oh you nosey old thing'. I think they're completely different from the Indians. You can get some nice people amongst them and some horrible ones – all different kinds.

On living in Athol
I think we've got too many Indians in our school – definitely too many.

I'd like to move out of Athol myself. The Indians have got most of the houses in the street – although they haven't got any on our estate at the moment but they're coming down our road and they'll try and get houses down there.

The Indians bring these germs over and diseases – they should have stopped them when they were first coming over and so we would have half as many as we've got now.

Indian people smell of curry. You can always tell an Indian house by the smell and by the way they paint it. It's usually red or blue or they just cover over the bricks with a black sort of paint. You can always tell them, they have bright colours.

Once I was going down our street and this walker – an Indian – stepped out like, and my dad nearly ran him over because they just step out or just pull out in their cars. It's terrible, you know, they just take advantage of everything.

When I used to go out at night I was frightened something was going to run out at me and so I used to run down the road. I hate coming down here and having to pass the houses round here.

One day my mum was taking Colin for a walk and we had got some fish and chips and were going to sit on a bench in the park down here. There were all these Indians sitting on the grass playing cards and they were throwing a knife and aiming it between the feet of the others. They were playing that game. My mum got the police but they said there was nothing they could do about it.

Sometimes you see these white girls down the street with Indians. I suppose they like them – everybody's got their own taste. I don't like them – and wouldn't go near them.

The Indian children even chase your cat – they chase it all over the place.

On frightening things that happen to me and to others
Elaine relates how frightened she is of the dentist and tells a story of how a man died from too many injections at the dentist. She has a

cousin and recounts in detail how she is an epileptic and bites her
tongue during a fit. She is only twelve years old. She describes how a
boy at school broke his arm and 'it was hanging out of his shirt'.
Another boy at school had a fit and 'he went through a glass window
and he died, you know; it seized all his neck off nearly and he suffered
from claustrophobia and the hospital tried to do everything for him
but they couldn't – he died and it said in the paper "accidental death",
but it was done by himself like – oh, I felt sorry for his mum'.
Another boy at school had a mum 'who suffers from nerves and she
went to get a cigarette and she fell in the fire and he tried to treat her
with cold cream and TCP and she died.'

> Now he's got nobody, you know, and he's getting
> scruffy – all his hair is down to here like. You feel sorry, don't
> you?

She tells a number of vivid stories about injury to others involving
their limbs – legs being broken, a thumb coming off and being sewn
on again, arms broken. Feet pre-occupy her. She had a wart on her
foot and had to have it burnt off, Colin has funny toes, her dad
dropped something on his foot and went to hospital and couldn't
walk. 'They all got something wrong with their feet'. She spends a
great deal of time in her interviews talking about shoes and
describing them in such detail that it runs to many pages.
When she sees an accident she exclaims:

> Oooh – look at that – and you're really enjoying the
> accident.

She dreads the idea of a car coming crashing into the house:

> Cor, just think you might be having tea and you find a whole
> wheel or something, coming charging in.

Death is very frightening to her:

> Anyone who's going to die like – this frightens me.
> When my nan was ill, I was frightened and started crying. My
> dad goes 'Don't cry', so you get frightened, you know.

She is frightened of going fast in cars, also of going on Johnny's
scooter.

She is frightened of thunder and lightning and also of heights.

Self-description

> *How would you describe yourself?:* I'm always giggling. Yesterday I was making all these animal noises like cocks and ducks and I was singing. My friend goes 'Don't show me up – everybody is looking at us.' I guess I couldn't care less.

> *How might your best friend see you?:* Round the bend – a bit crazy.
> I like to be in fashion, but prices go up when things are in fashion so it's best to wait anyway until the prices go down. I like to get things a bit too big for me.
> I would like a house and three kids – girls – they talk quicker than boys.

Chapter 5

THE INDIANS REFLECTING: THE SINGHS' LIFE HISTORIES

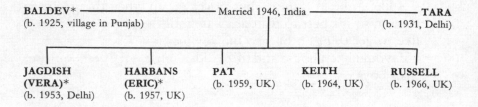

BALDEV* ———————————— Married 1946, India ———————— TARA
(b. 1925, village in Punjab)   (b. 1931, Delhi)

JAGDISH   HARBANS   PAT   KEITH   RUSSELL
(VERA)*   (ERIC)*   (b. 1959, UK)   (b. 1964, UK)   (b. 1966, UK)
(b. 1953, Delhi) (b. 1957, UK)

IMMIGRATION TO UK

Mr Baldev Singh: 1953
Mrs Tara Singh: 1957
Jagdish (Vera) Singh: 1957

* The research interviews were conducted from 21 February to 28 April 1971.
  The research subjects are indicated by an asterisk.

MR BALDEV SINGH: HIS STORY

I remember my father's death very well. I was only three years old and they were taking his body to the pyre – we burn our bodies in India, you know. So I was holding the hand of my grandmother and I said 'Where's my daddy gone?' She said 'He's gone to Delhi for treatment'. So I didn't exactly know my daddy was dead but I remember a lot of people crying. So I took what my grandmother said but it was still in my mind. I've told my own children this – they've asked me a lot of times about my own parents.

I only realised that he was dead when I was five years old and

I went to school for the first time and my grandmother sent me
to school and our custom in India is that the parents take you to
school and as I had no father, one of my next-door neighbours
went with me. And then I felt really sad that I had no father.

My mother died within a year of my father. She was not at my
village or in my house because when she was ill after the death
of my father, she went to live with her father – and I was left
with my father's mother – my grandmother.

My mother had some sort of medical treatment and she died
there. I didn't see her and I only remember her face very slightly
and I couldn't really describe her.

My grandmother gave me all the love and never let me feel
that I was an orphan. She was like a father and a mother and in
fact she was everything to me at that time. She lived for me.

I had a little sister too but she also died very young – very
young. I have only the slightest memory of her death.

It was just myself and my grandmother and we were only two
in a very big house – a two-storey house with lots of land
around it. She brought me up and she was a wonderful woman.
Very strong and six foot tall. My father was also very tall and my
mother had been like my wife, you know, medium size. My
grandmother brought me up very nicely – my parents could
not have given me all the comforts that she gave me.

She gave me a lot of money to spend – which is what
youngsters going to school want. I wouldn't say that she was a
wealthy woman because my father spent a lot of our money. He
was one of the very first educated men in our village. In those
days not many people went to school and he was one of the first
teachers in our village school. He went to college and had a
good education. When he became ill – there was something
wrong with his chest – he had to spend a lot of money on his
treatment and went to Delhi hospital – not many people would
go to a world capital but he went there for treatment. We were
comfortably off – with land – and my grandmother had a lot of
jewellery and my mother had brought a lot of dowry and so
there were no financial problems.

My auntie – my father's sister – was married and they were
also very rich people with a lot of estates. They are all judges
and magistrates in that family and had horses and stables and
thousands of acres of land.

My aunt's family and also her sons are very important
people – one of them is a member of Parliament in India, and is

a Minister in the government and some years ago one was President of the Olympic Indian team and he came over here and he stayed with us. They are so nice. But they are such *big* people that I shirk from them – but when they come here they are so nice.

And when I was in India as a child they were very kind to me – not only my father's sister but also my mother's brother – my uncle. They were very good to me and within the family I was the only child among my mother's family so naturally whatever I wanted, I got. I just had to say 'I want to buy a horse' and my uncle bought a horse for me – just imagine! He told his servant 'Oh, put the saddle on' and this sort of thing. So they were very good and kind people and I had very great generosity from them – all the time.

My grandmother was a very great woman and she loved me so much and she looked after me so well because my parents were dead.

She used to say 'Come on, get up, wake up, it's morning – go and have a bath and your breakfast will be ready for you'. She was not educated at all yet she taught me that the most important thing in life was education. She said 'Learn now and secure it for yourself in life'.

We are sitting in the upstairs bedroom which he and his wife share. We face each other over a small desk with a shelf of books above us and behind my back is the large double bed. The room has a pleasant, lived-in quality with pictures of Sikh religious leaders on the mantlepiece – and on the walls prints of flowers. He is a very tall, majestic and good-looking man who bears himself with dignity and pride. Clean-shaven and impeccably neat in a beige pull-over, he talks earnestly and seriously, crossing his legs and leaning back against the upright chair, keeping his eyes on mine with directness and friendliness.

We lived in a village where people of all religions lived – Hindus, Muslims and even Christians. I am a Sikh and it's not too different from being a Hindu. When I went to school, we all went to the same school. I used to be very religious when I was at school.

About five miles from the village where I lived, was the regimental centre where they stationed the English army. I remember seeing them when I was about fifteen years old and the English there seemed to be very decent people – in fact very, very decent. The people whom they sent to India – and especially the officers – came from really good families and were a good breed I should say. Of course they were the people to influence the Indian people and no matter what their internal policy was – how to rob and which way to rob our people, that's a different matter altogether – but as people they were of really good blood and were good officers and I liked them.

College and then the army

After matriculation I went to college for a month or so, but then the war broke out and I wanted to be adventurous and see new life and go to different countries. I was a very big boy, tall and about seventeen years old and they took me straight away into a clerical job in the army. One of the English officers – a recruiting officer – asked whether I wanted to go into a Sikh regiment and I said yes, I didn't mind. I wish I had joined the air-force but I just wanted to go somewhere and have an adventurous life and I didn't understand the full implications of it. If I had joined the air-force it would have been better for technical reasons and helped me with my life in this country.

I was given a clerical job and sent near the Afghanistan border and since the regiment was a fighting force we all had to have training even the clerical department. We had to get up at 6 o'clock in the morning and after a cup of tea, a quick shave and a wash we had to go for a ten mile run for physical training. I didn't take to it very nicely. My life with my grandmother was altogether different so I had to adjust myself. It took me a couple of months but I was alright after that.

I made very wonderful friends in the army. The regiment was going to the Middle East and I should have stayed in India as I was the most junior class of clerk. But the Colonel (who is now a Brigadier living here in Surrey) asked me whether I would like to go with them and I said 'Yes, sir, I'd like to go with the regiment'; then I was selected to go.

I made a lot of mistakes in my army days. One day I was drunk and disorderly and he just reprimanded me. Next day he came into my office and said 'Hello Mr Singh' I said 'Hello Sir'. 'Alright? How are you feeling now?' I said 'Oh very well Sir, thank you very much'. He told one of the senior Indian officers that he liked me very much because I was the only person there who had *volunteered* to fight – only one person! So naturally I was proud of that. I made a lot of mistakes but he let me go a lot of times.

When I was a Sergeant-Clerk I had my first experience of a fight with a British officer. He was Captain Fleming and that day he must have been fed up. I gave him all the reports on what was happening in the office, you know – all the routine work when all of a sudden, you know, while talking to him he said 'Oh! You are a bloody fool! Bloody fool!' – just like that, you see. I lost my temper and in the meantime I had learnt a lot of things. So I couldn't control my temper and I said 'If I'm a bloody fool, you're also a bloody fool, Sir' I said. He put me under arrest and took me to the same Colonel I mentioned before. On the charge sheet it said 'Indian clerk calling British Officer – bloody fool'. So I went to the Colonel and he said 'You are charged here with so and so' and I said 'Yes'. 'Did you address Captain Fleming like that?' I said 'Yes sir, I said it'. 'You want to say anything before I pass sentence?' I knew he couldn't do anything to me because I was a Sergeant-Clerk and he couldn't put me in jail for twenty-eight days. I said 'Yes, I want to say something. Why should Captain Fleming call me a bloody fool – because we are fighting for you?' He said 'Oh don't be like this Mr Singh. I know you are a very brave soldier' and he gave me all this flannelling. He said he had to reprimand me and he put on my sheet that I had spoken badly to a senior officer. I didn't care about that because I knew that I didn't want to make my career in the army but it hurt my feelings very much. But I was also happy because I had said that he also was a bloody fool if he called me one! Word went round all the regiment. All those Sikh soldiers were round my billet and so on. So the Colonel called Captain Fleming and said he should also put on his charge sheet something for talking to me like that. He said he had no right to call me that, since I was the only person who volunteered to fight. So he told him to be very careful in future. So I went to my office and I didn't care what reprimand was on my sheet and in came Captain Fleming. 'Oh, let's forget it Mr Singh', he said. 'Well, it's all forgotten,' I said and since that day he was such a wonderful friend. He would lend me his car 'Oh, just go out and have a night out and enjoy yourself' he'd say. And when my grandmother died, he was the person who sent me on leave back to India.

I was a good hockey player – and naturally the Colonel was

very happy with my sports ability because I was also a good runner in the army.

I will always regret that I didn't return to being a student – I wanted to be a lawyer but in the war you meet different people and start drinking and leading a carefree life.

The death of my grandmother

The saddest time in my life was when I was in the army and I received a telegram from India that my grandmother had died. I was very upset and that was the night I really cried. I had every opportunity not to join the army but I had joined against her wishes – she hadn't wanted me to go but she wanted me to carry on studying – but you know how it is – young people don't want to listen. So it was the very saddest moment of my life. After that my life has had it's ups and downs but it was not sadness so much as facing the bad times and learning how to face them.

Courtship and marriage

When my grandmother died I was given leave and I came back to my village. Now when I was away in the army I used to write letters to the man who became my father-in-law – just for curiosity's sake – for no reason at all even though I was not engaged. I had always wanted to be their relation because I knew my future wife's brother – he was at school with me, a very nice, beautiful boy and I knew they were a very nice family.

So when I returned to my village my future wife's family knew I was coming – they had known me before because I had gone to school in their sector of the village and they knew the background of my parents. In Indian custom we always look the family over to see if the parents are alright, the family breed is all right. So they knew my background and I knew their's and I was interested.

I had only once seen my wife but I knew from her brother – from meeting him and finding him such a nice and beautiful boy – that she must be very nice and beautiful. So I got an expectation that came to be realised.

The marriage was then arranged and in India in a family like ours the celebration goes on for three days. All my relatives go with me to the other village and they will entertain us for three days and nights continuously and next morning we have our religious celebration and we are then married in the eyes of God. And that is when I see my wife.

When we started our married life I was in the army. The war was nearly over and the regiment had come back to India and they asked me if I wanted to carry on in army service.

I had had enough of it so I took my wife with me to the North-West frontier where we were stationed. We had a nice bungalow over there and in those days money was no object and we really enjoyed our life – we dressed how we liked and had a horse and buggy.

I was about twenty then and she was fifteen. I think she was more sensible than me in a lot of ways and she had a lot of patience and also peace of mind. I didn't have patience at all – I used to blow up because service in the army spoiled me. She was quite the opposite to me. If I blew up she would listen and wouldn't say anything – there was no argument – no, nothing at all.

I had always wanted children. Because I had always been alone – the only child in my house – no sister or brother – I was so anxious to have a baby even in the first year. I wanted her to have babies and she said 'Oh no, there is a lot of time for children. It is one of Almighty God's blessings. When they, come, they come; when they don't come, they don't come. So this was my anxiety in the first period of my marriage. If a child comes, I would be very glad. If I had a son or a daughter even – makes no difference – but it must be a child.

It was six to seven years before Vera was born. It was not that I was worried in those years – because we were very young – but it made for a certain restlessness.

Sometimes I would say to my wife 'Oh I'll marry a second time' just like that, in fun – or sometimes seriously. I didn't mean it exactly because I had great respect for the parents of my wife. Naturally I didn't want them to feel that I treated their daughter badly.

Our marriage was without the guidance of parents because we lived – just the two of us – and if my parents had been alive we would have lived with my father and mother. It was a big house – so many rooms and only two of us. If my family had been alive, my wife would have had more company; as it was when I was out, she was there alone.

After a little while, we left my village and came to the city and we used to go out every night to the pictures and eat out and so on and we had a wonderful time – we had servants – but there was something missing. My wife was a very economical person and once she said to me 'Oh, why do we want two servants?' I said 'Oh, why not have two?' You see, she wanted to cook for me so that we could both sit and enjoy ourselves instead of servants coming and bringing our dinner and so on and I, in my own thoughts felt 'Oh no, let's have this nice posh life'.

Now I am a changed man and have a different opinion of life – I like to cook for myself and serve the children sitting round the dinner table.

In the early days of our marriage when I had worries I never used to tell my wife my worries although in my thoughts I wanted to. I wish I could have expressed my feelings towards her and told her all sorts of problems. She might have given me good counsel. It was only much later – when she came over here to join me, that I started expressing my feelings for her.

In those early days of our marriage I wanted her to be ready in a military kind of way. 'Oh, come and get ready – the buggy is waiting outside'. I wouldn't ask her, I'd tell her like that. Now I would ask her. In those days if she wasn't ready, I'd just shove off by myself and come home at midnight after some drinks or a party.

Work failure

He had gone into the film business with some other people and had invested his money in the business. But he was ignorant about how to handle his finances and this led to the downfall of the business. On the other hand, the men to whom he lent money went ahead and became very successful and although they returned his loans, he was very disappointed by the loss of his own business and his money, and by the fact that others with borrowed money had effectively used it to become rich.

It was a very great shock to me. I was broke and very disappointed. So I thought 'Well, let's go to England and see if I can be successful there.' My wife was already pregnant. I told her I had my passport and might like to go to England and that it might be better for us.

She advised me in those days. She said 'You are very extravagant'. Even though she didn't go to school as I did and she had not the same education as me, yet her brain was like her father's. He was a very educated man and so was her family.

She understood more about money than I did but she couldn't say much because the man is boss even with his own wife. Really, when I think back to those years when we were married, she gave me good advice, but I never paid any heed to her. I think really if I had listened to her advice, I should have been better off.

Thinking of going to England

When I was in the army, my officer who was British used to talk a lot about London – and I read books and papers about it because I was a student myself. I always had a notion in my mind that one day I would go to England and look around. A cousin of mine had been and he told me how nice it was over here, how nice the people are and so these stories strengthened my idea of going to England. When my film business was a failure I just wanted to come and look around here. I was twenty-seven when I came.

My first thoughts were wanting to look at London and see something of the world. I had no money troubles and so there was a lot of difference between people of my education and illiterate people who came to this country by boats, or by smuggling in or by helicopters illegally and so on. Their aim is to come and start work and earn some money, no matter in what condition they may live, but my thoughts were different. Their imagination made this a land of honey and gold – which is not true – and I did not have this sort of imagination. I had seen enough of good times and had enough money and position of my own, so my thoughts were not to go and start work – not at all – not the least thing in my mind. I wanted to see the world which I'd been studying and see how far it was true and also to have a change. I was feeling quite fed up with my own life – my personal life – my unsuccessful business and so I wanted change.

I came with some money from my inheritance and also my father-in-law gave me more than £300. He is a very generous man. So my wife went to stay with her parents and I came here by boat.

Early days in England

I had a friend who was living in Liverpool and I went to stay with him for a few days and then went to a cousin who was living in Essex. And then I came back to London to live with a few friends. They had a house over here in the East End and I used to wander around and see London – go to see the pictures because my main hobby was film work and I was interested in the direction of pictures and things like that. And it was very exciting being here. I went here and there – to Richmond by boat – Downing Street and Parliament – I used to wander around on my own because most of the people I knew here – Indian people – were quite working-class and my life in India was rather different from these people so I never mixed with them much.

So I wandered here and there and eventually after a month or so I got a bit fed up. I used to go to Hyde Park Corner and listen to the free speeches of people from the underdeveloped countries who were under British rule. This was also my hobby. But I was feeling a little lonely sometimes. And I missed my wife.

Those four years were very difficult for me because I couldn't settle down. There were not many Indians over here in those days — those who were here — well, even my cousin, he was a business man and he used to sell clothing in the market – and even the English people too – among whom I lived – well, many of them were very ignorant and were working-class, going to work, earning some money, going to the pub and that was their life. They wouldn't go a step beyond that.

I was very confused. I even wrote to my father-in-law that I would like to go to Canada but he wrote back 'Now you're there, you must do some technical course'. I was working in a company who were making some radio parts but I couldn't settle down and my mind was not on anything much. I could have taken a course if I wanted to but I was so confused. The life I was leading in coming over here – the money I had lost – the money I spent each week just on my expenses – whereas my fellow country-men and people from my own village used to spend two or three pounds a week compared with my £20 – and they would save some eight or nine pounds a week and I would only meet my expenses because I was a spendthrift. I was still in nice clothing and everything was still beautiful.

When Vera was born, I had only about £2 in my pocket that night. I was in a pub with a friend of mine and a cable came when I went home that a daughter was born. So in those days a bottle of whisky was thirty-five shillings, so I bought a bottle of whisky. I didn't have much of it – I was so happy – my other friend, you know, he was rather surprised. He must have thought I was a silly man . . . since generally an Indian drinks when a son is born – but I was so excited that I enjoyed myself.

I missed my wife. I knew she was with her parents and that she was better off there than in my house. I wanted her to come but at the same time I wanted to prove myself. I felt I shouldn't ask my father-in-law to spend more and more money on me but at same time I couldn't save money over here. So I was in a strained situation. I wanted to live like a gentleman – at the same time I wanted my wife over her but I was so disgusted with the situation, I couldn't save money. Those four years were the most unsettled years of my life.

After about four years like that I received a telegram. I had given up my flat in London and was leaving for Scotland where I thought I would try and settle down where nobody knew me. So my friend brought me this telegram to say my wife and Vera were coming – and all my relations over here – my wife's couple of relations, as well as my uncle over here and my other friends – they all sent me telegrams saying that if I won't be at the airport they will be there to meet her.

I was very excited but at the same time I did not have any money to welcome her in the way I wanted to, and she might have many expectations of me and I was quite broke. So I was happy but I was upset. I went and borrowed £15 from my uncle so that I could go to the airport and bring her back.

Re-union with my wife and daughter

She was quite pleased to see me and Vera was three and a half years old and she was walking and talking like a little one and I was really excited but at the same time I felt some sort of shame in myself, you see. Four years I had spoiled – at least I could have bought a house. Once I had saved £200 and put a deposit with an agent over here to buy a house but then I spent it on dogs, horses and good living.

I had lived nicely and had a wonderful time but you see I don't think they were very nice years of my life. Enjoyment is not the only thing in life when you have a wife and child who depend on you. It was a good job my wife's parents were rich people, otherwise what would have happened to my wife?

My wife – I don't know whether she pretended or not but she was so good and gentle and she just forgave everything but it was done . . . she was so kind and gentle. I even told her once,

I said 'I'm not a very rich man. I was different in India but now I am not.' She said 'Don't worry'. And she took half my worries.

I put my cards on the table that I was quite broke. So we started from there and she accepted it and she stood by me and she also played her part and I must say that credit goes to her. I learned my lesson. And I went to work at the steel mills – I had never worked hard before in my life and it was a terrible job to do and especially hard for a person like me who had never done any hard labour in my life. It was very, very hard hitting in those mills – sweating, 110 degrees of heat over there all the time – it was a terrible thing. And I was so tired and my wife would wash my hands, and put some vaseline on and that kind of thing 'Oh, you work very hard, you should have listened to me'. She only said that to me two or three times, but I just took all the money to her and said 'Here it is'. And I forgot the champagne and whisky and everything.

What kept me going was my love for my wife and my daughter and the time I knew I had wasted through my inexperience of life.

It was a very terrible job you see. I used to take a bath every morning and again every evening. My wife used to put the bath on – there was so much dirt and steel dust – and I always had to change my clothing in the morning and again in the evening. But I survived and I thought in my mind I must survive otherwise I'll regret it. So I had good will-power. If a person loses his will-power, then he is like a dead person – which I didn't want to be.

I always had at the back of my mind that this was a good lesson for me – that I was suffering but that God was giving me this punishment. So I accepted it – but I always thought that one day I would make a move. I felt I had to do it for a while and make myself feel a little comfortable, to buy my house, buy furniture and all sorts of necessities. Not on a lavish scale but just to make the house nice and decent.

Always in the back of my mind was the thought that this is not my job and I will make a move when the right time comes. I was working with people who were not educated – fathers and sons – they were mainly English people and a couple of Indians.

In those days when I worked at the rolling mills, there were no educated men among the Indians there and our Ambassador came out to those parts and I read the speech of welcome on behalf of the Indian community, and Vera made the presentation to the Ambassador's wife.

So the police came to know that I was educated and they contacted me and they asked if I could help them in court as an interpreter with the Indian people. I did so. The police are not bad – I think they're fair and if you're honest and a law-abiding citizen, the police will always clarify your problems, in my own view.

In my own good conscience while I was there, I helped an old Indian man whom I did not know, but the cost of that help was that I got the enmity of three other Indians. It was when I was working at the rolling mills and a man whom I knew – an Indian – brought a very old Indian man to my home. He told me that he worked in a factory and some Indians working there asked him for money to bribe the foreman so that he could keep his job at that place.

He did that but he was then given notice. I just took pity on him and I went up to the factory and saw the Personnel Officer who was white and I told him that these Indians who had taken the old man's money had wanted to bribe the English foreman. So he said 'Alright Mr Singh I'll look into the matter' and next day he sacked that English foreman on the assumption that he was getting the bribes and he also sacked those three Indians who were taking bribes for the sake of the foreman. Well a few days later – it was on Vera's birthday in fact – I had gone out to buy a cake and all of a sudden at least three Indian men jumped on me and we had a fight. They were all dead drunk and although I was very strong in those days and had a very good physique and I defended myself well, yet you cannot fight with three or four people. I was hurt very badly. They dragged me inside their house and they could have killed me there. I was hurt very, very badly and was in hospital for a long time. The police finally brought these people to court and they said they were drunk and were fined £25 and that was that. The man who had brought the old man to me wouldn't come to give evidence nor would the old man. I didn't know the man – I just took pity on him – and since that time I have said 'What is the good of helping these people? They have no character.' . . . The experience changed me a lot. Before that I would write letters for people, official letters – help people to go to solicitors, do interpreting jobs in court. But this was a very bitter experience. They definitely meant to beat me up because they were sacked on account of me and their business of getting bribes was stopped. It was the Indian people who did it – the white foreman doesn't know me or anything about me – I hadn't ever seen him in my life – it was the Indians and I object as a human being – with my dignity as a human being. So I don't have much liking for those sorts of people, you see – it was the bitterest moment of my life. From the beginning of my life I was very generous – when people come to my house, my wife will make a cup of tea and sometimes even dinner and so on and then I had this bitter experience and I think why should I entertain those people – I don't wish to eat with them you see.

Even my children know all this history – they will always remember it in their own life. Everybody knows, even my relatives know. And my wife knows all my mistakes. I didn't and don't hide anything. It was a really bad time.

Working for an airline company

He came to seek a post at Heathrow Airport with a large airline company. He was given the job of cleaning and sweeping in the catering section attached to a canteen – but he was fortunate since the lady in charge of the canteen was ill and he was asked if he could read and write and when he showed he could, he was given a job looking after some of the orders and supplies. He worked very hard and was very conscientious and then was given a better job in charge of issuing supplies of drink. It was a good job and he became aware that some of his English colleagues were envious of him. He was in the position to give others the occasional drink – there were always odd events – parties and celebrations and partly drunk bottles had to be finished, the remnants were not wanted back.

I can judge a person through his talk, through his looks. These people came to me for a little drink because I could give them free drink, even if they were bosses. But I could always judge their character. One of my friends there – he was my officer – a Mr West – he came over one day and said 'Hello, Pete, let's have a drink'. 'Oh yes, sir, have a drink'. There's a bottle of sherry on the table. We are both of us sitting together talking and finishing the bottle. 'Oh, when I was in Ceylon' he said 'I had a lot of coolies over there, you know'. You know he's an officer, he's my friend, he is still – but the psychological feeling of a man like that! I only say in my heart, he's not an educated person – he must have got the position he has but in

the back of his mind he still has to prove to himself he is
superior by talking to me, as a foreigner, in this way to prove
himself superior. But I quietly digest this and learn what sort of
people they are – still they're very nice. They recommended me
nicely and I got that job.

He was then appointed, despite stiff competition, as the first
Indian supervisor in the catering section and later made superintendent of technical supplies – a responsible post.

We don't allow anybody to come into the store because there
is a lot of valuable stuff here, some items are worth £10,000. So
it's always locked and only I am inside.

When I was working in the catering section, there were four
Indian labourers and there were also English blokes who had
the same status and work as the others. I would notice and feel
that even if the English chap did less of a job than the Indian, the
chef would come and bellow at the Indian 'Oh come on, look at
that – so and so is cutting the vegetables and you are just
cleaning the floor' – things like that you know. Maybe this is
part of their life – I don't blame them – maybe they think 'Oh
they're foreigners in this country' and they have a feeling for
their own people so that even if they do a little bit, in their eyes,
they feel that they're doing so much. 'Oh look – I'm so busy,
I've done this and that'. If the other person is Indian, he may
have done double that, but in the end the person will come to
him and say he's done nothing.

I really work hard. I used to bring home work without
charging overtime for it – so that I could speed up my accounts
and I thought in my mind unless I worked hard these people
wouldn't give me a better job unless I proved myself and
showed myself worth it. I believe in doing a job nicely, honestly
and faithfully. I think you will always find a break will come to
you if you do so but there are English people who are not used
to this sort of thing. I mean they tell tales to the
supervisor – saying he's no good, he's sleepy and so on. These
times should have gone.

A white person came over here and the supervisor said he
had to go and work at a store at night time and he said 'Oh no, I
want overtime – I don't want to go there'. He refused to go in
front of everybody. So the supervisor said 'Alright, you go
home then' so he went home. If it was me – an immigrant – he

would have sacked me, after all you're the servant of the firm and you have to work where you are told. But this Englishman came the other night and nobody said a word to him. He's as good as gold to them. Therefore the character of the superior officer is a little bit low – for rules and regulations are only used for immigrants and not for his own people.

But there are wonderful Englishmen who are my colleagues as well. One is my senior. He asked me the first day 'Do you know anything technical?' I said 'No, I'm quite blank, I was working in the catering section before this.' I told the supervisor the truth, you see. It is nice to tell the truth because when you tell lies, lies all the way, you have to change your statement – I don't believe in that. I tell my children not to tell lies – you always suffer and pay it back when you tell lies. So I told my supervisor I didn't know anything at all but I'd like to learn. I will work hard to learn and he taught me every small technical detail and I am very, very grateful. He's my very good friend that Englishman and he's an educated person. We drink now and again together and I go to his home and they ask me a lot of times because my wife does not feel very bright, so we couldn't go and join them and their wives, but I go to their homes and they are going to have the chance to come to my home. They told me later on 'We found that you were really interested to learn and you are a great man' and I have a high regard for them. They travel to Australia and New Zealand and they send me cards and bring presents for my children. They even went to Devonshire and brought half a pint of Devon cream for them.

All people can't be the same – there are very good English people and others but I have good judgement and can judge men straight away. There is a storekeeper who works with me and he talks of the Indians in India who were starving and this and that – and I said 'When I was in India, it was a good job that I didn't see you – I would have cut your throat!' This of course was all as a joke but I said 'People like you could not earn your living right here and so you had to go to a foreign country and then added your volume of expense to the economy of the other nation so that they had to pay you so you could survive. And now you are telling me that you were there to help us and teach us.' 'Don't tell me,' I said 'tell someone else'. You find people like that over here but why discuss things with these people who have hate for immigrant people? Only educated people might understand it. People who are really educated. These you will find – both sorts of people you find. And I'm not ashamed to answer the ignorant ones because I know these things politically and in educational methods.

My daughter Vera

Vera was born in India under the guardianship of my wife's parents. My wife's father is a very, very gentle man – very lenient and very well educated. He studied medicine and so on and I think his influence – the influence of both her grandparents – was very lenient and kind. By the time she came here to England, her kindness was like her grandmother's and she would do anything in the house to help. When we went anywhere – to relations for instance – she would like to offer her services too, nicely and politely.

I was not disappointed when I heard that Vera was born and it was a daughter and not a son because in my house my little sister was very young when she died. And my father's sister I had loved also.

She was a very little girl when she came with her mother to this country. She went to school and she was the only Indian girl in her school and later when she moved to another school there were only a few Indian girls. So her English is just like your girls or your children and I don't think she suffered any sort of prejudice. If she did suffer, she's a very tolerant girl and I don't think she would tell us. Although she speaks to us about all sorts of problems and she feels this country is becoming very racialistic and so on.

Eric now goes to the same school that Vera went to – a secondary modern school. It was a very nice school when she went there – she never complained of anything – the teachers were very nice. They still are because teachers are always good. It's the students who create all the troubles. Vera never had any problems but Eric tells me that there are always fights in their school now and sometimes the police come. They are between the English and Indian boys.

Once when my wife and I were in India, with the little girl, we left Vera and Eric here and Vera used to go to school. They looked after themselves but very good friends of mine used to come to our house every second or third day to ask Vera if everything was alright. They used to cook for them-selves – they were used to English food and it's not hard to make English dishes.

I wish I could impress on my children to work hard and to study – study. I don't know how far their brain goes – Vera could have gone further and done 'A' levels, even her headmaster told me so, but she said 'Oh no daddy, I want to work' and she got a good job – a very respectable job in the bank.

In my family, there's no contribution by Vera or others – whatever we have is all ours. Vera gives to her mother say thirty or forty pounds and she says to her mother 'I want these shoes and they cost £10 [laughs] and maybe she may spend £50 and she only gave £30 – but it's a pleasure – there's no feeling in her own mind that since she earns this money she should keep it – and she does not give any particular amount to the house – it's not like English people and pocket money – the money is always here. Lately she gave £35 to her mother and she took five or six pounds again. 'Oh mummy, I bought this, I bought that'. I told her recently 'You must save some of your own money now. Don't give it all to your mother' and so she keeps £20 in the bank for herself and she's saving those £20 to take us all on a holiday to a villa in Italy. She has rented a villa over there – she has sent them the money and she will pay all the expenses. I will get the airfares less ten percent – and she will pay the rest.

It is not how much she gives or earns in my view. I took the family once to France and Vera said 'Oh daddy I want to go to France again. It was very nice' so I said 'Alright, we'll both go to France'. So I took her again for a few days.

Vera has a girl friend who is English. She comes here for dinner sometimes and Vera goes to her house at lunchtime sometimes. The girl said 'Vera, how much money have you of your own? I have so much'. Then Vera said 'But how do you save it?' and the girl answered 'I give my mummy £20'. 'Well,' Vera said 'I give my mummy as much as she wants'. I know in this country you have to be independent but again when you are independent you lose some sort of love and affection from your mutual understanding.

Naturally we have to think of her when she gets married – anything she wants – maybe nice golden jewellery – I will buy her that. If she is working I'll leave her to save a little bit before she gets married. She's very lucky in the financial way of life because the wife's father will give her money when she goes to India.

Vera can marry at any time she wants to. I'd like to take her around the world first and then find some suitable young man for her and get her approval and then she can settle down. We have a lot of relations in America and Canada and they have family connections with other people and like, if they ask me 'Oh find some young man in this country' I will look around my friends and relations and then there is a sort of guarantee between those people. We don't believe in divorce and in the Indian way of life not many divorces come because the footing is very good. Whereas in this country you are going into a permissive society. 'Oh I love you so much' – they are madly in love but they don't know what they're talking about – in their view – in their eyes – love is just a physical movement of the body – that's all they're interested in.

They don't think of the consequences of children coming.

My wife's parents – we loved them so much – we would do anything for them in the world. That's what we want to create in our own family. What's the good of giving them love and affection if they don't love back. I don't mean that they must pay it back, you know.

If Vera goes off to Canada, she understands our feelings and is quite capable of looking after herself – she understands the honour of the family – respect, honesty and the future. She wouldn't like to upset her home. I think my children are very nice and we discuss things together and I ask Vera's opinion – even on marriage – we discuss these things. I don't believe in more rules than necessary.

I would like Vera to be a good wife to a gentle family and a gentle husband – to stand on her own feet and not to make the mistakes which I made in my life.

I wanted Vera to go to the university – to do medicine or teaching or something – but she didn't want to and she is alright in the bank.

My son Eric
Eric was born here. I was in the steel mills and on the right road, but my psychological feelings were different when Vera and Eric were born, because of my own life.

And then he was a boy. Now that he is growing up he may lose his temper uncertainly at times, but we bring him into line now. I'm very strict about these things, you see. Maybe he feels he's a boy and is growing up and so he argues sometimes with Vera.

I insist on Eric studying and working hard all the time instead of playing, you see. There's lots of time later in life for play so he doesn't have much time for his friends during the school terms. In the summer time he may take one of his friends to the Airways club and they play table tennis or something there.

Eric has got a few English friends in his class – they are very nice and they come to our house and he goes to their house now and again. He is a very reserved type of person but he also knows how to speak and how to go to other people's houses and behave there.

I try to help Eric and give him lessons myself. I sit down here in this room with all these books and so on and we do mathematics and English. I check his work. I wrote a letter to his teacher because he has had a very mixed-up situation. He has had asthma trouble and so we sent him to his grandparents over in India. He was born here but then when he was in India he started reading Indian languages and forgot English, but now he's catching up and his teacher is very happy because he is doing well now. I would like him to do his 'A' levels. I wish he would. He likes my thoughts. I don't care to say much.

Eric goes to a secondary modern school and I always go to the parents' meetings at the school. Unfortunately not many Indian parents come – there are more English parents than Indian although in the school there must be half Indian and half English children with less West Indians.

Eric is fourteen years old and is only in his third year at school but he tells me things when he comes home. I think I told you that there are always fights at their school although there never used to be when Vera went there. Since the Indians from Kenya came, they started these things and the West Indians and the bolder types of boys – they fight. Suppose someone is aggressive to me – either I have to stand up and fight or I tolerate it and let it go.

So these Kenyan Asians or West Indians also want to prove something. So they fight. The police are there and the other day a boy got hurt and went to hospital. They fight with fists or knives – anything – and even some boy hit the teacher but I don't know whether he was English or Indian. I always tell my son 'Don't take any part'.

One day Eric went to school and he told me when he came home that his own teacher – I would like to see him when next I go to the Parents' meeting – this teacher had said to him when they were all throwing javelins 'Oh, this is not a plate – hold it tightly. You are not holding a plate.' As if he was a dish washer you know. I'd like to see that teacher! I wanted to go next day but my wife stopped me. I wanted to go to him and see him because I can't accept these things when my children are behaving alright. I told Eric 'Why didn't you tell him, "Control your tongue – I'll bring my daddy tomorrow and you say the same thing in front of my dad – that I'm not a dish washer over here".' I mean these teachers, they make no distinctions and their minds are blank and they don't want to know. Maybe they're fed up, maybe they're fed up over the different races over here – I don't blame them but at the same time I don't want to accept these things for my children. My wife said 'Oh, why go? He may revenge himself on our son, de-throne him in his class or anything like that, so better let it go'. But next time I will go and see him. I would like to see that teacher again – the sports teacher – because he may be upset by the other Indian people – upset by other Indian boys and think that Eric is also one of them. But as a teacher, they should recognize that it is them who the people are paying. I always tell my children 'Always respect your teacher'. We used to call our teachers in India – our professor 'Sir'. Here you don't say 'Sir' to anybody – there's no respect.

In the papers you read now and again of a couple of English boys who hit Indians or Pakistanis – or of a couple of Pakistanis who catch hold of an English boy. These things happen now and again in our society. The Indian Association to which I belong, always tells people not to be aggressive – just defend yourself – and then there are also complaints that the others were defending themselves – so you don't know who is telling the truth, who is defending and who is attacking. So I don't allow Eric to go out very much. I rather like him to study at home and then at the weekends he can come to my club and play football there. I don't like him to mix with these sorts of people. I don't like it. At least I can prevent my own children from getting into trouble – I can't be a grandfather to the Indian nation over here. But if every parent did this then there would be no trouble.

I have to worry about my own children. I want to bring them up like good Christians or good Sikhs. If you have no faith in any religion or discipline or practice, then you are a lost person.

I like my children to have faith in God, and this free society and free love – this permissive society – I'm totally against.

I like to help people and I give to my children the same teaching to feel sorry in their hearts for people who are really hard up – or very old – or very little children who are in a desperate position. Vera and Eric used to go to help very old people with their flats and homes, papering their walls and things like that.

I am very proud of my wife, Vera, Eric and the three younger ones.

My wife

His marriage made him very happy and it was 'his first happiness in life – to have got married.' When his wife came to this country he kept going 'because of my love for my wife – and for my daughter – if I don't work hard, I'll let down my wife, my daughter and myself'.

Oh we talk about anything. Even when a letter comes from my parents in India – I call them my parents and consider them to be my parents – I'll read it straight away to my wife in English. Any letter that comes from anywhere – good or bad – or even bills – I always read them to my wife. When the childrens' reports come, we go to the school together to meet the teachers of the children and any problem we discuss together and then we take action. Rather, she decides because she decides better than me! I'm rather a hasty type of person. [Laughs] I take rather quick action but she is very comfortable in her thinking and is very neat and clear in her thinking and I follow her mostly.

I haven't got any friends whom my wife doesn't know. They all talk to her – they sit down together – English and Indian friends.

My thoughts on being Indian in England

If Indians or Pakistanis are educated they know how to behave in a free society like this one. They understand how to live in a foreign country and observe the rules and regulations. No educated Indian or Pakistani for instance would look at the legs of a young lady who is sitting next to them because in India our wives and daughters never keep their legs naked.

If people are good enough to earn their money in this country then in my opinion, they must be good enough to understand the rules and regulations and laws of the country. It is my own personal opinion – maybe other people think in a different way.

We must prove in this foreign country that we are as good as you are – not in colour but in educated manners, in society, in how we dress and in all sorts of subjects. To do this we must educate our children in the home – that's where education starts so as to bring them into the society to live on an equal basis. So if you don't find defects in your own children in your own home and put them right then when they grow up somebody else will find the defect and they won't like it.

I feel that the foreigners like Indians, Pakistanis and West Indians who come to this country, must adjust to the society over here. I don't mean in the bad ways of life – but in the good – to be good neighbours – a good working man – good lessons to the children – send them to school regularly, neat and clean clothing when they go to school – no curry smells – no oil heavy on the head, you know – things like that. The parents should do this training but they don't unfortunately. There is discrimination here but at least on the part of the immigrants, they must make their children perfect. If we were living in our country and the case was the opposite – the English living in my town in India – then they mustn't tell me what rules and regulations I should make.

I myself am a very firm father but a loving father. There's an old Indian saying that says you give your children your life, but you watch them with the eyes of a tiger – I will give anything to my children, but I will smack them with the paws of a tiger if they do anything wrong.

Some Indian families are getting out of step these days here. You see little children in the mornings – Indians, Pakistanis or West Indians – and they go into the nurseries. You will find mostly immigrant children there – their mothers go to work. I don't blame them going to work you know, but at the same time if they want to go to work they should not produce children. They must look after what they have. When the mothers have gone to work, they don't know what time the child comes home from school. They don't know so naturally in that sort of family they won't have much respect for each other, because naturally if I don't care for my children why should they care for me? These Indian families used to care for their children very much before – but nowadays they don't.

The other day I saw the son of a family I know and he was with the milkman and he should have been at school. I saw him and said 'Look, why don't you go to school?' He said his mummy had gone to the doctors – but meanwhile I saw her shopping in the shopping centre. How they tell lies – and the reason why they do it is they are ignored by their families, by their parents and their mothers don't know where their children are.

Indians and Pakistanis are very good hard-working people. And they are very punctual at work and that is why I'm very proud of them in their status as workers, you see. But the mothers who work don't care to dress their children properly according to the uniform of the school – they don't care about their breakfast, lunch or supper or whether the child's shoes are polished or not. They don't care about their children as long as they go to school but if by earning that money for the benefit of the family, the children suffer, I don't think the money is worth it, in my personal opinion. And this is what I don't like about immigrant people.

I could write a book about my own people you know, if I wanted to. They are so mixed up – they are very good at counting their money, so why not understand the other rules and regulations? There are always arguments with my people. There was a meeting some time ago about the people and their housing and problems of keeping the houses neat and clean. The sanitary inspector gave reports on Indian people living in this area. The people there were angry and said he was accusing us of doing this and doing that so I raised my hand to speak since I too was a member of this general borough. So I said 'You are all accusing the sanitary inspector. Are you really telling the truth that all your houses are clean – all of them?' I said 'There is dirt in your garden, stink of curry, smell of curry coming from the houses – even the gas or electricity people cannot give his nose to the kitchen. I don't say you shouldn't eat curry – I eat curry – but keep it nice and clean and good and comfortable for any visitor to come and visit here. How many people here really think the sanitary inspector is wrong when he gives a report on your house, or on overcrowding, or the police catching you shouting or disturbing the peace of the neighbours?' Of course, they didn't like my speech because it was against their interests. But it was true. I was very proud and I didn't care when all those people stood there listening to me.

But I'm not very proud of certain things that my people do like that.

Even the wife of our Ambassador, she told a lot of our people 'Try to live like these people – follow the example of clean living and being nice gentlemen – we earn the same money, why shouldn't we live nicely like them?'

Our people are only here to make money. It's as if they haven't seen a good standard of life in India so all of a sudden – oh! it's all gold. And they don't know where their children are going.

There's another thing I don't like about some of my fellow Indians – they are not truthful to the government. They tell lies to the officials over here. If they are not married, they will say they are married because of income tax. Now they are catching them but when they find once that people tell lies, then they will never believe them again. I don't blame the English people for that. In the factories some men say they have several children, maybe they're not married – they then claim the money for family allowances. Even when I came to this country and I had no children – Vera was not yet born – I was told by some that I was a fool and I should say I had two or three children. I said 'Well I haven't got any'. So I don't agree with my people. When living in foreign countries you must observe the rules and regulations of that nation and must try to be one of them. No matter how they may discriminate against you. At least you should be satisfied that you are doing right.

When the Teddy boys started over here, I read in the papers that a Lord Chief Justice said that they should be sent to jail to learn some discipline. You read in the papers now of Teddy boys among all sections of the population – who just kill for the sake of fun – English as well as immigrants. Some of the Indian youngsters are also like the English boys – they enjoy themselves, fights going on here and there – and the same applies to the West Indians. I think they're all the same. You read cases in Athol where a couple of Englishmen hit the Indians or their families – just innocent people – but things like this have lately quietened down. It's because the majority of the people are not educated, they just go to school and leave – they don't go to the army, they have no discipline or manners or etiquette. The English are as bad as the Indians.

There is justice in this country – justice is still here and all the people are not racialistic – there are very good people who are working for better community relationships – and naturally among them are also English people who are good-hearted and trying to tell the foreigners to learn good things in the school and at home.

The Kenyan youngsters are rather bad – our Indian boys were not so bad before but now, mixing in their company and living with them, these Kenyans say 'Well if the English skinheads do it, why shouldn't we?' A couple of times there was trouble between the skinheads and Indian youngsters, many of them Kenyan. The police overcame the situation.

The Kenyan Asians get on alright with us because they are very skilled people – better than our Punjabis – and there are good feelings between us. I am a Sikh and very proud of my people and their principles which I try and follow. These are to help the poor and defend the honour of the family and the honour of any woman who is helpless, and to share our earnings. We give ten per cent of our wages to any needy people or to our own temple. I give this donation now and again and over here my children go to church and give money there. I am very proud of my people but the world is changing – technology and scientific ways are changing the world and so naturally our people are also changing. My children over here, for instance don't know our own language. They don't read our language and they aren't very interested in going to the Sikh temple and learning about our religion. I don't force them because you don't have to go back, to take the past into the present but at the same time you must remember God and accept the old universal authority. God is one and he speaks to us all the same only in different languages and different people serve him in different ways. So I am happy that my children believe in God and worship God. I believe much in doing in Rome as the Romans do – and our Sikh religion tells many of the same things that are in the Bible, about marriage and love and adultery. I used to study the Bible a lot and I still remember a few things – that adultery is very sinful and true marriage is a good thing. Every religion tells the same things.

Living in Athol

Neighbours and friends: When we moved here to Athol, there were not many Indians. We bought this house in 1954 and there was an English family on one side and an Indian family on the other. They were very friendly people. When the English family saw my wife in the garden, they would say 'Hello, hello' and we would talk to them and when Eric had trouble with his asthma they told us which doctor was good and we went to the same doctor whom they had. They sold their house and an Indian family moved in.

We have Indian neighbours on both sides of us now. We don't mix socially – maybe I feel my standards are a bit better than their's – maybe they think more about money than the upbringing of their children – maybe our ideas are different but we don't mix with them very much. It's not a question of liking or disliking them but a matter of choice. Sometimes you find a large crowd in their house – noise and that sort of thing.

On the other side we say 'Hello' to each other but no more than that.

Two doors away from our house there lives an English couple. Their children are married except for one who goes to school with one of our younger children. They play together. When we moved in we got to know each other. And on a few occasions when my wife went to India and I had no motor car in those days, I would ask him whether he would mind taking her to the airport to catch the plane. He said 'Oh yes, willingly'. I always paid him a little bit but he didn't want to accept it, but I insisted on it. 'Oh no', he said – but I insisted. And so he took it. Gradually the friendship built up and when eventually Vera wanted to get her job in a bank, she needed some sort of reference – a bond you know – a form of security in writing, and I had known this man such a long time and he was so pleased to do it. I could have asked many other friends but I asked him and he said 'Oh yes, any time'.

When we were first settled here there were very few Indians here and we used to have very good English friends. If you went to a party and had a drink, everybody would speak to you – and you never know the insides of any man or woman because you don't know how they feel actually inside but we talked socially. I still have a couple of those friends since those days. Opposite the town hall there is a pub and that publican used to be very friendly with me. He and his wife were very good friends of mine. They were also good to my children and gave them each half-a-crown. Once long ago it was her birthday and I said 'Come on, it's your birthday. I'll buy you a drink'. They call me 'their friend Baldev'. But these days the pub is full of young people and there are no distinctions made between one and another. I don't blame these English people if they shrug their shoulders a little bit against the immigrants.

For example, on the opposite side of the road there was an old man and an old lady – an English couple – and next door to them lived an Indian family. When people are old they need a bit of comfort. One day he knocked at my door and I said 'Come in'. He said 'I must talk to you'. 'What can I do for you?' He said 'You know those Indians next door to me, their children are bothering me, they are making a noise and I can't sleep. They jump here and there' he told me. Poor man. I said 'Alright, I'll speak to him but I can't do anything because he's nothing to me, he's not my relative or my brother or sister – but I feel very sorry for you' I said, 'And I'll talk to that man'. He was an old man, after all, and you must prove yourself worthy, living as a neighbour to English people. I don't take the view of some 'Oh we bought this house for £5,000 – why should I care?' There was the old lady sitting in her garden on a deck chair and they had sat there for so many years in that house. So what happened after all the argument? The police came a couple of times but at the end the law is very soft in this country in certain respects. They couldn't do anything about it. The children were blamed and they couldn't do anything more about it. Poor man – he sold his house and he went away. And I am proud of my people, I am, in my way – but I can't tolerate these things. People who don't care for the comfort of their next-door neighbours. Of course, English children could also do it. You don't have to judge your next door neighbour as long as they let you live in peace and quiet. I mean you cannot change the world – even Lord Jesus Christ could not change it, could he? You can do a little bit and you must start from yourself.

A next-door neighbour of mine had a lot of lodgers including West Indians. It happened a couple of times that they brought a couple of girls and there was a party going on and the English friend next door to them was very upset by all the shouting and bànging all night long as the walls are very, very thin. So you feel uncomfortable in a situation like that. If the police come, then they say 'Oh because we are immigrants – they are harsh with us'. But I don't like that attitude personally. If they behaved themselves properly and went to bed at 10 o'clock and enjoyed themselves so as not to disturb their neighbours, that would be alright.

I had a very good friend – an Indian – we used to work together and although we meet now and again and we are able to talk on very deep subjects together, I eventually found out that his thoughts were near to communism with which I disagree altogether. So I don't have much life with him as a result.

There is a manager of a large store here – an Englishman who is a very good friend of mine. He came on my son's first birthday when we were having a champagne party and he gave £5 to my boy – he put it in my hand but I only kept £1 according to the Indian custom. I said 'I don't want all your money – it is nice to have a good friend' and he is still my very good friend. He comes here a lot of times and has a cup of tea with us. We often talk about mixed marriages and things like that. We can honourably discuss these things together. My feelings about mixed marriages are that I don't think the world is ready for them yet.

Athol as a community : When I came to Athol there were very few Indians here but gradually they are coming in and the English are moving out. They sell their houses at very high prices and I don't blame them because if I have to move out I also will sell my house at a high price – I don't object to that. In the whole area of Athol about a sixth or an eighth of it is occupied by Indians. You know our Eastern people have bonds with their own people. So our people like to go to a community where they are protected by their own community – rather like Jews in America or the Polish people go to their own community sectors.

My feelings about West Indians
When I started work with the airlines, there were a couple of West Indian porters there. I've had no West Indian neighbours.

My wife never liked to mix with them much. Don't take it wrongly but when I worked in the rolling mills, we rented a room out and someone suggested to me that we rent it to a Jamaican couple. I said 'Thank you, my wife never liked them and I wouldn't'. It isn't that I don't like them as human beings – don't take me wrong – but I didn't wish to have their company in my household.

They're very polite – and they're affectionate to each other. But these people are more backward than our Indian people.

Because in India there was a civilization centuries back and these people have not got so much civilization behind them – even countries like Kenya or other African countries – they may get their independence but that does not mean that they're all civilized. They can be Christians – Church of England or Catholics – but that does not prove that they're virtuous.

And then there was this next-door neighbour who rented his top room to West Indians. And there was this shouting and they were very noisy and the police used to go over there very often. We can't change the world but at least we can be respectable and we can want our neighbours to be too to give us peace of mind.

The 1971 Immigration Bill

I don't think you can judge the Immigration Bill thoroughly unless you read all the clauses of the White paper. If they require new immigrants coming in to register with the police – there should be no objection unless they start the same old thing – colour prejudice. 'Oh have you registered with the police? Check his identity. Have you got a passport? When did you come to this country?' And so on. People who, like me, have been living over here for some eighteen years feel in rather an awkward positon. If I took my children for instance and was walking around Piccadilly Circus or the Houses of Parliament 'Here's an Indian family – let's ask them who they are?' – this kind of thing can lead to unnecessary harassment. I'm afraid that people who have already settled down here, and who have made this country their home and are now part of the economy, might suffer.

The good will be for those people who have settled here who may have more opportunities than if there was a flood of people coming into this little island. People will get more education – more technical education.

The worst thing that I fear from this Bill will be the harassing of coloured immigrants. If the economy dwindles a little bit, then the competition for jobs will have a bad effect on the immigrants as the management has to appease their own nation first.

I watched Mr Maudling on television last night – he said that the government would not commit any harassment to the immigrants. It's nice to say that but if I go for a job to a factory they could say sorry no job for you but give it to an Englishman who is not as capable. What can you do? Nothing! It's only if the economy is booming that all people will be welcome.

I talk to a lot of Canadians at the airport and I think Canadians are more broad-minded than English people. In respect of colour prejudice, what is here may spread to Canada in a hundred years or might not come. There are troubles in every country but on the whole those of our people who went to Canada are still enjoying the same status as Canadian citizens and there is no prejudice on the employment side.

Because I have spent many years in this country and I have a pensionable job I would like to complete my time here and as far as my wife is concerned she naturally stays with me wherever I am. But for the sake of the children, they must get a proper education and technical knowledge over here, and then it's up to them but if they feel they want to go to Canada, I personally would love them to settle down there and make a life there. It's a wonderful country and a good country and they have a thousand times better chances than in this country.

Self-description

Without thinking too hard, how do you see yourself? :   If I were a rich person, I'd like to help the needy – I'd like to help my children – to give them a good education, to make them good citizens, I am a religious man in my own religion – quite fearful of God and believe in Him. I'd like to help God through the teaching of religious books to people of different nationalities.

I think money overcomes a lot of problems in the struggle of life. It is one of the most important things. To earn money, one has to work hard – it doesn't come through the roof. You have to make all kinds of sacrifices – now and again I do overtime, whenever it is available.

If I had had more education I should have been a different person – perhaps someone in authority maybe in India, in the diplomatic service maybe. I missed the boat after the army and didn't want to carry on further studies. I cannot go back on those years, you see, and I miss that opportunity very much. Because after all, it's only a working-class life now unless you are really somebody professional – a doctor, a professor, a psychologist, an engineer, a lawyer or barrister. I think I miss those opportunities very much.

MRS TARA SINGH: HER STORY

She moves delicately across the room in an elegant sari – a well-preserved middle-aged woman. Her face is sensitive, quietly humorous, tranquil and expressive. She gropes for words in a language which she understands better than she uses and as her need to convey subtleties of experience and emotional feelings is pressing, her facial expressions range widely across a large human canvas of feelings – her voice rises from its usual low soft tones to excited levels to express in pitch and in timing emotions as various as doubt and anxiety, hurt and pain, love and tenderness. Her hands convey a great deal too as they move to breathe life and inform meaning into the halting words; and her body becomes an expressive instrument with shoulders shifting uneasily upwards in tension or remembered fear – or again with outward, expanding breathing movements of her whole trunk she underscores memories of ease or joy. Her arms move to indicate disdain or contempt which her words phrase uncertainly.

We are sitting in the bedroom which she and her husband share – again, as in my interviews with him – we sit across a small desk in a quiet, darkly curtained room. The tape is only one receiving instrument in this series of interviews – for I am trying to understand her words by picking up their meaning from all that her body conveys to me. The words are the bones – but eyes, facial expression, voice, hands and body movements infuse the bones with meaning and with life. I try to put into words what her wordless communications evoke in me – to try out and seek from her the confirmation or disconfirmation of my reading of these multiple evocations. (The verbal material has been kept as near to the original as possible except for small alterations of grammar).

I was living in Delhi and oh! I was very lucky. I had a very nice father and he was very much loved by us children and by my mother. She was not very educated – she could only write our own language but he still respected her.

She was very kind – oh! I remember properly – she never hit me. [Laughs] I think I was changeable – but my mother had much patience and we had many neighbours and there were many girls my age and she always asked me to bring them home and not to go to their houses. But sometimes I went to their houses – and oh! their mothers were very cruel. They would say something – or do something and their mothers said 'Why

did you do that?' Their mothers were different. [Laughs] I
think maybe I was spoilt. [Laughs]

I had a little sister three years younger than me and also two
brothers. My sister died when she was about three and oh yes, I
remember when she died. I don't know what happened to her
but she was very sick for maybe three months. My daddy tried
to get her better. I don't know what the trouble was – maybe
she had TB. I remember when my sister died. The other day on
television there was a programme on *Little Women*. Oh, I started
crying at once because there were four sisters and one died. My
family said 'What is the matter with you? Why are you crying?'
I said 'Oh, I'll stop crying.' 'Why are you crying?' my young
child asked 'Is there some trouble?' 'Oh, I loved my sister' I
said. 'Oh,' she said 'You remember such a long time ago?' So, I
still remember. Oh she was a very nice girl. I think she looked
like an English girl. Yes she was very nice. We played together
and had little dolls. My mummy made me a doll with a nose and
eyes and we made a house for the doll.

My daddy was a graduate in India and he learnt so many
languages – Urdu, Sanskrit, Hindi and oh! his English was
very great and he was a graduate in English. But the British at
that time over there, never gave you a good chance – never
gave our people nice jobs. So he, at that time, was only working
as a night clerk for the *Hindustani Times* newspaper. He was very
good at writing but I don't think he was writing for the
newspaper. He was very young only seventeen or eighteen
years old and while he was still at school my brother was born
and three years later I was born when he was at college. When
he finished college my younger sister was born and then he
started work.

Later he got a job with the Indian Shell Company and we all
lived together in Delhi. It was a nice job. We all lived together
with my father's mother, my grandmother; my grandfather went
to Canada and lived there. He came back to India once and
wanted my father to go with him to Canada when he was young,
but my grandmother loved him very much and she wouldn't let
him go. My grandfather is dead now.

My mother and father were both very happy and sometimes
they would sit together and be talking all the time. Then he
would ask my mother to get ready and make the children ready
and we would go out. I was very young at that time and the
youngest little one would be in a little pram. And there were
English officers there, living in nice bungalows and I didn't

know why they were living over there. I didn't know at that time. So I asked my father once and he answered very properly. I said 'Daddy – dear daddy, where from have they come?' My daddy never answered me to shut up – he answered me very properly and said 'Oh, they are English – they are very nice people'. I said 'Oh, they are very nice white people?' He said 'Yes'. Oh! I thought they were very rich – with their villages and I saw an English lady and I liked her dress and she was wearing trousers and a little jacket and my father said yes, they had earned it, because they were ruling over there. And I said 'Why are they ruling here – in our country?' [Laughs] He said 'Oh, a long time ago they came only for business but they start now – they start to properly rule over here'. Oh! I was really shocked. And I stopped talking a little bit. He said 'Why have you stopped talking?' I said 'Oh, I am shocked!' He said 'Why?' I said 'Why have they come to our house – our country?' He said 'They are clever people – they've got brains'. [Laughs]

The English had a special park and playground. All the time I liked nice places and wondered why they could play in a different place and I couldn't go there because Indian children couldn't go there. One lunch time I was playing by myself on my own and I went there and was playing with the sand and an Indian servant over there came shouting saying 'What are you doing over here, little girl?' I said 'I've done nothing'. He said 'You've spoilt it for the Sahib' – he meant for the officers. I said 'I can't tell you what I've done'. My father came and he said 'Oh! You talk like this to my daughter!' and he slapped his face. [Laughs] He said 'This is one of your own people – how can you talk to a little girl like this?' I've never forgotten. He was only a labouring man and didn't know how to talk to a little girl and I mean – he used bad words – swore at me – called me bloody fool or something like that. But then I went with daddy and didn't go out of the park and the man never made trouble or asked me anything. He said that if I liked to play in a clean place, how could he stop me?

As I was growing, I was busy all the time. My daddy liked his daughter to learn as well as his sons – both his sons and his daughter – he never made a difference. Maybe he was anti-quated I don't know – because my husband says that over here, they make a difference between a girl and a boy but my daddy never made a difference between his children.

My brothers went to school – a boys' school and I went to a

girls' school but I was not a very long time at school. I stopped at the eighth class because at that time, when I was going to school, I had to pass the houses of Muslims – Oh! they are very bad. [Laughs] I'm a Hindu – a Sikh and the Muslims don't know if a girl is a little girl or a big girl. They looked with very strange eyes.

I don't know why they did that. My daddy thought that because I passed so many houses on my way to school, I should never be alone. So a lady came to call for me and took me to school, an Indian lady. It was not safe because maybe – like over here – they might have taken a girl and she would have disappeared. The Muslim men would have done this.

I tell the truth. I went once for a pencil, something to use in copying writing and I went to a shop and asked for ink and a pencil. He said 'Oh yes, come inside and I will give it to you.' I was only nine years old at that time. I still remember. I don't know whether he was a bad man but when I was in the shop he looked like this and he said 'Er . . . what do you want? What do you want?' and I didn't understand and I said 'Oh! I don't want it free. I will give you money.' And after a while oh! he started looking a bit funny and I understood. 'I'm coming back' I said and 'I don't want anything'. I came home and I asked my daddy. He said 'Oh! You are never to go to that shop. You ask me for what you want and I'll get it for you.' And my mother said 'Oh! Maybe she misunderstood' and he said 'You don't know. You stay in all the time and you don't know people'.

All the time my daddy did the shopping because at that time the vegetable shop was owned by Muslims and also the grocery shop and so he said 'Why should you go to shop? I've got lots of time to go shopping for you'.

My mother had lots of women friends [laughs] and people came to visit her and sometimes they came to eat and sometimes she was going to them. She was very friendly – not like me. [Laughs] I asked her shyly 'Why do you go out so many times? You go to so-and-so and why don't you stay at home?' She said 'Oh! I feel lonely [laughs] and I want to go'. I said 'Oh! You have a nice home and they come and they sit and they spoil it. Why are you inviting so many children?' [Laughs] The children came with the mothers and my mother was never fed up. [Laughs] No, at that time, I didn't like children. I liked only my elder and younger brother but I never liked other children. They were not very clean sometimes. My mother kept us children clean and at that time, when sometimes these other children came I said 'Oh! They are not dressed properly—they aren't nice children'. My mother said 'You all the time hear children' and she said 'After you marry I don't think you will have children because you hate children all the time'. [Laughs]

My daddy used to say 'I only regret that I didn't give you a good education because I think you've got a good brain like my sons'. And the only reason for this was we were living with very many Muslims over there. The living area was a bit Hindu but when I went to school and passed so many buildings, that area was Muslim. My father said 'I am dreaming badly. So many times I dream that some Muslim will take you away and make you dizzy'. He was frightened that I would be kidnapped by a Muslim. He said 'Maybe my dream will come true and what can I do?' Well, in those days, it happened to so many girls. I stayed at school for some time but he was worried that I'd be late home and he took me away. Then I did housework and needlework and crochet and learned so many things. [Laughs] Sometimes I didn't like it. But I didn't have any very good friends and so it was better to sit alone. And sometimes my mother and father were doing something. Well, my mother sometimes was talking to my father and she said 'I don't know about this kind of a girl. She's sitting alone hour after hour'. He said 'Never mind. Let her sit alone. Maybe she enjoys it'. One day I started a pullover for my father and I was finished it in one week [laughs] and he turned to my mother and said 'Oh! She likes that, why not let her do so?'

I was dreaming good things. [Laughing] I was dreaming that I want to learn this and I want to learn that and I saw other girls doing embroidery and I always asked my mother and said 'I want this – I want to do this' and she sometimes said 'Oh, you ask me the same things all the time. You don't want to play or go to places.' And then I asked my father to bring me some material and he brought me some coloured sash cloth and cotton and wools and he gave me lessons. He said 'Come, I will teach you to sew!' And he said 'You stitch over here and you stitch over there'. And my mother said 'Oh! She will learn nothing and what can you teach her?' And he said 'Never mind! – You never teach her.' He had a lot of patience and he said 'If a man wants to do something, he can do it.' He did not sew himself but he taught me how to sew.

Now I am not very clever at sewing. I do a little and a little knitting. Well, my father is still wearing my knitting – my pullover. And a little hole came and he asked my mother not to throw it away 'She will come again and she will mend it!'

My father also gave me lessons. He used to bring some books from the library. He read them first and gave them to me afterwards. He said 'Maybe something will be bad for you' and he didn't let me read it. [Laughing] One day I got a book from a friend. She gave it to me. She said 'Oh! It's very interesting. It's a love story'. I said 'Oh! I've never read a love story.' She said it was very nice and I started reading it and after I read it the first time, I fell asleep. My daddy came home a bit late and he said 'Who's reading this book?' My mummy said 'I don't know'. He said 'Oh! It's alright – maybe she's reading it, I'll ask her tomorrow'. The next day he said 'You're reading a book like this?' I was quiet. I knew he'd be angry. [Laughs] He said 'Where did you get it from?' I said I asked my friend to give it to me. He said 'You shouldn't read a book like this'. He was very cross. He was only cross with his eyes. He never hit children and I saw his eyes and I saw he was cross and I said 'Oh! I'm sorry. I'll never read it'. I went to my friend and said 'Don't give me any book like this'. [Laughs] She said 'Oh! Your father! My father never bothers!' I said 'Right. I don't know your father but my father is cross with me and I don't like it'.

My father always said 'If you've done something, don't tell lies. If you tell lies, again and again I will not be satisfied. If you have done something, you tell the truth'. I always believe my father and I tell the truth and tell my own children that if they do anything wrong, they won't escape their mother and father. They must tell the truth.

When I was young I lived near a Muslim girl and she was very friendly. She was older than me and all the time she came to our house and then they asked my mother if she would let me go to their house. She said 'Yes' because she thought I felt lonely. I went to their house and oh! there was quite a different smell. I don't know, maybe they had cooked meat and my father never ate meat and I only started to eat it after my marriage. My father didn't eat meat because he was sick. He was a vegetarian but my brother and I eat meat. So when I was in the Muslim house – they never stopped eating. And then their father came home and he didn't treat me like my father treats me or like my father treated my friends. He spoke differently. He said 'Oh! Who is she?' They said that my father was wearing a turban and a beard and that I was called a Sikh. Then he said 'Oh! Why has she come like this?' [Laughs] Yes, and oh! he touched my hand. I felt I don't know these Muslims, they look different and I never went into their house again. They asked me why I didn't come again and I said 'Oh, come to our house. We've got a big house. Come and play – I've got so many toys' I was pretending. I didn't tell her properly. I did not say that her house was not very nice and her father was not very nice maybe she would have agreed. [Laughs] I was very scared of her father. I was very lucky because I had got a very nice father. I was proud of him. At evening time he would say 'I am going for a walk' and he would ask me have I got friends? And I said 'Oh yes – so many' and he would tell me to ask them to get ready and sometimes he took twelve girls and sometimes twenty. He never asked me to cover my legs and I would have a little frock and knickers on and my mother said 'Oh! She's not a little boy, she's a little girl. You treat her all the time like a boy'. He said 'There's no difference' [laughs] 'no difference'.

My daddy has a very good nature and is a very nice person. He has a very good character and loves all children. He is very generous and he used to buy fruit and various other things and all the time he would bring home to us all these things. Some men enjoy themselves and never think of their wife and children. They go out and sometimes forget to come home. [Laughs] But my daddy was never late from work – he never came home late. Some men never tell the truth but he always told the family the truth.

Courtship and marriage

I was very young when I got married – only fifteen years old. My father's sister – my auntie – loved my father very much and her husband was the manager of the high school at that time. He was looking for a husband for me and he liked my husband and said 'Oh! He's a nice healthy boy and he's got nice manners and his background is very nice'. My husband's father was also an educationist. He was a teacher but he died very young. But my uncle was his friend before he died.

They never talked with me about it. They only talked together and my father said at one time – he said I had not got a man. I felt very shy and I said 'Why?' He did not ask me – he said that I will marry this man and they had made arrangements. I had not met him and had never seen him; that was the custom in those days. I felt like crying. These days it is better. Girls of eighteen or twenty marry now – it's not good if you are very young when you get married. I was only fifteen when I married and I ought to start to have children when I was sixteen. It's no good. I think it spoils a very young mother and she can't look after her children properly. She doesn't know how. I think it was a good job that I had no children at that age, but only after seven years.

So my aunt told me about my husband before I met him. She said he was shy and I said 'Oh stop talking silly. I don't want to marry anyone!' Then I thought to myself at that time, well maybe his father or his family – but then I said 'Oh! But I *know* he's got nobody.' Because he had no mother or father – nothing. Then I said 'Oh – it will be a lonely house.' My auntie told me he is a very good boy and is very gentle. I thought that made *her* happy because she had got a very big family – my auntie had married into a big family and had two brothers-in-law and two sisters-in-law and they were very rich people and very important – they had servants and they had everything. And she was not very happy. They all the time made trouble for her and she used to come home and say to my grandaddy and grandmother 'Oh! I wish I could die!' They made so much trouble and yes, she sometimes cried and even when I was a little girl she would say she had made a mistake and that she didn't want her mother-in-law or her father-in-law or her sister-in-law – that she was fed up with them.

So my auntie found me a husband with no mother and no father and no sisters or brothers and I felt I would be all alone and that maybe my auntie was wrong. Where I was going to was to a house – a lonely house. I never asked anything. I never said anything but I cried. And my mother said that you *did* cry when you got married and that she still cried whenever she had been in her parents' house and then came home, she started crying. I used to say 'Why are you crying?' and she said 'It's coming back – I don't like it'. Last year I was in Delhi and I was coming back here and getting ready and my mother – oh she was crying and my daddy said 'Oh don't cry. She'll be coming next year – stop crying. It's better to be happy. Why does she still cry?'

Early married life
I still remember . . . I was only fifteen years old when I married

him and he said to me 'Oh, I want a little boy'. I said 'Oh! a little boy?' I felt ashamed. I said 'Oh! I don't mind – I ask only my heart. I don't want a little girl or a little boy'. [Laughing] I was too young and did not want a baby yet. But I think because he was the only one child – he had no brothers or sisters, he wanted a child. After one or two years he thought maybe there was something wrong and maybe we would never have a child and he changed a bit and maybe wanted a boy or maybe wanted a little girl. He asked me 'Don't you want a baby?' I said 'Oh no – not now'. He saw other children and he bought toys for them – at Christmas time he gave them to children. He loved them very much and he wanted a family because he had no brothers or sisters.

Over there in India there is a golden temple and my mother, my mother's sister and my husband and I went over there. My mother said 'You wish something?' I said 'No' and then she asked my husband, 'You will give something?' and he said 'Yes'. She said 'Wish properly and God will give you something'. So he wished over there 'Oh God, I want a little baby. It makes no difference – a little girl or a little boy. If she gets a little baby, I will give money to the temple in the name of the child – for the praise of the child'. He did not say it loud but just in silence. I did not want a baby – not then.

And then later on I felt a little dizzy and I didn't know what had happened and I thought 'Oh there may be something wrong'. My friend next door said maybe I was expecting a child. I said 'No' and felt in a very bad condition – everything smelled terrible. I went to the doctor and he said 'Oh – there's nothing wrong – you're not pregnant'. I'm certain the baby was already living two and a half months but the doctor didn't know. He was a very good doctor and charged a lot of money to examine me [Laughs] and I didn't know why everything smelled so awful. 'What is wrong with me?' I thought. And just then my husband Baldev started going to England. He left and I didn't know what was the matter and I asked an old lady. She said it was maybe leukaemia and I said 'No, I don't shiver' And then I went to an Indian doctor and he felt me and said I was pregnant three months. He said 'Congratulations' but I wasn't sure. Baldev was already in England.

When a girl marries a boy, she must change – a girl has to be changed because there's a different house, different blood and different natures. Everything is different. Maybe in a Western country they don't change – I don't know over here but in India when you ask old people they will say 'Oh, it's a different life – there is the first life with mother and father in their house, and then there's the other life – the second life.' When I married many things changed. In my mother and father's house, my father liked very simple food – not many spices or hot things but plain fresh food. When I married, Baldev liked hot things and when I made something he didn't like it. He said 'Oh you don't cook properly'. [Laughs] I said 'Oh I don't know – when I cooked over there, my father was very happy.' He didn't like my cooking and I listened and I said 'What's wrong?' He said 'You don't put many spices – how can you cook like that? It's not very nice'. Well I made him happy. He had a different nature – not mean but just different. Sometimes he was shouting and talking and then went outside the house and it made me cry. I felt very sad. Well I then said 'Everyday it's like this and it's no good – must I change?' And he said he didn't mean it. He came home and he started laughing and it changed. I said 'I like your different face' If I had not changed, it would have made things worse. What made me angry then was he sometimes didn't tell me the truth [laughing] but he laughs about that time sometimes and he has changed from that time. Some men never tell the truth, they say they are going one way and they go the other way.

Baldev had a nice beautiful house there and I liked to keep it clean. I didn't care to eat breakfast or lunch sometimes if he wasn't home but all the time I cleaned this room and the other room because it was a nice house which his father had started to build before he died. I was never fed up over there. We still have that house in India – it is very big with three storeys and a little land but it is spoiled now because of the flood and things need repairs.

Her husband having gone to England, Mrs Singh returned to live with her own parents and remained there for four years during which time her daughter Jagdish (later known as Vera) was born.

Four years separation

My children when they were little, never screamed or cried – they only cried when something was wrong. I understood them and would say 'Oh something may be wrong'. When Jagdish was born I don't know why but the milk didn't come. I tried so many things – injections and tablets but they didn't work and I started to feed her with the bottle. She was very quiet and she slept a long time and my mother would say 'Don't let her sleep a long time, wake her yourself – maybe something is wrong if they sleep a long time'. I said 'Oh leave her to sleep' but my mother didn't leave her long.

And I gave her water and changed her and made her clean and she was very happy and playful and never cried unless she was sick. She was a very happy baby.

I had no worries over there because I had my father, mother and brother and before Jagdish was born my husband wrote from England every week. But after she was born I think he was disappointed – maybe he wanted a little boy and then came a little girl. Perhaps I misunderstood him but why did he not write properly? He wrote letters sometimes after a month, sometimes two months and I wrote every week.

I always wrote 'Please read this properly and don't put it in the dustbin – my letter!' [Laughing] I thought he would be saying 'Oh, you're not ashamed'. I thought it might click so I always wrote 'Oh thank you sir, I am only your servant'. Yes, I signed my letters like that because I needed him. I meant it really truly because I wanted to give him some comfort in his life – to wash and cook for him and because I was not working, I wanted to work for him. I felt very strange. I really never used to go out.

So he wrote letters when he liked and if he didn't want to write, he never did notice my letters. [Laughing] So one day I wrote him a letter. I said 'For nearly four years time, I have to live separately. How long must I live separate? Tell me the truth try to tell me the truth. Time is being ruined and I – about twenty-four years, am getting old.' [Laughs]

I would be an old rooster meeting him. Twenty-four years old! [Laughs] Well, the time came because my father and mother were also growing old and who could look after me and Jagdish who was also growing? I didn't want to depend on my brother.

I would think sometimes and my mother took notice and I think she also was thinking very much. All the time she said to my father 'You spend money to send her over there to England. She will be happy. Otherwise she'll become mental and something will go wrong and nobody will help her afterwards'. He agreed and said 'Yes' and so I came over here.

Arrival and re-union

I did not know where my husband was living then – he had left the one place and he had said 'Oh, I will never settle down. I'll find another job'. So I was worried because I did not know if he knew I was coming. My daddy sent twenty telegrams – to his uncle living in London and my cousin over here too and all the relations because he didn't know who could come to fetch his daughter. And he said 'When you reach over there, send me a telegram because I am very worried' I came over by plane and all the journey I worried. I said to myself 'I don't know – may be he comes not [laughing] and where will we go?'

He had not been very frank with me and had not given me good answers of what he was doing over here and I was suspicious.

I came here and he was at the airport and oh! I was so happy. [Laughs] And I said to Jagdish 'Oh there's your daddy' And she was very happy. Oh, she wasn't shy. She said 'Hello daddy, You never sent a letter for a long time'. [Laughs] 'Oh', he said, 'Who told her to say that?' And I said 'Nobody', 'Oh, she's very clever' he said and after that she became a little frightened because he sometimes talked – well, he didn't know how to talk to little children. She thought he would give the same sort of love like her grandad, because all the time he could love her and make her happy. And one day she started talking and she said 'Mummy, I don't like daddy'. I said 'Why?' 'I hate daddy'. 'Why?' 'I like my grandad. I want to go to Delhi and stay over there'. I said 'Oh, I can't stay without you. You stay with me and your daddy is like my daddy! I love my daddy'. She said 'Oh, your daddy is different from my daddy'. [Laughs] She was only three years old.

Oh, I was very worried that she was starting to treat him as no good and I said to my husband 'Oh, I ask you to treat her gently and make her a bit happy. She thinks of my own mother and father in India because she doesn't know you. That first impression is very bad for her and for you'. So he said 'Oh she doesn't like me and I don't like her'. [Laughs] I think it was because he had only got a grandmother when he was small and no brothers or sisters and no big family that he had no experience with little children. And his grandmother gave him everything to make him happy. I think she spoiled him very much.

When I was far away and thinking over this very new world in England, I thought it was maybe a very nice country and with nice gardens. Oh! I came to this country and well it looked stained because he had no proper house. He lived in a very big house – an Indian house and it had three storeys. It was in Birmingham and we had one little box-room. It was a lodging house and it was never kept clean and very many people lived there. Sometimes you could not even get into the toilet – they had only three toilets and about thirty people. And there was one very big kitchen and there were always many people wanting the kitchen and I always tried to find empty times. In the kitchen were standing so many men – and I wasn't used to this because I had got my own home in India. I didn't want to cook near men – standing near Pakistani men made me very nervous [laughs] and they never cooked properly because they were always staring at the person.

I was very sad and sometimes it made me cry. One day I asked Baldev 'What does it mean – lodger and landlady?' He said 'She's got the house and she's the landlady and you're giving rent and you're the lodger'. All the time he was calling me a lodger and I didn't like it. [Laughs] He was not very frank with me. I asked him 'What have you been doing over here?' and he never gave me a good answer and I got suspicious.

I tell you honestly that when I came here that first night and saw him – he had changed. He had not got good clothes on when I saw him at the airport. He had a suit – not very good and an old collar. I said to myself 'Now isn't this a pity – wearing clothes like this over here. What is wrong with him? He's changed'. I asked him and said 'You haven't got very nice clothes' and he said 'Oh my clothes are work-dowdy. [Laughs] My shirt has gone to the laundry and my suit to the dry cleaner'. I said 'When are they coming?'. I had seen another shirt at home not very good with all its collar gone. He said – laughing – 'Nearly a month'. And then afterwards he said 'Oh, I tell you honestly I've got no suit'. All his sweaters and shirts were broken – he had no nice socks – nothing. I said 'How much have you saved? I think you have saved too much'. [Laughs] I thought he had a big bank balance because he was greedy for money. He said 'Do you want to see my bank balance? [Laughs] I've got nothing'. I said 'Oh, don't worry – don't worry. You're healthy, you're alright. You've got two hands, two feet, you've got good health. Never mind, you can earn'. I was not despondent. He could earn – a man can do anything and make anything.

Maybe he had lost courage. I mean if a man loses courage, he can't do anything.

We left the lodging house and had one room. Old friends of ours from the Punjab gave us this one room. They were very friendly to us over there, and were old friends but they had changed over here. We didn't want to stay at the lodging house and went and asked if they could keep us there and they said they had got no room but they gave another person a room. She didn't want to give it to us because my husband had no money. Very frankly in the Punjab we ate together and went to pictures together, everywhere together but over here she had changed. She only gave us this room for two weeks and then said she had no room. She was very unfriendly. She also had a daughter the same age as Jagdish. We gave Jagdish an English name too and called her Vera in England. Well she gave her own daughter cereal and milk but for Vera only tea and toast. Oh, Vera was a very good girl and I appreciated her and I asked her 'Do you want something else?' 'Oh no Mummy, I'm not very hungry'. The lady asked me if I wanted to give something to my little girl and I said I did, so she gave me a cup of tea and toast and I gave the same food to Vera. Over in India she never took tea – tea is no good for children.

Well, I had no cow or buffalo any longer. My father kept buffalo and cows and would separate cow's milk for Vera. He would bring her special milk all the time. But when I came here, there was no fruit or milk. My husband started to work but there was not very much money – he brought home only six or seven pounds.

The Indian lady said we couldn't stay with her any longer and she found another room for us but without a bed. I had money – my father had given it to me – and my husband said he had no money and how could he buy a bed? I said 'I've got money' and gave it to buy the bed.

My husband had changed

My husband was very difficult at the beginning. He was not settled down in those days and sometimes I asked him 'Why have you changed?' and 'Why do you lose your temper so often? What is wrong? Do you miss something?' I asked him frankly 'Did you have a friend and do you miss something?' He said 'Oh no. I'm not a man like that. I only went to see the dog-racing and horse-racing and spent money when you were not here.' He was a rich man over there – well, he spoiled himself. He said 'Oh, I'm very ashamed because I'm not settled down'. He had wanted children but Vera came over here – the little girl – and he wanted to give her a good house and good toys and everything but he couldn't give it to her. All the time he spoke to me and I said 'Oh don't worry'. He took it in – I accepted everything.

But Baldev had changed in those four years. He was always saying 'This country is like this – this country is alright – this country I don't like it.' [Laughs] And all the time he was going out and saying to Vera that she must say, 'Hello lady', or 'Hello man'. I said to him 'Why do you tell her all the time to say this when she doesn't know these people?' He said 'In this country, it's the custom.' I said 'I don't like the custom. If you know the other lady you can say hello, but if you don't know her or the man why should you say it? You feel silly and Vera feels silly'. He all the time forced her to say 'Hello'.

It was very, very hard for me. He also wanted to change me. Sometimes I started washing. 'You are making a noise' he said 'Wash a bit slowly'. I said 'Oh'. He said I was doing this or that – and don't do it. I said 'Why?'. He said 'Oh, not in this country'. I said 'Oh!' [Laughs] 'All the time you tell me about this country, but you did not settle down'. I thought only to myself and never spoke to him about these things. I felt if I ask him something, he may be angry. Perhaps something is wrong. Nobody helped him over here because there was no one very near to him over here. So I thought that I should keep quiet all the time. I said to myself 'Never mind, keep steady and everything will be alright.' I think I was very patient at that time.

Early family life

She became pregnant again and felt miserable and sick much of the time. Everything smelled terrible and as they were living in one room she could not avoid various smells of fruit or oil or even soap.

I felt very sick and was thinking all the time that nobody was living over here – no sister, brother, mother or father. My daddy wrote letters and asked 'How do you feel over there?' I said 'I want to come home' He said 'Hold on – take it easy.

You'll be alright'. He didn't know what had happened at first when I came and he didn't know I was pregnant because I felt shy and couldn't write to my daddy about it. I couldn't write to my mummy because she could not write and read. Well my husband wrote one day to daddy and told him I was pregnant. Oh! I got cross with him. I said 'Oh, why did you write?' [Laughing] He said 'Oh don't worry – one day he will find out what you have got – a little boy or a little girl'.

One day my husband and I were standing near a gown shop. I was thinking 'Oh I want to buy everything for my baby'. He said 'Yes if you get a little boy, I will buy you everything' I said 'Oh! I am very shocked.' And I think that maybe if it's a little girl, maybe he will make a difference between a little girl or a little boy. I said 'Oh there's no difference between a little girl and a little boy because it's the same trouble.' [Laughs] And every day I was thinking. I never asked him 'Why did you say that if you get a little boy I'll buy you this and that?' I just said 'Oh God, give me a son.' [Laughing]

After five months we bought our own house. I never spent any money and Vera also had a very good nature. When we went shopping she never asked me for anything. She never said she wanted this and if you asked her if she wanted something she said 'No Mummy – you save money because we're going to buy a new house. I don't want to live in this house.' We had enough flea-bites there.

One day Vera was playing with a little Indian girl, eight years old and she pushed Vera into a coal shed and shut the door. After ten minutes I thought she hadn't come yet and something maybe wrong. I went outside into the garden and I said 'Oh Vera, where are you?' She was locked up inside. She said 'Oh mummy. Oh mummy'. I said 'What's happened?' and I opened the door. Oh! she looked blue. I held her and I'm not scared or anything. I asked her 'Who shut you up in here?' She said the girl's name. Oh! I was very angry and I called her and said 'Why did you shut her up? She was very scared my little girl – and you must never shut my little girl in, maybe she will die and then what can I do?' 'Oh' she answered 'If the little girl dies, it's no matter' I said 'No matter! I've only one little girl, and if she died at this time, how can I write to my mother and father? What will they be thinking?'. Oh, she said she was not responsible and if I shouted at her she would go and tell her mother. I said she could go and shout for her mother, I didn't care. Her mother had no manners – and all the time that I talked with her she talked with me like a servant talks. I never took any notice and said 'Never mind'. [Laughs]

When I got pregnant, after three months I said I must go to a doctor. It was the first time I had gone to an English doctor and also the first time I had gone to a man. In India I had an Indian lady doctor and a nurse. He was English and my husband said he would want to examine me and I said 'But he's a man!' [Laughs] He said 'Oh don't be silly – don't be foolish and if he asks you, don't feel shy.' I said 'Oh, I feel shy – I don't want men doctors – can't you find a lady doctor?' He said 'No, we are living in England not living in India. [Laughing] 'Oh, I understand'. When I went to the English doctor, he said he wanted to examine me and I was very worried and thought maybe he would kill me. It was very strange – it was a new country and I didn't know what would happen.

Well, he was a very good doctor and he gave me a letter for the hospital and I went there for examination and the Sister was a very gentle lady and she said she understood and that all Indian ladies go there and the doctors are very good and I must not worry. I was worried that my mother was over there, and I had no mother, sister or anybody here. 'Oh,' she said 'We all have no mothers or sisters. Don't worry about anything'. But I thought of it. This ward sister gave me very good courage and said that the doctor must see me – they examined my blood and everything. I was very nervous.

An English lady befriended her on her way to the hospital and went along with her. When she came home she told her husband that 'English ladies are very good over here' and he said 'I told you [laughing] that they're very good. If you ask something, they help you very nicely'.

But from that time, they've changed very much. At that time they helped you but I don't think in these days they give help to anybody – English or Indian – it's all the same.

A Home of our own – and children
My husband at this time was doing night work – shift-work at the steel mills. He looked for a house. It was not a very nice house – it was very old and no proper paper on the walls – no nice toilet or bathroom – nothing. If I wanted to see the house,

he said 'Don't worry, you can see it afterwards. I want to make it proper'. He was thinking that maybe if I looked at it, I'd turn it down because it was not a very nice house because we did not have much money at that time. He bought it and made a lot of plans and then some Englishmen, young, of the same age as Baldev came and said 'Oh Baldev, you bought a house. We'll help you.' It was an English man and he was engaged to a girl and they painted and papered it. My husband was one day talking to them and said 'My wife is very fussy and likes clean places. If she sees the house she will start crying and will say she doesn't want it. I just want her to feel a bit happy and to make the house clean.' They said 'Oh! We understand – all women are like that. [Laughing] Don't worry, we'll make her happy'. They painted the doors and windows and made a nice garden.

Then he said 'Now, do you like it?' I said it was very nice. He started to laugh and said 'Maybe if you had seen it before, you'd never have come'.

All the labour was English. It was a very nice place – and I felt lonely because it was a big house – three bedrooms, a dining room, sitting room and a very big kitchen and big veranda and garden. I felt confused. I didn't want to take anyone into my house but my husband said at nighttime I might want somebody to help me. He worked at night.

I liked living there. It was a very nice house and all our neighbours were English. Next door there was an English lady who was very nice and friendly – she was about sixty years old and in the house next to her was another English woman – a middle-aged woman called Miriam and she had an eighteen year-old daughter and a husband and they were all friends and came to our house for cups of tea. They had television and they asked Vera to come any time. Oh she was a very nice woman and she would bring things for me if I wanted anything. If I said 'I want a table cloth' then she would buy if for me and I gave her the money.

I was expecting Harbans then – well, we call him Eric as his English name – and next door to me on the other side was a very nice lady and a very good neighbour and she said 'I know your condition and if you need something, you knock on my wall and I will come to you'. She knew my husband was at work and sometimes was on night shift. She said 'Don't worry – I am thinking of you – don't worry'.

And next to her there was a shop with an English man and

lady and they were very friendly. They had two daughters – one of eight and one two year old and the elder one was going to school and when Vera started school, they took her along when she was four years old.

About four or five houses away there was one Indian family.

I was very happy there and one day I went to the doctor and I was expecting Eric and I couldn't walk as my leg had much pain and there was an English lady who looked at me and said 'What's happened? What's wrong with you?' And I told her my leg was aching and I had too much pain and she held my hand and she brought me home. My husband was at home sitting down and she said 'Oh, you shouldn't send her alone because if I had not seen her she would have been in a bad condition and might have fallen down and who would have looked after her?' Oh, he was very grateful and he said so many times 'Thank you very much – some other time I will buy you a drink' and she was very friendly and good – she had children and was from a respectable family.

All the time I asked Vera 'What would you like?' She asked 'Why do you go to hospital mummy? What's wrong with you?' And I said 'I want a baby for you to play with'. She said 'Oh, I want a little brother'. I said 'Oh, if you want a little brother, your daddy would be very happy'. She also said to me 'If you are going to hospital, you want some money' and she started saving [laughs] to pay for something for me. She was only four years old and at four o'clock in the morning we slept in separate beds and I called her 'Vera'. She woke up very quickly and said 'What's wrong, Mummy?' I said 'Oh, knock at the other room where Auntie Lucy is living.' This was the English couple who shared the house with us – we had given them a room. And she asked me why and I said 'Tell her I want her'. My husband was working at night and so Vera put the light on and opened the door and she went and said 'Oh Auntie Lucy, Auntie Lucy, my mummy wants you'. She came and said 'Oh, I must first ring Mr Singh and then the hospital,' and I got ready and she told me everything that I needed for the hospital – a nice dress and dressing gown and I made everything ready. It was a good job she came as I didn't know anything about what I needed and she could help me. There were so many things I didn't know over here about what babies needed because of the cold weather and different customs.

She made ready and came with me although she herself was

expecting a baby in two weeks time. Yes, she was a brave girl and it was her first baby she was expecting. The ambulance came.and there were two men there and I said 'Maybe there will be something wrong with me in the ambulance and what will I do?' and she said 'Don't worry, they won't mind you'. And I said 'Oh Lucy, go with me, I don't want to go alone'. She came with me and she wrote all the forms and then I think the ambulance men brought her home.

When I had Vera in India, I said to my mother I didn't want to go to hospital because the nurses were terrible – the conditions were bad and there was some shouting and joking and funny talking and I didn't like the hospitals. My mother said 'Don't worry. You can stay at home' and I had Vera at home. My mother was very frightened and went and brought other friends to help me. She said 'Oh God, give her anything, make her better'. She was very fussy.

But in England this hospital was different and it was very much better over here. The nurses were very friendly and they helped me nicely and nobody was shouting. Eric was born after five hours and they laid down a very good arrangement in the hospital. They gave me a separate room – it wasn't a big ward with so many women – and they brought Eric to me for feeding. He drank so much milk – maybe I was happy – I don't know.' [Laughing] I said to myself 'I'm dreaming – but oh! it's the truth but maybe it is a dream.' And I saw Eric and I said 'Oh – it's true and not a dream,' and I was very happy all the time and I held him and milk came – very quickly like a tap and they brought him to me – a clean boy and I gave him milk.

And at night time if he was crying or asleep I didn't know. But after seven days, the Sister said 'I will leave the boy here at night so you will know his habits and he will know you'. I said 'Alright' and he was a very spoiled boy because I picked him up and he slept. And when he woke he started crying and I remembered Vera and said 'Oh, she was ever so quiet and I gave her false milk but Eric drinks my milk and I don't know why he cries'. And all night I dreamed and I saw that all night I would carry him. And the next day the Sister saw me and she said 'Oh, you spoil him. Why do you hold him?' I said he didn't want to sleep and all the time he didn't let me sleep. She said 'You spoil him. Throw him out of the window.' [Laughing] She was laughing and I said 'I can't throw him – you throw him yourself' and she felt me and she said that I had a temperature and was not very well and she would not bring Eric to me that day. I said 'I give him up to you' and then she said to me 'Listen properly, you mustn't spoil him. I know Indian ladies love their boys very much and you carry him and he will get spoiled. He won't let you work. You must let him cry'. I said 'Alright'.

But after we were at home, I would let him cry sometimes and my husband would come home and he was very angry. He said 'You are making him cry and I'm very cross with you'. I was fed up sometimes because there was so much work left to do – sending Vera to school and giving her her lunch and my husband said 'Don't let him cry. I'll come home and help'. And he helped with carrying Eric and sometimes he didn't mind doing the washing and cooking.

When Eric was three months old I started to train him to sit on the pot and he loved sitting on it and I held him. I started this even earlier with Vera. My mother, she liked to keep children very clean. And Eric was very satisfied and he would sit and wasn't crying very much and I gave him so many toys and he watched me and Vera. Sometimes he was a bit late and would sit and cry on the pot and I still remember one day he was very upset and was crying and I said 'I don't know what will happen' and I felt it was my fault. He was very clever and he got into good habits.

Vera was a bit jealous of Eric. She felt that her daddy loved him very much and she said sometimes 'I hate him' and I said 'Why?' and she said 'Because you love Eric very much' and I answered 'Oh, I don't love him. I love my daughter'. So she said 'Why do you have him, why can't he love daddy?'. I said 'You misunderstand. Your daddy loves you very much' and she said 'Oh, he never loved me'.

I asked my husband and said 'Oh, speak gently to her and give her love'. He bought a lot of things for her but he sometimes spoke a bit roughly to her. I don't know – perhaps it was the military service he had done – or maybe becasue he had been a child alone. My father and my brother spoke very gently but my husband's heart was good but he sometimes spoke a bit short – not nicely and a bit roughly. She said 'My daddy speaks like this and I don't like him'. I said to him 'Don't hurt her. She has a very nice little mind and speak a bit gently and with love and she will understand; but if you talk roughly and with anger she won't understand. I know her nature'.

If she did something wrong, he would say to her 'Say sorry'

but she never said she was sorry and she is still the same. The other children born over here – if they do something wrong they say 'Mummy – daddy – sorry mummy – sorry daddy'. Oh, Vera never did that.

My daddy wrote a letter to me at the same time and said 'Don't ignore Vera. Maybe she will be jealous and you must care a little bit more for her and she will be happy. Otherwise she will be cross with you and she will feel hate for Eric'. And I thought 'Oh daddy, why did you write like that?' Afterwards I understood and I saw it all.

Eighteen months after Eric was born I had a daughter. She was born prematurely – a very tiny baby only 3 lb 10 ounces and I had oh! so many doctors when she was born. My feet were swelling and all the time the doctor said 'Don't eat salt' but my feet and hands were still swollen and I had too much blood pressure. I went to the hospital one day for an examination and the doctor said 'Mrs Singh, you go home and come again'. I said 'Why?'. He said 'You're not very well. You've got a lot of blood pressure and if you don't care for yourself you may die anytime'. I said 'Oh' and then laughing I said I felt alright, I said 'I've got a telephone number in my house. Please bring my husband and I'll stay here'. He said he would ring my husband and he told him my condition was not very good and they kept me in hospital, lying down all the time.

One day one doctor came – the next day another and I was very swollen and they took blood and gave me their own food but I didn't mind. I was only worried about Eric and Vera. Otherwise I was happy over there. I was in a big ward with so many ladies [laughs] – all English. I made friends with them and after a month they gave me an injection to start the birth. I talked to the doctor and asked him why they forced it and did not wait for the baby to be born naturally and he said 'I don't care for the baby but I care for you'.

All the time I was in hospital my husband was coming to see me and talking. I asked him about Eric and said 'Don't hit him – don't harm him he is a little baby. I miss him very much'. He said 'Don't worry, I take care' and he sent him to a good nursery for which he paid and he was there for two months – day and night. The nurse told him he was very good and sometimes he would call 'Mummy! Mummy! I want to go to mummy,' and they played with him and at night time specially he cried a bit and then he slept. My husband didn't want to go and see him because he said maybe if I see him he will start crying.

When he came home from the nursery – oh! he was very changed. A friend, an old man went to fetch the boy and he said to me 'You hide in the living room'. I said 'Why?' He said 'He'll be surprised that mummy is at home.' So I did and when Eric came my husband said he should call mummy. He said 'No. Mummy's not at home'. My husband said 'No. Mummy is still at home'. Eric then called 'Mummy, mummy, Eric's coming, mummy' and I said 'Oh Eric come in, mummy is coming.' And he was crying and holding me tight like this 'Mummy!' He was nineteen months old and was talking plainly. He said 'Mummy. Where are you?' And I said I was at home and he said 'I haven't seen you' I said 'No, I'm home now'. Then he asked 'Why did daddy take me away?' and he started crying. He threw this thing about and that thing about and he had so much excitement. Then he said he wanted to go to the toilet and he wouldn't let me help him when I brought the pot – he didn't let me. All the time he couldn't go on the pot. Sometimes my husband shouted at him and I said 'Don't shout and don't blame him. Maybe he misunderstands and thinks I am going again!' And all the time I said to Eric 'I'm not going anywhere'. They had kept the little baby girl still in hospital. I told him that.

I understand what happened to Eric. Here in London I have a next-door neighbour, an Indian girl and she had a little boy of three and she left him with her friend when she went to work and after she brought him home he was crying and protesting. She said 'What is wrong?' And he was shouting. I said I understood 'He shouts because he misses you – because you are working all day and he has to be in another house and he doesn't understand why you have left him'.

Since that time I still have trouble with swollen feet. And terrible migraine headaches. I was very bad last year and had to lie down all the time. The doctor gave me many treatments but could not find out what it was. Last year I went to India and my father found a good doctor there – a homoeopathic doctor and he said it was dropsy and gave me medicines. They made me feel very well. But here I saw many specialists and they took much blood and X-rays but couldn't find anything.

At times I felt so terrible. I was always dreaming. I felt 'Oh, I am going to die. What can the children do?' sometimes I felt like crying and then my husband would say 'Oh you stay and lie down' and then he would do something in the house. And he would go out with me and I would never go alone as I could not carry anything which was heavy.

I have a very good English doctor here. He is very good and his partner also is very nice. He looks strict but he's a very good doctor.

My husband

Over in India I was quite happy with my husband but when he came over here, he changed in those four years. And I felt he was not the same man. I never talk to anybody – anything in my heart I never tell it and so I saw him change. And then I did talk with him frankly and asked him what he was doing over here. But he never told me – he never gave me a good answer. Then I said to myself I don't care about a little hard time; maybe it will get better by waiting; maybe he will change.

Well, he has changed now and he is very good and I am very happy. But before, I tell you honestly, that he did not care very much. If I was a bit sick and something was wrong he did not care for me very much.

In this country he made so many friends. They were not very good – they had a good time and made a fool of him. Sometimes I would say to him that they were not very good and he said 'Oh you don't like anyone' and so I stopped. He used to bring them home for tea time and dinner time. They were not very educated and Eric was little and I would make dinner and they did not come for the visit itself but only for their own joy. 'Why is it all the time this entertainment?' I asked and he was angry and I said 'Oh, it's alright' and everyday – Saturdays and Sundays, there were so many crowds but not these days.

One day there was great trouble. An Indian man came to my husband. He did not know this man but he told my husband he gave a foreman at a factory £40 to get himself a job and after he was working there they gave him the sack and this man thought that maybe the men to whom he gave the money had accepted it but hadn't given it to the foreman. So after only two weeks he lost the job. These were all Indians except the foreman who naturally was English. So my husband went to the foreman and asked about it and he said he didn't get any money. So maybe the other men took it and they then decided to give my husband a lesson. Well, it was a Saturday and it was Vera's birthday, she was six years old. An Indian man came to our house and said to my husband that some men wanted to see him. My husband said 'Why do they want to see me?' I talked to the man and I didn't get anything from him. And I said to my husband 'Don't go outside. Maybe they will make trouble for you' And he said 'Well, it's Vera's birthday' and we had invited maybe twenty or thirty men and I was cooking all day and I asked him to fetch the birthday cake and some laundry.

Well, a police sergeant later on came to the house and I said to myself 'Why has he come?' Because all the time my husband interpreted for the police and they are all the time calling him to interpret. I thought maybe he had come for that. He said 'Mrs Singh? Your husband is in hospital and in a very bad condition. He has been injured in his eye and ear and there's blood. Indian men were fighting, they started to fight.' Well, I was shaking all over my body, My friend came and said she would go and see him while I look after the three children. She was an Indian who was studying over here and she came the next day and said 'I don't know what happened but his ear and face is all blood, blood, blood'. They had taken him far away to hospital and these Indian men had bit his ear almost off and they had dirty teeth and had been drinking and maybe that had started the poison.

What had happened was this. They had stopped him and asked him to drink with them and he had said 'Not this time – I have shopping to do'. They held him down and pushed him inside a house – men he had never seen before. Then they held him down and bit his ear and face – four or five men. They were mad and they were fighting and went into the garden. Next door was a little English boy and he saw and he told his mother. She telephoned the police. If she hadn't maybe they would have killed my husband and put his body in the soil and nobody would have seen him. When the police came everyone had gone only my husband.

He was in hospital a long time. He was many times a patient – six different times, because they took skin from inside and put it on his face and ear. It was terrible and he felt sick and dizzy. And it changed him. Before if the children were crying, he would hold them and make them happy but after this time, he was often very angry because he had been a patient so often, and if the little one was crying he would say 'Oh hit him hard' and I said 'Oh, he's only little, you can't hit him. It will make him worse.' I didn't like it. It never used to be like that.

It was very difficult because he was angry – much more than before. So I became very lenient to try and make him calm down. I said 'Oh stop' and then I ask the children to be quiet and go to their own rooms and not to answer back and he would then be alright. Last year I went to India and when I came back they said 'Oh mummy, he's been angry all the time.' [Laughing]

After my husband was taken to hospital, nobody came to the house to enquire after him. Everybody was talking bad things about him – maybe he took money – maybe this, maybe that, and everybody was talking down about him.

And all the time he had been inviting people and giving parties and giving food to friends but they never came and didn't ask about him. Over here, nobody is a real friend. Maybe people were scared of the other men. Even the first Indian man who came to tell my husband about the £40 never came to enquire. There were no witnesses but they caught them and they only . . . . only had to pay £25 fine each. It's not just.

Since that time he has changed. He does not trust others and he feels it's no good to help others. When the police asked him to help them interpret he didn't want to do it anymore. He guarded himself.

My children
I understand Vera's nature. You must speak a bit gently to her with a bit of love and she understands. She wanted a maxi coat and my husband said 'Oh don't buy a maxi – it looks like a gypsy'. She started crying. I said 'It's alright – I'll buy it for you'. Then he said 'Look, a maxi is no good, because if you are walking in the street and it's raining, you will spoil the shoes and the bottom of the coat.' Then she understands. He says that I spoil her and I say that I don't want her spoiled but children are different today and they want modern things and how can I stop her? She will be angry and upset.

She gives me all her money and she asks for what she wants. Oh, she has very good taste and she buys very nice things and sometimes I buy things for her when I see nice things. All the time I spend money on her because she is growing and I want her to be happy.

I like my children to be satisfied. I cook and ask them what they want. They all have different tastes my four children! Sometimes I get a bit fed up – they are not all saints. [Laughs] One wants this and another that. So I say I cook one day for one and the next day for another. I care also for my husband and sometimes cook him different food from the children. The children like English food very much and I cook both English and Indian food.

These days I am only thinking of my children. I like them to learn – to read and write properly and to be clever and to be able to stand on their own feet. I'm not greedy for the money they may earn – their father is earning for us – but I always say that they must never tell lies. They know my nature. They say 'Oh mummy never tells lies'.

My younger brother is living over here and sometimes he writes letters home and makes his own story. My father knows him and says 'Oh sometimes he is only making a story. But when she (that's me) is writing, I am more satisfied'. I think they believe me very much.

London and my neighbours

For the past ten years the Singh family have been living in London where they bought a comfortable five roomed semi-detached house in Athol.

When we first came here after eight at night, nobody was shouting in the streets. But now if you walk in the streets, there are Indian boys – young boys and oh, they talk very loudly and have not got very nice manners. I don't know about the English boys.

This street is a bit clean but if you go into other streets, they are very dirty and some of the Indians don't care – sometimes they put anything in the street.

I haven't seen any fighting in the streets here.

When we came here, next door there lived an English family with three children. She was very nice and soon after we came they started to sell their house. I asked her 'Why?' She said 'You have children and they are nice children. I don't want sell my house but next door to me, the Indian family makes so much noise. And I don't know what they are cooking, but oh, it smells terrible'. I said that maybe they were frying garlic and onion. And she said 'Oh sometimes, they make very much noise'. I said 'Maybe they are making a party because Indian people are all used to parties'. She was very friendly to me and I invited her to tea and she invited us. Well, after they went, they could think we are also Sikhs. Over here if one Indian does wrong, naturally you see me and write 'Oh she's Indian – the same' – but we are not the same. We are all of the same nation but we have not the same nature – we are not the same.

After that family went, another Indian family came next door and got a flat which had no light or gas. One boy came over from India first and later the family came. The son had no light and asked if we would kindly give him some electricity. I said they could fix up a wire from our house to theirs but not against the rules. They said nobody would see and I said 'Alright'. They used the electricity for one year and they never paid anything and after one year they said 'Oh, how much do you charge?' I said 'Oh forget it'. Then he took one pound and said 'Here' I said 'Oh no thank you'. It took them one year and they cooked everything and they took light. I didn't want to charge but they made no offers for a year.

I'm from the same country as them but they're not very nice. [Laughs] When our youngest was born they never came to see him – no little presents – no congratulations. If we see them in the street we are always smiling [laughs] but we are not very friendly.

I go to English shops because my children like English food. There is a shop at the corner and they are not very good people. The father and brother are serving and I wanted turnips and outside they keep them very nicely and inside they are not very nice but very damp. I said I didn't want the damp ones and he said I had to take them from there. 'Why are you asking me to take them from there? I don't want those. I pay you and I want the others' I said. The father started to talk very funnily and said 'You want *alu*' and started to talk Indian – *alu* means potatoes. I said 'You don't have to talk funny. I understand very well what I want. You better talk English'. He said he didn't care and I said if he didn't care, then nobody would care for him. 'Here are your turnips and give me my money back'. Oh, I shame myself and I was very angry. I came home and I felt very sorry for myself and I said [whispers] 'I'd better be going back to India.' [Laughs] I didn't want to go over to that shop and I told my husband. Sometimes I walk by and they say 'Hello' and I say 'Hello'. And sometimes I see something outside and ask Vera if she would bring it for me. [Laughs] They know it's my daughter and they always give us nice things because they know I don't like them.

I went also to a shoe-shop round here for shoes for my little girl who was then only three years old. The man showed me only one pair of shoes and I said 'Please show me a bit nicer shoes. If you have got something like Jumping Jacks. I always buy nice shoes' He said 'They are very expensive'. I said 'Never mind, I want an expensive shoe'. He then said 'You're an Indian and when you buy something as you are an Indian lady, then afterwards you change your mind'. I said 'I'm not that kind of woman. If I want shoes I can read your price myself. If I don't want them, I don't bother you. Please show me nice shoes'. Why do they talk like this? I think to myself. Maybe other women don't read the price and some don't know how much they cost and afterwards want the money back. Maybe it's their experience and they don't know who I am. Well, that man in the shop was very friendly – he was an Englishman and sometimes I go over there and he's very nice and I get shoes for the children there. But I thought about what happened and in these days many women are not educated and they don't read numbers and when they go shopping, they don't know anything. But if you can read and write, you are alright.

What being a Sikh means to me

The Sikhs are very courageous and our religion is a very brave religion. We are brave people and talk frankly and don't betray others. And the Sikhs always think about the poor and if somebody is hungry or poor, they give them food and let them sleep over without asking any questions.

The Hindus are not very brave and some things start trouble. But the Sikhs are brave and even if they have not much money and not a very nice home they are not very greedy for anything. But over here, in this country, they are greedy I think – for money especially. They are not satisfied. They work but they don't live very nicely. They are saving money to go home.

Self-description

Last year when I went to India my father said to me 'I'm very proud of you. You haven't any qualifications and are not very well educated but you are better than educated girls. I'm very proud that you went to England when Baldev was not settled down and you make him settle down without complaining'.

Without thinking too hard how do you see yourself?:   I'm an ordinary woman – I don't think I'm special.

Sometimes I talk to my husband and say 'I'm not very good because some women help their husbands a lot and go out and earn money. And I'm all the time at home and doing jobs at home'. But then I see other friends going to work and when they come home their children are back from school and they have helped themselves to food and the mother doesn't know what they have been doing. She may come home later after work and well, naturally the children are asleep and naturally she doen't even know whether they took a proper wash and bath and creamed themselves. If the mother is home, she must think of such things and give them food and they ask to go and wash and change.

I always think of my children first and sometimes my husband. If I am alone, I don't want to drink and eat by myself. I enjoy it more if I wait and eat with my husband and children.

I'm not satisfied because I have not got a very good education. When I was a little girl I very much thought I wanted to learn music – I played something like a harmonium and my father knew a little bit and taught me. At that time I was a bit shy and I never asked him to learn properly.

JAGDISH (VERA) SINGH: HER STORY

I came over here when I was nearly four and I remember living in India with my Mom in my grandad's house. It was light and very sunny and it was typically Indian with white walls and a courtyard and you could look down into the next person's kitchen and it was ever so friendly. You could call to each other all day long. I liked it there.

My dad was in England and I lived with my grandparents – my mother's parents – and two uncles and aunts and a cousin and my mom. I remember my grandfather. He was always much kinder to me than to my cousin because she didn't like to be cuddled – she was boyish – but I was always his favourite because he must have felt my father wasn't there. He used to buy me things and I always had my supper with him. I used to wait until he came home and just the two of us had supper together. I would moan and groan [laughs] in order to be there when he came home. Over there the women usually let their husbands eat first and then they eat afterwards – but he and I used to eat together.

My grandmother was such a cheerful person. I used to stay with her quite a bit because my mother went out with her brother and sister-in-law in the evenings and I stayed with my grandmother and she was willing to babysit. She was very good like that. She used to spoil me a lot. I always got my own way with her. She's so gentle that she couldn't be bothered to argue with anyone – she's good and she's like that even now. You just have to say something and she'll agree with you. I don't remember much about her when I was young except she was ever so pretty and used to wear white a lot.

I can't remember my mom very well when we were still in India. Except once we were going somewhere and I had to cross over a railway line and she fell over with me and I hurt myself. When we went home my grandfather thought she had hit me and he wouldn't believe that we had fallen over. I think she has told me this and, you know, they have spoken about it since. They were convinced that I'd been naughty and she had lost her temper. But really she had fallen over.

She never hit me – nobody ever hit me when I was a young child. Later on my dad spanked me a couple of times.

My cousin was a year older than me and we used to play together. I remember once she bit me on the ear. [Laughter] I'll never forget that because I always wanted her to play with me and she's a bit boyish and I remember after she bit me on the ear I was afraid.

I used to play with a brick which I wrapped up and carried about with me and called it my baby. [Laughs] And then my dad sent me a dolly from England. It was Christmas and the doll was a Red Riding-Hood with a kilt on. It was a nice doll and all the children from round about came to have a look at it. It was so life-like you know and the eyes opened and closed – and this doll was really lovely and I really loved it and my mom used to put it away at night and hide it in the suitcase and then one day I dropped it downstairs and the arm fell off and we couldn't get it repaired and I cried for ages. My grandad tried to get it mended everywhere but most of the toys came from Hong Kong and Japan and nobody could mend it.

I remember when we came over here and I had never seen my dad before and we were at the airport and my dad came forward and my mum said 'This is your Dad. Say "Hello" to him'. I remember that and then he sort of came forward and I didn't even want to talk to him because I missed my grandparents. On the way to England I've since been told, that I kept saying 'I want to go back – I want to go back'. I didn't want to come at all. My dad picked me up and said how skinny I was and how I had bent legs and he went on like that [laughs] – he still says that. And – I don't know – I didn't like him very much when I met him. I was frightened of him because he was so big and he lost his temper so quickly you know.

He used to sit there – and if you were quiet, he'd complain that you were quiet. And if you said something, then he'd say you were too noisy. I don't know – I could never please him. I was always frightened of him then.

My grandfather wasn't tall – he had a beard and a turban and he looked kind you know. If you look at my dad, he doesn't immediately strike you as being very kind – although he is – I have to say that – but he didn't look it when I first saw him.

She has returned from the bank where she works; it is early evening and she draws the pale blue curtains in the back bedroom which she shares with her younger sister before sitting on one of the two beds facing Sylvia Hutchinson who is seated on a small chair. Vera smooths the pink bed-cover in her initial shyness. She is an attractive eighteen year old with long, dark, well-kept hair and wide-set eyes, pleasantly dressed in a maroon skirt and matching sweater. She is stiff at first although eager to talk, and as her shyness gradually lifts she becomes caught up in the vivid memories of her childhood and her present concerns, and chats freely and confidingly, maintaining a constant flow of thoughts and memories. Each interview ends too soon for her needs. She has a friendly and engaging manner, her gestures are restrained and underplayed rather than dramatically expressive. As her young sister brings in a tray of tea and biscuits for Sylvia and herself she shares these with ease while continuing to relive her early memories.

The first place we lived in was the house of a friend of my dad's and I liked it there. He had a son and a daughter about my age and we used to play together. It was an Indian family and the boy was just a bit older than me and we got on very well and while his sister was at school there was just he and I during the day and my mum had company. I liked it there but it didn't last very long because my dad couldn't get a decent job and we hadn't enough money and we just moved.

We went to a huge house – there were many different families living there and there was an immense kitchen with two or three cookers. I remember all sorts of people there. There was a Jamaican lady and you know they do their hair in little plaits all over their heads and she did mine for me like that and I was so pleased with it. [Laughs] I had long hair then and it was sticking out all over the place when she had finished and I went to show my mum and she had a little laugh about it. I was always frightened by the Jamaican men because, I think – they seemed so big you know. I was frightened of my dad also because he was tall and huge.

There weren't any English people in the house – just Indians and a few Jamaicans. We had one room and I had to sleep on the couch and it was horrible and lumpy and I didn't like it very much. The room was ever so big though – it was downstairs and the stairs were always dark with worn carpets.

I was a quiet child then [laughs] and I didn't do very much during the day. I sometimes played in the garden or looked at books but I remember I was very lonely and I used to think of my cousin in India a lot even though she hadn't been particularly kind to me but at least she had been always there. And I remembered my grandparents and I used to feel sorry for myself. I suppose I was too young to actually cry much but I did cry at night.

I remember once we were sitting there and my mum was drawing the curtains and there was a girl passing outside and she waved to my mum and my mum waved back and I was lying on my bed crying because I didn't want to stay there any more in that big lonely house.

One day an Indian girl who was older than me and very spiteful locked me in a coal cellar and there was a cat in there and I was screaming the place down. You know, I was frightened of cats – I still am. She locked me in and there was a cat in the corner and I was frightened it was going to come at me and my mum came out to see what had happened. It was awful, I can still remember it – it was sort of dark and the cat's eyes were gleaming like they do. My mum let me out sort of shivering and my mum went and told the girl's parents and they told her off for which she got a hiding.

Sometimes she was friendly. I remember she took me to her school and I was ever so jealous because I wanted to go to school but I was only four. The teacher came home with us and said to my mum 'Well, I'm afraid she's too young – when she's old enough we'll take her on'. This girl used to tell me about school and make me feel jealous because I was a bit lonely then you know – just my mum and I and nothing much to do.

I had a money-box and I used to save up loads of money – my mum and dad used to give me two shillings at a time. I used to

say to them 'You mustn't take my money – that's mine' but I
was asleep and they opened it and took it all. My dad tells me
there was about £40 in it. They said 'Just imagine if we have a
house of our own! Then you can run about and we will have
people to live with us who have a little girl of your age'. I felt
happy then.

And then we bought our own house and I liked it a lot there.
We had a piano as well and although I couldn't play it, I could
make as much noise as I wanted to and didn't have to think
about somebody sleeping upstairs or that I shouldn't jump
around. We had a huge garden. I didn't like it at first because it
was so empty and then dad bought some chickens and it was
lovely. I really liked to play around with them all day. When we
were saving so hard for the house, I never had little dolls or toys
which everyone else had.

We had an English family staying with us in that
house – they had one of the back rooms and an upstairs room.
They had two girls – Phyllis and her younger sister, and we
were great friends because I wasn't going to school then and we
used to play about all day. I remember when her mum and dad
came the first time to look at the room and they were sitting
inside drinking tea and I was outside with Phyllis showing her
the garden and the first thing she did was take the lid off the
dustbin. [Laughs] It seemed such a funny thing to do you
know – her mum had her all nice and cleaned up and everything
and she had on a nice dress and her plait combed and then she
got all mucky.

Then they came to live with us and she was that sort of
girl – she used to get ever so dirty. The one time she looked
clean was five minutes before bed after her bath. [Laughs] She
was younger than me and when I went to school she was at
home all day on her own. We all lived together because we
shared the kitchen. They were ever such nice people and Phyllis'
mother was lovely – Meg her name was and they didn't have a
telly and we did so they used to come and watch every evening
and that was really good and they were ever so friendly. And the
husband – his name was Keith – he used to plant things in the
garden and we all used it, you know, and it was all right and ever
so friendly.

We've still got the house although it's up in
Birmingham – we thought we would keep it in case we ever had
to go back there and it's not used any more and it's overrun

with weeds and there are mice there – I'm dead frightened of mice.

Eric

Eric was born there. Our families feel that as soon as they have a son, they've just got it made. They always seem to want sons more than daughters in Indian families because the son carries the family name and when daughters marry they go away. But their sons are always with them. I was told that seven years after my parents married, my mum still didn't have any children and my dad and mum went to the Golden Temple where all Sikhs go and you make wishes and promise something. So dad promised so much money if he had a child and after I was born we went there – my mum and I – and that's where I was christened.

When Eric was expected I always used to tell my mum that I wanted a brother; maybe it was because my mum and dad wanted a son.

I was quite jealous of him. I remember once I had my hair cut short and had it done nicely and he hit me on the head with a plank and ruined it. I always remember that because I was in the back garden showing Phyllis 'Hey – look – how I've had my hair done' and he hit me because he was jealous I suppose. And then he had a rocking horse – something I never had – and a train set and lots of toys. And that Christmas they bought me a doll – a walking doll – and I was ever so pleased and Eric drew all over it's face. It was terrible [laughs] – he was so spiteful.

Eric was a nice-looking baby and everyone played him up and said how lovely he was and I also said he was, you know [laughs] but at one time I really hated him [laughs] and they were all saying how really nice he was. I wasn't allowed to hit him nor was he allowed to hit me – but we still did, you know. He was a lot of fun though but I was still jealous of him.

I remember when he was ever so young and he had a cot with little clowns and things on it and when I used to come to bed he could still stay up because he just wouldn't go to sleep until my dad came home and if dad was on late shift, Eric wouldn't go to sleep until he'd seen him. He was awful like that and if my mum turned the light out and went downstairs he'd still yell until she came. She would come and take him downstairs because he was spoilt – he really was. I didn't used to think I was spoilt then but when I think about it now I had lots of things then that the little ones don't have now.

Unless people speak to me first, I just won't speak and I wouldn't speak to my dad then. He always tried to get round me and I used to love this. He used to [laughs] say to me 'Well look, here's ninepence' and ninepence was great in those days and he would give me money and buy me things and I used to really love that because he could not bear to be ignored. But it's horrible, I just ignore people – I do.

And another thing I never apologise. If I got told off I'd never sort of give an excuse and I'd never say sorry. Eric and the others say it so quickly but I sort of feel belittled if I have to say sorry. I still feel this way. I find it so hard to apologise yet I feel sorry – I just can't say it. It just sticks in my throat. It used to annoy mum so because she would want some sort of an answer and I just wouldn't answer.

At school
It was quite a walk to infants' school and my mum and dad took me there for the first couple of weeks. After that I used to go on my own. I was the only Indian in the whole school at that time. I remember my first day and I wore a dress with flowers on it and everyone said how petty it was. When dad and mum went I didn't start crying. I liked being with all the other children there – I'd been on my own for so long.

The English woman who lived next door to us had taught me English and how to read and write so I knew things before I went to school and was more advanced than the other children. I used to like that, you know, because I didn't have to work hard.

I remember a boy in my class whom I liked. He was sort of puny and had big ears [laughs] and I sat next to him. I didn't feel any different from others and they didn't treat me as though I was different – we were all the same. I never came across anything like prejudice there – only here, when I came to London.

I don't remember much about school except one day when the school was on holiday and I didn't know about it. I probably had a letter to take home but must have forgotten to take it. So I had gone off to school at the usual time and I got there to find the gates were locked. I thought 'Oh – I'm late' and then I couldn't get in and I was staring at the gates when someone said to me 'Well, don't you know the school's on holiday this week?' and then I came home and cried all the way home. It was horrible you know – everyone was looking at me and I came in and yelled at my mum because she should have known [laughs], and then my mum went to ask the man at the corner shop who had a daughter at school and he said 'Yes – she's on holiday this week' and after that, if we were on holiday he used to come and tell my mum before – just in case I hadn't bothered to find out [laughs] because I didn't bother, you know. I didn't really care. But I will always remember that day – crying on the way home and everybody looking at me.

Sometimes I went to school on my own but there were a few girls who lived opposite and a couple from the corner shop who used to call for me and we used to go together. But since I was still in the infants' school and they were juniors, I came home on my own.

I remember there was a boy of my age at school and I was frightened of him and thought he was going to hit me or something. I can't remember why I was frightened of him because he'd never actually done anything. But just looking at him made me so frightened and I didn't like him. I used to take a long way home after school to avoid him but I never told anyone at home – it never occurred to me to say that I wanted mum to meet me after school. I didn't want that either.

One day my mum sent me to the chemist for dried milk for Eric and it was ever so dark and I'm frightened of the dark. And I had to walk up this long road – it wasn't late but it was dark and on the way back there was a Jamaican boy and an English boy both about seven years old, and they had a skipping rope and they tied it around me and I was so frightened and I started crying and they just tied it round me and ran off and left it wound round me a couple of times. I was crying and it started to rain, I remember, and I was frightened and there was a lady who was walking past and she stopped and helped me and brought me home. I didn't ask her to come in. I didn't tell my mother. I didn't like to worry her with things like that. Or perhaps I thought it was a weakness. I used to think about it late at night. I used to think I'd better not take that way tomorrow because he or others might be there.

I'm frightened of the dark and cats and dogs and things. We had an outside toilet and you had to walk out of the back door and once there was this cat there and you could just see its eyes and I screamed the place down – I don't like cats – they seem to scratch and spit.

English neighbours and friends in Birmingham
When we lived in our own house, we were the only Indian family in the neighbourhood. Everyone was ever so friendly and always willing to help. Ever so good they were. I never came across prejudice at all there.

I never found it strange to be only with English people. It is difficult to remember how I felt then but I was like a pet you know, because the girls opposite were all teenagers and they used to come over and play with me for a bit. I was their little pet and they were ever so kind to me and I used to like them a lot too. They were older than me and I used to feel sort of good being with them. They were nice people though – everyone was nice, especially the people who lived in our house.

School in London
When we moved to London I went to a junior school around the corner from where we live. I was in the top 1A Form and the teacher was a horrible lady and I really hated her. She was always yelling, shouting and screaming but only at Indian children. I noticed that and really hated it. We'd ask her something and she would yell at us and we wouldn't ask again. So then we wouldn't understand anything.

She would say that we don't know anything and how illiterate we were and things like that but at that time I really didn't understand what was going on and just felt there was a difference and that was it.

In Birmingham as the only Indian family in the neighbourhood we were treated specially – people were really friendly and nice, but here in London there are so many Indian people although there weren't as many Indians at school as there are now, there were quite a few more than I'd ever seen before. I just felt treated differently as a result and I don't know how I tried to put a meaning to it. I just felt it and that was it. I didn't bother to think why it was or anything like that. I realised it and just hated it from that moment on and I hated school as well. I hated the school because the teacher was there and I used to cry and wish to be back in Birmingham. I remember that plainly.

I never told my parents so they didn't know that I'd been crying and what was going on at the school. If I had told my dad he would have gone to the school and seen the teacher. I felt as if I were trying to protect my parents from it more than they were trying to protect me. I'd rather they hadn't known. It's funny because Eric is different and he'll come home and tell mum and dad anything but I never did.

In my class were an Indian girl and an Indian boy – he was a bit dirty. I was put to sit next to the Indian girl – I suppose because I could speak English or something. She was nice, I liked her at first but after a few days I didn't like her very much. She was a bit snobby. I had an English friend Miranda and we were friends right up until now. We were true friends. I never showed my feelings about being treated differently in class because I was an Indian. I don't think I ever showed it. I used to feel it and think about it but I never had an outburst about it. So I don't think Miranda ever knew. We were great friends and she used to come round and stay over here and we used to talk all night. And I used to go to her house and it was lovely because there weren't any small children.

It was only that particular teacher who was not nice and when she left I was so pleased. I had a rotten report that year as well. It could have been justified because I didn't like her so I couldn't ever work hard. My dad was very upset about my reports and that was something I really dreaded – bringing reports home because my maths were awful. [Laughs] I used to open them and then I'd be prepared for the worst. I would know whether to be all smiling because I'd got a good one or whether to be a bit meek because I had a bad one. And you know he used to sit there and read it to himself and then put it away and he wouldn't say anything.

After that year I had another teacher who got the MBE for having so many Indian children in her school, I think. Both for putting up with it and for dealing with it so well. She gave me a good report and put that my conduct was quiet in class.

I enjoyed my junior years at school and particularly remember a school trip to Kent. I was with all my school friends for two weeks and we stayed in a boarding house and Karen and I shared a room along with three others. It was really good and great fun and we went swimming and had day trips round Kent. It was the happiest time I remember at school. I didn't worry about anything at all. It was smashing and when I look back at it now, I feel sad. [Laughs]

When it was time to go to secondary school, I didn't want to go – I didn't think I could enjoy it. Miranda went to a grammar school and I was really jealous. We decided we would do homework together but didn't. She met a new crowd and that was it. But I went to this secondary school with some girls from the junior school and there were four of us who were friends. They were English.

I really hated my first year there because the girls at that secondary school were awfully prejudiced and were awful. In my class there were about four Indians, but there was a special class only for Indians with about thirty or forty in it and all the lower classes in the school had lots of Indians in them.

The Indian people seem to think they must do better than the English at school because if they do about the same, they don't really stand a chance because of prejudice. The Indians who had studied in India didn't know English but their maths was of a much higher standard than here because over there maths is one of the things that count above all others. If you don't know it in India, you're disgraced so that you jolly well learn it next time. My dad remembers that when he did maths at school, if he didn't know it he got the cane in front of the class which as you know is twice as embarrassing.

By the third year at that school, I was having a wonderful time with my friends but we didn't work. We just had a happy time. I really enjoyed that year and I got a rotten report and after that I thought I'd better work a bit. My dad was going mad about it – for weeks on end he didn't say anything to me. So I thought I'd work and have some peace and quiet. [Laughing] I took up shorthand at school but the teacher was horrible. During her first lesson she said 'I don't want any of you to think there's any difference in my mind between green, yellow, red or any other colour person. You are all the same to me and I don't have any favourites' and she rambled on and on but she did have favourites. People who start off saying they don't have favourites usually do. All the little goodies in the front were her favourites – mostly English but also an Indian girl who was older than me but marvellous at shorthand. She was her favourite but the funny thing was that she couldn't stand the teacher. Shorthand was a failure for me and I had to give it up because she said I'd never pass and I didn't like it anyway.

By the time I left school at sixteen, I had got to know some Indian girls at school but I'd largely grown up with English girls and my friends were English.

Work

I never really thought about work until a few weeks before I left school and then I went to the Youth Employment Officer and

said I wanted to work at the airport and she said it was difficult to get in at that time as it was late. I didn't really know
what I wanted to do at the airport. I could type but I didn't like
typing and thought I might do clerical work or something like
that.

She telephoned an airways company while I was there and
they said there were some vacancies and sent me a form. I filled
it in and sent it and while I was waiting to hear from them I went
to two interviews at different offices. One was a horrible biscuit
factory – like an old war building – and I didn't bother to take
the test which the man suggested and I just came home. The
Youth Employment Officer also sent me to a factory where they
designed furniture but it wasn't really my line to design
furniture and so I said 'No' to the person who interviewed me
and I just came home again. Meanwhile the letter from the
airways came and they said they didn't have any vacancies and
so I felt awful after that.

I didn't think that the Youth Employment Officer was doing
all she could for me – I don't know – maybe it was because I'm
Indian but I don't really know. The first time I went there I got
the impression she was very nice and she would do all she could
but next time I went there she probably thought I should have
taken the job and the next time also and so she wasn't very
interested and gave me any old thing so I didn't go back. She
really didn't help my English friends either. They just made it
on their own.

When I came back from the last interview at the furniture
place I saw my friend walking along and we started talking and
she was talking of her job with the Westminster Bank and said
'Why don't you apply?' I always thought banks were cold
places and stuffy [laughs] and we were walking past a branch of
the bank so I just bounced in and asked how to apply and the
Manager was ever such a nice man and gave me the address and
I wrote off and the interview came through. They were really
nice people and offered me a cup of tea and that sort of thing. It
was smashing but I was feeling a bit nervous going down there
the first day. I'm awful like that. [Laughs] At the last minute I'll
be already to go and then I sort of stand at the door waiting to
go and my mum would say 'Well, go on then' and I sort of stand
there and think – well, I don't really want to go. [Laughter] It's
horrible. And I feel such a big baby.

Anyway the letter came through from the bank and I was

really pleased and I thought well this is it – and banks are safe and secure and all that sort of thing and everybody's impressed. [Laughter]

The branch I'm in is a local branch because I didn't want to go anywhere too far away. I had told them I wanted to be near home.

There are no Indian girls in our branch but there are two Indian men. Indian customers were a bit surprised to see me there but they were pleased because they could talk and get across what they were trying to say. I can interpret since I speak both Punjabi and Hindi. In fact at work they are trying to get me a language allowance.

I have been working with the bank for more than two years now. I get on very well with the girls in the bank and an English girl called Selma, who started a week after me, is my special friend. Her dad also works at the airport but our parents don't know each other. Her mother's very nice. We've got the same sense of humour – Selma and I – and she's a bit silly but it's lovely. We work right next to each other.

It's nice because you do your job but if you feel like just sitting down for five minutes and talking you can. We always do. [Laughs] The people there are all like friends. I've been doing the same job since I left school and yet other friends of mine change their jobs every six months or so. I couldn't face strange faces every morning, you know. I have to feel there are people I know and have to feel secure and that's why I feel sorry for anyone new that joins us because it must be so horrible – you know, everybody else talking to each other and there you are thinking everyone is looking at you.

And it's not boring you know, because I get bored very easily if I'm doing the same old thing – you can change around. For instance, I've been machining for the last month or two – ledger keeping, you know, and now I'm going to do the standing orders.

Actually Selma and I are the oldest staff members there now – I mean of the junior staff – and there are about four or five new people who have come in and three more are coming so that pushes us up a lot. They trust us.

Maxine was catty and nobody liked her. She used to start talking about you and you could hear her and it was horrible and everybody dreaded going out of the ledger room because she was there. Or you would walk in and there would be a

deadly silence and you knew they had been talking about you
and that was horrible. It got so bad that I thought of leaving and
applied once again for a job with an airways company. But I
went along there for an interview and it sounded so boring and
it required Maths and I hate Maths and would never do it. Dad
is brilliant at Maths. I went home and was talking to my dad and
I said 'I don't think I got it' and he said 'Well, why's that?' and I
told him what a mess I'd made of the Maths questions they
asked me and he just laughed [laughs] and said 'Well, what are
you worried about? You've got a job, you know – you don't
need to worry about it'. I felt grateful really because I hated it
there. I seem to hate everywhere you know. It was such a relief
to get back to the same old faces at the bank and they all knew
where I'd been but no one really said anything. That's one thing
about our bank in particular – everyone who comes there says
how friendly it is. Everyone helps and is ever so nice, especially
since all the horrible people have left, including Maxine.

When I have to teach others at work I really don't know how
to put things to them. I don't want to feel as if I'm showing off
or telling them that I know it and they don't – although in fact I
do know it and they don't. I always think of the other person
and how he will take it if I tell him.

I don't really like teaching people because often the supervisor has asked me to teach people and I say 'I can't do it' and he
peppers me up a bit and says 'You know you can'. I might feel
differently, I think, if it was an Indian I was teaching – I might
feel more on the same basis and I don't think they would take it
differently. But on the other hand recently an Indian girl came in
with her mother to the bank and I was trying to tell her
something and she was going on and on as though she knew it
all and I couldn't stand that. She didn't know it all and she was
saying things which were complete rubbish and I was trying to
explain it to her but she wouldn't be told, you know. They come
over here and they think they know it all when they don't. I
know my job at least and have spent years trying to learn it and
in a few minutes someone else is dictating to you and you get a
bit angry. I try to keep my temper under control because I've
got a horrible temper. [Laughs] Now I haven't, but you know I
get a bit violent and start throwing things but I haven't done it
recently. Well, I was getting a bit ratty with these Indian
customers and the woman was carrying on and arguing about
her balance and this and that. You know people like that always

think they're higher up than you but then you get English people like that too who can't be told anything.

There was another girl who worked at the bank at one time whose father was West Indian and mother Scottish and you couldn't tell her anything either. When she left everyone was pleased. But I got on quite well with her you know. Then I thought perhaps they were being like this to her because she was half West Indian. The girls were nice in front of her but behind her back they all said 'Oh she thinks she's it' She did – but if you got to know her, when she got talking she forgot herself. She was a bit affected but when she talked to you and was on sort of equal terms, she was quite nice. I liked her and got on very well with her and they were really rotten to her. Selma and I told them and they made out they were sorry afterwards but it was a bit late because she had heard some of the things they had said. After she left she married a man from the American air force and sent an invitation to everybody in the bank which was laying it on a bit. No one went. I didn't either because I was doing something that Saturday and I couldn't tell whether no one went because she is like she is or whether it was because she was West Indian. It hurt me though when they did that – talking about her and ignoring her because I could just imagine it happening to me – when some of the old crowd at the bank were around – now it's different because there's a nicer crowd.

I haven't really had any very close West Indian friends before but there's a girl whom I know quite well. I met her through a friend and we meet sometimes by chance and often walk the same way to work. We confide in each other and if we've had a row, we tell each other about it and have found that our parents are much the same, row about the same things you know and all our brothers are the same nuisances. [Laughs] It was quite funny how I confided in her that easily. I think it was because she did in me so I trusted her quite a bit because I don't trust people very easily. So now when we see each other, we automatically exchange everything quickly. She's a very nice girl and is about the only West Indian girl that has been very close to me. Others whom I know aren't very close.

I have an English friend – who rambles on and on and she doesn't notice that you're not saying anything. I'm not naturally a quiet person but with this friend Joan I'm different. She had a brain haemorrhage or something and she seems perfectly normal but she does go on and on about her jobs and her accident and her doctor and I've heard it so often that it bores me to death. Sometimes she'll go on about our Indian way of life and our culture and this and that, and once I remember she said something about prejudice and she said 'Well, don't think I'm prejudiced, because I wouldn't be walking along with you if I were' and I didn't really know how to take that. So I said 'Oh no, I don't suppose I am. I wouldn't walk with you would I?' [Laughter] So she laughed about that you know. I'm very sarcastic if someone annoys me. I'm rotten. I couldn't tell whether she was being funny because she does say funny things sometimes.

Now with Selma, it's different. I think one reason why I get on so well with Selma is because she's interested in my Indian background and she'll ask me things. But she doesn't say 'Well, this is how it should be'. She won't try and change it. Well, she can't, can she? She asks because she's interested. But Joan will ask you something, and then she'll criticize. But Selma is interested, you know, and respects my views and I respect her views, you know, because it's more equal. But with Joan I always feel it's a bit condescending – or she'll say how superior she is to everybody else. It bores me sometimes but then I think she can't help it. [Laughs]

The girls at the bank never discuss things like colour or prejudice or what's happening in the country   they're more interested in their make-up and stuff like that. They're just not interested. They regard me – well – this amused me – they said to me 'We wouldn't think you were an Indian – you're just like one of us' and it didn't ever occur to them that I just don't want to be one of them, you know. I'm *me* and that's it. [Laughs] Or they'll say 'You're really English, Vera' but I don't *want* to be English. [Laughter] And then they say how odd it is that everybody else isn't like me – and what a shame – and how westernized I am – but they don't seem to realise that I'm not out to change the world, you know, and that it's just me [laughter] and that's it. If they like me, well that's good but I don't really want to be what they seem to imagine. They seem to feel it's a wonderful compliment. [Laughs] They probably mean it nicely   I've heard it so often: 'You're so English'. But I don't think it's a compliment – I just don't.

One day a relief cashier – a loud-mouthed and very rude woman who is getting the sack quite soon – came to work at the bank. And She was talking about this new race bill [The 1971 Immigration Bill] and this was the first time that this had ever happened at the bank. We were sitting there machining – three of us and talking about it and as we were talking about it someone came up and Selma said we were talking about the race bill and this person said 'How much is it?' or something silly like that. She didn't even know about it so that amused everybody but then this relief cashier said 'I don't see why these immigrants should all come over here and support their families in India – or why they should live off our National Health and do no work'. Now there's another woman at the bank who is English but who is married to a Pakistani. Her name is Joyce. She's a bit of a socialist because her husband's family are quite rich and they could live in Pakistan and be rich and have cars but she'd rather live here and work you know, and so she pounced on the cashier and said 'What do you mean – they don't work? And they don't live off the National Health', and this and that and the other and the cashier was quiet for once in her life and we couldn't believe it – because she's a big person and Joyce is tiny, really like a child, and you can't imagine her saying 'boo' to a goose – but this time she really pounced and the cashier was sitting there getting all red. We were quite amused, as she had just said a few things – normal things like 'Oh why do they all have to live in the same place?' and Joyce went on a bit and then I said 'Well, why is it alright for all you English people to go to Australia and take it away from the aborigines and go to America and take it away from the Red Indians – and go to South Africa and take it all away – and yet it's not alright for us to come over here, you know? You know you ruled over India.' And then she said 'What a poor country India was'. So I told her in actual fact it wasn't poor until we were ruled over and the English just took everything away – because it's true – I've been to see these things and there are huge holes in the walls where there were once jewels and they had been taken out. You know – like the Crown Jewels – these have mostly come from India. And she said that she didn't agree with that, which was a bit stupid because she really couldn't think of anything else to say. She became a bit quiet.

Joyce and I get on very well – we discuss Indian food which makes everybody else's mouth water. I don't see Joyce out of work – I'd like to ask her but I don't know what mum would think – because although she's English she's married to a Muslim and she's adopted the faith I believe. And my mum was frightened of them. She was going to school I think and she went to a shop and a man was trying to make her come inside to one of the inner rooms and it was all dark and horrid and she remembers the incident quite well and she ran away and was frightened. And I don't know whether it was because it was all horrible or because he was a Pakistani. I don't really know. But she's not very fond of them. She's not a prejudiced person really but she just hasn't got very pleasant memories and she saw things that went on around her which probably influenced her you know. But she never says anything unless you ask her. I did ask her. I'm not aware of Pakistanis being different at all – it doesn't matter to me at all you know. The thing is that I don't like to upset my mum because she hasn't been very well for some time. Anything you say to her, she'll start thinking about it and go on thinking about it. She used to get migraine and her blood count went down and she was ever so ill about two years ago and she'd be lying down and we had to help with the housework – so it was ever so bad. And she has been quite ill so we don't like to say anything to upset her because she might argue with you or she just thinks about things. You say something and she'll remember it a week afterwards, when you've forgotten it completely. She doesn't show she's upset but like a bad dream she keeps thinking of it all day and she's quiet you know. But you can see something's wrong and she'll tell you because you know she's not basically that sort of person – she's really friendly.

My dad has a few Pakistani friends and he talks about them and they send things over to him but he's never actually got around to asking them over either – perhaps for the same reason. I hope this is right because I hate to say these things if it's not so. My sister has Pakistani friends at school – which is more than I do because I don't know any Muslim girls at all.

I'm really more used to English girls and probably get on better with them because I know what to talk about – more than I would with Indian girls. Some Indian girls I see and I think 'Oh she's a bit like me' – but they seem sort of cold and they don't want to talk to you and I've never actually been one to just go up to people and start talking to them. I like them to talk to me first because I feel so silly. Also I think some of them are too Western altogether and I don't think I like it very much – they go to extremes.

There's a new lady who's come to work at the bank – she's an Indian from Kenya. I can't judge people at all just by looking at them – some people can. I liked her the first day but by the second day I was not so very struck with her. She has got funny little habits. She talks Punjabi because she speaks it and I speak it but others in the office don't understand. I think that's very bad because they don't know what you're saying and I understand how they must feel, because people can feel that 'Oh, they're talking about me' – or something. It's very bad I think. So when she talks in Punjabi I answer in English. I didn't the first week because I didn't know how to take it but now I just answer in English and hope she'll get the point. If she doesn't I shall just tell her because it makes it awkward for me really and I'm sure I wouldn't feel very happy if people were talking in a language I didn't understand. Her English is very good you know and she also speaks French and a series of Indian languages – and knows Latin. I think perhaps she's beginning to show off that she knows these other languages. I think she's creating problems for herself and it's not a good position to put me in. I don't think it's really fair. It makes it awkward and I don't know what to say. If tomorrow she starts talking to me in Punjabi again I'll say to her 'I've only spoken English in fact, because you know the others don't like it and I don't like it myself.' I shall tell her but it makes me feel awkward because I wonder how she might take it. She also talks to another man at the bank – the security man who also comes from Kenya – in another language which I don't speak. I think it's totally ignorant to do that and everyone notices it. She's a widow and when we heard that we were expecting someone quiet and inconspicuous but she's so flash and pretty – we were really surprised. Today in fact, she came to work in a sari – she's not wearing it because she won't wear English clothes but she's just wearing it for a change. I think it's very pretty but hardly something for work. That's why I think she's creating problems for herself there because the others don't really think it's quite the thing. She's from Kenya and from what we've heard the people out there are more or less like the English – they're more European than Indian. So I'd expected someone who was wearing quiet clothes and Indian women, once their husbands die, don't usually marry again and they are humble. But she's sort of loud – and sometimes she talks like a flirt.

Relationships with men
Indian boys think they're God's gift, you know – I'm reduced to laughter when I see some of them round here – they think they're so wonderful. I feel like screeching when I see them walking up and down the street. I don't know any Indian boys at all – only relatives and their friends but then I don't know any English boys either. I know Selma's boy friend vaguely – I've seen him and of course I know the people I work with but nobody apart from that. But these Indian boys whom I see in the streets, they come over here when they are about twelve and they grow up here and think this is it, you know – and they've made it and they haven't any jobs. Near where I work there are two little restaurants where they all hang out. You go past there and there are crowds of them and they don't do any work and they think they're wonderful. I think it's so useless. If they were in India they'd really have to work hard but because they're here they think they can get away with it – just doing nothing all day and being layabouts. These are boys of about sixteen to twenty and they seem to show off so much and are so loud. I expect they live off their parents or something.

It's changed round here since they all came in from Kenya. We hear that they're a lot more advanced than Indians from India and it could be that the Kenyan Indians are influencing the others quite a bit. And the girls are different as well. I can tell them straight away. They sort of walk along and think they are it – it's just the way they walk that really gets me – their whole personality and manner you can sense it immediately – there's lack of modesty. And other Indians, you see them whispering about them.

The girls at work talk about their boy friends and some days they're at the top of the world and they're so happy and other days they come in crying, you know, because they've broken up or something and it's the end of the world. So I'm glad I don't have to go through all that. I couldn't stand it all the time. I like to be in one mood and not go from one extreme to the other in the same day. I like to feel secure. I've never actually seen a boy whom I really like.

There's an English boy at work who gives me a lift home

sometimes and the minute I get out of the car you can see people standing there watching and thinking 'Yes, I know her.' So now I just say to him 'It's alright, I'll walk,' because I feel rotten. I don't want my parents to have to put up with these people talking about me when there's nothing to talk about. I'm just too lazy to walk. So there's no reason to put them in that position.

You don't see Indian girls with white men – but you do see Indian boys going out with white girls. For Indian girls it just isn't done. The majority are still very much with their parents – they aren't independent. And though I often think I could be independent, I'd hate to think what my parents would have to go through if I was because you know people talk. It's easy to say you should ignore what people say but I think it's very hard actually to come up against it and come out winning. So although I want independence, when I weigh it up I think I'd feel too insecure, you know.

If I had a boy friend, I'd like to be independent and not have to account for everything. But they'd probably ask me where I've been and this and that and the other and I couldn't bear that. I don't like to be questioned all the time and they would. Especially my dad – he's very Indian you know – and he'd hate it if he sees anything like that. He'd give me a long lecture about what happens to girls who go out like this – all the *News of the World* stuff you know – what would people say? And what will happen to my life altogether? And how they would just cut me off completely and all the unwanted children in the world – you know the usual arguments. But we've never actually come to that stage where I say 'Well, look, this is what I want to do'. I wouldn't dare say it – I think he wouldn't accept it if I said that.

My uncle has married an American girl and this is a great breakthrough in our family. I was very upset at the time because it wasn't long after my aunt had died so when he said he was re-marrying I didn't like her – I really hated her and it choked me a bit – he had even lost all his old photographs of his first wife. He came over here and had a tape of himself and his new wife talking to us and we didn't know what was going to happen – he just turned the tape on. It upset me an awful lot and I didn't like her, she was too sure of herself and my parents didn't like her at all you could tell. She's still in America and my mum didn't say anything but my dad said he wondered how my

grandparents were going to take it and I could see he didn't
approve at all. At first we didn't like her but last week we spoke
to her on the phone – we telephoned her up and she was ever so
grateful to hear from us.I talked to my dad a bit and said it's
hard enough coming into a new family without having all this
against you. She had been married before and had three children
and is white. In India a man usually marries again if he has
children but if a woman marries again if she has children, it's
the worst thing on earth, which is really silly. Anyhow I spoke
to dad and said 'If we're nice to her now she won't forget it you
know – it's going to be hard enough without making things
worse' so he seems to have accepted it now. Our grandfather is
very conservative you know – really Indian and if I said I was
going to marry an English boy I think he'd die on the spot. But
now hearing he's accepted my uncle's marriage, I can't believe it
you know. I'd like to actually *hear* him say it – not just what he's
written about it.

So if I think of myself and if I wanted to marry an
Englishman I think they'd hate it in fact. And I don't know if I
could hurt them in that way. If I get married I'd like them to
accept the responsibility and to me that's a sort of security
because then I can blame them. But if I get married like I wanted
to get married, then it would all be on my own head and if it's
wrong, then that's it. I think they'd cut me off completely and
they'd really hate it.

Also I wouldn't like to have in-laws that were too starchy. I'd
like to have people I could get on with – with backgrounds that
are a bit similar. But they couldn't be with English people I
don't think. I think there are a lot of odds against this sort of
thing. You have to really be able to take the talking of other
people because you see people turning their heads and saying
'She's cheap' if it's a white girl walking along with an Indian
man. They automatically don't like her. Both parties – the
Indians and the whites – think like that. If there's a white
woman pushing a pram with little Jamaican babies in inside,
they raise their eyebrows and wonder 'What's happened there?'
And, as I've said, you don't see Indian girls with white men
around here – but we've read about it.

A cousin of mine is marrying soon – it's an arranged
marriage – it's been fixed. He is a meek person – he's like a
girl – so he may allow it. I think arranged marriages depend on
how well you get on with your parents really. I wouldn't just let

mine choose anyone but then I don't think they *do* anyway. If you try hard enough you can make a go of anything really you know, and looking at other people's marriages that often break up I think that's awful. I don't believe in divorce either – if you take vows you should mean it.

I'm thinking of going to live in Canada in about a year's time. I probably will like it but I'm a little bit frightened. My dad is encouraging me but my mum hasn't said very much. I have relatives over there and I'm busy filling in immigration forms now. You tell them the work you want to do and they'll pick something suitable. When I think of going to Canada I think perhaps that one reason is wanting to be on my own there and try and work things out for myself. I know what I want to do and what I don't want to do but I don't really know why. I don't think I could live in a flat on my own – some people seem to manage it – they loosen family ties that way. When I go to Canada I'd like to try it on my own and be really independent but I'm not sure how my parents would take this – they would definitely like me to stay with a family – with relatives.

We've got family over there but I don't know them – they're just people in pictures who write letters and it could be just as bad living with them as it would on my own. A cousin of mine is supposed to be getting married and going over there but it's an arranged marriage and she's decided not to go so that's ruined it because I was going to stay with her.

If it doesn't work out in Canada I can come back on my dad's ticket and come home. But I'd be too proud to come home and admit that I couldn't make a go of it. But I think I'd be ever so lonely because I have to be with people. I can't bear being on my own. I get so bored you know after a few minutes. So I think I'd miss the family a lot but then I think I'll be older then and maybe I'll be able to do it.

At the moment I imagine that my relatives in Canada will welcome me with open arms – and I'm hoping it will be like that but sometimes I think they may be very cold and I'll go over there and no one will know me or want me.

I shan't go until I've got a job and I'll arrange that through Canada House and I'm hoping to meet some girls there with whom I could share a flat. I think my parents want me to stay with relatives but I wouldn't like to stay with another family because I'm awful – I would start comparing and I would compare them with my family and either if I find they're not half

as good or it they came up better, I'd hate it either way. So I'd
like to try it all on my own.

But they probably think 'Oh all alone in a big city – we can't
have you living on your own'. When I'm on my own I think of
what I can say to them and what they might say to me. I make
them answer what I'd like them to answer. But I think if I
actually said what I want to say they would come out with a
stronger argument than mine and I'd feel defeated because there
are two of them and one of me and I don't know if I could
actually take it then if they won. I would go down in their
estimation of me and I wouldn't like that either. I don't think
they know what I'm feeling about it. Perhaps mum
does – perhaps dad does even more because he reads and sees
things more than mum does. But because I never say anything
about my doubts and feelings they don't know. If they do,
they've never said and if they did say anything about it perhaps
I'd lie and not really say what I do feel because I don't know
how they'd take it.

It's difficult really and that's why I often wish that we did not
live here at all. That we were in India and then I wouldn't have
these feelings. It's very hard and I hate to see my sister growing
up like this – she's more docile than me – she's gentle and she
wouldn't say anything to hurt mum or dad. I feel she would do
the right things whereas I perhaps wouldn't do all the right
things. You know – they might say to me 'Well this is who
we'd like you to marry' and I'd say 'Well, I don't like him – I
hate him completely'. That's what's happening to my cousin.
Her marriage has been arranged and she's refused flatly and
will not go to India to marry the man – they were going to live
in Canada after the marriage. She's refused and my parents were
really shocked about this. I wasn't at all sorry. I was quite
pleased that she'd done this because it showed them that I
wouldn't just marry who they wanted me to. They wouldn't
expect me to I don't think – but I wouldn't have complete
freedom to pick out whom I wanted to marry. So I'm really glad
she did that. She ought to have more of a say – she'd only seen
pictures – I mean that's not much to go on at all. And she's met
her future mother-in-law and hated her on the spot. So I knew
something would happen but she never actually told me. She
might sort of weaken – weaken and give in to her father. I'm
going to write to her this evening and ask her exactly what she's
going to do because you know perhaps I can help her. It may do

her good to talk about it. My uncle – her father – doesn't know what to do – he wrote and said he didn't know which way to turn. He wouldn't force her – I know he wouldn't do that – but he doesn't know what to do because he's made all the arrangements in India with the future in-laws. She didn't like to tell him before because she didn't like to disappoint him but now I think it's worse. But then I feel – well, I might perhaps be like that – I wouldn't say anything at the beginning and then when it came down to it, I'd say 'Well, I'm not going to'. It would probably break my mum's heart or something.

I don't think my parents would behave in quite the same way but maybe that's why they want me to go to Canada so I can meet some of my relatives' friends. They've never said this to me but my mum was saying recently 'Well, we'll have to start thinking about getting you married now,' and I was completely shocked because I wouldn't like to get married until I'm about twenty-two or twenty-three and I'm only eighteen now. I'd like to see the world and that sort of thing. I told her and she said 'Oh really' and she hasn't said anymore about it. Often I don't know whether she's joking or not but she says 'I'm really worried about you now – I've never been worried about it before but all of a sudden you seem grown-up now'. I hope she's joking – it's got me quite worried.

A funny thing happened last week at the bank. I was standing there and an old Indian man came in – a really frumpy soul and he knows dad vaguely and he came to the counter and I'm nice to him and he said 'I'd like you to marry my son'. [Laughs] I had to try not to laugh, you know – it seemed so funny leaning over the counter and him saying this to me. Then he said it didn't have to be his son it could be his nephew! I didn't know how to take it! 'Well anyways', he said 'I'll see your parents' and he shuffled off. So I didn't know what to do – whether to laugh, cry or phone home. I told them and they just laughed. He hasn't been yet but it was only a few days ago and I was really worried afterwards. I told mum who laughed and said it was a very novel way of putting it. [Laughs] I just hope he doesn't come in again.

And he said to me 'If you don't want to, I won't think any the less of you – I'll still like you'. He's ever so sweet and I'm always nice to him because he's so sweet. 'You're just the sort of girl I want for my daughter-in-law'. It was so unexpected.

Indian girls don't get married so young any more. But when

my mum says to me that she was fifteen when she got married and 'Look at you – you can't do anything – you can't cook' she makes me feel really childish you know. She's prodded me so that I'm going to learn dressmaking just to show her. [Laughs] I don't think eighteen is old enough to be married – I don't like responsibility at all you know. Any little responsibility sort of nags me. I don't think I could take it.

When I sometimes say to dad I'll go over to Canada and he says 'Yes, we'll come over and help you get settled in a place' I don't really know whether he means a place of my own or not. I don't like to push it too far in case I can't go altogether. But I'd like it if they came to help me settle in because if I got a place of my own then he'd know what it was like and I wouldn't have to tell him and he wouldn't keep asking me because I think they tend to worry a lot. They'd worry about everything – if I shared with other girls they'd worry in case I was picking up bad habits like smoking – and going out all hours of the night and if I was eating or not – how I was living and whether I was living in a pig stye [laughs] – the usual things you know.

Some girls when they are young can imagine what it's going to be like when they grow up. I've never imagined anything like that. I don't know why. I can never imagine things happening. I'm planning to go to Canada and everyone around me is making these wonderful plans and this is going to happen and that – and they've got some idea of how they are going to make it work but I never can. When I was younger I used to think I'd never grow up. [Laughs] That used to frighten me that did, to think I'd be that age all the time. Now I'm there [laughs] I make plans sometimes but they don't come off. It doesn't worry me but it always seems as if I haven't got any future, you know. It always seems that way – I don't know why. It makes me feel different from other girls my age.

Since telling you these things dad actually said to me – he said 'Would you be prepared to try to live on your own?' and I said 'Oh yes'. And since he said that, it seems as if I wasn't so keen after all. It surprised me that he said that and it surprised me that he said I could go in the first place. He's offered to buy everything for me – buy me a place and get it furnished and everything. He said he didn't like to be indebted to our relatives over there because they're not that close and we don't know them anyway. But I'm frightened of being on my own really because I'd get lonely. I can't bear my own company. I could live on my own but as long as someone I knew was near. It's so far, you know – I feel a bit nervous. My mum's not happy – she hasn't wholeheartedly said 'Go' but I didn't really expect her to. She says she'll miss me and that sort of thing but you know I'll miss her as well [laughs] but I don't want to stay here and she realises this. I said as soon as we get a place and the younger ones have left school, she could easily come out there and live with me. The children definitely want to move to Canada – but my mum wants to go back to India I think because my dad has got land out there. I can't imagine it without her. I've always imagined us as being all together even though it may be in a different country. But I wouldn't go back to India – I could not stand the heat. I don't think I'd like it but if it's what mum wants, I'd like her to do what she likes. Eric wants to go to Canada, he wants me to go over so he can come later on and join me. He can't wait to leave school – so we can both go over. I don't know if the family will split up – it would depend on my dad and what he wants to do. I've often said to him 'Why don't you sell the land?' and he says 'Oh we've got it to go back to – it might be like Kenya over here' and that sort of thing. My mum doesn't want to sell the land because she says they want something to leave to us.

I'd like them to come to Canada. I want them to be there any way and as they get older I'd like them to live with me and that sort of thing. I'd like to take care of them. They hate this idea but I'd like to. They don't want to be dependent, they've seen so much of it, parents living with children and their children hating it and their parents interfering so they wouldn't want to be dependent on us you know.

If I think of sharing a flat with girls in Canada I'd probably get on better with Canadian white girls than with Indian girls. I wouldn't know the Indian girls there and would find it more difficult to get on with them because they'd probably think that I'm all on my own and living out there alone and what can my parents be like to let me live there. I don't think I'd like to be judged in that way. I think Canadian girls would be more similar to me than Indian girls.

My relationship with my mum

I get on very well with my mum – she's more like a friend and I can talk to her about anything. If we have an argument and I'm awful and won't talk of anything – she always comes over and talks to me which is more than anyone else will do. They think – if she's sulking then leave her to it. But you know you like to have people come round and say 'Are you angry?' and she'll do that. We get on very well and hardly ever row and if we do it's not over a serious thing – it's over silly little things that don't really matter like being untidy.

When I was in junior school and the people around me were saying what rows they had with their mothers and I didn't have rows with my mum, I'd come home and create something so we would have a row and I could say it as well. [Laughs] And she used to say 'You are acting funnily' which was wonderful and of course this set me off again 'Oh you don't understand me' and this and that. [Laughs] Oh that makes me laugh now because it's always interesting you know – the adolescence bit. There was nothing like that. We always got on very well.

She's calm you know and if you have a row with her she won't take it seriously, you know, unless of course it is really serious. Of course with dad we'll have rows and sit there yelling for hours and she'll come in and try and calm us down a bit.

When I started work two years ago I knew the girls around me were giving money to their parents so I said to mum I'd give her £12 a month and she said it was all right and I should give her less. She's saved it up for me. I always give her something because it's her who buys the food and she sees to everything and does my clothes for me.

She's never actually said what amount I should give her so I don't give her a regular amount and even now they say to me that I can keep my wages and they don't mind. I've had the advantage and I feel I owe them something and won't forget them when they are older. If you have too many set rules in the house it leads to rifts. If I want to borrow some money she'll give it to me and won't keep reminding me like other people tend to do. I don't borrow off my friends although they borrow off each other. There are always rows that they dare not ask their parents for money.

My dad

I row more with my dad than with my mum because we're so alike. Neither of us will give in. I feel like my dad because both of us are so quick-tempered and tend to rant and rave and then to be sullen for about three days or so. Well, he actually apologises. I don't ever go as far as that! We row about work sometimes. We all get pay slips at work and he's forever saying to me that I don't book my overtime and I say I do and he says 'Are you sure? If you booked your overtime, you'd get more money than this'. So I start hunting the ads for a new job which will pay more. [Laughs]

When we've had a big row, that upsets me a lot. I don't think he realises it. I try not to cry but if I do he sort of makes out that he doesn't see and he thinks I'm doing it to win you know. When really I'm crying because I can't think of anything to say. I don't cry easily and never in front of anyone – not like Selma who cries in front of me and others – it amazes me how she can do it. She often gets told off at work because she sits there chatting when she ought to be working – I don't like being told off for nothing but if it's my fault I don't mind. I spoke to my dad about it and he said 'If they ever made you cry, I'd get there like a shot'. [Laughs] That's really like him you know. That's the sort of thing he does – he's very protective. One day four of us were told off and it made me cry a bit because it upset me and he said 'Why didn't you phone me? I'd have come'. I was sort of amazed – but that is the kind of person he is and it would have been awful you know – like school. 'My dad's coming!' I'm glad I didn't tell him.

It's really dad's ways which annoy me – most of the time he's right in his views but it's just the way he says it which annoys. Afterwards my mum would explain it to me and I know he is right but it stings at the time. I never tell him – it's just his way – just the way he is. [Laughs] I love him. [Very softly]

The younger ones in the family come to me if they want me to approach dad – I don't know why. It depends on if I'm in a good mood then I'll put it properly. Sometimes they don't like to ask dad something themselves.

Dad and I often start off thinking the opposite of each other and it's often after a couple of weeks that I might come round to seeing it his way or he may come around to my way. Some of the things which really annoy him are my answering him back – but now if I don't answer back, that annoys him too because I'm not saying anything. He can't stand me being rude to my mum or if we complain about what we are eating because then he goes into a long history of people who haven't got anything to eat and how fortunate we are and that sort of thing and how other Indian people don't have what we have.

Once he got violent. I remember we were in the garden and I

had the radio on and it was a small one and Eric and I were having a row over it and dad brought a hammer and smashed it to pieces. I couldn't believe it because it was a birthday present. It was only small and not expensive but he got so annoyed. He just didn't say anything else you know – I'd never seen him like that before. It was awful and I was trying to piece it together. [Laughs] He didn't kiss me for days after that.

Eric

Eric started school over here and then went to the junior school in Delhi because of his asthma and he had to learn a whole different language and writing it and as a result his studies over here went a bit haywire. He's in the 'B' stream and we have all been in 'A' streams but his reports are very good and he comes third in his whole class.

Dad puts a lot of pressure on Eric to study and sometimes Eric – if he's feeling industrious – will go upstairs and study and at other times kick the ground and just wander off. Then mum interferes and takes Eric's side mostly and says 'Don't keep on at him. He's doing alright' which gives him a bit more confidence. He's really a very brainy boy but with this moving about it's been difficult for him.

When he was in India we heard he used to be rebellious and didn't feel his grandparents had the right to boss him and he was so independent.

Dad can be very awkward at times but at other times he and Eric get on wonderfully – out in the garden mucking about – or downstairs wrestling and they might only have been arguing that morning.

Eric is just like my dad – at any rate mum always says he is. They are both very stubborn and once they think something is right – that's it.

We get on quite well – Eric and I – he does tell me things and sometimes we talk quite sensibly – at other times we have a row and he says I'm bossy and that sort of thing. We can talk on the same level to each other.

My younger brother and sisters

The younger children in the family are like my mum – they always do everything right and you know, they are the sunshine sort of thing, but if they are annoyed they have got bad tempers. The other three children are a bit calm and very considerate. Pat is twelve now and she's the one that goes to church. Eric used to go to Sunday school until he was about nine but he doesn't go anymore and nor do I. My parents would like us to go but they never actually press the point. They think Eric and I are old enough to know whether we want to go or not.

Pat is very tidy and is a very gentle person. The two younger ones Keith and Russell, are quite attached to me and I spoil them quite a bit. If they are spoiled it's mainly my fault.

About myself

Without thinking too hard, how do you see yourself?:   I think of myself as being very selfish and stubborn. I never seem to think other people might want the things I want. It only occurs to me afterwards never at the time. I can also be a bit cutting and sarcastic and I like to get my own way. I've also got a bad temper.

I make friends quickly enough and can talk to people easily but I'm also a good listener.

It sounds as if I've a big head if I say anything nice. I'm hopeless. [Whispers] If I think of myself I only think of the wrong things about myself. If I sit down and analyse myself I feel – oh I'm selfish and I think about it but I never think – well, this makes up for it.

I can't think of anyone who dislikes me. I get on with everyone at work. When Eric and I are angry with each other he would see me as selfish and spoilt – that's his favourite phrase. 'You get everything and I don't – that's his argument.

I'm hasty and can say a lot of rotten things and afterwards feel sorry. I really hate to unpack myself like this actually you know.

I think a good life requires plenty of money. You can't do anything without money and I'd like to have a lot. I spend a lot so I'd like a lot so I can help my family. That's the most important thing to me.

I can be quite violent and break things – or throw things like a book or something – or just bang a door – it makes me feel good and I think to myself how childish it was – afterwards. [Laughs] I feel silly afterwards. It bothers me to fight with anyone and I think about it afterwards and think 'Well if I could have said this then, he'd have said that and we wouldn't have had a row'.

I was very unhappy when I moved schools – from junior to

secondary high school. I used to cry a lot because of leaving friends whom I had known well – I wanted someone I could be close to. I used to wish that I'd never had to move from the old school. When we left Birmingham I also cried at leaving – we'd been happy there and I cried for the things I was leaving behind.

I'm frightened of the dark – and rough people frighten me a bit as well – just ordinary rough people at school – physically rough people. And spirits frighten me as well. I don't know why this happens. I watched something on television once about a man who looked in a mirror and saw his own reflection and it wasn't his own but a spirit. And I wouldn't look in a mirror, I was so frightened.

I think, you know, it's better to be religious, then I wouldn't feel this sort of emptiness. I always feel I'm somehow in a corner with horrible things around me and closed in. Pat is very religious and she says I ought to pray. And so I set about praying but never sort of say anything. I like to feel secure all the way – so that I can believe in something and it won't let me down. Spiritualism really frightens me and I don't read about it because it makes it work. One of the dreams I had was about the house being all dark and these awful things around me and I'm frightened of the dark. Things which just move on their own. [Laughs]

I went once to a Billy Graham convention when I was in third year at secondary high school and I thought I felt something but it really was only the atmosphere with everyone around me saying 'This is it' and Billy Graham talking and the music and the prayers and everything. And when I came home next morning I didn't feel a thing. I can't explain what I'd like to feel, but I'd like to feel something. It's because I can't feel religious that I'm fond of spirits and that sort of thing. I haven't worked it out yet and it bothers me. I like to work things out and I try to forget it but the more I try and forget something the more I'm bound to think about it. None of my friends are involved in things like spiritualism.

Another thing which frightens me. Once I was on a bus and a man had a heart attack and nobody helped him or got up – no one moved. I can't really say it was their fault because I didn't move either. I was so frightened – I don't know why I was so frightened because the sensible thing was to get up and do something and in the end one lady got up and called out and everything was alright. But I remember I got off the bus and ran – I was about ten. I can't bear to see people in pain – or in that sort of condition – fainting or feeling helpless – I can't bear it – I feel the same thing.

I feel really angry when somebody doesn't listen to what I'm saying – when they don't attend – when I'm talking and they've sort of got their backs to me. I get angry also for being blamed for something I've not had anything to do with – for being judged.

HARBANS (ERIC) SINGH: HIS STORY

I remember when I was little we used to live in a big house in Birmingham and my dad used to keep chickens. We had a big garden and we used to play with the chickens. My dad used to work in a factory and Vera went to school and I used to be very jealous that I couldn't go with her.

Our house was divided in two. It was our house but we had an English family who were lodgers and they were our very good friends. They used to keep us company and they had two little daughters about my age. I was about two years old then. They used to keep mum company too because my dad used to work on night shifts sometimes and they didn't have a television so they sometimes used to come up and share ours.

I was the only son at that time and I was a little spoilt baby then. You know I used to get everything I wanted. Vera used to be sent to bed early and mum used to keep me up sometimes. She would put Vera upstairs because she was bigger and used to go to school. Vera was jealous of me and felt why should I stay up late?

Dad spoilt me and so did mum but mum would let me cry sometimes in my pram but dad used to get angry with her and say 'Why should he cry?' and he would pick me up. But mum used to have to wash up and didn't have the time to pick me up, you know.

Dad used to bring me quite a lot of toys. I had an electric train and a rocking horse and a rifle and quite a lot of other things. I think it was because I was the only son at that moment, you see. And then my little sister Pat was born. She's a year and nine months younger than me and I remember I used to hide her milk bottle in the piano because I was very jealous of her.

I was really spoilt then. Vera used to get all the hidings. If I had done things she used to get told off. I wasn't told off much then – but of course I am now. Well, I used to be jealous of Vera and I remember that one day she got her hair done at the barber's and I got hold of a plank of wood and put it across her head [laughs] because I was jealous, you know. Why should she have her hair done and why shouldn't I have it done also? I used to get jealous a lot about all sorts of things. If she used to have some sweets, she used to share them with me. I used to do that with her also but if she had, say, a ring or a girl's ring, I wanted it too. When we went to the same shop and she took some bangles home I wanted some bangles also. I wanted everything that she wanted. I also took her dolls away from her and all that and felt why should she have dolls and why should she go to school and not me? One day she took me to school but I can't remember much about it.

My mum had a blue box and we used to take money out of it sometimes. And one day when I was quite small I took about two shillings out which used to be quite a lot of money in those days. I went to get a lollipop and I gave the man the money and he gave me what I wanted and he then said he would keep the change and give it to my mum. [Laughs] You know he thought I might lose it and he told mum about it and mum put the box in a higher place and then I used to climb all over the place and try and take it. They just took it away somewhere else and didn't let me see it. They didn't give me a good hiding. I was really spoilt.

Living with the English in Birmingham

There was a very old woman who lived next door – an English woman called Susie and she used to have an apple tree and used to give us apples. All the neighbourhood then started calling me Eric instead of Harbans. My parents didn't mind because they wanted everybody's advice and it was easier to call me Eric. I also remember at that time that somebody living near us had a parrot called Polly and the parrot used to get jealous of the dogs and used to say all sorts of things about the dogs. He was very talkative.

I only remember a little about our next-door neighbours but I do remember the shopkeeper who was only a few yards from our house. He was English. We were the only Indian family living round there. I didn't bother about things like that then because I didn't know if there was any other place. I thought this was the only place and these were the only children.

We talked English as well as our own language. I think I

learned both languages at the same time. Because of our next-door neighbours we used to talk English, so that when I went to school I was accepted into the same class as English children.

Eric comes to the front door and greets Sylvia Hutchinson with a broad smile. The dark late afternoon winter chill contrasts with the warm and brightly lit interior, and on his return from school Eric's formal school uniform – dark blazer, black tie and well-pressed trousers – now have a more casual and comfortably lived-in air. She follows him upstairs to the blue and pink bedroom which his sisters share, his slightly chubby figure moving with speed and confidence. They sit facing each other on two chairs. He is a very good-looking boy of fourteen, at the beginning of his adolescence and neither his height nor the pitch of his voice have yet attained the adult potential which will be his within the next few years. Rather formal to begin with, halting and somewhat nervous, as the interviews progress Eric's eyes brighten and he loosens up considerably but still retains a certain awkwardness and formality in his bearing towards Sylvia. It is an intense and intelligent face which she sees, and as he talks of his father's taumatic assault his face reveals his involvement and concern.

When we lived in Birmingham, one day my dad went to get my sister's birthday cake. Dad spoke English well and the Indian people used to get jealous – saying why should he speak English and why shouldn't they? Because if Indians got involved with the police, the police used to ring my dad up and say 'Can you interpret for us?' and so a lot of people got jealous about this. Well, this day some Indian men said my dad should come and have a drink with them and he said 'No, because it's my daughter's birthday and I want to celebrate', and there were three of them and they attacked him very brutally and somebody ran for·the police and they were caught. And you know my dad's got a scar right across his ear and face from what they did to him. They were very jealous people.

We knew nothing about this and then a police-van came and the policeman informed us and my mum was shocked and it was Vera's birthday and none of us ate. Mum started crying. I wouldn't eat my dinner and Vera was upset. My dad stayed about three months in hospital because of these operations. He was very badly hurt and you know they had thrown a brick at his head and it had also hurt his head and gone into his brain.

There were three of them and they were quite big men. If there had been some witnesses they would have got at least five years' imprisonment but unfortunately there were no witnesses.

In those days my dad used to trust a lot of friends. But from that time he says 'Well, I will trust myself now. A lot of friends can betray you.' Before that, you know, my dad used to have a very nice face and good ears but now there's a scar across his face and ear.

We left Birmingham when I was about four and came to London where my dad got a job with an airways company. He thought he could get a better job down here because, you know, he's intelligent with his knowledge of Mathematics and English. And he got a job at the airport with a company and there were no coloured people allowed into that place at that time. And they gave my dad a job because my uncle had a job there but they were restricted you know – with no coloureds working there except my uncle and then my dad.

A trip to India

My mum said 'Well, we're going to India while you look around for a house', and so my mother, Vera, Pat and I went to India for about three months while my dad was getting settled down with his new job and looking for a house.

It was quite strange being in India. When we got there my uncle was a Superintendent of Police and he and my aunt came to meet us and they took us home. I didn't know my grandmother and when we arrived she was very sick and I could not go and be next to her. I thought she was an old woman. I didn't know her at all and I was very scared of her. I was scared that she might take me away and never give me back to my mum. When she was better, my little sister went to her straight away and put her arms out to her, but I didn't just go to her – I was scared of her. She was sick, you know, and I forget why I didn't go to her but I stayed with my mum because I knew her and couldn't go to anybody else. If anybody came whom I didn't know, I didn't go to them.

So I stayed a lot of the time with my aunt who didn't have a son because their first son had died of whooping cough. They always liked boys so they used to take me out and everybody used to think I was their son and they used to show me off. I used to go on my uncle's scooter and used to sit at the back. We used to go to a lot of places – old villages where my dad was born and mum showed me quite a lot of places. We stayed about a month with my uncle and aunt and then came back to Delhi to my grandad's place.

The weather was hot and it did look funny to see all sorts of coloured people and not to see white people. And the food was different. We used to have hot food – with lots of curry. My mum had brought me up on baby food and at first I didn't like the curry much but we got used to it.

Our home in London
We had quite a lot of fun and then when we came back to England our dad was there and, you know, we went to our new house straight away. We took a taxi and came here but because dad was at work he wasn't with us. We didn't have a key to the house so we knocked at our next-door neighbour's door and we first of all had to borrow money for the taxi because we only had Indian money, and then when we had given it to the taxi driver the question was how were we going to get into the house? Our next-door neighbours took us round the back and I had to get through the toilet window! It was funny you know but I got through and opened the door and got in. It was very strange as there was no furniture or anything. All our funiture was still in Birmingham and my dad had just finished putting in the electric light fittings and he had been working on the house. There were beds there. And straight away when I got home I had some corn flakes because it was such a long time since I had had any. We always want English food when we come home which is strange, isn't it? In India, my grandfather had bought corn flakes but they weren't the same.

Then dad came and welcomed us and we all liked it because now we knew it was our house and we could do what we wanted with it. An uncle and aunt were staying in London too and they brought presents for both Vera and Pat. I think they forgot about me and I was just looking and thinking 'Where's mine?' and then my mum told me to forgive my aunt because she forgot about me. I got very jealous. Well, she did bring me some old statue or something but I didn't want to play with it then.

My uncle and aunt came to stay with us because they didn't have a house of their own and stayed about two years. We could all fit in – there was enough room. I used to sleep with my dad because I was used to sleeping with him. When I was little we got used to it. You know he likes me. He used to love me and you know I used to sleep with him more than my mum you know. We all used to get on very well. There was no difficulty.

My little brother Russell still sleeps with dad sometimes. It's not really an Indian custom but you know a lot of people sleep with their dads when they're small.

My asthma trouble

When I was about two I started having asthma trouble – when we still lived in Birmingham and it wouldn't go away and we went to all sorts of doctors. I started school here and was very good at sums and everything – very good indeed. When I first arrived my teacher checked my English and she had on an orange jumper and she asked me what colour it was. I said 'Yellow'. 'Well', she said 'At least you know your colours!' But it was orange you know! She then asked me my name and I told her and she looked at my passport and saw it was British so she said they would accept me.

On my first day I sat next to a boy also called Eric. He was English and was looking at me and I was looking at him. He works in a shop now and goes to night school and I still see him there. Everybody else in the class was English but I felt quite at home. There was nobody like me, but they were very talkative and didn't show that they cared and so I didn't think about it.

I wasn't frightened because if I didn't understand what the teacher said I could say out loud 'I don't understand' but I understood what the teacher said. Then at playtime I went to Vera who was in the Juniors' at that time and I started crying that I didn't like people – I don't know why. [Coughs] I was very – you know – I had my asthma and had a very bad cough that day. And at lunch-time the school house-keeper said 'Well, you've got a bad cough alright and it would have been much wiser if you had stayed at home,' and I was coughing very badly and I went home for lunch and I stayed at home. And I still remember the drink I had. My dad said 'Give him what he wants,' and I had some Lucozade with ginger beer. The doctor came to our house and examined me and said I couldn't go to school for three weeks because I might spread the cough. It was like whooping cough it was so bad. I went back to school but in the first year I was away almost half the year because of my asthma. And then I started my second year and that year and the next I was really learning English very well and could read all the books and everything and was very good at it and better than the English boys sometimes.

But then my asthma started suddenly again – I had it most of the time but it got bad and I had to go into hospital – Great Ormond Street Hospital in London. It was that bad and they thought they could do something. I was there nearly three weeks and I didn't know anybody there and my mum and dad used to come and visit me. It was quite far for them to come but they came every day. My mum was at that time expecting Keith, so I was about six, I think. And it was quite hard for her to travel in trains you know. But I was lucky because my dad used to come to see me at 5 o'clock and I had to go to bed at 7 o'clock.

I was in hospital twice with my asthma – the next time I went to a hospital nearer my home.

On being sent to India
The doctors advised that I should go to another country because the weather here – being cold – was not good for me. So they decided to send me to India to my grandad's and I was seven years old and travelled on my own to stay with my grandparents.

I stayed there but I missed my mum and my dad very much because I wasn't used to staying away from mum.

I felt very bad. I was crying all the time you know. I cried at the airport but I couldn't really say anything because if I said 'I don't want to go', it was already too late because the seat had been booked. they could have cancelled it but I knew it was for my benefit. I wished I could be with my mum and dad but I knew I had trouble and had to get rid of my asthma.

The first time I went out to India I was flying alone and there was a man on the plane who was married to an English woman and they were my friends all the way. But when we landed at Beirut there was something wrong with the engine and we had to stay there. We were there several days because they had to fix the aircraft and there wasn't another one coming. The stewardess came up to me and told me that there was something wrong with the aircraft and I thought she was joking and I didn't want to stay in Beirut because I was very frightened. When I got off the aeroplane I was very worried about my suitcase and hoped that it would not get lost. And even if I had it with me

I kept on feeling I had to check my suitcase and if it got lost I'd have nothing to wear.

We travelled about Beirut looking at things – their old buildings and the mountains and everything was marvellous and if I was my present age I would enjoy it. But I was only seven and was really worried. We stayed there three days and I had to share a room with an Indian woman. I had a really bad name for her. It was a splendid room with a beautiful bed, a sofa, television, quite a giant of a room! She had two little kids with her and she made us all sleep on the floor with her – she was a wicked woman but I didn't really understand. If I was my age now, I'd go and put the television on and sit on a sofa and do what I wanted until 11 o'clock. But we all slept on the floor and I don't really remember much about it.

Life with my grandparents in India

And finally we got to India and my grandad was there to greet me. I lived with my grandmother and my grandfather and two of my cousins – both girls – who were at school. Their parents – my uncle and aunt – lived outside Delhi with their youngest child.

I didn't get asthma there. But I didn't really like it you know. The heat turned my colour also because my colour is quite white and like my dad's, but when I went there the sun turned me all brown because of the heat and when I came back here I was quite dark compared to my mum and dad.

When I was there my grandad used to write to my parents. If my dad sent a letter I always treasured it you know. And my mum came to see me after a while because she missed me very much.

I got on quite well with my grandparents but I was sad to leave my mother. My grandad understood me and we got on very well. If I wanted something he would buy it for me. He understood me best because he was well-educated, knew quite a lot of languages, and he could understand much faster and get the idea of things much better than my grandmother did.

But I was mostly unhappy living there with nobody of my own – no brothers and sisters and I could only visit my parents once a year and that was quite a lot of time to wait.

My grandad used to go out and work in the office and my grandmother used to go out and visit her friends but she was mostly in the house and I spent most of the time with her, apart from my cousins. It was quite boring staying with her. I liked her but I would rather stay with her now because I'm old enough now to look after myself but then I was a bit too young and so I didn't enjoy it. Now I would enjoy it very much and I wouldn't miss my mother and father because I am now capable of writing letters and would, you know. I was too young then but would like to go now on my own or with Vera. Pat is always sick in an aeroplane so she can't take it.

My grandmother was different from my mum. She was not as strict as my mum but then my mum should be, shouldn't she? It's different if you are with your mother and father and they tell you off, because then you understand them much better but if it's with somebody else, you feel different and I wouldn't listen to them. It's not that they felt I wasn't their son, but they knew in a way that if they told me off they might hurt me more. But they didn't tell me off because I never used to do anything. Maybe I did but I must have forgotten.

I went to school in India and my languages got very mixed up because I had to learn Hindi over there because I only knew how to count in English when I arrived. It was very hard for me there and then when I later returned here I had nearly forgotten all my English and had to learn English once again. I went to school with my two cousins – two girls who lived with my grandparents also. It was alright. I used to get on very well but I did miss my mother and father and when any of my relatives went to England, you know, I always wished I could go with them.

The ways of living were different. We didn't have the same beds as we have here because it's too hot a climate and the beds were made of rope and wood and we used to sleep outside where there were no roofs like these – and there were different ways of cooking.

We used to fight quite a lot, my cousins and I. And my elder cousin used to fight with her sister – of course, you can't blame her for that. They were both older than me and one used to hit me and run away and then I would come back and hit her. It was to do with little petty things – like she might nip my stool. But I used to get angry because they did not share things with me so I felt if they didn't then why should I share with them? So I often used to eat on my own.

When I first went to India, Vera gave me quite a lot of pencils and blotting paper, inks and nibs. Well, they used to nip these things from me sometimes. I used to trust them and they used to take them. Well I don't blame them you know, because they thought 'Well he has so many, he won't mind a little one'. But I did mind, you see. It's my nature and I still mind if somebody takes something from me. If they had asked me first I would still say 'No' – that's why they didn't ask. They used to give me nothing but they had nothing to give. It was my nature you know, not to want to give, but of course I have changed, because as you get older you start to change your habits. They were quite clever and would understand things very quickly. They used to help me with my education and with my homework.

Once my mother came to visit me with my little brother Keith and my cousins used to like Keith much better than they liked me. He was just an infant so they used to take him out and say this was their cousin from England and because he was from a foreign country he was much admired and I felt jealous but I also went out with them and also got a turn at holding him. We got on well when Keith came.

I was quite happy when mum came but when they were going, that was the unhappy part. I wanted to go myself but I couldn't. I wanted to leave, you know, but there was the difficulty of my asthma so I had to stay with my grandparents and they didn't mind keeping me.

Home! And return to India

After about a year my mother and father decided I was to come home. My dad said to my grandad 'I want him sent back to me,' and he sent a ticket for me, you know 'Come back'. But when I came here, on my first night, I got a very bad attack of asthma. Straight away I got it the first night here and my mum was very upset you know. The weather here is really bad and my dad was planning to send me back again that same night. They said the weather does not agree with me and the doctor came and he agreed with them. You know, he's been our doctor for more than twelve years now and he told them that if they sent me back again I'd be alright. So dad planned it and I went back to India – back again. You know I didn't really . . . I felt very . . . you know, when I came back home I thought they would keep me. I was so happy about it and it was good to leave India but you know they treated me as well as any grandparents could. Everything was alright in India and I could speak my own language. It was not really difficult, not even the money – but I wanted to stay with my parents and Vera and everybody. I wanted to stay with them and then I had to go back to India the second time.

I cried, you know. I told my mother that I don't want to go but she said it couldn't be helped and that if I could get rid of the asthma it would be good for everybody and they wouldn't have to stay up with it all the night. I got the impression that she was saying it for my own good.

Well, I went there the second time and my mum came to visit me with Keith once more. It was a long time since I'd seen him but I still missed him and he didn't know I was his brother because Vera and Pat were always at home with him. But then they woke me in the early morning and I was looking out of the window and crying to myself because I wanted to go home with them – but you know, my mum went back and then they sent me a ticket. And again I returned to India and finally the fourth time when I got back to England I said 'I don't want to go any more' and my mum said 'No, we're not going to send you any more. Because we miss you too much.' I was quite strong then. And I stayed here and started school here once more. I don't get asthma very often now you know.

And home for good!
I had been away in India about two and a half years, from about the age of seven to over nine. And I started school again – back to the same school. I was put in the second year and it was hard to try and understand English. But they didn't put me in the top class but in the secondary bunch – the 'B's. I had got English mixed up with the Indian languages. It was quite hard.

School in London
When I went back to the school they did not recognise me and then I told them who I was and then they all mobbed me you know – all in one go. There was a West Indian boy who lived over there across the bridge and I knew him and I told him 'I know you and that girl'. He said 'How do you know me?' And I said 'It's because you used to be in Miss Weston's class,' and I reminded them.

English, Indian and West Indian boys
At that time there weren't any 'immigrants' at school. Nobody

used the word immigrant and we didn't even know what the word meant. And then there were no prejudiced people at school, not like now when they all fight.

But you know, my dad says 'Don't fight'. My dad says if you go to school you go to learn something there, you don't go to fight you know. If you want to fight then you must pick your own time because otherwise you'll get the cane from the headmaster. 'And if you *do* get the cane, I'll give you double punishment,' he said. He means what he's saying because I do go to school to study and not to fight. You know I try to keep out of trouble all the time.

I'm in my third year now and will be doing O-levels next year. A lot of big boys pick on me but I don't take any notice. They are Jamaicans and English. If you start taking notice then there's trouble.

In my class there are about eight English boys, four Indians and one West Indian. There's a group of English boys who stick together and the Indians stick together also. If I don't say anything then they haven't got the right to say something to me. But if I go in there calling them names and want to pick a fight, then they have got a reason for doing me in. I've got a few English friends but they don't stick with you – they call you names and so why talk to them? That's what I think, you know, and a lot of Indian boys don't talk to them. They've got a group of their own and they're always fighting. I try and keep out of trouble. I would always go away if English or West Indian boys started with me.

I used to have friends among the English boys but, you know, once they start to call me names, then I don't want to know. When new boys come to the school these English boys gather around him and they say 'You've got the choice of either fighting with the Indians or fighting with us'. This is what they say to the West Indians.

If I walk home with this Jamaican boy in my class, they start to fight with him and when Indians see me with that boy, they say 'Well, he's thick with him'. They want to cause fights and they would probably pick a fight with me. So I said to myself 'Nice – you know!'

And if I am with an English boy then when other English boys appear that English boy would call me names. And if we meet Indian boys, the English boy would call the Indians bad names.

You know, there used to be quite a lot of friends amongst us all but now, nobody wants to know anybody.

The Indians are small, and the English and the West Indians are big and they pick on us. They are very prejudiced against Indian boys. I mean, we've got every right to say that we've had enough because I didn't say a thing to them. So I just don't want to know anyone because they call you names and if you still want to be a friend of theirs, then you are stupid. So I just don't want to know any one and I get on with my work. I don't say anything to anybody and they don't say anything to me – that's my opinion of how it is.

Other Indian boys feel the same as me.

A West Indian boy came to our school from another school and he carries a knife with him – that big – and if you go and tell the teacher, he might knock you off or something. If you shut your mouth and keep quiet, you're alright.

Of course he walks with a knife because he wants to act big – but I doubt whether he would use it because if he did, he would be charged with murder. Even if he threatened somebody, we could get the police – could phone the police up and so the police would pick him up.

If an English boy came and hit an Indian boy, then the Indian boy has every right to hit him back.

You know it's very bad at school – little boys smoke – and they stick those nudes right up in our class. The English boys don't care about the school. They enjoy themselves, have their fights and muck about and play and they don't care about bashing you up or anything.

Indian boys pay more attention to their work than the English. English boys could take it seriously if they wanted to but they just can't be bothered. They chat most of the time. If they paid more attention to their work they could be much better than they are, but now at the moment, nobody pays attention and they're keeping us behind in class. In English now, everybody keeps on disturbing us and we don't get on with our lessons.

I'm in 'B' class because of all the time I spent in India. I would rather leave my class because I can't really learn anything in this class. They're so ignorant and they just don't care. Half the time we don't do anything because of their nonsense. Even our English teacher gets mad especially with one English boy who makes a lot of noise and is babyish and behaves stupidly. The teacher doesn't like that. This boy doesn't take things seriously and doesn't care what he is going to be nor what he is going to do. So we don't really get a whole lesson because the teacher spends half the time telling him off.

He upsets our lessons and today he kept bullying me with my work. He bullies everybody but mostly me because he knows I'll say nothing to him. He wouldn't bully an English boy. It's unpleasant because our class was alright before but now it's not nice. It's unpleasant and you don't want to even work any more.

But my teacher says I'm working very well and I'm doing alright at the moment. I got an 'A' in Chemistry last year and an 'A' in Physics and also in Maths, and I got a 'B' in English. I'm planning to take Physics, Maths, and English at O-level and perhaps become a radio mechanic or a television mechanic.

I'd like to go to Germany. I've been doing a very big project at school on the river Rhine, I've also done France – the Riviera, Brittany, the Bay of Biscay and Paris – Paris Bois and everything like that. We're also learning about the coloured people and the French. You know, how they came to Europe and how Europeans came to Africa and took parts of Africa.

I'm very good at copying – map drawing and things like that. And I got an 'A' this time for my project. You know the more practice you get, the better it is. So that when it comes to getting a job, it will be good.

The English boys are so dumb, you know. They don't know anything about politics and if you asked them they would confuse Scotland with Switzerland. All they really care about is fighting, you know. Because it's their country they can get a job anywhere. But if an Indian who knows a hundred times more than an English person wanted the same job, they'd still pick the Englishman because of his colour.

All the English boys do is go to school, have a few fights and go home, have their tea and play football.

What I want to become
I have to study now because I'm aiming to be something and I must be something. My dad says if you want something then you must go after that thing and it isn't easy to aim for things but you must try as hard as you can. I want to be a radio mechanic and it's quite a hard subject but my dad said that if I did well he might send me to university or to college. So I hope I can do that.

If my dad says that I should become, say, a car mechanic, then I'll follow my dad's orders because he knows better than I and he's more in the trade than I am. You know my grandad advised my uncle and gave him good advice and I might need something similar.

You see, the English boys have got nobody to guide them like my dad guides me. He says 'If you get an 'A', son, then 'A' stands for something big'. He says, 'I don't want you to stick around school unless you study,' and I do what he says.

If you want to be something, you've got to go through all the hard things, you know. It's not easy come and easy go. My dad didn't have any mother or father and he wanted to be a lawyer but then the war came and he had to go to the war. But I've got my mother and father to guide me now and I'm very lucky, you know. Anybody would be. Whatever they say is good for me, that's what I also think.

But the English – not meaning you of course – nothing like that – all they want to do is poke around and if they can make a pound, they like that. They may work in a shop and get about five pounds and they think it's alright because they can get food and other things. But when they grow up and have to raise a family, they have become nothing. Now is the time to start the future. My dad says that if you take an ignoble trade like sweeping the roads, in a few years' time they will invent a machine that will do it and one must think of things like that. If they can land on the moon they can do a lot of things and it's best to go into the technical line. My dad's got a technical trade and he thinks that's what I should do too and I like the idea.

The teachers at school

The teachers at school are very fair. They've got every right to get angry with boys who don't behave but it's not done unfairly. If fights start, then the teachers don't do anything about it. They let it go on because of 'He started! He started!'.

Sometimes a particular teacher is very prejudiced. The other day in Chemistry one of the English boys started to whistle out of the corner of his mouth so you couldn't see who it was. She looked up and said 'Well, if I wanted to buy a cheap Indian pariah, I wouldn't buy one'. She had a nice way of saying it – you know – insulting us you know. We all got a very good picture of what she meant. You know, she didn't realise how prejudiced against Indians she was being. She was just taking us when our own teacher was away.

Last year during History the teacher asked an Indian girl a question and she wouldn't speak up and the teacher said something which meant all the Indian people. She said 'Well, if you don't know anything, you should stay in your own country.' Well, I mean to say if the British came and ruled in our country we can't say anything to them. I mean we could if we wanted to, but we didn't want to make trouble. In my grandfather's time all these British came and took everything they saw. I don't mean you – I'm not saying anything against you – but they came and now they have the right cheek to say we shouldn't come to this country. She should really look at the whole problem.

Race prejudice in this country

I like this country because it's very good educationally. It's better than India I think and you get every sort of facility here. But as soon as I grow big – about nineteen, I'm not going to care about this country. I'm going to Canada and will settle down there. That's what I'm aiming at because my dad says that when this country goes into the Common Market, it will be really bad for everybody. And it's become so prejudiced against Indians. I mean they take an English boy who doesn't know anything and give him a job and leave the Indian boy who's passed all his A-levels. So that's what my dad says and I feel it's true and this is what is happening in this country.

Kenyan Indians

The reason why there's more prejudice now is because of all the Indian people coming in from Kenya and you know there aren't any tags on people to say where they were born, whether in this country or Kenya, and the English think we're the same as others. You can't prove it unless you go up to them and say 'Oh yes, I was born in England so you're the same as me and it's just a colour difference'. There's such a lot of prejudice against us.

When all the Kenyans came from Africa, that's when the English started boiling up and felt 'Why should they come to this country?'. That's when the prejudice started and that's when the word started being used you know. That's when Enoch Powell really boiled up and that's when it started. If they had been kind it would have been alright you know. I like you and you like me. But as soon as the Kenyans came, well, they're not either English or Indian. They're mixed and they've made trouble for everybody.

If I came from Kenya I wouldn't like to be sent back to India without a job for my father. I really shouldn't speak up for them but in my opinion the British should check on them. There are too many you see, and they will spill over anyway.

In Kenya, if they don't want the Indians to stay in their country – well, why should they? You know every country has got its own right to decide this. For instance Egypt would not want Americans to stay there – they've got their own country so why shouldn't they get out? So Kenya has the right to get them out but not in one year because if it's all in a minute – then as you know, the headlines were saying 'They're coming – coming – coming'. And then some English said they were very against this and they should stay in their own country. But you can't really say where they should go to because there are no other countries. They might not like India. The Indian government might not accept them. They speak English in Africa and they will be able to speak the same language here, you know, so everything might be alright for them here. I mean if they went to Belgium to make a living they would have to learn the language and also in Holland and this would be very difficult. But why should they come into our country? They wanted to go to Kenya in the first place so they should stay there. So it's really a problem now. But the thing is, it's good for us if we get out of the country first before they settle down here. Our plan is to go to Canada for a start and to get a job.

Meanwhile the English are selling their houses to the Kenyans at a big profit because the Kenyans want to settle down straight away. So it's really their own fault – the fault of the English who sell their houses – because if they didn't sell their houses, they wouldn't be in this area now. And if they had no houses they would have to go back.

Things are getting worse at our school between English and Indians because of these Kenyans. The English think because they are coming into this country, they can blame us for it. There didn't used to be any fights in this school before these Kenyans came – but it's all different now.

Now all these Kenyans have come we have to move out. We feel bad about this you know, but we can't do anything about this Kenyan business because now all the British people are prejudiced against us. They can't tell the difference between us and them – that's the trouble. You must have seen it on television – so much publicity – so I really have to settle down in Canada with my sister. We want to go there.

I haven't any particular friends at school. I play with friends at school but I'm not really fond of them. They are not too close because I don't trust any of my friends. I had my fortune told this year by a man who works with my dad and he tells fortunes. He's a very rich man and he uses astrology and he said that I shouldn't trust my friends because they could betray me. Well it must be the truth as he is a very good friend of dad's. He told all of our fortunes. He's told the fortune of many famous people and predicted their future. He is also very charitable and believes in God.

With English friends, we might talk to one another or we might play with one another but we're not quite related. We are not close. There's no one close to me except my family.

Living in Athol

Athol has changed very much in the last years. There are more Indian shops here now and many more Indian people walking in the streets. On Saturday you go out shopping and there are hundreds of people in the streets. They walk anywhere, they bump into each other, they've got no manners to say 'Sorry' and this is true of everyone – English and Indians and West Indians. It's a shock. If you went back five years they would be saying 'Thank you' and when you go into a shop they would say 'Good morning' but now they don't want to say it to you. There are so many people here that everybody has forgotten their manners.

There are many more Indian than English shops now. And all about this street, there's a lot of mess everywhere. It used to be well cleaned and now instead of a few Indians living in this road, there are a few English and the rest Indians. A lot has changed in these four years.

There is no fighting in the streets. If people did that they would get into trouble with the police. But the English boys fight each other – the skinheads and the greasers. You know, the greasers wear German uniforms with lots of crosses and great big banners on their backs – jackets with a lot of tassles coming down. They stink, they say, because they have long hair and don't have to wash themselves. They drive motorbikes – sort of rocker-boys. But the rockers used to wear old flash cards but these are a German appendix.

The skinheads and the greasers fight and there are pictures of them in the papers here. The skinheads are running out of the park and the greasers are hitting them. Then the skinheads are beating the greasers out of the park and they are running and the skinheads are picking on them.

Skinheads, you know, have very 'crooky' hats and you only see a little bit of their hair and they're all bald and got great big rubber boots on and if they kicked somebody in the mouth, that would be a serious accident. You know, they would be able to take somebody's teeth out – the way they fight. They are clean and they've got nice clothes on and they drive motorbikes and they fight all around the seaside. They go and fight there. The skinheads have got these crew cuts and bovver boots. I haven't seen them – I've only heard about them.

I think they're stupid, you know. I mean, instead of going with the space age and everything, they are thinking about times past. They cause a lot of trouble – smash windows and fire soot all over cars and spoil their paint.

If they beat up people, then the police would take over. Normal people can't fight them – there are too many of them to fight off.

There was one Indian boy who used to be at our school and he was a bit of a skinhead. If they attacked Indians he would get up and bolt – he would not fight the Indians.

I don't think the streets around here are dangerous at night. I don't happen to go out at night – I expect it's a bit of a rough area, but I don't really know as I'm not out at night. When Vera comes home late, dad always picks her up by car so there would be no danger.

My dad

My father understands me quite a lot but he's got a hot temper. Sometimes when I ask my father something he might say 'No' at first but if I ask Vera she might be able to convince my father. But I feel in the end my dad would always tell me the right thing. If I'm in the wrong he would say so.

I go to my parents and talk to them if there is something I can't figure out for myself. I go to them for help.

I'm really more like my dad than like my mum because I also lose my temper sometimes. My father understands me quickly so I also understand others quickly. I don't like wasting time on something, which is also like my dad.

Actually I'm different from all the family – everybody in the family is something like mum or dad except me.

Vera and my dad understand about earning and politics and things. They know how a person has to work for his livelihood and they understand about those things.

My mum

She's a very nice mum. She's a Sikh and you know other mothers usually go to work and mum stays at home. It's important to a child's life because when other people's mothers go to work, in time the children grow up and also go to work and then they no longer care for their mothers and fathers.

A lot of Indian mothers work now in factories and all sort of places. I mean they're not educated so they can't get jobs in offices and have to work in factories. But our mother cares more about us than about other things. That's what I think.

My mum understands me and if I was worried about something I'd go to my mum because my mother wouldn't lose her temper that hard and I'm something like my mum too. I sometimes do something and she would agree with me you know.

At the moment our aunt is sharing the house with us and so she has my room and since dad is on night shift, Keith and I sleep in mum and dad's room. Mum has her own bed. And Keith and I have our own beds.

Vera

Sometimes if I want something Vera understands me better than anyone else and if she's in a good mood I'll ask her. She may say it's no use to approach my dad in which case I'll leave it. But sometimes she can convince my father.

We used to quarrel when we were young but we don't quarrel now. She's grown up and you must have respect for elders and I can fight with the young ones but not with the older ones. [Laughs] We get on well and talk to each other if we're in a good mood. When we talk to each other then Pat gets jealous and says we're leaving her out of everything and then a quarrel starts. Vera then tells her off.

My parents certainly treat me the same as Vera even though she is more educated than I am and she knows and understands more. I'm given the same rights in the family to speak and say what I think.

Vera is very like our granny you know – who is eighty now.

She's generous in a lot of things and she doesn't just tell you off, doesn't just natter about things. She's reasonable about things.

I love all my sisters and brothers.

Pat, Keith and Russell

Russell is spoiled now because he's the youngest. He's very shy and always quiet.

Keith and I are much the same, except for our ages. He plays as good a game of football as I do.

Pat is as shy as Russell and she's keen on her education. She is doing well at school and is now in the top class. We help one another. If I do something wrong to her, she tells me and we get on alright.

If I quarrel with any of my brothers and sisters, it's usually with Pat because she's older and she can understand so if I say something to her and she understands and I tell her how stupid she is or why doesn't she get lost – well, then she comes and hits me. The younger ones wouldn't fight me for anything.

Leisure time and hobbies

I like watching good programmes on television. During the school holidays I was watching *War and Peace* and also some historical films on Napoleon and Russia.

My dad belongs to a club to do with his airways company and sometimes we go there as a family. They have table tennis and colour television and a big football pitch and you can play there if you want to.

Sometimes dad, Vera and Keith and I may go to the cinema if there's anything on that's really good.

I go on my bike sometimes to do the shopping for my parents.

I'm really keen on photography and want to get a really good German camera. I also like making model planes and am keen on collecting stamps.

He has travelled a great deal in Europe because his father obtains concessions from his company. He has been to Switzerland and Greece and also re-visited India after he had permanently returned to England. He enjoys new experiences and the presents which they acquired there.

What I think about Indian and English family life and marriage

If an Indian couple have a quarrel – husband and wife – even if it was a bad fight they wouldn't divorce each other because once you have won a husband the woman must stay with him. We don't believe in divorce but the British do and if an English woman quarrelled badly with her husband then she might leave him and apply for a divorce.

In the whole of our family – my grandad, uncles and everybody, nobody has had a divorce.

If a man goes out at night and comes back, you know, very late and his wife stays up for him – well in the old days the wife couldn't say anything. But if you take an English woman, she would of course quarrel with her husband and say 'Why not me? Why can't I go out? Why should you just enjoy things?' and all that. But now women are so advanced – even Indian women – and they feel they have a right to stand with the men.

Indian people believe that once you're married, you must stay together.

Also Indian women wouldn't leave their children or run away like most English people do. I see them in films and I read in the newspaper about this French man married to an English woman and they had a baby girl. The man beat her up and she ran away and so he took the baby away to France. You know he had every right to do that if she left her baby alone and couldn't care less about it. Well the man has every right to keep the baby and although judges in France and England are considering the case, I think the man is right because he said that when she grows up he's going to tell the child that her mother left her but he kept her. I think that's as good a reason as any other. Once you're married you shouldn't leave your man unless he's done something to hurt you.

When you're an Indian girl you have to change all your nature, habits and everything when you are a wife.

Boys are not supposed to go out with girl friends among the Indians. But these Kenyans that have come in here, into this part of Athol, they use filthy language and you know, they don't look up to girls.

I haven't reached the stage yet when I want to get married. I'm not sure when that will be but I must get settled down first – get a job and everything. If you marry before you get a job then you can't really have a house.

Arranged marriages have changed and advanced. I mean, in the old days, marriages were arranged but now they discuss it and ask you what they think of their choice and if it's alright. If something goes wrong after that, well you've got your mother and father to blame because they made the wrong choice.

If you make your own choice, well then you have nobody to blame if it goes wrong.

Before I marry, I want to be something first – do something. I want to go to Canada and over there my mum's uncle lives. He's a very old man by now – he must be about a hundred and we've got many relatives there. That's one good thing about the Indian people. The family always thinks of you – it's like a big tree and then the new leaves fall and big branches cover them. That's what we think, you know, and there are always big roots which start from the grandparents and everything like that. So you know we believe in staying together not like the English people. We love our grandparents and uncles and aunties.

In our family boys and girls are treated the same. We get the same things which our sisters get. We all get the same. But different things are expected of people because the son of the family leads from his father and his father expects him to stay honourable and all those things.

I would want my son – if I had one – to do the same as my father wants me to do and my grandfather wanted his son to do and so on.

A son has more jobs than a daughter because he keeps the family name and must not drop the name down but always keep it high. Keep his head high and do a good job and everything.

I wouldn't set up on my own. I wouldn't leave my mother or father on their own. I'd stay with my mother and father even more than with my wife. If your mother and father have given you good care then you should give them the same. So when they grow old and if they can't fetch the water, so you go and fetch it for them. But the English way is not to care about their old parents. They don't even write letters to them you know. In two years' time, if they're dead, well, they're dead, but in our family if anyone dies we know and feel very bad about it.

If I bought a house I would keep them with me. When Vera marries of course, she has to do the same for her mother-in-law, as my wife would also serve my mother. That's what I think.

When I marry I think it will be to an educated woman who is handsome, and good and honourable. She mustn't spend too much money on clothes but should save up things for a house and car. Also I would like her not to leave her children and she shouldn't go off and do a job but stay at home.

My upbringing has been different to the English boys around here, because my mother and father care for me and so I've been looked after better than they have.

Their mothers and fathers wouldn't have given them the line of education which mine have. I am not as ignorant as they are and I'm better behaved. And if I wear school uniform, I wear it completely but they may have a school tie but not the rest of the school colours. Also they might speak to the teachers in an ill-mannered way but I respect the teachers.

I think that I feel very much like other Indian boys – many of us have come from the same sorts of homes. But the English are different.

If there's anything unreasonable I want to do, my parents would say so and then I would agree with them and say 'You're right'.

Indian mothers didn't used to work but it's only since these Kenyan Indians started coming because they wanted jobs to obtain mortgages so both man and wife started working in order to get a house. It's a bad influence on the children. I suppose they think that their mother doesn't love them because she loves money more, and instead of her giving them a good hot meal, they just have to have bread and butter.

I think it's good that Indian girls are not allowed to go out with boy friends. I mean anything can happen. You know what I mean? And then she can't marry for all her life and her life is all the way bad. Then she has to live with it. But these English girls, they don't care. They walk around with their boy friends and everything. I think this is bad because a man would not want to marry her and would say she could marry one of her boy friends but of course they won't care about her because they're just enjoying themselves. So that's what I think. The Indian girl should not be allowed to do that and she should wait for her husband then he can take care of her only. And it's the same with the husband. So both have to keep away from the opposite sex until marriage.

Canada or India?
I would prefer to go to Canada rather than settle in India. There are more things to see there and these Western countries are much more modern. India really has only started to come out now – mostly it's been in the dark.

But there's quite a lot of money in India too for skilled people and in politics and all those things.

If Vera goes to Canada, then I could go there and you know, slowly all the family could come over and settle there.

Self-description

Without thinking too hard, how do you see yourself?:   I want to be something . . . I don't want too many friends. I like to keep to myself.

I like travelling in my dad's car and I like going to foreign countries. I want to see more of Europe.

You couldn't say I was kind.

I don't like to go in for big fights.

I like to play football and if I like a subject and can do it well, then that makes me happy.

What makes me unhappy? If somebody didn't take me away with them – if they went on holiday and I didn't go, that would make me unhappy. Also if I didn't get the right share of everything.

And if I was learning something and couldn't do it – that would make me very unhappy.

And I get angry if I don't get my own way, or if someone breaks something of mine.

Chapter 6

INTRODUCING THE IDENTITY ANALYSES

The life histories reveal differences between the twelve subjects, highlighting how each has come to develop distinctive attitudes and feelings towards people of other races. In the next three chapters, detailed identity analyses of all the subjects will be presented, focussed primarily on two fundamental questions: first, what important issues bear on the identity development of each subject? and secondly, what relationship, if any, might there be between identity conflicts on the one hand, and attitudes towards racial groups on the other?

Conceptual tools for the analysis of life history material have been slow to emerge and as a result there have been few longitudinal studies on men and women as they grow into middle age and even fewer which show how racial, cultural and social class contexts may modify life experience and influence identity processes.

My method of approach has been to immerse myself in the interview material of one individual (the verbatim transcripts in full, and not the edited versions as reproduced in the preceding chapters), staying with the material for as long as necessary for my empathy and insight to grow from within the data itself, throwing light on the patterning of that particular life. This took a fair amount of time, involving the re-reading and studying of the diffuse, complex and intricately textured material. The life histories, therefore, were not approached with any formal, pre-set categories into which the data were to be fitted and compressed; instead, I remained as open as possible to what the material might suggest to me about the individual's personality dynamics, the unfolding of that life, the constantly changing and interactive pattern of experiences, feelings and conflicts all set within social and cultural contexts. In short, I tried to be sensitive both to the overall integration of separate motives and conflicts within the living whole, but also to the continuities and changes in the course of the natural history of each individual.

Although I have not approached the material with pre-set categories in mind, this does not mean that I did not bring

conceptual ideas to bear upon my approach to the analysis of the
material. Naturally, all that I have learnt and thought about
throughout a varied professional career in three continents has been
brought into play but not in a consciously pre-determined way.
These identity analyses draw upon my particular experience and
insights and they therefore rest on such interpretive and integrative
abilities which I may have, as well as on shortcomings in these
respects. The conclusions to which I come are affected to an
unknown extent by my primary areas of sensitivity, unwitting
personal preferences and differential awareness. These problems are
specific neither to me, nor to this research task, nor to this particular
research method. If I had chosen to set up, in advance, precise
categories into which the life history material was to be analysed and
squeezed, the choice of such categories inevitably would have
reflected my personal preferences.

To a large extent I have approached the research material as
projective data and tried to discern patterns of meaning in the life
histories including the part played by unconscious factors.
Unconscious motives were inferred by such things as the consistent
repetition of ways of relating to people, obsessive concerns and
themes, over-emphatic assertions, pauses and hesitations in relation
to associated ideas, slips of the tongue, casual comments slipped in
and also the actual sequence of the material and the associations
underlying such sequences.

Many of the concepts used in the analyses have originated from
clinical work with patients, and because of this tend to be associated
with pathological processes. But as is well known not every conflict
is neurotic. A certain amount of conflict is both necessary to, and an
essential aspect of healthy functioning.

Defence mechanisms are everyday mechanisms. They are not
necessarily regrettable or abnormal in themselves. It is only by
studying each individual that it can be ascertained whether
various defence mechanisms are being used for constructive ends in
the service of the ego and to facilitate ordinary life, or whether they
are being used pathologically as part of a fixed and neurotic pattern.
Processes referred to in the identity analyses, such as depression and
splitting for example, are not in themselves necessarily unhealthy for
they can, at times, be used appropriately for surviving a crisis and as
aids towards further growth and recovery.

This is an exploratory study primarily concerned with evoking
fresh insights and hypotheses rather than with their validation. I
have made the best sense which I can of the data. My main reason for

including the lengthy life histories is to afford readers the chance to reach their own interpretations of the material and perhaps to redress emphases which I am placing. For the same reasons, I have cited in these next chapters considerable material from the life histories so that in the context of my interpretations, the reader can see in a general way how I have reasoned from the data.

Chapter 7

IDENTITY AND RACE IN A WEST INDIAN FAMILY: THE JAMES'

Frederick and Geraldine James and their children Johanna and Adrian were born in Barbados in the West Indies. It is within the constraints of the historic and cultural past of their people that certain aspects of their identities must be viewed.

This past exposed the forefathers of the James' to three centuries of slavery, forcibly dispossessing them of their language and original African cultural traditions, violently severing and fracturing their family lives and traditions and subjecting them to personal degradation and humiliation. When, in 1834, these Afro-Caribbeans were emancipated from slavery they came under the influence of British colonial governments which continued to dominate West Indian affairs until the early 1960s when independence was finally achieved. These twin events of slavery and colonial rule have influenced many aspects of West Indian life and left their imprint on the identities of its people.

The period of colonial government provided a cultural legacy which established Britain as the mother country and as a result she became the model for aspects of social, educational, religious and cultural life. Many of the administrators of the colony were middle-class, and social patterns characteristic of Victorian England came to be valued and internalized by the people of Barbados. Since the pace of economic and social change has been slower in the West Indies than in Britain, many of these Victorian values, attitudes and traditions have remained more deeply entrenched there than in Britain itself.[1]

To West Indians, Britain was felt to be home and when immigrating here, 'the West Indian made an inward movement, a journey into his cultural womb',[2] as Hiro has described it.

The humiliation and degradation of slavery, followed by a period of colonial rule during which power and privilege were retained by the British in their own hands, led to feelings of deep conflict in the West Indians towards the British. On the one hand, the British were hated and feared as the source of their suffering and exploitation, and on the other, the West Indians were dependent upon the British for security and material support. Furthermore, they became models from whom to copy and learn in the face of the enforced fragmentation and collapse of much of their original parent culture. The British were also the source of envy and jealousy for their power, privilege and material well-being.

What effects did these deep currents of feeling, involving race, have on the four subjects? The task of this chapter is to try and trace how each person forged a personal and unique sense of identity, to identify the issues affecting that identity, and to illuminate current unresolved identity conflicts, exploring the relationship between these and racial use and misuse.

1 MR FREDERICK JAMES

Issues Bearing on The Formation of His Identity

Early family relationships

It is in the family that the individual first develops feelings and ideas about the world and who he is. Frederick James' mother played a central part in his life. He loved her and in turn felt her to be loving, generous and capable of considerable sacrifice for all her children. She also saved him, on occasions, from the physical attacks and punitiveness of his father. His first burgeoning identity seems to be rooted in a warm and trusting relationship with his mother.

His father's presence is shadowy in the life history apart from a severe disciplinary role. What emerges is a picture of a much-loved mother and a father more absent than present, a situation familiar among Negro families of the Deep South as well as in parts of the Caribbean.[3] The historic exploitation of the black man, both by slavery and by a colonial system which stripped him of the full dignity and status as father and head of the family, affected the stability and structure of the black family as a whole. As a result, it was in the black mother that most strength and responsibility became vested and Frederick's recollections of his parents fit this well-documented model.

Growing up

His early recollections include recognition of both colour and social class differences within Barbados. His father worked for an 'English gentleman' and white people were a familiar part of his early background. At adolescence, relationships with a white woman employer and her nephew played a significant part in his later development.

At an age when the development of technical skills give an adolescent youth a feeling of growing competence, young Frederick was taught to ride a bicycle by his closest white friend, the nephew of the woman who later employed him. Confronted by a younger boy more adept and skilled than himself this could have been a wound to his self-esteem. But it was ego-enhancing, culminating in the white youth saying 'You see, you can ride by yourself'. In this way Frederick recalls the achievement as his own because his young teacher did not use the occasion either to patronize him or to inflate his own ego. When this bicycle was given to Frederick by the white woman, the gift can be seen as one symbolizing prowess and control.

What was it, in the relationships between Frederick and this white family, that seems to have lessened the gap between them, so that the space in which destructive envy might have had free play was reduced?[4] It seems that these experiences did not stimulate hate and resentment but acted as a steady spur to him and as a stimulus for further growth and sustained effort.[5] He valued and appreciated what had been shared with him (and chose a life-career connected with motor-vehicles, culminating in his present one as a bus-driver). His mother's care and love are likely to have made it possible for him to feel grateful for these good experiences, which, in turn, mitigated feelings of destructive envy and consequently he was able to learn from these white people and internalize them, in part, as models.

The relationship also depended on how these people felt and behaved towards Frederick. Both the white woman and her nephew were able to share food, material possessions and skills with apparent generosity which in no way demeaned the dignity and self-esteem of the recipient. When he became the woman's chauffeur this increased his self-esteem and assisted a developing sense of masculine identity and adult competence.

It is interesting to speculate that while Frederick was consolidating his relationships with this family, he was still under the rigid and often fierce discipline of his father who flogged him for coming home late at the age of seventeen. Perhaps it was the white 'mother and father' who, in this instance supported and upheld a maturing adult dignity and it was his black father who reduced his status to that of a child.

As a result Frederick established with the white family good parental, as well as sharing sibling, relationships. Unfortunately, we know little of Frederick's actual relationships with his own siblings. When later he considered emigrating, the white woman expressed concern as she felt he was too thin (and so might need more feeding from the nurturant, maternal part of herself), that it would be too cold for him (away from her warm protection), and that she did not think he could stick it out (over-protection, perhaps, but also putting into him her need for his continuing presence and appreciated service). She was a protective and caring figure in his life but it was also she who taught him to drive a car on which ability his career has been based. When he finally came to Britain he retained a warm affection and regard for her but was not dependent on her to the extent that her misgivings about his emigration undermined his own resolve to go. [After the study was complete, and when asked whether I had reminded him of anyone else in his past, Mr James said he associated me with this white lady. See a discussion of transference effects at the end of this chapter.]

Later when working in a garage in Barbados, he was ironically bitter and jealously angry when a white man fresh from school was given a chance to train abroad. He commented, 'The ordinary people – the West Indians – we would be there for all our lives. They wouldn't think of sending us on a course'. Outwardly he was fatalistically resigned. 'We just took it for granted at that time – it was just the way we had found it, I suppose. We thought it was the way it would be.' There was no good and fair mother to mediate as in his recollections of childhood, where his mother made sure that each child had a fair share. He felt he was among the disfavoured, and he turned the anger back against himself leading to a mildly depressed reaction, not acute enough to lead to self-denigration or paralysing self-punishment. For soon after this when he considered going to Britain, his healthy assertiveness acted for him in a positive and self-enhancing way when he said, 'I want to do better than this . . . I want to get somewhere . . . I will go and try . . . I want to make a better living. That's why we all do things – with hope.' This is healthy aggression used in the service of recovery from narcissistic injuries which had threatened his self-esteem. Rochlin (1973) has written pertinently on this point:

> Some of our worst failures more often than our successes may compel exertions to change. . . it is in the regenerating of ourselves that we find ample confirmation of the powerful incentives to recover from the countless disappointments, frustrations, and displeasures we never really wholly

accept. What affects self regard affects narcissism, compels us to act, to venture, to risk . . . Often our development gains.[6]

His motivations for leaving Barbados are important. They affect the way in which he perceives and interprets what happens to him in Britain and the relationships he makes. He might have left Barbados in anger as a gesture of hostility toward his home or towards the white people there; or he might have left feeling hurt and bruised and gone to Britain as the mother country, hoping unconsciously for bountiful love, welcoming arms and support. If the depressive effects of his life in Barbados had weighed more heavily on him, he might never have found sufficient energy and emotional resource to have made such a decisive move. His actual decision to leave, while prompted by a variety of inner and outer factors, was characterized by a movement toward something new, regenerating and hopeful. For him, it was a new beginning.

Colour and social class

Each person's answers to race and identity are singularly his own for each confronts questions of who he is at particular points in time, at different stages of psychosexual development and always set within the context of a specific society. Questions of identity emerge, however, not only in relation to race, but also in relation to social class. A central component of the sense of identity is how people place themselves and are placed by others in the social status systems of their society.

Barbados was stratified both by race and social class. West Indians, disadvantaged by slavery and colonial exploitation were to be found disproportionately among the working class. Frederick's early recollections are a recognition of both colour and class differences and illustrate how he saw them as going together. He went to different schools from white boys (many of whom went to private schools), but he played with white boys after school although there was no intimacy of contact. He asked himself, 'Why is it that the white man seems to have the best of things – gets the best of everything?' In Britain he later felt elated.

> I felt very good and very happy when I came here because in
> my country . . . you see the white people only with their cars
> and their servants and their elaborate homes. But when I came
> here and saw them – they *all* have to work . . . we will all be

walking with our own kids here and we will all be going to
work . . . I felt a kind of equality.

He accepts *social class* differentials in the new society and his relief
lies in that white men also can be workers.

There is little in his life story to throw light on how he experienced
his skin colour in contrast to a white skin – nor what its deeper
meanings might have been for him since these are never neutral.
From where he viewed West Indian society, he saw that West Indians
like himself had to do the 'dirty part of the work and the white man
only walked with his hands in his pockets, showing and telling me
what to do'. His resentment and envious anger are class-based as well
as being directed against racial discrimination in Barbados.

Marjorie McDonald[7] in a recent psychoanalytic study on skin
colour anxiety and personality development among both black and
white young children in Ohio, has shown that there is a critical
overlap of the developing awareness of racial differences in skin
colour at the same time as the child confronts conflicts which occur in
the anal phase, when the child is learning to devalue his dark faeces
and reject them as a needless part of himself. It is during this stage
that brown temporarily becomes a bad colour and anything bad gets
rejected as of no value. The colour results in an identification with a
'bad, out of control dirty person' and the whole constellation of anal
phase conflicts are displaced onto the darker skin shades. McDonald
further found that the *actual* skin colour of a child's *own* skin made no
difference at all to these conceptions of a dark skin colour since it is
the colour of the child's faeces which brings these reactions.

There are three points in Mr James' life story where skin colour
anxieties seem to manifest themselves. The first is his allusion to dirty
work. Later, when in Britain, he mentions two painfully upsetting
incidents involving aversive reactions, possibly to his skin colour.
The white children on his one-man bus avoided contact with his
hand when taking their change; and the fat white lady whom he went
to help when getting onto the bus rebuffed him and it was physical
contact involving touching which he felt led to her response.
Although studies on skin colour anxiety seem to have been done
primarily on children, it is more than probable that many adults,
both white and black, have failed to deal with these unresolved
problems which can be unconsciously stirred up by the sight of
people of different skin colours or by their physical contact. It is a
factor which should not be disregarded.[8]

It is impossible to know whether Mr James is expressing his own unresolved problems or whether he is sensitive to the attributions and attitudes which whites project onto black people, arising in part from unresolved skin colour anxieties of their own. Both could be at work. In any event, two of these occurrences which aroused his sensitivity were inflicted on him by behaviour emanating from others.

Managing separation problems

By the time Mr James decided to emigrate, he was married with three children. It was he who decided to come to Britain, stimulated in part by the large numbers of fellow West Indians who also were coming, but he was also prompted by positive needs of his own to extend and widen his capacities as a provider for his family.

In the process of leaving one's country, there is an inner and an outer sense of loss involving the wrench of separating from the intimate things which mean home, including familiar relationships. Mr James knew he soon would be re-united with his wife so found it more difficult to leave his children as the period of separation was unknown. His acute separation problems were, however, experienced in relation to his mother. The children whom he left behind, especially Adrian, lived with his mother and for thirteen years when Adrian stayed with her, Mr James felt that a rich part of himself was still there with his mother. When he was re-united with Adrian in London he said

> 'I'm glad to have you,' I said 'but even now I can't get over the feeling of knowing that I am not over there. Whilst I was not there *you* were there, and I knew that a part of me was with my mother. But now that you are not there, I feel as if I have done a wrong. I have left her all alone, you see.'

And later he commented 'When he was there, I felt he was there. And my mother knew he was there, so if she felt lonesome some part of me was there'.

Mr James seems to have managed his problem of separating from his mother by splitting-off a part of himself in phantasy, and by a process of projective identification[9] he put these split-off feelings in phantasy into his son, with whom he then became able to identify. It was through this identification and by using his son as a proxy that he continued to feel in close contact with his mother, gratifying his wish still to be with her and to bring comfort to her. He partly recognised what he was doing. 'When I brought him here, I felt there was no link at all there. I would only have to write'. He had not emotionally separated from his mother when he emigrated and experienced the pain of separation only when Adrian came to Britain. At that time the part of himself which in phantasy had been lodged with his mother, was brought back and re-integrated into himself, leaving him with doubtful feelings of having taken away from her that loving bit of himself.

In this way, Mr James took one of those important steps in the lifelong process of identity development by which parts of oneself which are lost, are re-found and re-integrated. His identity was now strengthened by being able to experience the pain of the separation – an aspect of reality previously denied by his phantasy – and by the fact that he was now able to link his past with his present and his childhood dependencies with his growing adult ego. When during the following year, his mother died, he was able to experience his grief and sadness and his real mourning for her began.

Although Mr James defended himself against the anxiety of separating, nonetheless this was not a depleting process for him. On the contrary, while an important part of himself was in phantasy with his son and his mother, he was meanwhile living a full life in England and coping realistically with problems in the new country. So the split between the projected part of him obtaining vicarious gratification with his mother, and the more adult part of himself in London, was not one which either emotionally cut him off from Barbados or one which drained the life from him in London.

It is possible that this process only worked because Mr James, his mother and Adrian all unconsciously colluded with these vicarious needs. The loving son part of himself which he projected into Adrian enabled father and son to keep in live emotional touch with each other during those thirteen years meeting both their needs. His mother probably felt that she had not lost her son but gained, through her grandson, her son anew. In this way, Adrian could gain a 'mother' in Barbados, while retaining close contact with a father whose good son part he was re-enacting and re-living, and Mrs James (senior) could retain 'her son'. Adrian re-joined his family in Britain when his grandmother relinquished him in his best interests. Her health was declining and she put his needs above hers and was a good 'mother' to the end.

This discussion on how Mr James handled his separation anxiety is of fundamental importance in understanding how he coped with the stress of immigration and what his internal resources were when he came. For in the process of leaving, parts of the self can be left behind in phantasy, while other parts are brought into the new society. Some people leave their hope behind and bring their despair, their helplessness, or their rage. If, with his close attachment to his mother, he had not been able to resolve this problem in the way in which he did, it is possible that acute ongoing homesickness for those left behind might have so impoverished his life in Britain that he could well have needed to blame someone or something for his distress; and it is in situations like this that scapegoating and dehumanizing of other races can occur. Or, alternatively, apathy and depression might have drained his capacities for work and love. In any event, he not only made a bridge between his child, his mother and himself, but he also brought with him into his life here a sturdy enough ego, able to cope with the reality of a new life. Since one of the concerns of this book is to try and throw light on how each individual handles such critical transitions in life, and to trace whether these positively enhance the development and growth of the individual or conversely lead to destructive effects particularly in the inter-racial area, it is significant that Mr James managed this major turning point with benign results both for him, his family and for his race relationships in this country.

Positive and negative elements in identity

Positive and negative identity elements are present at each stage of an individual's life. Negative identity elements are all those which an individual tries to submerge in himself as undesirable, as parts of himself which he may know, or fear, or has been told he is but tries not to become. Erikson has suggested that every person's identity contains a hierarchy of positive and negative elements which arise from socialization experiences which present the individual with ideal prototypes of behaviour as well as evil ones to be feared and avoided.[10] At all stages in an individual's life, positive and negative identity elements are in dynamic interaction and often in conflict. Negative identity images, however, do not only arise from within; individuals and groups who disown aspects of *their* negative identities often project these in exaggerated form onto others.

As part of Mr James' positive identity, he brought with him moral attitudes favouring ideal standards of integrity and honesty in personal and public life, consideration, kindness and helpfulness. Nor were these surface attitudes. When the fat white lady rebuffed his helping hand as she struggled to get onto the bus, he felt hurt and decided he would not help anybody else again 'but being the type of person I am, I couldn't do that. Since that day I continued to help people . . . I just couldn't stay and see someone struggling and not help'. He stands firmly behind his own sense of values, rebuff or no rebuff, his positive sense of identity is solidly based on being kind, helpful and supportive and in the face of what he takes to be a racial rejection, he is caring enough to continue to help other white people. He treats them as individuals and shows them a quiet respect.

His values also give positive weight to being quiet, restrained, moderate and polite. He believes in hard work, the exercise of technical skill and self-discipline, and he wants a good education for his children. He is prepared to work hard, to defer short-term satisfactions in order to secure a home of his own where he and his wife can be re-united with their children.

These values, no doubt, emanate from the foundations of trust and loving care which he received from his mother. But having also experienced these in relation to the white family in Barbados, involving contacts across both racial and class barriers, he is better prepared to exercise these qualities when he meets them again in coming to England.

As a bus driver in London with an accident-free record of ten years, he derives a positive sense of identity from a job consistently well-done. He is not given to idealising a situation nor to overlooking its problems and is realistic about his job, characteristically reflecting. 'It has a good side as well as a bad side'. Work is part of his positive identity, bringing him a sense of achievement, security and respect.

His role in the family further strengthens his masculine identity. As the head of the family, major breadwinner and decision-maker, his assertive role is complemented by other gentle qualities of nurturance, warm concern and care for his wife and children. He derives satisfaction and pleasure from his marriage, and from his children.

He has strong feelings of pride in the mutual help which West Indians give to each other, the generous ties of family life which sustain his people, and in the recent independence of his country.

On the ship going to Britain, he was given advice which he found helpful by an Englishman on board – encouraging adaptability, getting along with all kinds of people, and in particular meeting the needs of landladies in respect of coming home at a reasonable hour, being tidy, 'nice' and not loud or noisy. This advice evokes parental constraints. It also reveals negative stereotypes attributed to West Indians by the English, and it is striking how these preferred behaviours emphasize aspects of the anal character – control, pliancy, orderliness, tidiness, and avoidance of loud explosive sounds. In the light of McDonald's work[11] (and Mr James' confirmation that the advice given was accurate according to his West Indian friends), it is possible that the requirements of landladies in regard to West Indian tenants are over-determined by projections onto West Indians arising from unresolved anal phase conflicts, unconsciously stirred up in white people by contact with black people.

The Englishman is incidentally conveying to him how West Indians are perceived; these are the images projected onto them, which then have either to be denied by them, or lived down, or lived *with*. They constitute aspects of an attributed negative identity of the West Indians – that which they are told, explicitly or implicitly, that they *are*, and which they then have to try *not to be* – noisy, untidy, out-of-control, making trouble or having rows.

The friendly Polish landlord presented Mr James with another benign white father-figure, who saw him as tidy and clean, doing what he (the landlord) liked and not being noisy or giving trouble. He was valued for these very things. 'If he told me what he liked, well, I did it, you see . . . . I never gave anyone any trouble'. He contrasts his attitudes with those of other West Indians, some of whom he sees as refusing to come to terms with other people's needs and unable to compromise.

It is possible to interpret Mr James' responses as confirmatory of studies which have pointed to Negro lowered self-esteem and tendencies towards compliant obsequiousness and defensive adjustments in behaviour, to meet with dominant white majority expectations,[12] and to question whether Mr James' behaviour reflects acceptance of, and reaction to these negative identity projections. In his particular case I do not think it is so simple. His positive identity is securely and consistently built around these very behaviours and personality qualities. He is naturally quiet, peaceful and adaptable, able to respect others and earn respect, considerate of other's needs as his whole life story exemplifies. His bearing with family members, the occasional visitor and with me throughout the interviews, confirm this picture. There is a natural 'fit' in his case between his temperament and personality and those qualities which landlords want from their tenants. As he himself says, 'Everyone says I'm very friendly and quiet . . . easy to live with . . . I know of some people who get objections but I have never had any. But then I myself don't like loud noise. I like quiet and peacefulness'.

It is the balance between positive and negative elements within his personality which throws light upon this. The negative identity elements do not, in themselves, propel his behaviour or personality into a false conforming pattern since these patterns are already a firm part of his sustained identity. But what they do is to constrict within narrow limits his feelings and behaviour into these particular patterns and to fix them. Spontaneity is reduced and that which authenticates himself to himself is ever more firmly anchored in these particular ways of behaving and feeling.

Managing loss: experiences with some West Indian males
The 'shocking conditions' which he found on arrival, linked with a sense of outrage that the West Indian liaison officer was exploiting his own people, did not lead Mr James to feel unduly persecuted or to develop paranoid projections against the English or his fellow West Indians. He was able to use righteous indignation and ironic humour to cope with the situation, realistically observing that others managed differently. He steadily put his aggression to work for him in positive ways, improved his housing conditions and immediately got himself a job.

Three other incidents, all involving exploitation or loss incurred at the hands of West Indian men, are similarly revealing of his ways of coping. Not belonging to this country by birth, newcomers have impelling inner needs for a home of their own, which can help to anchor them in the new society and give them an intimate feeling of belonging and a sense of 'being at home'. For Mr and Mrs James a home also meant that they could be re-united with their children. When Mr James was defrauded of his savings of £200 by the West Indian estate agent, he was angry and felt that the man 'was a fool and a crook'. In the face of this prodigious loss, he started to re-accumulate money and to find constructive ways to buy a house which he finally did. Later, West Indian friends on two separate occasions borrowed small sums of money from him which were not repaid. In these three cases, although angry and bitterly disappointed, he nonetheless felt secure enough in his identity as a man not to be inwardly depleted by these real losses to the point of feeling emptiness and despair. His potency borrowed or stolen, he could forgive and start once again to make good the losses. Characteristically, disappointments are not denied, anger is experienced and he is able to transform these into positive and active ways of tackling and surmounting problems. As a result he does not need to blame others or feel unduly persecuted. He acts and grows in the process.

He shows a capacity for adequate reality-testing and accepts that simply by being alive and trying to make a path for oneself, there are inevitable losses, defeats and reversals of fortune. He has a sense of the tragic in life. 'Everybody has problems. Many of my friends have had set-backs. Considering the amount I lost and everything, I think I got off fairly well'. He sees beyond the personal to man's common experience, and by accepting this and then being able to act, he makes steady ego growth, his identity becomes consolidated and he feels himself to be a man who can surmount loss and disappointment and in the face of it continue his own long-range plans.

These four experiences – all with male West Indians – may re-evoke for him his original father but the attacks on his masculine self are not experienced as overwhelming, and inside he seems to have internalized a sturdy and viable masculine identity.

The English
Although the English are experienced as good and friendly and, on the whole, are seen as father or mother figures, he does not seem dependent upon them and just as he made up his own mind about emigrating when the white woman demurred, so he seems to go his own way in Britain too. He experiences easy relationships with white people, treats them as individuals and does not resort to group stereotypes. He makes a clear distinction between white children on the bus who are troublesome, and their different behaviour inside their own homes where, he feels, 'you can speak to them.'

At the political level, he was thrown into despair by the Immigration Act,[13] and whereas previously he had known Enoch Powell as a politician who expressed prejudicial views towards coloured immigrants, now he feared that his views were prevailing in the country as a whole. He feels attacked and bewildered both by the Act and by Powell's speeches, and his feelings are bruised. It is striking that it is solely in the interview which followed the passing of the Act and a speech by Powell that he moves towards a global 'they' when discussing the situation created. 'They start bringing things up and I wonder why I came here?' he says bitterly. He makes no distinction between political parties in Britain. By arousing his insecurity and anxiety, the Act leaves him defenceless in the face of his anger and hurt. He cannot find anything practical and active to do – apart from the thought of returning to Barbados, but he realises that this is no solution as he wants his children to be educated in England. In short, his usual capacity for translating frustration and anger into constructive action cannot be used and he has no weapons. If he was involved in party politics in Britain, he might have been able to express his wounded feelings by appropriate political action. Since he is not, he used the only means he could, and for the first time in his life history interviews resorted to verbal stereotyping and scapegoating of another minority group. He expressed dismay at how many Indians had entered the neighbour-hood, noted how crowded everything was and speculated with gloomy foreboding about the thousands of Kenyan Asians whom he felt were waiting to come to Britain. So he joined in the 'numbers game' which Enoch Powell started playing in Britain and which was picked up by others. His fear of being overwhelmed and invaded by alien others is his defence against an Act and political speeches which made him feel alien, unwanted and attacked. The mood of despair passed, however, and by the next and following interviews his own sense of moderation and balance had returned.

Self-description

At the end of the study, Mr James was asked to briefly describe himself. He saw himself as 'very quiet, decent, fairly even-minded and as loving everyone and not hating or envying anyone'. He was also asked how someone who might not like him might see him, and he said '*so* quiet . . . a very quiet fellow . . . I don't know, I can't approach him . . . he seems *that* quiet'.

Although he is a person who seems able to love and is not riddled with hate or envy, his affirmation of loving *everyone*, and his denial of *any* hate or envy, suggests that he may be defending himself against the normal amounts of hate and envy which we all experience. His fears and anxieties about himself focus around the problem of his unapproachability.

It is these two aspects of his identity conflicts – the unconscious need to defend himself against any hate or envy, and doubts concerning his approachability, which are linked with, and find an unconscious outlet in his attitudes and feelings toward Indians.

Unresolved Identity Conflict and Race

Mr James' contacts with Indians as neighbours are formal but friendly. Language barriers keep communication to a minimum. However, it is in his general experiences with Indians in the community that his emotional feelings become deeply involved. There are three themes which emerge from his life story:

1   Indians are felt to be unapproachable and unreachable.

They seem so *different* . . . so cast away as if they want to be by themselves . . . most of them don't seem friendly at all . . . they seem to stay *beneath* . . . they always seem to be far away from others.

2   They use their language to exclude others and this is felt as personally rejecting, annoying and rude.

> Though they can speak English, they don't do so . . . . They always 'nat, nat, nat' in their language and you are the odd man out. It's so annoying and not polite . . . they should learn to speak more English and speak it amongst people in crowds . . . . I don't think it is nice to carry on in a different language in a crowd when you can speak the language others speak.

3   They have a different culture and their folkways and social habits are alien and strange. But some of these are changing under the impact of acculturation to the new society. He cites their different cultural patterns which accord to parents the right to tell children what to do and whom to marry, their clannishness, their unwillingness to adapt themselves, congregations on the pavements so that pedestrians cannot pass freely, men embracing and hugging each other.

At all stages of life individuals experience unresolved conflicts of identity – what he wants to make of himself, how he thinks of himself, where he is going and his inner resources for doing it. These are conscious and unconscious processes. Mr James projects onto Indians his uneasy feelings about himself as being unapproachable and unreachable. Fearing that he is too quiet and unapproachable, he rids himself of these unwanted parts of himself and attributes them to the Indians. He finds their language rudely excluding and their cultural patterns different and strange. Deeply buried in the racial past of his own people, three centuries of slavery have left their unconscious imprint and understandable envy enters here, the envy that West Indians might have for people who have retained their *own* language and culture when *their* African language and cultural past has been wrenched away from them and abruptly severed at the roots. Such feelings would be deeply buried and unconscious, and in making this interpretation I am taking into account that envy and hate have played only a very small and normal role in his everyday life, although both could have been stimulated by the gross disparities in fortune between himself and others. His explicit denial of envy and hate in his self-description can now be understood in the light of these hidden envies and hates for a people – the Indians – who can proclaim their language as an audible mark of their cultural identity and in so doing exclude someone like Mr James from participating with them and understanding them. When his language is the language not of his *own* ancient cultural heritage but of those who were the slave-owners and the exploiters of his forefathers, then, by contrast, there is indeed much to envy in a people who can use their language and visibly communicate a viable culture. Erikson has drawn attention to how American Negro writers have almost ritualistically affirmed their inaudibility, invisibility, namelessness and facelessness 'a void of faceless faces, of soundless voices lying outside history' as Ellison puts it.[14]

In the steady growth and development of his personal identity, Mr James was able to handle, and apparently handle well, the usual experiences of envy and hate by which everyone is confronted. But it is his racial identity as a West Indian which shapes his feelings toward Indians. Had he been younger and politically motivated to join in the ranks of the black power movements where 'black is beautiful', such ideological commitments might in turn have acted to diminish envious feelings of Indian culture and language through the recovery and reclamation of his own African heritage and past. But those centuries of slavery are a stark and bitter period of history and they have left cruel legacies behind them.

Of course, there is a social reality 'out there' which conforms in part, at least, to his perceptions of the Indians. This is not being overlooked or denied. But the question that remains is the apparent 'fit' between Mr James' areas of conflict about himself and how these then are pegged onto Indians rather than onto any other persons or group. [It is worth noting that the interview in which Mr James discussed Indians preceded the interview in which he gave his self-description by almost a month.] Indians are not only visibly identifiable but they retain many cultural customs and, of course, use their own languages, so are appropriately chosen as the target group to be used as a repository for these feelings of Mr James. The English after all, share the same language with him and a common cultural traditon although each shapes these in distinctive ways.

His envious feelings and irritability toward the Indians are not extreme and his attitudes towards them are not rigidly fixed or stereotyped. He constantly comments on changes in their behaviour to which a more prejudiced person would be impervious, and is hopeful of the direction in which change is occurring.

Vicious and virtuous cycles in race relations

Throughout his life, Mr James' identity has shown a steady progression, characterized by a growing sense of coherence and wholeness with a sense of continuity over time. 'Living in this country hasn't changed me as a person in any way at all. I think I'm still the same'.

It takes a well-established identity to cope with the major stresses which he has faced, and the ways in which he tolerated and managed these throws light on his inner strengths and his coping patterns. He came with hopeful feelings and steadily extended and developed a sense of competence to deal with difficult situations which, in turn, led to the quiet but steady recognition which others around him bestowed upon him and which were both gratifying and in turn helped him to grow and develop still further. In this way a series of benign cycles were initiated so that each hurdle overcome led to steady increase in ego strengths which, in turn, facilitated his handling of the next critical transition.

Small variations in behaviour can generate chains of events which are seen as leading to benign or virtuous cycles – or to their pathological opposite – a vicious cycle.[15] What generates these cycles exactly and how under certain circumstances these become reversed is one of the concerns of this study. Some of the major critical transitions which Mr James traversed, showing the type of cycles generated and their implications for his race attitudes are:

Managing envy of white people: Envious feelings lessened by good experiences, leading to introjection of kindly, generous white figures as role models, leading to reduction in destructive envy and acting as a spur to further growth and development. *Potential source of destructive feelings towards whites overcome by benign cycle.*

Overcoming disappointment and shock at housing conditions on arrival in Britain: Shock at conditions leads to reality-testing and ability to put aggression to work purposefully thus minimizing need to scapegoat, leading to successful attempts to improve housing, enhancing self-esteem so reducing need for scapegoating still further. *Potential source of destructive feelings towards the English overcome by benign cycle.*

Recovering from loss of savings: Narcissistic blow and loss of material potency compensated for by using aggression to achieve goal, avoiding wasteful energies of hate and stereotyping as well as depressive reactions, leading to success through renewed savings and appropriate action, increasing sense of self-esteem and feelings of potency. *Potential source of destructive feelings towards his own racial group overcome by benign cycle.*

Skin colour anxiety in relation to prejudice: Provocative, hurtful racial rebuffs by whites dealt with by maintenance of reality-testing, affirmation of own values of self-respect, helpfulness and concern for others, irrespective of race. *Provocative destructive feelings towards the English switched into benign cycle.*

Withstanding political developments within the UK, involving feelings of racial attack: Under pressure of Immigration Act and Enoch Powell's speeches, anxiety aroused and feels attacked, resorts to scapegoating of another minority group (Kenyan Asians) with some attempts to recover reality-testing at a later time. *Political developments lead to vicious cycle with some reality-testing to mitigate it at a later stage.*

Mr James' ego strengths show in his capacity to tolerate anxiety and frustration and cope with disappointment. He is able to delay fulfilment of his goals while finding some satisfaction and relief in the active pursuit of that which he wishes to achieve. He attempts to alter situations by active mastery and aggressive attack on the problems involved. A person with a weaker ego would not be able to sustain this degree of anxiety. By turning passive into active means of adaptation, he both avoids regressive pulls in the opposite direction and overcomes his problems. The implications for race relations are vital since by acting as he does he does not need to resort to destructive ways of misusing racial groups.

By being able to tolerate ambivalence in himself and in others, he does not need to split off good from bad with consequent tendencies to stereotype racial groups.

It is only under the temporary but dislocating pressure of the Immigration Bill and the Enoch Powell speeches that he resorts to using Kenyan Asians as scapegoats. Although this was a passing mood, nonetheless it should be taken seriously if a man of his balance and moderation could be pushed into racial misuse of this kind. If pressures of this type mount in England, Mr James could well be driven to finding scapegoats for his sense of insecurity and feeling unwanted.

His *racial* identity can best be described as a *surrendered identity*[16] – an identity waiting to be recovered. Unlike highly creative and articulate black writers, Mr James is not consciously determined by an inner need to be 'heard and seen, recognised and faced', but nonetheless at an unconscious level, this is his conflict.

2. MRS GERALDINE JAMES

Issues Bearing on The Formation of Her Identity

Early recollections

Mrs James recollects her mother as being a very good woman and a 'woman of peace' who *never* had rows or quarrels with *anybody*. A picture emerges of a woman apparently frightened of her angry and destructive feelings who tried to keep these separate from her good and peaceful feelings. She appears to have defended herself against these fears by the avoidance and denial of all kinds of aggressive attack and turned her fears and anxiety into their opposite. 'Even if somebody tried to pick a quarrel with her, she would just go away and if she felt like singing, she might just sing'.

She brought her children up to deny and avoid any hurtful, verbally aggressive attacks which might be made on them personally or directed at members of their family, or their race. Mrs James was taught not to answer back when a friend insulted her and not to reveal in her bearing or behaviour that she might be angry or upset at anything she had heard, and if she did answer back, her mother linked such behaviour with that of a prostitute.

From a very early age, Geraldine James saw provocations and attack from outside as being sufficiently frightening to require their rigid denial, and in any event she was taught to keep aggression and anger under severe control.

While she remembered her mother as very good and peace-loving, she also recollected how she had lashed her children, not without cruelty. These two images of her mother exist side by side but with no discussion of their contradiction, as if she keeps her picture of her alive by blocking-off the negative features and keeping those separate from the more idealised aspects.

Her father she recalls as a quiet and peace-loving man. 'I never heard him quarrel or swear at anybody'. He died when she was ten years old and whatever his role in her life had been, his place in her identity formation remains unchanged as a good father, unmodifiable by any chance of later reality-testing. Both parents are therefore remembered as ideally good.

Klein[17] has shown that the separation by infants of the mother into a good and a bad one is an essential stage in their emotional development which allows loving feelings to be attached to the person who brings good and soothing experiences, and destructive and angry feelings to the mother who frustrates. In a normal, smooth development, the infant in relationship with an accepting and tolerant mother is helped to bring these phantasies together and so experiences the mother as both good *and* bad, and this helps to develop a growing perception of reality. The infant's angry feelings toward the frustrating mother are weakened by the reassurance received that the mother is able to survive the destructive phantasies, and this, in turn, helps the child to accept his aggressive feelings with increasing tolerance, cope with feelings of ambivalence, and confirms and deepens his capacity for constructive loving relationships.

If, however, development does not go smoothly and the relationship between the infant and mother is less than optimal, a reluctance to accept a normal share of hateful feelings can result. In such a case, the bad feelings tend to be split-off from the good feelings, and the belief in the ideal goodness of the self is retained while the bad feelings are attributed to others by a process of projection. It is a precarious balance to maintain, ensuring the experience of one kind of attitude at a time, while omitting all that is at variance with it out of conscious awareness. In the process it depletes the individual by impoverishing his range of emotional feelings (e.g., ambivalence), but it also diminishes the full human stature of the other person into whom the bad feelings, which have been disowned, have been evacuated.

Mrs James has a tendency to split-off the idealized feelings felt for her mother and father, from the destructive, angry feelings which are displaced onto her brothers and sisters. She sees her siblings as quarrelsome, with hot tempers and hurting each other – with only one exception, a brother. She feels herself to be different, a view confirmed by the community, which she perceives as seeing her and this brother as the best in the family. Her self-esteem and early sense of identity are built on this contrast between herself and her siblings.

She thinks of herself as taking after her mother. 'I just ignore people . . . Where I'm concerned, I don't care what they say because words are wind, and wind is cheap because you don't have to buy it! I turn my head and tell them I don't hear anybody say anything.' She avoids hurt and provocation by 'not hearing' and denies and represses any resulting feelings of anger which the narcissistic injury to her self-esteem justifiably evokes. The same defences are used in relation to insulting remarks made about her own race. 'I hear a lot of very dirty remarks that people make about the coloured people, but it never bothers me because they aren't talking to me personally.'

These aspects of her inner world provide the undertow for many of her later relationships, especially in relation to race. Her need to keep the feelings of love and hate somewhat separate and the rigid control of aggression which it requires, influence her perceptions of reality.

Growing up

She grew up among white people and felt accepted as one of them. She played with white children. 'It was not as if I was outside in the yard and they were in the house. No – all the mothers and fathers cherished us in the same way and they more or less used to look upon us as one of them.' She identified with the white children, and their parents became her alternative good parents.

Her experiences with three consecutive sets of West Indian employers after she left school were deeply frustrating and she felt exploited. She had very strong motivations to learn and acquire technical skills and her fruitless search for ways of acquiring these made her especially sensitive to being exploited.

By the time she started working as a nanny for white employers her self-esteem was low. The West Indian employers had failed to teach her. They had been bad 'parents' who were experienced as undermining her health and indifferent to, and unconcerned with her as a person.

Working for white people: becoming a nanny

A crucial turning-point was reached when she became a nanny. She gravitated into a role familiar to many West Indians at that time in Barbados, and it served diverse conscious and unconscious needs. A period of more constructive growth commenced and her self-esteem felt enhanced. 'You are more or less in the best position in the family because everybody looks up to you as you are caring for their child.' Her uniform, which she liked wearing, was an outward symbol of her new role which confirmed her, in her own and other people's eyes, as a person of some significance.

A vital part of her growing identity was concerned with the acquisition of skills, doing a job well, being responsible and earning respect for her capability. These were ego-enhancing experiences and they helped to consolidate a sense of her own identity based on her adult effectiveness, her capacity for trust and being trusted, all confirmed for her by the white parental figures for whom she worked.

At the unconscious level the more dependent and childish parts of her were also expressed in her work. She liked to be taken care of and enjoyed the dependency aspects of the relationship. But she also turned passive dependency needs into their active controlling opposites, and in handling difficult white children, in the process she also became an effective nanny for her own needy 'child' inside her. At the adult level, she looked after everything for the white woman; banked her money, taught her about the currency and how to become responsible for her own monetary affairs despite the woman's resistance. It was she who was the teacher to the 'childish' white woman, and it was also she who decided, as a mother might, what the white woman should eat. It appears that her active abilities to control and manage, and her passive needs to be cared for and mothered are both polar aspects of the same unresolved problem – one pushing her toward constructive development and growth, the other feeding a somewhat regressive need to be a child once more. And in this period of her life the forward-moving, creative aspects of an adult identity built around work competence began to form.

Like her husband's experience, the scope for destructive envy seems to have been reduced by the reciprocal capacity of both Mrs James and her white employers to nourish and feed each other with good things and to be able both to appreciate each other and to be appreciated, so that envy acted as a spur for further good work, service and growth. She gave back to her employers valued skills which repaid their generous help to her.

Her attitude towards colour and social class problems at this period of her life was to deny any personal awareness of colour prejudice or racial discrimination, but to recognize class differences and to accept these. 'If they take you as a maid, then you *are a maid*. They don't refer to your colour. Sometimes one met uppity people, but even then they didn't say anything about my colour.'

Lost and found

Her reasons for coming to England (despite the wrench of having to leave behind her three children), were to join her husband and avoid the risk of his finding another woman and herself being 'on the outside looking in'. This theme of being rejected or overlooked as contrasted with being on the 'inside', loved and included, runs through much of her life story.

On arrival in London, she was separated geographically from her husband for almost a year. She was working at a railway canteen and became a resident in a railway hostel. Her world expanded. She tolerated her separation from her children and her husband well and did not seem to suffer very much distress. In fact, the part of her which was hungering for new experience and for being wanted and actively missed, was not displeased. And her widening social life and work experiences provided many compensations.

As the only coloured woman in the hostel (except for one other who was only there for a very short period) she experienced delight, elation and wonder at being valued and wanted *as a coloured*.

> I was the only coloured . . . it didn't bother me . . . They would never go out anywhere and leave me. They *never* did . . . I got along fine with them . . . The only coloured in the pub was me. Everybody wanted me . . . Nobody knew me, but even strangers bought me drinks and everybody started talking to me . . . They were all white. I was the only little coloured one.

Later on in London, she became a patient in a hospital and was the only coloured patient in the ward. 'Everybody makes a fuss when its like that. [Laughs] When you are *one* person you get more attention.' Here her sense of racial identity has a special value – a rarity value.

She seems to have an unfulfilled need to be the one and only child and have the undivided attention of her 'parents'. Since she was the seventh child in a family of eight children, it is understandable that she failed to get the attention she needed and why she derives pleasure from being wanted and found special by white people who evoke for her her own parental figures.

Illness and the regressive use of white parental figures

Relationships with white persons in authority have a special quality for her. In many different incidents, she projects the picture of a distressed, helpless and needy part of herself – a regressed 'child' – whose needs for lavish care, protection, concern, and wholehearted devotion, are overwhelmingly met by white people in different roles. These become idealized parental figures carrying out their professional duties with such exceptional care and devotion that the picture is evoked of a small, fragile baby, and very devoted parents whose only concern is for their child.

For example, she sees the hostel superintendent and her staff as waiting on her hand and foot when the doctor said she was not to do anything for herself during a severe bronchial infection. This was done 'with the greatest pleasure' and included all kinds of care which a mother would bring a child, including washing out soiled nighties.

The white man, visiting his wife in the bed next to hers in a hospital ward, held a cup into which she vomited. The ambulance driver would not let her walk to the ambulance although she felt able to do so, and he made sure that she would be fed at home. The doctor who attended her during childbirth, finally confronted her with the two aspects of herself – one adult, able, competent and strong, and the other helpless, weak and regressed – when he said to her 'We are not going to help you, you are very strong.' To which she retorted 'That's what you think!'

During illness, the disruption in the continuity of well-being often brings to the fore aspects of dependence and of an impaired self, which can stir up angry feelings in a patient. Mrs James' unconscious defence against these feelings was to become the helpless but good child whose needs were met by these idealized and devoted custodial figures who attended to her. It is a way of using illness to vicariously support an image of herself as an ideal child with ideal parents in neither of whom can any aggression or bad hurtful feelings be found. The idealization serves to cover up any underlying hostility or fear of attack. It is the illness which brings out the tenacious clinging to these more childish parts of herself which have otherwise been largely repressed, and which then re-assert themselves at a time of regression and dependence.

But the rigidly repressed fears of aggression emerge as themes connected with death. The white doctor who attended her at the hostel said she should not move from her bed 'else I will have your death on my hands'. Earlier the superintendent had threatened to smack her because 'you could have killed yourself'. The white husband of a fellow-patient in hospital said 'I pulled you through – I thought you were going to pass out on me', and the white sister talks of having to take the possible responsibility for her death. These themes of death seem to be evoked because she fears her ordinary angers to be unduly powerful and even lethal because they have had to be so severely repressed.

Through these projections of herself as helpless and the white figures as inordinately helpful and caring, both are reduced in stature. The English are not credited with their full range of ordinary feelings which include ambivalence, irritation, anger, detachment, as well as a human capacity to err. And she undermines herself by temporarily losing touch with the adult, capable, person she is whose full range of emotional feelings should include anger, fear, disappointment and an acceptance of reality. It is a defensive manoeuvre which enables her to avoid facing her split-off aggressive feelings.

Work competence and relationships with white people

In England, it is through work that Mrs James' identity as a technically competent and efficient person becomes consolidated. She has well-sustained work motivations and obtains pleasure in achievement for its own sake. It stands her in good stead at various points in her life and not least in the incident with the white tramp in the railway canteen.

The white tramp provoked her and precipitated* an explosively aggressive response which she felt unable to control. She turned to the white manageress and the white charge-hand appealing to them to control her. 'From the time I have known you . . . I have never been disrespectful to either of you . . . I am asking you now please don't let me be because I don't want to be.' Her internal controls are weakened and it is to these two white women she appeals in order to harness their help as super-ego figures. She offers to put away her overalls 'very gently' – a reversal of the anger which she is experiencing. When the tramp held her, her anger erupted and she grabbed the knife and threatened to 'drop him dead'. The policemen who are called in and who embody parental images of authority and conscience, go away again, however; her value as a conscientious worker is upheld by her employers. They do not want to lose her. It is striking that when her anger is precipitated and expressed rather than denied, it becomes possible for her to find a varying range of feelings inside her towards the tramp. She reveals compassion, and sees him as a nuisance rather than a bad man. By rigidly holding on to her aggressive feelings, she tends to make others into cardboard figures, totally good or totally bad. But when her anger explodes, though in the process she terrifies herself, it is found after all to be containable and less lethal than she had feared, and her self-esteem and adult identity get a boost from her indispensability as a worker. This incident, while not precipitated by issues of race, since she says that the tramp also hated a white woman who failed to buy his fish, nonetheless throws light on her inner struggles to contain her

---

* It is only possible to speculate on some of the factors which might have led to the extreme reactions which Mrs James had to this particular incident. The tramp had tried to sell her fish and there are several places in her life-story where *fish* figures in contexts of emotional significance. One of her brothers was a fisherman and she has ambivalent feelings toward her siblings. She remembers being given fish as a gift because people liked her mother. A fish bone once stuck in her throat requiring hospital treatment. Apart from the feelings evoked by fish in this incident, a dirty cap thrown into her lap could have evoked unconscious sexual feelings of a disturbing kind.

aggressive feelings, and these have implications for her patterns of racial misuse.

Her working relationships reveal characteristics of her attitudes and feelings towards white employers. She is able to deal with them on an adult, person-to-person basis as when she gave in her notice to the superintendent of the hostel because her transfer never came through. This was forthright. When she discovered that the superintendent had been consciously withholding her transfer, she was able to accept her explanation and forgive her.

She describes her present white employer as very nice and 'never saying a cross word', and she uses an aggressive, teasing, bantering humour with him which he reciprocates, so that latent hostility is discharged in sublimated forms. Because her aggression is handled in this socially acceptable way, she appears to be relaxed in this relationship. She talks to him and finds him receptive, understanding and helpful.

Another dimension in her relationships with white people expresses the controlling nanny in her which manifests itself from time to time, strikingly so in relation to white men in the canteen bar who try to hurry her up in supplying them with drinks. She lectures them as children, and exerts her power to control their behaviour with apparent effect. These are the two sides of her dependency on white people the passive aspects already examined, and the active aspects which enable her to take control when the situation invites it and to do so in a humourously hectoring manner.

In recent years she has developed in ways which enhance adult status. A contributory factor might well be her growing capacity to express normal aggressive feelings through an acceptable humour which reflects a reduction in the rigidity of her previous controls.

Her overall capacity to handle a full-time and physically demanding job, run an attractive home, care for her family, including two very young twins, is impressive. Her home is spotlessly kept, and she is justifiably proud of its appearance and the high standards of its maintenance for which she and her husband both can claim full credit. Her babies seem healthy and lively, and she enjoys cooking and seems to feed her family well. In all these respects, her capacity to handle a wide range of demands, while also giving time to this research study, is impressive testimony to her energy, capability and over-all efficiency.

West Indians as siblings
Idealization of white parental figures represent one part of Mrs James' tendency to split; the other part involves the projection onto

fellow West Indians of those feelings which are experienced as totally bad.

She did not like working with West Indians. She found that

> some of them were so touchy. . . . there were always rows and
> confusion, bad behaviour and language . . . they couldn't hear
> anything and let it slide . . . they think they own the
> place . . . the supervisor was a hard nut to crack . . . she used to
> drive us like slaves . . . I couldn't stand the shouting and
> hollering.

These vignettes evoke her quarrelling siblings, always having rows. They seem to contain a revived memory of her mother's lashings, those cut-off and repudiated aspects of her idealized mother-image 'driving us like slaves'. Her defences in the face of this work experience were characteristically to 'pass and hear things and just go on as if I'd never heard'. She removed herself and sat alone with a few quiet people. In contrast to her pleasure when she was included as a member of the white social group in the hostel, and her delight in being specially noticed and valued there, in this situation in the ice-cream factory she felt she was neither known to the other West Indians, nor valued by them, and so she could not bear to join in and become part of the group. By removing herself, she alienated herself from, and contrasted herself with, them as she had previously done with her real siblings. She felt that she was not what they were, and her identity became crystallized. She saw these fellow West Indians as aggressive and hurtful siblings, who embody for her the feared aggressions, which, as part of her negative identity, she denies and projects on to West Indian fellow workers. As a result she is able to retain her self-image as a quiet restrained person whilst offloading unwanted aspects of herself on to these sibling substitutes.

Coping with colour prejudice

In her life in Barbados, denial and avoidance were used to cope with colour prejudice. When she came to England she did not expect colour prejudice. Her way of dealing with it suggests that she tried to keep very separate her own *personal* experiences with white people (felt to be good) from those experiences of other West Indians with the English (felt to be painful and anger-provoking). She also rigidly separates and contrasts the period soon after she arrived in England (the late 1950s and early 1960s), which she felt was bad from the colour prejudice point of view, with the present situation, which she sees as being so good as to suggest that idealization may be at work.

The experiences of her West Indian acquaintances and friends in relation to whites are described as painful, insulting and anger-provoking. 'The first thing they (the whites) referred to was your colour – you black so-and-so.' Ideas of dirt and defilement are attributed to the coloured people by the white people. 'If you pass *here*, as you pass they wash it away with water because they feel you have left something on it.' At the pub, glasses were deliberately broken after coloured people had used them. These are powerful images, conveying an association of dark skin with notions of dirt and faeces, and again raise the part played by unresolved anal phase problems in relation to skin colour, discussed earlier in this chapter.

Although she recounted with considerable feeling how coloureds were excluded from the Anglican church when they first arrived, she personally denies having suffered painful and humiliating experiences. Her use of denial protects her from the reality of the world about her and so makes it possible to control her resulting anger. 'If I found awkward people who said things which were not called for – well, I just ignored them and didn't bother about them.'

But she was unable to maintain the split between what was happening to her, and what all other West Indians seem to have been experiencing, and when it started to break down she increasingly resorted to isolation and avoidance to protect herself from the cruel reality. She stopped going out and kept to herself. 'If you don't have anything, you can't lose it, so since I didn't choose to go and mix with people, they couldn't do anything to me.' Through restrictions of her social life, she retreated from the possible pain of narcissistic blows to her self-esteem and the threat of resultant indignation and anger. Within the community at large, she felt she was indistinguishable from other coloured people and her sense of identity was vulnerable and had to be protected. 'All coloured people look alike to the English'. The pleasant feelings which she had in the hostel of having been valued as an individual and as a coloured, are endangered within the wider community. And since she felt herself to be different from her own siblings and from their symbolic representatives in the community (her fellow workers in the ice-cream factory) she could no longer protect her identity except by withdrawal, and restriction of her world to the small setting of her own home. 'I used to say I just don't feel like walking out . . . I just kept to myself.' By doing this she acted to protect her *personal* sense of identity as the person she felt herself to be, from the encroachment of a projected *racial* identity thrust upon her.

What emerges in Mrs James is the use of defensive manoeuvres which her forefathers adopted as a necessary means of survival. Withdrawal, denial and avoidance have been shown to be character-istic defences among Negroes in North America, in their response to racial prejudice and discrimination.[19] Her mother also handed on to her daughter these chosen, unconscious modes of defence. In the contrasts which she draws between life in London when she arrived and now, she distances the painful to a remote past, where she is able to deal with it as long as the present can be kept nearly perfect. 'Now everybody is happy . . . everybody is together now, more or less . . . we are all one big happy family . . . now everybody is hand-in-hand . . . now everybody is one.' Although this may be so – that the present is better than the past – nonetheless her perception of the present is idealized.

In a more reality-oriented mood she speaks from her heart and with adult conviction when she says,

> I always say that respect is due a dog. If you've got a dog, you'll treat it with respect and that dog will then always respect you. . . . But if you keep hitting it and kicking it about, whenever that dog sees you, he will bark and be ready to jump on you . . . As long as we're here, you must accept us for what we are because we don't change. Our customs are the same as yours, the only difference is colour . . . we are all human you know . . . starting from *now*, we must learn to live together and settle down.

Although her interviews took place during the period when the 1971 Immigration Act was passed and Enoch Powell made speeches on race, she did not refer to these events at all, and at the end of the study I asked her what she felt about them. She said she had had no time to watch television or read the newspapers and knew nothing about either the Act or the speeches. As for Mr Powell, 'I don't know Mr Powell'. So the critical experience, through which her husband seemed to be passing, she dealt with by avoidance and denial.

Feelings toward Indians

Unlike her husband, Mrs James is not emotionally preoccupied with Indians. They appeared minimally in her life story. She sees her neighbours as good, concerned and well-meaning. They play into, and incidentally support, her chosen defences. 'They talk in their own language but what you don't know, doesn't hurt you . . . they don't bother me and don't trouble me.'

Her identity as wife and mother

Although fond of her children, they figure relatively little in her life-story and then only in relation to issues of feeding, control and sex.

She is fond of her husband and their relationship includes humorous banter and teasing threats. He is able to answer her humour with his. She needs his nurturant qualities and depends on him in many ways. He is the decision-maker in the family, but he also spoils her in lovingly indulgent ways and she adds 'how he is – thank God for him.'

She has a lot of spirit, is extravert, ebullient, and needs to be in the centre of the stage which complements his quiet restraint. Her passionate and exuberant style contrasts with his economy of expression. Some of the more caring and tender qualities in the marriage he supplies, while she provides a good deal of drive and energy.

As a mother she exerts a firm, nanny-like control, with emphasis on behavioural conformity rather than on feelings.

Unresolved Identity Conflicts and Race

The process of identity formation is a life-long and continuous one, and each person's progression through various stages of the life-cycle differs. In Mrs James' case, identity formation seems to have been uneven. On the one hand, she has steadily consolidated her identity, over time, maintaining a sense of direction and purpose, remaining true to her values as a person and she is confirmed by those around her as the person she largely feels herself to be. On the other hand, she has been hampered by the cut-off and encapsulated aspects of her identity, which are the unconscious source of her anxieties and of her unresolved identity conflicts. These press upon her and at times they limit and impoverish her, representing *foreclosed* aspects of her identity (an interruption in the process of identity formation involving a premature fixing of self-images and the avoidance of alternatives involving ambiguities, interfering with the development of other potentials for self-definition).[20] At times of stress these fore-closed aspects become most evident. Her early internalization of her mother's attitudes toward aggression, and her defences for dealing with her angry feelings, have become a fairly unchanging part of her internal world. It is these which seek unconscious expression and in the process involve the misuse of racial groups.

Her major unresolved identity conflict is how to retain a sense of her own goodness and self-esteem while controlling her ordinary angry feelings which she experiences as unnecessarily frightening and dangerous. This conflict is exacerbated by cultural factors. In growing up, children have different opportunities to identity with real or fictitious people, and to avoid anti-heroes who are held up by family or community as people whom one should *not* be like. Because of the political and economic history of the West Indies, there were few, if any, positive models among West Indians at that time, who could show a healthy and appropriate use of assertiveness and aggression.[21] Mrs James' mother offered no basis for positive identifications in this respect. And there is no evidence of anyone else having served this purpose for her. It is, as if, any healthy assertion of her angry feelings could only be experienced as negative and part of a disowned negative identity.

As I have shown, her patterns of racial misuse, both of West Indians (seen as siblings), and of white people (seen as idealized parents), stem from these unresolved conflicts.

Given such a set of inner and outer dynamics, why did Mrs James select these *particular* racial groups for the attempted resolution of her inner conflicts? It is important to remember that this process started early in her life. Her siblings, who had deprived her of being the 'one and only' child, excited the usual feelings of sibling rivalry. Their aggressive dispositions made them appropriate repositories for carrying her disowned aggressive feelings, whilst she retained for herself her own goodness. Later on, other West Indians serve the same functions for her, especially when aspects of their behaviour give some reality foundation to her projections. The fact that they are the same race as her siblings means that they provide appropriate figures for the displacement and transfer of feelings from their original objects.

Her choice of white people as idealized parental substitutes is understandable in relation to the society within which she grew up. It was paternalistic and roles of authority and power were vested in white people. Her early experiences with whites were as parent-substitutes who cherished their own children but also cherished her. As employers they were good and caring and contrasted with her bad experiences with West Indian employers, so her intrapsychic needs and external reality converged.[22]

The Indians play no part in her inner world because her foreclosed identity was formed very early in her life in Barbados. There were no Indians there. The inner drama with its split roles. was already cast with players carrying out their assigned parts before she came to England. These same groups continued to serve her inner needs well enough in England, because in both societies there were white figures in power and authority and there were fellow West Indian workers.

These split images of whites and blacks, tend to emerge most often during periods of stress (as in illness), or under provocation. Alongside these patterns of racial misuse, she has been steadily moving towards a more realistic perception of the English and is able, at times, to use her attacking sense of humour as a way of handling her ambivalence towards them, so reducing earlier idealization patterns. The difficulty is that these more mature insights may not yet be stable enough to withstand any further regressive pulls which stress can evoke under similar circumstances. West Indians may still be judged unduly harshly and devalued as a group – a deflection of her own perilous self-esteem back towards her own group.

Vicious and Virtuous Cycles

Mrs James' misuse both of whites and her fellow West Indians, constitute infringements of *their* identity processes. To be seen as idealized and too-good is a denial of the humanity and ordinary imperfections of white English people; and to be devalued as quarrelsome and divisive, is to stereotype her own group, and negatively diminish their range of qualities. In her inter-racial encounters, by avoidance and denial, she shuns the possibility of confronting these stereotyped images with revised versions of reality. In this way, while her racial attitudes avoid confrontations, nonetheless they feed, in a general way, potentially vicious cycles in that her attitudes, by their negative imputations, impinge on both racial groups.

3 MISS JOHANNA JAMES

Issues Bearing on The Formation of Her Identity

Early family relationships

Johanna's early childhood was punctuated by separations. Her father left Barbados to come to England when she was six years old, followed some months later by her mother. When she went to join her parents in England at the age of thirteen, she left behind her two brothers, Neill and Adrian, and faced new separations from her grandmother, with whom she had been living, and from other members of her extended family in Barbados.

Her early memories are of a warmly devoted father; they are memories of delight in being treated as a feminine little girl by an effective father who loved her. She recollects how she jumped on his lap, how he taught her to swim, took her out in his car, and bought her dolls. She was clearly fond of her mother but also remembers being controlled in irksome ways and sensed that her mother had difficulties in separating from her children and seemed dependent on them for her emotional needs. 'She didn't think we were able to do without her.'

On the departure of her father, she seems to have felt the pain and the anger of separation and she missed him a great deal. When her mother left, this led to anxiety and she recalls her attempts to control her feelings of loss. 'I thought it over to myself and felt that this was going to mean an awful lot of loneliness.' She was able to experience their loss with a capacity to grieve, neither denying their absence nor projecting badness into them. All of these things, taken together with a tolerance for her own ambivalent feelings felt towards her absent parents, suggests that she had managed earlier developmental phases reasonably well and had reached what Klein[23] has described as the depressive position.

As she moved into a new life without her actual parents, she was able both to mourn their absence and to preserve good feelings for them, while concurrently enjoying her life with others and expressing to them the love which had been given to her. Her affection for her grandmother was deep and enduring as also her love for her aunt. And the warm bonds of the extended West Indian family helped to cushion the pain of separations.

Her relationship with her young brother Adrian, aged two, was a warm and concerned one. She felt close to him and when she came to London and had to leave him, his distress upset her greatly. But, nonetheless, she was able to relinquish her responsibility to her granny and her warm interest in him continued.

Contacts with white people in Barbados
Her mother's white employers were good to her and what she recalls about them are evocative of her father's relationship with her – the husband used to take her out in his car with his own children, and the wife bought her dolls. Although these were white parental figures, Johanna, unlike her mother, had no internal need either to idealize them or to use them as enduring parental models or substitutes.

An early memory involved noticing the differences in skin colour between herself and white people and, although too young to understand her granny's explanation, she observed the differences, reflected on them, and they were neither denied nor avoided.

At secondary school, her anxieties focussed on the fear of not being liked. Experiences recounted to her by adult West Indians had led her to expect unpleasantness from whites but she found the white teachers and children friendly, and, at a body level, was loaned a swimsuit by a white child on her first day.

When the father of Paul – a white school friend – referred to her as 'that coloured girl' her initial response was to turn down an offered lift. Paul's father, by attemping to give a partial but friendly explanation of his remark, made it possible for her to show *her* flexibility and trust and to accept the lift. What might have become a destructive cycle between herself and a white family was changed to a close and continuous contact between them, showing her capacity to turn a potentially vicious cycle into a benign one.

While able to enjoy mutual visiting, friendship and acceptance by white children, nonetheless Johanna recognised differences between them. 'I never felt left out and they made me feel one of them although I knew I wasn't, but I just never gave it a thought.' Her capacity to hold these two things together – the unity and the separation – contrasts sharply with her mother's difficulties. Johanna neither brushes differences aside, nor does she feel an inclination to dwell upon them.

In visiting homes of white friends, social class differences became apparent to her when she met their coloured maids. She felt angry and envious that white people did not do the dirty jobs but had the 'smart' jobs, like office-work. She noted that white Barbadians tended to look down on West Indians as past slaves and thought they were stupid; she believed it best to ignore them in the hope that they would in time feel and think differently. She was aware of the position ascribed to coloured people in her society, noting social class as well as racial distinctions.

A new life in England

Her re-union with her parents in England was affectionately welcoming. For the first time she had a room of her own, which had special meaning for her, and as the only child at home she was able to enjoy being 'the one and only' for the first time in her life.

Her experiences at an English school, approached with a certain anxiety, were extremely important for the development of her identity and her race attitudes. She made friends easily and was well liked by both staff and students, all of whom were white. The critical experiences with Susan, the English girl, who accused her of smelling, throws light on her ego strengths and her ways of coping with attack and humiliation. When confronted by this accusation, she first questioned herself and decided that she did *not* smell. In her search for an honest and realistic appraisal, she asked an English fellow-student and was told that 'It's just a thing which some people say about coloured people'. She felt depressed. This negative identity which was thrust upon her with all it's associations of anality, she reacted to with sadness and anger, which she controlled and turned back against herself. But above all, by holding on to the reality that she did not smell, she was able to ignore Susan who became merciless in her attacks. Finally, Johanna turned to a white teacher who gave her support. Humiliating treatment followed from the girl and from her mother who called her a 'wog' and a 'little black thing'. Exposed to this provocation, she was still able to retain a realistic and positive image of herself. When Susan finally made a friendly overture, Johanna characteristically and thoughtfully needed to know and understand what lay behind such shifts in behaviour. Susan's explanation of being unhappy at home and taking it out on Johanna was acceptable to her, since they later became good friends.

In this series of events, three things are especially important from the point of view of race relations: first, the other English girls gave Johanna their moral support; secondly, Johanna had sufficient ego strength and self-esteem to initiate an approach to white girls for their comments on whether in fact, Susan's accusations were correct or not. This is reality-oriented behaviour characterized by openness, flexibility and an overall courage; and thirdly, at no stage was Johanna provoked into negative stereotyping of white girls in general and so scapegoating was avoided.

Her strengths lay, not only in being able to see the distortions in Susan's attitudes and beliefs but also in being able to affirm her own sense of identity which included an inherent dignity, integrity and feeling of being a worthy and respected person. In the process of affirming her positive identity and withstanding the pressures upon her, she also gained the support of the teacher. The negative attributions which Susan tried to attach to Johanna were weakened, and finally collapsed when Susan apologized. As a consequence, Johanna's identity became enhanced, both in her own eyes and in those of fellow-students and staff. Again, what could have become a vicious cycle of hostile projections and counter-projections was tipped over by Johanna into a benign and virtuous cycle characterized by a friendly set of relationships.

Johanna's sexual identity was meanwhile becoming more securely established and confirmed. The interested attentions which she received from the boys at the neighbouring school, made her aware of her sexual attractiveness and her father's love for her (symbolically expressed in his welcome-home gift to her of a nightdress case) also acted to support a growing femininity and sense of identity as a woman.

By the time she left school, her ability at school had been acknowledged, her leadership qualities recognised by being made a school prefect, and her high standards of deportment had led to an image of herself in other people's eyes as being, if anything, 'too good'.

Trying to cope with racial discrimination
In trying to obtain employment as a clerk-typist, Johanna approached five firms on different occasions and was rejected by all of them, apparently on grounds of colour. After the first rejection, her parents recognised her unhappiness and urged her to go on trying. After two more rejections, both felt to have been made solely because of her colour, she experienced a deep sense of depression. 'I never really got angry . . . I just felt I wasn't wanted.' Her anger is turned back against herself; she gave up, stayed at home for two weeks and did not bother to look for a job. 'I then felt that wasn't good enough, and I would make another try.' She pulls out of the depression, turns her anger into positive action and again seeks work. But once more she is rejected on spurious grounds of 'health' which are not convincing and she is angry and hurt. And when the fifth interview leads to harsh rejection and abrupt rudeness, she becomes extremely depressed. 'It was nearly driving me out of my mind.'

Her search for work which would give her an opportunity to show what she was capable of doing, was being cruelly denied to her. A negative image of how West Indians were regarded by English employing bodies was being thrust upon her. Deeply shaken, she remained true to her inner nature and instead of retreating into an angry self-punitive withdrawal, she faced the ugly situation which she confronted. Summoning renewed courage, she set about finding a small, personal setting within which she could work and so restore the damage to her self-esteem which these humiliating rejections had aroused.

Within the protected confines of an English home, she found a job. 'It wasn't fantastic – it was just a house – just her home – but at least I thought I might be happy there.' She had exercised choice, her ego strengths enabling her to endure the acute anxiety of seeking acceptance from yet another potential English employer. She risked the apprehension for the sake of an active movement towards self-actualization and growth.

Although nervous at the outset, it is striking that when treated with acceptance and as a person in her own right, she was able to respond with warmth and genuine feelings. Her bitter experiences of racial discrimination did not elicit an inner need to stereotype negatively English people in general. On the contrary, she remained open to the interest, respect and affection of the entire white family, and was able to reciprocate these same qualities. They were three very happy years during which she could give back, out of gratitude, that which she had received. She came to feel part of the family and when after three years she decided to leave, she grieved at the pain of parting but the decision to move on was her own; her ego strong enough to face potential blows to her self-esteem. From the point of view of her identity development, this period served as what Erikson has termed a psychological moratorium[24] – a period of delay when Johanna needed to experiment with new roles and flexible self-images, when no irreversible decisions were made. It was a home-based apprenticeship in work skills and in exploring her relationships with an English family.

From the race relations aspect, let us consider the path she chose. By reacting as she did to the corrosive effects of racial discrimination on her self-esteem, she used her freedom, limited and circumscribed though it was, to select a setting within which she could develop. Frankl has called the ability to choose one's attitude in a given set of circumstances, the last of human freedoms left to man.[25] She used this freedom, but what alternatives did she have?

Her anger and frustration could have led her to assume that very negative identity which English society was thrusting upon her by its rejections and discrimination. She might then have chosen to become aggressively that which she was implicitly regarded as being – socially inadmissible, rejected and unwanted, undesirable as a person and without value as a worker.[26] This could only have fed a destructive spiral in race relations by which the discrimination of the white employers would have led to an angry embodiment in Johanna of their negative stereotypes, further stimulating white prejudices and hostilities so that attitudes on both sides would have escalated in destructive ways. Another path which she might have taken would have been to withdraw into depressive inertia, a burden to herself and her family and an angry accusation implicitly levelled at the society which had failed to value her. The loss would have been both to her and to society. There were other possibilities, including one of turning her anger into a purposive attack on the foundations of racial discrimination and those segments of English society which allow or tolerate discrimination on the basis of colour. She could then have joined others in political pressure groups to try and alter existing injustices. None of these alternatives are mutually exclusive. Instead, her leading tendency was to use the painful series of incidents as something on which to reflect so that it became part of an inner experience. It also acted as a trigger for a seriousness of search, a decision and a choice which facilitated her personal growth. But what is most striking is once again, her capacity to turn a potentially malignant cycle in racial misuse, into a creative and constructive spiral.

On prejudice and discrimination

Having achieved some impressive 'heart work' on her own prejudices, reaching an inner state of respect for individuals as individuals, her comment that 'Laws to make people unite won't work. It has to be something from the heart' carries conviction. Job discrimination rouses her greatest sense of outrage. 'If people want to make things better, they should start by seeing that coloured people who are qualified should be given the positions which they merit. Job discrimination is what annoys me more than anything else.'

Feelings of despair are also rooted in her belief that race relations will deteriorate still further in England. Enoch Powell is seen as a destructive politician. 'If anyone's ruining the chances of us all getting on together, he's going about it the right way.' Her defence in the face of all these political and social issues is to choose non-involvement and to try not to think about these issues. She knows it is there but feels impotent to do anything about it.

Moving in mixed world

Her present post is a 'smart one,' as she once described such office jobs when she lived in Barbados. She more than doubled her salary by moving to a West End medical practice. This upward occupational mobility, linked with the recognition of her competence, has helped her self-assurance and further consolidated a positive sense of identity. Initial nervousness at the thought of working with

English girls has now abated. She feels at ease with them and is no longer preoccupied with racial differences. Her natural charm, attractive personality and sex-appeal are responded to by her English employers and her colleagues – especially male, white colleagues. The significance of this for Johanna, previously rejected for jobs on grounds of race, lies in the re-affirming of a healthy narcissism with a consequent shift in her feelings of racial identity in a more positive direction.

Jealousy and envy are openly expressed by the white girls because she attracts the men and 'takes them away' and they challenge her about being too nice to people. Her reaction is quiet affirmation. 'But I don't go out of my way to be – it's just me.' Since they continue to be friendly, they seem to have been able to sustain this potential threat to their relationship.

Johanna's social life has been moving steadily towards widening social contacts with people of all races. Indians are related to as individuals and she has an Indian friend with whom she partly identifies, both having difficulties with their parents, caused by cultural shifts and emphasis on conformity and control. Race is forgotten and transcended and it is the individual who matters. She has been actively searching for a wider identity, appearing to by-pass black power, and 'black is beautiful',[27] for what Erikson has called a more inclusive identity, where those who previously depended on each other's negative identities, join their identities so that new potentials are activated in both.[28] She becomes an innovator, helping her English colleagues at work to 'take the plunge' and come to West Indian parties, where she gives them psychological support re-membering her own feelings of self-consciousness. People are welcomed in her home, irrespective of race, and valued for themselves alone.

It is in the street and in public places where Johanna's more inclusive identity is put to a stern test. When she is out with her friend Roger (who looks white although he has a black parent) or when she is talking to any English male acquaintance, she becomes aware that English people tend to be sexually curious as to the nature of their relationship. It is an invasion of her privacy and distastefully embarrassing to find herself the object of others' vicarious needs to uncover her private relationships. Since her contacts with the Englishmen are those of acquaintances, and her relationship with her boy friend is not an intimate one either, she rightly resents this and tries to escape from it. 'Oh my God, let's get out of here.' She not only protects her own rights to privacy and freedom but consistently respects the rights of others; she is furious when she sees a West Indian boy pestering a white girl who was not interested in him.

Unresolved Identity Conflicts and Race

The distressing incident with the waitress throws light on environmental provocations of racial prejudice, and how these press on unresolved identity conflicts in Johanna.

When, on account of her colour, she was treated with humiliating contempt by the white waitress in a West End restaurant, this provoked a reactive and righteous rage which she could not allow herself to express. 'Oh God! I'd just love to tell her what I think of her but I just can't be hostile to people – I just can't . . . I always stop myself.' Her anger is literally experienced as choking; she cannot eat, because of the wrath which she has swallowed back into herself. When the Englishman at the next table not only expressed his empathy, but also his shocked surprise at her lack of overt reaction, it is as if he voiced for her, part of her own inner dialogue. His voice says – for her – that she should have said something to the waitress, she should not have just sat there and taken this attack. To which, her inner voice answers, 'I can't – I stop myself'. To him, she denies the inner rage, 'I'm getting used to it – I just can't be bothered.' This is an outward denial of the bottled-up feelings inside her.

On sharing this upsetting experience with her English colleagues with her characteristic openness, one of them spontaneously goes to challenge the waitress for her rudeness to 'the polite young lady'. On her return, when she questions Johanna as to why she stays in a country like England where she is subject to such rudeness, Johanna's answer reflects her awareness of the tragic and ironic aspects of life, as well as her capacity for trying to overcome things. 'Our life is full of whys and buts and ifs, but it's no good thinking like that.'

The pain of the incident continues to weigh heavily upon her and her undischarged anger becomes relentlessly self-attacking. She stops going to that restaurant and wishes she did not exist. She phantasies annihilating herself as the anger finds no legitimate way of expressing itself and becomes turned back against herself. This is the root of her depression and underlies her tensions and headaches. She has, however, a capacity for seeing a reality whole and being able to recollect different and more benign experiences, and so she is able to recall very good treatment she has had in other restaurants. In this way her self-esteem becomes somewhat regenerated.

She explores her phantasied fears of what might have happened to her if she had answered back and expressed her indignant feelings to the waitress. She draws upon actual experiences of people known to her in order to project the imaginary scene – a big row, nasty and degrading, the police come and she is falsely accused of saying things which she has not said and so 'everybody would have been against me'. This inner phantasy has sufficient persecutory aspects to strangle any expression of her justified indignation. But the inner debate and conflict continue to pre-occupy her. 'Many of my friends don't just sit back – they fight back. I suppose it's not a bad thing, fighting back – but there's no point in fighting if you're not going to get anywhere – it's like hitting your head against a wall'. But there is the other side of it too. 'We're all made differently. Some people can take things and some can ignore them and I'm one of those who can pretend that I have never heard things if I want to. But if I really want to take action, I can get pretty worked up about it.'

Of course, the ability to be angry is found in all healthy personalities and the major problem is not only to learn to control it but also to learn under what conditions and in which ways it can legitimately be expressed. It is often necessary to express righteous indignation, to be forceful in one's own self-defence and also to be capable of voicing protest at unwarranted treatment as a form of self-affirmation. For Johanna, however, such behaviour is felt to be threatening to her own integrity and self-image since it is experienced as indistinguishable from evil, destructive rage.

Her dilemma is complex since many things are happening at once, and there is a dynamic interplay between her unresolved identity conflicts, her experiences of life, the social and environmental realities, and the provocative pressures of this specific situation. All these aspects overlap and modify each other as different facets of the whole. For purposes of clarification, however, they need to be talked about separately.

At the intrapsychic level, she does not find it easy to express aggression and within this particular family there is a style of dealing with such feelings which has certain consequences. It must be kept under rigid control or else self-degradation is felt to follow, public shame and humiliation occur and there is the betrayal of one's inner sense of identity and firmly held values. Johanna's ability to pretend that she has not heard things, evokes her mother's way of coping. Difficulties in handling aggression and common styles of dealing with it are traceable through three generations, if we include Mrs James' own mother (as reflected through the eyes of Mrs James), Mrs James herself and Johanna.

Socialization processes affect the expression of aggression. Storr has suggested that the way a child is handled within a family may determine whether predominantly paranoid or depressive mechanisms are used for dealing with aggression.[29] Johanna uses depression but does not do so to an extreme extent. She feels that right is on her side. Her depression turns into tension headaches and other somatic complaints. In this choice of defence-mechanisms she is closer to her father (and therefore perhaps to the grandmother who brought them both up) than to her mother, who tends to use predominantly paranoid means of dealing with her angry feelings. 'It is not I who am violent and destructive, but they.'[30]

Probably the absence of available West Indian models with whom Johanna can identify in situations of this kind add to her difficulties. Her parents are no longer appropriate because of generational differences which parallel vast changes in the social, economic and political climate, and there are rapidly changing racial identity images among black people themselves. Her world is politically different from the familiar one that her parents faced during their late adolescence. In the context of this discussion, she requires models who can stand firmly for the right to be treated with respect, and do so with integrity, dignity and quiet but robust self-assurance. As social and communal changes come about, so new role models emerge. Through identification with new models, the pace of further change quickens. Johanna seems to lack such models for identification. In recent years, the United States has produced several outstanding examples of black leaders who have been able to do precisely this for their own people. There is no evidence in Johanna's life story that anyone has come to serve this function for her. And yet it is a fundamental need if her own understandable problems in this area are to find a new resolution.

Historic factors also play a part since social and political realities have long inhibited Negroes and Afro-Caribbean peoples from openly expressing their negative feelings. Under conditions of slavery and colonial rule, such self-control had an important preservative and adaptive function. Before a child is conscious of how and when to express angry feelings, he is affected by the stress of his parents in their efforts to control the display of aggression in relation to white people. Messages are unconsciously picked up, transmitted from one generation to the next, consciously and unconsciously, and so enter the inner experience of each succeeding generation. As a result, overt rage and its expression have become dammed up and in their place have come guilt, shame, fear, self-hatred and recrimination.

For Johanna, her past presses upon her and she finds within her one small voice which echoes her mother's defences of denial. But the formidable negative images of how her people are stereotyped by the English community confront her. Some of these images are conveyed verbally, as when the waitress finally came to apologise to Johanna said 'What surprises me is that you didn't blast off which most coloured girls would have done'. It is against such negative stereotypes that she consciously and unconsciously defends herself when she comments that it would not be worth it to assert herself in a situation such as the one she confronted, as it would be degrading. She feels terribly embarrassed at public displays of shouting and abuse. She is affected by these English stereotypes of her people and fears their self-perpetuation if any behaviour of hers adds support to these negative identity images. Her fears act as a brake upon her freedom to show her indignation as it wells up inside her, and so she is unable to test out realistically whether these fears are justified or not.

At home she feels that her parents treat her as a child and she resents their restrictive control. She realises that part of this is the over-protection which characterizes the attitudes of West Indian parents toward their daughters but also senses that her mother perceives the world as a dangerous place, people as untrustworthy, and that these underlie her mother's control of her. Her wish to take care of herself is constantly confronted by her mother's inner fears and consequent needs to control her. 'It's an awful way to be.'

It is not only that she finds this frustrating but she is actively striving for autonomy and freedom. 'I like to feel free . . . I don't feel like an individual since I'm not free to do as I want . . . I prefer to have freedom and then if I get hurt . . . I've only myself to blame.' By their failure to recognise and support this insistent need, her parents fail to confirm her adult identity and constantly convey, by their control, that they see her as immature and dependent. Her bottled-up frustration and resentment are not directly expressed. They become converted into tension headaches.

Two different issues appear to act as restraints upon her. Since the family have only recently been re-united, their present unity as a family is felt to be relatively fragile, and she fears that direct confrontations with her parents on these issues might fragment the group from within. She assumes a responsibility to keep the family together. In addition, the strong emotional bond between her and her father with its oedipal overtones, seems to lead both of them into an unconscious collusion aimed at retaining each other for the present, rather than letting each other go.

Different psychologists have used varying terms for processes of growth moving toward fuller functioning, such as autonomy, individuation, self-realization or self-actualization, and although each puts his own emphasis upon it and theoretically explains the process in different ways, I find Maslow's approach useful[31] for understanding Johanna's strivings and the conflicts which she has.

To Maslow, healthy people are those who have sufficiently gratified their basic needs for love, safety, belongingness, respect and self-esteem so that they are motivated primarily by trends towards actualization of their potentials and a fuller knowledge and acceptance of their own intrinsic nature. All of these then tend toward a greater unity and integration within the person.[32] Self-actualization is, of course, an ideal which few people, if any, actually approach. But Johanna's life and development are, I believe best understood both in relation to the active processes which steadily propel her nearer towards her goals, and to those forces which impede her further growth.

Because she wants to conserve the warm bonds which the family currently provide, she has been unable to combine her search for autonomy with the retention of their love.

These difficulties within the family are exacerbated by conflicts in relation to racial prejudice and discrimination. She rightly requires to be valued with full human dignity and respect which she herself accords to others of all races. Because of all the factors previously discussed, she has not yet been able to reconcile her compassionate understanding of others with a justified indignation and anger which can be vented on her own account, in defence of herself. Maslow has shown that self-actualizing people *can* give expression to their justified indignation and disapproval *more* wholeheartedly and with less uncertainty than average people. 'Anger does not disappear with psychological health; rather it takes the form of decisiveness, self-affirmation, self-protection, justified indignation, fighting against evil, and the like.'[33]

Johanna's anger is largely a reactive one to the social and political forces which confront her. It is not primarily a welling-up from inside her of unresolved conflicts from her past. Her fears in venting her feelings spring largely from the social consequences which she imagines may follow. She lacks adequate models who show healthy anger, neither destructively sadistic nor motivated by malice, but reactive to a lack of respect and freedom denied on grounds of colour. If she could find a way of expressing her indignation, movement toward personal autonomy would be facilitated. Her personal strength would be affirmed in her own and in others' eyes, her identity strengthened. It is offensive to her to be treated as only an anonymous part of a general category of persons since it denies her individuality.

Her self-description confirms that she has a fairly realistic awareness of her positive aspects, as well as those human shortcomings and difficulties which she shares with others. She is largely able to accept herself as she is without either self-idealization or self-denigration. Her conflicts in expressing her anger and irritability are faced at a conscious level. 'People get on my nerves sometimes . . . I sometimes want to shout at people . . . I never really get angry . . . I try not to get into arguments.'

By holding back her anger and keeping it bottled up, she pushes it back inside herself. It impedes her, limits her spontaneity, makes her feel less well physically and is depressive in its effects. It also makes her appear excessively good which she knows she is not and this is disturbing and alienating. She retreats into her room when the going gets tough, becomes quiet and lives 'in a world of my own'. She is aware of what is making her angry and frustrated. She cannot yet solve the problem of what to do about it.

In no way does Johanna try and resolve her problems unrealistically. She knows they are her problems and understands that they emanate from a society which shows prejudice and discrimination, as well as from her relations with her parents. Since she sees people as whole functioning human beings, she neither splits her objects nor projects onto racial groups her unresolved identity conflicts. If anyone suffers, it is she at this stage.

She has a good perception of reality and is interested in thinking through problems, trying to understand them by self-searching and a lively curiosity. She accepts that some are insoluble; that we all live with conflict, doubts, suffering and anxiety and that we all have human shortcomings. So she neither reaches for an ideal perfection for herself nor requires it of others. Like her father, life is sensed with tragic overtones.

As a result she shows acceptance and regard for others and has a capacity for warm and meaningful relationships with all sorts of people. Her spontaneity, while curbed in areas touching on control of anger, is still available to her in a capacity for joyous delight. Her striving for autonomy and the consistency and integration of her behaviour over time, suggest a strong, well-developed ego is at work and identity development is steadily occurring.

She is not a narrow product of her cultural or racial past; but is a person who potentially transcends the secular boundaries of both race and social class.

Vicious and Virtuous Cycles

Johanna is one of the three subjects in this study who does not resort to racial misuse, and consistently and impressively converts potentially vicious cycles in race relations into their oppo- site – constructive spirals of racial accord. These have been dis- cussed in detail, starting with her earliest encounter with Paul, the white schoolboy in Barbados, her handling of Susan in an English school, her way of dealing with the traumatic effects of job discrimination by seeking and finding work in an English home and finally her confrontation with the waitress. In each of these contexts, Johanna transcends the pitfalls of feeding prejudice with prejudice, and while showing resilience and resourcefulness, moves each cycle away from its destructively escalating course towards a final resolution which, while maintaining her integrity, evokes positive feelings of regard and respect in the others.

This is a striking achievement to which I return in the final chapter of this book.

4 ADRIAN JAMES

Issues Bearing on The Formation of His Identity

Early family life: coping with separations

Adrian was separated from his parents at the age of two when they left for England. He was fortunate to have his paternal grandmother, already a familiar figure, to love and care for him and she played an extremely important part in his life as a mother-substitute from that time on until he re-joined his parents at the age of fifteen. These vital early separations were only the first of a steady stream of other separation losses which occurred as one loved parental-substitute after another left, in each case except one, to come to England.

His aunt, who he felt to be like a mother to him, was a member of his grandmother's household and he was very sad when she too deserted him. He was seven years old at the time. His earliest memory, interestingly enough, does not concern the loss of his parents, which he could not recall, but appears to be a displacement or screen memory of that separation. When his aunt took him to school at a very tender age, he remembers vividly how he cried inconsolably all through that first day because I did not know where I was and she'd gone. And all the teachers tried to lift me up and said 'Hush, hush' and I did not pay them any mind. I'm crying and crying and want my aunt . . . and I sat there all day, wailing and crying, crying, crying. And when my aunt came back for me I was still crying.

His tears were surely for his missing parents as well.

An uncle who was a 'kind of a father' to him, left for England at about the same time, and a few years later, when he was nine his sister Johanna, to whom he was devoted, set sail to re-join their parents and he watched her leave with intense feelings of sadness, abandonment and rejection.

> Well, they don't care about me, they don't like me. They sent for Johanna and they left me here for all this length of time . . . At the airport I called out to her because I didn't want her to go. I knew then I wasn't going to see any of my family until I grew big . . . when I saw other children going to the park and I couldn't go, I'd just sit and cry and say 'I wish my sister was here; then I could have also gone.'

Finally, his brother Neill, who had become a more and more distant figure, totally disappeared from Adrian's life and when they met by chance some years later in a shop, Neill gave no sign of recognition although it subsequently became clear to Adrian that he had known who Adrian was. This was a deeply hurtful experience.

Throughout his life in Barbados it was his grandmother who from the time his parents left until his re-union with them some twelve years later provided a continuity of love and care. But the bonds with his own parents were kept alive; his grandmother often spoke to him about his father, revealing to Adrian how deeply she loved his father and missed him. The letters which maintained a link between Adrian and his parents, and in particular those exchanged with his father, were very important to him.

> I thought a lot about my dad and my mom after they left. They used to write to me and send photographs of themselves. . . . When I was old enough to write, I wrote as if I was just talking to my dad in front of me. It seemed as if my dad was there and I was talking to him. I loved him a lot although I didn't know who he was.

The contacts maintained through letter writing were not, in themselves, sufficiently sustaining for Adrian to feel in touch with his unknown parents and loved by them. But at the same time, as discussed earlier in this chapter when analysing his father, deeper forms of interaction between Mr James, Adrian and his grandmother were unconsciously maintained through projective identification. Mr James obtained unconscious gratification of his needs to stay in touch with his mother by using Adrian as that part of himself which had remained behind in Barbados. His mother – Adrian's grandmother – apparently unconsciously colluded with this by retaining, through Adrian, some sense of her own son's continuing presence. And Adrian, by sharing the same 'mother' with his father – also appears to have unconsciously conformed with his father's and grandmother's unconscious perceptions of him. By collusion, he sustained these mutual projections by feeling himself to be the container of aspects of his father. In these ways, Adrian may have been helped to feel loved and to be the possessor of specially unique meanings for both his father and his grandmother. It was only when finally he re-joined his parents in England that he could be seen more fully by them as the person he in fact was, and some of these projections could then start to be withdrawn.

It is difficult in Adrian's case to know how much damage these separations may have caused. The extended family system of West Indians would in any event have compensated for some of the worst consequences of early separations. Adrian had a substitute mother, already familiar to him before his parents left, and what emerges from all four life stories of the James' family, is that his grandmother was a remarkably devoted, consistently reliable and loving person. She was certainly one of the most important people in his life. His continuous relationship with her would have been a sustaining one, mitigating some of the ill-effects of his separation from his parents.

Splitting Processes

Melanie Klein in tracing how unconscious phantasies of the child and external reality each affect the other,[34] has pointed out that when bad environmental experiences occur to a child these are more likely to leave him with a sense of his own 'badness' if at the same time his inner world is coloured by phantasies which are angry and attacking. The developmental stage at which separations occur is therefore extremely important and since Adrian's parents left before he was three years old, he was then at a developmental phase when fears normally arise from inner phantasies of destructiveness, stimulated by the necessary absences and frustrations of the mother; and when, as in his case, both parents disappear, he may well have feared that he had driven them away because of his own phantasies and thus because of his 'badness'.

A way of coping with such anxieties is to split off the loving and good feelings from the frighteningly bad ones, so keeping his conflicting emotions of love and hate as separate as possible. Such a split is considered by Klein[35] to be an essential stage in the development of the young infant and under the multiple stresses which Adrian was experiencing, it was one way of helping to maintain both his hope for himself and his future (by keeping both himself and his parents idealized and very good) and by thrusting out and projecting onto others his hurt and angry feelings, stimulated by the actual loss of his parents and his feared 'badness'. The introjected figures of his parents serve, in phantasy, to keep inside him powerful, good, ever-present parents to act as barriers against his inner persecutory fears and anxieties. While at the same time, his own self-image remains a very good one, but one to which he clings rigidly – a defence against the feared aggressive feelings.

Adrian's idealization of his father may have been further consolidated by his grandmother's evident love and admiration for him, and by the fact that there was no basis for reality-testing available between father and son other than through their letters. The constancy with which Mr James wrote to his son and sent him such money as he could afford, further upheld Adrian's positive feelings for him.

> I know some fathers don't care about their sons, but I always saw him as a father who loves his sons – loves his children and would try his best for them. If I needed money and he didn't have it in time, he would try to get it to me as fast as he could. He would write once a month and send money . . . . I saw my mom more or less the same way as I saw him. I felt she was the same. She used to write every two weeks.

There were also other factors which contributed towards Adrian's tendency to split off his good from his bad feelings. The identity analysis of his mother also revealed her tendency to split. Adrian's earliest years were spent with his mother and it is likely that, by the time she left, he was more than usually vulnerable to experiences which, while emanating in the external world (his parents' departures), also echoed her possible handling of Adrian. Furthermore, his own child rearing by his grandmother and uncles seems to have strongly favoured the curbing of aggression, since its outward expression was disapproved, and a high degree of self-discipline expected. His grandmother played an extremely important part in encouraging him to achieve through work and to recognise that it took hard and diligent effort. For all these reasons, the weight of Adrian's upbringing was strongly disapproving of the expression of aggression and emphasized, by contrast, diligence, control, reliability and obedience.

While splitting processes continue to be in evidence in Adrian's life, there is also a capacity realistically to express his pain at the separation from his parents and his ambivalence of feelings. He is aware of feeling deserted and is not out of touch with the full reality of his position. After Johanna left and he felt rejected, he commented 'I couldn't give up, you know, and I had to write to them just to keep in touch. Well, after Johanna had gone, my dad said "Don't feel downhearted – I'll have you down here one of these days." Well, after that I began to cheer up.' And later, when talking about Neill, it is possible that he was unconsciously reflecting his real feelings about his parents. 'I like him but he does certain things which I don't like. He should not have left and gone to live on his own as if he didn't care and could leave his relatives like that.'

Under the provocative stress of multiple separations, Adrian's tendency to use splitting as a defence strongly manifests itself, but not to the point where it becomes an extreme and rigidly held pattern since there are signs of a capacity to recognise his feelings of rejection and abandonment and so to experience ambivalence.

Keeping the good away from the bad – school days in Barbados
Unlike his sister, and indeed his parents as well, Adrian's school experiences in Barbados were almost entirely among fellow black West Indians. He had no contact with white people in Barbados except one person in his church. His tendency to split therefore, was worked out in Barbados on a canvas entirely composed of members of his own racial group.

On the one hand, he maintained an image of himself as being rigidly good, hard-working, unaggressive, morally correct, meeting adult requirements of him both at home and at school, and being liked and well respected by his teachers. On the other hand, the denied and feared 'bad' aspects of himself contained all his understandable feelings of anger arising from the deprivation of his parents and the blow to his self-esteem which this had occasioned. He denied these aggressive feelings and projected them onto West

Indian peers at school who expressed then for him those bad, impulses to do with destructiveness, bullying, stealing and aggression.

In incident after incident he feels himself to be rigidly guarding and protecting his good self, the boy whom the teachers liked and of whom they approved, the captain of the form and the hard-working and able boy who got the highest marks in his class. He was also guarding the boy whom his grandmother could love and respect. He fears his understandably angry feelings and his resentments, and cannot admit these into his conscious self and so they appear in his life story as frightening aspects of bullies who assault him and treat him roughly. Again and again, he is wrongly accused of acts of which he is innocent. The bullies become persecutory figures. 'Their ways are so different, they are more like dogs'. What is at stake seems to be his own inner goodness, as time after time he is accused of various misdemeanours, minor acts of arson, bullying, talking in class, sexually 'interfering' with girls, and stealing. When he is wrongfully accused, he is able to exonerate himself in one of two ways; either he acts directly, by appealing to a man in authority, seen as benign and fair-minded – these are father figures (a headmaster, a police-man) and in each case they find the real culprit and clear Adrian's good name – or, alternatively, he escapes and outwits his adversary. There is not one incident related where he willingly accepts the role of victim, masochistically phantasying himself as unable to take action on his own behalf and so vicariously gratifying some need to be the martyred victim.

He projects the badness; and at times, his own fear which is denied, is attributed to the delinquent boys and 'I tremble for them'.

There are three incidents which have a slightly different symbolic quality, all of them involve stealing fruit, two of them round, juicy fruits (coconuts and guavas). In these incidents the same adult man – an evil persecutory figure – accused him of stealing what was not his and in each case the punishment had a nightmare quality. A bull is let lose to chase him, five dogs are set on him, and at another time the man himself hoists Adrian onto his shoulders and is riding him off to the police station when Adrian escapes. These incidents have oedipal overtones, as if he is symbolically stealing 'mother's breasts and milk' and an irate and angry 'father' catches him; he explains in each case that he was entitled to what he took as he had permission to do so – or that he had been falsely accused. It seems as if, having felt denied of his own mother's presence and her continuing love, his phantasies of stealing this back confront an angry father and guilt is aroused.

His reputation was under attack by the bully boys. He perceived them as trying to 'make my reputation drop' and since he was known as the best behaved boy in the school with an excellent record of achievement at school work, resulting in the respect and liking of his teachers, he felt the boys bore him a grudge. His defence against these attacks was to use denial, splitting and also avoidance of the boys in so far as that was possible. But as we have seen his ego resources were sufficiently sturdy for him to act on his own behalf to enlist parental figures who could protect him and uphold his reputation. He is greatly concerned with how adults perceive him and far less concerned with his peers' judgement of him. This is understandable in relation to his absent parents. By contrast, his sister Johanna was able to turn to her peers for re-assurance but for Adrian his sources of support and re-assurance are adult figures. It is parents who know, who are powerful, who can both blame, praise and exonerate. It is peers who can befriend (a cousin) but who can also be frightening persecutors.

In a number of incidents recounted, emphasis is put upon the theme of his smallness and hence his feelings of vulnerability and helplessness in relation to the bigger boys. Since he was an able student, he was, in fact, often in classes with boys considerably older and bigger than himself. This in itself, may also have served as a way of supporting a denial of his own aggressive feelings as he must have felt even more vulnerably aware of their bigness and persecutory strengths.

Re-union with his family

In coming to this country, Adrian left behind a familiar world and his beloved grandmother and he brought with him his phantasies of his unknown parents and their new twin babies as well as his actual memories of Johanna.

He was welcomed by his parents and his sense of relief was great as he was haunted by the fact that since he did not know their voices, he could be claimed by anyone. It was not as difficult as he had feared; his delight with his new home and London generally, and his re-union with the family, was mixed with a realistic assessment of the adjustment which he had to make. 'My family got used to me pretty quickly but it took me bit of time to get used to them because, you see, my ways were different. I did things differently and then my mom would tell me it's wrong and I would do it her way and try to get used to her.' It was the first time since the departure of his aunt and uncle that he was living under the same roof as a married couple. He was fifteen when he arrived and was already involved in adolescent change and starting to feel and experience his own developing sexuality.

Having lived in a small Barbadian town where he had no personal contact with white people apart from one member of his church congregation, he was suddenly plunged into living in a huge metropolitan city, in an ethnically diverse community and going to school with boys who were English and white, Indians and Pakistanis and also some West Indians. Cultural adaptations must have posed greater problems for Adrian than for his parents, both of whom had worked for middle-class white people in Barbados and had been to school with white children. Johanna, too, had had close friendships with white schoolmates, so Adrian had the narrowest range of inter-racial experiences of all four members of his family and had to make the largest adaptations in terms of cultural values and attitudes.

He starts to explore his new environment absorbing and observing. He samples new experiences with his father. He goes to dances with his father's friends, not minding that he is with older people, as if he is allowing himself some preparatory experience of being his father's son and using his father as a model in these social situations.

His identity development seems to be temporarily suspended between the young man who left his grandmother in Barbados and the young man who is slowly growing and clarifying who he is, where he belongs and what he is moving towards. In his situation at home and also at school he is feeling his way, deeply absorbed in taking in the situations which confront him, observing with acuity and sensitivity, and in the process trying to sort out his own position. 'At fifteen, with my mom and dad, it means actually a lot to me . . . it's a new phase . . . I begin to enjoy myself.'

Within the family, Adrian gets on well with the twins and picked up his relationship with Johanna. His mother took firm control of him and although he made efforts to adapt his ways to those of the family, and to do things like the English, he found it 'pretty awkward' at times.

At the contact interview, Adrian seated himself on the periphery of the circle, took no part in the discussion and answered minimally only when addressed. Often his mother answered questions which were directed to Adrian. By the time the study had finished however, he was relaxed and at home within the family group and took his own quiet but natural part in the discussions.

Unresolved Identity Conflicts and Race

The splitting processes to which Adrian resorted in Barbados involved West Indians exclusively for his attributions, but in the multi-racial situation within his London school, these same splitting tendencies find expression by being invested in different racial groups. The English and the Indians are the two racial groups chosen.

The interviews with Adrian commenced about six months after his arrival in England when his chosen role seemed to be that of an observer, more accurately that of a participant-observer. He found himself in a marginal situation at school where a small group of West Indian boys were outnumbered by much larger groups of both English and Indian boys. He tended to remain on the sidelines in these early months.

The English boys initially rejected him and did not want to play with him. At the same time he found to his distress that they could not understand his accent and as a result he had to resort to writing down what he had to say. This must have resonated most painfully the earlier lack of direct verbal communication between himself and his parents when he was young, and revived a sense of isolation and rejection.

He perceived the English boys as rough, destructively aggressive, undisciplined, wild, shocking and sexually provocative. This group of English boys seems to have unconsciously served as a repository for his disowned and frightening aggressive feelings, while the Indian and Pakistani boys were idealized and seen as very good and admirable, apparently serving the function of keeping alive for him his own ideal self-image. In Barbados, he was able to express and have confirmed, his good and able self whom the teachers liked and approved. But as a newcomer to this overwhelmingly complex society, unsure of himself and under the stress of his uprooting and his re-union with his family, he was not yet in a position to express himself and find, by confirmation from peers and teachers, his own worth. The Indians and Pakistanis were ambitious and hard working students with 'very good reputations' and by admiring and idealizing them, they unconsciously kept alive for him during this period aspects of his own ego-ideal – his ambition and capacity for hard work.

He saw the English boys as bullies with ways very different to his own, for whom he could not feel sorry as 'they bash you up, get their cuts and then they go back and bash you up again'. In this way he distanced himself from them as well as from his feared and denied aggressive feelings, which they now carried for him.

With marked insight, Adrian noted that envy played a part in the ill-feeling between the English and Indians.

> They grudge the little Indian boys what they have . . . The white boys feel very bad about the Indians outclassing them. Like if a white boy sees an Indian tomorrow with a new pair of shoes on, he would say 'Oh – his shoes – how cheap!', and . . . in this way they actually crush the Indian boys. Its probably that the English boys want what the Indians have accomplished. They can do it if they try hard enough to learn, but they don't. They just come to school and talk about girls . . . half the prefects and form captains and librarians at the school are Indians and they have a good reputation for behaviour. I think the white boys actually feel a grudge against the little Indian boys for what they have accomplished. The Indian boys usually come top in their form. . . . That might be why some of the English boys don't like them. . . . To me, the Indians and Pakistanis are not different from others in the school. In some ways they are even better than some of the white boys . . . The Indians actually outclass the white boys in everything at school. I hope no one will dislike them – I don't dislike them.

In Barbados, he felt he had been envied by the rough bullies for his accomplishments and that they had tried to destroy his reputation. Now he sees the English boys trying to do the same to the Indians. Although his identification and empathy go out to the Indians, he does not see them as passive victims any more than he saw himself in that role in Barbados. He recognises that it is because of their *positive* accomplishments that they are attacked, and he identifies with their continuing capacity to pursue their objectives in the face of these attacks.

His Victorian background in regard to sex contrasts with the values and attitudes of the permissive society into which he is now plunged. With so many things demanding of his commitment and involvement, his consciously expressed feeling that he is not yet ready for any sexual involvement with girls is understandable in the light of his more pressing needs to work out a place for himself in his new society and establish his relationships at home and at school. But, nonetheless, there is some denial of his sexual feelings and an attempt to separate them off from himself as possibly too anxiety-producing at this stage. As a result, he seizes on these interests of the English boys to express his moral disapproval.

At the time that he is clarifying his attitudes towards the English boys, Enoch Powell's speeches directed against coloured immigrants in this country were also having some impact on him. 'What he's trying to do is to make all white people hate the coloured people. I don't hear of any black people causing trouble in this country. If there's any trouble, it's probably some stupid white man.' This confirms for him at a political level, what he is already feeling and expressing in his racial stereotyping of the English boys. They are stupid, trouble-making and provocative.

Adrian was studied at a critical and rapidly changing period of his life. His fragile sense of security and his unresolved identity conflicts led to splitting processes, to which he had resorted earlier in his life, when in Barbados. In England he seizes upon and distorts certain social characteristics of these two racial groups and converts their qualities into racial stereotypes. The Indians are 'very good' and the English are 'very bad'.

Adrian, as an able cricketer was put into the school cricket team soon after his arrival and the 'headmaster was proud to have a new boy playing in the school cricket team'. During his first year at school, he was promoted three times in class, tackling his work with energy, purposiveness and evident pleasure. And at the Anglican Church, of which he was a member, he was the only coloured in the choir and was then honoured by being made the Chief Crucifer in a largely white congregation. These achievements, and the re-cognition which they brought, earned him respect among his peers, the staff and in the community, all of which helped to secure a more sturdy sense of identity as an able student, a good sport and well-respected. After the study was complete – eighteen months after his arrival in this country – Adrian was made a school prefect.

As a result of these changes he was able to value his abilities as worthwhile and feel his own 'goodness'; so he gradually became able to 'take back' into himself his previous idealizations. This, in turn, started to make him feel stronger inside and so steadily lessened the need for further splitting with its resulting stereotyping. Perhaps his re-found parents and their love for him also meant that he no longer needed to cling so tenaciously to rigidly held ideas of himself as 'good'. He was loved and accepted as he was and the inner angers which arose in part from his separations from his parents and his feelings of rejection were assuaged and so could be further deployed by seeking expression in constructive work. He was able to convert his aggression into active channels – sport, work and play. Consequently, the racial stereotypes which had served such a dynamic function in his life at particularly stressful periods, became less necessary. After the study was complete and we returned to clarify with Adrian some of the points raised, he revealed a shift in his feelings; some of the English boys were really 'quite nice' and had become his friends and although he still liked and respected Indians, he saw them more as individuals and capable of being both good and bad.

The potentially destructive cycles of escalating racial hostilities in which Adrian was immersed at the beginning of his school experience in this country, were switched into their opposite by two different factors: first, by Adrian's skills and achievements which dramatically altered his status and position in the school; and secondly, by his increasing inner security arising from his re-integration into a loving family.

Considering his early experiences and deprivations, Adrian's identity development has proceeded relatively well and is moving in a positive direction. Arriving in this country at the critical point of adolescence, he displayed a similar kind of inner intuitive wisdom to that which Johanna also had shown. He, too, needed a resting phase – a psychological moratorium – to allow him to take in and absorb all kinds of new relationships and situations, changed cultural patterns and attitudes. He was not ready to fix his roles or to prematurely commit himself. He used this period fruitfully and as the study drew to an end there were already signs of steady identity crystallization. His stage of development might be called that of an *emergent* identity. Assertiveness and constructive use of aggression are emerging in the field of work competence, sport and play. His splitting tendencies are diminishing. There is also some evidence of a growth in his sexual identity; his career plans are shifting from an earlier interest in accountancy (with possible anal associations), to being a pilot with an emphasis placed upon control, risk-taking and the need to 'be on target' (as he puts it); all of these suggest a shift towards a more genital orientation. His choice of career also reveals positive identifications with his father, since he too wants to control a large machine but not a bus, an aeroplane.

His relationships at home have worked out well thus far, although it is likely that the firm control which his mother exerts over him, upheld as it is by West Indian cultural patterns, may become an area of conflict in the future.

At the inter-racial level, unresolved identity conflicts could have been inflamed by the initial racial prejudice which he experienced from the English boys at his school. However, it seems likely, that whereas they didn't want to 'play with *him*', by his prowess in the cricket team, he managed to turn what might have become a vicious cycle in race relationships into a benign one. He had a specific skill which was valued by the whole school. And so he ended up playing with *them*.

His capacity to admire the Indians and Pakistanis for their positive abilities enabled him to identify with them until such time as he could find within himself similar areas of competence on which his identity development is now steadily basing itself.

At the time of the study, the major identity conflicts confronting Adrian were those general to adolescents in our culture, exacerbated by his uprooting in mid-adolescence and being catapulted into a 'new' family and new society. These included how to find within himself the competence and goodness which was his, while expressing a legitimate amount of anger and aggression. In Barbados, his West Indian peer group carried the 'bad' parts of himself, while the 'goodness' was carried both by the idealized father-images and by his own idealized self-image. In England, his English peers carry the 'bad' projected bits of himself; but now that he has been re-united with a good and loving father with whom he seems to have a positive relationship he no longer requires an idealized father-image; his ideal self-image is now attached to peers – the Indians and Pakistanis.

Why, since there were West Indian boys at his London school, did he not use them for carrying his disowned 'bad' feelings? It seems possible that they were not powerful enough within the school to carry as much relevant weight as did the 'English bullies'. Furthermore, since his Victorian values had been outraged by the white boys' aggression and also their personal habits of smoking, swearing and talking about sex, the West Indian boys at his school did not lend themselves as appropriately as did the English to serve his unconscious needs.

And why were the Indians chosen for the projections they received? It is generally recognized that Asian students in this neighbourhood are noted for their educational aspirations and achievements, more of them proportionately going on to 'A' levels than do their fellow white students. Adrian's choice of racial groups unconsciously fits some of the social characteristics of English and Asian boys but by distorting and exaggerating these qualities and giving them a global generality, he turns them into social stereotypes to serve his unconscious needs.

Finally, a word about his own self-description. He emphasises, at the positive level, those same qualities which run as themes throughout the self-descriptions of his father, mother and Johanna – he sees himself as kind, generous, helpful, honest and 'with a good conscience'. His negative self-description brings out the feared 'badness' against which he has been defending himself for so long. It relates to past memories in Barbados. He remembers a coloured woman who disliked him and who saw him as black, ugly (= bad?) and a no-good thief. It seems that his fears as a deprived child were that he was unloved and unloveable, and that he had been left because he was 'bad'. His fear of stealing appears to connect with what was said earlier in this chapter in relation to early stealing incidents – that what he longed for and took in phantasy was his mother's love of which he had felt deprived.

Vicious and Virtuous Cycles

The potentially destructive cycles of escallating racial hostilities which Adrian became involved in feeding in his early months in this country, were altered dramatically, and converted into benign cycles by two different factors: first, by Adrian's gifts as a cricketer and his school achievements both of which dramatically altered his status and position within the school as well as giving a boost to his self-esteem; and secondly, by re-integration into a loving family his tendencies to split were diminished, and the anxieties which underlay his defences, were allayed.

TRANSFERENCE AND COUNTER-TRANSFERENCE EFFECTS

Although we anticipated that we might meet with some hostility and suspicion on account of being white, from the outset the James' response to us both was friendly and welcoming and the relationships got off to a good start. Some of the factors contributing to this have already been discussed in general terms (see Chapter 2).

Over and above these general factors, the previous good relationships which both Mr and Mrs James had had with white people in their past, and Johanna's unusual capacity for making close friends with white people and welcoming them to her home, meant that all three were open to friendly and trusting relationships with us. Over time these became consolidated, building on the earlier foundations. Adrian was the only member of this family whose contacts with white people were extremely limited apart from the schoolboys in Athol who carried his negative projections. Sylvia Hutchinson, being young, warmly acceptant, friendly in her approach, and attractive in appearance and personality, afforded a non-threatening relationship with Adrian, contrasting in every way with his relationships at school.

For all four James', it proved possible to use us as trusting confidantes and friends with whom they could share their experiences and attitudes towards the English, some of which were hostile. Johanna's life story reveals that she has often done this in the past with her white friends – trusted them with the details of unpleasant and painful encounters which she had had with other English people. So her response to the research relationship was confirmatory of the inner evidence in the research material. Their general air of relaxed informality contributed to ours, and helped us to feel increasingly at ease with them; and no doubt, *vice versa*.

Each of the four related to us in distinctive ways. Mr James, reserved and shy at first, soon talked more freely, sharing feelings, doubts and uncertainties. His manner was quietly reflective, confiding and at times inwardly searching. In the terminal interview, he said that I had reminded him of the white woman in Barbados with whom he had had an important and positive relationship. Although these are his conscious transference effects and he would be unaware of the unconscious associations nonetheless they confirm my own feelings that he was using me during the interviews as a representative of a good internal object, a trusted friend. He allowed me to see his grief when his mother died, as well as other vulnerable aspects of himself, expressed humour and many different facets of his personality; what was not shared however, or expressed were signs of hostility or anger, whether overtly or covertly. That this was not specific to his relationship with me or to whites in general is shown by his life story which reveals a man not easily moved to anger – an accident-free record at the wheel over ten years confirms this too.

His wife used the interview situation very differently. An exuberant personality, words tumbled out fast and experiences were re-enacted and dramatized rather than explored reflectively in greater depth. I felt placed in the role of audience to her performance. If I put a question to her, she often had difficulty in taking it in because of this absorption; but her identity analysis has shown that one of her defences against anxiety is not to hear, and to treat 'wind as cheap'. She said in the terminal interview that I had reminded her of a white woman whom she had known – her closest friend at the railway hostel when first she came to London, a friend who had taken her out to pubs, made her feel good and helped her to become one of a group of white friends. This confirmed my own feelings during the interviews that she was not idealizing me as a doctor, para-medical or related professional as her life story might have suggested, but as a peer and friend.

Johanna and Sylvia Hutchinson established a warm and easy relationship. There were only a few years difference in age between them, both were personable and attractive and Johanna seems to have been able to identify in part with the interviewer and use her as a trusted confidante. Characteristically, she did not feel at the terminal interview that Mrs Hutchinson had reminded her of anyone else; throughout the study, Johanna emerges as someone who responds to individuals as individuals.

Of all the families studied, the James' reacted to us with the greatest warmth and acceptance and conveyed the least covert hostility and nothing that we noted as overt. We are likely to have further consolidated their original positive feelings towards white people and no doubt in so doing, their unconscious feelings towards the English may have shifted in the course of this study in a more positive direction – a by-product of the research process, affecting the research data – a not unusual phenomenon with other research methods.

At the counter-transference level, Mrs Hutchinson and I explored with each other, before and after each interview, the feelings stirred in us by our research task with these particular subjects, and what in the relationship or the research material was pressing on sensitive areas of our own. To the extent that we became conscious of these, we were able to minimize some of their effects on us as interviewers; but of course, only some of the unconscious aspects were able to surface – others remain unknown.

At the level of interpretation, for which I am solely responsible, there is always the risk of selective attention, differential sensitivity to certain issues while being relatively indifferent to others, and other sources of subjective bias. This is one of the impelling reasons for the length of this book – for taking the decision to present as much of the raw life history material as possible as well as my interpretations of it, so that readers can make their own interpretations of the data, or modify a special emphasis if it is felt to be unfounded. My interpretations represent the best sense which I have been able to make of the material, but there are many different ways of conceptually approaching the data and interpreting it.

DISCUSSION

In the final chapter of this book (Chapter 10) the findings from all the identity analyses are pulled together and theoretically organized; here I will briefly comment on some of the salient features which have emerged from the analyses of the James family.

1 Among three members of the family (Johanna is the exception), there is a striking relationship between unresolved identity conflicts on the one hand, and patterns of racial misuse on the other. Racial groups serve as repositories for unwanted, or for longed for but as yet unrealised, aspects of the self. Johanna is one of the few subjects in the study who does not resort to racial prejudice; her frustrations are largely turned back against herself.

2 The choice of racial groups made by the three members of this family differs, each one unconsciously chosing specific racial groups which make a 'fit' with the vulnerable areas touched off by the underlying conflicts.

3 Specific racial groups selected as repositories can be substituted for by other racial groups under specific conditions involving social change (e.g., Adrian's use of *West Indian* bullies while in Barbados is served in England by a choice of *English* bullies).

4 There are some areas of vulnerability constituted by these unresolved conflicts, which are shared in common by various members of this family. While the source of unresolved identity conflicts lies within the inner world of individuals, nonetheless attributions and pressures emanating from the environment powerfully modify identity processes so that what starts as outer can become inner. Reviewing the conflicts of all four James', many of these emanate from racial discrimination and prejudice, either past or present, which exert an influence upon them. The roots of Mr James' attitudes towards Indians lie in the historic past of his people; his current anxieties in this country, as well as his painful experiences from aversive reactions to his skin colour, all stem from current racial discrimination and prejudice. His wife's fear of her aggressive feelings and her methods of coping by resorting to splitting processes, denial and avoidance, while these are individually

determined, are nonetheless also common coping patterns evolved in the course of adjustment and survival of black people in response to their historical exposure to racial discrimination within specific social contexts. No doubt these coping patterns played some part in Mrs James' socialization. Johanna struggles against confirming stereotyped negative images of black people as aggressive, and this prevents her from venting her hurt and angry feelings at the prejudice and racial discrimination which she encounters. She fights against an attributed identity foisted upon her. A lack of appropriate West Indian models for identification, able to express restrained anger, also is a product of their people's history in relation to race. Although Adrian's major unresolved conflicts stem from earliest childhood experiences of separation and feelings of abandonment, he too is exposed in this country to the exacerbation of existing inner conflicts by racial prejudice in the form of physical threats of attack by white boys.

5 Certain patterns of coping with anxiety and conflict are shared in common by several members of the family. Both Mr James and Johanna express depressive anxieties (without being clinically depressed), and so tend to turn aggression largely back against themselves; while Mrs James and Adrian both tend to use defences stemming from the paranoid-schizoid position, characterized by splitting and attempts to keep the bad and the idealized separate. These defensive ways of coping directly affect their race attitudes.

6 The members of this family share in common positive and constructive ways of attacking and solving stressful life problems. They are all able to use active and realistic means of tackling stressful situations; they are competent, make progress in reaching set goals through constructive efforts; despite set-backs and frustration they persevere with what they set out to do, containing their anxieties well and using them to harness their active efforts. And they all have a diversity of channels through which to express themselves and their unresolved identity conflicts – in work, play and in their relationships – and as a result the racial arena is only one of many. They are able to be flexible and are capable of change. All of these, as I show in Chapter 10, are basic to the concerns of this study.

BIBLIOGRAPHY AND NOTES

1 Hiro, D. *Black British, White British*, Eyre & Spottiswoode, London (1971).
2 *Ibid.* p. 17.
3 Hauser, S. T.*Black and White Identity Formation*, John Wiley, New York (1971),

p.68. Hauser found that Negro mothers were described by their sons with the strongest superlatives as advisers, exceedingly nurturant, providers and bosses. Any problems could be solved by them.

4 Klein, M. *Envy and Gratitude*, Tavistock, London (1957); Joffe, W. G. 'The unenviable preoccupation with envy'. *Psychiatry and Social Science Review*, 4, No. 14 (1970), 8 December.

5 Schoeck, H. *Envy: A Theory of Social Behaviour*, Harcourt Brace, New York (1970).

6 Rochlin, G. *Man's Aggression: The Defence of the Self*, Constable, London (1973), p.22.

7 McDonald, M. *Not by the Colour of their Skin*, International Universities Press, New York (1970), p. 127–130.

8 Ibid. p.129. McDonald believes that it is normal and desirable in a multiracial society for children of all colours to have the opportunity of realistically disentangling confusions about skin colour and problems arising at a time when the ego is busy with anal stage developments in relation to faecal colour, cleanliness, control and valuableness. She contends that through the over-lapping in time of skin colour anxiety and anal problems, there is gain if both are worked through and finally experienced as separate and unrelated.

9 Zinner, J. and Shapiro, R. 'Projective identification as a mode of perception and behaviour in families of adolescents' *International Journal of Psycho-Analysis*, 53 (1972), 523–530.

10 Erikson, E. H. 'Identity and the life cycle', *Psychological Issues*, I (1959), 1–171; Erikson, E. H. 'Psychoanalysis and ongoing history: problems of identity, hatred and non-violence', *American Journal of Psychiatry*, (1965), 241–250; Erikson, E. H. *Identity: Youth and Crisis*, Norton, New York (1968); Erikson, E. H. 'Autobiographic notes on the identity crisis', *Daedalus*, (1970), Fall, 730–759.

11 McDonald, M. (1970), op. cit.

12 Kardiner, A. and Ovesey, L. *The Mark of Oppression: A Psychosocial Study of the American Negro*, Norton, New York (1951); Proshansky, H. and Newton, P. 'The nature and meaning of negro self-identity', in Deutsch, M. Katz, I. and Jensen, A. R. *Social Class, Race and Psychological Development*, Holt, Rinehart & Winston, New York (1968); McCarthy, J. D. and Yancey, W. L. 'Uncle Tom and Mr. Charlie: metaphysical pathos in the study of racism and personal disorganisation', *American Journal of Sociology*, 76 (1971), 648–672.

13 Immigration Act, 1971.

14 Erikson, E. H. Identity: Youth and Crisis, Norton, New York (1968), p. 25.

15 Wender, P. H. 'Vicious and virtuous circles: the role of deviation amplifying Feedback in the Origin and Perpetuation of Behaviour', *Psychiatry*, 31, (1968), No. 4.

16 *Op.cit.* p.297.

17 Klein, M. *Our Adult World and its Roots in Infancy*, Tavistock, London (1960).

18 Dollard, J. *Caste and Class in a Southern Town*, Doubleday Anchor, New York (1957), third edition.; Kardiner, A. and Ovesey, L. *The Mark of Oppression*, Norton, New York (1961).

19 Hauser, S. T. *Black & White Identity Formation*, John Wiley, New York (1971), p.34–35.

20 *Ibid.* p. 67.

21 Dollard, J. *Caste and Class in a Southern Town*, Doubleday Anchor, New York (1957), third edition, p. 124. Dollard has pointed out that the Southern negroes' love and loyalty to his white master, built up in slavery times, tended to carry over to new employers and that this was the basis for the idealization of the master symbol of whiteness.

22 Klein, M. *Our Adult World and its Roots in Infancy*, Tavistock, London (1960).

23 Erikson, E. H. *Identity: Youth and Crisis*, Faber & Faber, London (1968), p. 156–8.

24 Frankl, V. E. *Man's Search for Meaning: An Introduction to Logotherapy*, Simon & Shuster, New York (1963).

25 Grier, W. H. and Cobb, P. M. *Black Like Me*, Houghton Mifflin, Boston (1961); Erikson, E. H. (1968), *op.cit.* p. 172–76.

26 There may be several paths to the same goal of achieving mutual respect and tolerance of racial groups for each other. To find a conscious pride and identity through black power and identification with 'black is beautiful' can lead to a positive valuing of one's own group making it easier to value another; conversely, to find a more inclusive identity first, can later lead to a fuller valuing of one's own racial identity and the racial identity of others.

27 Erikson, E. H. (1968), *op.cit.* p. 314.

28 Storr, A. *Human Aggression*. Allen Lane, The Pneguin Press, Harmondsworth. (1968).

29 *Ibid.* p. 109.

30 Maslow, A. H. *Toward a Psychology of Being*, Van Nostrand, Princeton (1968).

31 *Ibid.* p. 25–26.

32 *Ibid.* p. 162.

33 Segal, H. *Introduction to the Work of Melanie Klein*, Heinemann, London (1964), p.4.

34 *Ibid.*

Chapter 8

IDENTITY AND RACE IN AN ENGLISH FAMILY: THE CHATTAWAYS

The Chattaways are English and Athol is their home. Rebecca Chattaway's mother lives in Athol and she stayed with her before her marriage to Charles. The first period of their married life was spent in Athol and although they moved to another part of London for a short period, they subsequently returned to settle there in the mid-1950s, where all three of their children were born.

To understand identity processes in the Chattaways, they too must be seen against the historic and cultural past of their people, not only the events of the past and the present, but the related ideas, images and myths to which these give rise. Of course, it is impossible to do more than very briefly indicate some salient aspects of these which bear upon the themes of this book.

Since both the West Indies and India have had important historical bonds with Britain enduring over the past centuries, we may ask what legacies these have left behind which influence and affect contemporary feelings and attitudes of the British towards West Indians and Asians.

As the leading slave-trading nation in the world, by the middle of the eighteenth century Britain's profits from slavery were so considerable that the concept of the African slave as an economic commodity had taken a firm hold. By the time slavery was finally abolished in 1834 many of the basic attitudes towards black people had already taken shape, the British feeling themselves to be inherently superior, and the masters. The colonial plantation patterns later established in the West Indies, embodied and typified these sets of relationship and their associated myths and ideas, and further consolidated them in structural ways.[1]

Towards the end of the eighteenth century, the focus of Empire shifted away from the American colonies and concentrated on India. A British historian writing in 1792 described the Indian people as a 'race of men, lamentably degenerate and base, retaining but a feeble sense of moral obligation ... governed by a malevolent and licentious passion'.[2] The Indians at that time were commonly

379

referred to by the British as blacks[3] so that attitudes and prejudices emanating from the period of African slavery as well as from Indian rule both tended to reinforce each other. By the time that the functions of government were transferred to Westminster following the Indian mutiny, the attitudes of the British towards the Indians tended to be exclusive, those of a conquering race.[4] As a result, both in India and in the West Indies, the image of the British in their own eyes was an exalted one while their image of West Indians and Indians was one of diminished worth.

Although the Colonial Empire has of course ceased to function in its old form, nonetheless attitudes and images do not just disappear, as indeed the beliefs in the inherent inferiority of the Negro did not crumble with the abolition of slavery. When, in the 1950s, the number of colonial coloured immigrants steadily increased in Britain, the prevailing attitudes of racial superiority towards West Indians and Asians came up against, and confronted, values held within British society, according to its citizens regard for the equality and human dignity of all, irrespective of race or colour. Previous to this, when viewing the colonies and their indigenous peoples, the British had been able to consider themselves racially liberal and fair-minded in their own country, while retaining attitudes of superiority towards people of colour overseas. But as the presence of people of colour became more noticeable in Britain, a new situation was created within the society between these two sets of ideas, which had been conveniently split on geographic lines until then. The inner contradictions between these two sets of attitudes have increasingly become more apparent and can no longer be avoided.[5]

But this is only one of the inner changes which this society is undergoing. British people, who until recently have been brought up and educated with secure notions of the Empire, are having to adjust to the vastly changed reality of being citizens of a relatively small country with few overseas possessions. The inner adjustment required, on both these fronts,[6] is a taxing one for British people, involving considerable shifts in cultural identity about which we still know very little indeed. For just as notions about black people emanating from earlier periods die very slowly, so the British, historic, cultural and national identity is only slowly changing and it will take time for new crystallizations of identity to emerge.

It is against this background that each of the Chattaways has forged a personal sense of identity and it is to these four people that we now turn.

1 MR CHARLES CHATTAWAY

Important Issues Bearing on His Identity Formation

Mr Charles Chattaway had a difficult and tragic childhood, suffering a double deprivation early in his life. He never knew his father and although his mother visited him from time to time and seems to have indulged him, she was not readily accessible and did not live with her infant son except for very short periods. He spent the first years of his life with aged grandparents (whom he felt to be somewhat severe and puritanical) and with some uncles and aunts. It was not a home to which he ever felt he could bring his friends.

His life story reveals anxiety, hurt and resentment, not uncommon in the reactions of those who have been deprived of a secure sense of parental love and attention,[7] and although he defends himself against feelings of need and dependency by the use of denial, his deprived childhood has exerted a potent influence upon him and his subsequent identity.

In the ordinary course of events, children receive love and care from a mother and so incorporate within themselves a firm sense of being lovable. This not only stands them in good stead in times of trouble but it is the base upon which their self-esteem becomes established. But if the infant's earliest experience of his mother is such that he has not acquired a feeling for her essential goodness, he will then find it extremely difficult to achieve any conviction of his own essential goodness or lovability, and will possess little inner sense of self-esteem upon which to rely.[8] Charles Chattaway seems to have had this unfortunate background. He shows vulnerability to feelings of rejection which re-kindle his anxieties about his own worth and produce difficulties for him in coping with resultant feelings of anger for the way in which he has been treated. Having an insufficient sense of his own lovability and goodness, he finds it very difficult to easily admit his angry feelings and hostilities.[9] Yet, as Rochlin has commented 'Whatever injures self-esteem, unconsciously intensifies and generates aggression in its defence . . . injured self-esteem endlessly creates a menace'.[10] Bowlby's work on children separated from accessible parental figures, has also shown that they tend to respond aggressively, expressing anger, which only sometimes is the anger of hope but often it is that of despair.[11]

Melanie Klein has noted that when an infant misses his mother and his needs are not satisfied, her absence may be felt to be the result of his inner angry and destructive feelings and that this occurs as a normal part of infant development.[12] Since there is an inability to distinguish between internal and external experiences in infancy, Charles, as an infant, might have felt anxious in case his inner angry feelings and phantasies had actually driven his parents away. In the absence of a 'good-enough' mother to act as a barrier against such frightening phantasies, his sense of inner destructiveness might not easily have been mitigated and angry feelings towards his absent parents could in turn have stimulated fears of their retaliation so adding to a sense of anxiety and persecution.

An additional burden exacerbating Charles' feelings of low self-esteem arose from his perception of the district in which he grew up as 'a terrible quarter' where one was regarded 'as a prostitute or a thief', if one came from there. This no doubt added an additional negative aspect of his self-image to be internalized and coped with in the course of socialization in that community.

This combination of early life experiences seems to have left him with a sense of diminished worth, mobilized his anxieties, provoked outbreaks of anger and stirred in him feelings of persecution. His story reveals the efforts he made to deal with these largely unconscious problems. At times he seems to have repressed his powerful anger and denied it, but projected it into others, for it is not unusual to feel the hostility of others easier to bear than the experience of one's own aggressive impulses. Harboured aggression however, when repressed and denied, can lead to conflicts and disorders which sap energy and some of the later signs of depression, apathy and despair in Charles Chattaway may well stem from these impotent feelings of anger which are partly turned back and directed against himself. Although these self-critical attacks manage at times to curb and control his aggression, there are other times when his feelings of hostility and rage erupt and express themselves in ways which further burden him with persecutory anxieties and in turn act to deflate his self-esteem anew.

What aspects of his life story add support to these interpretations? His needs for love and dependency are rigidly denied.

> It didn't bother me not knowing my father – I didn't think about him . . . . I mean to say, my father never bothered about me. Why should I bother about him? . . . I mean I've got hardened . . . It never bothered me that my mother didn't live with me. She was alright. I mean to say, she left me a penny a day for sweets and that sort of caper, you know.

He valued the independence of mind which his childhood

experiences exacted. 'I had to think by myself as a child. It was over to me', he said but ruefully admits that he did not know how to take care of himself properly and suffered as a result.

He was a physically energetic child with strong drives and growing up in an environment which he described as 'rough'; aged grandparents may not have accepted the more rough-and-tumble aspects of his healthy exuberance and so they may not have helped him to feel his aggression was acceptable and could be contained. Instead he seems to have been terrified of it. It erupted with violence during his primary school days when, perhaps to overcome his own fear of attack and humiliation, he attacked a young boy and 'crippled him'. When he was called vicious by the headmistress this could only have added to his sense of persecution and confirmed his worst fears about himself, stemming from likely early phantasies of anger and destruction towards his rejecting parents. This episode at school remained to haunt him throughout his life, and at the very end of his life history interviews when he was talking of what he dreaded most, he added 'Seeing blokes who are crippled. It upsets me, you know'. [The full significance of his marriage to Rebecca whose father was a cripple cannot be explored here, but it is noteworthy nevertheless.] His anger having been let loose, he was left fearful of his destructively violent feelings. The full weight of his feelings of guilt – however denied – led him to rationalize this episode as a case of self-preservation, only one person could survive, the other had to go under. This philosophy of a simple power struggle and this mode of relating to people, more as objects than as human beings with feelings, needs and conflicts of their own, continues to reveal itself at later stages in his life and especially in his race relationships.

This outburst of violence left scars on him and later in life he sought to protect, with concern and love, his own children from his feared destructiveness. Immediately following his comments on how cripples upset him, he went on to say

same as I can't hold new babies – that's a thing I can't do. I never held any of mine, only Colin, and that was a great struggle. But the others I couldn't hold. I get nervous – you know what I mean – or I grip them . . . and Rebecca says 'Ooh, it's too hard'. I forget, you know and I'm frightened I could hurt someone, so that's why I very rarely pick a baby up. When they get older I do . . . I'm frightened, you know what I mean. I forget myself but I did hold Colin, but he was the only baby I did hold. I've got more relaxed, see, because I'm getting older, so I'm more able to take things a bit easier, you know.

This deeply moving inner struggle is aimed to protect his loving relationships from an overwhelming fear of his 'badness', his destructiveness and what he fears his hands might do. At one point in his life story, he said 'The only aptitude I've really had is using my hands'. They express his use of creative aggressive impulses as well as his feared destructiveness.

At the age of ten, following his attack on the schoolboy, his perilous sense of security was further undermined when he was evacuated from London to Cornwall during the war. When his grandparents' home was bombed, he later returned to live with an aunt and uncle in a different part of London. For the first time he shared substitute parents with a 'sibling', his cousin who was a few years older than Charles. Envy and jealousy were aroused and he particularly felt the absence of a caring, guiding father's presence. 'He's got his own house and everything now . . . I don't know, I suppose his father stood behind him and could read him. With myself, as I say, my mother was not very career-minded . . . she wasn't the type of person who had been around a lot or knew anything much about work and all that'.

It is not difficult to understand that in the face of the frequent separations and changes of mother figures and his parental deprivation generally, his anger and despair also manifested itself in minor delinquencies of stealing fruit from barrows. But these became more serious as he started stealing motor cars, coal, lead and copper ingots. He protests and denies any sense of guilt. 'It wasn't a crime nicking, you know, the crime was getting caught.' He was never caught for any of these acts and although such delinquencies were widespread in his community and 'everybody used to do it all the time,' nonetheless, they seem to have burdened his conscience as evidenced by the revealing way in which they emerged towards the end of the study. I asked him if there was anything which he had not yet talked about and which he felt he might like to tell me, either in connection with his present life or his past life. The question was wide open and he said 'You mean – like getting into bother and all that sort of caper?' After avowals that he had not done anything which others also had not done, he then revealed, for the first time, how he stole motor cars before his marriage and also spoke about his other delinquencies and added 'I've been lucky'.

In the army he had a number of minor brushes with army officers, leading to disciplinary action on at least five occasions. All of these are suggestive of feelings of depression, low morale and apathy (slovenly behaviour, dirty boots, accusations of malingering, etc.) or they involve some outbreak of aggression (hitting a NCO). After he was demobilized, anxiety and depression again expressed themselves in oral forms by over-eating, excessive drinking, gambling and the stealing episodes already mentioned. It was only when he married Rebecca and was able to find a stable relationship with a warm maternal woman, that his deep needs for love and security started to be met, and he gave up drinking, brought his weight down to normal limits and stopped gambling.

What channels could Charles Chattaway use for integrating and expressing his feelings of aggression positively and constructively?

After a childhood deprived of a sense of home, his passionate feelings about houses and homes are understandable. A potential area for constructive effort – to acquire a home of his own – although one of the objectives of his life, remains unfulfilled. His first three years of married life were spent with his wife and infant son in two small rooms with no water taps and he finally ended up living in his present Council house. He feels regret that when he could have bought a house of his own he 'Couldn't be bothered'. He is in touch with his feelings. 'Let's be honest about it. I myself couldn't be bothered to buy a house – that was my attitude – when I had the chance.' It is revealing of his deeper problems that he could not manage to mobilize his energies for this purpose although his earning capacity during the childrearing years seems to have been relatively good and maintained steadily over time. His anger of despair seems to have run deep. Since he experienced a sense of shame and failure at not having a home of his own, this further reduced his self-esteem and increased depressive feelings and apathy.

Work is a vitally important area for the active expression of aggressive energies. There is evidence that in earlier periods of his life Mr Chattaway was able to express his masculine identity positively and productively through work, and that this brought him much satisfaction and also recognition. But at the time of the study this had unfortunately ceased to be an effective and constructive channel for commitment or self-expression. In fact, the reverse was the case. It is in relation to work that his present sense of demoralization, depression and apathy finds its clearest and most symptomatic expression.

When as a young man he found that he was entirely dependent on a welder to do some of his work for him, and that this man could keep him waiting (with possible evocations of an infantile relationship with a partly absent mother who also kept him waiting, and a father who never appeared). His fear of dependence goaded him into a constructive use of his aggression and for three years he studied to become a welder which he successfully became.

> If that particular incident had never happend in my life, I wouldn't have bothered about learning to weld . . . but if I go anywhere now and people want to be funny, I haven't got to ask them to do anything for me. I can do machine work, welding, pipe fitting, I can do all of them now. It doesn't bother me.

His fear of dependence turned his industry to good effect, steadily increased his skills and eventually he became a foreman with a number of men under his control, confirming his identity as an able, responsible, competent man upon whom others could depend – a healthy use of reversal.

But at the time of the study, when he was forty-one years old, he was out of work for the first time in thirteen years and although he had offers of employment, he was not motivated, showed a deep sense of depression, low morale and apathy. He did not want the responsibility of being a foreman again, felt caught in the middle between management and men, between being responsible for others (a father) or accepting a more dependent role.

> I always used to be conscientious – be at work on time . . . it's done me no good. So I thought – well, I'll just get a job, plod along, why should I bother? They asked me if I wanted the foreman's job, and I said 'No – I've had enough of it, responsibility over people'. I wouldn't mind if you didn't have to chase them, but you get these blokes who just don't bother'.

His inner world and the work scene on which he is commenting are so inter-related that what he attributes to others is also a projection of his inner state.

> 'I'm ashamed to admit it, but I don't care about working hard or well any more . . . I sort of plod along. What's wrong with me is what's wrong with the whole country. I think it's apathy . . . I was conscientious then but I've changed now . . . I think the trouble lies with the general relaxation of discipline

not only in homes between parents and teenagers but also discipline has been relaxed in industry.

His conflicts in relation to aggression manifest themselves in work. Being a foreman requires self-assertiveness and the exercise of authority and power but he either feels that he is too indulgent or too ruthless towards those under his supervision. By relinquishing power because he fears he may use it too ruthlessly, he exposes himself anew to being under someone else's domination, subject to other people's whims and favours and so drifts towards accepting a dependence which he most resents and fears. What has prompted this shift?

Jaques[13] in descussing the mid-life crisis has pointed to psychological changes characteristic of the stage of life which Mr Chattaway has now reached, and for our purposes the re-arousal at this age of unconscious depressive anxieties seems to apply most pertinently to Mr Chattaway. He managed his early adult phase of active working life with successful and energetic efforts but his underlying and unresolved problems in coming to terms with hateful and destructive impulses and bringing them into focus with his loving and constructive feelings are thrust forward with additional force during this phase of his life. What is required for working through this mid-life crisis successfully is a capacity to accept ambivalence in himself, admitting and coming to terms with his own shortcomings and destructive impulses as well as feeling in touch with his good and positive feelings and so also in turn being able to accept imperfections in others. But his earlier infantile difficulties in integrating love and hate, make this phase of life a specially hazardous one for him.

> 'When the prevailing balance between love and hate tends more towards the side of hate . . . there is an overspill of destructiveness in any or all of its various forms – self-destruction, envy, grandiose omnipotence, cruelty, narcissism, greed – and the world is seen as having these persecuting qualities as well',[14]

writes Jaques. Mr Chattaway turns these renewed feelings of anger towards himself in self-destructive attacks which form the core of his depression and these produce his present state of demoralisation and apathy. But his aggressive cruelty, envy and anger are expressed with feelings of special intensity and omnipotence towards the Indians and Pakistanis.

The mid-life crisis arises from the natural consequences of ageing which begin at birth but make themselves felt at roughly the ages 35 – 40 when degenerative processes are observable to the trained eye. According to Cath,[15] there is 'an inner awareness' of these depleting physiological processes which affect the body, influencing feelings of narcissism and deflating self-esteem. This can mobilize compensatory feelings of anger. Mr Chattaway was concerned with his health – he mentioned it as the most valued possession and it's absence as something which he most dreaded. 'Bad health – you have got to sit around and watch life go past you and you can't do anything about it.' To him, awareness of ageing processes was experienced as depressing, compounding the other sources of depression already discussed.

But the mid-life crisis in not only involved with physiological changes and intrapsychic processes, but also with each person's role and position in different life contexts such as family, work and community. Like adolescence, it is a critical period of development when either potential growth continues, or stagnation and regression occur. Some people cope relatively well, mastering anxiety and stress and as a result develop still further; but if earlier experiences in infancy and childhood have failed to lay the foundations for a sense of inner security and trust, this phase of life may lead to serious aggravations of earlier difficulties and to regressive problems.

Mr Chattaway's situation within his family, both his pattern of relationships and his role within the family, have all undergone change at this period in his life. His mid-life crisis overlaps in time the coming to sexual maturity of his children. John is a sexually mature man and his daughter Elaine, although a late developer, is now on the threshold of her menarche. He is necessarily moving towards ageing with aspects of future sexual decline. This produces anxiety and strain in a family, altering roles and affecting the interaction of both parents with their maturing children. Mr Chattaway has reacted to this phase by becoming more sensitive to the special bonds of understanding which he feels unite his wife and son John while at the same time his relationship with Elaine is somewhat overlaid with ambivalence and anxiety. The relationship between his wife and John, which he senses is a close one, provokes his jealousy and gives him a feeling of being excluded and of being pushed out.

With family life generating fresh sources of strain at this time of life, some men find counterbalancing dividends in work, the creative efforts bringing compensations for other areas of inner loss. But Mr

Chattaway's depression expresses itself in relation to work. As a result, he denies himself a vital source for the confirmation of his masculine identity, and a vicious cycle is set in motion by which his low self-esteem and depression are further aggravated both by his unemployment and by his subsequent refusal to accept posts of responsibility. This plunges him into work which reduces his social status and power and increases his dependency, diminishing still further his feelings of worth. So work both expresses his demoralization and regression, and also further accelerates the downward spiral. His inability to resolve critical identity problems concerned with love and hate, exacerbated at each point by his mid-life crisis and the reactivation of the depressive phase, results in his angry feelings being turned back against himself, so that instead of being able to liberate these energies for constructive efforts, they are dammed up inside him in a potentially explosive way.

Not only is his own social status tenuously held, but his attitudes towards the changes occurring in Athol are also coloured by fears of deterioration, decline and downward drift in the social status of the community. His place within the community and his images of Athol bear directly on the difficulties he has in managing to sustain and handle the stresses of mid-life. As a result of the influx into the community of West Indians, Indians and Pakistanis, he believes the community to be deteriorating, feels that Athol is known far and wide as a place where English people would not want to live and he experiences a sense of shame to be living there. He fears, and deeply resents, the territorial invasion of his community by coloured immigrants, citing how they have taken over the cinemas and pubs, obstruct movement on the pavements, have brought violence to the streets of Athol and diluted standards of education in the schools. He feels psychologically pushed out of his community and the pleasure he used to derive from drinking at the local pub, going to the cinema or shopping locally, have all been sacrificed since he does not like going there now that each of these places is felt to be taken over and invaded by coloured immigrants whom he perceives as noisy, obtrusive and culturally or socially alien. They have become a persecutory element in his community life, felt to be depriving him of what should be his, impinging upon him and pushing him out. So at his mid-life crisis, when sources of support and anchorage for him might lie in having a recognized role and secure place in his neighbourhood, he feels his territory to have been invaded, geographically and culturally, and he withdraws from one modest communal activity after another, until his life in Athol solely consists of transporting himself by car through its streets en route to work or to shop in other districts.

Although his English friends are leaving Athol or have already left, his needs seem to be served by staying on there. This is because of the unconscious satisfactions he derives from his misuse of the various racial groups in Athol to work out his unresolved identity problems. If he were living in an all-white neighbourhood he might not so easily be able to avoid confronting those aspects of himself which he finds frightening and which he cannot easily face. As it is he uses the visibly different and culturally diverse racial groups for the off-loading of his deeply buried and denied conflicts and so he remains in Athol, continues to attack bitterly what has happened to the community, but his needs appear to be served by the very groups whom he is attacking and who provide unknowingly the screen which protects him from seeing himself more clearly and indeed from seeing them as they are. These external social realities and the meaning they have for him, expose him to threats of impingement by strangers visibly different in appearance from himself and with different life styles. These intensify feelings of inner persecution hostility and insecurity.

Experiences of loss and ageing, under optimal conditions, can stimulate people to shift their libidinal investment into new relationships or activities which can then serve as shields against regression.[16] What avenues can Mr Chattaway use? There seem few indeed; the most hopeful signs lie in a new-found ability to use his relationship with his wife with greater trust and companionship. He asks for her views and advice not without some ambivalence as he wonders aloud as to whether he is 'getting soft'. His need for some replenishment and for a renewed sense of belonging is expressed in his relationship with her, but apart from this he has seriously constricted his other sources for re-establishing self-esteem and his identity as a man. He is withdrawing into a depressive phase, marked by shame and guilt, but he also betrays an oscillation between this and his needs to compulsively act out his hostile feelings, particularly towards Indians who draw his split-off angry feelings. Granting himself a license to be destructive towards them, this creates further conflicts and increases both his need for punishment and anxiety over the consequences of his actions – an interpretation further developed later in this analysis.

Unresolved identity conflicts in relation to race
Mr Chattaway's major identity conflicts revolve around the following

issues : First, a deep sense of deprivation and dependent needs which seem to conflict with inner demands to realise his adult identity and be a responsible father and husband. Secondly, he is struggling to protect his good loving feelings and relationships from his angry feelings and destructive aggressive drives. Thirdly, he is trying to re-establish his feelings of worth in the face of a mid-life crisis which has eroded his self-esteem and aroused feelings of shame and guilt at his delinquencies and shortcomings. These are burdensome problems, many of them a legacy from his infancy and childhood. By means of various defence mechanisms, these unresolved identity conflicts seek unconscious expression and they manifest themselves in his relationships with Asians and West Indians, and also with the police and intellectual members of the middle class. What links his identity conflicts with these various groups?

By the unconscious process of projecting his undesirable feelings and attributing his hostility to others, he describes vividly and with intensity the violent assults, knife fights, hostile attacks made by Indians and Pakistanis against white people within the community. By attributing the origin of these hostilities entirely to these groups, his aggressive feelings become more bearable and capable of denial. It is, of course, true that within this community there are indeed acts of violence and some of these originate within the groups in question, but of the twelve subjects studied it is striking that only Mr Chattaway and his son John give a picture of these events with frequency, and they see them as always starting within the black community and as being acts of special ferocity. As attempts to rid himself of his inner conflicts, the Asians appear to be seen as more violent and dangerous than perhaps they are.

By means of projective identification with his son John, his hostile feelings also seek vicarious expression when he comments that John's gang – the skinheads and their rival gang – the rockers, ought to combine and 'have a go at the wogs . . . they must stick together else the coloureds will get the upper hand and they won't be as tolerant to us as we've been to them'. He is fearful of retaliation fed by his own suppressed hostility.

But apart from the projection of his destructively aggressive feelings, his guilty stirrings about his delinquencies are also unconsciously projected onto the Indians and Pakistanis. He perceives them as having criminal records, being corrupt and dishonest, preying on their own people like leeches and breaking the laws of the land. This so enrages him that he violently acts out his hostility in repetitive acts which he can no longer contain against the pedestrians, perceived as solely Indian or Pakistani, who cross at the end of his road against the lights. To drive his car is one of the few acts of freedom which he feels is left to him within Athol. By their actions, he is brought to a stop and has to wait until they have crossed the road. This seems to evoke in him such rage that for the past six months, he has taken upon himself to punish them for their disregard of the laws of the land, in violently omnipotent ways. He drives across the pedestrian crossing when the lights change, regardless of whether anyone is in his way. He admits that he has bruised a few people and if he should kill someone he would regard himself as being technically in the right. The psychological significance of these frightening acts seems to be twofold: it is a way of punishing fiercely and without compassion, others' transgressions when his own delinquencies have gone unpunished and for which he appears to feel a deep but unconscious sense of guilt. And he chooses a racial group whom he dehumanizes and for whom he feels no empathy. The Indians and Pakistanis are seen by him to be living within the structure of his society but not fully integrated with it and his own repressed desires have a similar dynamic and are a working model of the same kind of split-off function. (When asked how he might behave if one of the pedestrians was white he answered that white people did not cross against the lights.) This is a situation in which either the motorist or the pedestrian need to defer to the other. Each is affected by the presence of the other. He sees the role of these Indian and Pakistani pedestrians as powerfully controlling, another of those situations which he perceives as an 'either/or. His anxiety and anger at being controlled by their actions is so overwhelming that he uses his motor-car as a hostile and aggressive projection of himself to move against those who so transgress. It is with his hands on the wheel and through their work that he expresses his violent anger.

These immigrant pedestrians evoke in him feelings of being invaded, his territorial rights are felt to be impinged. Storr commenting on territorial *animals* has said that

> aggression . . . has now come to serve the function of putting a distance between itself and its neighbour: . . . animals suffer from something which may be compared to repressed aggression in man if the individual distance between them is reduced. There can be no doubt that man, also, is a territorial animal. Even in circumstances so far removed from the primitive as contemporary Western civilization, the country-side is demarcated by fences and hedges many of which carry

notices stating that 'Trespassers will be prosecuted'; . . . The presence of a stranger in the garden is generally regarded as a threat, or at least as a circumstance requiring investigation; and, on a national scale, the invasion of the homeland by an enemy evokes a more passionately aggressive response than does a battle with the same foe on territory which belongs to neither.[17]

Mr Chattaway has seen his neighbourhood amenities taken over and invaded territorially and his car moving through the streets of Athol has been one of the last ways in which he felt free to use and claim his territory. It is perhaps not without significance that it is the masculine assertive symbol of the car which is used by him in this way. His despairing anger at what is happening to him in many areas of his life seems to put his feelings of masculine identity in jeopardy.

But motor cars belonging to Indians and Pakistanis have symbolic meaning for him too. He feels passionately angry, claiming that they have no indicators on their cars or that they fail to use them. The cars are experienced in his inner world as being 'all over the place', invading monsters who have taken over his territory and nobody knows where they may be going to next. The cars are seen to be 'bashed up' and this rouses his anger because the owners 'don't bother – just like their own country which is going to rack and ruin'. He projects into the Asians, their cars and their country, his despair in relation to Athol and what he feels is happening to it, but he also unconsciously reveals through these projections his inner state and current integrity as a man which he fears is damaged, directionless, running down and with which he is unable to cope. His attacks on the Indian pedestrians are violent and despairing and reflect his feelings about his own run-down, out-of-control, depressed and directionless state and the disintegration of his familiar community world.

He tries to soothe his injured feelings of self-esteem and to buttress them by convincing himself that the clear-cut identity of the Indians and Pakistanis is generally inferior to his own. The echoes of historical themes and images explored at the beginning of this chapter are not difficult to find in Mr Chattaway's current attitudes. To him, most Asians are backward and illiterate and cannot compete in a developed society. They run shops with a low standard of hygiene, and the men are more likely to accost women in the streets than would Englishmen. Jahoda has written

to the extent that early insecurity remains, a person experiences the visibly apparent clear-cut identity of others as evidence of his own personal failure which is deeply resented. If he can convince himself that the other's identity, even while clear-cut is inferior, the comparison is easier to bear – at least he is not an Indian or a black however uncertain he is about everything else.[18]

Linked with the need to see the Indians as inferior is an awareness of their different culture and ancient traditions which he partly seems to envy. He wishes that the Indians would accept integration which he interprets as a giving up of their own culture and language and accepting English cultural patterns. The cultural differences and the clear-cut identity of the Asians is what he finds goading and they stimulate his envy. They have what he lacks – membership of a closely knit group, sustained by warm family bonds – and he both envies and denigrates it and wishes to see it submerged in an integration so that English cultural patterns can envelop the Indians and Pakistanis in a familiar and non-threatening cloak. His own identity is insufficiently established to be able to accept the Indians' culture without feeling it as invasive of his own.

Mr Chattaway therefore uses the Indians and Pakistanis to psychologically 'carry' for him certain denied aspects of his own unresolved identity conflicts. Some of his perceptions may fit some Indians or Pakistanis accurately enough. Some are sure to be aggressive, violent, ignorant, delinquent, backward as other people also are; but the intensity of his need to stereotype them rigidly as a group in global ways, and the unconscious processes underlying these needs, are central to the concerns of this book.

What of his attitudes towards West Indians? To a certain extent, Mr Chattaway makes sweeping statements about 'coloureds'; but he does distinguish, on the whole, between West Indians who share a common language and culture with the English, and the alien Indians and Pakistanis who do not. It is this fundamental difference in the cultural integration of the two groups which makes the Indians and Pakistanis the more fitting targets for his projections. He is more tolerant towards West Indians although he sees them as noisy, boisterous and lacking in discipline, and betrays general attitudes of social superiority toward them. But his major hatred and antipathy is reserved for Indians and Pakistanis.

It is striking that he has worked as a colleague with members of both groups and that within the context of work he accepts them as fellow-workers, respecting them for their contribution and not faulting them in any way. The work sphere and his inter-racial contacts within that sphere are encapsulated, and kept separate from his otherwise racially prejudiced attitudes. It is possible that since the area of work has until recently been a source of satisfaction to him, he has been able to accept coloured immigrants as colleagues without rancour or need for negative projections. It is of course impossible to guess whether his changed present attitudes towards work with his current disinterest and apathy, may lead, in the future, to changed perceptions of his coloured colleagues. What is known, however, is how his good feelings for his fellow-workers are kept separate from his negative feelings towards the same groups in other social arenas. What seems to be decisive is that where he shares the same role with coloured immigrants as providers and contributors his feelings are those of acceptance and respect. It is as consumers of facilities, and users of public space where they seem to be in competition and where prejudice enters. This point is fully discussed and elaborated in the final chapter.

White groups are singled out for stereotyped attack as well. By a process of displacement and substitution for his primary relationship with his missing, rejecting father, he perceives the authority symbols of his community as unfair, punitive and persecutory towards himself but protective towards immigrants. They are neglectfully 'absent' towards the native-born English. He feels victimized by this, deprived of support and protection from feared and frightening violence, and is outraged that there are 'favourite sons' whose misdeeds can be overlooked by the police while others, felt to be innocent like himself, are severely treated or are overlooked indeed, deserted by these father-figures. Dicks[19] has discussed how policemen in society can embody parental images. Mr Chattaway's attitudes toward the police seem to be a re-evocation of his father's desertion of him. His feelings are intensely hostile, 'I could have killed those coppers . . . I could have torn those coppers to bits.'

To a lesser extent, he also directs hostility towards the middle class and especially 'those intellectuals – the upper crust', who are noted for their forthright stance on race prejudice and discrimination. Mark Bonham-Carter and Jeremy Thorpe were the two whom he named most frequently. He resented the fact that the middle class, while personally insulated from the intrusion of coloured immigrants into their privileged communities and schools, were felt to be foisting onto the working class, coloured immigrants who then 'invaded' their communities. This is generally speaking an accurate social observation as there *are* class differences in exposure to the mass effects of immigration. His strength of feelings, however, are likely to have been exacerbated by the pain of the past; somewhere there are leaders, seen as parent figures, who look after themselves but neglect their sons.

His feelings of victimization, of persecution, of defensive anger and hostility are directed towards male figures, the police as standing for male authority and named male political figures. Nowhere, for instance, does he attack immigrant mothers – it is always the men – men who are standing on the pavements holding hands, men driving cars, men crossing against the lights. This suggests that it is his father and his sense of angry deprivation at the hands of this unknown father who lies at the root of his bitterness and feelings of having been unfairly treated. (This may also account for his capacity to co-operate with me, despite my middle class affiliations – a point to which I return later on when I discuss transference effects.)

To summarise: his hostility and aggression, expressed both in acted-out forms and verbally, is directed towards Indians and Pakistanis; his feelings of low self-esteem are buttressed by his denigratory attacks on the same two groups, and to a lesser extent on West Indians; and his deep sense of aggrievement, deprivation and neglect by his father are displaced onto the police as a source of society's authority, and to a lesser extent onto some notable public personalities within the middle class.

Why has he unconsciously chosen these specific groups for these precise purposes? The cultural background, home language and outlook of West Indians he accepts as being more like his own whereas the Indians and Pakistanis are experienced as more alien. As a result, he feels the Indians and Pakistanis to be more distant from him, more separate, so that he is able to dehumanize them more readily to the point where he feels no concern for them as human beings.

By appropriate symbolic displacement his emotional feelings toward his missing father are carried by his own white group and by those who exercise the symbols of parental authority – the police.

Vicious and virtuous cycles

Mr Chattaway's attitudes are of the vicious cycle type. His early infantile problems, sense of deprivation and resultant feelings of anger, his low self-esteem are all exacerbated by his mid-life crisis, the deepening of his depression, his unemployment and downward social mobility; while at the environmental level, the influx of coloured immigrants into the community strains his low tolerance for sharing and brings incursions into his already deprived sense of territory and home. To deal with influxes of strangers into one's own community can be a creatively stimulating experience for individuals who have a secure sense of a well-established identity, a feeling of having inside the self early experiences of a 'good-enough' mother and father. Without these, intrusions of strangers are unlikely to be met with interest, curiosity or flexibility but as a threatened source of deprivation, straining the original feelings of having had too little of early inner securities. It is as if siblings have appeared without prior preparation and before there has been enough good mothering or fathering for the child to be able to share.

In the few years preceding the study, and contemporaneously with it, Enoch Powell delivered some of his more racially provocative speeches. Mr Chattaway expressed positive views about these speeches which strengthened and supported his own racialistic views, making it easier for him to own his attitudes without undue guilt or inhibitions. Hiro has commented that following these speeches by Enoch Powell 'Voices were no longer lowered. Coloured workers were often taunted by white work-mates with "When are you going back home?" In some places white hostility did not stop at words.'[20] Mr Chattaway felt less concern or guilt about treating Indians or Pakistanis in the way in which he did when a man of such prominence in British life – Enoch Powell – could express extremely negative attitudes towards black people and have his views widely publicized through the mass media.

Mr Chattaway, although disclaiming membership of the National Front (or the British League of Fascists), was a regular reader of their pamphlets and news material. He enthusiastically supported their views on colour and race, pressing their literature on me. Although the National Front was not strong then, it nonetheless afforded a formidable source of support to Mr Chattaway in confirming and maintaining his rigid attitudes on race.

One of the vicious cycles involving race traverses the following loops:

1 His sense of deprivation, difficulties in handling his anger, and feelings of low self-esteem are alerted (in ways already described) by the presence of large groups of culturally different, visibly distinct Indians and Pakistanis.

2 By a process of projection, his hostilities, delinquencies and shortcomings are attributed to these groups and they then become increasingly persecutory figures to him.

3 The sense of persecution leads him to violent, overt expressions of his feelings.

4 His sense of guilt and fear of retaliatory punishment are further stimulated, which increasingly deflates his sense of self-esteem.

5 The more his self-esteem falls, the more intense does his need to attack the same groups become. The cycle is inexorably re-enacted.

Another vicious cycle is set in motion by his depression:

1 The anger which he turns back against himself leads to an increased difficulty in coping with major responsibilities at work.

2 This lowers his evaluation of his own worth in his own eyes.

3 His depression deepens further.

4 In this way, more and more of his anger is trapped in ever-diminishing circles, or it spills over into overt action of a violently explosive kind. And whichever course it takes, his race attitudes become more hostile as a consequence. His self-esteem is either increasingly deflated by this process so encouraging defensive manouevres of finding Indians and Pakistanis even more unworthy than himself; or, if the anger is turned back against himself he cannot contain it and it finally erupts, again going towards the Indians and Pakistanis in hostile actions as already described.

What sources of change or flexibility are there in either Mr Chattaway or in his situation which might produce shifts in these vicious cycles and so initiate any reversal of them? The one hopeful direction in which to look is the small but nonetheless promising turning towards his wife with both a need and an enhanced capacity for mutual care and companionable understanding. If his mid-life crisis can be weathered with her emotional support, his work energies may once again find a constructive outlet. This, in turn, could reduce the pressures which at the time of the study are pivoting him into these vicious cycles. If his self-esteem can be re-built, some of these loops might possibly be reversed.

He said at one point 'I am getting more relaxed because I am getting older.' Although he said this in relation to holding Colin as a child, it may be that with advancing age his strength of drives will diminish sufficiently for anger to be reduced and his relationship with his wife could help to ameliorate some of the stress he experiences.

However, at the present time, there is little sign of these vicious cycles breaking down or changing direction. The fixed attitudes and behaviour patterns are being sustained both by his deep intrapsychic conflicts and the pattern of social forces; and while the present circumstances continue to support them, his unresolved identity conflicts prompt acute forms of racial misuse.

2 MRS REBECCA CHATTAWAY

Issues bearing on the formation of her identity
Although Charles and Rebecca Chattaway both come from broken families, their early lives and critically important relationships with their parents were very different as were consequent effects upon their later identity development.

Unlike Charles, Rebecca spent the first six years of her life with both her parents and when they separated she lived with her father and her paternal grandmother, both of whom gave her loving care while her mother continued to see Rebecca and their emotional bonds seem to have been well sustained. When she was ten and went to live with her mother and new step-father, she felt accepted as one of the family. Her step-father was 'very, very good to me – marvellous – a cracker-nut!' She became part of a 'proper family' where all the children, herself and her brother and their three step-sisters and brothers were treated the same way, with love and acceptance and also with firmness. Her mother made Rebecca's friends welcome at the house and they all came and enjoyed her step-father's card tricks and other attempts to amuse them. This sense of having been securely cared for by two 'fathers' and two 'mothers' pervades her life history and a happy childhood shines through her life story and is the foundation upon which her identity has been formed.

She loved, admired and respected her mother and these feelings continue to the present time. As a child she felt her mother to be 'a splendid mother . . . always nice', who treated all the children generously, fairly and with loyalty. Her words were law and they knew how far they could go with her. Rebecca saw her as hard-working and admirable and from the age of ten, when she rejoined her mother's household, she identified strongly with her mother, finding it both natural and gratifying to work hard and also help run the household and look after the children.

> No one could convince me that I was a drudge to my mother – no one. I just thought that she worked all day like I did. I used to come home from school at dinner time and cook the midday meal and the breakfast things were there and the curtains still to be drawn and I had to do all that but I never thought less of my mother – No! I went back to school and

I called in at the nursery where my mother was cook and she would tell me what shopping to get and I had it all prepared by the time she came home from work.

She was able to give back in gratitude the love which she had received and very early she took on the role of a caring young mother, but was able to express some grievances and resentments at having had to look after the children – her step-siblings – and having had to put their needs before her own. But her capacity to accept the good with the bad, the normal frustrations of life alongside the warmth and pleasures, sustains her into her adult life.

Both her identification with her mother and a precociously early assumption of a mothering role are striking. Although the situation partly demanded this of her, she very readily responded to the role of the little mother and this remains as an essential core of her identity as a woman. She brought to the role qualities of warmth, concern and responsibility, and to a large extent she has been partly parasitical upon this role ever since, so that her wider personal identity is more difficult to discern than is her identity as mother.

When she married Charles, for instance, and they were spending their honeymoon at her mother's house, she found it natural to take her young step-brother Jackie along with them when she and Charles went to the cinema. 'Charles' face as long as you like', as they sat in the back row accompanied by a ten-year old. During that same honeymoon week, Charles bought her a special treat of strawberries and icecream, seeking to enjoy the intimacy of something shared just between the two of them and he asked her to eat them in their own room. But Rebecca shouted down the stairs 'Charles has brought some ice cream – do you want some Jackie?' 'He used to turn green and I couldn't understand why he didn't want to share it. He was an only child and he made a big thing of having treated me and me only but I could never see it. I used to take my lump of ice cream and give them all a bit.' This revealing pattern must have been repeated many times in their early life together. To Rebecca sharing comes naturally. She notes how her mother always treated all her children in the same way and does so to this day.

Her mother was able to love and share her good feelings and generosities and Rebecca in turn is able to do the same. When she married, however, the role of mother conflicted with the more intimate role of a wife. Her need to treat her husband in a motherly way might well have satisfied some of the unconscious needs for mothering which Mr Chattaway had missed in his early life, but at the same time he wanted to have a special relationship with Rebecca. 'He wanted to be my number one. He's as happy as a sandboy, my husband, when there's only me and him. I'm his wife but I'm also mum to these three. He likes it if we are alone together.' Her primary identity as a mother seems to have contributed to some of the difficulties within the family, as well as having provided some aspects of love and security.

Her close relationship with her mother (who lives around the corner) continues to the present time and they see each other frequently, a not uncommon working-class pattern in England. Rebecca's difficulties in emotionally separating from her mother in turn affect her relationships with her children who also show signs of difficulty in working through separation problems from their mother.

Her life is emotionally bound up with her children – John, Elaine and Colin. When asked to give a brief self-description, she said 'I'm a good mother to my kids. I like to know that they're alright' and she went on to recount how a friend had told her that she did not express enough of her own needs and personality. 'You're alright sorting out other people's problems, but you don't push for yourself'. Her personal identity rarely emerges but in a recent row with Charles, something new seems to have crystallized for after having asserted her viewpoint, she added to Charles 'this is *me* this time'.

What aspects of her *personal* identity can be discerned? Her work life before marriage was relatively short. She did office work for a period but after marriage she has worked part-time cleaning offices or houses and although she started a course in typing before Colin was conceived, after his birth this too was necessarily abandoned for the time being. Work as a creative means of expression outside the home has not been an aspect of her identity and indeed by choosing the particular part-time work which she has done, she has maintained a domestic role so underlining once more her chosen identity as a mother and housewife.

Rebecca is an able, warm-hearted and likeable person with a capacity for empathy and understanding. 'I'd rather sympathize than say "Oh, you shouldn't have done it!" I don't pick people to pieces, not because I'm lah-di-dah, we all have a little bit of scandal in us, but it's nothing big in me.' Her life history bears out this insight. She is not given to feelings of persecution and seems to have little need to be distrustful of others. She can express her ordinary angry feelings and does not seem to be unduly plagued by them. 'I'm not bad to get on with but I can lose my temper, but I don't like my own way all the time in any argument'. She prefers to explore difficulties and 'have them out' so she cannot bottle things up, and feels uneasy with others when they are angry and fail to say what it is all about. When Charles sulks, for instance, she finds this unbearable and would much rather that he said what was on his mind.

Her longings for a home of their own have gone unfulfilled but she is philosophically acceptant. 'We've never been able to save up enough deposit . . . I love this house but I would like to have one of my own but I can't see us ever being able to do that'. She characteristically blames no one for things which have failed to go as she might have wished, but manages to accept things as they are with a fair degree of balance and good humour. 'I really am quite content to go along as I do. I've never been one to want to go out . . . I like to go to a show now and again but only if we can really afford it.'

Her worst fear is of being ill and dying and 'leaving my kids. I think that's tragic'. Again, it is the mother in her which is uppermost.

Unresolved identity conflicts and race

Since her identity is rooted in a sense of her own worth as a warm, understanding and basically good mother, she is secure enough in this aspect of her identity to also accept as good mothers West Indian and Indian mothers at Colin's school.

> I know they are good to their babies – they're good mothers. I've never seen them knock their children about – they seem to have a lot of patience with them. The children are always beautifully dressed and they're always clean. The mothers are all friendly and they always say 'Hello', but we don't have anything – you know – no conversation.

She can identify with them as mothers revealing herself as tolerant, open-minded, friendly and fair.

In her interpersonal contacts with immigrant children her maternal generosities and warm concerns are readily evoked. When, for the first time, an Indian child joined Elaine's class when she was about eight years old, 'I told Elaine to talk to her because I said "Ah, be kind to her. Don't push her out". Elaine invited her to her birthday party and Mrs Chattaway encouraged Elaine to tell the other children that the Indian girl was expected. Everybody came. Some four years later the girl's distraught mother came to ask Mrs Chattaway for help in searching for her daughter who had failed to return home from school at the expected time. She took over with characteristic energy and concern. 'I said to her "Well, you go home and I'll look for her"," and when she eventually found her she performed a mother's task and 'gave her a good telling-off' and took her back to her mother who did the same.

Another incident which resulted in her arriving slightly late for her fourth appointment with me, throws light on how her maternal attitudes transcend racial barriers. She gave money to a young girl who was crying bitterly in the street and whom she did not know. '"I've lost my money and I've got to get some peas with it and my sister's going to hit me if I don't find it and I've looked all over!" So I said to her "Here, don't cry any more. Take your two bob and get your shopping," and I thought "There's not much in my purse, mate," but I couldn't see her breaking heart.' Questioned as to who she was, she said she was coloured; 'I don't know whether she was Indian or curly-headed – she had an anorak all around here – breaking her heart! "My sister's going to give me such a smack", she said'.

She expressed some pleasure in her childrens' personal relationships with West Indian or Indian friends, noting how an Indian colleague of John's had shaken hands with him with 'great feeling'. And she notes with enjoyment that Colin had made friends with a 'little coloured girl' at school.

> I put Colin in this play-school. For one reason he was lonely, and for another, there are no coloured children round this estate but there will be in his class and I don't want him to have such a shock to know that there's another child who is a different colour. So he mixes with them now. He gets on *ever* so well with a coloured little girl. She adores him and she gives him all the teddies and I don't know her name. I've asked him but he doesn't know.

An additional context within which she has had direct personal relationships with Indians and West Indians is when she has been ill and required medical attention. Both doctors to whom she turned in relation to gynaecological complaints were Indians, partners of her English doctor. Although the first doctor was competent but not unusually helpful in explaining the meaning of his diagnosis to her and its implications, the second doctor 'was ever so nice. He did me a drawing of the womb and . . . told me about his mother's fibroids' and spent time telling her in detail about what was happening to her insides. To her, doctors whether black or white, 'have all got such a lot of sympathy and kindness. I mean, they must have because they must see a terrible lot of suffering so they've got to be kind'.

Her confinement with Colin was at home and she felt bitterly about the unavailability of a bed in hospital. She was uneasy about the twelve year interval between Elaine's birth and the forthcoming birth and aware that West Indian and Indian women were occupying a large number of hospital beds because in many cases their living conditions did not make confinement at home as easy as in her case. But despite this genuine sense of grievance, her response to the West Indian midwife who delivered her (and it was a very difficult birth) was a very warm one. She was 'marvellous and she showed kindness', and even when Mrs Chattaway felt that the techniques used by the midwife had afforded her less support and help than her previous experiences in hospital had given her, she separated her critical judgement of the professional approach adopted by the midwife from her feelings for the woman herself and from her attitudes towards the racial group of which she was a member.

These incidents have been recounted in detail because they illustrate how Mrs Chattaway relates to people, irrespective of race. She reveals trust and good feelings as well as being open to reality-testing. These express positive aspects of her identity and are a sturdy and important part of her personality. However, her feelings towards individuals, as individuals, contrast with some of her attitudes towards racial groups. Her prejudiced attitudes arise first from her primary identity as a mother, and secondly, they emanate from her inner world and the effects upon her sexuality of her mid-life crisis, a forthcoming hysterectomy and from unconscious conflicts in family relationships.

Her identity as a mother

Because Mrs Chattaway is emotionally bound up with her children and tends to identify with them and see their problems through their eyes, and because each child is involved with different racial groups in distinctive ways, she too becomes emotionally involved with these racial groups. Some of her racial attitudes emanate from these maternal preoccupations and might be seen as *secondary* attitudes rather than as primary personal views arising in depth from her own inner life and experience. She becomes an active protagonist on her childrens' behalf.

But her identity as a mother is involved at a deeper level as well. The area of their behaviour where her helplessness is at its greatest is in confronting and coping with the destructively hostile feelings which her husband and her children express towards each other, the defenceless cat, and to others in the community. These affront her and arouse her anxiety, they burden and frighten her and contrast with her own more relaxed, friendly and generally kind interpersonal approach. It is, of course, possible that her husband and her children 'carry' for her, her own denied feelings of aggression. This may be so. But nonetheless, having devoted her life to being a 'good' mother, when confronted by aspects of their destructive hostility, her conflict lies in how to maintain her loving supportive feelings for them (with which so much of her positive self-image is involved), and yet also remain true to her own values of tolerance and kindness.

She, too, can erupt in anger; she knows this about herself and accepts it, preferring to express anger rather than bottling it up; and she seems more capable of maintaining balanced relationships which include aggression than the other members of the family. Her anxieties are especially aroused when the quantity of hostility and its intensity increases within the family. But she is not rigidly defensive so does not wholly deny the reality which confronts her. She faces some of the pain and distress of the 'nastiness' but if she wholly admitted this into consciousness her identity as a good mother would be sorely undermined. 'We are what we love', as Erik Erikson has said[21] and too great a part of her self-image and her feelings of worth are bound up with her achievements as a mother and as a motherly-wife. She needs, therefore, to find some more glaring examples of the *same* kind of behaviour and attitudes, but located outside the family circle, so as to externalize the feared 'badness' and then, by comparison, her own family can be found to be more acceptable to her. It is, of course, an unconscious maneouvre to retain her self-image and sense of identity as a more-or-less-good mother and to restore her family as a more-or-less-good family. The greater 'badness' is located elsewhere.

This pattern can be traced in the phrases and emotionally tinged themes, indeed even in the specific words with which she first describes her husband's or her children's behaviour and later uses these identical words, phrases or themes in relation to behaviour negatively attributed to West Indians or to Indians.

She exclaims, for example, at the '*spitefulness*' which skinheads and rockers show to each other and how they attack each other savagely and kick and destroy each other's moterbikes, and since John is a skinhead she is talking about her own son. On another occasion, she describes with evident distress Colin's persistent '*spitefulness*' to the cat. 'He'll pull it's tail as he passes, as it's lying there quietly – ding-dong he goes. I know other children do it but Colin does it more. He's so *spiteful*. Her picture of West Indian men include the attribution of 'a *spiteful* streak . . . I think underneath them they would really be *spiteful* and knock you about'.

Her concern over Colin's behaviour illustrates especially well the point which I am making. She notes how all three children have bad tempers but Colin's causes her the greatest anxiety because he is

> an awfully *aggressive* child – he shouts and hollers, he screams and speaks so aggressively from the back of his throat . . . he is so aggressive in the mornings – he is terrible when he comes downstairs, he drives me potty . . . I don't know which way to turn. He shouts 'Shut your mouth, shut up', and he shouts at his gran and grandad.

If she puts him in a room by himself

> he goes on screaming and hollering . . . he shouts and hollers at you . . . he's so cheeky and lippy . . . he's aggressive, I mean he wouldn't think anything of kicking you . . . Ooooooh, he's so aggressive, terrible! . . . He's so emotional and gets het up and bad-tempered!

She is driven to despair by the situation with Colin, her existing means of coping with him have proved ineffective and he worries her greatly. [After the study was over I referred Mrs Chattaway to the local Child Guidance Clinic for help with Colin.] Her self-image as a mother has been threatened.

> You'd never believe he was mine . . . I don't know whether I should try to be kinder or try another system with him or what . . . but everytime I give him a good smack on his bottom, he's sick . . . . I don't know whether it's because I'm older, that I'm giving in to him, but inside, I *rave*.

It is because of the *extent* of this anxiety and her impotence in the face of it that she displaces and projects onto West Indians especially, these disturbing qualities in Colin's behaviour with which she cannot cope.

> They are different to us because they're aggressive. I mean they're boisterous, they shout, they holler and shout, they fight and the screaming and shouting before they start fighting,

it's really awful . . . The way they talk, you know, it's as if
they're always in a bad mood all the time . . . it's the tone of
their voices . . . . I've always made my kinds have respect for
me – they're not going to talk to me like a bit of dirt but West
Indian parents don't seem to bother when the children get
older, they let them be shouting and bawling and boisterous and
if they calmed them down indoors, they wouldn't be mouthy
outside. West Indians are very much more mouthy than
Indians – they shout and bawl, couldn't be quiet to save their
lives . . . . Their aggression, it's like a streak in them, like
Colin's got a bad temper and that's his streak.

She recognises, up to a point, that the aggression is not confined to
West Indians or Indians and she uneasily tries to cope with the
painful awareness that John is capable of violence and may also be
destructive in the same ways as she attributes to other racial groups.
She is, for example, absorbed by the symbolic threat of knives (which
will be discussed in further detail in relation to the area of her
sexuality) and she describes how 'a darky had a great big knife down
his trousers, all with a jagged edge', but she reassures herself that
'Johnny doesn't [carry a knife] because I begged him not to, because
I said "You'll come up against one of those darkies – he'll bring his
knife out and you'll bring yours, and you'll come off second best".'
When referring to the noise and aggressive disturbance created by
West Indians at Elaine's school dance, she again tries to reassure
herself that the West Indians are worse than John.

It's always the coloureds. I know the white boys can do it. I
mean the likes of my Johnny could go to a dance . . and they
could be a bit funny. I just hope that Johnny never throws a
milk bottle through a window because he'd have to answer to
me, let alone the police, if we found him doing things like that.

She cannot avoid knowing about John's potential violence since,
as a skinhead, he has frequently been involved in group fights and
attacks on rockers and on Asians. She, however, tries her best to
control him and hopefully focusses on the worse excesses of 'the
coloureds' in order to retain her image of her son as 'good' and not to
concentrate on the possibilities of his serving as a target for the more
feared violence of 'the coloureds' towards him.
Although her relationship with Charles seems to be improving
and is somewhat softened by the mid-life crises through which they

both are passing, nonetheless there are aspects of the relationship which add to the stress of interpersonal friction within the family.

> I do dread rowing with him because he sulks afterwards . . . he gets me to such a pitch . . . . I'm not frightened of him – I used to be – but now I'll have a go with him. And it's the afters – that's when he's going to sulk, come in and eat his dinner and slosh the cat . . . we've got to such a pitch when he's sulked over a simple thing that . . . we've had a terrible row.

She relates how these vicious rows have often been followed by threats of separation, until he finally got her to breakdown point, and then withdrew. She told him '"We're either going to be happy or we're going to part. This is *me* talking this time". I'm not saying that anybody can get on with me, because they can't, but it's just that he's so *bombastic* with it all.' In a different interview she describes the West Indians down the road at the local pub in the same way 'They are so *bombastic* – they shout at each other and you'd think there was going to be a fight any minute.'

Her feelings for Charles are further complicated by her husband's attitude towards John. She has a very close oedipal relationship with her eldest son. Her husband's dealings with him upset her greatly although she recognises the underlying jealousy.

> I know that Johnny's asked for it but he [Charles] goes on and on and how it hurts me, and he says 'Wait until that boy comes in', and my tummy goes right over, right over. I don't want him to get onto John and I don't want Charles to have the miseries because when he starts – Oh my God – he makes my life a misery. He forgets there are others apart from himself. I can't *bear* the way he talks to John – I can't take it. I don't like it. I don't know if it worries John or if it hurts John, but it worries me.

The constant stress of interpersonal friction which these relationships impose upon her and their apparent intractability, pervades her. The negative feelings and tensions generated by the high level of intrafamiliar aggression, she projects and displaces onto West Indians and Indians.

Sex and her inner world
Her relationship with Elaine is of a different order from her

relationship with the male members of her family. As a daughter on the threshold of her menarche, she tends to identify with her, unconsciously using Elaine to express for her some of her own emotional frustrations and sexual anxieties.

She longed for her to enjoy her first dance and when the West Indians broke it up and the headmaster banned future dances, her response was passionate.

> She thoroughly enjoyed herself at the dance . . . and now they can't have any more because of the coloureds. I think it's a shame. Elaine never goes anywhere in Athol because of them . . . . There's always trouble. It makes me wild because – well – there's no more dancing. She was so excited. It's always the coloureds because they are so aggressive.

She felt that the police should have provided better protection at the dance. 'There are enough of them driving up and down here all night, looking to see if the likes of my Johnny are behaving themselves.'

It is through Elaine that Mrs Chattaway reflects her intense concern and anxiety over the related problems of aggression, sex and knives. She is concerned about her daughter's dawning sexuality and the threats which she feels are posed by the sexual and aggressive behaviour of Indians (rather than West Indians) within the community. These also stimulate her own sexual anxieties, arising from her mid-life crisis, with its threatened loss of sexual attractiveness, and from a forthcoming hysterectomy which she incorrectly fears may curtail her sex life. Since she has a lively and apparently satisfactory sex life with her husband, she is struggling with the anxieties of an impending loss of this important part of her life. In addition, her repressed oedipal feelings for John, while denied and unconscious, nonetheless tend to make her specially sensitive to sexual reverberations in general. For all these reasons, Elaine's problems in coping both with the fears and reality of aggressive sexual advances seem to symbolize for Mrs Chattaway *her* denied desires and fears.

Indians are largely perceived as the potential sexual aggressors. It was an Indian youth who had accosted Elaine in the street and 'asked her to come to bed' and Mrs Chattaway on occasions has also been approached by Indian men in the street, which understandably had angered her.

Forbidden and denied desires emerge in her advice to Elaine.

> 'Don't let a West Indian bring you home', because I mean, some
> of them are lovely looking boys – you've got to admit it – and I
> think the girls get flattered to be asked to go out with them
> because on the one side they have got charm, but underneath
> that charm they're more aggressive, I reckon, than a white man,
> definitely.

The story, previously quoted about the 'darky with a great big
knife down his trousers', is followed by the following comment: 'I
told him [i. e., her brother who recounted the story] that he should
have told a copper. If my Johnny had a penknife, they'd have had
him. The police would probably just say to the darky "Don't wear it"
and he'd say "It's my religion'. Well, if it's his religion, he wants to
keep it done up, not bring it out'. The phallic symbolism seems
apparent.

In several places she links these ideas of West Indians or Indians
being sexually forward, and aggressive, with having knives. She has
never actually seen anyone attacking with a knife, but insists that she
has heard of such incidents. To her, West Indians are considered the
more aggressive, loud, exuberant and bombastic but Indians are
cunning, quiet, stealthy and sly. 'They're quiet – they would bring a
knife out only to look at you.' [sic] But she seldom distinguishes
between West Indians and Indians.

> Coloureds are very aggressive. They don't know how to have a
> clean fist fight – always threaten with knives, come out with
> their knives straight away . . . They're a terrible lot at Elaine's
> school. I think they're ever so fierce. They're not like my John's
> crowd – I mean John's lot may have a fight but they never
> bring knives and things out. The coloureds don't think
> anything of having knives. It doesn't worry them at all.

There are some aspects of West Indian and Indian behaviour which
are, no doubt, accurately perceived and described by Mrs Chattaway,
for example, the break-up of the school dance and the Indian youth's
approach to Elaine. Her response to incidents such as these would be
little different if the perpetrators had been white and English. In both
cases, she would have sought to ensure her daughter's goals (i. e., in
the one case the continuation of school dances with adequate police
protection, and in the other case Elaine's freedom to walk in the

streets of her community unmolested). However, the particular nature of the racial stereotypes which she advances and their intensity, with their emphasis on the shouting, noisy, angry aggression and fights, and the sexual aggression and dangers seem to stem from two unresolved current identity crises:

1 The first is related to the anxiety and concern generated by the intensity and quantity of hostile and destructive feelings which pervade relationships within the family. These arouse her fears and throw doubt on her worth as a good mother and threaten to disturb her feelings of love for, and acceptance of, her family. Her negative racial attitudes, largely directed towards the West Indians, have the function of siphoning off these negative feelings which otherwise she fears might damage her family. They also have the function of saving her from openly expressing her aggressive and destructive feelings under the provocation which her family provides. By these imputations and projections onto the West Indians, she acts to conserve her identity as a good mother and wife, and her relationships with her family are protected from further erosion. It is the West Indians who suffer.

2 Her mid-life crisis, with the anxieties which it raises about sexual attractiveness and performance, the intensity of her repressed oedipal feelings for John, her daughter's approaching menarche and sexual awakening, the forthcoming hysterectomy (incorrectly understood to herald the end of her sex life) have all led to the unconscious stimulation of her sexual interests as well as to the strengthening of her defences againt their expression or conscious recognition. The West Indians are perceived as being sexually attractive but also dangerously aggressive and frightening, embodying not only a threat of attacks with knives but also of being – in phantasy – sadistically knocked around.

These racial displacements and projections serve the function for Mrs Chattaway of diverting her oedipal guilts and anxieties to safer territory outside the family and to an alien racial group different from the racial group of her son.

Vicious and virtuous cycles in race attitudes

Mrs Chattaway's *personal* relationships, as we have seen, are all remarkably free of racial prejudice. In her life history, are there any incidents when a potentially virtuous cycle in race relationships is twitched into a vicious cycle – or *vice versa*? There seem to be no instances of this. On the contrary, at times where a provocative situation potentially exists, she is not influenced in the direction of prejudice. For example, her good feelings for the West Indian midwife were not reversed when she found herself insufficiently helped during labour. She showed herself open to reality-testing . It was not the race of the midwife not her personality but the use of a particular set of professional practices to which she objected.

When Colin's behaviour distresses her, she at no time attempts to forge a link between this behaviour and, for instance, his association with West Indian or Indian children at his school. She is able to focus on certain aspects of Colin's relationship with his brother and sister and question her own failures. In these and other incidents, Mrs Chattaway shows an unusual capacity (given the family values which surround her in relation to race) for establishing interpersonal bonds with persons of other races and of being able to sustain them. The vital elements in her personality dynamics which make this possible, stem from her early infancy and childhood which gave her a healthy capacity to weather the fears centred on infantile persecutry anxieties. She does not resort to splitting the good from the bad, is not given to paranoid projections, and seems able to tolerate ambivalence.

It is only when the *quantity and intensity* of aggressively destructive feelings within the family reaches a point beyond her capacity to maintain her image of herself as a good-enough mother and her image of them as good enough – both vital to her sense of identity as a person – that she resorts to *group* stereotyping, emanating from the stress which engulfs her. In her case, it is probable that social conformity pressures within the family play an important part in her group projections. Her stereotypes of the West Indians and Indians, while they have a personally unique stamp, also have similarities with some views of her husband. Involved as he is with racial issues, she is exposed to many of his ideas on race.

Her personality dynamics, *in themselves,* do not seem to drive her towards racial projections of a negative type; situational stress emanating from the family dynamics, and inner stress emanating from a multitude of sexually-tinged conflicts press for a release outside the confines of the family system. If she too expressed more of her aggressively hostile feelings towards the other members of the family, it might be more than the family system itself could sustain. For the family to cope with the aroused oedipal problems would be impossible because of the incestuous threats. In each case, the stress requires her to externalize her conflicts and she chooses racial groups to bear the displacements and projections of these unresolved identity conflicts.

Finding herself living among immigrants

Living among immigrants in Athol has meant for Mrs Chattaway facing loss – loss of her 'beautiful Athol' which she loved and which she now feels is a 'run-down, dilapidated area [which] started with the coloureds letting things go and now . . . white people aren't bothering because they can see that the Indians and the coloureds are getting a lot of their own way and people are just giving up'. Loss and change confront her, change necessitated by the sense of impingement and invasion which she experiences in relation to the *number* of immigrants within the community. 'There are definitely, definitely, too many coloureds in Athol – definitely'. She feels their presence everywhere.

She now shops in a small local section of Athol and has stopped going to the High Street because she dislikes their presence on the pavements where they stand and

> jabber, jabber, jabber and won't move when you want to get by. Once upon a time you could go along and say 'Excuse me', and they would move, but they're too ignorant. They look right through you, you know, and you've got to more or less push your pram into them to move them. They've got no manners anyway.

The spatial invasion of public highways and pavements is what draws the anger and irritation of both Mr Chattaway and his wife. While Charles is trying to run immigrants down as they cross against the lights at the pedestrian crossing, using his car as an aggressive weapon, Mrs Chattaway is provoked to overt action of a provocative kind in pushing her pram into them –'more or less'. In each case what has provoked them is the obstruction of a predictable and familiar freedom of passage and the visibly different bodies, racially distinguishable, which usurp public space in ways which they feel are contrary to their established mores.

A similar sense of invasion and impingement by coloured immigrants has curtailed her occasional visits to the local pub where once in a while the whole family went to have a drink in the garden. They no longer go. In these ways her life has become even more centred on the home than previously; and since Colin's birth, less than three years ago, necessitated her returning into the closed family setting from work outside the home, these feelings of impingement act as additional constraints upon her freedom of movement, albeit self-chosen constraints. She has withdrawn back into her home and it is only through Colin's school that she makes contact with groups of mothers, presumably a cross-section of the community.

From what has been said earlier, Mrs Chattaway has been exposed to increasing anxieties and stress as she senses the rise in aggression within the family and within the community. But she has additional fears, which arise not only from what the immigrants might do to members of her family, but also arising from what the members of her family might do to them. These also perturb her. Her husband with his car at the cross-roads arouses her anxiety and she expressed concern when she recounted how her husband and John had gone to 'beat up' the Indian youth who had accosted Elaine. She voiced her fear that her children might be the victims of knife attacks one day and be 'cut up'. All of this adds to the tension and stress under which she lives and, as already shown, it is the increasing inability to tolerate stress which leads to the racial misuse to which she then resorts. These create a vicious cycle. Inter-racial tensions create stress and stress leads to a greater inner need to offload that tension; in an effort to protect her family, she displaces these sources of tension outside the family, chooses racial groups as repositories and so exacerbates racial intolerance still further. It is an inexorable process.

The noise and shouting, 'bawling and hollering' which she attributes to West Indians may, or may not be, as loud as she says, but to *her* these auditory impingements touch on exposed and sensitized nerves reducing her tolerance to cope with her own small son and his 'hollering and shouting'. Again, these in turn create vicious cycles in racial intolerance by imposing additional strains on her capacity to tolerate whatever noise levels reach her from the West Indians; each exacerbates the other – the noise within the family and the noise without.

The presence of West Indians and Indians in Athol has led her to believe that the police are more hesitant to arrest coloured immigrants and more likely to look out for young white men like John. She projects a similar picture to the one given by her husband. This may or may not be accurate. This study is not constituted to answer that question, but as she believes it to be so, it leads to a sense of fear in her. Since she is already uneasy about John and his activities as a skinhead, this only increases her concern and she uses the police as a focus for her sense of anxiety. The West Indians and Indians are felt to be favoured while John is an exposed target for police harassment.

In conclusion, Mrs Chattaway's major identity crises at the present time arise from her inability to cope with both the quantity and the intensity of pressures acting as *overloads* in three different areas of her life: there is too much aggressive hostility both inside the family and also outside the home in ways which involve her family members; the intensity and quantity of sexual anxiety, which she is trying to cope with, seems to be more than she can handle; there is too great a sense of impingement and invasion within Athol by different racial groups for her to feel unaffected. Each of these threatens her with loss of an essential part of her identity. The first is intrinsically linked with her identity as a good mother and the loving feelings for her family which she needs to conserve; the second is concerned with her sexual needs and vitality which are part of her identity as a wife and as a woman; and the third is concerned with her identity as a woman living in a familiar and loved neighbourhood, confronted by what she perceives to be deterioration, invasion and massive change, threatening her sense of security – which derives from the familiar.

Her attitudes towards racial groups arise from each of these three sources of identity strain. If the quantity and intensity of each of these threats to her identity were either to shift or to be reduced, it is possible that Mrs Chattaway could maintain, within the community, that greater level of interpersonal tolerance towards West Indians and Indians at a group level which she already displays in all her relationships at a person-to-person level. As it is, she is goaded and pressed by overload in these three areas, and racial groups within the community act as available and accessible repositories for the displacement and projection of her conflicts.

JOHN CHATTAWAY

Issues bearing on the formation of his identity
John Chattaway's early memories are extremely meagre and impoverished. At eighteen, he remembers nothing of his early years, no memories of his father nor of the birth of his sister and his one recollection is of his mother taking him to school. Although his earliest relationships have either left little mark on him or are unavailable to him, he recounts in minute detail an overwhelming number of accidents and incidents, all connected with body injury. Some of these happened when he was very young; others span his eighteen years of life. In most, it is he who is injured but on occasion he relates incidents where his friends are the victims. Some incidents are recounted as if they were humorous pranks, but many are acts of impulsive cruelty involving body violence.

It is, of course, impossible to tell whether all of these accidents and incidents actually happened. There is some internal evidence which suggests that John takes phantasy for fact. But whether they are accounts of his actual experiences or of his phantasies, nonetheless they occupy an immensely important part of his inner life and to him they appear to be real. They preoccupy him inordinately and figure prominently in each interview.

Certain patterns can be discerned. They are all concerned with violence done to the body and the major preoccupation is with the body damage. There is no concern with motives, feelings, or possible factors which might have led to the occurrence. The bodily zones which are damaged are predominantly the head (including parts such as the tongue and the ear, etc.) but also arms and legs. These are injured, scarred and marred but nonetheless they recover and continue to function, even if somewhat impaired. All of these body parts appear to serve symbolically as phallic displacements. The violence which occurs is often the result of cars or motorbikes being out of control, or it originates in the impulsive, sadistic and sometimes bizarre 'humour' of John or his friends who do extraordinarily hostile things to each other. The persons involved in all these occurrences are men.

Although some of the incidents are horrifying and frightening, John recounted them without any affect, betraying a striking lack of involvement and concern. 'I don't like accidents but I don't mind them when I am in them . . . If I get smashed up, that doesn't affect me.' He also showed no concern for others who might be involved.

By far the largest number of injuries refer to the head area and it is striking that he is a *skinhead* – the word itself linking this area of major traumatic injury and anxiety to the enveloping skin, which in the detailed descriptions he gave of his many injuries was frequently described as scratched, bruised or as having been stitched. His description of the *skinheads*, and their rival gang the *greasers* (or *rockers*), emphasises differences between them in relation to how hair is cut and dressed – their 'head- dressing' – as well as differences in relation to the possession of motorbikes or scooters, those aggressive objects which figure in his accidents as the means by which body injury is produced.

Which came first? Did he become a skinhead and because of the gang culture become so sensitized to the head that he recollects or phantasies innumerable head injuries? Or was it the other way around? This seems the more likely. By joining the skinhead gang, multiple deep needs are unconsciously satisfied in him, one of which is his preoccupation with heads and their injury.

These incidents and accidents appear to be expressing castration anxiety. It is, of course, only possible to speculate as to the sequence of events and their unconscious meaning. An early series of head injuries might have exacerbated existing castration fears but it is also possible that the castration anxiety produced an accident-proneness or indeed a wanton invitation to such accidents which in turn further increased the anxiety. (For example, a recent accident on his scooter produced serious concussive effects because, among other things, John was not wearing a crash helmet.)

Many of the incidents and pranks which he related depict himself as the victim, or his mates as victims and he as one of the perpetrators. The phantasy being repeatedly re-enacted depicts a situation where the victim is rendered impotent and immobilized (welded to a bench, locked in a cupboard, welded to a ball and chain, impaled, gassed, etc.) They are images of acts which create impotence at the hand of another. It is as if there is a castrating father with power and malice and an impotent son. As later discussion will attempt to explore, it seems as if the real 'crime' is oedipal and the immobilized person is one who in phantasy or reality, can no longer sexually transgress. If these incidents happened in reality, they certainly follow a similar pattern which suggests that John unconsciously contrived or colluded in involving himself in just such situations. If they are more phantasy than fact, they serve the unconscious purpose of punishment and the enactment of phantasized constraints upon revived oedipal strivings re-aroused during adolescence.

By combining the sparse information available from John's life history with some material derived from those of his parents, the following picture of his early life emerges. He was the first-born and his early years were spent with his mother in circumstances where their housing was so cramped and hemmed in by constraints on noise and movement, that he had little opportunity for being a physically active child. Nothing is known of actual injuries, whether at the time of his birth or afterwards. His father had little contact with his young son and his predominant bond was with his mother and this remains, as we have seen, a close, intense relationship on her side. John's life story, meagre as it is about family relationships, suggests that he sees his mother as the person who 'wants him to stay' at home, when during fights at home his father might angrily tell him to get out and to 'clear off'.

Until he was eleven years old, Mrs Chattaway took him, hand-in-hand, to school because he was reluctant to go and although John was teased by other boys, nonetheless he continued to go to school in that way for many years. His mother's picture of him at that stage was that he was a slow learner and a fairly isolated child. Exposed to humiliating dependence on his mother, his relationship with other boys must have been very difficult.

His life history reveals a deep and all-pervading sense of intellectual inadequacy and failure which he attempts to mask by its opposite – a defensive need to assert and boast of his high ability, outstanding intelligence and creativity. The quality and content of these inflated claims hauntingly reveal how painfully inadequate he must have felt (and indeed, still feels) and with what difficulty he tried to take hold of problems posed by school work. His phantasy at the end of the study was that 'In ten years time, I think I'll be famous – I'll invent something . . . I haven't thought about it yet, but I'll invent something. You don't have to do anything, just something simple to be famous.' The sense of inadequacy lurks uneasily under cover of this heroic day-dream.

> I didn't want to do well. I could have, you know, but I just didn't want to go to class. In mock exams I always used to come near the top but in real exams I used to come about twentieth because I never used to want to go up to the next class . . . If we had an hour for an exam, I finished it in quarter of an hour and went home and I came second in class.

These seem to be attempts to salvage a faltering and tottering self-esteem. He had to cope with the laughter of his peers, exposed as he was to his mother's escort and to the fear which in the first place had led to that escort. It is understandable that he experienced a sense of humiliating dependence on his mother, visible for all to see, and that his masculine identity must have felt in jeopardy. It is equally understandable that all of this stimulated feelings of hostility and angry defencelessness.

As a means of coping with these anxieties his peer group became more and more important to him. He became part of a gang at school which he was more able to manage than close personal bonds and revealed enough rudimentary capacity for sharing and empathy which allowed him to take part in gang life. His capacity for identification with equally phallically assertive youths goes just so far, but does not extend to having concern for their welfare or the welfare of their victims. He reveals little capacity for personal affectional ties and meaningful relationships and seems largely unaware of, or indifferent to, the feelings of others. The gang provided him with support against the oedipal threats, strengthened his masculine identity and affirmed some sense of his adequacy. It filled an inner void and provided a potential haven of group security, and relief from the pressure of four related and largely unconscious problems: his incapacity to make meaningful personal relationships, his feelings of intellectual inadequacy, his fears about his masculine identity and the revived oedipal strivings which aroused his castration anxiety. It brought him a clearer sense of group identity which hid his diffuse and unformed personal identity. Through the gang, he was unconsciously seeking a disengagement from his primary ties to his mother. By committing acts of destructive aggression and hostility in concert with others, he proclaims his masculinity with vengeance and is afforded the security of the group.

This pattern of gang membership and identification with values which emphasise gang warfare and violent attacks upon others, was maintained after he left school when he became a member of the skinheads. Erikson has said, 'Isolated sufferers try to solve by withdrawal what the joiners of deviant cliques and gangs attempt to solve by conspiracy'.[21] In John's case, the conspiracy is a desperate acting-out of violence and treating others as things without feeling or compassion.

Images of potency may be grandiosely inflated by the exploits of the *skinheads*, both towards their rival gang the *greasers*, and when both gangs combine and attack the Pakistanis; but there is no sign in John of guilt, self-reproach, self-questioning or compassion. It is only the outward acts which count – the aggressively cruel attacks; he apparently remains unnervingly unafraid both of his own hostility and of others' violence towards him.

The hostility is directed both towards groups and towards individuals, especially those in authority. At school and later at college, he reacted to punishment with increased inner rage and he beat up the teacher. 'I just got hold of the teacher and belted him one. I just got up and lost my temper with him. He sort of fought back but I had the upper hand.' He was expelled the next day. He was always in trouble at school and had angry confrontations with the headmaster. He is also contemptuous towards women, treating them as things. 'They come after me. I don't bother about them. Once I had three girls going at once and we had a kind of game with my mates as to who could keep going longest without getting caught. It was making me broke.'

His attitude towards his mother and father is mostly overlaid with aggression.

> They said to me 'You're not going to have a scooter'. I got a scooter. They said 'We'll put a hammer through it', and I said 'I'll put a hammer through your car if you put a hammer through that', and that was that . . . . . My dad and I sometimes have a punch-up – he punches me maybe once a year – something like that – mostly when the coppers come round and I'm in trouble. I hit him back if he hits me and then he stops when he knows I'm going to hit him back.

John appears to express and act out for his father those negative identity elements which his father fears in himself. When he gets into trouble with the police, his father is angry 'because he doesn't want me to get into trouble. He was in trouble, you know, but not really anything for him to worry about'. When John brings the coppers to the door of the house, both parents are angry.

He has almost nothing to say about his feelings for Elaine or Colin, but during interviews exchanges between Colin and John were mostly about being beaten up – Colin asking John to beat him up – a partly humorous, but also aggressive, exchange.

John talks little about his work or his career plans and has difficulty in envisaging a career with a future for himself. He is working as an apprentice gas-fitter and his major pleasure seems to lie in macabre fun and games with his mates. He has a passionate interest in scooters and owns three and is obviously skilled in the instrumental mastery of his machines, deriving pleasure and power from his skills. His exploits and accidents on these scooters, however, are so numerous as to suggest that they – and the cars of his friends – serve the function of acting out his castrational phantasies. When as a skinhead his attacks on greasers take place, there is a savage delight in destroying and damaging their motorbikes, 'smashing them up' as well as attacking the greasers as people.

Identity conflicts and race

John is currently facing four identity conflicts which are critical for his future as an adult. Each of these is linked with his passionate hatred of the Indians and more particularly of the Pakistanis.

First, under the pressure of revived oedipal threats and his resultant castration anxiety, he feels persecuted and acts by attacking the potency of others suspecting that otherwise they will do the same to him. He was with Indians and Pakistanis at school and from that time on he has disliked them and perceived them as potentially dangerous, because he believes that they all carry knives which they would not hesitate to use.

If I was walking along with a crowd of my friends – say about six of us and we get pulled up by the police and get searched, if I've got a comb on me or a sharp pen or something with a top on it, they do me. But I can guarantee that if you pull up practically any Pakistani, he's got a knife on him because at school they all used to have knives and stuff that you can stick into someone. [Interviewer: Do you ever carry a knife?] If I do, I always get rid of it before the police come.

He sees the Pakistanis as not only dangerous because they use knives but as provocatively violent. He cites an incident when about seventy Pakistanis were 'chucking bricks' at about thirty skinheads and finally 'we went back and got the blokes with cars and we really gave them a hacking, you know. We swung one through a shop window and smacked them really up.' He attributes to others the same malignant hostility which simmers away inside him and it no doubt is an escallating process.

Secondly, his feelings of inadequacy and fears of dependence are uneasily provoked by the contrast between his own intellectual struggles and the ability of some of the Indians and Pakistanis. He understandably envies them and consequently resentfully mocks their overall ability, competence and independence, their ways of working alone and their desire for responsibility. By scorning their achievements as hollow, he is trying to cope with these envious feelings by denying any need for envy. By deriding them, it helps his faltering self-esteem.

Thirdly, his need for his father's regard and interest and for his father to serve him as a model for his personal identity growth as a man, is indirectly and painfully revealed by the jealousy which the Indians and Pakistanis excite in him as he perceives them being indulged by teachers at school and treated as specially-liked children. He feels they are favoured by being let off work, assembly, and games. They are favourite sons allowed to wear any clothes they like and given special food. And when there are disturbances between the white English boys and the Indians or Pakistanis, he feels that the teachers blame the English for the ensuing fights. John seems to be longing for attention from his father and the kind of interest and support which Mr Chattaway may find very difficult to give, having himself lacked a father's interest in his own life. The situation is further exacerbated by the close present bond between mother and son.

And finally, the frail sense of personal identity which John has is put under great strain by the 'otherness' of the Indians and Pakistanis who have their different culture and language and distinctive physical appearance, and this seems to be something which John cannot tolerate since it throws into relief his doubts and sense of a frail and diffused identity. For this reason, he asserts that it is not the race or colour of the Indians or Pakistanis to which he objects because where their attitudes, use of language, food and other cultural habits are European, he accepts them as one of the gang. He feels the same towards West Indians. It is the alien *culturally* different and distinctive identity of the Indians and Pakistanis which mark them out for John as a target group for his own tottering self-esteem, a group which can be isolated and himiliated, beaten and attacked as a way of propping up his own deep sense of inadequacy and frailty.

These identity conflicts have come to a peak during his adolescence but the problems to which they relate are deeply embedded in his personality and are only now being mirrored with a special intensity. His need to revenge himself for past humiliations will only be assuaged if he can achieve some positive goals for himself, enabling him to feel some security and positive affirmation of his identity as an adult male. His apparent prowess on a bike, and his interest in it may provide a possible basis for future skills, but as yet, positive goals of the kind indicated are not yet in view.

His personality growth and development has been stunted in certain vital respects which have important implications for race relationships. He does not seem able to experience concern, depression, self-reproach or guilt nor does he reveal a capacity for forming enduring affectional ties. These all make the prognosis for his racial attitudes a specially depressing and negative one. Since his social situation is one where he is surrounded by different racial groups and his personality dynamics impel him to blame others for his frustrations and failures, it is likely that even if he were to cease being a member of a gang such as the skinheads, his inner needs and unresolved identity problems would inevitably involve him in the misuse of racial groups as receptacles for his chronic and deep-seated conflicts.

Vicious and virtuous cycles
John's overt behaviour and attitudes towards Indians and Pakistanis are provocatively hostile and destructively aggressive. There is little in the social situation in which he finds himself and – more importantly – there is little in his personality dynamics, which might

suggest a possible shift towards more benign race attitudes. On the contrary, the vicious cycle of gang warfare between the skinheads and the Pakistanis was escallating at the time this study was done. As he himself comments, 'I wouldn't feel anything if it was a Pakistani [whom I killed] but I wouldn't kill anyone else if I could help it. I don't like Pakistanis and they'd kill you if they had the chance'. They are dehumanized, made into things, and are therefore felt by John to be fair game. The vicious cycle spirals downwards. John comments that the police are increasingly constraining any gang attempts at assaulting Pakistanis, And these may well come under firmer control. But as John comments, 'If I go out tonight and see any of them, I'll have a go at them'. His propensity for acting out his violent hostility towards Pakistanis, the impulsiveness with which he acts, these are triggers which keep the vicious downward spiral of destructive race relationships ever escallating.

Finding himself living among immigrants
The numbers of Indians and Pakistanis in Athol expose John to stressful competition, which, at school, certainly exacerbated his problems. For an individual like John, with a diffuse sense of identity, to be confronted within the neighbourhood by persons with a clear-cut alien culture, distinguished from the English by appearance, language, religious differences and innumerable patterns of behaviour is to be endlessly confronted by his own lack of a clear-cut identity.

He might well have settled on a negative identity as a member of a gang intent upon destructive gang warfare, even if there had been no *racial* groups other than the English within the neighbourhood.

> We skinheads don't like the greasers . . . . you have got to have a go at someone, haven't you? If there's no one else, we'll have a go at them. But none of us like the Pakistanis and we join up with the greasers to get them — and once we've got rid of them, we start fighting the greasers all over again . . . . There were about seventy skinheads and they beat up all the Pakistanis — just beat them up, and they put loads of them in the hospital and if it wasn't for the police, you know, they would have killed them all if they had the chance.

The presence of Pakistanis gives John a gradation of human targets — first choice for attack are the Pakistanis, but if that is made difficult, the greasers are the next. John is likely to *search* for target groups who can be attacked with impunity with a ruthless disregard for the feelings of the others concerned. In conditions of economic, ethnic and religious marginality, identifiable groups who are at a disadvantage will be especially vulnerable for selection as potential scapegoats.

To summarise: John's identity problems lie deeply entrenched in his personality dynamics and throw up questions of early damaging experiences in his socialization, with the possibility of additional constitutional and perhaps organic factors which have combined to produce a young man with characteristics which lead him to act out his hostilities. Whereas the target groups – the Indians and Pakistanis – whom he selects for his aggressions and hatred are felt to have specific characteristics which inflame his unresolved identity conflicts, nonetheless this is a young man who has deeply embedded inner needs to overtly express hostility with an unusual disregard for the feelings of those concerned. The groups whom he may attack may change, but his personality dynamics are less likely to undergo a major shift and to that extent it is more than likely that he will continue to seek out suitable repositories for his inner unresolved conflicts.

When asked at the end of the study how he saw the future, he answered 'It's going to get more and more tense. It's going to boil over – there will be guns and stuff like that because people are getting tired of the Indians now. I know they are.' His projection of a growing tension in the country reflects his own tension and the erupting feelings inside him, the explosive hostility which he cannot easily contain.

4 ELAINE CHATTAWAY

Issues bearing on the formation of her identity
Elaine was fifteen years old when studied – a late developer who had not yet reached her menarche, she was in a class with girls of all races, the majority of whom were likely to have achieved sexual maturity at eleven or twelve years of age.

She is the middle child, a daughter sandwiched between two sons. She was twelve years old when Colin was born and she vividly remembers the day. Her mother was confined at home and labour was difficult, Colin's arms got stuck; but eventually all was well and she came into the room and insisted on holding her infant brother. She then sat at the end of the bed and was there each time her small brother was fed. From her life story it seems that she identified with her mother but experienced a considerable amount of envy and jealousy – envy of her mother's ability to make and also to feed the baby, and jealousy because of the attention and love Colin received from her mother. Themes of envy, jealousy and her delayed sexual maturity are important in her identity formation and are expressed in the identity conflicts which confront her at the time of the study. They also play a fundamental part in her race attitudes.

She does not remember much of her earliest years and was sparse in her comments on her parents. However, she gives a picture of an easy joking relationship with her mother which also has teasing aspects. It seems to be basically an affectionate one although as her adolescence confronts her, she has become resentful of her mother's attempts to control her. 'She's sort of got it planned for me, like.' She feels criticized by both her parents at the present time but recognises that this is part of her adolescence.

Her father's attitude towards her is experienced as critical and often hurtful, but he is supportive of her in relation to her work at school. He berates her for being stupid and clumsy in language which affects her self-esteem and makes her struggles for an emergent femininity much more difficult. 'Oh, you stupid . . . . stupid mare, always knocking something over . . . . clumsy . . . . you never learn . . . . you can't do anything, can you?' Since Elaine is on the heavy side, and already sensitive to being both plump and a late developer, these remarks are doubly wounding especially coming from her father at a time in life when she needs a father's regard. Elaine's fears and distress about her late development are therefore exacerbated by her father's clumsy criticisms.

On the other hand, he encourages and actively helps her with her school work and prods her into working harder. He is ambitious for her and wants her to undertake further studies when she leaves school, which she does not want to do and so does not specially value his help. He seems to be expressing, through her, his own lost ambitions and drive. She is also deeply resentful of what she feels is his selfishness in demanding the sole use of the shed and so displacing her bicycle, and of his angry retorts that she should build a shed of her own. She feels that 'everything is for his privilege'.

Her relationship with John has sadistic features. He twists her nose round and round and savagely hurts her; he practices judo on her and roughly hurts her arm, he belittles her in front of his friends (just as his mother describes his father as doing to him), and he calls her 'stinker'. Although they fight a great deal, nonetheless she feels she can depend on him in an emergency requiring his physcial protection and she shows a maternal concern about him when he is injured, hoping that he 'has not damaged himself, an arm or something'.

Elaine, like John, is also obsessed with body injury but her concerns are almost entirely to do with arms and legs. Throughout her material there are innumerable stories and an obsessively morbid fascination with details relating to limbs which have been broken, severed, hang limp or been twisted and deformed, and in one case she dwells excessively upon the loss of a thumb which a child at school sustained, the part actually having been severed. Unlike John, Elaine's accounts of body injuries are almost entirely connected with others and rarely with herself. These injuries express a great deal of anxiety apparently arising from unconscious castration ideas and an undue preoccupation with damage to, and loss of organs, symbols for a penis. Freud's investigation into fetishism in relation to the castration complex showed that instead of acknowledging evidence of castration, a fetish can arise which substitutes for the missing penis.[22] In this way the valued object is displaced to another part of the body. For Elaine, her feet and shoes serve this function. Innumerable pages of detailed interview material relate to feet and to microscopic descriptions of shoes – her shoes, shoes she would like to have, their colours, forms, materials, and problems associated with buckles and other adornments. In not one, but several, interviews this fetish takes over suggesting both condensation and displacement of a valued but missing phantasy penis to the non-sexual part of her person. The major relevance of this for our purposes lies in recognising the feelings of castration anxiety which she has, their effects upon her attitudes and fears concerning her femininity, and how these in turn, manifest themselves in racial feelings.

She both resents her youngest brother Colin and yet is fond of him. 'I thought he would change us all and he does . . . . we've got to keep our eyes on Colin . . . . he gets his own way . . . . everyone always used to give in to him and now he takes it for granted . . . he really screams for things he wants. He always shouts and gets his way'. She is jealous of him and is tormented by jealousy of girls at her school. She is extremely vulnerable to feeling overlooked, and is painfully aware when her chosen friends prefer other girls' company to her own. Exchanges are aggressive. 'Oh, I didn't see you', comments her friend. 'You couldn't miss me, you rotten old cow.' She fears that people do not listen to her and that others only use her for convenience. This hurts her feelings, undermines her sense of self-esteem and, 'it makes me wild'. Her hatred for a rival is secondary to her intense need for love for herself, attention (which she feels Colin is accorded at home) and being valued for herself alone. She usually copes with jealousy by denial. 'I couldn't care less', is her usual hurt response. Her friends' perceptions of her, as seen by Elaine cruelly emphasize her present lack of femininity or charm. 'My friend says that when I whistle I sound like a navvy.' A girl calls after her 'Old grandma, keep doing your knitting.' Her late development affects the way in which both her parents and her school friends see her, adding to her inner difficulties. Her anxiety to reach sexual maturity and catch up with her peers makes her feel 'not proper'. She longs, understandably, to be feminine like her friends; feels left out and childish in relation to their absorbing interest in boys as well as their capacity to attract them. She has not yet gone out with boys and would like to, but she ruefully comments 'I'd feel a drip, you know, walking round as young as I am'. It is an awareness of her social immaturity which she reflects which of course rests upon her sexual maturation.

It must also be specifically galling for Elaine that her mother proclaimed *her* evident femininity by producing Colin at the very time when Elaine's menarche might have been expected. The sources of envy within her were probably sorely aggravated by this event and by the continuing mothering which Mrs Chattaway accords to Colin. Elaine coped with this by an identification with her mother in the maternal role and some of her care for Colin is an expression of this aspect of her emerging identity as a woman.

Doubt cast on her sexual identity seems to evoke despair against which she defends herself by manic behaviour and a manic use of words. She proclaims a negative identity for herself built on the images of that childishness which she so longs to transcend and transform into the sexual maturity of womanhood. She takes that which she is, debases and distorts it to emphasise and proclaim the immaturity. Her description of herself reveals this negative identity. 'I'm always giggling. Yesterday I was making all these animal noises like cocks and ducks and I was singing. My friend goes "Don't show me up – everybody is looking at us". I guess I couldn't care less.' She thinks that a best friend might see her as 'round the bend – a bit crazy'. Her interviews and her self-description both suggest manic defences as a denial of the underlying anxiety.

Unresolved identity conflicts in relation to race
Elaine's inter-racial experiences were very limited in her early life.

Her one Indian friend at junior school was mentioned in passing. She went to the young girl's house, and 'she gave me sweets, apples and we got on all right at school but you know I don't like to mix with them'. At the same school her jealousy was aroused because Indians and Pakistanis came to school by coach which to her signified that they were being accorded special privileges by the authorities.

At her present secondary modern school in Athol, her fellow students are Indians, Pakistanis, West Indians and white English and although her first school dance – an event of great importance in her life – was most disappointingly broken up by the violent and disruptive behaviour of some youths ('My friend's brother says it was a crowd of Jamaicans who did it') she does not use this unhappy event as a trigger for racial stereotyping. Her identity conflicts do not primarily involve her relationships with West Indians. She sees them as amusing people, some of them funny in a pleasant way but also 'lippy' (verbally aggressive) and aggressive in general. Since Elaine's exchanges with her friends and her recollections of how both her father and her brother address her are all aggressive in tone, West Indians no doubt carry some of her projections.

But her major unresolved identity conflicts express themselves in envy, jealousy and anxiety in relation to her femininity, which are powerfully resonated by the Indians and Pakistani girls in her class. Primarily it is these young women who excite her destructive envy. Because she sees them as feminine in appearance, using make-up, adornments, elaborate clothes and special shoes to enhance their already desirable femininity, she is roused to hatred of these Indian and Pakistani girls. They are felt to be flamboyantly displaying that which Elaine so longs for for herself but which, at the present time, she is denied.

> The Indian girls at school – well, they sort of overcome themselves. Like this one girl who came to school the other day in a black sort of sparkly dress, with sort of silver stuff on it and grey stuff around the arms – and lots of make-up on like this, you know – and up here, her hair is tied back. And then they wear tights so that you can see their bums and things like that, you know. And they wear high-heeled shoes . . . . The Indian girls who dress up like this are younger than me, you know – they're about thirteen years old . . . . Whenever you go in the toilets they go in, and they're all there doing their hair and their eyes – they put mascara on – you know – black stuff on their eyes . . . They go out with much older boys than we

do. Sometimes these Indian boys come into our school and they whistle whenever an Indian girl goes by – and this and that and they go off with them. They don't do that to the white girls at all – if they did I'd kick them, but they keep staring at you though.

She not only envies them their appearance and the attentions she believes they get from older Indian boys, but they seem to have money which make some of the feminine attire more easily available to them than to her.

This Indian girl at school used to have a different pair of tights every day, carrying them in her bag. She had a ladder once, so she took them off in the toilet, put them in a bin, just in the dustbin, nothing round them or anything you know – all cheesey-like – and she put another pair of tights on, just like that. We can't afford tights. I laddered mine once at school. I used to carry a bit of cotton around with me if I had to sew them up. I can't just take them off and put them in a bin, just like that. I can't afford it.

Indian boys also are seen as having money. 'They have everything nice . . . have lots of money.' One has a car and 'nice patent shoes', and they can afford to buy clothes in bulk which she contrasts with her father's more modest wardrobe.

Her jealousy extends also to the teachers' attitudes towards the Asian students in her class. English girls are not allowed to wear eye make-up, nor can they wear high-heeled shoes or even flat Scholl's sandals, but 'Indian girls come to school with their flat-heeled sandals and they go click-click-click, you know, as they walk along and nothing's said. English girls are not allowed to wear rings, but Indian and Pakistani girls can.' She is jealous of the special attention paid to Asian students as compared with the English and observes with feeling that in class the teachers help the Asian students and 'won't help us', that they are given homework which the English are not required to do. She is jealous of the care and concern, the helpful attention which she fears the others are getting and which as an English student she feels she has been denied.

Her fears and anxieties are alerted by Indian boys with knives who terrify her and she recounted several incidents when she was frightened. She recalled hearing of a violent attack which an Indian boy made on one of John's friends, stabbing him in the back with a screwdriver; and on one occasion she ran away from an Indian who had a knife. Although we know from both her mother and her father that Elaine was once approached by an Indian youth in the street with a sexual invitation, Elaine did not mention this episode.

To summarise: Elaine reacts to her sexual immaturity by envying the Indian girls their appearance, the ways in which they enhance their femininity, their worldliness, money and sexual appeal for Indian boys. She hates them for having what she longs to have. The teachers at the school, seen as parental surrogates, provoke her jealousy by according favoured attention to Asian students. And her fears for her safety and castrational anxiety are focussed on the aggressive intentions of Indian boys who carry knives and who she believes would not hesitate to use them.

Why is it that Asian and not West Indian girls excite this degree of envious resentment? On the whole, Indian and Pakistani girls are feminine in their style of dress, tend to be slender, and culturally, adornment is important and emphasised. Many West Indian girls are inclined to be heavier in build, like Elaine herself, and feminine qualities are not *specially* enhanced in these particular ways. Since Elaine sees herself, as well as West Indian girls, as funny she seems to identify more readily with this group.

Vicious and virtuous cycles
The Asians siphon off Elaine's unease about her delayed sexual maturity so that her attention is focussed on their displays of femininity, which she then denigrates. At an interpersonal level, no actual confrontations are described and it is probable that her stereotyped pictures of Indians and Pakistanis act to maintain a social distance between herself and them. When Elaine finally reaches her menarche these attitudes may no longer be as vitally necessary for her.

Finding herself living among immigrants
Like the other members of her family Elaine feels that there are too many Indians and Pakistanis in her school and in her neighbourhood as a whole. She would like to leave Athol and live elsewhere.

TRANSFERENCE AND COUNTER-TRANSFERENCE EFFECTS

In our relationships as interviewers with the Chattaways there were some areas of difficulty which it is important to discuss as openly as possible, and although these arise in relation to this particular family they also have relevance to our relationships with the other two.

The first of these concerns the type of 'fit' made between ourselves as interviewers (with our styles, approach and personalities) and each of the families, distinguished by common cultural values and patterns. The 'fit' affected their ways of regarding us and responding to us, and also affected their styles and emotional patterns. As already described, we made a good 'fit' with the James family; although a useful working relationship developed with the Chattaways, there were difficult elements in the relationship which made these relationships less comfortable.

The Chattaways communicated to us, at the outset, some guarded suspicions about the study and ourselves, which we later came to see was their way of relating to the world about them. With the exception of Mrs Chattaway – and even at times with her – they gave a sense of living in a present where something awful and unexpected could easily happen. These feelings communicated themselves to us, making us at times ill at ease, somewhat more vigilant about stepping over a boundary or putting a foot wrong least we upset them.

In acknowledging our different ways of relating to the James' and to the Chattaways, I am acting on the assumption that the notion of an aseptic relationship in the field between interviewer and respondent, with the facility to replicate interviewer responses with different respondents, is an illusion. Friedman, among others, has shown that even after rigorous training of experimenters with human subjects, each one was unable to replicate verbal and non-verbal behaviour with different respondents despite laboratory conditions.[23] Koch also has described, what he calls the 'simplistic theories of correct scientific conduct', as 'the dogma of immaculate perception'.[24] Although I realise that there are *always* differences in relationships with different respondents, nonetheless within the cultural context of this study, I wish it were not so! I am bound to recognise a struggle within myself with this illusion – the notion of an aseptic relationship in research dies hard.

Differences in the ways we related to these three families were in part necessarily, therefore, compounded by our prejudices as interviewers, including any racial prejudices we might have, and particularly those of which we were not aware. The important issue is the *extent* to which these influenced the data, and our *readiness* to be alert to these factors.

It is probable, however, that certain affinities between interviewers and respondents facilitate or impede the research task and in the process different feelings are released on both sides, conscious and unconscious. If we had studied several families in each of these three racial groups, it might have been possible to probe the dimensions of our reactions on racial or cultural grounds, as distinct from personality ones. As it is, we are left with three very different families; and it is not clear how many of the differences we experienced derived from factors of racial or cultural prejudice or 'fit'.

There is also the issue of the personal values and moral attitudes which each one of us, as individuals, have and although my professional training helps me to try and prevent one state of feelings from taking over the other and not to betray them knowingly to the respondents, nonetheless at an emotional level some of the disclosures by Mr Chattaway, notably his actions at the crossroads with his motor car, aroused in me feelings of deep disquiet, anger and fear. Fortunately the information emerged in the interviews after I had had time to develop feelings of empathy for him as a man, recognizing with some compassion his vulnerability, and how hurt and damaged he had been by life and the serious deprivations he had suffered. As a result, my feelings for him supported my professional training in trying to preserve my capacity to accept him and his feelings as *his*, and different from those that I approve of in myself. And my scientific curiosity was deepened by the need to try and understand the roots of this man's despair which underly his acts against the Asians.

Sylvia Hutchinson had similar feelings aroused in her when John related his gang activities as a 'Paki-basher', but since he had early proclaimed his identity as a skinhead, she was not surprised at these activities since there had been press publicity relating to similar events. She did not think that these revelations made it difficult to listen to him, as she was aware of his confusions and vulnerabilities and this made it easy for her to feel compassion for him.

DISCUSSION

Within the Chattaway family what emerges is a direct relationship between the misuse of racial groups on the one hand, and unresolved identity conflicts on the other. The family share in common certain sources of underlying conflict which account for their patterns of racial prejudice.

1 Three members of the family (Mrs Chattaway is the exception) face unresolved conflicts arising from *unmet dependent needs for love and care*, connected with the father rather than with the mother. These unmet needs provoke feelings of envy and jealousy of different racial groups, perceived as favoured or indulged by parental custodians of society (police and teachers). It is not known whether there are significant differences in reality in the way racial groups in Athol are served by these custodial figures. What is known, however, is that this is how the three Chattaways view them, and it is their perceptions which trigger-off and re-kindle earlier fears of deprivation of parental love and care. The racial groups in question are then feared and hated as jealous rivals. Central to these common issues is Mr Chattaway's original deprivation of his father, which makes it much more difficult for him to meet his children's needs for protection, love and firm support since he, too, has spent his life in need of just these same things.

2 *Threats to self-esteem* affect all four members of this family but for different reasons. For Mr Chattaway they are triggered-off by his mid-life crisis, his unemployment and pervasive feelings of shame and guilt at his short-comings and delinquencies. For Mrs Chattaway, they arise from the challenge to her image of herself as a good mother and the shocks to her self-esteem provoked by the behaviour of both Colin and John. For John, low self-esteem originates from his intellectual difficulties and sense of inadequacy, aggravated by demands made on his abilities as he assumes an adult working role. And for Elaine, her sense of inadequacy is increasingly prodded by the frustration and delays in her sexual development. Lowered self esteem easily excites aggression and it is these angry feelings and resentful envies which can so often lead to attempts to denigrate other racial groups and to diminish the worth of their achievements and characteristics.

3 Conflicts emanating from *feared destructiveness, hostile aggression and persecutory fears* that others will attack them, are also common to all four members of this family. These conflicts powerfully confront both Mr Chattaway and John but also play a part in the inner life and phantasies of Elaine. Although they are also present in Mrs Chattaway, such conflicts do not seem to spring from the deeper recesses of her inner life but more from the aggravation of these anxieties by the other three members of the family, who may be carrying some of her own unexpressed aggressive drives. Their preoccupations with hostile aggression and destructive attacks lead the Chattaways to the projection of these feelings, which are then

experienced as emanating from racial groups and coming towards them. This creates inexorable vicious cycles.

4 The members of this family are all facing quite severe conflicts connected with *body damage and associated fears and phantasies*. Mr Chattaway feared his violent and destructive impulses could be body-damaging – his past experiences haunting him into the present. John and Elaine are inundated with fears apparently related to castration anxiety. These three members of the family are confronted with conflicts emanating from intrapsychic sources. For Mrs Chattaway, the forthcoming operation is perceived as a severe threat to her body integrity and her sexual capacity, the source of her conflict being not so much an inner welling-up of unresolved conflicts as the response to a situational stress. In all cases, they are unable to contain their anxieties and they latch onto distinct body images of members of racial groups other than their own, whom they attack either physically or verbally.

5 *A cultural threat to their frail sense of identity is* posed for all four by the *territorial and culturally* alien impingements of immigrants. None of these individuals – with the possible exception of Mrs Chattaway – is secure enough to hold firmly to their own sense of identity and as a result they are exceedingly vulnerable to feeling overwhelmed by the clear-cut identities of people who are racially and culturally distinct.

6 In contrast to the James family, the Chattaways have not been able to express in their current lives active achievements in the field of either work or play. Each seems unfulfilled as a person, physically active or even restless yet without a focus of constructive effort for that activity. Furthermore, for all except Mrs Chattaway, close relationships and bonds seem lacking in their lives and for John and Elaine these are particularly crippling handicaps. For all these reasons, this family has *limited sources of flexibility* for diverting their inner tensons and unresolved conflicts away from racial channels and into constructive alternative channels.

In the final chapter, the issues raised by the Chattaway family in relation to race are further explored as they bear on the wider concerns of this study.

BIBLIOGRAPHY AND NOTES

1 Hiro, D. *Black British, White British*, Eyre & Spottiswoode, London (1971). Part I.

2 *Ibid.* p. 299.

3 *Ibid.* p. 299.

4 *Ibid.* p. 301.

5 *Ibid.* p. 305.

6 Dummett, A. *A Portrait of English Racism*, Penguin, Harmondsworth (1973), p. 266.

7 Bowlby, J. *Attachment and Loss, Vol. II: Separation, Anxiety and Anger*, Hogarth Press, London (1973); Rochlin, G. *Man's Aggression: The Defence of the Self*, Constable, London (1973), p. 48.

8 Storr, A. *Human Aggression.* Allen Lane, The Penguin Press, Harmondsworth (1968), p. 77.

9 Bowlby, J. (1973) *op. cit.*, p. 246; Storr, A. (1968), *op. cit.* p. 78.

10 Rochlin, G. (1973) *op. cit.*, p. 120.

11 Bowlby, J. (1973) *op. cit.*, p. 246.

12 Segal, H. *Introduction to the Work of Melanie Klein*, Heinemann, London (1964), p. 3.

13 Jaques, E. 'Death and the mid-life crisis', *International Journal of Psychoanalysis*, 46 (1965), Part 4.

14 *Ibid.* p. 511.

15 Cath, S. H. 'Some dynamics of middle and later years: a study in depletion and restitution', *in* Berezin, M. and Cath, S. (eds) *Geriatric Psychiatry: Grief, Loss and Emotional Disorders in the Ageing Process*, International Universities Press, New York (1965), p. 24.

16 *Ibid.* p. 44.

17 Storr, A. (1968) *op. cit.* p. 33.

18 Jahoda, M. 'The roots of prejudice', *New Community*, IV (1975), No. 2, 179–187.

19 Dicks, H. V. *Licenced Mass Murder*, Sussex University Press in association with Heinemann Educational Books, London (1972), p. 31.

20 Hiro, D. (1971) *op. cit.* p. 234–235.

21 Erikson, E. H. *Identity: Youth and Crisis*, Faber & Faber, London (1968), p. 138.

22 Freud, S. *The Splitting of the Ego in the Process of Defence*, Standard Edition, Vol. XXIII (1940).

23 Friedman, N. *The Social Nature of Psychological Research*, Basic Books, New York (1967), Chapter 7.

24 Koch, S. 'Epilogue', in Koch S.; (ed). *Psychology: A Study of Science, Vol. 3: Formulations of the Person and the Social Context*, McGraw-Hill, New York (1959), p. 749.

Chapter 9

IDENTITY AND RACE IN AN INDIAN FAMILY: THE SINGHS

The Singhs are Sikhs from the Punjab and their historic and cultural past contrasts vividly with the other immigrant family in this book, the West Indians. As we have seen, slavery fragmented and almost entirely annihilated the original African culture of the West Indian peoples and British colonial rule eroded it still further. By contrast, the Indian people fared much better under British rule, maintaining their ancient and rich cultural heritage and retaining their religious practices and language, sustained by largely undisturbed family and social structures.

But it is not only the difference between a lost culture and a continuing and thriving one which distinguishes these two peoples. Under slavery, the British planters and their slaves in the West Indies had close personal contact since their daily lives were often interlinked. But in India, the elitism, detachment and aloofness of the white man tended to emphasise social distance and promote in the Indians some sense of awe of the British. They were felt to be alien, with different customs, language and religious observances. As already noted, West Indians coming to Britain came in search of their mother country; Indians came as to an alien land whose people belong to a very different culture.

Migration from India goes back to about 1834 when the first batch of indentured Indian labourers arrived in Mauritius. Deprived of slave labour in the colonies, Indian labour was imported and this was followed by similar waves of migration to Ceylon, South Africa, Malaya and Burma. These served the interests and economic needs of British economic expansion and growth. Wherever the Indians went, however, their culture went with them; they maintained their cultural identity fairly intact, clinging to their traditional patterns of community and family life and to their cultural values, upheld and supported by their history and their religion.

Much of this early immigration came from the Punjab, where the Singhs originate. The Sikhs have a martial history and a tradition of bravery and military discipline and a very large number of them were therefore attracted to join the Indian army. This brought them in touch with British officers, and when some of these men later migrated to Britain (Mr Singh is one), their path of adaptation was eased by familiarity with certain English cultural values and attitudes learnt from British officers.

Sikhism is a religion dating from the sixteenth century. Male Sikhs traditionally wear their hair long, have beards and turbans but the beard and turban have been abandoned by many Sikhs in England and Baldev Singh is one of these. His hair is cut no differently from an Englishman, he has no beard and although his devotion to the Sikh religion is a deep one, outwardly nothing about him, apart from his fine and impressive height and stature, might outwardly suggest his Sikh identity. Although the Sikhs repudiate caste distinctions, there is evidence to suggest that these did not disappear entirely but that their place was taken by the non-structural differentiations of class.[1]

Mr Singh came to Britain in 1953 when there were relatively few Indian or Pakistani immigrants in this country, and those already here tended to be professional people who spoke English, many of whom had served with the army in India. After 1960 however, the number of Asians entering the country increased, and the type of immigrant was more often rural in origin, less familiar with the English language, or the culture and values of its people and many of the immigrants had less education than earlier immigrants.

The very early days of Baldev Singh in England were days when there were very few racial incidents between the English and the Asians. But racial trouble started developing in the mid-1960s and it reached a climax and became headline news during the spring of 1970 – a year before this study commenced. Violence between skinhead youths and Asians erupted in several urban centres, including Athol. By this time, however, both Mr and Mrs Singh had been in this country for some years so they had had earlier experiences with which to contrast the violence which then started to surface.

The family plays an extremely important role in Hindu and Sikh society. It is a joint family system binding its members together through the sharing of property, a common house, religious and cultural beliefs and practices. It is a patriarchal family in which the father has the major power but the mother wields silent and subtle pressure. Social ties are based on consanguinity in the male and not the female line, so that a joint family would also include married brothers and their families as well as unmarried brothers or sisters, all living under the same roof, that of the eldest male member of the family. Living in a large family group is part of the cultural tradition.

This meagre outline is not intended to do more than point to a few of the salient historic and cultural factors which provide some background against which to view the Singh family. It is to Mr Baldev Singh that we now turn.

1 MR BALDEV SINGH

Issues bearing on the formation of his identity
Baldev Singh suffered a double deprivation early in life. Both his parents died before he was five and although he remembers his father's body burning on the funeral pyre, he was not told at the time that it was his father and he was not helped to mourn his death. He remembers little of his mother's death which took place shortly afterwards. The Sikh extended family afforded him love, security and support. He lived with his grandmother who was devoted to him. She was a well-to-do woman and, although uneducated, taught Baldev to value education. He loved her dearly. She died when he was a young man and he was heart-broken.

His earliest identifications with family members reveal a deep sense of pride in the social standing of his wider family, their educational attainments and community prestige. He revered his father for having been not only a man of means but also the first educated man in his village and a teacher. And he respected other family members for their social standing, wealth and educational achievements (judges, magistrates and a member of parliament). Understandably, since his father died when he was three, he has little in the way of personal memories of the man himself, so that these external aspects of his father's achievements serve as unchanging inner models for his early ego-ideals. At the age of fifteen, he came to know British officers stationed near to where he lived, and he also perceived them predominantly in terms of these chosen values. They embodied for him, in somewhat idealized ways, social standing and eminent worth. They 'were from good families . . . of good breed, good blood . . . very, very good people'.

When the war came, contrary to his grandmother's wishes, he abandoned his law studies; he volunteered to join the British army and was seconded as a clerical officer to a Sikh regiment. His close association with British officers, further strengthened his chosen identifications with persons of prestige and standing.

An incident in the army, when he was called 'a bloody fool' by a British officer is revealing of his attitudes at that time. He retorted 'If I'm a bloody fool, Sir, then you're also a bloody fool', a self-assertive and angry response to being demeaned. The outcome of this incident was favourable to Baldev in every way; his fellow Sikhs admired his courage, and although reprimanded by the Colonel, he had made his point and the officer in question subsequently became his friend.

This incident throws some light on two aspects of his identity: first, despite a close identification with British officers and their values, he at no time accepted these slavishly at the expense of his dignity as a man; and secondly, having openly and angrily confronted a superior, he was flexible and open-minded enough – as was the officer – to facilitate the building of the relationship on a friendly basis.

In the army he began a correspondence with his future father-in-law, long before any question of marriage to Tara had been raised. Sikh cultural patterns provide for families mutually to choose and approve of each other before marriage arrangements are entertained. Baldev had known and admired Tara's brother at school, liked the family and corresponded with his future father-in-law, a man of high education, considerable means and esteemed within the community. But his choice was not made solely on these grounds, as he sought and found integrity, maturity of judgement, generosity and a gentleness of spirit in this man. His own family background being found acceptable, at the age of twenty Baldev married Tara, whom he had not previously seen. She was fifteen years old. Both families held positions of some importance in the community, were well-to-do and valued education highly. His identity as a person of social standing was now enhanced by his marriage to Tara.

If he had had parents of his own, or if his grandmother had been alive, it would have been traditional for his wife to have lived with his family. As it was, he left the army and they set up their home together 'without the guidance of parents', living alone in a large house with servants. Looking back, he reflects that he was 'impatient and explosive', pursuing shallow values of wanting 'a nice posh life'. He recalls, with regret, that he used to order his wife around 'in a military manner'; although he wanted to share his feelings with her, he could not manage to do so.

She advised me a lot, even when I had a lot of money she said 'You are extravagant'. She understood more about money than I. She couldn't say much because the man is the boss, but really, when I think back to those years when we were first married, she gave me very good advice, but I never paid any heed. If I had listened to the advice she gave me, I should have been better off.

She wanted to get rid of the servants and live a simpler life but he resisted.

She was more sensible than me in a lot of ways. She didn't go to college or to high school but I think she has a lot of patience and peace of mind. I didn't have any patience at all. I used to blow up because service in the army had spoiled me and she was quite the opposite. If I blew up she would listen, wouldn't say anything, no argument, nothing.

He was restless and anxious for a child but his wife was in no hurry to have children so young and after six years of marriage and a disastrous attempt to put his funds into a film enterprise which failed, he decided to go to England. The failure of this enterprise was of critical importance to him. His high ego-ideals were rigid and idealized, containing, his positive identifications with family and with British army officers. His failure to live up to his standards – of attainment, wealth and social status – left him feeling an acute sense of shame,[2] exacerbated by a comparison between his failure and the success of his colleagues in the same enterprise. Although his wife was in the early weeks of pregnancy with their first child at last, he left her behind in India and went to England. He left behind him not only a wife and unborn child, a familiar culture and country, but he was also in flight from himself – his shame and sense of failure. But at the conscious level he saw his trip to England as a positive voyage into a new life.

Arriving in London long before the main bulk of Asian immigration commenced,[3] he was filled with curiosity about England, and the desire to enlarge his view of the world. He had money from his inheritance and his father-in-law had given him a couple of hundred pounds.

He spent money freely, lived well, gambled, bought new clothes and enjoyed himself, living the life of 'an English gentleman'. But his life was lonely and as his resources dwindled he found himself unable to maintain this chosen life-style. He was confused and frightened, felt shame and self-disgust at the situation he faced and yet was reluctant to settle for an ordinary job. During these years he clung to class attitudes as an essential core of his identity and as he steadily became poorer, he continued to contrast his own class identity with working-class Indians and Pakistanis whom he regarded as somewhat ignorant and limited in outlook. Nonetheless, he recognised that they could save money whereas he was a spendthrift, barely able to meet essential expenses. He wanted to prove himself, did not wish to ask his father-in-law for more money, but he wanted his wife and daughter with him.

It was into this steadily deteriorating situation that his wife and young daughter Vera came. He and his wife had been separated for four years during which time letters were irregular and not very informative. She had been living with her parents and backed by their financial and moral support she came to England to see what was really going on with her husband. When he heard she was arriving imminently, he was excited but deeply ashamed. He had no money and had to borrow in order to meet her at the airport. It took him a few days before he could tell her fully what his situation really was. 'I don't know whether she pretended or not – she would know that better in her own mind – but she was so good and gentle and she just forgave everything. I chose my wife well and if it had been otherwise, she would have run away and I would not have blamed her for that.'

Her support was strengthening to him; his capacity to share his most vulnerable feelings with her revealed inner courage. He took responsibility for what he had done and for that which he had failed to do, and she rose to the crisis in their relationship with steady resources of love, generosity and rare inner strength. He started the long grinding haul to re-establish the security of all three members of his small family, obtained a gruelling job in the steel rolling-mills where he worked at exhausting physical labour for the first time in his life. 'She took half my worries. I was so tired and she washed my hands and put some vaseline on, that kind of thing. "Oh, you work very hard – you should have listened to me." She only said that two or three times, but I just took all my money to her and said "Here it is".' He settled down and worked very hard, gave up his 'champagne and whisky', and started to save steadily and provide for his wife and small daughter. He saved enough to buy a modest house, which with the help of new English friends, he put in good order.

This turning point in his life came when the values by which he had lived until then, were judged and found wanting – by himself. His wife played a most vital role in this. He felt the support of her acceptance of him as he was, and her faith that he could change. He accords much of the credit for his subsequent achievements to her but is also sturdily able to acknowledge his own strength. 'I had good will-power. I survived. I always had at the back of my mind that this was a good lesson for me. I was suffering at the mills, but God was giving me this punishment so I accepted it.'

Piers has commented 'Behind the feeling of shame stands not the fear of hatred, but the fear of *contempt*, which on even deeper levels of the unconscious spells fear of *abandonment*, the death by emotional starvation'.[4] For Mr Singh, his worst fears were put to rest; his wife did not abandon him but stood firmly beside him and continued to love him. Shame for him, took the form of needing to claim the defeat as his own – he had done it to himself, nobody else had done it to him. This was his way of protecting his narcissistic feelings.[5]

In the period which followed he steadily re-built his life and regained his self-respect. When the Indian Ambassador visited the city where he lived, he was asked to give the speech of welcome. He was active in community affairs, recognised as a well-educated, intelligent man; police used him as an interpreter in court when necessary.

His community devotion, however, led to the traumatic assault on him following his intervention on behalf of an Indian whom he did not know. By intervening at the factory and drawing attention to corrupt practices, he drew the wrath of three Indian workers and was set upon by these three drunken men, who assaulted him gravely and savagely. Left alone, shocked and with mutilating injuries, the police were alerted by a young English boy next door to the house where the men had dragged him. He was in hospital a long time requiring several operations, and felt understandably bitter, particularly since the man whom he had helped failed to appear in court to give evidence on his behalf.

> And since that time I have said 'What is the good of helping these people? They have no character.' I just took pity on that poor man, but when you have an experience like this with people of your own nation, you don't want to help anyone because they are not worth it. The experience changed me a lot. Before that I would write letters for people, official letters – help people to go to solicitors. . . . From the beginning of my life I was very generous. It was a most bitter experience. . . . I object as a human being – with my dignity as a human being.

Although sorely hurt and disillusioned, Mr Singh's values still continue to express themselves in modest ways. He is active in Parent Teachers Association meetings at Eric's school, and he talks at local meetings in the borough where issues relevant to immigrants' lives are discussed. At a recent meeting, he had sufficiently recovered from his frightening assault to speak critically of his fellow Asians on matters bearing on their social-class behaviour (cleanliness in general, hygiene in the home and curry smells emanating from their kitchens, etc.).

After some years in the Midlands and having consolidated his family and community relationships, and after Eric was born, he came to London with his family. He made a very modest start as a cleaner with a large airline company, but he quickly worked his way up to positions of increasing responsibility. His career has been gratifying to him, culminating in his appointment to his present responsible post as a storeman in charge of major technical supplies. He is the first Asian to hold such a position and works very hard.

The need to be recognised as worthy of respect echoes throughout his life story. His early identifications with family members have now been re-worked and integrated at a more mature level, and he realises that respect is not accorded automatically but through the integrity of hard work. What he had tried to acquire without effort in the past – as if it was his birthright – is now struggled for and worked at unremittingly, with full conscious effort and commitment. He regrets that he did not acquire the kind of education which his grandmother had wanted for him and which he should have pursued when he was younger, but he hopes and expects his children to achieve educationally what he failed to do. 'If I look after my children and make them good and give them a chance to grasp these things that I missed, I think I will achieve through them.'

Early habits of self-indulgence and high living have been replaced by simple pleasures in family life. Although money is still highly valued it is now recognised as a means to an end, and he realises how hard he has to work to secure it, according it a lesser place than personal integrity and respect.

Work has played an extremely important part in his identity formation; it expressed his downfall and humiliation, and it has been his pathway towards establishing himself as a competent, intelligent, extremely hardworking and reliable man, as well as providing him with friends. His aggression expresses itself constructively through work and although angry outbursts are still a problem for him, and he keeps himself on a tight rein, they are less of a problem than they used to be.

Baldev Singh is able to accept his positive as well as his negative qualities and he relates well to others, accepting them as individuals, irrespective of race. He greatly values, loves and respects his wife, is sensitive to his past failings in their relationship and now recognises how different yet complementary they are. His wife seems to 'carry' for him those aspects of himself which he finds difficulty in owning or expressing, such as the gentler, more peaceful aspects of himself as well as clear-thinking and decision making. 'She decides, because she decides better than I. I'm a hasty type of person. I take rather quick action but she is very comfortable in her thinking and is very neat and clear and so naturally I follow her mostly.' He realises how great has been his debt to her. 'She played her part to bring about what we are now. I must say that credit goes to her.' It also, of course, goes to him, not least for his generosity and inner strength in openly admitting his debt to her.

His identity as a father is of vital importance to him. He is fiercely protective of his children as well as supportive, appreciating and valuing their individual qualities.

His religious attitudes are tolerant and of crucial significance to him. He sees God as One, speaking to different people in different languages but His voice is the same. He has brought his children up to choose whether to be good Christians or good Sikhs – he does not require of his children that they have to 'take the past into the present', but that they should have faith in a religion is vital to him. Even more important is how people live by their religious faith. 'Lately I believe much in doing in Rome as the Romans do. Where is the difference if you remember God and worship God? It is the same thing in every religion. Our Sikh religion tells us the same things that are in the Bible.'

At the age of forty-seven, Mr Singh has re-worked some of his earlier unresolved conflicts, come to terms with his short-comings and destructive aspects, and seems to have weathered his mid-life crisis well. The road he has traversed has been a long and demanding one and he has accomplished difficult and impressive inner work. He still, however, sets idealistically high standards for himself and his children whom he tends to control somewhat firmly. The permissive society of present-day England he hates and fears.

Unresolved identity conflicts and race
Mr Singh's most pressing identity conflict arises from, and is sustained by, the continuing experience of being an immigrant in England. It revolves around the following issue: how can he

distinguish himself – and how, in turn, can he be distinguished – from the mass of Asian immigrants in London, so establishing in his and in other people's eyes, his social standing, education, character, integrity and worth as a human being, thereby
confirming for him major aspects of his identity and affirming the
recognition and respect in which he is held? These have been the
salient identity issues for him throughout his life. In his cultural past,
social status, education and achievement are highly valued and are
linked with his original family of origin and his wife's family. His
personal reaction to this cultural past has been to invest these aspects
of identity with special importance, and uprooting has made them
even more salient for him. If he had remained in India, these aspects
of his identity would have found their natural confirmation in his
familiar setting. But in this country, things are not so simple.

When he first arrived in Athol from the Midlands, he was accorded
special recognition by English people as a neighbour, client or
friend. But as the numbers of Asians have increased and their social
class backgrounds become more diverse, he is increasingly
confronted by English people who are unable to differentiate
between him and other immigrants. As a result, he can be lumped
together with groups who differ from him in their social origins,
status, educational levels, and their understanding of English ways
and culture.

Having re-built his self-esteem after his critical first years in
England, he is left with a wound which, although healed in many
ways by his own achievements and the steady tackling of inner and
outer tasks, nonetheless leaves him especially vulnerable to issues
concerning his self esteem, respect and recognition by others. When
confused in other people's minds with negative identities attributed
by the English to the Indians and Pakistanis, this is a painful
experience, stirring in him those anxieties and humiliations which he
faced in his early days and against which he so splendidly struggled
and finally overcame.

His vulnerability is two fold: if other Indian or Pakistani
immigrants behave in ways which he personally finds distressing, or
of which he legitimately disapproves as an individual, their
behaviour or attitudes constitute a threat to him, because, in turn, he
can be seen as indistinguishable from these others. This source
of vulnerability is related to the second. Baldev Singh, as an individual, believes in distinguishing between people as individuals,
irrespective of race. But he notices that some English people are
unable to do this, particularly those who are ignorant, uneducated or

prejudiced and who have negatively stereotyped attitudes towards Asians. He feels especially threatened by such people, and his vulnerabilities are prodded by Asians whose behaviour and attitudes feed and confirm these negative identity images.

Both of these sources of vulnerability make him cling even more rigidly to his personal high standards which verge on the idealized and unattainable. He expects these standards both from himself and from the members of his family, but also from his fellow Asians. His ego-ideals become increasingly high as he feels threatened by the lower standards of behaviour and values of immigrants of his own race but of a lower social class.

He sees the English as not broadminded in relation to race, feels there is more colour prejudice in England than there used to be, and more than in Canada – a country to which he is greatly attracted and where he would like his children to settle. He also observes that, at his place of work, Englishmen in authority have double standards; they will accept from their fellow English lower standards of performance, an unwillingness to work, low productivity and a slight bending of rules and regulations, whereas if the workers are coloured immigrants they will be judged by far more exacting and rigid standards and fired. Mr Singh may have accurately described the situation; or, by a process of projection, he may also be putting into such Englishmen those critical standards which he himself adopts towards his people. Both may be true, but they have the same psychological effects upon him for each can only make his expectations of himself, and his expectations of other Asians, even more rigid and demanding than before. To feel that he and his fellow Asians are being judged by more exacting standards than are others requires him to ask more and more of himself, his children and fellow immigrants of his own race.

He has unstinted admiration for Indians and Pakistanis as good workers, but it is in their family lives that he feels working class Asians fall short and these pose a threat to him.

> The mothers who work don't care to dress their children properly according to the uniform of the school – they don't care much for their breakfast, lunch or supper or how the child goes – their shoes aren't polished because the mother goes to work and does not care for the children as long as they are at school. They earn that money for the benefit of the family and yet the children are suffering with these little things. I don't think the money is worth it, in my personal opinion. And this is

what I don't like about immigrant people. I don't say they shouldn't work here. They should work, but at the same time they should look after their children.

He is concerned about the noise which certain Indian families make and which disturb their neighbours, and is specially vigilant that within his own home when curry, for instance, is cooked that the house should not retain the smell and that it should not spread to the neighbours, and he criticizes some Indian families for not doing the same. He is also sensitive to the tidiness and general state of repair of Indian homes within the community.

It is because these questions pose a threat to him, that he feels that he must voice his criticisms as a citizen and he does so at a public meeting. In other ways, his philosophy of life is that each person should be responsible for his own life and problems. 'I don't have to judge my nextdoor neighbour as to what sort of person he is, as long as he lets me live in peace and quiet. I believe in this. You cannot change the world, even Lord Jesus Christ couldn't change it, could he? You can do a little bit and you must start from yourself.' He *has* started with himself; as a worker, parent, citizen and householder, his standards are high, his struggles to meet these standards noteworthy.

I don't like other things about Indians and Pakistanis because . . . . they tell lies to the officials over here . . . . in order to get various allowances . . . . The English . . . . believe people in the first instance, but when they find out that these people are telling lies, they don't believe them again. I don't blame the English people . . . . I'm not very proud of our people who tell lies . . . . no matter how they discriminate against you. On your own part, you should at least feel satisfied that you are doing right.

It is these negative identity images against which he defends himself. And when the English fail to notice the difference between himself, his family and the mass of immigrants he feels hurt and angry. When confronted by attitudes of racial superiority on the part of the English, he is capable of angrily pointing out the fallacy of the arguments advanced and challenging the person concerned. If, however, he believes the individual to be ignorant and uneducated, he feels that it is not worth bothering with him. 'You find people like this, but why discuss these things with people who have hate or dislike for immigrants? Only educated people might understand – people who are really educated. These you will find. You find both sorts of people.'

He has many English friends, including his senior storekeeper, who taught him everything, and to whom he is very grateful; also other supervisors who helped him a lot. 'They are educated people.' They visit each other's homes, exchange gifts and are close friends. He also has a very close relationship with an English neighbour, who stood security for Vera when she took up a post as a cashier at a local bank. Their children play together and the families are very friendly.

He is basically a fair-minded man, recognising faults both in his own race and in other races, and does not project blame onto any specific group.

> You hear and read in the papers that a couple of English boys hit an Indian or a Pakistani, or a couple of Pakistani boys caught hold of an English boy. These things happen now and again in our society. The Indian Association always tells people not to be aggressive but just to defend themselves but it's difficult to know who was defending and who was attacking.

He sees the police as basically impartial. His attitudes towards the Kenyan Asians are open and without prejudice. 'They are a very skilled people, better than our Punjabis although they originally came from the Punjab . . . . I have very good feelings for them.'

The West Indians play no part in his life. They hardly figure in his life story. He sees them as polite and affectionate towards each other but has no personal bonds with them and in general feels them to be below his standards of education and culture – the judgement of a man with an ancient cultural heritage confronting a people whose cultural heritage has been broken off at the roots.

To summarise: Mr Singh's unresolved identity conflict arises from a fragile sense of his status and self-esteem within this English setting. This unconsciously drives him to seek respect and recognition from the English. These are often denied him, because: first, the English cannot readily distinguish between one Asian and another; secondly, the attitudes and behaviour or some working class Asians give support to negative stereotypes of them; and thirdly, these stereotypes are then attributed indiscriminately to all Asians, including the Singhs. To defend himself against this conflict, Mr Singh raises his own ego-ideal standards and expectations for himself and his family even higher than before, and becomes increasingly critical and judgemental both towards his fellow

countrymen, many of whose standards fall below his, and towards
the prejudiced and ignorant English.

His dilemma lies in the fact that he is basically a fair-minded man
who does not believe in judging his neighbours. But the core of his
identity conflict lies in his dependence on others for the confirmation
of his identity. The price which he pays for his unconscious attempts
to resolve his identity conflict is that he makes very heavy demands
on himself and on others, his standards tend to be very high with the
result that he has to deny, in part, his human frailties and those of the
members of his family. He is caught in a vicious cycle: as his own
ego-ideals become more rigid and exacting, and as his denial of his
own human frailties increase, so his fellow Indian and Pakistani
immigrants are likely to be judged by even more exacting standards.
As they fail to reach his standards, he becomes more vulnerably
exposed which tends to raise his ego-ideals still further.

Vicious and virtuous cycles in race relations
Mr Singh's patterns of coping with face-to-face, inter-racial
confrontations are different from the defensive measures to which he
resorts in the face of the group pressures already discussed. At the
interpersonal level, there is no instance in his life story where his
attitudes or behaviour have the effect of exacerbating racial tensions
or where vicious cycles are initiated or kept in motion.

When he was brutally attacked by the three Indians and let down
by the unknown Indian man whom he had befriended, he learnt a
bitter lesson about people and their shortcomings and he withdrew
somewhat from his previous involvement in helping others. But he
never conducted any personal vendetta against his assailants nor
against the unknown man. Neither did he make light of the full
meaning which the incident had for him.

When he first came to England, the four years of regressive decline
showed him going through the following loops, deeply revealing of
the man and his characteristic way of solving problems:

1 He failed in a film venture in India whereas his friends thrived
and succeeded in the same venture.

2 He left India and came to England, partly rationalized as a new
chance.

3 He squandered his resources, led a life of idleness and luxury,
experienced shame, humiliation and feelings of lowered self-esteem
at his poverty, false values and character deterioration.

4 On the arrival of his wife, he faced up to these things in himself,
told her all, and so shared his shame and humiliation.

5 With her emotional support, he started to rebuild his self-

esteem, re-establishing his identity as an able, reliable husband and father, and re-secured his family's economic future.

6 He achieved this by facing up to his shortcomings, accepting himself as imperfect and consequently able to accept others more readily, irrespective of race.

It is at the group or community level where the vicious cycle operates; it is directed both against those English who are ignorant and prejudiced and against a social class segment of his own people.

2 MRS TARA SINGH

Issues bearing on the formation of her identity

Tara Singh was born into a respected, well-to-do Sikh family and grew up in a happy home in Delhi where she felt loved and sensitively understood by her parents. At the time of the study, both parents were living in India and her relationship with them continues to be an important and satisfying one.

She recalls her mother during childhood as being a very kind and patient woman, whereas the mothers of her friends were both impatient and somewhat cruel. Her mother kept her children well dressed and very clean and when she entertained her friends and their children, Tara resented this intrusion. 'Why do they come and spoil your nice home?' she asked her mother. She did not like the children, commenting that 'they were not very clean sometimes. My mother kept us children clean and they were not dressed properly. They were not nice children.' In India, where dirtiness has been ritually projected onto the Untouchable castes, concern with cleanliness reflects not only matters of ordinary personal hygiene but also an awareness of caste and class differences. This incident also throws light on other identity issues. She seems to have wanted to have her mother to herself, free from jealous rivals – the unclean, not nice children – but also she wanted to keep the home inviolate from invasive outsiders. These themes return in her life story.

She greatly loved and admired her father, a graduate and a versatile linguist. He plays an extremely important part in her life and she remembers him as being gentle, warm and loving, firm and able as well as being widely respected in the community. She recalls her first sight of white people when she was very young – and her conversation with her father about these British officers. He told her the English were ruling their country. 'Oh, I was really shocked and I stopped talking a little bit. He said "Why have you stopped talking?" I said "Oh, I am shocked . . . . Why have they come to our house, our country?" He said "They are clever people – they've got brains".'

Apart from the image of the English projected here as intelligent, exploitative people who have earned their wealth and their high standard of living through their brains, this conversational exchange echoes Tara's earlier theme of intruders into her home, her country, her territorial domain. She is expressing an image of an inner hearth, a boundary which she feels encloses her domain and which should not lightly be invaded by outsiders. Her imagery of both home and country is a territorial one – an inner sanctum. When as a young married woman she was later to leave both her country and her home, this need for a personal centre was one which she could not easily find and this exposed her to great pain and suffering before she could re-constitute it.

Another early incident throws further light on images of territorial space felt to be inviolate when, as a little girl, she invaded a park specially set aside for English people. Her father's handling of the incident highlights caste and class differentials within India at that time which enabled him to secure for his small daughter a special concession. While Tara as a young child was judging the children who came into her home as usurpers, as 'not clean' and so beneath her social status, she, in turn was treated by the Indian labouring man on behalf of the society which he served as someone who could defile and spoil the playground for the English. A hierarchical ranking of class emerges from these early perceptions of herself and others – the English were at the top, but the Indian middle class from which she came could establish their rights to privilege and respect. And at the bottom of the hierarchy are the working class.

Her father was a highly educated man, well respected in the community, and he in turn respected her mother although she was less well educated than he. He valued education for all his children, sons and daughters but Tara's formal school education came to a premature end because of her father's haunting fears that the Muslims in Delhi would kidnap his daughter because she was a Sikh – a Hindu. 'I am dreaming badly – so many times I dream that some Muslim will take you away and make you dizzy . . . Maybe my dream will come true and what can I do?' Her father arranged for her to go to school accompanied by a middle-aged woman as chaperon, but after an incident when Tara went to a Muslim shop to buy a pencil and the owner started 'looking a bit funny' and frightened her considerably, her father removed her from school. Tara's own thoughts ran along the same lines as his, 'Oh, the Muslims are very bad. I'm a Hindu – a Sikh – and the Muslims don't know if a girl is a little girl or a big girl.'

She retired into her home, her world an inner one of her own thoughts and solitude and a family world within which she was loved and protected. Her father would not allow her to go to Muslim shops and indeed he bought all the provisions for the family to protect both his wife and daughter from the threat of Muslim attentions. In this way, aggressive sexuality was located outside the home and attached to the Muslims.

And while she was alone

> I was dreaming that I want to learn this and want to learn that and I saw other girls doing embroidery and I always asked my mother and . . . she sometimes said 'Oh, you ask me the same things all the time. You don't want to play or go to places.' And then I asked my father to bring me some material and he brought me some coloured sash cloth and cotton wools and he gave me lessons. He said 'Come, I will teach you to sew' '. . . and my mother said 'Oh! She will learn nothing and what can you teach her?'. And he said 'Never mind – you never teach her.' He had a lot of patience and he said 'If a man wants to do something, he can do it.' He did not sew himself but he taught me how to sew.

He also gave Tara lessons and kept a vigilant eye on the kind of books which she read. She accepted this control of her activities because of her love and respect for him and her deep desire to please him, and was proud of him, recognizing his 'very good nature'. Throughout her life to the present time, he has expressed his love for her, his confidence in her and the pride which he feels about what she has accomplished in her life. His only regret has been that she could not have had the same high education which he provided for his sons as he recognises her intelligence is as high as theirs.

This relationship between Tara and her father was a very close and important one and played a vital role in confirming for her her growing sexual identity as a feminine, sensitive young woman. He removed her from the sexually aggressive threats posed by potential Muslim abductors and by retaining her at home, his importance to her became intensified. His assumption of aspects of both the father and mother role, by instructing her not only in ordinary educational matters but also helping her to acquire feminine skills in sewing and embroidery, can perhaps best be understood in relation to this specific culture. Erikson in a study on Gandhi has commented on aspects of bisexuality among Indian men[6] feeling it to be a deep and national trend. The total image is one in which it is difficult to allocate masculine and feminine identifications.[7] Tara's father is expressing in his combined mother/father role a culturally familiar pattern. The greatest importance, however, of the role he assumed in teaching her to sew is that he gave her a splendid example of a willingness to tackle unknown problems in the service of a devoted love for another person.

Her father was the emotional focus of her early adolescence and critical in her later identity development. He made her feel valued and respected and his patience and persistence were aspects of his personality with which she seems to have identified. He recognized her individuality and respected her as the person she was-in-the-process-of-becoming. This also reflects the Hindu view of life, which sees *dharma*, according to Erikson, as being a highly personal life task in which the individual is immersed and which is affected by previous lives as well as by acquisition and choice.[8] 'Better one's own *dharma* [though] imperfect, than another's well performed; better death in [doing] one's own *dharma*; another's *dharma* brings danger.'[9] Tara's father while recognizing his daughter's *dharma* continues doing his own *dharma*.

In coming to feel her home and background to be an essential part of her, she was repudiating the alien and disturbing aspects of the Muslim world from which she had been largely protected but which she tentatively explored in a visit to a Muslim schoolfriend. She found the Muslim father scared her and the cooking smells strange and unfamiliar and never wished to go there again, returning to her home and feeling that she was very lucky because she had a 'very nice father'. Home was familiar and a beloved father a part of that world.

The strong oedipal overtones of her attachment to her father, in other cultures, might have been a hazard to later relationships in marriage. But the Hindu approach to life facilitated Tara's transition into marriage and into a close bond with her husband. The Hindus distinguish between several stages of life, in each one of which a different life style and the acquistion of different strengths is cumulatively added to one's maturity and re-integrated at the succeeding stage.[10] The stage of Tara's protected young adulthood at home can be seen as the first stage in the Hindu lifecycle where the development of competence in basic skills is part of the apprenticeship of that age; this is followed by a different shift in life patterns where adulthood is seen as linked with marriage, the development of a family and community involvement. This second stage in Tara's life was facilitated by a culture pattern where the parents actively choose, and are chosen by the parents of the future spouse. In this way, Tara's father actively blesses her union with *this* specific man, a man of his choice. The transfer of sexually-tinged feelings from the oedipal father to the man whom he has delegated as the life partner for his daughter is emotionally facilitated. But, in addition, the culture, ritually provides for the young woman to marry at an early age (fifteen in Tara's case) and to move away from her parental home into the home of her husband's parents, and so structures a marked shift away from the oedipal parents and into a new family situation. She married Baldev. Her family had chosen him because he was a 'nice healthy boy' from a respected and good social background and with exemplary manners. She had never seen him before she was married, a customary practice. She felt like crying and this was made worse by her knowledge that Baldev was an orphan, which meant she left her father's house and went to live with Baldev alone, an unusual circumstance which frightened her with the prospect of the loneliness ahead. 'So my auntie found me a husband with no mother and no father and no sisters or brothers and I felt I would be all alone. Where I was going to was a house – a lonely house. I never asked anything. I never said anything but I cried.'

Culturally accepted and defined, this major transition in a woman's life was seen by her mother as a time when crying was part of the pain of separation – and as a crisis of change in the life of a woman. 'When a girl marries a boy, she must change. A girl has to be changed because there's a different house, a different blood and different natures. Everything is different . . . . There is the first life with mother and father in their house and then there's the other life – the second life'. This surely must correspond with what Erikson has written about as *grhastha*, the second life stage.[11]

She found Baldev different from her father – he had a different nature 'not mean, but different'. She found his more explosive temperament and his capacity for expressing anger upsetting and it made her cry and feel very sad. She consistently worked at pleasing him, recognizing the need to change. She came to like the large house, wished to live there with Baldev without their servants because of a need to truly serve him and cement the intimacy of their bond. However his will prevailed and she got pleasure from keeping the home clean and cooking for him. But she noted that he lied to her on occasions which angered her, her own upbringing having been very strict on this point. 'My father said, "Don't tell lies. If you tell lies, again and again I will not be satisfied".

When Baldev decided to leave India for England, he left behind not only his wife but also his daughter-to-be, since neither Baldev nor Tara knew at the time of his departure that she was then pregnant with Vera. She returned to her father and mother and for four years lived there with her small daughter. At first letters kept her in touch with Baldev but as the years dragged on, his lack of response to her letters caused her growing concern and sadness. But her primary commitment to him as her husband was the focus of her life. 'I needed him. I wanted to give him some comfort in his life – to wash and to cook for him. I was not working. I wanted to work for him. I felt very strange.' But finally when she could tolerate it no longer she wrote to him. 'How long must I live separate? Tell me the truth – try to tell me the truth. Time is being ruined and I – about twenty-four years old – getting old.' With inner strength and the support of her parents, she took the courageous step of coming to England without any confirmation from her husband that he would welcome her and be there to meet her. She left the sanctuary of her familiar home, her culture and her country, and with her three-year old daughter came to a new land whose language she did not know. She came to a husband about whose life and life-patterns she had known little for the past four years. She was leaving behind her father, her mother and brothers and seeking the re-establishment of her family life with her husband. Her hope lay in the re-union and in the chance of family building and consolidating.

She confronted a very changed husband, poverty-stricken without a job or a home, no promise of security for herself and Vera. Yet this gentle, quiet woman who had lived an extremely sheltered and protected life, rose to the critical test of her husband's shame and demoralization with an inner calm, impressive resilience, courage and, above all, a quietly sustaining love, grounded on hope. When she discovered that he had no savings, no job, a few tattered clothes and that for the past four years he seemed to have squandered his time and his inner resources, she said to him '"Don't worry, don't worry. You're healthy, you're alright. You've got two hands, two feet – you've got good health. Never mind – you can earn". I was not despondent. He could earn – a man can do anything and make anything. Maybe he had lost courage . . . if a man loses courage, he can't do anything.'

Her earlier experiences had laid the formation of a sense of inner security and trust which now stood her and her husband in good stead. Her sense of self-esteem was sturdy enough to meet his crisis with inner strength and love, and she did not falter when confronted with his failure, although it exacted from her all her resources of strength and courage. Earlier experiences had left her with inner feelings of an essential goodness, which helped her to believe that Baldev could re-find *his* goodness. Her hope and trust carried them both through this major crisis. She was sad, cried when alone and suffered and missed her parents and her brothers very much indeed, and when asked by her father in his letters as to how she felt, she confessed she wanted to come home. But he said 'Hold on, take it easy. You'll be alright', and although he did not know any details of their major crisis, nonetheless these words helped to sustain her. She withstood the privations of extreme poverty, the anxiety and fear, and coped with prodigious problems of adjusting to an alien culture, a vast urban environment and a new language.

Having lived in comfortable homes, relatively insulated from the outer world, she found herself living in a huge house as a lodger, confined to a tiny boxroom with her husband and small child, and to make things worse sharing bathroom facilities and a communal kitchen with Muslims. Her childhood fear of Muslim men now had to be contained in this strange and bewildering world.

Among the stressful problems she faced were the re-establishment of her relationship with her husband as well as the difficulties which Baldev and Vera were having in being together for the first time. In both situations she seems to have been aware of her ambivalent feelings in which love predominated, and to have some acceptance of the ambivalent feelings of both Baldev and Vera. She recognized that Baldev's past life had made it difficult for him to know how to approach small children. 'He had only got a grandmother when he was small and no brothers or sisters or a big family and he had no experience with little children . . . He sometimes spoke a bit roughly to her . . . I don't know, perhaps it was the military service he had done.' But she also understood Vera's past relationship with her loving grandparents and how she longed to return to them and away from the somewhat clumsy first encounters with her father.

In coping with the multiple stresses and strains, her chosen means of weathering the crisis were to contain the stress within herself. 'I thought that I should keep quiet all the time. I said to myself "Never mind, keep steady and everything will be alright". I think I was very patient at that time.' She listened to her husband and understood his feelings of shame. But he was very difficult in those early years, short-tempered and unsettled. 'All the time he spoke to me, I said "Oh, don't worry".' But it was very hard for her because in addition to other burdens, Baldev wanted her to conform to the cultural habits of the English, even in small ways. 'Sometimes I started washing. "You are making a noise", he said, "Wash a bit slowly". I said "Why?" and he said "Oh, not in this country". I thought to myself, "Oh, all the time you tell me about this country, but you did not settle down".' She felt that if she raised matters with him he would be angry.

She gave her moral support to him in his exhausting work at the steel rolling mills and they saved every penny which they could. Their goals co-incided; she needed to re-create a home, her own sense of bounded space, and he needed to prove himself able to provide for his wife and growing family and so secure his masculine identity as a husband and father. During this testing time, they were not only helpful to each other, but her parents in India were also morally behind her. Much later, after a trip to India, her father told her how proud he was of her. '"I'm very proud of you. You haven't any qualifications and are not very well educated, but you are better than many educated girls. I'm very proud that you went to England when Baldev wasn't settled down and you made him settle down without complaining".' Her father's recognition of her courage, as well as her impressive capacity to tolerate frustrations and disappointments without either indulging in self-pity or apportioning blame, throws light on the nature of their relationship and how her father confirmed for her these dominant aspects of her identity.

The loving support which she had received throughout her life from both her parents also helped her in turn to fulfil herself as a mother. She was devoted to Vera, appreciative of how she too helped in small ways to hasten the day when they could buy their own home, by making no demands on her parents for toys or special food, both of which she had previously taken for granted in her life with her grandparents.

Their first home of their own in England was in the Midlands and was in a suburb of a large city where they were surrounded by English people. All their friends and neighbours were English and they were met with acceptance, friendship and kindness. She was able to ask, at times, for the guidance and concrete assistance which she needed, reciprocated with appreciation and acts of hospitality.

Her pregnancy with Eric and her subsequent pregnancy with her third child, plunged her into a period of very poor health which still remains one of the current anxieties of her present situation. This brought her into contact with English doctors, hospital staff and fellow-patients, and she felt well cared for and valued, and was appreciative.

She was sensitively insightful as a mother, coping with Vera's jealousy of Eric. Her father wrote to her after Eric was born '"Don't ignore Vera. Maybe she will be jealous and you must care a little bit more for her and she will be happy. Otherwise she will be cross with you and she will feel hate for Eric".' Her initial reaction was disbelief but afterwards 'I understood and I saw it all'. When she was pregnant with her third child she had to be urgently hospitalized for some months before the baby was born (prematurely). Eric, who was then eighteen months old, was taken to a residential nursery. During this period his father felt it best not to visit the little boy in case he would become more distressed and after Mrs Singh returned from hospital, Eric's reaction to the separation was sensitively observed by her; without any knowledge of psychological studies on childhood separations from a mother, she recounted what she had observed:

> When at nineteen months he returned home he asked me, 'Why did daddy take me away?' and started crying. He threw this thing about and that thing about and he had so much excitement. Then he said he wanted to go to the toilet [Mrs Singh toilet-trained (pot-trained) her children from the age of three months following her own mother's example. 'My mother liked to keep children very clean.'] And he wouldn't let me help him when I brought the pot. . . . Sometimes my husband shouted at him and I said 'Don't shout and don't blame him. Maybe he misunderstands and thinks I'm going again.' And all the time I said to Eric 'I'm not going anywhere'. . . . I understand what happened to Eric.

As her family grew, her capacity to value each child and to respond to their individual needs emerged. Her fulfilment lay in her home and family and her identity as wife and mother was expressed within the setting of the home. 'Sometimes I get a bit fed up – they are not all saints.' Her children like English food so she cooks both Indian and English food. As her health continues to give concern and her mid-life crisis increases her anxieties, it is of the children that she thinks. 'At times I feel so terrible . . . I am always dreaming and have felt that I was going to die . . . What can the children do? . . . I like them to learn, to read and write properly and to be clever and to stand on their own feet'. To a certain extent, she now expresses through her children, her unfulfilled educational desires.

At the core of her values as a parent are those of integrity and moral standards. Her children must never tell lies. Her feelings as a

Sikh are also reflected in her role as a parent. She is proud of her people's courage and bravery, capacity to talk frankly and to be honourable towards others as well as their generosity to the poor. Her identification with these qualities of courage, openness and honour could well have served as additional sources of support to her during her years of critical adjustment. She sees herself as 'an ordinary woman. I don't think I'm special'.

The relationship with her husband has greatly improved since the early days in the Midlands. He has changed, is helpful, caring and supportive. But after his traumatic physical assault, which happened before they left the Midlands, and his many resultant operations, she noticed how these had changed him as a person. 'Before, if the children were crying, he would hold them and make them happy but after this time, he was often very angry because he'd been a patient so often . . . it was very difficult because he was angry – much more than before.' He also naturally felt let down by his friends after this assault. 'Since that time he doesn't trust others – he's changed and feels it's not good to help others.'

In their marriage, complementary interactions between Baldev and Tara express contrasting aspects of their personalities. Differences are not avoided but used, so that each expresses for the other the feelings and emotions which each may find difficult to acknowledge in themselves. It is Baldev who is able to show the anger, hurt and disappointment probably because he unconsciously knows that she will continue to express the patience, gentle accommodation and acceptance of frustration and suffering. Each uses the complementary identity of the other, and what each has become is because of what the other is able to be. Through Baldev, Tara remains in contact with the aggression in herself although at the conscious level much of this has had to be disowned. Her physical illness may also be an expression, in part, of her unexpressed frustrations and angry feelings, particularly the migraine headaches and the high blood pressure. And it is through Tara that Baldev remains in touch with the gentle, clear-thinking, patient and courageous parts of himself.

Tara has only a limited number of channels through which to express herself. She is the only woman among the three wives studied who has never worked outside the home and whose present activities are almost entirely confined to the home. The psychological space of her home is the arena within which all her feelings, relationships, needs and anxieties have to be contained; and as her mid-life crisis, and the maturing of her two eldest children, require from her some shifting of her libidinal investment to other channels she is very restricted indeed. This is perhaps why her anxieties about her health may be exacerbated and why she now longs to have learnt a musical instrument. She is a person who suffers her frustrations, mostly by sad but philosophical acceptance of them, but she also turns them back against herself. Her depressive tendencies stop her from any need to scapegoat others for her mounting sense of frustration. Her ways of handling anxiety enable her to endure, at a cost to herself, rather than to blame and punish others.

Unresolved identity conflicts and race

In her life story themes of inviolate space recur. She is absorbed with inner space, an emphasis on interiors envisaged as peaceful and where intrusion is seen as a threat.[12] Her identity as a woman, wife and mother is apparently fulfilled within the home and it is within that setting that her race attitudes largely are meaningful. As a child, she resented 'the unclean Indian children' who violated her sense of home; they were usurpers of her private space. Her judgement upon them was a social class one.

By extension, her country – her wider home – was felt to have been invaded by the English. They might be rich, clever, elegant and clean but they were invaders of her country and their presence in this inner citadel shocked her. They, in turn, tried to exclude her as a young girl from their playground, seeing her as a potential defiler of *their* clean space. In her present life in Athol, neighbours can potentially invade her privacy of home in two ways: first, by intrusiveness of noise against which there is little protection; and secondly, by their physical presence.

The noise in the streets has worried her increasingly. 'When we first came here at eight at night, nobody was shouting in the streets. But now if you walk in the streets, there are Indian boys, young boys and oh! they talk very loudly and have not got very nice manners. I don't know about English boys.' *Her* neighbours have also on occasions had their problems with noise from *their* neighbours. This has made her fearful that Indians causing the noise will feed negative identity elements which, in turn, may be attributed by the English, to all Indians. The English family next door recount their troubles with their Indian neighbours on the other side of them, complaining of noise and 'terrible' cooking smells.

She was very friendly to me and I invited her to tea and she invited us. Well, after they went, they could think we are also

Indians. Over here if one Indian does wrong naturally you see me and write 'Oh, she's an Indian – the same', but we are not the same. We are all of the same nation but we have not the same nature – we are not the same.

She was also upset when her immediate Indian neighbour moved in and exploited the Singhs' kindness in allowing them to take a lead from their electricity supply because their own house had none; having used the electricity for a whole year they made no offer to pay. 'I didn't want to charge but they made no offers for a year. I'm from the same country as them but they're not very nice.'

It is the threat, posed by the attitudes and behaviour of Asians of a lower class than herself, which arouses her anxiety. She does not, however, berate them angrily or criticize them harshly; rather she notes the problems, uses her discriminatory standards of choice and judgement with which to assess their behaviour, and decides with whom to associate. Her positive sense of identity is linked with standards of integrity, good manners, consideration for others, kindness, quiet bearing and cleanliness. Where these are transgressed by others, she disapproves in her quiet way and exercises her options of choice, but largely because – as an immigrant – each Asian is felt to threaten *her* image in the eyes of the English.

As a consumer and shopper, her forays outside the home expose her to such situations. Two experiences reveal her personal qualities and throw light on the negative identity images which the shopkeepers project onto her. The first incident occurred when she asked the English shopkeeper to give her fresh vegetables displayed outside the shop. When he wanted to give her damp inferior ones from inside, she demurred. He then patronized her, assuming she could not speak English and did not know what she wanted. To which she replied ' "You don't have to talk funny. I understand very well what I want. You better talk English".' After an angry exchange she came home and felt angry and ashamed of herself. 'I came home and I felt very sorry for myself.' She did not want to shop there again but sometimes she sees something outside and asks Vera to buy it. '[Laughs] They know it's my daughter and they always give us nice things because they know that I don't like them.'

In the other incident, she wanted shoes for her youngest child and against the resistance of the shop-owner, insisted on being shown an expensive shoe.

He then said 'You're an Indian and when you buy something

then afterwards you change your mind'. I said 'I'm not that kind of woman. If I want shoes I can read your price myself. If I don't want them, I don't bother you. Please show me nice shoes'. . . Well, that man in the shop was very friendly . . . . sometimes I go over there and he's very nice and I get shoes for my children there.

She reflected on her experience and commented 'these days, many women are not educated and they don't know anything . . . they don't know who I am'.

In both these incidents, Mrs Singh held her ground with firm dignity and a sturdy sense of self-esteem. In the first incident, the shopkeeper resorted to patronizing rudeness as if she was un-educated and ignorant; in the second case, the negative identity thrust upon her was also one which linked Indian women with associated notions of ignorance and not knowing their own minds. She is aware that the English shopkeepers cannot distinguish between someone of her intelligence and background and the uneducated mass. And although this is the same problem as her husband's, her response is different. She recognises the problem, reflects on it and understands some of its roots, but she steadfastly continues to be herself, firm and dignified but angry and resolute when necessary. She does not resort to stereotyping the English, on the one hand, or the Indian masses on the other. Each can be understood in terms of their problems and backgrounds.

As far as destructive aggression is concerned, since the Muslim men were her repositories – and her father's – for these feelings during childhood and adolescence (*likely* to be a common stereotype at that time which other Hindus shared), these feelings were projected outside the family. It seems likely that Tara Singh does not need to project her destructively aggressive feelings onto racial groups since the childhood use of Muslim men for this purpose was more her father's need and may well have been general in that community. Instead, angry feelings are contained within the marriage (as already discussed) by the complementary bond with her husband. He can express the anger and she placates him. But as already said she also turns back any angry feelings against herself in the form of headaches and possibly her high blood pressure.

Her relationships with the English in this country have been friendly, mutually respectful, and at times spontaneously warm. Since she has not been well in recent years, and has had several babies since coming to England, her contacts with the English have not only been as neighbours and shopkeepers, but also as doctors, nurses and fellow-patients in hospital. Her experiences have left her with friendly and positive feelings. The English doctors, of whom she was initially very frightened (because she had never been examined by a man before), have turned out to be 'very good'. She likes her doctors and respects their judgement and skill. During her stays in hospital, she appreciated the kindness of the Sister and how gentle she was. She comforted Tara when she felt bereft of her mother and said, '"We all have no mothers or sisters – don't worry about anything".' English women, whom she met en route to the hospital, befriended her with concern when she was not well. She has been deeply grateful for these kindnesses and appreciative of their spontaneous nature. When, after Eric was born, the Sister warned her that Indian women tend to spoil their sons, Tara took this to heart and tried not to pick up Eric each time he cried. She valued the advice given.

She is a person with a sturdy sense of her own self-esteem, feels herself to be both lovable and worthy of respect and, in turn, is able to love and respect others. Her childhood relationships with her parents helped her to resolve early conflicts of love and hate for the same person with a largely favourable outcome. Love is dominant over hate in Tara Singh and she is capable of experiencing sadness and showing concern for others. By carrying inside herself an inner source of her own goodness, she is able to sustain periods of frustration and disappointment aided by feelings of trust and hope. Ambivalence in herself, and in others, she tolerates reasonably well and as a result has little need to split-off good feelings from bad, resort to idealizations or massive projections of her disowned feelings onto other people.

Vicious and virtuous cycles

Mrs Singh is one of the few subjects in this study who do not resort to racial misuse. It is revealing to re-examine her handling of the two incidents with English shopkeepers. In both, she stood her ground as a consumer, insisting on her rights to select merchandize and be served conscientiously. When, in the first incident, she was treated with rude condescension, she withdrew her custom, expressed her anger and demanded to be treated as an intelligent consumer. In withdrawing her custom, she did not carry this to excess since she noted that when Vera bought things on her behalf, the man gave her good quality food as if in delayed respect – and expiation. She is fairminded and able to laugh at herself at the compromise she adopted. The shopkeeper learnt presumably to respect a woman like her – recognition of how firmness and angry dignity can bring rewards. In the second incident, her polite firmness also brought rewards, both to the shopkeeper and to herself. She won enhanced respect from him as an intelligent consumer who knew what she wanted and he gained her continuing patronage.

What had threatened to be difficult inter-racial confrontations, potentially able to escallate destructively, became trading bonds with benign inter-racial consequences. In each case, respect for Mrs Singh was achieved; although in the first case, it was respect indirectly acknowledged through a third party – Vera. And in both cases, Tara Singh reflected on those difficulties which less educated women of her race might have.

She shifted the potentially vicious spirals of ordinary trading encounters between Asians and English into a constructive direction. And she did so by affirming her personal identity.

3 MISS VERA SINGH

Issues bearing on the formation of her identity
The first years of Vera Singh's life were spent in India with her mother, grandparents, uncles, aunts and a young cousin. She recalls her life in the extended family with images of a sunny, cheerful and typically Indian house where 'you could look down into the next person's kitchen and it was ever so friendly . . . you could call to each other all day long'. She looks back on those earliest years with nostalgia for a cheerful and devoted grandmother, a gently loving grandfather who made her feel a favourite and 'special', and the warmth of being part of a friendly and companionable group.

When she left India at the age of three she went reluctantly with her mother and remembers how she longed to return to India, which feelings were intensified after her first meeting with her father. He left her feeling inadequate and somewhat unloved as he commented on meeting her on her 'skinny and bent legs'. His striking size and appearance and more passionate and volatile temperament contrasted vividly with the gentle, short, bearded and turbanned grandfather whom she had left behind and whom she loved. 'If you look at my dad he doesn't immediately strike you as being very kind, although he *is* – I have to say that – but he didn't look it when I first saw him.'

She felt deprived of the love and security which had been hers, was lonely and used to cry to herself at night, missing her grandparents and the lost home. Perhaps these early experiences of loss left her with some residue of feelings of basic mistrust so that her way of coping with her sadness and loss was to keep her feelings to herself. She cried alone at night and did not turn to her parents for comfort.

Within that first year in England, her brother Eric was born and this exposed her to feelings of intense jealousy. Her relationship with her father was a difficult one at that period. Her conflicts about her missing grandfather, combined with her father's inner struggles to cope with a re-union with his wife, his shame and sense of failure and the energies which he poured into his exhausting work at the steel rolling mills, all seem to have militated against the establishment of a solid basis of love and warmth between them. When Eric was born she witnessed the joy with which Indian families greet the birth of a son, especially the first-born son. 'Our families feel that as soon as they have a son, they've just got it made . . . They always seem to want sons more than daughters in Indian families. I always told my mum I wanted a brother, maybe because my mum and dad wanted a son.'

Instead of being the favourite and 'special' as she had felt in her grandfather's home, she now watched *her* father favour his newly born son. 'Eric was a lovely baby and everyone played him up and said how lovely he was and I also said he was, you know, [laughs] but at one time I really hated him. I was quite jealous of him.' Her envy of his masculine identity must have been intense. She recollects how he would not go to sleep until his father came home and 'he was spoilt, he really was and always got his way'. Two incidents which she remembers as showing Eric's 'spitefulness' both appear to be connected with her feelings of being a little girl. She had had her hair done nicely and with narcissistic pride was showing it to her friend when Eric hit her on the head and ruined her hair. The second incident concerned her new doll, a Christmas present from her parents and symbolically something which she could use as a fiction of her motherhood to make her envious feelings towards her mother more bearable. But Eric drew all over its face and 'ruined it'.

She kept her feelings to herself, and learnt the power that came from not answering or responding. 'Unless people speak to me first, I just won't speak and I wouldn't speak to my dad . . . he used to try and get round me and I used to love this . . . I really used to love this because he could not bear to be ignored. But it's horrible – I just ignore people, I do.' She also resented and resisted apologizing.

These may well have been early defensive manoeuvres to gain attention from her parents when her envy and jealousy of Eric were at their height. They served to establish patterns of controlling others as well as punishing them. In the light of her ambivalent relationship with her father, her loss of her grandfather's love, her mother's pregnancy occurring so soon after her arrival in England, and the birth of Eric, she seems to have felt overlooked and neglected. By a process of reversal, she turned from the passive experience of being neglected to the active role of avenging herself on her parents. By arousing their anxiety by her behaviour she obtained special attention. It was an unconscious manoeuvre which succeeded but it left her feeling 'horrible' and uneasy. Her inability to apologize might have originated in this period when she may well have felt that it was her parents who should apologize to her. When the situation required her to be sorry, she could not express this because her angry hurt feelings towards her parents were crying out to be heard. But these were held back in silence. 'It just sticks in my throat.' Her feeling that 'it was horrible' perhaps make sense in terms of the aggressive impulses which she was controlling and denying. She could feel in touch with her sadness at the loss of her Indian childhood; she could experience her angry jealousy but her anger towards her parents was denied and she was not fully in touch with it.

Because she felt she could not trust her parents to love her and give her the fullness of their attention, she dared not risk confiding in them about her fears and anxieties. It may well have seemed to the small Vera that there was nobody in whom she could fully confide and to whom she could turn with her feelings. They remained untold and unshared.

It was to her small English friends and their parents that she increasingly turned for her sense of inner security. Her earliest experiences of living in the big lonely house in the Midlands (where they first lodged) were soon replaced by a happy period when they moved into their own home. The English family who lived with them and shared their home had two young daughters who became her great friends. She enjoyed their companionship, the freedom of the garden, and her warm and relaxed friendly relationships with the girls' parents. They were all sharing the house and its amenities and these re-evoked for her her earliest experiences of being one of a happy family group – her Indian past.

These relationships were the first of many warm, secure friendships with English children and adults. It was an English woman – a neighbour – who taught her to read and write before she went to school. As the sole Indian pupil in the school, she felt no differences between herself and the others, was accepted and experienced no prejudice of any kind. As the only Indian family in the neighbourhood, Vera became 'the pet' of English children older than her and of their parents. She felt happy with them. 'They were ever so friendly and always willing to help.' In losing the role as her grandfather's favourite, she had found compensation in becoming her English neighbours' 'pet'. She felt special and loved, was happy and enjoyed being a member of a friendly group.

An important source of her developing sense of identity lay in the social acceptance and group relationships with her English peers. Her membership of the group served as an important source of strength for her and gave her the security and approval which she sought. When the group, by chance, failed her, as when she went to school on a public holiday only to find the gates locked, she returned home crying bitterly and found to her distress that in the streets 'everybody was looking at me'. Without group support, she had several frightening incidents during her early days at school when young boys tormented her, in one instance tying her up with a skipping rope and leaving her alone in a dark and rainy street. She was helped through the intervention of an English woman who untied her and brought her home. 'I didn't ask her to come in. I didn't tell my mother because I didn't like to worry her with things like that; or perhaps I thought it was a weakness. I used to think about it late at night'. The group of English peers represented security and friendly support to her; her own inner fears and anxieties she kept to herself and felt unable to turn to her parents for their emotional understanding.

Feeling closely identified with her English schoolfriends, it was a second traumatic loss to her when she had to leave the Midlands and the warm security of group life and be exposed, not only to this loss but to the harsher realities of a school in London. She left behind her, once more, a home, a neighbourhood where she was made to feel special and a group of good friends. And she came to a situation vastly different from that which she had left. Far from being special and in a unique role, she was one Indian pupil among very many at the school, and experienced racial prejudice for the first time.

She met this crisis, characteristically, alone. Her closest friend, an English girl called Miranda, was never told of her feelings about being treated differently because of being an Indian. Her desire for support and understanding was very great but she was frightened that it might not be forthcoming and so she dared not risk exposing her vulnerability. This difficulty in trusting others was in evidence in her early childhood relationships with her parents and it continued to be her way of coping with loss and distress, even with her closest friends. The following year at school was happier – her teacher was pleasant and showed no prejudice, she worked well and at the end of the year a school trip to Kent, lasting a fortnight, gave her the 'happiest time I can remember . . . I didn't worry about anything at all'. She had re-established a sense of security with her new group of English schoolfriends.

But another separation was imminent when her closest friend went onto a different secondary school from her. She hated the separation and was very unhappy in her first year at the secondary school and once again, she experienced racial prejudice in the classroom. However, characteristically, she gradually made new friends and once more started to enjoy school, although she worked very little. At no time did she resort to stereotypes about racial groups. Her English teachers are seen as individuals, some racially prejudiced, others not. She is fairminded in her comments on them. Although the Youth Employment officer did not assist her to find suitable employment, she recognized that her English school-friends had fared no better. By the time she came to leave school, she had never had an Indian school friend; all her close friends had been English girls. She had gone to their homes and slept overnight there as, in turn, they had been entertained and welcomed overnight in her own home. Colour prejudice was what distinguished one individual from another but was not, to Vera, a quality of any group.

When she came to leave school, her sense of identity was too diffuse to enable her to actively choose a vocation and pursue it with any commitment. She lacked a sense of direction and had given no thought to what she wanted to become. As a result of a chance encounter with a friend she entered the bank, but what was decisive for her in accepting the post as cashier was that working for a bank meant to her a place which was 'safe and secure and everybody's impressed'. Her identity needed both the security with her peers and group approval. She felt re-assured by the warm and friendly reception she received and the familiar glow of security. 'I couldn't face strange faces every morning. I have to feel there are people I know and I have to feel secure. That's why I feel sorry for anyone new who joins us.' She had now been in the job two years and has had several promotions. As well as being the only Indian woman cashier she also has the unique advantage of being able to speak several languages (English, Punjabi and Hindi) and draws an extra language allowance which enhances her sense of worth and her feelings of self-esteem. At one time she tried to obtain work at the airways but she returned with relief since she disliked the other prospects and felt 'relief to get back to the same old faces'.

Her sense of who she is and her wider racial identity are clarified both by what she actively asserts and feels herself to be and by what she repudiates. The girls at the bank don't think of her as an Indian but 'just like one of us' . . . and

> It didn't ever occur to them that I just don't want to be one of them. I'm me and that's it . . . . Or they'll say 'You're really English, Vera' but I don't want to be English. [Laughter] And then they say how odd it is that other Indians aren't like me – and what a shame – and how Westernized I am. But they don't seem to realise that I'm not out to change the world, you know, and that it's just me [laughs] and that's it. If they like me, well, that's good, but I don't really want to be what they seem to imagine. They seem to feel it's a wonderful compliment – they probably mean it nicely. I've heard it so often 'You're so English!', but I don't think it's a compliment–I just don't.

She stands poised between two cultural worlds and can value both the Indian aspects of her heritage as well as the English culture within which she had been socialized, and she recognises that she cannot be understood or responded to as either all one – or all the other. Her English friend Selma is liked for many qualities but especially for the way in which she is able to interest herself in Vera's Indian background, asks about it, but does not express views whose aim is either to modify or alter Vera's cultural values. Both Vera and Selma have respect for their own cultural background and for that of the other. By contrast, another English friend of Vera's revealed her patronizing attitude when she observed '"Well, I don't think I'm prejudiced, because I wouldn't be walking along with you if I were"'. To which Vera responded ' "Oh no, I don't suppose I am either else I wouldn't walk with you, would I?" ' They were both able to laugh.

Because Vera is able to value herself, she can also respect the English as equals. But any attempt on their part to patronize her or to perceive her as a blueprint of themselves, is repudiated. In her late adolescence, and having been exposed throughout her life to considerable cultural conflict, her identity problems express intrapsychic conflicts characteristic of the developmental phase of late adolescence, as well as conflicts aggravated and defined by these two cultural pulls.

At the intrapsychic level, her desire to steadily assume an adult independence and autonomy conflict with her strong feelings of dependence upon her family. Basic to her identity development has been an intense longing for security which, in part, has been expressed through her peer group; but a major part of this has represented a regressive pull back into unmet childhood needs. The Indian traditional family, with its close-knit relationships and stable core, afforded her a source of security. She wants independence and autonomy but clings regressively to the security of home.

> Some girls when they are young can imagine what it's going to be like when they grow up. I've never imagined anything like that – I don't know why . . . When I was younger, I used to think I'd never grow up [laughs] and that used to frighten me . . . . to think I'd be that age all the time . . . Now I'm there, I make plans . . . but it always seems as if I haven't got a future. It always seems that way, I don't know why. It makes me feel different from other girls my age.

Her plans to leave England and go to Canada to settle, represent a forward movement in her identity development where she seems to want to test out her independence but her inner doubts assail her. She characteristically keeps her doubts to herself. 'I never say anything . . . so they don't know how I am feeling. If they do, they've never said and if they did say anything about it, perhaps I'd lie and not really say what I do feel because I don't know how they'd take it.' She cannot risk exposing these anxious fears to her parents in case they fail her and as a result, she will feel that she goes down in their estimation. This difficulty in risk-taking seems to be linked with her early insecurity when she first came to England. When she envisages possibly staying with another family in Canada, an Indian family, she is fearful that in comparing them with her own, it would be hateful if they turned out to be either less worthy or more worthy than her own. So she would like to avoid exposing herself to that risk.

Similar issues of independence arise also in relation to her present social life in London. She has unfortunately no social relationships with men, whether Indian or English, at the present time, and never has had any.

> You don't see Indian girls with white men – but you do see Indian boys going out with white girls. For Indian girls, it just isn't done. The majority are still very much with their parents – they aren't independent. And though I often think I could be independent, I'd hate to think what my parents would have to go through if I was because you know how people talk.

It's easy to say you should ignore what people say, but I think it's very hard actually to come up against it and come out winning. So although I want independence, when I weigh it up, I think I'd feel too insecure, you know . . . . If I had a boy friend, I'd like to be independent and not have to account for everything . . . I don't like to be questioned all the time and they would. Especially my dad—he's very Indian, you know—and he'd hate it if he sees anything like that. He'd give me a long lecture about what happens to girls who go out like this . . . and what people would say . . . you know, the usual arguments.

She projects some of her own doubts into her parents so that she can make them, in part, the reason for her inability to pursue actively that independence which attracts her in various fields. She does not like to upset her mother because she has not been well and she tries to protect both her parents from other people's gossip should she fail to conform to expected Indian patterns. She carried this consideration to such an extreme that she ceased accepting ordinary, friendly and perfectly innocent lifts by car, offered by an English male colleague after work, since she felt that she did not wish to expose her parents to the neighbours' talk especially since there would be no foundation for any gossip.

In her dilemma of whether to conform to her peer group and its values (and her peer group is an English one) or to conform to her parents' expectations and the wider Indian cultural patterns in which she sees them embedded, she weighs both up with ambivalence. Where her choice lies with her parents – as in the case of the turned-down lifts – she seeks to justify that choice by stressing consideration for her parents' feelings.

Vera's ambivalence in relation to her wish for independence, also surfaces in her reasons for wishing that her parents might play some part in the choice of her final husband. If they helped to choose him, this would mean that they accept the responsibility and 'to me, it's a sort of security because then I can blame them if it does not work out well'. On the other hand, the conflict expresses itself in her relief that her cousin has refused, at the last moment, to go through with an arranged marriage, and in her identification with her cousin she comments 'It will show my parents that I wouldn't just marry whom they want me to'.

Her inner fears of being sufficiently able to stand by the emerging adult inside her, are exacerbated by her mother and her mother's cultural values. Mrs Singh was married at fifteen and undertook adult responsibilities from that time. To her, Vera must seem to be grown up and yet Vera lacks many adult domestic skills and her mother prods her so that 'she makes me feel really childish, you know'. She will learn dressmaking 'just to show her'. In short, some of the movement towards her adult identity growth is emanating from a shaming process instituted by a mother who expresses cultural expectations which have ceased to be culturally relevant for Vera, but which were critically important skills for her mother as a very young woman.

At work, the conflict also manifests itself. She is disinclined to teach others the real skills which she has mastered in her work. She fears it will be like showing off 'telling them that I know it and they don't'. She recognises that she does know it but it frightens her to affirm that she is adult enough to have competence and skill and to be able to guide others. Lacking a sturdy sense of her own adult worth and fearful that she might be thought stupid or ridiculous, she is caught between a self-image of herself as 'childish' and the adult self to which she is aspiring. When she envisages teaching others, she fears that she might be seen as 'cocky and know-it-all'. She balances precariously at the present time between the childishness which she fears, and yet to which she partly clings, and the adult independence and responsibility which she wants but is too frightened to risk. 'I don't like responsibility at all . . . any little responsibility sort of nags me'. Her image of herself includes an awareness of how she is able to make good friends and retain them and her capacity to talk to people easily and to be a good listener. But she has doubts about her worth as an individual. 'If I say anything nice about myself, I feel as if I've got a big head . . . I'm hopeless . . . If I think about myself, I only think of the wrong things about myself. I don't ever think of the compensating things.'

At the level of her racial identity, she has a sturdy sense of who she is, her worth and her feelings of straddling the two cultures. Yet she has no models with whom to identify. Her sense of racial identity is being forged from her unique personal experience. 'It's difficult, really, that's why I often wish that we didn't live here at all. If we were in India, I wouldn't have these feelings. It's very hard and I hate to see my sister growing up like this.'

She is troubled by her temper, feels that she is hasty and can, on occasions, be violent and 'break and throw things'. This exposes her to feeling childish. She thinks about it afterwards, wondering how she might have avoided these clashes which are usually with her father. Her swings in mood trouble her because 'I like to be in one mood – I like to feel secure'. It is the unpredictable, the unknown, which troubles her; the familiar, the safe and sure are what she seeks but these in turn trap her because they engulf her in past patterns. The conflict remains: how to go forward, risking new experiences in the face of her need for security and safety.

Her relationship with her mother has been a very good one. They have got on very well and even during her adolescence she had to contrive rows with her in order to feel some identification with her English peers, all of whom recounted rows with their mothers. 'Oh, that makes me laugh now, because it's always interesting – the adolescent bit.' She sees her mother as calm and with a sense of humour so that if she had a row with her mother, she would not take it seriously, unless, of course, it was of some intrinsic significance. She feels her to be a friend with whom she can talk about anything and if they do have an argument and she lapses into her usual quiet sulk, her mother makes the first approach more than any other person does. 'You know, you like to have people come around and say "Are you angry?".'

Her relationship with her father is a more difficult one since she feels that they are so alike in that both of them are quick tempered and neither will give in. But the big rows upset her considerably which, characteristically, she does not let him see. She feels that most of the time his views are right, but it is his way of going about things which she finds difficult. 'It's just the way he says it – just his way, the way he is . . . [very quietly] I love him.' As the elder sister, she is used by her brothers and sister as an intermediary in their difficult dealings with their father.

Unresolved identity conflicts and race
The identity conflict with which Vera struggles at the present time is her desire for autonomy and independence, for adult responsibility and growth, and the fear that this entails risks, uncertainty and the undermining of strong needs for security and dependence on the familiar and known.

Throughout her life, Vera has coped with problems by a retreat into herself; she cries alone, is sad and lonely, wrestles with her problems alone as best she can. Nowhere in her lifestory does she resort to blaming others, or idealizing others. There is little evidence of either scapegoating or tendencies to split-off her good from her bad feelings. To this extent, she is not a person who finds the resolution of her identity conflicts in a gross projection of these conflicts onto racial groups.

The core of her major identity conflict goes back to her earliest uprooting – the loss of her Indian home, and the loving sense of security which she had known. As each loss occurred in her life, she dealt with it by a regressive longing for the period which had preceded it. She wanted to go back. The roots of her security are with her Indian family and her relationships with her parents. But she has grown up in England and with a rare capacity for friendship she has made close friends with English girls. It was the English who made her their 'pet' and took over her missing grandparents' role of loving and spoiling. Life has brought her many satisfying experiences, pleasant and enduring companionship with the English. In the Midlands, she did not go to school with any Indians, nor did she have Indian neighbours. So her familiar world is an English one; her family world an Indian one.

At the bank too, her friends are English and her relationships with them seem secure, forthright and robust so that she has little hesitation in challenging their racial attitudes with humour but also with straight and firm talk. She affirms, just as her mother and father also do in their different ways, a pride and respect for her Indian historic past, her traditions, and for the person she is – an Indian caught in a changing cultural world but nonetheless one who values her race, her culture and her past.

Her challenge to an English relief cashier at the bank who made remarks about Indian immigrants in England was to the point. 'Well, why is it alright for all of you English people to go to Australia and take it away from the aborigines and go to America and take it away from the Red Indians and go to South Africa and take it all away—and yet, it's not alright for us to come over here, you know? You ruled over India!' Later when the woman commented on what a poor country India was, Vera commented that 'in actual fact it wasn't poor until we were ruled over by the English. They just took everything away because it's true – I've been to see these things and there are huge holes in the walls where there were once jewels and they have been taken out, you know, like the Crown jewels – these have mostly come from India.'

The tone and inner conviction with which Vera speaks affirms her beliefs and political attitudes. She is not afraid of risking her relationships with her English friends, since they seem to be secured on the basis of a mutual respect and tolerance for each other. However, when the Indian woman from Kenya started talking to Vera in Punjabi, Vera found this was not only an ignorant thing to do but was causing her embarrassment and making things also awkward for her English colleagues. She resolved to talk to the Indian woman about it.

The English are seen as individuals, and she is able to choose those whom she likes as her friends. However, her contacts with Indian girls of her own age have been much more limited. She has no close friends among them and to a certain extent she uses them to carry aspects of her negative identity. Her identity conflict in relation to adult responsibilities at work evoked in her the fear that if she taught others she would be seen as 'cocky and know-it-all'. This is how she sees Indian girls. They are often 'know-it-alls . . . they come here and think they know it all, when they don't'. Since this is how she tends to see Indian girls, they carry these negative images for her. This, in turn, makes it more difficult for her to overcome *her* fears of being 'cocky' if she feels that she might so be judged by her English friends.

She partly identifies with Indian girls in another respect – also an area of unease in herself with which she is fully in touch. 'I think they are a bit like me . . . they seem sort of cold and they don't want to talk to you. I've never been one to just go up to people and start talking to them. I like them to talk first because I feel so silly.' This keeps her approach to Indian girls limited since neither are able to make the first contact.

Indian youths draw from her aggressive laughter and scorn. Her early feelings of jealousy and envy towards Eric as the first born son, may be influencing her present perception of these Indian youths. 'They think they're God's gift. I'm reduced to laughter when I see some of them round here – they think they're so wonderful. I think it's so useless . . . they seem to show off so much and are so loud'. Unconfirmed in her feminine sexuality by her lack of contacts with men, she needs to see these Indian youths as carrying a brash, arrogant yet empty masculinity. Her isolation from men must be painful for her, working as she does with English girls who have boyfriends. Her scoffing attitudes towards these youths no doubt conceal her longings for a boy-friend of her own.

She has one West Indian girl friend who made the first trusting overtures to her.

> We confide in each other and if we've had a row we tell each other about it and have found that our parents are much the same, row about the same things, and our brothers are the same nuisances. It was quite funny how I confided in her that easily. I think it was because she did in me so I trusted her quite a

bit because I don't trust people very easily. So now when we see each other, we automatically exchange everything quickly. She's a very nice girl and is about the only West Indian girl that has been very close to me.

Vera is one of the three subjects in this study who is not racially prejudiced.

Vicious and virtuous cycles
Her race relationships initiate and sustain virtuous cycles. Without idealizing the English she has made good friends, and they have mutual respect and warmth of feeling for each other. The relationships are robust enough to allow for discussions on race and culture and Vera is able to affirm her values and attitudes in ways which seem to increase respect for her. Her contacts with Indian girls and youths are very limited and there are no instances in her life story of personal encounters.

She deals with people on a fairly reality-oriented basis, is not given to stereotyping racial groups, and sees individuals as individuals and responds to them accordingly.

4 ERIC SINGH

Issues bearing on the formation of his identity
Eric was too young to remember his first separation from his parents but his mother's life story includes a vivid account of how at the age of eighteen months he was put in an institutional nursery for two months, because she was unexpectedly hospitalized prior to the birth of her next child. He was a greatly loved first son and by all accounts, including his own, over-indulged and spoilt. When his wife suddenly disappeared into hospital, Mr Singh took his young son to the residential nursery, and felt that it might only aggravate the child's distress if he went to visit him there. So Eric was unprepared for the disappearance of both his parents, and for two months he was deprived of all contact with his family and must have felt abandoned. On his return home, his mother's sensitively observed comments reveal how angry and hurt he must have felt and his resultant insecurity manifested itself in various ways, all expressive of a lack of trust and feelings of rage. This severely stressful experience for the small boy was followed soon afterwards by the first manifestations of his bronchial asthma which required him to go into hospital on two different occasions for fairly

extensive stays. On neither occasion could his mother stay with him but he was visited often by both parents. By the age of seven, he had been separated from his parents on three different occasions, all of them linked with severe physical and emotional stress. But more was to follow. His asthma was so badly affected by the English climate that as a desperate measure his parents sent him to stay with his grandparents in India in the hope that this might help his condition. He travelled alone to India where he was to remain for two and a half years, although his stay was punctuated by tantalizing visits to England, each of them linked with the hope that he might remain with his parents permanently. But each time his asthma returned with such severity that he had to face another separation and leave once more for India.

When he returned home from the residential nursery, he had to get used to a new baby sister; and when he was in India and his mother came over to visit him, she twice brought with her the youngest child, Keith. On these occasions, understandable envy and jealousy were aroused. His life story reveals some of his awareness of these feelings, which could have been provoked by separations from his parents, and the severe bronchial asthma which may have left him feeling relatively weak and helpless compared with more robust siblings, leading to jealousy of their association with his parents of which he was often cruelly deprived.

He recognizes both the parental indulgence and the jealousy

> Dad used to bring me quite a lot of toys . . . . I think it was because I was the only son at that moment . . . . And then my little sister Pat was born . . . . I used to hide her milk bottle in the piano because I was very jealous of her . . . I was really spoilt then . . . . Well, I used to be jealous of Vera and I used to get jealous a lot about all sorts of things . . . . I wanted everything that she wanted.

Similar themes recur throughout his life story. He also had difficulty in sharing and giving, recognizing this in himself and neither attempting to avoid or deny it.

Whatever unique combination of psychological and physiological factors contributed towards Eric's asthma we cannot know, but present knowledge suggests that asthmatic conditions are produced by a combination of emotional factors interacting with an underlying allergic condition. Certain psychodynamic patterns tend to reappear as central features in these conditions and most studies have focussed on the relationship between the child and the mother.[13] How, in Eric's particular case, his threshold to the susceptibility to asthma was lowered by emotional factors, we cannot precisely know, but whatever its cause the consequences of the asthma in Eric's childhood were not only these frequent separations from parents and siblings but also his geographic and cultural uprooting, with all that that implied for his socialization experiences in two vastly different cultures.

Born in the Midlands, he spoke English and Hindi at home. He recalls the house in which he lived with a sense of pleasure – not only the large garden and the freedom to play which it gave him, but also the friendly English family who shared their house and whose children became his earliest companions.

His admiration and respect for his father are evident and his feelings towards him are warm and personal. 'I slept with my Dad because I was used to sleeping with him. When I was little we got used to it. You know he likes me. He used to love me and I used to sleep with him more than my mum, you know. We all used to get on very well. There was no difficulty.'

His attachment to his mother is also strong and he missed her greatly and knew that she also missed him when he went to India.

> I felt very bad. I was crying all the time. I am always crying at the airport but I couldn't really say anything because if I said I didn't want to go, it was already too late because the seats were booked. They could have cancelled them but I knew it was for my benefit. I wished I could be with my mum and dad but I had trouble and had to get rid of my asthma.

He lived with his grandparents in India and felt that his grandfather understood him. 'But I was mostly unhappy living there with nobody of my own . . . . I got on very well but I did miss my mother and father and when any of my relatives went to England, I always wished I could go with them.'

Since he had had to relinquish so much, it is understandable that he clung onto his few possessions. On his flight to India, plane trouble brought him down for a few days in Beirut and he recalls clinging onto his suitcase with the greatest anxiety lest he be separated from it. In India, he lived with young cousins and he remembers angry fights because 'they did not share things with me so I felt if they didn't, why should I share with them? . . . It's my nature and I still mind if somebody takes something from me. If they had asked me first I would still have said "No". . . it was my nature not to want to give.' Having had to surrender his daily contact with his parents and siblings, and leave the security and love of his home, his sense of deprivation and a lack of satisfying experiences may well have stimulated in him a powerful sense of possessiveness and wanting to hold onto what he had, not wishing to share this remnant with others.

Each time his mother came out to visit him the parting was extremely painful for him, and he might well have felt persecuted by his condition; each time he saw her disappear taking a young brother with her. When, after a year, his parents decided he should return, on his first night home in London he had such a bad attack of asthma that he had to return to India. 'I cried, you know. I told my mother that I don't want to go but she said it couldn't be helped.' The cycle repeated itself. His mother and Keith came to visit him again and 'it was a long time since I'd seen him, but I still missed him and he didn't know I was his brother because Vera and Pat were always at home with him'. And when they left 'I was looking out of the window and crying to myself because I wanted to go home with them.'

At the age of nine and a half, he finally returned to live in London with his parents, where he has remained ever since. Having been deprived of his family for so long, his bonds with his parents have become intensified. His emotional life is greatly bound up with home and his feelings for his father are strong. Even before he went to India and the brutal assault on his father occurred, his recollection of that day and its aftermath, show powerful feelings of empathy with him.

He identifies with his father, sharing many of his attitudes and values, modelling much of his behaviour upon his. Whereas Vera sought her security by turning towards her peer group, Eric, whose contacts with his peer group were broken by his two and a half years in India and who had suffered much dislocation and uprooting, found his security by an intense cementing of his bonds with his family, predominantly with his father. His relationship with him shows signs of some idealization. He admires his dad's career experience and his intelligent grasp of economic and political affairs. He cites his views and aligns himself with his dad's expressed viewpoint.

He says 'If you get an 'A', son, the 'A' stands for something big . . . I don't want you to stick around school unless you study', and I do what he says . . . I have to study now because

I'm aiming to be something and I must be something. My dad says if you want something then you must go after that thing and it isn't easy to aim for things, but you must try as hard as you can. I want to be a radio mechanic and it's quite a hard subject but my dad said that if I did well he might send me to university or to college. So I hope I can do that.

His ego ideals and his father's are extremely close. He values the role played by his father – and also his mother – in helping him to shape his goals and clarify his values.

His school career which had started well, suffered a set-back after his stay in India where he was educated in Hindi. By the time he returned to England, he had lost ground and had to be placed in a lower stream than his ability would otherwise have merited. He is in a class with boys, many of them less intelligent than himself and likely to be less motivated to work. His attitudes towards his fellow scholars – English, Indian and West Indian – need to be understood against that background. At the present time, he describes his classroom situation as being comprised of two conflicting groups – the one English, the other Indian. 'When new boys come to the school (who are West Indian) these English boys gather around him and say "You've got the choice of either fighting with the Indians or fighting with us".' He perceives the English and West Indians as being big and persecutory, the Asians small. 'They pick on us. They are very prejudiced against the Indian boys'.

The picture he gives of the Indian and English groups at school is strikingly similar to that which Adrian James described in the first year of his stay in London. [See Chapter 7, pp. 367–8.] The Asian students pay more attention to their work than the English, they take it more seriously, are more highly motivated and 'try and get on with things'. The English *could* take it seriously if they wanted to but they 'just can't be bothered'. They chat and smoke and

> stick up nudes in the class – they fight and don't care about bashing you up or anything, and they are largely disinterested in class work . . . The English boys are so dumb, you know. They don't know anything about politics and if you asked them they would confuse Scotland with Switzerland. All they really care about is fighting, you know.

In particular, the group of English boys in the B stream with him are felt to be 'very ignorant, full of nonsense and just not caring . . . . all the English boys do is to go to school, have a few fights and go home, have their tea and play football'. He sees their problem as being partly the failure of parental guidance. 'You see, the English boys have got nobody to guide them like my dad guides me.'

In order to cope with his past insecurity and his feelings of envy, jealousy and ambivalence towards his parents, Eric resorts to splitting, denying his ordinary bad feelings, idealizing the good and keeping them separate from each other. His preferred self-image and father-image are both somewhat idealized and these are kept separate from negative and disowned identity elements, which are also likely to be somewhat exaggerated and distorted. He clings somewhat rigidly to ideals of goodness and high aspirations for himself and these are also extended to other Indian youths like himself, but *not* Kenyan Asians. And at the negative pole, the English are seen as *utterly* lacking in these ideals and values, as being lax and undisciplined in their impulses. He attributes the differences between the two groups to parental guidance; Indian parents seen as providing invaluable moral guidance and firm control linked with loving care and high standards. By contrast, English parents are seen as neglectful, disinterested, unable or unwilling to care for their children in appropriate ways, and lacking the high ideals and motivations of Indian parents. Although social and cultural differences between Indian and English parents in Athol may account for some differentiations along these lines, Eric rigidly stereotypes both Indians and English with an all-or-nothing quality. Eric has anchored his emerging identity on a close identification with his father, and therefore seeks to retain the goodness for his parents, himself, and his Indian group. Since his father's own ego-ideals and expectations are exceedingly high, Eric's intrapsychic needs to split and idealize are supported by the model which his father provides. That which is repudiated as bad, feared and unworthy is split-off and attached to his English school fellows; it is one way of dealing with uncertainty in oneself.

Eric tries to cope with the perceived hostilities between Indians and English at school by avoidance and withdrawal. 'I don't say anything to anybody and they don't say anything to me . . . . My dad says "Don't fight." My dad says if you go to school, you go to learn something there. You don't go to fight.' His father threatens him that if he is caned for fighting at school, he will get double punishment from him.

He means what he says, because I do go to school to study and not to fight. I try and keep out of trouble all the time . . . . A lot of big boys pick on me, but I don't take any notice. They are Jamaicans and English and if you start taking notice, then there's trouble.

His father's bitter experience at the time of the brutal assault on him, and his consequent lack of trust in his friends, is not unlike Eric's feelings about his friends.

'I haven't any particular friends at school. I play with my friends but I'm not really fond of them . . . . I don't trust any of my friends . . . I had my fortune told this year by a man who works with my dad . . . and he said that I shouldn't trust my friends because they could betray me. Well, it must be the truth as he is a very good friend of dad's . . . With English friends, we might talk to one another or we might play with one another but we're not quite related. We are not close. I have not really got close friends. There's no one close to me except my family.

This lack of trust appears to be a deeply-seated aspect of his personality and part of his identity. His early experience of having been abandoned in that residential nursery could well have accounted, wholly or in part, for this degree of basic mistrust. But like Mrs James and Adrian James, Eric also seems to have anxieties and defences which stem from the early stages of development, characterized by Klein as the paranoid-schizoid position.[14] Eric has difficulties in bringing love and hatred close together and managing ambivalent feelings, so he resorts to splitting as a way of handling persecutory anxiety.

Eric's capacity to use withdrawal and his inability to be close to his peers, both reflect impaired feelings of trust which surface when his expectations and hopes are rudely upset and disappointed. The classroom situation which he describes could well undermine such feelings of trust as he may have, and push him back regressively into a mistrust of all peer relationships. The original tendency could be a legacy from his earliest developmental stage, but the situation within the school with its emphasis on conflict, suspicion and group hostilities, exacerbates and further emphasizes this trend.

I used to have friends among the English boys but once they start to call me names, then I don't want to know . . . .

> If I walk home with a Jamaican boy in my class, they start to fight with him . . . . And if I am with an English boy, then when other English boys appear, that English boy would call me names. And if we meet Indian boys, the English boy would call the Indian bad names . . . . You know, there used to be quite a lot of friends among us all, but now nobody wants to know anybody . . . So I just don't want to know anyone.

He recognizes how much he owes to his Indian parents and their cultural patterns.

> My upbringing has been different to the English boys around here, because my mother and father care for me and so I've been looked after better than they have . . . . Their mothers and fathers wouldn't have given them the line of education which mine have. I am not as ignorant as they are and I'm better behaved . . . . Also they might speak to the teachers in an ill-mannered way but I respect the teachers . . . . I think I feel very much like other Indian boys – many of us have come from the same sorts of home. But the English are different.

He conforms to his father's views on the permissive society in England, agreeing with him that Indian girls, for instance, should not be allowed to go out with boy friends and Indian men also should not go out with women; both should keep away from the opposite sex until marriage. His views on marriage, divorce and sex are conservatively traditional and do not differ from the views which his father expressed in his interviews. It is impossible to know – since this study was not designed to throw light on this problem – whether the rather rigid over-identification with his father is characteristic of father – son relationships among Sikhs, where attitudes and roles are handed down from generation to generation and upheld by a richly articulated family culture, or whether Eric is unusual in this respect. Eric is the youngest of the male subjects studied. His present rigid self-restraint may start to shift under the impetus of increasing sexual feelings during adolescence.

Unresolved identity conflicts and race
Eric's identity conflicts arise from early insecurity and deprivation and feelings of frailty connected with his asthma. To cope with these, his defences take the form of splitting ideal parents and ideal self,

from those bad others – his English peers and their parents. The unacknowledged parts of himself – his negative identity elements, those feared bad feeling – are projected onto the English group of schoolboys, whose behaviour make them an apparently appropriate repository for these feelings. The reality is distorted into a stereotyped picture, whereby all the English boys are felt to be stupid, lazy, aggressive, badly behaved, sexually free and lacking in drive and ambition. His positive sense of identity is inextricably bound up with his parents' expectations of him, and centre on ideas of hard work, ambition, self-discipline, good manners and behaviour, sexual and aggressive control and restraint.

Just as his ideal self-image incorporates idealized attitudes towards his parents, his negative feelings towards English peers also include negative stereotypes of English parents. While his split-off negative identity feelings attach themselves to English parents, his views on English teachers at school are not stereotyped. They are seen as individuals varying from those who are highly racially prejudiced, to those who are objective and fair-minded in relation to race. Teachers are not seen as parent substitutes; his unresolved identity conflicts are concerned with linked pairs – ideal parents and ideal self as one linked pair, and English boys and their far-from-ideal parents as the other linked pair. His early ambivalence about his parents from whom he was separated on so many occasions, with resultant feelings of uncertainty about his lovability, have apparently led him to split-off ideal self and parents from their opposite, the abandoning, non-caring parents and their resultant English offspring.

It is important to Eric that he be seen and responded to as the person he feels himself to be. The entry into England of many Kenyan Asians is felt to be a threat to him. He fears that there are 'too many of them' and that in other peoples' eyes, he may be confused with these Kenyan Asians. He wonders why they should come to England; this may reflect his early childhood problem about sharing what he has. He believes that the English are wrong to sell houses to them, for by so doing they encourage them to settle in England. Their presence is felt to be a persecutory one, affecting his own sense of 'home' and security. He blames the Kenyan government, the Kenyan Asians and the English people for the increasing prejudice which he senses is building up in England against Asians generally. He realises that if this is so, he too will suffer as a consequence.

What particular behaviours or attitudes of the Kenyan Asians does he feel are a threat to him? He specifies only two issues: the apparent sexual freedom of the young men and the fact that mothers go to work and so neglect their children with resultant effects upon the children's behaviour. Again it is the linked pair – neglectful parents and their neglected children. If the English cannot tell the difference between one Indian (from India) and another (from Kenya) then all that he struggles for in his personal identity will lack confirmation and recognition by others. He fears he can be confused with the anonymous mass.

Despite this, he *is* in touch with some of his less admirable qualities which are common to most. He knows he is greedy, does not like to share, is ungenerous, unkind at times and untrusting; and although he does not like to fight, he can get angry if he does not get his way. But despite these self-insights, he seems to cling tenaciously to his high ideals and a rigid preferred self-image. It is his inability to share and capacity for unkindness which moves him to blame the defence-less Kenyan Asians. They have been banished from their own country and have sought a tenuous security and refuge in England. Yet he resents their intrusion into his world. As a child he was denied the security of *his* family home, so now he feels deprived by others who, homeless themselves, try and join the 'family circle' – his recently regained English homeland. His answer to this threat is to plan to withdraw – to migrate to Canada and to get out of the country. It is his chosen line of defence and it fits in with both Vera's and his parents' plans. They feel that Canada is likely to be better for Indians than England – the Kenyan Asians are felt by them to have exacerbated prejudice in an already prejudiced society.

Eric, his father and mother seem to have similar problems in relation to the identity threat posed by other Asians in this society. They all want to be recognized and acknowledged for their *personal* identity qualities but as the number of Asian immigrants has steadily increased, their personal identities are challenged by negative *group* identity images derived from the other Asians in this society. Eric, in turn, holds unfavourable stereotypes of the Kenyan Asians, and fears that the English may attach the same stereotypes to him.

Vicious and virtuous cycles in race relationships
In inter-racial encounters within the classroom, Eric resorts to avoidance, withdrawal and isolation. By so doing he expresses his chosen unconscious defences but he is also incidentally meeting his father's expectations of him – not to fight. By the act of withdrawal, he is able to invest even more energy in his work, so strengthening his positive sense of identity. If the classroom situation is accurately

perceived in its essential characteristics (and Adrian James' description tends to confirm its *general* accuracy), then Eric has not many alternatives open to him except to engage in open conflict with English boys, so meeting fire with fire. By not choosing to do this, he avoids a vicious cycle of aggression and counter-aggression. Although his feelings and attitudes are negative towards the English boys, his behaviour fails to reflect this in overt form but his silent disapproval may well come across. His basic sense of mistrust, makes him less vulnerable to deep hurts at the hands of his peers; but these hurts re-inforce his already established philosophy of mistrust.

Although his *overt* behaviour may not feed a vicious spiral in relationships with the English, nonetheless he cannot initiate virtuous spirals either. He is trapped in a split world involving group stereotypes; and his emotional blockages in relation to close friendships, keep him encapsulated, so that nothing new can happen at the inter-racial level.

But he does feed vicious spirals in his patterns of racial misuse of both English and Kenyan Asians; these may not take overt behavioural forms, but antipathy and negative stereotyping are impingements on the identity processes of the groups so misused.

TRANSFERENCE AND COUNTER-TRANSFERENCE EFFECTS

Both our role as social scientists and our association with the University of Sussex markedly influenced the way in which Mr Singh related to us. At the time of the initial interview he took a dominant role and expressed enthusiastic interest in the research and willingness to become a subject. In contrast with other respondents, from the outset he viewed us with marked respect and deference and since I was the one to interview him personally, and was the older and more senior of the two of us, he increasingly accorded me a more and more elevated status. During my interviews with him, the idealization became more apparent as did the veneration. I later came to realize that these qualities with which I was invested, had always been an extremely important part of his own values and inner life. I came to symbolize for him the achievement of his thwarted educational ambitions, the status and community recognition which he had always sought and which had been salient values throughout his life.

I felt increasingly uncomfortable and restive at being idealized and placed on this pedestal of learning, particularly as my major research task in the field was to relate to him personally and help him to feel comfortable within the relationship so that he might talk freely about himself, his experiences and feelings. The part of himself which needed to use me in this way, was the part of himself which hid behind formidable intellectual defences. It was also the self-idealized part of himself which by projective identification he put into me. I did not feel that he related to me as the person I am, but as an ideal object unconsciously used for identification purposes.

At the transference level, Mr Singh unconsciously used the interview situation to meet two related inner needs. First, association with English people who were obviously motivated to learn about him personally and about his family as individuals, contrasted with his many negative experiences with other English people, unable or unwilling to distinguish one Asian from another. This aspect of the study he clearly enjoyed and valued. But what interests me is that while he rightly objected to an ascribed and distorted identity based on race, foisted onto him by ignorant English people, at the counter-transference level I was aware of his ascribing to me an idealized identity based on occupational role and status, to which I was inwardly objecting. Secondly, what I came to see was that in elevating me, he was, by association and by processes of projective identification, elevating himself. Association with scientists who were middle class and invested by him with very high professional status make him feel valued, appreciated and respected which his life story shows is what he has sought throughout his life.

At times, in the series of interviews, I succeeded in getting Mr Singh to talk freely and personally about himself and his feelings but most interviews also included lengthy and highly generalized accounts of his views, attitudes and moral preoccupations. At the terminal interview he commented, in answer to the question of whether I had reminded him of anyone he had known, that I had not but added that 'he had enjoyed my company', and went on to add additional accolades.

His wife's relationship with me was very different. Unable to use English with fluency, her feelings and her life story were expressed not only through words but also through expressive mime and body language. She related to me personally and directly and with apparent emotional involvement. Her interviews always required from her quite strenuous efforts, both in concentration and the expressive aspects of her material. I found myself very fully used in each interview, bringing into play all the insight which I could find to understand what she was trying to convey to me. I felt absorbed in the process and able to feel empathy for her as a person. At the terminal interview she commented that I was 'like a sister' to her.

Sylvia Hutchinson experienced both Vera and Eric as somewhat more defended in their responses to her than were the West Indians. Although both Vera and Eric related well to her, neither ventured so readily into deeper levels of reflection. Some of the content which each brought up in their interview material happened to touch on conflict areas in herself, which might have made it more difficult for her to feel wholly at ease, and this perhaps communicated itself unconsciously to them. She was aware of these sensitive areas which were being prodded, and to this extent they are unlikely to have affected the material to any marked extent. She did not remind them consciously of anyone they had known but Eric commented 'I like her; she's very good at listening and understanding'. And Vera, feeling that she had spoken so much wondered why Mrs Hutchinson had not fallen asleep?

DISCUSSION

Within the Singh family, two members – Mrs Singh and Vera – do not resort to racial misuse, while Mr Singh and Eric both do and in their case, there is once again a direct link between their unresolved identity conflicts and patterns of racial misuse.

Mr Singh and Eric (and also Mrs Singh) all seek confirmation from the English of their personal and social class identities. Each feels a sense of identity vested in status, intelligence, educational achievement, integrity, character and moral values on which their self-esteem has been grounded. To the extent that the English are seen as being racially prejudiced and ignorant, they are also perceived as unable or unwilling to differentiate between one Asian and another. As a result, these three members of the family feel denied that which they seek, and in addition are threatened by an ascribed inferior identity based on race, derived predominantly from stereotyped images of lower class Asians in England. These images include notions of lower standards in personal and family life, in character and moral qualities than they personally feel they have achieved. Whereas Mr Singh and his son Eric handle this conflict in somewhat similar ways both involving racial misuse, Mrs Singh deals with it differently.

Both father and son share in common high ego-ideals (with some self-idealization) and these become increasingly elevated as a way of distancing themselves from images of lower class Asians. As their standards become more demanding, these in turn affect the standards by which they judge the mass of Asians in this country (or in Eric's case, the Kenyan Asians). Because they are found wanting, each feels impelled by the negative attributions which are coming towards them from the English, to increase their expectations of themselves still further. This creates a vicious escallating spiral. Splitting processes are also involved by which rigid self-idealization and family idealizations are kept separate from the bad aspects of lower class Asian life (or in Eric's case, bad aspects of life among the Kenyan Asians). These idealizations being rigid and too exacting, in turn, create a need to offload onto others failures to live up to such high standards.

Mr Singh misuses both the English and lower class Asians whom he denigrates in different ways; Eric contrasts idealized self and idealized parents with bad English parents and their children, seeing these English pairs in stereotyped and negative ways along with the Kenyan Asians. Both blame the English as the cause of their resultant feelings as they are unable to differentiate between one Asian and another; both perceive different groups of Asians as posing threats to their self-image.

Mrs Singh is much more in touch with her good and her bad qualities and is able to sustain ambivalence. As a result, she does not stereotype racial groups but deals with the negative identity attributions which are foisted onto her by firm, reality-oriented personal confrontations, based on her role as a consumer and shopper. Racial misuse is not called into play. Like Johanna James, she turns back against herself her frustrations and suffers psycho-somatically as a result.

Vera's unresolved identity conflicts take a different form from the rest of her family. Embedded in her family culture and yet socialized in a peer group culture which is English, she resists all racial identity attributions. She wants none of it, but demands to be seen as the individual person she has become. She is the only Singh family member studied who seems relatively indifferent to class issues. While major unresolved identity conflicts in the men of this family are worked out through two racial groups, the West Indians play virtually no role in the inner life of this family with the exception of Vera who has a close West Indian friend.

Like the James family, the Singhs cope with the stresses of life through active strivings for competence and mastery in the area of work. Mrs Singh's chosen arena is the home. In all cases, their energies tend to be harnessed to constructive and positive goals which are ego-enhancing. All four Singhs are able to stand up for themselves and affirm their personal values and worth. In personal inter-racial encounters the three older members of the family will challenge someone of another race if their personal identity has been assailed by racial prejudice. The form of challenge is firm, dignified, angry but restrained. It is only Eric who tends to avoid the confrontation, but the encounters he has to deal with are of a physically violent and provocative kind, demanding a different response.

BIBLIOGRAPHY AND NOTES

1 Hiro, D. *Black British, White British*, Eyre & Spottiswoode, London (1971), p.144.
2 Piers, G. and Singer, M. B. *Shame and Guilt: A Psychoanalytical and Cultural Study*, Charles C. Thomas, Springfield, Ill. (1953).
3 Hiro, D. (1971), *Op.cit.* p.122.
4 Piers, G. and Singer, M. B. (1953), p.16.
5 At the time of the initial interview, Mr Singh told us in detail the humiliating aspects of these years and how he finally came to face these shameful parts of himself. This was said in front of his four children, the two younger ones having, by then, joined the family group.
6 Erikson, E. H. *Gandhi's Truth: On the Origins of Militant Nonviolence*, Faber & Faber, London (1970), p.402.
7 *Ibid.* p.36.
8 *Ibid.* p.305.
9 *Ibid.* p. 37.
10 *Ibid.* p. 37.
11 *Ibid.* p. 37/38.
12 The University of California study showed that girls and boys when asked to construct a scene with toys on a table, used space differently. The girls revealed an absorption with interior play scenes, sometimes being intruded upon by animals or dangerous men. Boys concentrated on high towers, exterior scenes, accidents, dangers and collapse being the hazards. Erikson, commenting on the meaning of this study, suggests a profound difference between the sexes in the experience of the ground plan of the human body, relevant throughout life and affecting the elaboration of roles for men and women. See: Erikson, E. H. *Childhood and Society*, Norton, New York (1963), second edition, Chapter 2.
13 Alexander, F, French, T. and Pollock, G. *Psychosomatic Specificity – Experimental Study and Results Vol. 1*, University of Chicago Press, Chicago, (1968), p. 12.
14 Klein, M. *Our Adult World and its Roots in Infancy and other Essays,* Heinemann (1963).

Chapter 10

RACIAL SPIRALS

In Chapter 1 it was argued that by choosing to study unresolved identity conflicts an essential point of entry is gained into the spirals of reciprocity and interaction between the races, which is the central task of this study to explore. The preceding three chapters have focussed on the individual and, as a result, the incessantly interactive and reciprocal nature of the processes at work between the races could not be held effectively in focus long enough to enable them to be described and understood in general terms. In this final chapter I move away from the individual life as a focus to concentrate on those general processes which seem to be at work.

Since the processes concerned are exceedingly complex and in constant flux – as well as being interlocking – it is difficult to present them clearly. It seems only possible to do it bit by bit, so that cumulatively the parts of an intricate pattern are assembled into a rough theoretical model which, however inadequate, may nonetheless serve the useful purpose of depicting what has emerged from this study about the interactive relationship between unresolved identity conflicts and racial misuse. Despite the inherent human interest and rich variety of the twelve life histories, the essential contribution of this investigation lies in the development of ways of thinking about identity and race, about the theoretical questions to which it gives rise and about their implications.

The generic processes which are seen as linking unresolved identity conflicts and the misuse of racial groups are not thought of as being substantially different in kind from those which might be discerned if the study had focussed, not on racial groups, but on (for instance) social class or religious groups in societies where such categories were highly distinctive and invested with emotional significance. In communities with or without multi-racial populations, but where there are well-defined group differences, similar links may well occur between unresolved identity conflicts on the one hand and, on the other the misuse of such social groups. The interlocking spirals of destructiveness in Northern Ireland or the civil war between Muslims and Christians in Lebanon, to cite only

491

two examples, both point to deep conflicts within a society where race is not the issue. But since the major concern of this book is with race, the model (although it indicates where other group processes of the type suggested may occur), nonetheless is specifically directed towards showing how identity conflicts and race processes relate.

1 INDIVIDUALS AND GROUPS

We are all social beings, living within social structures, and throughout life we constantly interact with others and react to what is coming to us from these others. Depending upon how we are constituted we, in turn, make use of this. Among these cumulative interactions are those involving interactions with social groups. All societies distinguish between groups in terms of their status, power and social characteristics, and each person belongs to a number of ascribed groups, membership of which become an important part of identity. We are all members of a racial group, whatever our views on racial categorizations may be, and we are therefore likely to be seen by others to be part of such a group; but at the same time we also are placed in a number of other social categories to do with social class, religion, occupational role and whatever other social groups are relevant within a particular community. Some of these groups are fluid and informally constituted, such as those designated by local lore, for example, as the 'goodies' or the 'baddies', the intellectuals, the drop-outs, diverse groups in fact based on different ideological bases and different life-styles.

All these groups serve important functions, both consciously and unconsciously, in our lives. They provide a means, however grossly misleading and however we may in some contexts deplore this, of differentiating and distinguishing between people and their ascribed characteristics; these, in turn, help people to locate and define themselves in various ways relative to others. Our group affiliations become aspects of our identities, while at the same time crystallizing how we may differ from, or resemble, people in other social groups. Whether we accept or rebel against a group into which we may have been born or graduated by choice, chance or achievement, nonetheless this process serves as a way of clarifying identity and by means of a process of comparisons and contrasts, leads to a sharper sense of one's own identity and, developing alongside, an improved awareness of certain aspects of the identity of others.

In the context of this study, the most important function served by groups is largely an unconscious one. Throughout development, but especially when under stress, we all at times use social groups as repositories for our projections, providing a way out for the individual from experiencing inner conflicts that he would otherwise consider too disturbing or painful to face. These projections do not emanate only from the bad and denied parts of the self but also from the idealized parts of the self. Sometimes this process is sanctioned by society, whether openly or covertly. When it forms part of an explicit social ideology or during times of war or incipient group conflict, the process is open and overtly sanctioned. A lot of the time it merely receives covert acceptance within one's own reference group. This may be a regrettable aspect of social life but it is nonetheless a constant feature of the way we all use groups. The groups chosen as repositories are felt to be 'safe' in the sense that they are unconsciously regarded as fitting receptacles to 'hold' the anxiety and contain it. Since racial groups outwardly differ in appearance, the choice of a racial group as a repository for unwanted and denied aspects of the self is particularly seductive, because it gives the added advantage of putting a wider visible social distance between the person acting to offload denied aspects of his identity and the racial group chosen as a receptacle.

2 RACIAL GROUPS AS POWERFUL SOCIAL MAGNETS

Although race constitutes only one kind of socially differentiated group within society, nonetheless racial groups possess distinctive and unique aspects which make them more susceptible to exploitation by others for the unconscious working-through of unresolved inner conflicts. It is above all else the visibility of skin-colour differences, physical type and appearance which distinguish one race from another. These act as visual signals and they very easily become associated in people's minds with a range of social characteristics, status factors and roles which, while not part of racial differences as such, often become linked with racial groups by the process of association. Pervasive cultural differences expressing differences in attitudes, values, traditional habits, ways of emotionally expressing oneself in both words and gesture, and moral codes, are all part of cultural learning and tend to vary between one racial group and another because of common cultural backgrounds and traditions. As a result of the high visibility of racial appearance, these become falsely perceived as part of a racial difference. In addition, where historic, economic and political factors have led to patterns of racial discrimination within a society, these in turn express and facilitate an institutionalized racism within a society so that certain racial groups suffer different degrees of deprivation in regard to education, wages, health, housing and employment. These disabilities, because they occur disproportionately within certain racial groups, all too readily become falsely linked and confused with the outer visible insignia of race. As a result, not only do racial groups become concentrated within certain social classes, but also, for the same reasons, occupational roles are disproportionately held by certain racial groups, which adds to the racial stereotyping. Striking among such occupational role differentiations are those often filled by the disadvantaged, namely the menial and dirty jobs or those involving shift work, which others in the society tend to avoid. Race therefore acts as a powerful magnet, cumulatively drawing into its net a variety of realistically perceived cultural, social, economic and educational differentials which become falsely but inextricably perceived as part of a racial difference.

In addition to all the above features, skin colour differences *per se* stir up unconscious images within different societies, by which symbolic qualities and notions attributed to both black and to white as colours tend to follow universal patterns which have endured over time.[1] This leads some people to link a particular skin colour unconsciously with specific psychological attributes which the individuals of this group may or may not have but which arise from symbolic associations with colours as such. McDonald[2] has studied the role of skin colour with its attendant anxieties and associated ideas intensively and shown the effects these have upon both black and white children in the United States. Primitive mechanisms are aroused by skin colour, so that a different coloured skin may not be recognized for what it actually is, with the result that its owner cannot possibly be recognized for his or her human and uniquely individual identity. Brown and black are colours in many racially mixed societies which are associated with ideas symbolizing death, dirt or danger while white tends to be attached to notions of purity, goodness, chastity, innocence and cleanliness. These ideas of course, are rarely conscious within the context of racial encounters but they reverberate at a deep and disturbing level and add their weight to other currents of feeling.

3 CONCEPTUAL 'SHAPE' OF THE MODEL: A SPIRAL

The shape that the processes take in this model is thought of conceptually as being a spiral rather than a circle, since while there is constant movement in the interactive and reciprocal cycles, nonetheless these are not mechanically repetitive. Although the interplay between identity processes and the misuse of racial groups may seem at times to follow inexorably repetitive behavioural patterns of action and reaction, nonetheless, both in respect to the multiple meanings which these have and the effects to which in turn they give rise, they are viewed here as cumulatively developmental and everchanging.

Conceptually, spirals can be thought of as ascending and benign or descending and vicious, and also as capable of changing course from ascending to descending and *vice versa*.

4 THE BARE ELEMENTS OF THE INTERACTIVE SPIRAL

At the outset the conceptual spiral is presented as a bare skeleton set within a particular environing society with its own history in relation to race and with its distinctive, social, economic and political structure. Bit by bit the flesh will be added (see Diagram I).

The diagram has three interactive constructs. Firstly, there are the unresolved identity conflicts which arouse anxiety in the individual and, by putting an individual's feelings of security in jeopardy, may cause him to deny or avoid the painful nature of various identity conflicts by resorting to a variety of defence mechanisms. We all, whether healthy or neurotic, use defence-mechanisms and since identity conflicts are also universal these are normal everyday processes.

Disowned aspects of identity are all too readily projected by individuals onto racial groups, imposing on them these denied images. These and other defensive manoeuvres, which will be fully discussed later in this chapter, establish a link between unresolved identity conflicts and racial misuse; and although this link is subject to other influences to be developed shortly, for present purposes the point I am making is concerned solely with three interactive constructs and the way the processes move. The target racial groups which are used as repositories for the projections of the primary racial groups are provoked into protecting themselves from these impingements upon, and infringements of, their identity processes. This in turn, modifies and affects *their* unresolved identity conflicts and so leads them in turn to use defence mechanisms also and thus to resort to the misuse of racial groups. This impinges back

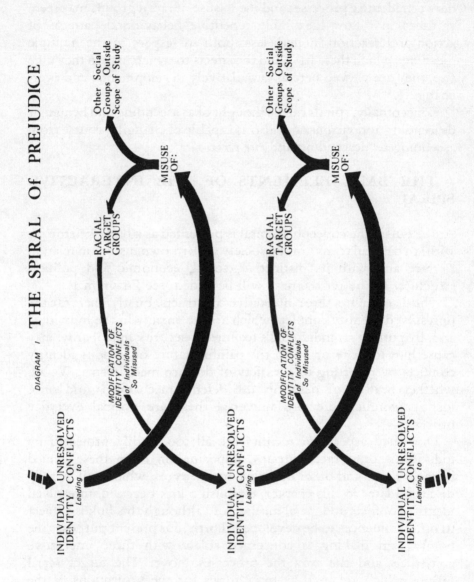

DIAGRAM I · THE SPIRAL OF PREJUDICE

upon the primary groups, and begins to promote a further twist to the spiral. This is the essence of the spiral, interlocking processes linking unresolved identity conflicts with racial misuse.

In short, the theory advanced here is that part of the ordinary life of multi-racial communities involves us all in the use of racial groups in these ways, and in turn we also are so used by others in the course of their attempts to handle their unresolved identity conflicts. There are important differences in the type and extent of racial misuse resorted to, in its intensity and fixity and in the relative positions of power and influence of the racial groups concerned, which make the powerful less vulnerable and the powerless excessively vulnerable to these forms of racial misuse.

Hauser[3] in a study on identity development among white and black lower-class youths in the United States has shown how differing racial, social and cultural conditions affect identity issues among both whites and blacks. But although he exposed how identity issues are modified by impingements upon them of the projections made by other racial groups, he did not follow this through to explore how, in turn, these identity conflicts continued to be reflected in, and to alter race relationships.

Although much excellent work has been done to show the cruel impingements on the individual and the conflicts to which these give rise in black minorities,[4] the other side of the spiral has received little attention. Even in those countries where there is a dominant white population, as in the USA, South Africa or Rhodesia, the racial projections which are being 'beamed' towards the white man may not be received loud or clear because of the coercive pressures of institutionalized racism and the penalties and consequences for the minority of making their feelings explicit. The 'black consciousness' movements, in these countries have arisen however, because of the identity impingements and infringements to which their subordinate status cruelly and consistently exposes them; what is being proclaimed is their response to that assault on their identity. This is part of the spiral process by which racial misuse has led to identity issues and their resultant conflicts, which, in turn, move the momentum of the racial spiral forward into a new cycle.

5 TRANSITORY OR FIXED PROCESSES

These processes can, at best, be only of a transitory nature: fluid, dynamic processes which are part of normal and healthy trial and error transactions in the service of conflict resolution and potential growth, with enhanced capacities to deal more effectively with reality at a later stage. In such cases the individual is using an emergency device to distance an ill-defined something from the self. However by the very act of distancing, it acquires definition, so that what has been attributed to a racial group 'out there', may later on be able to be re-integrated and more readily accepted as part of the self, the person remaining unaware of the intervening emergency step which had been taken. When this happens the process has been a fruitful one for the person concerned and he or she can now move forward again towards a greater wholeness and be more fully in touch with his or her feelings. Moreover, if the process is transitory and not too violent in its attributions or in the behaviour to which these may lead, no great harm may have been done to the racial groups so used.

But under less favourable conditions, instead of a fluid and short-lived process, stereotyped images are attributed to one or more racial groups with fixity and rigidity, and intense and often deeply destructive processes are set in motion. Aspects of individuals become inextricably tied up with the racial group and people are unable to test ideas against reality. As a result these fixed images cannot be withdrawn and the defensive energy keeps the process going. The racial repository has become a permanent, locked safe. Identity conflicts in an individual cannot shift readily when parts are locked up in another racial group. Once this happens individuals tend to justify the racial prejudice with all its distortions by finding something to despise and denigrate in the group so chosen in order to reduce feelings of guilt. Attitudes are rationalized in order to gain social approval; and rationalizations conceal the deep underlying function which such racial prejudice serves. Once a choice of racial groups has been made, processes of closure tend to make the selection permanent and help to sustain the stereotype. Later in this chapter the problem of why some individuals are more prone than others to use transitory or fixed receptacles among racial groups will be discussed.

6 THE 'FIT' BETWEEN VULNERABLE AREAS IN THE INDIVIDUAL AND RACIAL STEREOTYPES

Identity conflicts are ever-present but they vary in intensity and significance from one period to another. They are particularly provoked under the pressure of various forms of stress such as developmental changes during adolescence or the mid-life crisis, the upheaval of immigration, or having immigrants move into an area previously without them. Unresolved conflicts constitute particularly *vulnerable areas* in the personality. Under the stress of anxiety these vulnerable areas can be easily 'touched-off', resonated or stimulated, by one or another of these factors:

1 Realistic features of different racial groups, which are seized upon by the individual and distorted.
2 Prevailing stereotyped images of these groups.
3 Phantasy ideas arising from the imagination.

What seems to happen in the case of each of the first two factors is that the individual's vulnerable areas are unconsciously resonated or stimulated by specific images or features of the group which most readily offer the opportunity for an unconscious 'fit'. Selective attention is shown to just those features which 'fit' the vulnerable areas. But these specific features, by being taken out of the whole complex pattern of which they form only a small part, are seized upon and elaborated into stereotyped images to justify the usage, and in the process undergo distortion and exaggeration. The individual, as a way of rationalizing the function which this is unconsciously serving, uses these specific features, now elaborated and distorted, and applies them as absolute, falsely applicable to all members of the racial group concerned, in a blanket condemnation. In such cases reality testing is resisted and inadequate.

An example of the way in which vulnerable areas are initially resonated by the first factor – *realistically* perceived features of another racial group – would be, for instance, Elaine Chattaway's delay in menarche, making her especially vulnerable to aspects of femininity which she sees as a feature of young Asian women, their saris, physical grace and feminine make-up contrasting with other racial groups within the school. Her perceptions may be accurate ones but her reaction is an intensified one, leading to resultant distortions and disparaging blanket condemnations. This process facilitates stereotype-building because attributes of a group become the focus of distortion and of intensely perjorative imagery, containing the projective elements which emanate from the preoccupations of the individual concerned.

Long-established racial stereotypes – the second factor – unfortunately abound in many societies and to a greater or lesser extent are afforded some social sanction, however covertly. There are a vast range of stereotypes other than race which are in common use to maintain equilibrium as for example those of social class, gender roles, child and adult roles, and stereotypes of various occupations. As a recipient for certain projections but not for others, once a racial stereotype exists, that group is readily exploited as a repository for those specific projections. For example, Mrs Chattaway's vulnerable areas, constituted by unresolved conflicts arising from her uncontrollable and aggressively noisy young son and her overtly aggressive elder son, John, and the conflicts these cause her as a mother, as well as her vulnerable areas to do with revived sexual anxieties, seize upon the existing stereotypes of blacks which tend to cluster around their imputed aggressive feelings and superior sexual performance, both of which she links with ·West Indians.

In the third category – phantasies – belong those racial groups who are relatively unfamiliar with each other and it is they who are more likely to attract to themselves varied primitive and often bizarre projections of those parts of the personality least adequately integrated into an abiding sense of identity. In this group would fall those phantasy features and ideas arising from ever-active remnants of childhood longings. Many of these have a quality of wish-fulfilling day-dreams expressing deep longings for an unfulfilled 'Golden Age', a 'Garden of Eden'. People in this group are filled with profound feelings that other racial groups have internally achieved and possess that which they have not, abundant sources of love, care and inner contentment. Perhaps Elaine Chattaway is the subject who comes closest to this kind of phantasy since she sees the Indians and Pakistanis as having all the love and attention from teachers as well as wealth and clothes and a life of ease.

Whether or not racial stereotypes fall into any of these categories they are always, by their very nature, in error because of the distortions; they are also dehumanizing in their effects because they are applied absolutely to all members of a racial group without distinction. They attribute to that group aspects of unresolved identity conflicts which preoccupy those resorting to the stereotyping. Furthermore in most stereotypes there are false causal imputations, either explicitly or implicitly stated, by which racial variables are held to account for differences which lie in historic, cultural, social-environmental and psychological areas.

7 THE CHOICE OF PARTICULAR RACIAL GROUPS AS REPOSITORIES

In Chapters 7, 8 and 9 it has been shown why each individual subject chose one racial group rather than another for those unacknowledged parts of themselves. These choices are unconscious, the vulnerable areas constituted by the unresolved conflicts acting as if magnetized, propelling themselves towards a likely repository; and if none suitable is available, the individual uses phantasy to re-make reality. Only a longitudinal study could throw light on what happens as new identity conflicts occur. Are the same racial groups used or is there a shift to more 'fitting' ones?

Among our subjects, Adrian James (the West Indian youth), affords a striking example of how an unresolved identity conflict may continue over time and within two different societies (Barbados and Britain), different racial groups serving as repositories for the same vulnerable areas sensitized by unresolved conflicts. While in Barbados, he was struggling to contain understandably hurt and angry feelings arising from fears of abandonment, and fellow West Indians – boys bigger and older than he – were used as a group to carry his disallowed aggressive and frighteningly destructive impulses for him. When he came to this country, white English boys at his school came to exemplify for him these same qualities of out-of-control bullies, bent on aggressive destruction. But as he steadily developed stronger inner resources and became re-integrated into a loving family he was able to express successfully a socially acceptable form of aggression both in sport and within the classroom, so gaining the recognition of both peers and staff. He no longer has the same anxiety about his angry feelings, nor are they likely to be as strong as in the past. He is able to withdraw his projections from the English boys and can to see them as individuals more like himself.

Those defence mechanisms which a person habitually uses play a decisive role in the actual choice of racial groups. For example, if the major unconscious need served by using a racial group as a repository is to offload certain feelings or attributes, denying that they belong to the self, then the group to which these are attributed through projection and displacement will be selected to afford as great a contrast as possible to the individual's racial self-image. The group chosen is felt to be alien and different. In this way maximum psychological distance is sought from the choice of group.

Individuals who are particularly prone to resort to envy and jealousy will select a group whose relevant qualities, under ordinary circumstances, would arouse positive feelings of regard or even admiration which envy and jealousy then convert destructively into something negative and deplorable. For instance, John Chattaway, heavily burdened with anxieties and conflicts relating to intellectual adequacy, focusses on the high aspirations, potential ability and work achievements within the school of Asian schoolboys (a relatively high proportion of whom proceed to 'A' levels), attacking them with envy and so converting these into something negative.

By contrast, those people who, under the stress of anxiety, habitually resort to splitting in order to keep the ideally good qualities and the people who symbolize them as far apart as possible from those which are felt to be exceedingly bad, choose two contrasting racial groups to serve these purposes. They seek groups whose stereotyped images resonate each extreme. Mrs Geraldine James, for example, selects the idealized, too-good, nurturing parental figures as stereotyped images of the English group and contrasts this with the too-quarrelsome divisiveness equated with her siblings and which she, in turn, ascribes as stereotyped images to her own West Indian group, particularly to peers in a working situation. (It is interesting to note that at work they are under the control of supervisors so images related to the family – parents and children – emerge in both parts of the split.)

8 THE SAME PERCEIVED ATTRIBUTES OF RACIAL GROUPS RESONATE DIFFERENT RESPONSES

It follows that since the contents of stereotyped images are partly projective of underlying conflicts, they tend to be symptomatic of inner determinants within individuals, and so the same attributes of racial groups mean different things to different people. The identity analyses have yielded many examples of this, of which three are cited here: 1 Whereas both Mr and Mrs James observe and reflect on Indians who talk in their own language, to Mr James this at times meant exposure to what was felt to be rude affronts to his self-esteem, leading to feelings of exclusion and rebuff. Underneath his response was an envious regard for those who have a language of their own which had not been forcibly wrested away by the historic events of slavery, forced uprooting and colonial exploitation. To Mrs James, however, Indians talking in their own language did not upset her because they played into her chosen defences of avoidance and denial. 'What you don't know, doesn't hurt you – they don't bother me and don't trouble me.'

2 In the Singh family, Mr Baldev Singh and his wife Tara both resent what they see as the incapacity and unwillingness of the English to make an effort to distinguish between one Indian and

another, one social class and another; and they both react sharply to not being seen and responded to as the individuals they rightly feel themselves to be. They both repudiate the projection on to them of the racial stereotypes which they experience as imputations coming from the English. To Baldev Singh these in turn lead to stereotyped images which he holds of the English as ignorant and indifferent to the individualities of others like himself; but he is also prodded by this situation towards increasingly rigid idealized self-images as a way of compensating for his bruised feelings. Mrs Tara Singh however, does not stereotype racial groups and possesses a more stable and well-integrated sense of her own identity. She is able to handle these situations with a quiet affirmation of who she is, firm and dignified and with no resultant tendency towards racial prejudice.

3 The attributions of being hard-working, intelligent, ambitious and aspiring are accorded to Asian schoolboys by both Adrian James and John Chattaway and yet to Adrian these qualities are admirable and embody an aspect of his own positive self-image but one which he is unable to experience and make real for himself at that point in his life; as a result he idealizes and admires the Indians for these very qualities, while John, handicapped in life by a fragile grasp of his own more slender intellectual resources, disparages and attacks these attributes in envious destructiveness.

9 PSYCHOLOGICAL FUNCTIONS SERVED BY RACIAL MISUSE: UNRESOLVED IDENTITY CONFLICTS INVOLVING THE MISUSE OF RACIAL GROUPS

What is it that people unconsciously seek to gain by racial misuse and the prejudice which it expresses? Racial prejudice occurs so universally and is so widespread in different societies that it clearly serves a psychological need, however deplorable this may be from the point of view of society and of those misused. What it seems to do for the individual is to protect and preserve his identity and bolster a psychological equilibrium which is felt to be precarious; and although the positive gain of holding anxiety temporarily at bay is bought at a very high price, both to the individual expressing the prejudice and to the victims, nonetheless there are short-term gains.

In the preceding three chapters the multiple and frequently contradictory determinants of each person's feelings and attitudes towards racial groups is traced in detail. From this it emerges that prejudice does not always arise in the same way.

Patterns of racial misuse differ in the psychological functions which these serve and they vary widely from person to person. By bringing these twelve identity analyses together, six different types of unresolved identity conflict are found to account for the 'spillage' into the racial area. Each of these involves distinctive defence mechanisms which have certain consequences both for the individuals employing them and for the racial groups used as repositories. I will now present these six types of identity conflict, but in so doing I am not in any way suggesting that everyone experiencing such conflicts is necessarily, and always, propelled towards racial misuse. What I am saying however, is that in the life history material it is these conflicts which spill over into the racial area and which account for all the examples of racial prejudice found. Later in this chapter I will be looking at the three subjects, who, while they experienced conflicts similar to the six types to be presented, nonetheless did not take them out on racial groups, and I hope to demonstrate what distinguishes these three people – Mrs Tara Singh, Vera Singh and Johanna James – from the rest of the subjects.

If a person experiences and has difficulty in resolving any of these identity conflicts it does not follow that racial prejudice is inevitable. It is not a question of the presence or absence of conflict. A far more complex picture emerges, involving a pattern of interactive inner and outer forces. This underlines the view taken throughout this study that in human behaviour there are seldom direct lines of cause and effect by which the simple presence or absence of certain inner conflicts will mechanically lead to specific outcomes. The position taken is that each of us attempts to negotiate between complex, changing and often conflicting inner and outer forces, many of which are interactive and amongst which issues of choice also play some part.[5] Essentially in all that follows, the processes which I am discussing are *normal* processes, which we all use in one context or another to varying degrees. Since this book is about race, all the examples are of people who misuse racial groups. Many of us may use the same processes but work them out through other social groups.

(i) Unresolved conflicts between positive and negative identity elements
The positive and negative elements contained within a person's identity are often in conflict. This can be seen in many of our subjects who are at war with themselves, struggling and wavering between an acceptance of themselves as they are and a degree of self-hate. Some

degree of being at war with oneself and some degree of self-hatred or guilt is taken as normal for people who attain competence in their social relationships. What is crucial however, is the fierceness of this being at war with oneself, and its ruthless quality. If the conflict is experienced as too painful and too cruel, splitting and projection result.[6] The core of the difficulty lies in the pain of accepting one's imperfections. These conflicts between positive and negative identity elements manifest themselves in the life history material in two distinct ways: in one the negative elements are repudiated as being part of the self, in the other the ideal and longed for positive identity elements are felt to be temporarily out of reach of the self.

(a) There are those who are unable to tolerate in themselves qualities which they consider deplorable or undesirable and they project these onto racial groups, so attempting to re-arrange reality and disguise it in ways more bearable to the self. What are the qualities which are disowned and repudiated by our subjects? They include an unconscious fear of their own aggressive acts or intentions, moral inadequacies, failures which a person has difficulty in accepting, personality qualities considered unlikeable or reprehensible, intellectual inferiorities and lack of competence, and finally images of the body as bad or damaged. By seeking to get rid of these aspects by projecting them onto other racial groups, the discomfort and conflict of facing these imperfect aspects as part of the self are avoided. The issue here is predominantly one of individual capacities to tolerate feelings of ambivalence. The greater the capacity to weather ambivalence, both towards oneself and others, the less is there a need to project feared bad qualities outside the self. People have varying levels of self-acceptance, often uneasily maintained against the pull of underlying feelings of self-rejection. It is a balance of forces which can readily be upset by stress and the persistence of environmental provocation. The more an individual feels able to trust his good and loving feelings, the greater will be his capacity to accept shortcomings in himself as well as others. It is people who have had their self-esteem severely undermined who find it very hard to hold on to a belief in the satisfactory aspects of themselves and are more liable to project negative, denied aspects of their identity on to others.

A racial group, different in physical appearance and in socially and culturally acquired features may be seen as a psychologically 'safe' area for such projections since it is far removed from oneself. Let us see what examples of this type of unresolved conflict occur among the subjects.

Mr and Mrs Chattaway and their son John all tend to deny their hostile aggressive impulses and project these on to Indians and Pakistanis and to a lesser extent on to West Indians. 'To feel the hostility of others, originating outside ourselves, is far more bearable than the experience of our own aggressive wishes' says Rochlin.[7] Mr Chattaway, by means of projective identification with his son, seeks a vicarious expression of his own hostile feelings by urging skinheads and rockers to combine and 'have a go at the wogs'. Mrs James repudiates not only her own quarrelsome and aggressive feelings but also her siblings who embody these qualities for her. She projects these aspects of herself on to her own racial group from whom she then has to distance herself in a working situation. Eric Singh whose rigid self-image allows for little flexibility in the expression of ordinarily legitimate aggressive feelings splits off these feelings from his self-image and sees the English boys at his school as unqualifiedly aggressive, destructive and badly behaved.

Moral inadequacies and shame at his own delinquent acts emerge from the interviews with Mr Chattaway and lead him, in turn, to a passionate attack on Indians and Pakistanis as delinquent, corrupt and dishonest, breaking the law of the land. By trying to run them down with his car at the traffic lights, he avoids his inner shame and guilt and converts them into a potentially murderous attack on an alien racial group whose members then 'carry' for him these negative identity elements with which he would otherwise be internally at war. He converts an inner battleground into one on the streets of his neighbourhood.

Mr James choses to see a certain unapproachability as a defect in his personality and fears that he could be seen by others as unreachable. He, in turn, projects on to Indians and Pakistanis his uneasy feelings, leading him to see them as both unapproachable and unreachable and so makes his personality more bearable by contrast.

John Chattaway has difficulty in facing up to areas of intellectual impairment and this burden is lessened by attributing similar shortcomings to Indians and Pakistanis. Eric Singh, who makes very heavy demands on himself to be hard-working, ambitious and self-controlled, has difficulty in accepting ordinary needs to be lazy, indifferent, spontaneous and even at times out of control; and these negative elements are projected onto English schoolboys while he steadfastly enacts in his own life their extreme opposite.

Mrs Chattaway, while trying to save her image as a good mother, offloads her childrens' quarrelling outbreaks of anger and aggression on to West Indians. By extruding these outside the family and attributing them to other racial groups she distances them from herself. Although she does not deny that they also form part of her family repertoire of behaviour, by exaggerating their occurrence outside the family and locating them in different racial groups, by contrast her self-image becomes more convincing to herself.

Both John and Elaine Chattaway have deep anxieties in regard to their bodies, feeling that something has damaged them and the apparent body integrity of visibly different racial groups unconsciously triggers off the projection and acting out of these fears. In John this takes the form of violent body attacks on Asians, particularly on Pakistanis, attacking in them what he fears may be damaged in himself.

In all these cases there is a measure of denial underlying the use of projection. 'It is not I who am at fault, but it is them.' If the other can be perceived as destructive, or as inferior or wanting, then by comparison the person feels his own imperfections are more bearable. These ways of handling unresolved identity conflicts have consequences both for the individual concerned and for the racial groups to whom these qualities are attributed. The loss to the individual lies in avoiding facing up to his human limitations and imperfections. It is only by an acceptance of our human shortcomings that we, in turn, can accept the shortcomings and frailties of others. Racial tolerance is enhanced in direct proportion to the struggle of each of us to face up to and accept what is less than optimally desirable but is humanly possible in the self.

But although the loss to the individuals is in itself a deprivation of *their* growth potential, by offloading their negative identities onto racial groups, gross infringements of identity in the target groups occurs. And whether the target racial groups accept these, consciously or unconsciously and so collude with the 'aggressor' or whether they use energy and resource to withstand these psychological onslaughts, either way they are being affected and their identity conflicts will in turn reflect these. And the spiral movements continue.

(b) The second way in which intrapsychic conflict between positive and negative identity aspects manifests itself is in the attempt by an individual to retain and keep alive longed-for and somewhat idealized aspects of identity which are felt to be difficult to hold onto because of negative identity elements within the person which threaten to deny them full expression. Such people at particular points in their lives may find it hard to believe anything good about themselves and to retain inner feelings of love, goodness, ability, competence or talents. These positive attributes are then experienced as aspects of other racial groups. Positive aspects of identity are extended into another racial group and, by a process of identification, the person can then admire and love in others what they so want for themselves and feel they have not got. Unconsciously this process can be a hopeful one for the individual because in this way he may remain to some degree in touch with these qualities which at a future time may well be re-claimable as part of the self. This too, is a normal process which we all at times use, mostly in our closest relationships with marriage partners or close friends. There is a danger however that by splitting off and denying one's own positive qualities and attributing to others these positive qualities, they too undergo distortion and become highly idealized. These qualities, although positive, by their idealization and distortion also act as impingements on the target groups so chosen for what is being projected are more than average expectations and qualities and these elevated expectations act as severe constraints and impingements on the identity processes of members of the target racial groups.

Mrs James and her son Adrian both use this type of idealization, the former choosing white parental figures who are seen as inordinately helpful 'good, good, good' and caring, keeping her from harm and bringing her through various crises with unabating love and excessive devotion. In this way she unconsciously keeps in touch with excessively loving parents, who in turn make her feel lovable, valuable and good. It is interesting that she manifested this most vividly when she was alone in Britain for the first time, living apart from her husband (but not by choice), cut off from her children, and at last sorely ill. Her depressed feelings evoked regressive longings. Her need for reassurance that she was both lovable and loved must have been intense. Her son Adrian also resorted to idealization at a critical period in his life when he first arrived in England and was facing multiple sources of stress including a reunion with parents whom he hardly knew, the shift from a tiny community to a huge metropolis and entry into a large multi-racial school after years of living solely with fellow West Indians. By idealizing Indian schoolboys he was able to keep his ideal self-image alive, attributing to them those qualities which previously had been an intimate part of his own sense of identity. Under the multiple stresses of uprooting and the upheavals through which he was passing, he could not retain for himself a sturdy self-image as a hard working, respected boy of some achievement. By idealizing the Indians he was able to keep in touch with these same qualities until such time as he no longer required this emergency action and was once again able to integrate these as part of his identity.

(ii) Unresolved sexual conflicts

These can be differentiated as follows:

(a) The arousal or the re-arousal of incestuous and oedipal anxieties which threaten to break out in the family, especially during adolescence, is handled by some of the subjects by the denial and displacement of these anxieties as far away as possible from the family by attributing them to racial groups. By these means attempts are made to ward off incestuous and oedipal anxieties which, while emanating in the family are not ordinarily consciously available to people and can neither be openly expressed or resolved there without gross damage to family relationships.[8] These feelings are deeply buried and passionate and add an intensity to their diverted expression.

Among our subjects these particular problems can most readily be discerned among the Chattaways. Mr Chattaway's sexual anxieties in relation to Elaine have overtones of a deep emotional involvement. This may account both for the especially virulent attempts he makes to try and beat up the Indian youth who verbally accosted her in the street, and for his aversion to Asians because of their feared sexuality.

Mrs Chattaway's intensity of feeling for her son John, with its renewed oedipal threats and overtones, increased by her own mid-life crisis, unconsciously heightens her sexual awareness as well as her anxiety in relation to sex. The attractiveness of West Indians as well as her strengthened defences against them displaces outside the family arena, her oedipal stirrings. John, too, siphons off his renewed oedipal feelings and unconscious feelings of guilt by castrational and persecutory anxieties which are connected with body damage and which lead to his participating in physically violent gang attacks on Indians and Pakistanis and on rival white gangs.

(b) Unresolved problems in sexual identity lead some subjects to hate in other racial groups what seems to be troubling and fraught in themselves. Adolescence exacerbates sexual identity issues and insecurities since it is then that they predominantly become the focal developmental task. Disgust and fascinated envy, linked with shocked disapproval at actual or phantasied sexual activities of other racial groups, come to serve as a vicarious experience for disallowed sexual strivings and unresolved aspects of sexual identity. Both Adrian James and Eric Singh unconsciously envy, and consequently bitterly attack, what they see as the sexual permissiveness and sexual provocativeness of English boys. This shocks them but preoccupies them nonetheless. Elaine Chattaway, who has painful problems arising from a delayed sexual maturity, and who feels inadequate in her sexual identity as a result, is inflamed, disgusted and yet absorbed with the Indian girls at her school, their sexual attractiveness and seemingly successful sexual relationships.

(iii) Identity conflicts arising from low self-esteem and feelings of inadequacy
Racial misuse stemming from conflict in the area of low self-esteem and feelings of inadequacy takes four different patterns among our subjects. I will deal with these separately, although there is some slight overlapping between them.

(a) There are those subjects who, whilst denying their feelings of personal inadequacy, lack of accomplishment or abilities, fervently wish for these as incomplete aspects of their identity and resort to envy and jealousy of racial groups credited with these same abilities, accomplishments and cultural gifts. Mr James, as a West Indian with a broken cultural identity, feels hidden envy towards Indians who have their own language and culture and who can proclaim that language as an audible mark of their identity. Mr Chattaway, whose childhood life with his family was so severely deprived, leaving him with feelings of inadequacy, reveals hidden envy of Indian patterns of culture for their clear-cut identity, ancient traditions, and the close-knit quality of family bonds. He denigrates these in envious attacks and argues that their culture should become submerged and diluted by full integration into English culture.

John Chattaway mocks and derides the overall ability and competence of Indians and Pakistanis, their capacity to shoulder responsibility and be independent, and enviously labels these achievements as hollow because he is sorely burdened with his own intellectual struggles and feelings of inadequacy.

(b) Some subjects, while denying their inadequacies, try to bolster and inflate their self-esteem by disparaging and diminishing the worth of other races. In this way impoverished individuals seek to convince themselves that if the identity of other races is so inferior and tarnished, then, by contrast, they themselves are not as bad as they had feared.

Mr Chattaway, buttressed by his injured feelings of self-esteem, deflated by depression, unemployment and low morale, tries to cope with this by convincing himself that the clear-cut identity of Indians and Pakistanis is inferior. They are seen as mostly backward, illiterate and unable to compete in a developed society. John Chattaway derides the Indians and Pakistanis, as we have seen, in order to reassure himself that his own capacities are not so bad. Mr Singh is very preoccupied with social class values and with the challenge to his self-esteem posed by the English inability to distinguish between a person like himself of education and standing, and lower-class Asians; so he attacks and vilifies lower-class Asians, thus enhancing his bruised self-esteem.

(c) A third variant of how lowered self-esteem triggers off racial misuse arises from deprivation and rejection in childhood which engenders fears of having been unloved and found unloveable. These fears in turn stimulate a need to blame someone, particularly parental figures who draw towards them anger and resentment, and give rise to envy and jealousy towards sibling surrogates. It is as if a Garden of Eden is felt to exist but it exists for people of another race. Anger and resentment at these early and deep wounds to self-esteem seem to be assuaged by resentful attacks on surrogate parental figures of a different racial group and their 'favourite' sons and daughters who are felt to be greatly indulged by this parental love.

Eric Singh suffered frequent separations from his loving parents, starting as an infant when he was put in an institution because of his mother's unexpected hospitalization, followed by many geographic separations caused by his severe asthma and his return to India to escape the climate. Now he splits off his need to blame his own parents for any of these painful experiences of abandonment (since logically he recognises that these were in his best interests and inescapable) and to protect them he directs attacks on English parents who are felt by him to be lacking in love and care for their own children, and basically rejecting. By misusing another racial group in this way, he is able to conserve a good if somewhat idealized image of his own parents.

Mr Chattaway, with a deep sense of deprivation as a result of his tragic infancy and childhood (it will be recalled that he never knew his father, and his mother left him in the care of aged and rather formidable grandparents), tends to equate authority figures unconsciously with parental images. He perceives the police as having favourites among the Asians and as understanding and indulging them, treating them in fact with special concern and compassion. Indians and Pakistanis are felt to be favoured and protected 'sons' and are enviously hated as a result. The police are viewed as being unfair and unjust parental figures, depriving him of his rightful needs for protection and care, while giving these to other racial groups.

John Chattaway's need for a father's regard, support and

consistently reliable care is not felt to have been adequately met and so he, in turn, angrily blames teachers as parental surrogates for favouring the Asians whom he then attacks with envy and jealousy. He too sees the police in the same way as his father.

Elaine Chattaway, who understandably craves love and attention for herself in the face of strong competition from her youngest brother Colin, a very demanding child, also feels incensed by the teachers' indulgence of Asians in the classroom whom she enviously and jealously attacks.

In all these cases the person is denying his or her own vulnerable feelings and sense of deprivation of parental love. It is striking to note in passing how the original deprivation of parental love for Mr Chattaway, in turn makes him unable to give to his children effectively that which he never received. For all three these problems are played out in the racial arena.

(d) The previous types have in common that fact that they deal with issues of low self-esteem which emanate from a steady ongoing inner state, revealing how the individual unconsciously feels about himself and his adequacies at the deepest level. The fourth and final variant differs from the three already discussed because feelings of esteem are powerfully challenged and eroded by onslaughts and attacks made on the worth and esteem of one's own racial group. These emanate from outside the self in the first instance and come from members of other racial groups. Variations in the type of onslaught suffered, the personality dynamics of the individual concerned, particularly ego strengths and styles of coping, together with social ideological values all play a part in influencing responses to such challenges by different subjects. Four different styles of response can be discerned in the case material.

1 A pattern of response which meets the hostile racial attack by a reactive anger, openly expressed. This is a powerful response which attempts to restore self-esteem. Mr Singh was able to show anger when, on several occasions, racial prejudice was openly shown by Englishmen towards Indians, wounding his self-esteem and driving him to a reactive anger. His wife also shows a capacity for righteous anger when treated by English shopkeepers in ways which she finds demeaning and unacceptable to her self esteem. Both Mr and Mrs Singh have sufficiently robust identities to be able to use this direct response. Adrian James could express to the interviewer his angry feelings towards Enoch Powell for his attacks on coloured immigrants, reported in the press and through the mass media.

2 A pattern of response which denies that the hostile attack is

legitimately being aimed at the 'right' racial group, namely one's
own group, and suggesting that it should properly have been
directed at another racial group. This device aims to deflect the attack
and use the third racial group as a scapegoat. By this manoeuvre the
individual seeks to affirm the self-esteem of his own group and his
own at the cost of the self-esteem of another group. Mr James affords
a good example of this when, in response to the anger and anxiety
provoked by Enoch Powell's speeches on the Immigration Bill he in
turn felt so attacked and insecure that – for the first time in the course
of all his interviews – he engaged in some scapegoating of the
Kenyan Asians. Eric Singh, under the same provocation, also uses
the Kenyan Asians as a scapegoat group. They, at that time, were the
most recent wave of immigrants and so were most vulnerable to
being used for such scapegoating purposes. A variant of this pattern
is one which uses a different social class within one's racial group to
deflect an affront to self-esteem. Mr Singh, while recognizing the
hostile attacks on his race, denies that they apply to his own social
class and reference groups but says they apply to a lower class group
within his own race.

3 A pattern of response which denies that hostile attacks on one's
own racial group have ever been sustained by oneself personally but
admits that this is an experience of one's peers within one's own
racial group. In this way the individual denies the need to react
personally to the provocation in a direct way and displaces both the
incidents and the feelings onto peers, to whom, in turn, reactive
feelings are attributed. Mrs James, for instance, reacts to the painful,
humiliating, insulting and anger-provoking behaviour and remarks
directed by white English people at West Indians by denying that
such things had ever happened to her, though they had often
happened to her friends. Since Mrs James' mother had taught her to
do just that, namely to behave as if she had not heard insulting or
humiliating remarks, these styles of response lie deep in her earliest
socialization experiences and are an intrinsic part of her personality.

4 The fourth pattern, although not involving racial groups as
targets, nonetheless arises from racial attacks on self-esteem, and
belongs here because of its vital implications for race attitudes. The
hostile intent behind the racial attack is correctly recognized but is
not met by counter-attack. Racial groups are spared from attack, but
in the process some of the aggression meant for others is turned back
against the self.[9]

Johanna James best illustrates this way of handling humiliating
attacks as her experience in the restaurant with the white waitress

well exemplifies. She 'swallowed' her anger. Part of her conscious rationalization for doing this was not to add corroborative behaviour which might strengthen an existing stereotype, that which sees West Indians as aggressive, noisy and lacking in restraint. Inwardly she turns her anger against herself, leading to depressive feelings and some psychosomatic complaints. She suffers but protects racial groups from her attacks.

(iv) Identity conflicts arising from wounds to a personal sense of identity through being found indistinguishable from other people of the same racial group and having a projected racial identity thrust upon one
Especially vulnerable minorities singled out for discriminatory treatment experience the projection and offloading of negative identity elements onto them which have the effect of denying to each individual his or her personal identity. Struggling against this is the desire of individuals to be recognized as the people they feel themselves to be rather than as interchangeable units.

Three members of the Singh family provide examples of this conflict. Mr Singh's need to be confirmed by the English as an individual of good character, some social standing and ability is threatened by the ignorant views of some English people. This leads him to a deep sense of hurt which in turn makes him contemptuous of those English and acting to protect his narcissism and self-image, he attributes these same features to Asian Indians of a lower social class than himself. Eric Singh follows substantially the same course when he becomes fearful that he may be confused with Kenyan Asians. He splits off the projected identity elements attributed to his group and by projecting these onto the Kenyan Asians he is enabled to retain his own feelings of identity, striving for ever higher standards for himself, so that by contrast the gap widens between him and the group to which he attributes the negative qualities. Mrs Singh, as mentioned earlier, shows little tendency to stereotype any racial group, so when shopping she firmly, and with dignity but angry resolve, continues to be herself, quietly insisting on her personal right as a consumer to be treated as the person she feels herself to be.

Mrs James, the West Indian, when she becomes aware that 'all coloured people look alike to the English', uses withdrawal and self-restriction as a way of protecting her personal sense of identity from the encroachment of a projected racial identity. Johanna, when confronted by indifference to her competence and personality qualities in her search for employment, reacts with severe humiliation and hurt, which trigger off angry feelings which she turns back against herself.

(v) Identity conflicts arising from spatial impingements and infringements experienced as threats to the territoriality of identity

In recent years increasing attention has been paid to the importance in identity of concepts of space and territory. Although space pervasively affects all our lives both consciously and unconsciously, until fairly recently it has been taken for granted and ignored. But within the last decade anthropologists, ethologists, architects, town planners and psychologists have increasingly turned their attention to the influences which notions of private space and territory have upon us all. Hall,[10] in two important works, has pointed to the impact of spatial relations upon us and shown how these vary between individuals and also between cultures. Although the conceptual framework in which different writers have approached this field varies, Hall, Horowitz, Landis, Sequin and also, at a more popular level, Ardrey,[11] all stress the importance of notions of space and territory. They see each of us surrounded by an outside space which we regard as our own territory. At the body-image level, the internal representation of this space is referred to as body-buffer-zones by Horowitz, and it is these which can be felt to be transgressed upon or invaded by others. Landis, whose work on ego boundaries opens up many exciting fields, has suggested that ego boundary attributes may relate to the different ways people experience and use the space around them, which in turn affects how they react to infringements of this space. He suggests a direct relationship between body-buffer-zone concepts and ego-boundary attributes.

In our material, identity conflicts arise from notions of the territoriality of identity and from spatial impingements and infringements which subjects experience. Since races are *visibly* distinguishable, territory can readily be seen to be 'invaded'. But it is not only the visual perception of territory and space which is involved; space can be invaded by other sensory impingements and the life history material reveals what a wide variety of forms these can take. Individuals differ in the size and shape of their body-buffer-zones and the extent to which they experience these as penetrated by a variety of different factors. For instance, one person may have very low tolerance for auditory impingements and react to his space being invaded by loud noise, while to another noise may be no problem but being touched may infringe his sense of space which alerts him to protective action. It is these variations in tolerance for sharing space and their related vulnerabilities which lead to unresolved identity conflicts for the person concerned. Each tries to maintain a personal sense of identity and its territoriality in the face of what are experienced as culturally alien impingements, seen as racial in origin. The types of impingements and infringements cover a wide field and are illustrated separately below.

(a) Territorial impingements: These occur when public places, cinemas, shops, pubs and open areas of street or park are felt to be excessively used by one or more racial groups whose domain they become. Such groups are then experienced as invaders.

Among our subjects, it is understandably the English family who experience this shift. They see their community amenities and territory being taken over by new and, particularly, coloured immigrants. What had been their own territory is now experienced as alien and invaded by newcomers. The familiar world feels as if it is disintegrating and both for Mr and Mrs Chattaway their previously 'beautiful Athol' is now felt to have changed, become run down and dilapidated. They stop shopping where they used to shop, they avoid the pubs and cinemas and by avoidance and self-constraint they curtail their previous activities within the neighbourhood, so depriving themselves of what they had enjoyed and taken for granted in their lives. They feel angry and aggrieved at their loss. Whereas when the West Indians or Indians leave their countries of origin to migrate to England, they are able to retain inside them an image of what is lost as still *there* and still potentially recoverable, the Chattaways cannot do this. They are daily confronted by change and what they painfully experience as serious loss.

These territorial impingements are linked with quantitative factors, since it is the number of racially different people who are felt as inundating the territorial space, so leading to feelings of being swamped by the sheer weight of numbers involved. In addition to the four Chattaways, Mr James as well as Eric Singh feel that there are too many immigrants.

(b) Spatial impingements curtailing freedom of movement: Four subjects experience impediments to freedom of movement and passage on the pavements of Athol which previously they had taken for granted. Three members of the Chattaway family and Mr James all blame Asians for gathering in small groups, conversing intensely in their own language, blocking freedom of movement and being

seemingly indifferent to the obstruction they are causing. This excites a variety of reactions, but all express fairly intense irritation and hostility. Mrs Chattaway, for instance, is sufficiently worked up about it to push her shopping trolley into them.

Although Mr Chattaway's deeper underlying conflicts account for his reasons for using his car as a violent means of attack on Asian pedestrians crossing against the traffic lights, nonetheless the actual provocative stimulus which outraged him was one which constituted an impediment to his freedom of movement. If the Asians were crossing against the lights, by so doing his freedom to drive his car was controlled by them. His anger at this situation leads him to act out his asserted right to freedom of movement by putting in jeopardy the lives of those who might be crossing in front of his car.

(c) Auditory impingements experienced as a sensory assault on notions of identity space : Excess noise and shouting attributed to specific racial groups is experienced as an infringement on the territoriality of identity. There are, of course, wide cultural variations governing conventions in volume of voice, pitch, loudness and softness of speech as well as tolerance for outbursts of shouting and explosive laughter. On the whole, the English tend to be restrained in these areas by contrast with more exuberant and expressive cultures. Auditory impingements assail the senses and permit few ways of taking avoiding action apart from physical distance. Although the Chattaways' sensitivities in this area may well be inflamed by Colin's shouting, Mr and Mrs Chattaway and Elaine nonetheless complain of excessive noise and shouting attributed to West Indians. Mr and Mrs Singh also complain of the same thing for which they blame both West Indians and some lower-class Asians. In all cases the irritability and aggression is expressed as part of a racial stereotype.

(d) Visual impingements experienced as an aesthetic affront by unpleasing, dilapidated, untidy exteriors of houses, gardens and cars: Where visual qualities are attributed to racial groups, notions of style and upkeep of one's territory are assailed. To Mr Chattaway, the run-down dilapidated cars belonging to Indians irritate him because they act as a displacement symbol for his own run-down state. Mrs Chattaway complains that the curtains of Indian houses are always recognizable and 'sleazy', while Mr and Mrs Singh, in attempts to maintain their own sense of identity based on high standards, are assailed by the lower standards of upkeep of homes and gardens by some of their compatriots.

(e) Olfactory impingements experienced as distasteful caused by unfamiliar cooking and food smells: The alien intrusion into familiar identity space of smells which are not part of a childhood past appear to act as infringements on identity. In our material curry and garlic create the major problems. To the Chattaways they are unpleasant smells but more important, they are reminders that their territory is no longer their own but now includes other races and cultures. Mr and Mrs Singh, who manage to cook traditional foods with sensitive regard for their neighbours' privacy regarding smells, react to their compatriots who fail to take these precautions with critical class-stereotyping.

(f) Germ and dirt impingements experienced as a threat to health and a hazard to identity survival: Poor hygiene, hazards like spitting in the street and dirty and unkempt backyards lead some of the Chattaways and Mr and Mrs Singh to express concern lest they be invaded by germs. In all cases blame is attributed particularly to the Asian group, or to specific social classes in that group.

(g) Impingements experienced as invasions and intrusions into the privacy of personal relationships by the undue curiosity and gossip of people in the neighbourhood, stimulated by inter-racial associations of the sexes in the street: Notions of privacy and the private space within which it feels comfortable to function are assailed, for both Johanna James and Vera Singh, by the intrusiveness into this private space by the watchful looks, gossip and destructive comments on inter-racial contacts between both of these young women and the few acquaintances and friends they have among white men. Whereas Johanna resents this angrily as an intrusion into her privacy and her unassailable right to freedom of choice, and wants to escape physically from the scene, Vera sees this as an unpleasant social reality which she must respect for the sake of her parents and so discontinues to accept lifts home from work – a perfectly innocent arrangement. In both cases unresolved identity conflicts, occasioned by this intrusion into their private space, trigger off legitimate feelings of outrage, resentment and despair at racial prejudice within society.

(h) Identity issues aroused by threats to newly achieved and vulnerable territoriality of identity: Because immigrant groups have only begun to put down their roots in this country, their identity is grounded primarily in their original countries of origin. Their newly achieved

territoriality of identity is put in jeopardy by political speeches and
pronouncements which attack the presence of growing numbers of
coloured immigrants in England and urge the curtailment of their
numbers ·or even their repatriation. We were in the fortunate
position of doing the field work for this study while Enoch Powell
was making some of his notorious speeches attacking coloured
immigrants and passionately pressing for repatriation. The shock of
this to the subjects is reflected in the case material of Mr James,
Johanna, and Adrian, who showed mounting despair and anger.
Linked with these speeches, the passing of the Immigration Act[12] led
the Singh family to such uncertainty about their future that they
began to consider Canada seriously as a new territorial base for Vera
and Eric and perhaps themselves after retirement. The threat to their
newly achieved sense of territory led to the expression of anger and
hostility towards the English, particularly to the politicians and
political parties involved, but it also brought about the scapegoating
of the Kenyan Asians who, as even newer newcomers, were felt to be
less entitled to a place within 'their' space.

All of the impingements separately dealt with above, act both
consciously and unconsciously on the sense of space and territory
and lead to racial misuse and stereotyping where boundaries are
overstepped and body-buffer-zones infringed. Penetrability of the
buffer-zones is heightened under conditions of stress and conflict,
especially when the symbolic nature of the infringement is counter-
pointed by the inner psychodynamics of unresolved identity conflicts. Thresholds for the penetrability of body-buffer-zones vary and
our subjects are thought of as having contracting or expanding
vulnerabilities as their inner state and situations jointly determine.

*(vi) Avoiding and resisting processes of identity change and growth by
resorting to racial misuse as a diversion*
We all resist identity change to one extent or another and it is only a
matter of degree whether this creates a serious blockage in growth
processes. Individuals use racial issues as a means of avoiding
anxiety-provoking changes in identity. All the examples in this entire
section could well be included here since they all involve a diversion
into the racial area of unresolved conflict. But there are some subjects
who vividly illustrate this particular way of resisting inner change.

Mr Chattaway dislikes living in Athol because of the coloured
immigrants and could well have left the area and lived elsewhere. But
if he had done so, he would have had to confront his acute conflicts in
relation to work and unemployment, his feelings of aggrievement

and resentment at the way his life has worked out, and conflicts emanating from his mid-life crisis. By avoiding these, his feelings of frustration and demoralization are channelled into an intense preoccupation with race and with the politics of race as his support for the forerunners of the National Front indicates. These provide him with an outlet, but at the expense of the Indians and Pakistanis – who are his main targets – and to a lesser extent also the West Indians. Furthermore these offer no prospect of an attempt to grapple with and face his inner problems. Society loses and so does he.

Johanna is able to see insightfully the destructive aspects of race relations in the community and how these cheat her of being seen as the mature, responsible and intelligent adult which she is. By concentrating her energies on this important community issue, to an extent she drains-off energies from the taxing developmental task which faces her. She needs to establish some inner separation from her parents in order to shift her identity within the family to one which fully recognizes her mature adult status. By concentrating on the one, the personal growth challenge while admitted, is nonetheless not yet fully engaged.

10 ACTIVATORS AND CONSTRAINTS

Up to this point, the ideas presented have been largely concerned with understanding the psychological relationships between unresolved personal conflicts and racial misuse. We see that racial misuse does not arise from inner causes alone but that these are powerfully modified and affected by a whole range of social, environmental, situational as well as psychological factors which act to exacerbate or to reduce identity conflicts, so functioning as *activators* which encourage racial misuse and prejudice, or as *constraints* which discourage conflicts spilling into the racial area. These activating or constraining factors interact either singly or cumulatively with the steady ongoing levels of unresolved identity conflicts; and it is these interactions which, taken together, account for racial misuse. A solely psychodynamic explanation of racial prejudice is as unsatisfactory as one which puts emphasis upon purely political, economic or sociological factors. In this model, the activators and constraints either facilitate the social evil of racial prejudice, or constrain its expression and growth and move people towards an inner respect for their own separate identity and a full respect for the identity of others, irrespective of race.

I now wish to consider six different categories of activators and constraints, five of them acting upon the agents of prejudice and the conditions which affect them, and one concerned with target racial groups singled out as victims of racial misuse. I will begin with the broadest and most generally pervasive of these, namely activators and constraints embedded in the *social ideologies of society*, then move to consider the *stress of change* as an activator and *continuity* as a constraint, then a consideration of what makes racial groups more or less *vulnerable and accessible as targets*, followed by an analysis of *social situational* activators and constraints, then an analysis of how the *family* functions in these contexts and ending up, where the analytical chapters of this book began, with the *intrapsychic factors*.

(i) Social ideology and its institutionalization

Societies differ in their explicit and implicit presuppositions and ideas regarding racial groups, and although these have historic roots it is quite beyond the scope of this book to explore them. These social ideologies are part of the structure of a society and are usually reflected in its institutions, laws and practices.

Several points arise in relation to social ideology. First of all, there is tremendous power in the explicit social ideological forces which permeate a society, especially if these are reinforced by strong agencies within the society and given sanction by its laws. These can, on the one hand, canalize the ferment of unresolved personal conflicts in ordinary citizens into 'false solutions' involving racial prejudice and the dehumanizing of other racial groups. On the other hand, they can be channelled into a respect for the fellowship of man, the common humanity of man. A social ideology can have the effect of giving cultural license to the dehumanizing of selected scapegoats within that society, individuals given social saction and support for such racial misuse and the distorted images which these embody. Only rarely will people, under these conditions, examine and challenge their own feelings and motivations.

Where the ideology is egalitarian and democratic and where stress is laid within the society both on the outlawing of racial discrimination and prejudice and the fellowship of men, and where these are backed up by institutional procedures and the full weight of the law, the ferment of unresolved personal conflict if especially pressing may still impel some to seek out racial groups as repositories, for reasons already described. But the powerful support of the wider society will be denied to those who choose this course and they will be swimming against the tide rather than carried along with its insidious currents.

Since racially prejudiced attitudes will not be widely sanctioned or shared, the person who is prejudiced cannot rationalize his attitudes as being either respectable or justified.

The people who swim with the tide, taking their cue from the social ideologies of their society, are involved in different inner tasks dependent on whether the ideology *activates* racial misuse or *constrains* it. An ideology which activates racial misuse is aided and abetted in its destructive task because of two factors: first, it is easier to blame others than to find the fault within oneself; secondly, the level of anxiety and fear in relation to painful identity conflicts constitutes a ferment which is a constant hazard. A social ideology which provides acceptable socially sanctioned repositories for denied aspects of ourselves exploits these human vulnerabilities and seeks to make racial misuse acceptable.

Three separate studies published by the Columbus Trust, one by Norman Cohn,[13] one by Henry Dicks[14] and the third by Leon Poliakov,[15] have explored the conditions under which extreme forms of racial persecution, mass killings and national exterminations occur. And although each of these books is directed at quite different problems, nonetheless they all point to the conclusion that most individuals intimately involved in violent persecutory acts during such periods (e.g. the holocaust) were not generally found to be grossly pathological in their psychological make-up. Individual psychopathology was found to be less important in accounting for their actions than the overwhelming importance of a dehumanizing ideology, institutionalized and accepted within the society. People in high authority play an extremely important part in pushing an ideology. Under such conditions, these studies show that there appeared to be no lack of people prepared to carry out the deeds of gross dehumanizing or indeed the extermination of specific races selected for destruction. These are extreme cases, yet governments through their access to propaganda and the use of the mass media, can expound their goals in ways which make them appear positive and morally sound and little explicit attention need be given to the groups who may have to be sacrificed and who are the hapless victims.

Stanley Milgram's experimental work[16] on individuals in various strata of life, not only in the United States but also in Munich, Rome and Australia, has shown how willingly people will comply with authority to inflict pain and suffering on helpless victims so long as their behaviour is legitimized by people in power whose status is respected. In such situations, individuals become thoughtless agents of action. Milgram comments that 'the culture had failed almost entirely, in inculcating internal controls on actions that have their origin in authority'.[17] He notes how his work in the laboratory, confirms the findings of both Cohn and of Dicks.

But what of societies like Britain? She upholds a social ideology based on democratic and humane principles, an egalitarian society which seeks to treat all its citizens fairly, irrespective of race, and in support of this, Race Relations Acts[18] have been passed to uphold these rights by law. These are the explicit core of the social ideology in this country and for such an ideology to work successfully full commitment to a multi-racial base for the society is required and imaginative efforts and strong determination to provide ways of making such a society work. These issues cannot possibly be done justice to in this book, but there are two points which I wish to make.

The debates on immigration were at their height during the time this study was being done and they have continued to be matters of major policy debate. Discussions focus on the undesirability of more *coloured* immigrants entering this country, the debate not being conducted in terms of economic realities so much as in terms of tolerance for people who are black or brown entering the country. These statements of policy which, overtly or covertly, express attitudes towards coloured immigrants (including some who talk of repatriation of coloured immigrants) convey that coloured people are less acceptable as people, less desirable as citizens or neighbours, and alien and unwanted. These attributions cannot be compartmentalized. Since these images permeate society in a powerful way, they are at variance with protestations at the highest level in the land that this is a multi-racial society in which each man is accorded the same dignity and respect. The implications of these attitudes towards *coloured* immigrants give covert sanction to the use of coloured groups as repositories and the danger which this potentially creates is that these groups are now marked and stigmatized as unwelcome. If the society undergoes periods of severe economic stress or political instability, these groups may well be put at hazard as racial repositories for aggravated personal conflicts. Politicians and political parties can elevate or diminish levels of prejudice and can manipulate and exacerbate people's sensitivities and feelings of self-esteem in relation to race. These influential pronouncements give momentum to downward racial spirals. Nothing stands still. To deflate the self-esteem of coloured immigrants *affects* the racial spirals, so that response and counter-response flow from major pronouncements which have the backing of political parties.[19] It will be remembered that it was in response to Enoch Powell's speeches about immigration and the idea of repatriation of coloureds that the James' expressed their fear, anxiety and anger and Mr James was temporarily driven to scapegoating Kenyan Asians. Eric Singh reacted in the same way, also choosing the same group to carry his uneasy and insecure feelings. And the Singh family started to think about migration to Canada.

The second point is that although the extremely important Race Relations Acts have certainly helped as major constraints to diminish levels of racial discrimination within this country, nonetheless a recent study[20] – which brings together the findings of a whole group of research projects on racial discrimination in this country – reveals considerable and widespread evidence of discrimination in respect of employment and job levels, earnings and housing. This was found to be based on a generalized *colour* prejudice which makes little distinction between black and brown people of different ethnic groups. To this extent there is still a long way to go if the Act is to constrain the expression of racial discrimination fully. An important finding of this study was that minority groups were found to be the last to recognise an injustice due to racial discrimination. This means that in our life history material such discrimination as is reported is likely to be only a small part of what the West Indian and Indian subjects might well have been exposed to without their knowledge.

What social and political ideologies emerge as important for our twelve subjects? Although in general the James' and the Singhs hope for a society without racial prejudice or discrimination and Johanna has a positive vision of a good society, none of them volunteered information on their political beliefs and it is doubtful whether any of them belong to political parties or espouse particular political causes. Mr Chattaway admires the National Front organization, reads its literature and felt sufficiently committed to their viewpoint to press their literature upon me. This organization provides him with a feeling that he is not alone in his racist views and it gives him the sanction which enables him to justify his actions. It acts as an activator on his deep and underlying unresolved conflicts. The saction this provides him with makes it virtually impossible for him to consider revising any of his views on race.

John Chattaway sought and receives similar sanction and support for his violent attacks on Pakistanis by identifying with and actively joining the 'skinheads', a gang committed to 'Paki-bashing' and by their acceptance of him into the gang he is given a license to continue to attack Asians with group support. He does so with impunity.

(ii) The stress of change as an activator: continuity as a constraint
Change in the life circumstances of our subjects activates anxiety and
insecurity which, in turn, plays upon unresolved identity conflicts
increasing tendencies towards racial misuse. In a recent paper Marie
Jahoda has observed:

> Any change in our external life circumstances brings us face-to-
> face with the question of our own identity. In the lifelong efforts
> to acquire, maintain and develop one's personal identity,
> familiar external circumstances are useful props . . . Any sud-
> den change, for better or worse, removes these props and
> gives rise to insecurity and anxiety about one's identity. In such
> psychological states the seemingly clear-cut identity of others is
> envied and resented. Well-defined and visible social groups
> become an easy target.[21]

Reviewing the identity analyses of the twelve subjects, major areas
of change which operate as activators on racial prejudice are:

(a) Developmental changes: Both adolescence and middle-life are
periods of heightened stress due to social, psychological and bodily
changes which increase the salience of identity issues. In both these
periods there are inner and outer tasks which involve conflict and
choice. The way in which these are handled will either augur well for
further growth and constructive consolidation (this outcome will act
as a constraint on racial misuse) or badly if stagnation and
regression are the outcome as these will then be more likely to
activate projection, and splitting processes and increase racial
stereotyping.

Both Johanna James (who was aged nineteen at the time of the
study) and Vera Singh (eighteen), are the most racially tolerant of all
the adolescents and both seem to have passed through the most
turbulent phase of adolescence. Adolescent turmoil for John Chattaway (eighteen) has excited deep-seated anxieties, centred in his
body, as well as confronting him with the wide gap between his
omnipotent and unreal phantasies of fame and success and his
current and hampering difficulties in relation to work and achievement. These, in addition to his lack of satisfactory relationships with
others, all activate his racial hostilities. His sister Elaine (fifteen),
suffers the anxiety of a delayed sexual maturity arousing feelings of
inadequacy in her in relation to her peers, as previously discussed.
Both Adrian James (sixteen) and Eric Singh (fourteen) are in the early
stages of their adolescence and both deal with the heightening of their

sexual drives by denial and projection, offloading onto their English peers attributions of sexual license, sexual aggression and laxity of morals which are, in part, a displacement of their own growing sexuality. These stereotypes of English boys are also strengthened in Eric by his image of the permissive society, perceived as negative. Among these four adolescents, John, Elaine, Adrian and Eric, envy and hostility towards the body integrity, sexual freedom and adequacy of racial groups other than their own, are activated by their own developmental changes. For John and Elaine Chattaway it is the Asians who mostly carry these projections, but for Adrian and Eric it is the English.

The mid-life period involves a re-anchoring and re-securing of identity in the face of developmental changes. Most important of all this mid-life crisis re-arouses unconscious depressive anxieties with the possibility of a re-working of the early depressive position.[22] What seems to be most important for weathering this stage constructively is the capacity to come to terms with one's own shortcomings and destructive impulses while also remaining in touch with the good and positive qualities within. It is a time for accepting ambivalence in both oneself and others. However, at the same time the somewhat depleting physiological processes associated with ageing are also changing the body and shifting feelings of self-esteem, and with adolescent children in the family there is also the re-arousal of oedipal problems and the hightening of sexual anxieties. These are some of the inner changes and hazards; but alongside these the individual is also re-assessing his position in various life contexts within the family, at work, and in the community.

The ages of all six adult subjects are remarkably close, all were forty or forty-one at the time of the study with the exception of Mr Singh who was forty-six. For both Singhs and for both James', work and family satisfactions continue to serve as stable anchors. It is Mr and Mrs Chattaway who are most at hazard. Mr Chattaway's unemployment, whether chosen or not, nonetheless brings with it deflated self-esteem, low morale and depression. He feels somewhat excluded by his son John's close bond with his wife and all of these things activate his racial hostilities. Mrs Chattaway's threatened hysterectomy arouses her anxieties which serve to activate racial stereotyping.

(b) Changes due to immigration or to finding oneself among immigrants : The stress of uprooting involves feelings of loss, not

only of the familiar patterns, values and relationships of the past but also of being known and recognised, seen as the person each feels himself to be.

The James' family responded to the stresses of immigration as a challenge, tackling problems realistically and with active ways of coping and a purposive commitment to the resolution of problems. Under stress they reveal inner resources of considerable strength and diversity and the results are both constructive and impressive. In their case, immigration as such did not exacerbate their unresolved identity conflicts to the point of racial stereotyping or racial misuse. Their strengths in rising to the challenge and achieving the overcoming of obstacles have tended to act as constraints on such racial misuse.

The Singhs, after Mr Singh's initial devastating few years alone here, also display active and constructive ways of tackling their adjustment problems, bringing to these robust and sturdy aspects of their identities with the exception of one area of special vulnerability. This involves their deprivation, because of immigration, of recognition by a community which, not being theirs by birth, is unable to give them that which they feel they merit. This is a highly sensitive area for all of the Singhs, except Vera, and patterns of racial intolerance are activated in both Mr Singh and Eric by this painful lack.

The changes to which the Chattaways have been exposed in finding themselves living with immigrants have combined with other vulnerable areas in their personalities insidiously and powerfully to activate an intensity of racial hostility and prejudice in three of them, and a less intense pattern of racial misuse in Mrs Chattaway.

(c) Changes due to the vicissitudes of life: Insecurity and anxiety aroused by unexpected misfortunes and life events serve as activators of racial prejudice when individuals are forced to confront who they are and this often exacerbates tendencies to blame racial groups for their misfortunes. Among our subjects, stress-evoking events include the ill-health of Mrs Chattaway with the threat of an impending major operation leading to the exacerbation of her racial stereotyping, recurrent illnesses for Mrs James in her early years here stimulating splitting processes involving racial groups, Eric's chronic asthma and the profound effect this has had upon his life situation and his inner world, unemployment for Mr Chattaway with its depressive consequences with downward social mobility and deflated self-esteem all exacerbating his racial hostilities, and the brutal assault on Mr Singh leaving him with permanent body injuries which affect his feelings towards his fellow Asians.

(iii) Activators and constraints which make racial groups more or less accessible and vulnerable as target groups

Over and above the activators and constraints which have already been discussed which make target racial groups especially vulnerable to be used as social repositories and the 'given' perceptible physical differences in appearance which, of course, are unalterable but nonetheless serve as activators as shown earlier in this chapter, the most important of all activators is the association between social disadvantage and racial identity and it is this which must be broken if racial misuse is to be constrained.

To do this, Marie Jahoda has spelled out what the policy lessons for Britain might be[23] and although I cannot do full justice to her important and constructive recommendations, she has pointed to the need for a common language, 'English at least as a second fluently spoken language', a policy of continuous active concern with creating chances for the social diversification of various minority groups, and most important of all, the severance of links between racial differences and socially inferior positions. 'To destroy this link where it exists, to prevent its establishment where it is in danger of forming, should be a major aim of race relation policy.'[24]

(iv) Social arenas: specific social situational contexts as activators and constraints

I come now to a fundamental question posed by the case material. Why do individuals, with known racial attitudes, feel, and apparently behave, differently in contrasting social settings? In other words, how are identity issues played out in different *social arenas* and what is it within these arenas which activate or constrain these from becoming mixed up with racial attitudes?

Four social arenas account for the major contexts within which inter-racial encounters occur among our subjects, namely the school, health and medical settings, the place of work and the street. I am struck by the way each of these social arenas differentially elicits, stimulates and provokes in individuals only a partial and highly selective range of their repertoire of racial attitudes and in each of these four social arenas, the range of attitudes and behaviour patterns so resonated, are contrasting and distinctive. Furthermore the patterning of group processes *between* the races differs widely within each of these four social contexts. I now want to look at each of these arenas in turn, identifying the overt and the hidden processes which seem to be at work. Since I rely for my interpretations on insights derived from the life-history material and did not do an exhaustive analysis of these social contexts in their own right, what follows must be viewed as speculative and exploratory.

(a) The school: All six adolescents spoke vividly of their secondary school experiences at local schools, and although there is a great deal that could be considered in relation to the role of the school as a social arena, I will concentrate almost entirely on a particular descending spiral in race relations which emerges from the material. It would appear that within two schools in this working-class comunity there is at work a self-perpetuating vicious spiral in race relationships with the English students and the Indian and Pakistani students each enacting highly contrasting positions within the school and the West Indians hovering uncertainly in the middle, veering one way or another according to personal choice or pressure of forces.

The Asians and the English express different and contrasting aspects of their identities while offloading on to the other group those denied, disowned and repudiated aspects of their racial identity. But each group symbiotically depends on the other to represent for them these disowned identity aspects while continuing to express in somewhat over-emphasised forms their chosen image of themselves. This interaction, I believe, is one based on mutual projection and expresses unconscious collusion between the two groups. To illustrate this: I am attracted firstly by the notion that the values of Asian students, as well as their role as newcomers into a complex, competitive and highly industrialized society, combine to place a high and almost puritanical value on educational achievement, and the hard work, diligence and responsibility which this implies within the school system. In addition the cultural values and the structure of the Asian family lead Asian students to accept the authority of the teacher, with outward respect and deference while continuing to apply themselves well. Trist[25] has suggested that such values may relate to specific stages in industrial society and that these very attitudes characterize societies moving towards increased levels of industrial complexity (such as India for example). Furthermore, a strong incentive for migration of Asians to this country is the regard that they have for the high standards of education here, which, in turn, would be particularly valued by Asian adolescents and be an important focus of their life in the new society. As a consequence of

this, disproportionately high numbers of Asian students within these
two schools proceed to 'A' levels, compared with other racial groups
in the community. West Indians too, share some of these cultural
values, particularly those which accord high status to education, and
those Victorian attitudes which invest great respect and authority in
teachers. By contrast, English working-class values within the same
schools suggest a different contemporary cultural picture. In Trist's
terms, Britain is moving towards a post-industrial period where the
emerging values are self-actualization, self-expression, interdepen-
dence and capacity for joy.

Trist's views now appear to be unduly optimistic about post-
industrial society. Both North America and Western Europe
(including Britain) confront ever-rising inflationary trends and
serious levels of unemployment. But for Asians and for West
Indians, coming from societies which are in the early stages of post-
colonial growth and development and where industrialization is still
rising, education is seen as a longed for opportunity and one, which
in their parent societies, is not readily available to all. To members of
these racial groups higher education brings the promise of enhanced
standards of living, job security and rising social status. However,
many of the English – who have long taken universal education for
granted – feel disenchantment towards notions that higher education may lead to these economic and social advantages. A realistic
look at present trends in rising unemployment, not least among
graduates, brings many a sense of disillusion that education does not
by itself solve these aspirations for a higher standard of living and job
security. To West Indians and Asians, therefore, education is both an
important opportunity and represents the chosen route towards a
better life but to the English working class, who have seen how
current problems within this society have not been surmounted
despite rising standards in higher education and greater opportunities for all, disillusion and disenchantment leads many to turn their
backs on further educational advance. The case material bears this
out as English scholars at these schools are seen as having largely
eschewed ambitious educational aspirations, are keen to leave school
as soon as they are allowed to in terms of age, tend to be rebellious
towards parents and to challenge the authority of teachers openly,
the teachers being seen as parental surrogates. They are eager for
experiments in new-found areas of independence, particularly those
relating to aggression and sexuality.

While the English tend to disparage the Asians for their hard work,
and being conformist, 'teachers' pets' and well-behaved, the Asians

tend to despise the English for their lack of discipline, lack of motivated goals, uncontrolled aggression and rudeness to both teachers and parents and for their sexual experiments and loose, sexually-tinged language. Each group unconsciously seems to use the other as repositories for their disowned and repudiated identity elements, that which each has chosen 'not-to-be'.

The collusive patterns take the shape of a vicious descending spiral because the more the English despise or attack the Indians (and unconsciously envy them) the harder the Indians work, since this is their chosen line of self-defence. The harder they work, the more irritating this becomes to the English and the less in touch the Asians are able to be with their spontaneous impulse life, whether in areas of sex or aggression, since increased self-control is required from them to maintain these chosen defences. But since their impulse life is increasingly constricted and their independence limited by this chosen role, they secretly envy and hate the English for their apparent freedom and licence. However, by doing so it keeps alive for them those very instinctual forces which they have forbidden themselves at present. By the same token, the English keep alive, through their envious hate of the Asians, educational objectives and aspirations. The more the English see themselves perceived by Asians with these images projected onto them, the greater is their defensive need to continue to re-enact, ever more vividly and flamboyantly, these same patterns.

It seems to me that in these ways it is possible that the school as a social arena (whatever else it may do to positively enhance inter-racial good feelings, and I am sure some do a great deal) activates in both English and Asian students – particularly male students – only a part of their full repertoire of racial feelings, and these magnify mutual envies and hatreds. Each group needs the other to comple-ment their chosen identity images and to enact for them their negative identities.

To illustrate some additional points on the above themes, some interesting corroborative vignettes emerge. It is Johanna James, a West Indian who recognizes that at school she is regarded as a 'good-goody' and hates this constricting, and to her, false imputation. Adrian James splits off his positive identity of a hard-working achieving scholar and attributes this to Indians, whereas his disowned aggressive and sexual drives are ascribed to the English. It is Adrian who, with marked insight, notes that it is envy which leads the English boys to scoff at the Asians' new shoes because it is really their scholastic achievements and hard work which they covet and which Adrian recognizes could equally be theirs if they were prepared to work for it. Vera Singh is one of the three subjects in the whole study who does not engage in racial stereotyping, but it was she who in order to avoid being seen by English peers as dull and related happily to her family, engineered false fights with her mother to ensure that she too could be seen as having a turbulent adolescence. Eric Singh notes that Asians are motivated to work hard, but that the English cannot be bothered to take their work seriously. He sees them as mostly involved in smoking, fighting, drinking and in sexual adventures. Of course these are adolescents who are unsure of their identity, and who are experimenting with various roles within a school setting. It is a place where competition and rivalry is allowed, achievement expected and where teachers are seen as parental surrogates.

There are positive ways in which the school encourages inter-racial respect, liking and harmony and in such ways acts as a constraint upon personal conflicts moving into the racial area. Johanna James' experiences with white peers, both in Barbados and in this country, are vitally important in consolidating a steady, mutual respect and affection between herself and white students. It is because of this that she can effectively mobilize the support of her white peers when she was falsely told by one that she smelled. She knows this to be false and they confirm this and give her warm support. For both Johanna James and Vera Singh, school has been the source of close friendships with English girls. It is too early to tell with respect to Adrian James. Eric Singh keeps himself to himself and neither of the Chattaways, John and Elaine would wish for friends who are not white.

Two of the parents have extended their inter-racial contacts through the school. Mrs Chattaway has respect and regard for Asian and West Indian mothers whom she meets when she takes her youngest son to school. The 'good mother' in her allows her to recognize and identify with the 'good mothers' in others, irrespective of race. To this extent, the school constrains her from further racial stereotyping. It is also through the school and as a parent that Mrs Chattaway becomes involved in helping an Asian mother with her daughter, again giving full rein to her considerable qualities as a caring, warm-hearted maternal person.

Mr Singh is the only parent who is an active member of the Parent – Teachers Association and in this role he has made contact with other parents. But he is angry when Eric is exposed to a teacher's assumptions that all Asians are the same and will end up

doing largely menial work. In this context the school becomes a
further extension of the community for Mr Singh and yet another
activator of his anger towards the English who cannot differentiate
between one Asian and another.

Finally, I wish to comment on the specific psychological function
of teachers. Within this racial context, adolescents are highly preoccupied with inner developmental tasks connected with separating
from parents, and yet their emotional dependence on them is still
very important. Furthermore they are coping with the re-arousal of
oedipal strivings. In the case-material, teachers seem to be unconsciously equated with parents and are zealously observed lest they
accord more attention, and hence love, to one student rather than
another or to one racial group rather than another. This creates a
dilemma for the teachers because if immigrants need special help to
assist them with language or cultural adjustment problems, this may
well excite the jealousy of other groups. It is John and Elaine
Chattaway who experience this jealousy intensely; this, in turn,
activates their racial prejudice. However, we know that special
deprivations in their *particular* family have left them especially
vulnerable to this kind of teacher – pupil relationship. To what
extent this kind of jealous reaction may be more generally found, I do
not, of course, know.

(b) The work place :   Since all the subjects who work are engaged in
white-collar, skilled or semi-skilled occupations and none of them
are entrepreneurs, they are not in direct competition with fellow
workers but mutually dependent on each other for collaborative
efforts. The work place emerges from the material as a social arena
where actual work performance and pulling one's weight is the all-
important task and it is the major criterion by which each person
judges the other, irrespective of race. Each person brings to his work
place his own ways of coping interpersonally which becomes
reflected in his inter-racial contacts. Mr James, for instance, behaves
towards others, with sensitivity, restraint and self-regulating consideration and he appreciates it when others treat him in the same
way. Inflammatory issues touching on racial or political matters are
avoided in the canteen so that 'things are not stirred up'. This fits his
personality pattern. His wife healthily and constructively discharges
ordinary aggressive feelings (which are problems to her in other
contexts) in sturdy bouts of teasing, bantering and aggressive
humour with her present Jewish employer. Johanna develops close
and affectionate relations with the English women with whom she

works although she recognizes, with unease, that they are somewhat envious of her evident sex appeal and that they watch how men in the office respond to her. Mr Chattaway, who in other social arenas has deep-seated racial animosities, is able to identify with West Indian and Asian workers as fellow-providers and contributors as long as they work well. His wife has never worked with people of other races, and in her part-time work as a cleaner she is not deeply involved with fellow-workers in any event. Mr Singh is grateful to those Englishmen who have taught him technical aspects of his job but he notes that the English have double standards, judging work-output and quality of work done by coloured immigrants much more harshly than they judge English colleagues. Vera is respected as an equal within the bank, makes good friends among the English girls, and extends her first-hand knowledge of people of various races.

Work appears to be an encapsulated social arena among these subjects. Unresolved identity conflicts are not activated into patterns of racial misuse; work achievements and motivations act as constraints upon identity issues expressing themselves in the area of race. I am, of course, talking about what happens once a subject is at work; the traumatic effects of racial discrimination in obtaining employment, as in Johanna James' case, have been dealt with earlier.

(c) *Health and medical settings*: Within the health and medical arena, roles for medical personnel as well as patients are defined and crystallized and their encounters are rigorously structured by their respective roles and by the professional standards which govern health and medical practice. There is a complementary 'fit' between the professional skill of medically trained workers in the health field, their nurturing and caring approach to the patient and the anxiety, pain and at times regressed neediness of patients. Within this relationship, the patients' anxieties can be contained and helped, regression can be allowed for and some of the angry feeling elicited under stress can be tolerated. Injuries can be made good and fears of illness as inner 'badness' can be made 'right' with the help and skill of a practitioner.

All of the twelve subjects were potential or actual patients at one time or another and none of them are medical or health personnel. Most of them recount times when they have been ill or sought help from medical personnel and very often these experiences with doctors or auxilliary medical staff are with members of different racial groups from the patient. Irrespective of racial prejudice expressed in other social arenas, the encounters during illness create ascending spirals of benign inter-racial contact.

To cite a few examples: it will be recalled that for Mrs James illness brings to the fore the more helpless, regressed, clinging and childish parts of herself and white doctors, nurses, ambulance drivers and fellow patients (as well as their husbands!) are all found to be inordinately helpful, nurturant, caring and carry for her her split-off idealisations. Johanna James who turns back against herself angry hurt feelings provoked by racial discrimination and prejudice, takes her resultant headaches to the white English doctor who recognizes their psychosomatic base and gives understanding to the stress she is under and encourages her to 'let it out'. Mrs Chattaway finds, by chance, that she is discussing her gynaecological complaints on two different occasions with two different Indian doctors who are both 'ever so nice and helpful' and when she is confined at home with Colin, she has a West Indian midwife who is 'marvellous' and whose kindness she appreciates. Mrs Singh, who at first is reluctant and shy to be examined by a white male doctor, finds her many needs for medical and hospital care are well met by the English personnel and she notes their friendliness, gentleness and understanding.

(d) The street: Of all four social arenas, it is the street which activates unresolved conflicts most potently and provocatively so that these manifest themselves in feelings of anger, irritation, disgust, murderous hate and overt violence towards members of other racial groups. It is in the street, whether as motorist, cyclist, driver, passenger, pedestrian, shopper or shopkeeper that individuals of different races mingle and confront each other as anonymous, stripped of their roles, sources of social status and personal identities. It is the visibly different racial exteriors which most clearly define a group identity and which all too readily lead individuals to project on to racial groups those feelings which are stirred up in the street. What is it about the street which activates these feelings?

The street itself is a very neglected area for social and psychological study and in what follows I bring together some ideas which attract me as pertinent. First of all, the street is a place where people move and traverse space, usually with some destination or purpose in mind, so assertive action is expressed through physical push and movement. People are often in a hurry, vying for space, whether on the pavements of crowded inner cities or in the streets. As a result, physically aggressive feelings and overt actions to suit are very readily evoked, frustrations and irritabilities aroused. Secondly, a degree of depersonalization is probably inevitable in the task of navigating the relatively impersonal street as others will be encountered chiefly as impediments to progress or having priority in a queue. Thirdly, the street belongs to everyone and the space of the street is therefore not personally bounded as is an individual's home or work place. It is potentially boundary-free. Fourthly, following through on earlier discussion of Hall's work and also that of Horowitz and his colleagues on the hidden dimensions of space,[26] present knowledge suggests that each person is surrounded by a body-buffer-zone and within the street infringements of, and impingements to this, occur as was shown in the earlier discussion on territoriality of identity. What is transgressed is the deeply felt unconscious notions of what each person feels comfortable with, in other words what feels 'right' to them. Ideas of 'proper' ways of behaving in the street, of how people move, walk, stand, converse, gesture, look, the sights which are considered pleasing or distressing to the eye, the volume of sounds found bearable, what smells excite, invite or repel, all these can transcend and rupture invisible boundaries – and when that occurs, people feel these are unwarrantable intrusions on their sense of personal space and very strong feelings are aroused. Privacies are invaded by ways of looking, moving and touching which penetrate these invisible boundaries. Since cultures profoundly influence the distinctive ways in which one habitually learns to look, or not to look, to move and to touch, to talk in certain tones and at a particular pitch, to gesture and gesticulate within the common space of the street, different races expressing different cultural patterns unconsciously transgress the body-buffer-zones of others. Fifthly, the street as a social arena lacks the constraints seen in the three other social arenas where common goals can bring co-operation, or where roles can support and maintain a complementary or constructive relationship. Everybody is anonymous within the street; there are few rules, except those that define where we may move (driver, pedestrian etc.); there is an absence of personal identities and no shared tasks which lead to roles being interdependent. All of this activates and brings to the surface that which can be *seen*, namely racial differences in physical appearance. Sixthly, because there is no way of having one's individuality recognized, it is in the street that all members of a racial group are most exposed to the basic indignity of being regarded as indistinguishable from other members of the same race. Seventhly, Milgram[27] in looking at the socio-psychological aspects of city life has suggested that city life constitutes a continuous set of encounters with *overload*, that is the inability to process inputs from the environment because there are too many to cope with or because they come too fast. In trying to conserve psychic energy, he suggests, people in crowded cities reserve energy for carefully defined inputs. The ultimate adaptation is to disregard totally the interests, needs, and demands of those whom one does not define as relevant to the satisfactions of one's own personal needs, and to develop highly efficient perceptual means of determining whether a person falls into the category of friend or stranger. From this it follows that where there are large numbers and high density (as for example in Athol) racial groups may well be reacted to in the street as physical presences, as units, and not as individuals. As such they lie outside the orbit of either friendly feelings or of empathy.

For all these reasons, it is in the street that the sensitivities of almost all our subjects are highly inflamed in ways which activate conflicts in the direction of racial intolerance. Examples have already been given earlier in relation to a range of spatial infringements and impingements bearing on territory. In addition to all of these, some subjects perceive the street as a focus of anxiety, threat and physical danger. For many it is seen as the place where violence lurks and can erupt, a place where each man may harm others. Mrs James protects Adrian from the street. It is in the street that Mr Chattaway uses his car to punish Indians even though this may kill. It is in the street that John and his skinhead gang members attack and are attacked by Pakistanis. For Mrs Chattaway, the street is a focus of anxiety not only because of what her husband may be doing at the traffic lights with his car, but also because of what her son John may be doing and what, in turn, may be done to him. She fears that the children may become victims of unpredictable violence. Elaine Chattaway is also frightened in the street; she too is uneasy about what her father may be doing with his car at the traffic lights, but her fear also focusses on Indian boys 'with knives' and on incidents of overt violence between Asian and white English boys. It was just off the street that Mr Singh was gravely assaulted by fellow Indians, yet his life was saved by an unknown English boy, and Mr Singh is concerned and anxious as he notes instances of child neglect in the street by his own people, particularly the children of women who go to work. He also sees the street as the focus for English and Indian fights in which it is difficult to know who is attacking and who is defending. Eric Singh is exposed to being called names in the street by English boys and his anxiety is compounded by the fact that whoever he may be with is intimidated by this, and falls in with the name-calling too. It is in the street that he fears he may be mistaken for a Kenyan Asian which arouses special anxiety because he is involved in scapegoating them himself. The street is also perceived by some as the place where sexual confrontations and attacks may occur. The Chattaway family are particularly concerned about Elaine and the possibility of encounters with West Indians or Indians, their anxieties exacerbated by an actual incident involving her.

In all these ways, the street as a social arena activates racial prejudices and stereotypes. Are there any ways in which the street brings about constructive inter-racial feelings? In only a few instances is the street seen as a place where good things happen between people of different races. Mrs Chattaway is the only subject who tells of finding pleasure in unfamiliar exposure to new cultural experiences. She enjoys the Indian music from the Sikh temple. As she walks down a street some distance from her home, she hears it and likes it.

Four subjects find kindness and help in the street from people of other races. They all needed that help. Mrs Chattaway befriended the weeping coloured child who had lost her money, Mrs Singh was helped by a white woman when she was frail and ill, Vera – when a small child – was brought home by a kind white woman when she was very frightened, and her father's life was saved by the intervention of an English boy. All of these acts of kindness originate with the English. Why Mrs Chattaway, in contrast to her other racial attitudes, construes the street as a place where benign encounters can happen, is a fascinating question to which I return in the section on family dynamics which follows.

These are small constraints, but nonetheless important ones, in the face of the much more insidiously potent activators which propel many blindly towards racial prejudice and hostility in the streets of our cities.

(v) Family dynamics as activators and constraints
The family, with its characteristic patterns of relationships between members, habitual ways of interpreting and coping with experience, and shared system of values and norms, functions as a small social system which may either activate or constrain its members from racial misuse. There are two different ways in which this happens. There are those processes which originate *within* the family and subsequently spill over and find their discharge in the neighbourhood. And then there are those processes which arise from a dynamic interplay between vulnerabilities inside the family and the inter-racial tensions, excitements or harmonies within the neighbourhood. In such cases, what starts outside the family may be taken

into the family and once inside, may compound and exacerbate existing conflicts. It may stay within the family and be contained or 'held' there, or it may undergo modification or correction within the family. In short, the approach taken is to regard both the family and the neighbourhood as open social systems, interacting with each other through permeable boundaries,[28] so that processes both from the family towards the neighbourhood, and *vice versa*, can be traced as they oscillate back and forth.

In what follows, I will be looking at how the James family, the Chattaways and the Singhs function as three different families in relation to a variety of processes which appear relevant to the activation or constraint of racial prejudice. These three families differ not only racially but in their *cultural* origins and patterns. It is impossible to unravel what is *cultural* from those unique features which distinguish one family from another within the same culture. I am unable to draw any *cultural* conclusions on the basis of a study of one family from each of three cultural groups, since this study is not constituted to make such generalizations. In what follows, therefore, I want to emphasise once more that no inferences are being made about *the* English family, *the* West Indian or *the* Indian family. It is the processes which concern us and how these function as activators or constraints within three specific families – the James', the Chattaways and the Singhs.

(a) Common coping patterns within the family, as activators or constraints: The effects of socialization experiences on each of the subjects has been explored in the preceding three chapters. In the theoretical literature extensive coverage is given to the importance of parental attitudes in the determination of prejudice[29] and relevant portions of this have been referred to earlier. In what follows, I move on to consider those coping patterns within the family social system which function as activators or constraints.

1 Cognitive processes: The thought processes and style of thinking which is tacitly encouraged within a family affects and also reflects how its members interpret and construe their experience. Previous work on those thought processes which underlie racial attitudes[30] suggests that one of the major problems in racial prejudice is the tendency of some people to categorize groups prematurely and by over-generalizing, they move away from reality-oriented thinking towards exaggeration and stereotyping of group differences. Such cognitive styles differ from those in people who are able to cope with ambiguities, do not prematurely foreclose and generalize, are open to new information, and are capable of reality-testing. Some families show a high tolerance for irrational thought processes and premature group categorizations while other families continue to reality-test their observations, revising and changing earlier judgements. The James family is markedly reality-orientated in its cognitive style, probably partly under the influence of Mr James' mother who cared for Johanna and Adrian, and partly under that of Mr James himself. Mr James certainly has a striking record in this respect; we have seen how, after the rather shocking experiences of his first few days as an immigrant, which in another person could easily have stimulated persecutory feelings with consequent racial stereotyping, he realistically set about observing how other West Indians were faring, found that not everything was bad, and decided that he could improve his condition. He also showed a reality-orientated response to the loss of his house-deposit money which made it possible for him to begin saving anew. Johanna reveals a similar cognitive style in her responses to racial discrimination and prejudice. She feels outraged, hurt and angry but is able to assess the situation realistically and draw her own conclusions about the individuals and social forces involved without resorting to distorted and fixed racial stereotyping. Within this family, cognitive style acts as a constraint upon racial prejudice. It helps to modify and reduce the fixity of Adrian's emergency resort to group stereotyping under the multiple stresses of immigration, entry to a new society and reunion with a family which he hardly knew. It also helps to temper Mrs James' tendencies to split off 'good' and 'bad' objects. Of course under stress members of this family, in common with the rest of mankind, show tendencies towards irrationality but what is important is the overall *balance* of reality-orientated as opposed to irrational cognitive processes.

The Singh family, too, on the whole have more reality-orientation in their thought processes than irrationality. Mr Singh is able to distinguish between one individual and another and not to move to a hasty over-generalization. Reality features are appraised and kept in mind and these cognitive patterns are striking in both his wife and daughter Vera. Eric, who has had to cope with severe deprivations shows more tendencies towards stereotyped thinking than the rest of his family; this may also, in time, be tempered by the family style.

In the Chattaway family the balance of irrational thought processes is stronger than those which are reality-orientated. The dominant role played in the cognitive developmental patterns within this family is probably that of Mr Chattaway, who uses premature categorization of racial groups and stereotyped thingking, generalizing about racial difference with absoluteness. His effects on the family are pervasive, and his children seem to share his cognitive style. Mrs Chattaway is much more open to reality-testing than the rest of the family; within the orbit of the home she conforms to their style of thought but expresses greater freedom of judgement and follows her own reality appraisals in many inter-racial encounters outside the home. All the previous examples of this family serve to illustrate their cognitive style well. One only needs recall Mr Chattaway's insistence that no white people *ever* cross against the lights at his pedestrian crossing to underline his style of global categorization.

Whether the view is taken that cognitive patterns are the result of deep-seated inner conflicts, or whether they are viewed as primary processes which in turn affect attitudes, nonetheless they are of importance both in the development and in the maintenance of racial prejudice. In the James and Singh families these operate as *constraining* influences upon racial misuse, but in the Chattaway family they *activate* and entrench racial prejudice and gross racial misuse.

2 Ways of coping with stress: The three families differ in their characteristic patterns of coping with stressful situations. The James', when up against it, tend to pick themselves up, assess the situation realistically, mobilize *active* ways of tackling the problem, focussing upon the main target, and try again with marked courage, persistence and an ability to tolerate frustration. One has only to remember Mr James' responses to all his disappointments, or Mrs James' capacity to cope with her first year in this country when she was separated geographically from her husband and her children without losing faith, and Johanna's striking response to racial discrimination when seeking her first job. After each depressing rejection and feeling depleted and depressed, she was urged by her family to 'try again'.

The Chattaway family, with less ego-resources available to them, and with a different cognitive style, deal with stress by first of all proportioning blame for its occurrence outside the family and so avoiding a realistic assessment. The counter-attack when it comes is not directed at the source of the problem but takes the form of often frenetic activity discharged against groups felt to be responsible. There is apathy and depression too, as when Mr Chattaway is out of work but turns down offers of employment and nurses his grievances. But he projectively continues to identify with John in his attacks on Asians as a vicarious outlet for himself. With his car he also indulges in overtly violent attacks on Asian pedestrians. Although activity is expressed by the Chattaways in relation to stress, it is not channelled towards the achievement of ego-enhancing life tasks but used negatively to destroy, punish, and attack groups who are felt responsible for the stressful situations, and since there is a high intensity of feeling within this family the ways of coping with stress are charged with passionate and feverish conviction, based on a minimum of reality-testing.

The Singh family divides on sex lines. Both Mr Singh and Eric share, to an extent, common patterns for coping with stress and Mrs Singh and Vera behave very differently. The male pattern under stress is to resort to demand even more of themselves, thus their ego-ideals become higher, and greater self-control and ambitious striving after goals is required of them. Their style of coping tends to lead to compartmentalizing; the striving for goodness leads to some splitting, in that others are seen as having lower standards. Under stress, activity is harnessed to exert pressure upon the self. It is the self which is felt to be the answer to the overcoming of problems, but some rigidity of controls in turn leads to racial (and social class) stereotyping. However, reality-testing proceeds alongside this too; having explored the possibilities of Canada as a better environment from the point of view of racial tolerance, Mr Singh is able to work actively towards this on behalf of members of his family. If the conditions for the exertion and recognition of the self are not available in one setting, then active measures are taken to *remove* the self to a setting within which it can function better. Mrs Singh copes with stress by being enormously supportive and helpful to her husband and family if they are in difficulty. She may pay for this with psychosomatic problems, although the picture is less clear here. Vera deals with problems by active means and her plans for going to Canada are realistically engaged.

By their ways of coping with stress, the James' patterns act as consistent and important constraints upon racial misuse, the Chattaway's patterns serve as powerful activators of racial stereotyping and gross racial misuse, and within the Singh family the picture is a divided one, the women acting as constraining forces, the men activated in part towards racial stereotyping.

3 Capacity to tolerate ambivalent feelings: Families differ in their general ability to admit and sustain feelings towards each other which ambivalently combine both love and hate. Some families are able to weather dissensions, rows and tensions without the solid undertow of good loving feelings being endangered. They are able to tolerate their own ambivalence which in turn allows them to tolerate this in others. But there are families who are more impoverished and less able to trust their loving good feelings; arguments and dissensions leave them feeling more depleted inside and their worst persecutory fears rise to the surface. Their inability to cope with ambivalent feelings is of fundamental importance for race relations. The good feelings are split off from the bad and this leads to the stereotyping of racial groups.

Mr James and Johanna show a marked capacity to accept their ambivalent feelings which in turn helps them to accept these in others. They can 'hold' their feelings within themselves and within the family and find these to be ego-strengthening. Mrs James and Adrian, for different internal reasons, resort to splitting under stress. Adrian still has to use racial issues to balance his account during his early years in this country. But it would seem that the high tolerance of ambivalence in Mr James and Johanna and the use of humour as a way of expressing ambivalence both within the family and outside it by all its members (Mrs James' relationship with her white employer for example), seem to ameliorate the intensity and potential rigidity of these splitting procedures. As stress abates for both Mrs James and her son they both move away from rigid racial stereotyping towards a more tolerant position.

With the notable exception of Mrs Chattaway, the three Chattaways have little capacity to trust their loving feelings and are unable to tolerate ambivalence in themselves or others. The serious deprivations and early childhood history of Mr Chattaway, as well as his experiences at school when he seriously injured another boy make it understandable how endangered his good feelings seem to be by fears of an inner 'badness'. He and his two children project their worst paranoid fears on to racial scapegoats, unable to weather their own ambivalence. Once again Mrs Chattaway, with a quite different family background, has more capacity to trust her ambivalent feelings but these are put under severe strain within the family and she seems to outwardly conform more often than not.

The Singh family again divides along sex lines. The male members show difficulties in coming to terms with ambivalence but the women are both strikingly able to trust their loving feelings, to weather storms and quarrels, and to accept ambivalence. Within the family the calming influence of Mrs Singh particularly, exerts a restraining and ameliorating influence on the compartmentalizing towards which the male members of the family tend to incline.

To summarise : in their capacity to tolerate ambivalence the James' predominantly, and to a lesser extent the Singhs are *constrained* from racial misuse; by their incapacity to preserve loving feelings with lots of ambivalence mixed up in it, the Chattaways' feelings of love are endangered and the threat that its absence creates it to *activate* racial prejudice and gross racial misuse.

4 Projections outside the family :   What is capable of being tolerated and worked out *inside* the family system and contained within it affects that which is projected and has to be extruded into the neighbourhood. That which cannot be confirmed, validated or even expressed within a family may often lead to it being sought by necessity outside the family. It is this balance between the inner dynamics of the family system and the psychological use made of the neighbourhood which helps to explain why the Chattaways, who so intensely dislike living in Athol with Asian and West Indian immigrants, nonetheless continue to live there. They need these racial groups to maintain their chosen defensive patterns. By offloading their denied and unresolved identity conflicts on to these racial groups, the equilibrium of the family is sustained by these projections and it helps to hold the family together. The equilibrium they have achieved, although deplorable from the point of view of society and the racial groups so grossly misused, serves the needs of this family by siphoning off the intra-familial tensions. This may throw light on what might happen if this family did move to another neighbourhood; they would have to confront and face up to their individual conflicts and aggravated sources of tension within the family, or they would have to continue to find scapegoats, either racial or other social groups, even if these were not to be found within their neighbourhood. Membership of anti-immigrant organizations such as the National Front, for instance, could serve some of their defensive purposes but not all.

This way of looking at the Chattaway family throws light on why some other white families within Athol may also choose to remain there although imbued with both hate and fear of their black and brown neighbours. An equilibrium is achieved through the unconscious interaction between the inner family dynamics and the misuse made of racial groups, the family needing to have racial scapegoats whom they can massively blame for their inner uncertainties and tensions. To survive without them is to face inner tasks which are overwhelmingly difficult for such families. To remain, builds into the society collusive patterns between inter-racial scapegoating and a family homeostasis, patterns which are deeply destructive of inter-racial harmony and bought at the cost of some family stability, the sickness being extruded into the community. This is what the Chattaway family are doing.

Turning to more specific emotions and feelings, the case material shows that what is kept within the boundaries of the family, there sustained and tolerated by its members, directly relates to that which is extruded into the neighbourhood. The experience of envy and jealousy is strong in Mr Chattaway, John and Elaine and also in Eric Singh. Within the Chattaway family (with the possible exception of Mrs Chattaway) feelings of envy and jealousy, along with other powerful feelings, are kept hidden and denied. As a result all three express unconscious envy and jealousy outside the family circle, and the police and teachers as well as racial groups are used for the dramatic re-enactment of scenarios which unconsciously reproduce family groups of parents and favoured children, each of the Chattaways identifying with the children who are by-passed.

By contrast, envy and jealousy appear to be openly admitted and apparently tolerated within the Singh family. Eric in his life history repeatedly identifies his feelings of envy and jealousy, and Mrs Singh shows a singular appreciation of these feelings and how they manifest themselves within family relationships. As a result Eric seems more able to trust his envious and jealous feelings which are expressed, contained and understood *within* the family circle, and so he is not impelled to re-enact these vicariously through surrogate parental substitutes or surrogate siblings within the school context.

Denied, hidden and avoided conflicts within a family can therefore act as *activators* for these same conflicts moving outside the family orbit where they are offloaded onto other racial groups. Where a family is able to face up to its major conflicts and tries to deal with them, however inadequately, with some openness and tolerance, this in turn helps to *constrain* them from finding expression in racial misuse.

5 Identity confirmation within the family and outside the family : If the family is able to give some recognition and confirmation to each of its members in terms of their unique identities and their struggles to express themselves as the people they feel themselves to be, there seems to be less need for these members of the family obsessively to *demand* identity confirmation outside the family. Of course they will also seek the ordinary confirmation of their identity within the community at large but an obsessive demand to wrest identity recognition and confirmation from the neighbourhood is another matter. It is possible that Mr Chattaway's need to be confirmed within the family as an assertive and powerful figure is insufficiently met and that this leaves him feeling vulnerable, humiliated and impotent to control and influence the members of his family in effective ways. He does not take this need to be seen as a man who can control others to his place of work, where he explicitly rejects the opportunity offered to him to control others, but he obsessively acts out this need at the traffic lights with his motor car. Here indeed he feels power over the life and limbs of Asian pedestrians.

Johanna's struggles to secure active confirmation of her adult, mature – and therefore sexual – self within the family exacerbates her need for that same adult recognition in the community and makes her especially aware of how racial prejudice and discrimination deny her this full confirmation.

6 Alternative channels to racial groups: the diversity of channels through which identity can be expressed: The conditions of everyday life create hazards for all the subjects in their attempts to maintain a rewarding image of themselves and secure their identities. Instead of using racial groups for bolstering identity, what other options do these three families have for protecting their identity and in what positive ways are their aggressive energies being utilized?

Aggression is not only brought into play as an urgent defense against threats to identity and feared hostility or provocation, but it may positively serve to raise self-esteem through a wide range of constructive activities. The steady pursuit of work goals, the pleasure in achievement for its own sake, the mastery of skills, the development of hobbies, the participation in active sports and a wide range of satisfying social relationships harness aggressive energies. Constructive and creative ways of tackling the problems of everyday life all call upon reservoirs of aggression. The three families differ in the diversity of channels which they have at their disposal for expressing aggressive energies. The greater the number of optional channels and the richer the use made of these, the more powerfully they may constrain racial groups from being misused to bolster identity. Rewarding experiences, which in turn lead to the enhancing of identity, are facilitated by the fullness of use of alternative channels.

The James family use a wide variety of channels through which their active healthy aggressive needs are expressed. For all four of them work is a major source of satisfaction involving the active pursuit of work goals, the mastery of different skills and the pleasure in a job well done. They work constructively and well, using considerable energy which they are able to sustain and in turn they each receive the satisfaction of meeting their own standards as well as the pleasure and satisfaction of having their effective performance recognized. The home which they own is another channel for much purposive, constructive and creative effort. They garden, decorate, furnish, fix and repair and are rightly proud of what they have achieved. They all have friends; Adrian's late arrival in this country has meant a slower development in this direction, but he too shares family friends. Social relationships are important to them all and they lead an active social life with occasional parties and dances to which they go, often as a family. But, in addition, they each have friends of their own. For Adrian sport is an active area for the channelling of his energies, and membership of a church a sustained area with active participatiion in the choir and in other duties.

The Chattaways have sparse and limited channels. Work for Mr Chattaway has ceased to be meaningful at the present time and he has withdrawn from it, feeling inwardly dejected and demoralized. Work outside the home has never been of much importance to Mrs Chattaway and it occupies only a few hours each evening. It is her work as a wife and mother which serve as the principal channel for her constructive energies. John does not seem to be strongly motivated towards work goals and uses work largely as an arena for pranks. Elaine cannot wait to leave school. The family has very little social life; the parents' leisure patterns were largely passive ones in the past—going to the pub, playing cards or bingo—but these seem to have fallen away, partly due to the birth of their youngest son and partly because of their feeling that community facilities have been taken over by coloured immigrants. Elaine sorely lacks stable friends and longs for them. John as a member of a gang has the fellowship of his gang members, but even these serve only to channel his energies into highly destructive attacks on Pakistanis or on rival white gangs. The Chattaways' home, in contrast to the other two families, does not belong to them but to the Council and although it is well maintained, it does not act as focus for constructive or creative energies of family members. Hobbies do not figure very much in the family except for Mr Chattaway who reads largely political and ideological material which serves to cement his negative views on coloured immigration and animosity towards coloured immigrants. John's interest and passion for motorbikes, on which he roams the streets of Athol in search of trouble, are also a means of facilitating racial attacks. These severely limited channels for developing and maintaining self esteem, linked with what appears to be apparently high energy levels among members of this family, create a reservoir of highly labile unfocussed aggression, prodded and stimulated by unresolved conflicts; it is this which spills over into the racial area. As a result, there are very few constraints against the use of racial groups for the bolstering of self-esteem. By the singular lack of alternative channels, and the intensity with which the few channels involving racial misuse are used, racial prejudice and racial attacks are activated.

The Singh family have a widely diversified range of channels. Mr Singh is a man of considerable intelligence, energy and ambition and invests a large part of himself in doing his job well, even to the extent of night work which he undertakes to increase his efficiency. He derives great satisfaction from this and also from the respect and recognition accorded him by his superiors. Vera at the bank and Eric at school both attack their work with energy, diligence and a sense of responsibility and also derive pleasure from their efforts and the recognition afforded to them. Mrs Singh has never worked outside the home and obtains her satisfactions from her family life and her role as a wife and mother, which she takes seriously and from which she derives satisfaction. The family vests her role with importance and this helps to sustain her. Their home, which they own, is a very important focus for their family life. It is well cared for, but mostly its importance is as the very hub of their family relationships which are all-important to them. They have friends and entertain them at home and also use the club facilities connected with Mr Singh's employing body. It is here that they use sports' facilities and have social contacts with fellow employees and their families of all races. One of the side advantages of Mr Singh's employment enables the family to fly abroad at very little cost and they enjoy family holidays in Europe where they all share a villa. These activities have widened their horizons and extended their interests, solidifying family bonds, each member drawing much nourishment from their relatively full family life. All of these diverse channels serve as constraints upon the misuse of racial groups.

The diversity of optional channels in relation to the strength and intensity of aggressive needs is of major relevance to inter-racial patterns. The Chattaways are the one family with both a very limited range of channels and yet high intensity of aggressive needs. It is this combination which creates a *fixity* of patterns in relation to race: the projections on to racial groups are pressured because of lack of spread across diverse channels. This puts their attitudes and behaviour largely out of the range of reality-testing. What each of them has put by projection into racial groups seems to be stuck there and becomes rigidly fixed.

In summary: a large variety of options for reconstituting security can act as constraints upon racial misuse. Very little diversity of channels linked with intensity of aggressive needs powerfully activates and fixes patterns of racial misuse.

7 Values within the family: Families express their shared values in many different contexts of life, throwing light on how they orientate themselves to the world. One way of identifying these family values is to trace in the life stories how each family tries to protect their good objects, namely something or somebody whom each cares for and is experienced as benevolent.

Whereas the James family stresses positive values in interpersonal relationships such as concern and care, consideration, kindness and being helpful towards others, the Chattaways tend to think in terms of restraint, of *not* doing something and so curtailing or avoiding doing harm to the other. They place the emphasis on curbing oneself. Mr Chattaway's need to protect his own children from his feared destructiveness expresses itself in *not* holding them as babies. Since *doing* can bring destructiveness to the fore, ways of protecting those whom each loves involves exerting constant vigilance and control. This may throw light on the fact that work, which once meant positive things to Mr Chattaway, is now a 'not-doing' area. The emphasis in this family is therefore on control and constraint and anxiety is an ever-present feature. Positive values are not explicitly striven for.

The Singh family is markedly influenced by religious and moral precepts of what each person *ought* to be and how each *ought* to behave. Emphasis is upon love and mutual care, on being a respected and good citizen contributing to the common well-being of all, working hard and being respectable and respected, considerate to others and above all responsible for one's own way of life. Mr Singh's catastrophic first few years in this country, when he felt that he betrayed his own firmly held standards and principles, are openly faced by him and discussed with all the members of his family including his youngest children. He points out his own weakness in that period – his moral failure to live up to his own values – and then proceeds to show how he resumed full responsibility for his situation and fought back to regain his self respect, and in the process, the full respect of his wife and family and others in the community. Of all three families, this family consistently emphasizes *moral* values and attitudes, an emphasis which is of course related to the severe standards which the male subjects set themselves. As a way of expressing their love and care for each other and for others whom they value, the giving of gifts, whether of money, food, clothes, jewellery and other good things of life, symbolize gratitude and love. This is not solely the parents' privilege. Vera, for instance, pays for part of a family holiday in Europe out of her own savings, taking with her her parents and some siblings. To give within the Singh family is to love and to appreciate, and to receive is to know you are loved.

The Singhs believe that they each assume responsibility for what happens to them in life, for the choices which they make, for their actions and for the consequences. The James', too, although not spelling this philosophy out in the same articulate ways, nonetheless also show by their actions and values that each holds himself accountable to achieve that to which he aspires. The Chattaways (with the notable exception of Mrs Chattaway) at present appear to view themselves as largely *acted upon* by those with whom they interact. They show a lack of attributed responsibility which in turn makes few internal demands on each member, and whatever damands are made seem to be largely external in origin. They are concerned with the avoidance of harm and the use of denial to throw the blame elsewhere, rather than assuming it as part of their own responsibility.

These different value systems serve to constrain both the James and the Singh families from the misuse of racial groups, but play into the hands of the Chattaways by activating their racial prejudices; vigilance and control is within the family only and even there it has its limitations; outside, in the inter-racial arena, their values do not help them to curb their racial animosities.

In all the ways already analysed, each family is influenced by the compounding of activators or constraints which re-inforce each other in self-perpetuating cycles within the family. In the James family, each one of the areas discussed above reveal family patterns which constrain racial misuse. These cumulatively strengthen the influence of any one pattern by its combination with others acting in the same direction. And so constraints against racial prejudice within the James family are *stabilized* and *re-inforced* by cumulative constraining factors. The Singh family, to a lesser degree, also reveal a similar compounding of constraints against racial misuse. The Chattaways' self-perpetuating cycle moves in the opposite direction. Each of the patterns discussed above show how that family system activates racial prejudice and misuse, *stabilizing* and *re-inforcing* its *destructive* path.

(b) Family dynamics and race dynamics: How does the inter-racial situation in the neighbourhood become mirrored inside the family? And how do inner family patterns latch on to specific inter-racial aspects of life in the neighbourhood?

Inter-racial relationships in the neighbourhood vary from relatively good and constructive to those which are bad and destructive. The first example, showing a fluid inter-change between family and neighbourhood is taken from the James family where Johanna's white friends, made at school, church and work, come to stay at her home. Here the inter-racial values within the home, the general orientation and family patterns confirm and further strengthen these bonds of inter-racial accord, solidifying them so that Johanna, in turn, is strong enough in her own convictions to later help her white friends to 'take the plunge' and go to parties where people of all races mix freely and in friendship. What is initiated in the neighbourhood in terms of friendship bonds, moves into the home where these are further strengthened, and Johanna then takes her re-inforced feelings of inter-racial friendship back into the community to work in ever-widening fields.

The next three examples are drawn from the Chattaway family and exemplify how specific vulnerabilities or hazards within the family lock into matching features of race relations within the neighbourhood, there compounding and exacerbating the original feature with direct implications for race relations.

The strong bonds between Mrs Chattaway and John, which have evident oedipal features, leads Mr Chattaway to feel jealous and to feel excluded and pushed out by his son. When John borrows his tools without permission, he is outraged at this invasion of his shed and the threat to his possessions. This, and similar events, make him even more sensitive to issues of jealousy and of being invaded or pushed out of his community space by coloured immigrants which in any event he is also experiencing in his neighbourhood. But this, in turn, lowers his threshold for dealing with his son's behaviour realistically as each of these 'invaded' areas – both within the family as well as outside the family, aggravate the vulnerable inner core of his conflicts, thus compounding them. The wheel turns . . .

Another example drawn from this same family concerns the high incidence within the family of severe conflicts associated with body damage and related fears and phantasies. The apparent body integrity of visibly different groups in the community unconsciously triggers off their own body fears and among the male Chattaways this leads to physically overt attacks on the others' apparent body integrity. These, in turn, stimulate renewed anxieties and persecutory fears of retaliatory body harm which may be inflicted on themselves, so compounding the original sense of damage to their vulnerable selves. The cycle continues inexorably.

Finally, the shouting and out-of-control aggression of Colin, the youngest child, exacerbates vulnerabilities to shouting and aggressive noises of racial groups within the community and to any apparent lack of self-control which they may reveal. Thresholds of tolerance for all of these impingements are lowered. The less they are able to cope with Colin's difficulties, the more exposed they are to noise and aggressive displays in the neighbourhood. Each impingement lowers their capacity to deal with the other realistically, and the cycle continues, ever in the same direction.

Turning to the Singh family, Mr Singh's shame and humiliation at how he failed to live up to his own standards in his early years in this country was followed by gigantic efforts to rehabilitate himself and he impressively succeeded. When the English are seen to perceive him and his family as indistinguishable from ignorant Asians of no particular achievement or worth, that which the family has so zealously fought for is put in psychological jeopardy and their reaction towards the English is compounded and exacerbated by this inner family struggle. This in turn leads the male Singhs to higher and higher ego-ideal standards for themselves and more rigorous controls which in turn made them even more vulnerable whenever they are regarded as indistinguishable from other Asians. The pressure on them grows, as does their sensitivity to the affronts to their achievements, and to their personal identity.

(vi) Intrapsychic activators and constraints

Some people under the pressure of unresolved identity conflicts misuse racial groups and others do not. What is there within the make-up of each person which, *in interaction with other activators and constraints*, may cumulatively account for these differences? The identity analyses have provided some insights into the part played by intrapsychic factors in each of the subjects and these are now pulled together in general terms.

(a) Early childhood influences and determinants: The extent to which

the child's needs in early life are more or less adequately met significantly affects the potential for later development. Where basic needs for love and security are met by reliable care, and where a sense of belonging and being valued has been established, it seems that these are most likely to enhance later possibilities for tolerance and respect towards others. But a great deal will depend on the other activating and constraining factors. When there has been deprivation of these basic needs, the inner foundation on which tolerant behaviour is based may be largely lacking.

Let us look first at those subjects who suffered an evident deprivation of these basic needs. No less than seven of the twelve subjects were exposed to stressful experiences in early childhood arising from the early death of a parent, gross deprivation of parental love and care, or from long separations from parental figures. Of these seven, three subjects suffered especially grievous losses and serious deprivations.

Mr Chattaway never knew his father and his mother did not live with him and only saw him occasionally. Brought up by austere grandparents, he does not know who his father is to this day, and the double deprivation of both parents as reliable, caring figures left him with apparently ungratified needs and wounds to his self-esteem. Maslow[31] has shown how such early deficiencies in love and care can lead people in later life to treat others primarily as need-gratifiers, not as the whole individuals whom they are but rather as interchangeable units. Mr Chattaway's racial feelings appear to originate in these early and very painful deprivations which aroused inner anxieties and unconscious fears and left him with a damaged sense of his own worth.

Eric Singh suffered many separations from his parents. At the age of one and a half, and after an infancy where he was greatly loved and indulged by both his parents, he was precipitately removed to an institutional nursery when his mother was unexpectedly hospitalized. It will be recalled that his father thought it best not to visit his small son; and as the boy was too young to understand, his world suddenly changed catastrophically. Later, when he developed asthma as a very small boy, he had two fairly long bouts in hospital. At the age of seven, when severely ill with asthma, he was sent to India because of his health and there he remained with his maternal grandparents for nearly three years. He missed his parents and siblings acutely and the devoted care of his grandparents seemed to do little to assuage his painful feelings of loss, deprivation, loneliness and suffering. These severe early deprivations have left their mark on his later relationships, notably those involving race where he shows the least tolerance of all the members of his family.

Adrian James was separated from both his parents at the age of two when they emigrated from Barbados, and although he was left in the care of an exceptionally warm and devoted paternal grandmother, he lacked a father's presence and had to wait until he was fifteen years old before his parents could afford to send for him to join them in this country. This created severe stress and inner anxieties and he early resorted to splitting processes as a way of coping with these. His re-union with his family gradually led towards an enhanced inner integration, although in his first year or two in this country he still resorted to splitting processes. After the study was complete, a return visit revealed that racial stereotyping had virtually ceased.

These three subjects are the ones who suffered most grievously and it is striking that they are among the most racially prejudiced of all the subjects (although Adrian's presence in the group is transitional).

Another four subjects also sustained deaths of parents and separations from parents during early childhood, but all were fortunate to have unusual sources of compensatory love and devotion from a surviving parent or from grandparents. Johanna James, from the age of six, was cared for by an already familiar and beloved grandmother. Vera Singh, separated from her father for the first three years of life was cared for not only by a cherishing mother but also by two devoted maternal grandparents. Mr Singh, both of whose parents died before he was five, was brought up by a grandmother who committed herself entirely to his care; and although he too lacked a father's presence, the extended Sikh family provided him with alternative paternal figures in addition to the warm and consistent devotion of his grandmother. And finally, there is Mrs Chattaway, who lived with both her parents until their divorce when she was six, and thereafter was cared for by her father and her paternal grandmother, both of whom she loved; but she also kept in close and continuous contact with her mother, of whom she was very fond and with whom she went to live when she was ten, thus acquiring not only a much-loved mother but also, in the process, a stepfather of whom she was extremely fond. In all four cases, these alternative sources of love seem to have given inner sources of security and stability and to have acted as a constraint upon racial misuse. (Mrs Chattaway's racial prejudice expresses conformity to the present family pattern, as her interpersonal dealings are remarkably free of racial prejudice.)

The subjects who show the greatest intensity of racial prejudice are Mr Chattaway, John Chattaway, Eric Singh and Adrian James (transitionally). Since Mr Chattaway lacked a father in his life, and since he unconsciously felt himself to be destructive and was fearful of what he might do to his children, this in turn seems to have deprived John of a sense of inner security and stability which Mr Chattaway was unable to give and still sorely lacks in his own life. These four subjects all sustained serious deprivations and it is these which *activate* their patterns of racial misuse.

At the other polar extreme, the subjects who show an impressively high racial *tolerance* are Mrs Singh, Vera Singh, Johanna James and to a somewhat lesser extent, Mr James. It is striking that the two Singhs and the James' shared in common a 'mother-figure' who was responsible for their early care. Mrs Singh's parents were responsible for her early care and for the early care of Vera; Mr James' mother also brought up her son and in turn, Johanna. These care-giving and apparently nurturant parental figures appear to have consistently contributed to the positive qualities of these four people, helping them through their earliest developmental phases in reasonably healthy ways, making it possible for them to feel loved and valued, which later shows in their evident capacities for racial tolerance.

It is the *quality* of relationship between a mother-figure and a young infant which helps to determine how a child weathers the earliest developmental phases. The outcome of these early phases is viewed as critically important for the concerns of this book since the way the paranoid-schizoid and the depressive phases[32] are handled will help to shape, for example, how people later come to terms with separation and loss and whether they may experience their inner world and the outer environment as overwhelmingly threatening and unmanageable; or, if the outcome is reasonably good, how well they are able to tolerate, in themselves and in others, feelings of ambivalence. If however the outcome is poor, individuals feel too impoverished to trust themselves with ambivalent feelings towards others and their paranoidal anxieties lead them to evacuate their bad feelings onto others, splitting off their bad feelings from the good and keeping these rigidly separate and often lodged in different racial groups.

From the identity analyses, the four most tolerant appear to have resolved their early developmental phases reasonably well. They are all people who incline towards showing depressive anxieties while not being clinically depressed. Under stress, they tend to turn their anger and aggression inwards against the self and as a result they spare others. This is the core of their racial tolerance. Inclined to be thoughtful, aware and somewhat reflective, each seems to have a certain capacity to be alone and to be able to face up to some of the uncertainties as well as the inevitable pains, losses and ambiguities of everyday experience. Strength has been found in coming to terms with misfortunes and each has largely done this alone by inner 'heart-work'. But by turning the aggression back against the self, they pay a certain price for sparing others their hostile feelings. For at least two of these subjects, Mrs Singh and Johanna James, this creates some psychosomatic complaints. To a certain extent, of course, we all have propensities for either of these extreme reactions (depressive or paranoid-schizoid). These are to be found in every individual to a degree, but it is question of where the greater or lesser emphasis lies and the intensity with which these tendencies manifest themselves.

Turning now to the *most prejudiced* group of subjects – Mr Chattaway, John Chattaway, Eric Singh, Adrian (transitional) and probably Mrs James, all appear to show some unresolved elements from the paranoid-schizoid phase. Adrian and Eric experienced severe separations in their earliest years which no doubt increased anxieties and difficulties at that phase. The chosen defences among this group of subjects are denial and projection, and they each turn their anger and aggression outward against others. They tend to avoid facing their negative identity elements, are unable to tolerate ambivalence in themselves and in others, and so resort to splitting processes. Of all these subjects, however, it is Mr Chattaway and John Chattaway who are the most extreme and the most prone to paranoidal anxieties and fears with consequent needs to violently project their 'bad' parts. It is the intensity and the violence of these projections which leads to the rigidity and fixity of racial prejudices.

It would appear from this discussion that the way in which early developmental phases are weathered is of great importance in establishing pre-conditions for potential racial tolerance or pre-judice. Where there is a reasonably favourable resolution of both early developmental phases, the pre-conditions for tolerance in later life may have been met but nevertheless racial tolerance does not automatically result. The effects of other activators profoundly affect outcome. This is particularly true of social ideologies and the group processes common in hatred and maintained by them. Cohn has pointed out that in various parts of the world today citizens, ordinary soldiers and bureaucrats become involved as participants in massive persecutions and exterminations of other racial groups, swept along unquestioningly and automatically as they act on behalf of their governments.[33] No doubt many of these people had reliable and loving care as children and weathered their early developmental phases well enough, but this, it seems, is insufficient to enable them to withstand the conformity pressures which grip them as passionate social movements of an ideological kind turn with inhumanity or violence on a particular racial group when this is backed up by powerful group forces within the society. The laboratory work of Milgram[34] has demonstrated vividly how ordinary people can commit acts of apparent inhumanity and cruelty towards others when ordered to do so in a setting where power is vested in those controlling the experiments.

Tajfel examines why it is that in many societies innumerable people, in innumerable social situations, have not shown anything approaching autonomy and are buffeted here and there by powerful social forces beyond their control inflicting suffering on others.[35] He believes that these are not extreme cases but merely the end of a long continuum and that we behave in unison because of the influence of our reference groups. Childhood influences however benign, do not appear to be sufficiently potent in themselves to counteract these corrosive forces. It is the interactive combination of early childhood determinants with other *constraints* which is vital in determining racial tolerance, and not any one factor taken by itself.

Perhaps this precarious combination of factors accounts for the relatively low incidence of racial tolerance in society. Norman Cohn has commented that 'in one part of the world or another tolerance and respect for members of what are regarded as "outgroups" is not at all the norm but, on the contrary, is very rare both in history and in the world today.'[36] A poor resolution of early developmental phases as well as deprivation experiences appear to hinder the development of those potentialities which underlie racial tolerance. Unresolved paranoid-schizoid elements are powerful activators propelling individuals struggling with unresolved identity conflicts towards racial misuse.

(b) Low self-esteem: Self-esteem can be injured by childhood deprivations, by the failure of important relationships, and by humiliating experiences of all kinds. These damaged feelings can arouse aggression as Rochlin[37] has shown. 'When narcissism is threatened, we are humiliated, our self-esteem is injured and aggression appears.' But aggression is only a means to an end, namely to restore self-esteem and to relieve the feelings of indignity which have been aroused. Aggression takes a variety of forms. It can impel people towards hostility or violence, anger and irritation or it

may be the spur for gratifying achievements in work, positive and challenging activities and creative endeavours, or in working for an ideal or a cause. The question of which way aggression will be used in the defence of one's identity depends on a combination of factors. Perhaps the most important of these is the capacity to turn passive into active ways of coping as a means of defence. This involves a direct attack on the problem itself so that aggression is harnessed to the pursuit of goals, and self-esteem is enhanced by the integrity of the work itself as well as the possibility of goal achievement. We have already seen that both the James and the Singh families show their ego strengths in these ways.

Where wounds to self-esteem are experienced as very severe, however, humiliation may be too crippling for the individual to be able to respond in positive ways. Furthermore, if the balance of paranoid-schizoid elements is heavy, the aggression aroused will most likely take the form of attacks on those who are felt to be the cause of the damage to self-esteem. This serves as a defence against the anxiety of feeling a passive victim of another's cruelty or neglect.

If pervasive attitudes and social and psychological expectations within a family convey that each member is responsible for his or her own actions, and if the family stress the *active* part that each child may play in his own socialization, then it is likely that each feels some sense of responsibility for his actions and the way that others behave and feel towards him. The world is perceived as something that can be managed and the individual feels he can exercise some choice and control over what happens to him. When exposed to blows to his self-esteem, such a person may be more able to convert aggression into active ways of coping since the environment is not felt as overwhelmingly threatening. However, where individuals are socialized in families where there are strong authoritarian pressures and controls, and where these are linked with an absence of notions of delegated responsibility to the growing child, he is more likely to feel a lack of responsibility for his own actions, both in relation to his own goals and in his relationships with others. He is likely to make fewer internal demands on himself and his environment is experienced as physically more threatening and less susceptible to control or change.

These two contrasting modes of responding to the world are not unrelated to the balance of personality features within the individual already discussed. Where these incline more towards the depressive side in their overall emphasis, responsibility for oneself is a goal sought; where the balance is more towards the paranoid-schizoid pole, notions of being an object unpredictably acted upon by others are more likely to be aroused, linked with an absence of self-responsibility. In the face of attacks on their self-esteem, Mr Chattaway and John Chattaway are the most vulnerable subjects and least able to convert their aggression into active constructive goals. They both disclaim responsibility for their actions, make few demands on themselves and certainly experience their environment as physically threatening. Their patterns of coping with blows to their self-esteem involve racial misuse. Members of the James and Singh families are able to convert the aggression released by attacks on their self-esteem largely into active channels, with high investment in the work area.

In other words, blows to self-esteem do not *necessarily* activate racial prejudice. The aggression released may indeed go in that direction but will be dependent upon the personality make-up of the individual, the intensity of the humiliation caused, the degree of anxiety aroused, the socialization emphases, and the resolutions of early developmental phases.

(c) Other socialization factors: In addition to the earlier points made about the crucial role of the family in the development of racial attitudes, there are three additional aspects of socialization which operate as activators or constraints.

1 Body-identity: Deep-seated conscious and unconscious attitudes towards their own bodies are communicated unconsciously by parents to their growing children. Self-debasing and self-rejecting feelings towards one's body are not confined to any racial group but where a society discriminates against people on the basis of their race, and in this society it is the black and brown racial groups who are singled out for such invidious treatment, these attitudes necessarily contaminate body-identity feelings. 'Black is beautiful' gives back pride and easy acceptance of body-identity to groups who have suffered from racist humiliations in the past. However, these deep-seated feelings in relation to skin-colour and body-identity are handed on unconsciously by one generation to another and can endure as a negative legacy of the past.

McDonald[38] in a fascinating and important study found that skin colour conflicts lie at the root of racial attitudes among white and black children and that being helped to work these through psychologically in a multi-racial nursery school, the children become progressively able to separate skin-colour conflicts from early

developmental conflicts, which are happening at the same time. This
provides a basic foundation for a later realistic accommodation to
racial differences among both white and black children. She has
shown how skin colour anxiety – if successfully resolved –
promotes growth and psychological development, whereas an
unsuccessful resolution potentially supports arrests and fixations in
development.

It is difficult to find examples of such skin colour anxiety in our
case material since it is an elusive, diffuse and largely unconscious
anxiety. That does not however mean that it does not potently exist
among the West Indian and the Indian subjects.[39]

2 Inter-racial contacts and experiences: The opportunity for inter-
racial contacts during the formative years of childhood varies from
subject to subject. These early encounters influence later ones by
stirring memories and shaping expectations. It is not the encounters
as such but rather how these are handled at the time, and the
consequences which they produce, which potently affect later
experiences with the same racial groups. These have been individually traced in the last three chapters. Each individual's
experience is unique and even within the same family, siblings are
exposed to different varieties of inter-racial contacts when young.
For instance, Johanna James went to an inter-racial school in
Barbados where a potentially divisive and anxiety-provoking experience with a young white schoolboy was handled by them both in
ways which later led to trusting and warm relationships with white
peers at school, progressively increasing in number and depth. Her
brother Adrian went to a solely black school in Barbados and had no
experience of white peers on which to draw until he came to this
country at the age of fifteen. Vera and Eric Singh also differ in the
continuity and friendliness of their relationships with white peers,
Vera's being consistently positive and warmly sustaining while
Eric's bonds were constantly undermined by hospitalization and
lengthy stays in India.

3 The part played by parental attitudes: The extent and character of
the parents' involvement in the child's racial socialization and the
part played by parental attitudes towards race, act as activators or
constraints on racial misuse. The child absorbs the attitudes of his
parents by direct instruction, explicit attitudes and the unconscious
covert communication of feelings towards racial groups. By unconscious imitation of parental attitudes and identification with either or

both parents, the child takes into his internal world, the parents' own social attitudes, social ideologies and stereotypes which may be revised later in life. Since siblings do not necessarily share the same racial feelings, parental attitudes by themselves are unable to account for differences in racial attitudes among children. But they still act as activators or constraints combining with other factors.

4 The peer group: Of particular interest as a reinforcing and stabilizing force is the peer group. Individuals have different inner needs and accordingly use the peer group differently. Johanna James turns to hers for support when a white classmate humiliates and insults her. They uphold her and reinforce her attitudes of good sense and inner conviction. But her mother's need is to isolate herself from her peers – her fellow workers at the ice cream factory – and so keep her values distinct from theirs. To this extent, isolation serves to crystallize for her *their* values *and* her own; and by rejecting theirs, she is able to clarify where she stands. In a similar way, Vera Singh's close bonds with her English white peers serve to reinforce her good inter-racial feelings, but when they seek to attribute an English identity to her, she psychologically uses this as a means of clarifying, for herself, who she is, where she stands what she believes in, in contrast to her peer group.

The peer group does not appear to function as an activator or constrainer of racial prejudice so much as a reinforcer or stabilizer of previously held attitudes. John Chattaway for example, *needed* to find the skinheads who then reinforce his level of racial intolerance. They did not make him into a skinhead, or shape his intolerance; he psychologically needed to be found and to find them. Similarly Johanna was not influenced in her opinions by her peers; she took a stance which then required confirmation and support and she was able to ask for it (an unusual strength) and then to be given what she needed.

11 THE COMPLETED MODEL

The model can now be completed, incorporating the activators and constraints. This model (See Diagram II) essentially deals with how processes move; it shows how constraints *eject* the unresolved identity conflicts away from the spiral, out of the field of race relationships, whereas activators perpetually feed the vicious interactive spiral of prejudice and keep it in constant movement.

It must be emphasised that the research and the ideas underlying

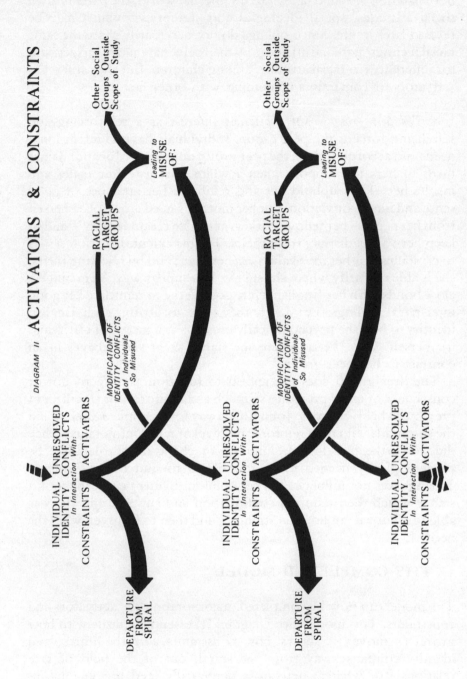

DIAGRAM II   ACTIVATORS & CONSTRAINTS

this model are those derived from a culturally limited sphere, namely the values and attitudes characteristic of liberal traditions within Western culture, particularly those of the late twentieth century. The model is therefore only relevant to such Western societies. In applying it to different communities of this type, it is the weight and relative strength accorded to each of the activators and constraints which will vary form one societal context to another. For example, in a society like that of South Africa, the social ideology of *apartheid* and its massive institutionalization in political, economic, educational, legal and social forms is obviously of the utmost importance as a dominating and compelling activator which also potently affects the other activators as well (e.g. the stress of change among blacks, family dynamics and social arenas). Since racism is embedded in the overall economic structure of that society, mass communications and overt and covert forms of racial indoctrination potently structure and act to maintain existing racial stereotypes and prejudices. However within the same society constraints also operate, distinguishing one family from another, one social arena from another and one individual from another. The model is broad enough to encompass both the vicious spiral of continuing and deeply embedded racial prejudice and misuse and to raise questions, largely unexplored, of how *apartheid* in turn bears upon the identity processes of the black, Indian and coloured people and how they, in turn use and misuse both the white groups and each other while being in turn, of course, also massively misused.

The model, although derived from a study of a very small number of individuals sharing a common inter-racial neighbourhood, where each person's daily life necessarily involves a wide variety of forms of inter-racial encounter, should also be applicable to communities which are *not* racially mixed, but nonetheless are part of a wider society including various racial groups. In such cases it may well be that resort to racial misuse is still engaged in although face-to-face contact is limited. In Britain at the present time, there are large areas which remain almost wholly white and yet the debates and issues relating to race preoccupy many within such areas.[40] In any event the model allows for the possibility that groups other than race are used in similar ways under the pressure of unresolved identity conflicts.

12 VICIOUS AND BENIGN SPIRALS

What has been revealed in the course of this study on the factors leading either to vicious or to benign spirals in face-to-face encounters between individuals of different races? Repeated actions and reactions do not, of course, fit a uni-directional causal pattern and as a result they are not easy to analyse and do not readily lend themselves to simple generalizations. This is why they are best dealt with intensively in each of the individual identity analyses. Nonetheless some general observations can be made.

First, the model of racial spirals already presented is applicable to face-to-face encounters.

Secondly, the processes which initiate vicious downward spirals are of two types which are distingusihed by the *relative* weight and intensities of the contributory forces. There are those spirals which arise from an upsurge of *urgent inner* pressures from *acute* unresolved identity conflicts which can be catalysed by a variety of appropriate environmental provocations – not particularly provocative to other people. Then there are those spirals which spring from *incessantly aggravated* and extreme forms of *environmental provocation* and it is the unremitting pressure of these upon individuals which arouse their latent unresolved identity conflicts, since we all have vulnerabilities which can be inflamed. Numerous examples of the first type have already been cited; Mr Chattaway and John Chattaway best exemplify how the first type of downward spiral operates.

Environmental provocations which trigger off downward spirals may occur most frequently during mass periods of unemployment when deprivation, disadvantage and loss of status all act to create uncertainty and stress which will increase the incidence of vicious spirals in race relations. In this study the environmental provocation which most insidiously but potently affects the vulnerabilities of almost all the subjects are influential pronouncements by leading politicians, notably Enoch Powell's inflammatory speeches against the coloured immigrants in this country, urging their repatriation. Deep anxieties and insecurities are created among the immigrants and scapegoating of other racial groups – notably the Kenyan Asians – is evident in at least two of the subjects (Mr James and Eric Singh), and there is reactive anger, waves of insecurity and despair in almost all the other immigrants with the notable exception of Mrs James who knew nothing about the speeches (a characteristic defence in her case). Acts of racial discrimination are also potent provocations, because the pain and the anger of such humiliating indignities arouse latent vulnerabilities. The case material abounds with a variety of responses to racial discrimination and prejudice. Johanna James suffered intensely from racial discrimination but because of her personality structure, depressive tendencies and chosen values, was able to withstand the inner pain at considerable personal cost and so avoided initiating a vicious spiral. Adrian James' experiences at school, exposing him to racial prejudice, might have stabilized and reinforced his existing tendencies towards racial misuse so feeding a potentially vicious spiral. However, his skills as a cricketer and his achievements in his school work increased his standing with his peers and his resultant self-esteem, so a potentially destructive spiral shifted into a benign one. Eric Singh's reaction to racial prejudice at school, although not overtly feeding a vicious chain, nonetheless since it includes withdrawal, avoidance and isolating defences, is also unable to initiate a benign spiral. At the interpersonal level Mr Singh's behaviour does not exacerbate racial tensions, but because of the invidious attributions of a racial identity imposed on him by the English, he becomes trapped in a vicious spiral which in turn makes him both more critical of the English and of his fellow Asians.

However, it is important to distinguish the forces which initiate a spiral from those which continue to sustain it. What sustains it exists more in the present than in the past – which is not to under-estimate the role of unconscious motivations but to point to present circumstances which stabilize and reinforce behaviour patterns once these are initiated. For instance, although neither Mr Chattaway nor John are influenced initially by Enoch Powell's speeches to act as they do towards other racial groups, nonetheless his words sustain and confirm the social acceptability of their general outlook and this gives support to their behaviour, stabilizing and reinforcing the downward spirals. The full range of activators can potentially combine to reinforce downward spirals once they are initiated; constraints can act in the same way to maintain and support benign circles.

What is striking in a review of all the vicious and benign spirals found, is how often *potentially* provocative inter-racial incidents are ignored and as a result become benign spirals. Examples abound; they include the white woman on the bus who insultingly rebuffed Mr James for his proferred help, to which his response was deliberately to continue to help passengers of all races; Mrs Chattaway's good feelings for the West Indian midwife were not reversed when she felt insufficiently helped during labour, which she attributed to differences in professional practice rather than to racial differences; Johanna James' striking response to the white English school girl who accused her falsely of smelling; Vera Singh's reaction to the white employment officer who failed to find her a job, was to realise that this was happening also to her white friends; Elaine Chattaway's disappointment at the West Indians' disruption of her school dance was not an occasion for attributing blame to a racial group. All of these show that potential sources of provocation within a multi-racial society may often sensibly be ignored.

13 THE INNER AND OUTER WORLDS OF RACE

As members of the same society we are inextricably affected by each other, and as members of one or other racial group within this society, we both use and misuse racial groups and in turn are used and misused by racial groups other than our own. It is, I believe, the unresolved identity conflicts which generate the ferment underlying this misuse and since identity conflicts are universal and continue to manifest themselves throughout life, we are never without the possibility of unresolved identity conflicts raising their uncertain heads. But the latent ferment is aggravated in intensity by fluctuating environmental stresses, such as mass levels of unemployment, falls in the standard of living, political instability or any increase in group disaffection specifically affecting one part of a community.

Of course, there are many conflicts which are resolved and lead to continued development and growth for the individual and do not constitute a problem in race relations. But where the inner turmoil of unresolved identity conflicts interacts with powerful combinations of *activators* in the absence of balancing and equally potent *constraints*, the individual is propelled or nudged towards racial misuse. However, we are not passive pawns in this process except under rare and exceptional circumstances involving massive, inexorable pressures. We are mediators of the conflicts and forces which press upon us and although it is true that at times we feel relatively helpless, nonetheless we do have choices and options for re-constituting our security. To assume that people are all victims of circumstances does not square with the evidence of this study which has shown how some subjects, when exposed to both inner and outer stresses, have nonetheless managed to avoid the easy option of racial intolerance.

What seems to be needed is a widespread recognition and understanding of the twin conspirators in the field of racial prejudice. There is the underlying *ferment* which is found in all modern societies and this can contract or expand in extent and intensity under varying conditions. And because historical, economic and political factors – as well as racial discrimination – have led to inequalities between racial groups in most societies, racial groups constitute particularly potent social magnets drawing into their field a variety of physical, social, cultural, psychological and economic differentials. As a result they act as specially *seductive repositories* for denied, disallowed and unwanted aspects of identity. It is when these twin conspirators get together, that the consequences are inflammatory and racial misuse results.

Because the processes linking racial groups are incessantly interactive and take a spiral form, whatever alters or influences any of the racial groups or one or other of the *activators* or *constraints* within the *spiral*, however small such modifications may be, may create expanding cycles of modifications. This is because each twist of the spiral feeds back its modifications which add to the initial stimulus.

Those initiating racial misuse inexorably become subject to misuse by other racial groups with resultant impingements upon identity processes for all the racial groups concerned. The more powerful, dominant and numerically superior of these groups are the least likely to become *aware* of these massive impingements, but the relatively powerless are much more at hazard and more vulnerable to these impingements. Their sense of identity is more readily infringed by others, their ways of feeling and being themselves are more profoundly exposed to what others do and do not do. And this of course is fed back into the spiral.

Because of the rapidity with which Britain is moving towards becoming a multi-racial society and because of the decline in its position as a world power, the British are, of necessity, struggling to crystallize their own sense of who they are, where they have come from, where they currently stand and what they stand for. To the extent that their present sense of cultural identity may still be unstable and needing to be vitalized by continual clarification, so will the immigrants in this country – particularly the coloured immigrants – be more likely to be blamed not only for such uncertainties and insecurities, but also for current social ills. A striking illustration of this occurs at the time of writing, when the leader of the Conservative party is on record as attributing to the very small proportion of coloured immigrants within the country the potential for culturally 'swamping' the English. Statements such as these are not only a powerful *activator* of racial prejudice but reveal inner uncertainties and frailties of a cultural identity.

What, if anything, can be done about the apparently inexorable movement of vicious racial spirals? The procedures and techniques by which one seeks to tackle creatively vast and infinitely complex social problems such as this, would seem to require the same kind of attention to detail which this book has given to the underlying causes of racial tolerance and intolerance. It is beyond the scope of this study to do more than point very briefly to a few of the fundamental issues which need to be tackled. First of all, since the ferment arises from inner causes, any person or group engaged in racial stereotyping or any form of racial prejudice, needs to face the challenge of self-scrutiny and ask himself 'What is being avoided by this racial prejudice? What am I not facing, in myself, that such recourse to racial misuse is happening? Why is this happening *now*? What would I have to do in my own life-space to make it more bearable to face my own problems?' If public figures with political power engage in any form of racial misuse, however concealed, we, as citizens, are entitled to ask of such individuals or of a political party which espouses these views 'What is being avoided? Why? And why now? What are the hidden gains of racial misuse, and what is lost by avoiding a productive attack on the real underlying problems?' The need to divert attention from the actual source of these problems should alert us all, both individually and collectively so that at no point should racial misuse be condoned.

Of course, this is very easy and glib to say and extremely difficult to do, or to press others to try and do. Nonetheless this seems to me to be the obvious starting point. What is required is the *open* ventilation and *free* discussion of racial prejudice in ways which lead to a widespread growth of insight within the community as to how these unresolved identity conflicts, to which we are *all* prone, may manifest themselves and why they move as they do towards racial groups. And how these same processes also may involve other groups differing in religion, social class etc. If a concerted attack on this problem were made at all levels in the community, starting with the family, moving to schools and the work place and involving professional care-takers such as teachers, nurses, community workers, the police and doctors so that people were able to talk openly of their feelings and be helped to see the dynamic link between what is inner and what is outer in the field of race prejudice, then in time this might lead to racial misuse losing at least some of its forbidden and veiled power.

It was striking that during the course of field work four or five of the subjects casually commented in their life history interviews on incidents which they spontaneously and correctly interpreted as instances of scapegoating. All of these were interpersonal incidents occurring within their own racial group. This type of insight now appears to be widespread in many sections of the community (including those who do not read seriously or in relevant fields). What is urgently needed is to spread equivalent insights in the field of racial misuse, skilfully, steadily and deliberately within the community. It is not only knowledge and facts which are required, although these have their rightful place, but the need for emotional re-education through small groups in face-to-face encounters. What emerges from this study is, for instance, the need to help people of all ages and all races to find within themselves a more ready acceptance of their own imperfections and particularly of their ambivalences, so that the need for resorting to racial prejudice is mitigated. The strengthening in each of us of our own individual identities, both personal and cultural, sharpens and clarifies for each person who he is and enhances his inner security. It is only when such feelings are secured that others can be responded to and respected.

The responsibility which rests on us all is very considerable. We not only have power as individuals in relation to our own lives, but as citizens we need to invigorate a social ideology which embraces multi-racial harmony as a desirable goal. We need to back this up with steady and informed support for constraints within society which outlaw racial discrimination and reveal racial prejudice as the destructive evil which it is.

There are no perfect people, no perfect choices and no perfect solutions to the conflicts which we all face. But there are a variety of ways in which we can each act responsibly to constrain ourselves, others and our societies from the destructiveness of racial prejudice. Instead of hiding our imperfect selves and our imperfect solutions from the light of day, we need to open them to further scrutiny and exploration.

BIBLIOGRAPHY AND NOTES

1 Group for the Advancement of Psychiatry, Committee on Social Issues *Psychiatric Aspects of School Desegregation*, Report No. 37, G A P Publications Office, New York(1957); Coles, R. *Children of Crisis: A Study of Courage and Fear*, Faber & Faber, London(1968); Reiser, M. 'On origins of hatred toward negroes', *American Image*, 18 (1961), 167 – 172.

2 McDonald, M. *Not by the Colour of Their Skin*, International Universities Press, New York (1970).

3 Hauser, S. T. *Black and White Identity Formation: Studies in the Psychosocial Development of Lower Socioeconomic Class Adolescent Boys*. Wiley Interscience, New York (1971).

4 Davis, A. and Dollard, J. *Children of Bondage,* American. Council on Education, Washington (1941); Elkins, S. M. *Slavery*, Grosset & Dunlap, New York

(1963); Pettigrew, T. F. *A Profile of the American Negro,* Van Nostrand Reinhold, New York (1964); Kardiner, A. and Ovessey, L. *The Mark of Oppression.* Norton, New York (1951); Grier, W. H. and Cobb, P. M. *Black Rage.* Basic Books, New York (1968); Fanon, F. *Black Skin, White Masks,* Grove Press, New York (1962); Malcolm X. *Autobiography of Malcolm X,* Grove Press, New York (1968); Cleaver, E. *Soul on Ice,* McGraw-Hill, New York (1968); Proshansky, H. and Newton, P. 'Colour: the nature and meaning of negro self-identity', in Watson, P.(ed) *Psychology and Race.* Penguin, Harmondsworth (1973); McCarthy, J. D. and Yancey, W. L. 'Uncle Tom and Mr Charlie: Metaphysical pathos in the study of racism and personal disorganization', *American Journal of Sociology,* 76, (1971), 648–672.

5 Hudson, L. *The Cult of the Fact,* Jonathan Cape, London (1972); Hudson, L. *Human Beings,* Jonathan Cape, London (1975).

6 I am indebted to Dr R. Gosling for his helpful clarification of this point.

7 Rochlin, G. *Man's Aggression: The Defence of the Self,* Constable, London (1973), p. 119.

8 Pincus, L. and Dare, C. *Secrets in the Family.* Faber & Faber, London (1978).

9 Rochlin, G, (1973), *op. cit.* p. 158.

10 Hall, E. T. *The Silent Language,* Doubleday, New York (1959); Hall, E. T. *The Hidden Dimension,* Doubleday, New York (1966).

11 Horowitz, M. J., Duff, D. F. and Stratton, L. O. 'Body – buffer zone', *Archives of General Psychiatry,* 11 (1964), 651–656; Horowitz, M. J. 'Body image,' *Archives of General Psychiatry,* 14 (1966), 456–460; Sommer, R. *Personal Space,* Prentice Hall, Englewood Cliffs, (1969); Seguin, C. A. 'The "Individual" Space', *International Journal of Neuropsychiatry,* 3 (1967), 108–117; Landis, B. 'Ego boundaries', *Psychological Issues,* Vol. VI. No. 4. Monograph 24; Ardrey, R. *The Territorial Imperative,* Atheneum, New York (1966); Kinzel, A. F. 'Body – buffer zone in violent prisoners'. American Journal of Psychiatry 127 (1966), 99–104; Newman, O. *Defensible Space: People and Design in the Violent City,* Architectural Press, London (1973); Rudofsky, B. *Streets for People: a primer for Americans,* Doubleday. New York (1969).

12 1971 Immigration Act.

13 Cohn, N. *Warrant for Genocide,* Eyre & Spottiswoode, London (1966).

14 Dicks, H. V. *Licensed Mass Murder: A Socio-psychological Study of Some S S Killers,* Basic Books, N. Y. (1972).

15 Poliakov, L. *Aryan Myth: History of Racist and Nationalist Ideas in Europe,* Heinemann, London (1974).

16 Milgram, S. *Obedience to Authority: An Experimental View,* Tavistock Publications, London (1974).

17 *Ibid.* p. 147.

18 Race Relations Acts 1968 and 1976.

19 None of these comments are intended to argue the case for or against mass immigration. This lies outside the scope of this study. But whether this country acquired its racial minorities by deliberate policy, accident or even lack of foresight nonetheless they form part of this society and my concern here is to examine how they are treated and the implications this has for them and for everyone in this society.

20 Smith, D. J. *Racial Disadvantage in Britain: P E P report*, Penguin, Harmondsworth (1977).

21 Jahoda, M. 'The roots of prejudice', *New Community*, 4. (1975), No. 2, 179–187.

22 Jaques, E. 'Death and the mid-life crisis', *International Journal of Psychoanalysis*, 46 (1965), 4 203–314.

23 Jahoda, M. (1975), *op. cit.* p. 186.

24 *Ibid.*

25 Trist, E. L. Urban North America: the challenge of the next 30 Years', in Hollander, E. P. and Hunt, R. G. (eds) *Current Perspectives in Social Psychology*, Oxford University Press, Oxford (1976).

26 Hall, E. T. *The Hidden Dimension*, Doubleday, New York. (1966); Horowitz, M. J. 'Body image', *Archives of General Psychiatry*, 14 (1966), 456–460.

27 Milgram, S. 'Experience of living in cities', *Science*, 167 (1970), No. 3924, 1461–8.

28 Landis, B. 'Ego boundaries', *Psychological Issues,* Vol. VI, No. 4. Monograph 24.

29 Adorno, T. W. *et al. The Authoritarian Personality*, Harper & Row, New York (1950); Christie, R. and Jahoda, M. (eds) *Studies in the Scope and Method of 'The Authoritarian Personality'*, Fee Press, New York (1954); Katz, P. A. 'The acquisition of racial attitudes in children', in Katz, P. A. (ed) *Towards the Elimination of Racism*, Pergamon Press, Oxford (1976); Pushkin, I. and Veness, T. 'The development of racial awareness and prejudice in children', in Watson, P. (ed) *Psychology and Race*, Penguin, Harmondsworth London (1973), p. 23 – 42.

30 Allport, G. W. *The Nature of Prejudice*, Addison-Wesley, Reading, Mass (1954); Kutner, B. and Gordon, N. 'Cognitive functioning and prejudice', *Sociometry*, 27 (1964), 66–74; Tajfel, H. 'The roots of prejudice: cognitive aspects', in Watson, P. (ed) *Psychology and Race*. Penguin, Harmondsworth (1973), pp. 76–95.

31 Maslow, A. H. *Toward a Psychology of Being*. Van Nostrand, Princeton, (1962), p. 202.

32 Segal, H. *Introduction to the Work of Melanie Klein*, Hogarth Press, London (1973).

33 Cohn, N. *Warrant for Genocide*, Eyre & Spottiswoode London (1966); Poliakov, L. *Aryan Myth: History of Racist and Nationalist Ideas in Europe*, Heinemann, London (1974); Dicks, H. V. *Licensed Mass Murder: A Sociopsychological Study of Some S S Killers*, Basic Books, New York (1972).

34 Milgram, S. *Obedience to Authority: An Experimental View*, Tavistock Pablications, London, (1974).

35 Tajfel, H. Social Psychology and Social Reality. *New Society* (1977), 31 March, 653–654.

36 Cohn, N. personal communication (1978).

37 Rochlin, G. (1973), op. cit, p. 1.

38 McDonald, M. *Not by the Colour of their Skin*, International Universities Press New York; (1970) Kubie, L. S. 'The ontology of prejudice', Journal of Nervous and Mental Disorders, 141 (1965), 265–273.

39 Skin colour anxiety is likely to exist both among West Indians and Indians

since a light brown skin in both countries has been regarded as a mark of status originating in the white skin of Aryan conquerors or colonisers.

40 Cohn, No (1978) op. cit. This is not unusual. Norman Cohn has pointed out that studies on anti-semitism in the 1930s and 1940s found that that form of ethnic prejudice was often very strong in areas where there were few or no Jews. And when Shakespeare created the character of Shylock there had been no Jews in England for some four centuries.

INFORMAL GUIDE LINES FOR INTRODUCING THE RESEARCH PROJECT TO A FAMILY

Who we are

Research workers from the University of Sussex, social scientists interested in understanding people – their experiences and feelings – how they come to be the people they are.

What we are doing and why we are here

Although human behaviour has been studied for a long time, we still know very little about people in our own society – and less about the different groups in our community – people who have been born and brought up in different countries and who now live here together.

Politicians, TV and radio people, as well as journalists, often express opinions about the different groups and races in our society and how they think about things, but very little work has been done scientifically on how families in all these different groups live, what their experiences are, how they feel and think, and what life looks like through their eyes.

This is why we are doing the research. We have no connection with TV, radio, newspapers, politicians, the government, the local council or anybody official. We are scientists trying to get the facts.

We are working with English, West Indian and Indian families and they are working with us to help us to understand what happens to them at home and at work, at school, whilst out shopping, in the street, in the pubs, etc.' and how they feel about these things.

So we have come to ask you if you will also work with us and take part in the study – help us by teaching us what has been important in your life – what you are experiencing right now in the present – teaching us of your life through your own eyes.

We may be rather slow and clumsy because we may not understand your background and ways of thinking, and we hope you will tell us if we blunder and make mistakes or get hold of the wrong end of the stick.

573

What is involved

We want to study two generations in each family – both parents and two adolescent children, a daughter and a son, so we can learn how each generation may have different experiences and points of view.

We realise you are leading busy lives so we visit families in their homes, by appointment, at times to suit each person.

To get to know your life and your feelings takes a bit of time, so we want to visit you quite often.

Since we are scientists we won't be taking sides or judging what you tell us as good or bad. We all have likes and dislikes and feelings that are both good and bad, and this we have learnt to understand about ourselves and will understand it in you also.

We know how mixed up we all can get at times in our feelings, so that sometimes we may like neighbours and on other occasions we may dislike them, and we do not expect you to be different from ourselves and other people. We know that feelings change from time to time and we will be trying to understand these feelings and trying to understand what makes them change.

Confidentiality of material

There are two of us working on this research and we belong to the Columbus Centre of the University of Sussex.

All the things we learn about a family will be private and confidential, and right from the first interview, the family can choose a different made-up name for itself and that is the name that will be on any of the notes that we keep – the made-up name. Only the worker who visits your family will know your real name and your real address. Otherwise, all the material that is collected will just have on it for example, the 'S' family, the 'T' family or the 'P' family and the names that you make up for yourselves.

What we want from you

We think it is a big decision to make to decide whether or not you would like to be one of the families in this important study, and so we would like you to talk about it and think about it before deciding whether you will join or not. We can return in a day or two for your decision and will understand and respect you for whatever decision you make.

FACE SHEET FOR EACH INDIVIDUAL INTERVIEW

FAMILY

Ethnic Group . . . .
Interview No . . . . . *with* . . . . . *Date* . . . .
Interviewer (s) . . . .
Other interviewers present . . . .
Place of interview . . . . *Time and duration* . . . .
Others present?. . . . .
If so, what relationship to respondent were they?. . . . .
. . . .
Did interruptions occur?. . . . .
What were they and how did they seem to affect respondent? . . .
. . . .
How did they affect you? . . . .
Relationship with respondent . . . .
How did you feel befor coming to interview anout *this* interview
with *this* respondent? . . . .
. . . .
Rapport and emotional quality of this interview as a whole?
. . . .
How did respondent behave?
(a) At the beinning of the interview? . . . .
. . . .
(b) During the main part of the interview?. . . . .
. . . .
(c) In bringing the interview to a close?. . . . .
. . . .
How did you behave and feel?
(a) At the beginning of the interview? . . . .
. . . .
(b) During the main part of the interview?. . . . .
. . . .

(c) In bringing the interview to a close?...................

....

Any special circumstances that might have affected responsiveness of the subject?.......................................

How does respondent feel about another interview, do you think?

....

How do you feel about another interview with this respondent?

....

TERMINAL INTERVIEW WITH THE FAMILY

FIRST SECTION

1 How have you felt about this study?
2 Has this study changed you as a family in any ways you can think of?
3 Has the study led you to discuss different things among yourselves?
   What sorts of things?
   What kinds of feelings have been stirred up by this study?
4 Has it changed your feelings about being:
   West Indian?
   English?
   Indian?
5 Has it changed your feelings about life here? In what ways?
6 (Only for West Indian and Indian families) Has immigration changed you as a family?
   What things have changed?
   How?
7 What sort of a family did you think of yourselves as being before you immigrated?
   Now?
8 How did other people in your own country think about your family before you left?
9 How do you think other people who know your family, think of you as a family now?

TERMINAL INTERVIEW WITH THE FAMILY

SECOND SECTION

1 What have either of us done or said here which might have struck you as odd, or silly, or upsetting or annoying?
2 In what ways could we have done it differently or better?
3 How have you thought of us?
4 Is there anybody that we have reminded you of? Anyone you might have known in the past perhaps?

INDEX

579

INDEX TO AUTHORS CITED